Educational Communities of Inquiry:

Theoretical Framework, Research, and Practice

Zehra Akyol
Independent Researcher, Canada

D. Randy Garrison
University of Calgary, Canada

Managing Director:	Lindsay Johnston
Book Production Manager:	Jennifer Romanchak
Publishing Systems Analyst:	Adrienne Freeland
Managing Editor:	Joel Gamon
Development Editor:	Myla Merkel
Assistant Acquisitions Editor:	Kayla Wolfe
Typesetter:	Alyson Zerbe
Cover Design:	Nick Newcomer

Published in the United States of America by
Information Science Reference (an imprint of IGI Global)
701 E. Chocolate Avenue
Hershey PA 17033
Tel: 717-533-8845
Fax: 717-533-8661
E-mail: cust@igi-global.com
Web site: http://www.igi-global.com

Library of Congress Cataloging-in-Publication Data

Educational communities of inquiry: theoretical framework, research, and practice / Zehra Akyol and D. Randy Garrison, Editors.
    pages cm
  Includes bibliographical references and index.
  Summary: "This book is an extensive reference that offers theoretical foundations and developments associated with the CoI theoretical framework"--Provided by publisher.
  ISBN 978-1-4666-2110-7 (hardcover) -- ISBN 978-1-4666-2111-4 (ebook) -- ISBN 978-1-4666-2112-1 (print & perpetual access) (print) 1. Blended learning. 2. Internet in education. I. Akyol, Zehra, 1980- editor of compilation. II. Garrison, D. R. (D. Randy), 1945- editor of compilation.
  LB1028.5.E325 2013
  371.3--dc23
                        2012013056

British Cataloguing in Publication Data
A Cataloguing in Publication record for this book is available from the British Library.

All work contributed to this book is new, previously-unpublished material. The views expressed in this book are those of the authors, but not necessarily of the publisher.

Table of Contents

Section 3
Administrative Issues and Organizational Support

Section 4
Emerging Research and Practice Issues

Detailed Table of Contents

Section 1
Theoretical Foundations and Epistemological Insights

This chapter discusses the epistemological assumptions and theoretical foundations of the Community of Inquiry (CoI) framework. Specifically it addresses the central concepts of community, collaboration, constructivism, inquiry, discourse, metacognition, co-regulation, and motivation. The primary goal is to reinforce the CoI's theoretical coherence and enhance its practical utility in providing direction to the study and practice of e-learning in a range of education contexts.

This chapter addresses, in psychohistorical, philosophical, and educational terms, the emergence of and prospects for the practice of a specific form of philosophical pedagogy in an online environment. It explores a form of structured group dialogue known as "community of philosophical inquiry," a communal critical thinking discourse that reflects the ongoing transformation of the contemporary information environment into a hybrid zone which combines the literate, the oral, and the imagistic.

This chapter focuses on metacognition in relation to learning and cognition and discusses the potential of the Community of Inquiry (CoI) Framework to guide metacognitive development in online and blended learning environments. The commonality between metacognition and the community of inquiry is presented and the metacognitive construct developed using the CoI framework as a theoretical lens is introduced. The chapter also provides the strategies and activities to support metacognition in a community of inquiry are provided.

Chapter 4

This chapter discusses the role and place of the Community of Inquiry (CoI) framework within the history of distance education. The review of the history reveals two important factors for changes in distance education: the effect of leading learning theories of each era and technological advancements. Distance education has moved from a behavioristic, teacher–centered, correspondence study concept, first to an independent learning model, and then to the current student-centered, socio-constructivist, and community-based online learning. In this latest era, the post-modernist age, the CoI framework provides online instructors with a functional framework for designing and teaching their courses more effectively.

Section 2
Design and Implementation

Chapter 5

This chapter examines the importance of various indicators of teaching presence from students' perspectives for their success in online courses. The chapter begins with a review of the CoI research associated with teaching presence in the context of the other presences. The top two indicators that students perceive to be important are making requirements clear and being responsive. These findings and future research directions are discussed in the chapter.

Chapter 6

This chapter provides an innovative CoI perspective on blending synchronous and asynchronous online learning. Issues associated with asynchronous online learning are discussed and a blended online learning design approach is explored to mitigate some of the challenges. It reports on effective ways to engage graduate students attending virtual seminars in real time, based on the findings of a qualitative doctoral study that took place in five Francophone and Anglophone North American universities. Perceived differences between faculty and students were identified and design and delivery solutions explored.

The focus of this chapter is teaching presence through examining the impact of a redesign of a CMC
environment, which by increased instructional design and organisation provided a more explicit scaffolding of the learning phases for learners. It was hypothesised that learners in a redesigned Optima
environment would reach higher levels of cognitive presence due to clearer scaffolding. By comparing
4000 contributions to discourse using two content analyses schemes in a longitudinal perspective, the
research results reveal that Optima participants contributed less to cognitive presence from the beginning
of the course onwards, in particular to integration of argumentation.

Chapter 8

This chapter presents a coaching approach to promote higher-order discussion skills in synchronous
chats. Based on a review of the concept of coaching, the chapter explores how two types of coaching
can improve online discussion and cognitive presence. Indicators of teaching presence were seen to be
useful in implementing functionalist coaching and practical suggestions for coaching using the teaching
presence categories are provided.

Chapter 9

The chapter presents strategies and techniques for fostering greater cognitive presence in asynchronous
online discussion forums. More specifically, the chapter outlines the four stages of cognitive presence
while offering strategies and question prompts to engender cognitive presence in online discussions. A
quick reference guide is included as a discussion aid, suggesting ways to recognize the stages of cognitive presence as well as providing question prompts for engendering greater cognitive presence and
critical thinking.

Chapter 10

This chapter provides an extensive review of critical thinking, cognitive presence, collaborative learning
and technologies that support collaborative learning. The findings from a recent multiple-site study to
explore the extent to which teaching and social presence and other factors contributed to the development

of cognitive presence are discussed. The participants used an innovative online resource and participated in online discussion forums to assist them in learning about educational research and developing research proposals. Through examining the participants' use of this resource, the strategies contributed to improving cognitive presence are discussed.

Chapter 11

Jennifer C. Richardson, Purdue University, USA
Ayesha Sadaf, Purdue University, USA
Peggy A. Ertmer, Purdue University, USA

This chapter addresses the relationship between types of initial question prompts and the levels of critical thinking demonstrated by students' responses in online discussions. The chapter is framed around a research study involving discussion prompts that were coded and classified using Andrews' typology for question types and Practical Inquiry Model (PIM) for their level of critical thinking. The chapter provides important implications for instructors who teach online, especially those looking for general guidelines regarding how to structure discussion prompts to elicit high quality student responses.

Chapter 12

Christine E. Nickel, Regent University, USA & Old Dominion University, USA
Richard C. Overbaugh, Old Dominion University, USA

This chapter presents the results of a study that investigated the differential effects of cooperative versus collaborative instructional strategies and blended versus fully online delivery methods on various aspects of academic community. Results suggest that cooperative and collaborative strategies in online and blended environments are equally effective in regard to individual achievement, but that blended cooperative learners perform significantly poorer on group projects. The course module design highlights the essential elements typical of design strategy based on typical instructional design processes, while using the Community of Inquiry as a theoretical framework that enables "operationalization" of the instructional design process.

Chapter 13

Ana Oskoz, University of Maryland, Baltimore County, USA

This chapter reports on a study that examined the construction of a community of inquiry in a blended, foreign language, undergraduate, lower-level course. Students' asynchronous discussions were analyzed to explore their level of social, cognitive, and teaching presence. The results indicate that the blended environment promoted different types of social interactions than those previously found in exclusively online discussions, with a lower presence of cohesive and affective indicators. The discussion of the findings and implications for foreign language blended courses are provided in the chapter.

Chapter 14

Yoshiko Goda, Kumamoto University, Japan
Masanori Yamada, Kanazawa University, Japan

This chapter presents the application of the CoI framework in a foreign language (EFL) context through a research study that explored the relationships among EFL students' participation level, satisfaction with online discussions, perceived contributions to the discussion groups, English proficiency, and interactions during the discussions in a community of inquiry context. Overall, the results suggest a positive impact the CoI elements developed in the EFL context on students' participation and satisfaction level. The authors provide suggestions for the application of the CoI framework to design computer-supported collaborative EFL learning environments.

Chapter 15

Katrina Meyer, University of Memphis, USA

This chapter reviews the research on the CoI framework and student retention and relates the CoI framework to existing retention theories developed for the pre-Internet world and for online learning. The ability of the CoI framework to improve student retention is discussed as well as the relative impact the framework may have on retention, given other influences on retention as captured by several retention theories. A theoretical link between the CoI framework and retention is proposed, through the intermediary of student learning.

Chapter 16

Norman Vaughan, Mount Royal University, Canada

This chapter focuses on assessment and introduces a triad approach to assessment – integration of self-reflection, peer feedback, and teacher assessment practices. Through a research study, the chapter demonstrates how the CoI, combined with the use of collaborative digital technologies such as blogs, wikis, and other social networking applications in higher education, can provide an opportunity to reinforce the principles of good assessment feedback.

Section 3
Administrative Issues and Organizational Support

Chapter 17

María Fernanda Aldana-Vargas, Universidad de los Andes, Colombia
Albert Gras-Martí, Universidad de los Andes, Colombia
Juny Montoya, Universidad de los Andes, Colombia
Luz Adriana Osorio, Universidad de los Andes, Colombia

This chapter describes an institutional Pedagogical Counseling program-assessment and systematizing initiative, in terms of an adapted Community of Inquiry framework. The process includes ample opportunities to discuss and reflect on key counseling design questions, explore counseling programs from a pedagogical perspective, and implement and evaluate new tutoring designs. This chapter describes the inquiry process and the lessons learned from the implementation of the Pedagogical Counseling inquiry exercise.

David S. Goldstein, University of Washington Bothell, USA
Carol Leppa, University of Washington Bothell, USA
Andreas Brockhaus, University of Washington Bothell, USA
Rebecca Bliquez, University of Washington Bothell, USA
Ian Porter, University of Washington Bothell, USA

This chapter describes the use of the CoI framework to design and deliver a ten-week Hybrid Course Development Institute (HCDI) for faculty members from a variety of disciplines. The faculty experienced a blended format and developed courses based on the three components of the CoI framework: cognitive presence, teaching presence, and social presence, the last of which is particularly challenging to achieve. This chapter provides an overview of the HCDI structure, content, and assessment, and suggests ways to foster social presence in and beyond a blended learning institute for faculty members.

Martha Cleveland-Innes, Athabasca University, Canada

This chapter discusses the impact of philosophical and pragmatic changes on teaching practice and the role of teacher. A principled approach to teaching is introduced for faculty to stay on track of teaching requirements, regardless of delivery mode. The principles are to support new teaching practices but, if adopted, will also change the way the role of faculty is configured and executed in the higher education context.

Dodzi J.-A. Amemado, University of Montreal, Canada

This chapter presents a research that was undertaken in fifteen Canadian universities to explore teaching requirements as university education shifts into the digital era. The results are interpreted in the light of the CoI theoretical framework. The responses of the participants indicated that the frequency of some indicators were higher than others, such as information exchange, discussion and collaboration. The chapter argues that some categories, such as group cohesion, should be given a greater consideration in the CoI framework for online/blended teaching and learning.

Section 4
Emerging Research and Practice Issues

Chapter 21

This chapter provides a creative and innovative look at an analogous area of knowledge workers through examining each of the CoI presences in terms of knowledge workers and communities of practice. Emphasizing the hidden wholeness of a CoI, the chapter argues that this is not that different from what a knowledge worker might experience in the workplace. The phenomenon analogous to teaching presence in online learning is a knowledge worker's ability to create and disseminate knowledge. Communities of Practice provide a measurable phenomenon analogous to social presence. Finally, data-driven decision-making's use for evaluation, coupled with innovation, serve as phenomena parallel to cognitive presence. Together, these three measures, developed in parallel with teaching, social, and cognitive presence, provide an effective framework for evaluating online work, which is quite similar to online learning.

Chapter 22

This chapter provides an interesting discussion on emerging technologies and how these technologies may influence the CoI framework. Innovations in digital publishing, multi-screen, multi-user virtual environments, on-demand education, adaptive learning environments, and analytics are discussed, with a focus on how advancements in these areas may require rethinking and realignment of some aspects of the CoI framework.

Chapter 23

This chapter examines how a community of inquiry develops in a multicultural environment. The results of a two phased research study are presented in the chapter. Phase one comprised creating intercultural competency indicators to test how they developed and expanded existing teaching and social presence indicators; and phase two involved augmenting the 34 item CoI survey instrument. The results reveal that instructor intercultural competence in the form of efficacious facilitation and open communication strategies can compensate for the lack of an instructional design that is culturally oriented and inclusive. A revised version of the CoI survey for online intercultural teaching and learning environment is also provided in the chapter.

This chapter describes ongoing design-based research being conducted in the Master of Arts in Teacher Leadership program at the University of Illinois Springfield. After an initial Quality Matters review and redesign, semester-to-semester implementation issues identified by the CoI survey form the basis for ongoing course improvements. The chapter reports the efficacy of using this design-based, collaborative approach to building communities of inquiry in online courses. Preliminary findings indicate learning outcomes significantly improved across time and that the design based approach provides methodological flexibility while focusing on both theoretical and pragmatic course improvement goals.

This chapter describes the conceptualization and implementation of an international cyber-learning environment as a community of inquiry through application of design based research methodology. The cyber-learning environment aims to foster engagement among faculty, staff, and students of 13 medical schools from Sub-Saharan Africa and their partners around the world. The chapter addresses key environmental constraints and how these constraints guided operational decisions during implementation and discusses challenges and solutions as well as lessons learned.

Foreword

This book is a welcome addition to the growing body of literature based on the Communities of Inquiry framework.

Full disclosure: I was a member of the small group of researchers at the University of Alberta who developed the Communities of Inquiry framework in the late 1990s. At that time online learning was still a rather suspect innovation in higher education. While it did allow for interaction among groups of learners, which some earlier forms of distance or distributed learning had not, there were still questions about the quality of interaction within online learner groups. "Communities of Inquiry" was our attempt to build a framework within which these questions could be investigated.

Soon after the seminal papers describing this framework were published I "went over to the dark side" – i.e., took on administrative roles in higher education. In consequence, I now spend more time thinking about the macro level background activities that must occur in support of the learning experience. I am currently the President of the Canadian Society for the Study of Higher Education, which provides a forum for research directed mainly to these broader issues.

However, I am still very much aware that the front line activity of directly fostering learning is the whole point of higher education. And I'm also well aware that the proportion of learning in higher education that occurs online is steadily increasing. So I have noted with great interest the steadily increasing group of scholars, centred around Dr. D. R. Garrison, who have adopted and adapted the Communities of Inquiry framework to study various aspects of online learning.

This theoretical framework is particularly apt for the study of online learning. In this leaner communicative context, student learning is dependent on deliberate actions by instructors (Teaching Presence, in the Communities of Inquiry framework) to build a collaborative and constructivist learning process (Social Presence) that will assist students to achieve the desired learning outcomes (Cognitive Presence). However, I believe that this framework can also be applied to higher education in general, and can inform faculty development even in contexts where most or all of the teaching is done face-to-face. The present collection should, therefore, be of value even to educators whose interests are not primarily related to online instruction.

This book summarizes and builds on the past decade of research using this research framework for the investigation of online learning. It will be a must read for those using or planning to use the Communities of Inquiry framework in their own research. It will also be of interest and value to those of us who are not at the moment on the front lines of teaching in higher education, but who need to understand the overall context of higher education as it incorporates a larger and larger proportion of online learning.

Walter Archer
University of Alberta, Canada

Walter Archer *is currently (2012) Associate Dean (Interim), Engaged Learning in the Faculty of Extension at the University of Alberta, President of the Canadian Society for the Study of Higher Education, and Editor-in-Chief of the Canadian Journal of University Continuing Education. From 1988 through 2001 he held appointments in the Faculty of Extension as Assistant Professor, Associate Professor, and Professor. From 2001 through 2007 he was Dean of Extension at the University of Saskatchewan before returning to the University of Alberta in 2007.*

Preface

There have been significant theoretical developments in the field of distance education in the last decades that have provided enhanced understanding of teaching and learning in distance and online learning environments. One of these theories is the Community of Inquiry (CoI) Framework developed by Garrison, Anderson, and Archer (2000), which focuses on higher level learning processes. Since its first appearance, the CoI framework has become a credible and coherent theory with the contributions of many researchers and critical reviews. The CoI theoretical framework represents the process of creating a deep and meaningful learning experience through the development of three interdependent elements – social presence, teaching presence, and cognitive presence.

The CoI theoretical framework provides well-structured guidelines and a set of principles to develop effective learning environments and assure and sustain successful educational experiences. The guiding philosophical premise of the framework is to create a collaborative and constructivist learning community. Through the development and maintenance of mutually interacting and supporting social, teaching, and cognitive presences, the framework aims to reach deep and meaningful learning. Social presence provides the sense of belonging through the development of climate and interpersonal relationships in the community. Cognitive presence is the description of the progression through the phases of practical inquiry to construct and confirm meaning through sustained discourse. Teaching presence provides the design, facilitation, and direction throughout a course of study. It is only when all three elements are developed and balanced in a collaborative learning environment that we can be assured of deep and meaningful learning.

Many research studies have provided evidence of high levels of learning in the context of a community of inquiry. The potential of the CoI theoretical framework has been widely recognized and the principles and strategies have been applied to various learning contexts including K-12, higher education, work place settings, as well as online and blended learning environments. The CoI theoretical framework has also been investigated in various disciplines and fields (e.g. nursing, divinity, social sciences, adult education).

Recognizing the growing interest in the CoI framework, there have been many publications in prestigious journals, presentations at worldwide conferences, and a special issue of the *Internet and Higher Education* journal. These developments in the last decade also resulted in a second edition of the "E-learning in the 21st Century: A Framework for Research and Practice." This book is largely an introductory text and was only able to give an overview of recent CoI research and theoretical implications. As such, there was still a need for a book to collect recent research and provide in-depth theoretical interpretations and developments arising from a range of different contexts. The editors of this book, xviii

Educational Communities of Inquiry: Theoretical Framework, Research and Practice, aim to meet this need by providing an important contribution to the literature on e-learning and representing the first extensive reference book of recent research and practice associated with the CoI theoretical framework.

The target audiences of this book are both researchers and practitioners. Graduate and undergraduate students in the field of educational technology as well as adult and distance educators who are interested in learning about and using the CoI theoretical framework will benefit highly from this book. Researchers in most fields who wish to conduct studies investigating aspects of teaching and learning in online or blended environments will benefit from the insights in this book. In particular, those who wish to further explore and contribute to the CoI theoretical framework will find this book invaluable. The editors hope that this book will also allow researchers to lead them to explore new areas of research. It will also provide practitioners direction in terms of designing and delivering online and blended learning experiences. Faculty who are willing to teach courses using the CoI framework will welcome this extensive resource of research and practice. Finally, practitioners and policy makers (i.e., instructional designers, teachers, professors from K-12 to higher education to corporate institutions) who are interested in applying the principles of the CoI theoretical framework to plan, design, deliver, and evaluate courses or training programs in online or blended learning environments will be attracted to this unique resource.

THE STRUCTURE OF THIS BOOK

The first section provides an extensive exploration of the theoretical foundations of the CoI framework.

The goal of the first chapter is to strengthen and clarify its philosophical and theoretical assumptions and principles. Through an analysis of community and inquiry the unity of shared discourse and personal reflection are explored. The work of John Dewey is central to the epistemological foundation of the CoI framework although the connection and contribution of other educational and learning theorists are identified. The connection and place for concepts such as metacognition, self-regulation, and motivation are also briefly explored.

The philosophical roots of the CoI framework are more deeply explored in the second chapter. This chapter provides a philosophical analysis of communities of inquiry that makes an important connection to previously unexplored fields of study relevant to pedagogy in online learning environments. The chapter looks at important concepts such as the "ideal speech situation" and the role of the facilitator that is crucial to a deep and meaningful community of inquiry. These issues are then explored more deeply in the opportunity for "hybrid discourse" that mixes the literate (text), oral (verbal speech), and visual means of communication. The complexity and dynamic interplay of the constituting elements of systems like communities of inquiry are also analyzed.

The crucial place of metacognitive awareness in a community of inquiry is identified and addressed in depth in the next chapter. Chapter three is an example of an important theoretical exploration associated with the development of the CoI framework. It discusses the value and role of metacognition in a community of inquiry by mapping the origin of the concept and contextualizing it within a collaborative learning environment. Specifically, it defines the construct in terms of knowledge, monitoring, and regulation of cognition and explores its place in the CoI framework. Finally, the practical support of metacognition and how it can be developed is described.

The fourth chapter provides an interesting and valuable historical perspective of communities of inquiry from the perspective of distance education. This is important, as the authors note, because online distance education has become an important strategy for higher education. Moreover, research suggests that online communities create a sense of belonging which leads to satisfaction and persistence. The evolution of distance education and its associated technologies from independent study to collaborative approaches is described. Interaction and the online learning community are explored before describing the Community of Inquiry framework.

The second section of the book is devoted to design and implementation issues of the CoI framework.

The first chapter in this section, chapter five, focuses on the central role of teaching presence for the success of online courses. The chapter begins with a review of the CoI research associated with teaching presence in the context of the other presences. The top two indicators that students perceive to be important are making requirements clear and being responsive. These findings and future research directions are discussed.

Chapter six provides an innovative CoI perspective on blending synchronous and asynchronous online learning. Issues associated with asynchronous online learning are discussed and a blended online learning design approach is explored to mitigate some of the challenges. Like the previous chapter, attention is drawn to the importance of teaching presence. Perceived differences between faculty and students were identified, and design and delivery solutions explored. A summary of effective teaching presence practices is provided.

The relationship between teaching presence and cognitive presence is explored in chapter seven. In particular, the chapter reports on a study that looked at the balance of teaching presence essential to students moving to the integration and resolution phases of cognitive presence in a problem based learning design. Using a rigorous mixed method quasi-experimental research design, the CoI framework was extended to study two levels of explicit scaffolding and its effect on the quantity and quality of cognitive presence. Then came the somewhat surprising finding that too much explicit scaffolding (a form of teaching presence) led to reduced cognitive presence. The temporal development of a CoI was also discussed.

Chapter eight also focuses on the relationship between teaching presence and cognitive presence. Specifically, it looks at ways to promote discussion skills in a blended learning course design using the CoI framework. Based on a review of the concept of coaching, the chapter explores how two types of coaching can improve online discussion and cognitive presence. Indicators of teaching presence were seen to be useful in implementing functionalist coaching and practical suggestions for coaching using the teaching presence categories are provided.

Chapter nine provides a practical discussion of how to nurture cognitive presence and foster critical thinking. The chapter begins with a thorough discussion of each of the four phases of cognitive presence and its development. Strategies and question prompts are provided for the phases of cognitive presence (i.e., Practical Inquiry model). A valuable guideline for identifying and eliciting cognitive presence based on the practical inquiry descriptors and indicators is provided.

Cognitive presence is also the focus of chapter ten. Using the CoI framework, this study explores how teaching and social presence contributes to the development of cognitive presence. The chapter provides an extensive review of critical thinking, cognitive presence, collaborative learning, and technologies that support collaborative learning. The rest of the chapter provides evidenced based strategies to promote cognitive presence in online discussion forums.

Chapter eleven explores question prompts and levels of critical thinking that operationalizes cognitive presence in the CoI theoretical framework. The chapter discusses the importance of question prompts for higher critical thinking and notes that only a small number of studies have explored the role of initial question prompts. Nine types of question prompts were rigorously studied and analyzed. The relationship between type of response and phase of inquiry as well as those that promote the highest levels of critical thinking are identified and recommendations discussed.

In chapter twelve, the CoI framework is used to operationalize the instructional design process and to study blended and online approaches using cooperative and collaborative strategies for group projects. A discussion of the distinction between cooperative and collaborative learning is provided along with a description of the elaborate research design. Differences were found on group project grades (but not individual grades) that used a collaborative compared to a cooperative group strategy with a blended approach. An interesting and insightful discussion of the four treatment effects and each of the CoI presences is provided.

Chapter thirteen explores the development of social, teaching, and cognitive presence in a blended foreign language course. The analysis of asynchronous discussions indicated that students were able to create an environment that encouraged reflection and meaningful interactions in online discussions. However, the study yields different types of social interactions in the blended learning environment than those previously found in exclusively online discussions with a lower presence of cohesive and affective indicators. The discussion of the findings and implications for foreign language blended courses are provided.

Chapter fourteen also focuses on the application of the CoI framework in a foreign language (EFL) context. The study explored the relationships among EFL students' participation level, satisfaction with online discussions, perceived contributions to the discussion groups, English proficiency, and interactions during the discussions in an community of inquiry context. Overall, the results suggest a positive impact the CoI elements developed in the EFL context on students' participation and satisfaction level. The authors provide suggestions for the application of the CoI framework to design computer-supported collaborative EFL learning environments.

An invaluable review of research on the CoI framework and student retention as well as a discussion of the CoI framework in relation to the existing retention theories are provided in chapter fifteen. A theoretical link between the CoI framework and retention is proposed through the intermediary of student learning. Emphasizing the overall difficulty of overcoming the influences of external factors on retention, Meyer argues that the principles of "academic integration" and "utility" can be maximized by using the CoI to design courses that require active student learning, consistent and challenging involvement with the content, and efforts to connect what is learned with the student's current and future professional or practical needs.

The last chapter of the second section, chapter sixteen, focuses on a substantial issue – assessment. The chapter introduces a triad approach to assessment – integration of self-reflection, peer feedback, and teacher assessment practices. Through a research study, the chapter demonstrates how the CoI, combined with the use of collaborative digital technologies such as blogs, wikis, and other social networking applications in higher education, can provide an opportunity to reinforce the principles of good assessment feedback.

The third section includes chapters about administrative issues and organizational support.

The first chapter of the third section, chapter seventeen, describes an institutional pedagogical counseling program-assessment and systematizing initiative through the adaption of the CoI framework. An inquiry through pedagogical-counseling experience-exchange process was set up to analyze, assess, and potentiate ongoing support activities by the staff members of the Center for Research and Development in Education (CIFE) in counseling projects of undergraduate and postgraduate programs. The CoI framework adapted to conceptualize CIFE staff's review, and it was found that the CoI framework was crucial to framing the pedagogical counseling experiences and shaping the role of the various players within the overall exercise; in addition, it provided a route map for the future of the pedagogical counseling program.

Chapter eighteen explores how the CoI framework can be used to design and deliver a ten week Hybrid Course Development Institute (HCDI) for faculty members from a variety of disciplines. The faculty experienced a blended format and developed courses based on the three elements of the CoI framework: cognitive presence, teaching presence, and social presence. The data from both faculty and the students in blended learning courses developed indicate the challenge of developing a well-balanced social presence. The authors argue that faculty members come to cognitive presence and teaching presence a bit more naturally, but social presence demands careful and sustained consideration when designing blended courses and curricula. The suggestions for ways to foster social presence in and beyond a blended learning institute for faculty members are provided.

In chapter nineteen, the focus is on teaching presence from an institutional perspective. The chapter discusses the impact of philosophical and pragmatic changes on teaching practice and the role of teacher. The author suggests a principled approach to teaching for faculty to stay on track of teaching requirements, regardless of delivery mode. The principles are to support new teaching practices but, if adopted, will also change the way the role of faculty is configured and executed in the higher education context.

Last chapter of the third section, chapter twenty, presents the results of research concerning the ramifications of teaching requirements as university education shifts into the digital era from the perspective of teaching center managers and IT specialists. Using the CoI framework as a theoretical lens, it was found that even though all three elements of inquiry were found important by participants, the categories of social presence such as group cohesion were indicated as more crucial and should be given more weight toward the pedagogical requirements for online/blended teaching and learning. The authors suggests that group cohesion could be facilitated and reinforced by appropriate role models played by all participants in any online intellectual activity, especially teaching and learning in a university context.

The last section of the book presents chapters that discuss emerging research and practice issues.

Chapter twenty-one provides a creative and innovative look at an analogous area of knowledge workers. The chapter draws parallels to each of the CoI presences in terms of knowledge workers and communities of practice. The author begins by emphasizing the hidden wholeness of a CoI and argues that this is not that different from what a knowledge worker might experience in the workplace. A major part of the chapter explores the tenets of knowledge management and its impact on academic institutions. The point being that we can generalize the CoI framework to the world of work and use its presences to help define processes inherent in knowledge work. The author notes that learning management systems that we have become so familiar with has the potential to provide educators with a practical appreciation of knowledge management systems. The chapter concludes with a call for more research that explores the utility and connections of the CoI framework in a variety of contexts and cultural settings.

Chapter twenty-two provides an interesting discussion on emerging technologies and how these technologies may influence the CoI framework. The authors introduce the innovations in digital publishing, multi-screen and applications, multiuser virtual environments, adaptive learning environments and analytics, and explore their potential impacts on the CoI framework to evolve and account for new types of learner and instructor interactions. The importance of sound pedagogical principals of the CoI framework in order to adapt the emerging interaction styles as a result of these affordances is emphasized.

The CoI framework in a multicultural environment is explored in chapter twenty-three. The chapter reports a two phased study. Phase one comprised creating intercultural competency indicators to test how they developed and expanded existing teaching and social presence indicators; and phase two involved augmenting the 34 item CoI survey instrument. The results reveal that instructor intercultural competence in the form of efficacious facilitation and open communication strategies can compensate for the lack of an instructional design that is culturally oriented and inclusive. A revised version of the CoI survey for online intercultural teaching and learning environment is also provided in the chapter.

The last two chapters of the final section introduce design-based research methodology for CoI research. Chapter twenty-four demonstrates an ongoing design-based research being conducted in the fully online Master of Arts in Teacher Leadership program. After an initial Quality Matters review and redesign, semester-to-semester implementation issues identified by the CoI survey form the basis for ongoing course improvements. The chapter reports the efficacy of using this design-based, collaborative approach to building communities of inquiry in online courses in which learning outcomes significantly improved. It is indicated that the design based research perspective provides methodological flexibility while focusing on both theoretical and pragmatic course improvement goals.

The final chapter provides a combination of an emerging research method and context. The chapter describes the conceptualization and implementation of an international cyber-learning environment as a community of inquiry through application of design based research methodology. The research presented in the chapter involves the development of the cyber-learning environment to foster engagement among faculty, staff, and students of 13 medical schools from Sub-Saharan Africa and their 50-plus partners around the world. The chapter addresses key environmental constraints and how these constraints guided operational decisions during implementation and discusses challenges and solutions as well as lessons learned.

CONCLUSION

Educational Communities of Inquiry: Theoretical Framework, Research, and Practice offers readers a valuable resource by providing a comprehensive overview of trends and issues related to the research and practice of the CoI theoretical framework. The first section of the book explains the philosophical insights and theoretical underpinnings of the CoI framework and clarifies some of the issues with regard to its role on learning and place in e-learning world. The second section of the book informs both researchers and practitioners about the strategies and tools to develop an effective community of inquiry which in turn impact learning and retention. The third section represents the innovative uses of the CoI framework to approach administrative issues and to support organizational development. The final section gives the readers an opportunity to envision the future issues and trends of the CoI research and practice.

The editors believe, with the diverse and comprehensive coverage of educational communities of inquiry, this book will contribute to a better understanding of the concepts, research, and practice of the CoI framework. All the contributing chapters in this book are instrumental in expanding the body of knowledge in the e-learning field generally as well as the CoI framework specifically. They hope that this publication will be a good reference resource for all stakeholders who seek better ways to teach and learn in an e-learning environment through the development of effective communities of inquiry.

Zehra Akyol
Independent Researcher, Canada

D. Randy Garrison
University of Calgary, Canada

Section I
Theoretical Foundations and Epistemological Insights

Chapter 1
Theoretical Foundations and Epistemological Insights of the Community of Inquiry

D. Randy Garrison
University of Calgary, Canada

ABSTRACT

This chapter discusses the epistemological assumptions and theoretical foundations of the Community of Inquiry (CoI) framework. Specifically, it addresses the central concepts of community, collaboration, constructivism, inquiry, discourse, metacognition, co-regulation, and motivation. The primary goal is to reinforce the CoI's theoretical coherence and enhance its practical utility in providing direction to the study and practice of e-learning in a range of education contexts.

INTRODUCTION

Theoretical credibility of the Community of Inquiry (CoI) framework is essential if it is to continue to grow in use and provide direction for the research and practice of online and blended learning. The theoretical foundation for the CoI framework is an explication of its fundamental assumptions, concepts and values with regard to a worthwhile educational experience. An educational experience must be directed to purposeful learning that develops personal meaning while confirming shared understanding and public knowledge. The theoretical foundation of the CoI framework is generic to the ideals of a higher educational experience.

A recent critical analysis of the CoI theoretical framework offered valuable guidance for strengthening its philosophical and theoretical underpinnings and provided guidance to the discussion in this chapter (Jezegou, 2010). To begin, Jezegou (2010) noted that the CoI framework is the most advanced e-learning model to date, but "the authors do not really develop the theoretical foundations of their model" (Introduction, 2nd paragraph) that would "give it wider theoretical scope" (Conclusion, last paragraph). More specifically, Jezegou identifies a need to elaborate on the epistemological bases, particularly concepts such as community, collaboration and constructivism as well as related concepts such as metacognition, self-regulation and motivation.

DOI: 10.4018/978-1-4666-2110-7.ch001

Before addressing these constructive suggestions, it should be noted that much of this critique was based on the book, *E-learning in the 21ˢᵗ Century*, which was published in 2003. This was the first attempt to summarize the four original studies. While Jezegou (2010) has provided a valuable service to strengthening the theoretical foundations of the CoI framework, it should be noted that much research has been published since 2003 that has addressed many of the theoretical concerns voiced by Jezegou, especially with regard to understanding the conceptualization of the elements (see for example, Swan, Garrison, & Richardson, 2009). Moreover, a comprehensive update on CoI research has been published in the second edition of *E-learning in the 21ˢᵗ Century* (2011). Another work of seminal conceptual importance on metacognition and self-regulation has been published recently (Akyol & Garrison, 2011) and expanded upon in this volume (see chapter three). That is not to say that more work is not required. Explicating and validating such a comprehensive framework is an ongoing challenge. This chapter is a contribution to clarifying and updating the theoretical foundation of the CoI framework.

UNITY OF DISCOURSE AND REFLECTION

We begin our discussion here with an exploration of the epistemology of a community of inquiry. That is, in its simplest terms, an exploration of what constitutes knowledge and how is it justified in a collaborative constructivist community of inquiry. We focus on each of the constituent components before exploring the inseparability of the individual and group in achieving a community of inquiry worthy of a higher order learning experience.

Community and Collaboration

Learning in an educational context is a social enterprise. The social nature of an educational experience draws attention to a specific kind of learning that is inherently community based and collaborative. The first challenge is to describe what we mean by community and what the nature of collaboration is in a formal educational community of inquiry.

Community is defined by context and purpose. The essential elements of community are described by Rovai (2002) as having "mutual interdependence among members, connectedness, interactivity, overlapping histories among members, spirit, trust, common expectations, and shared values and beliefs" (p. 42). While these elements do apply to an educational community, there are other characteristics that need to be explored. The first obvious characteristic is a focus on learning but not just any kind of learning. In an educational community the academic goals are greatly influenced by societal knowledge and expectations. This introduces a purposeful and formal focus to learning. The values and beliefs of the discipline must be respected but there must also be pedagogic leadership that creates a sense of belonging and personally meaningful academic collaboration. Learning in an educational sense is socially worthwhile but must be personally meaningful. Also, unlike individual knowledge processes, an inquiry process (discussed subsequently) requires a common interest if it is to be of concern to all members (Petrie, 1981). This sets up an interesting dynamic that is central to the concept of a community of inquiry.

Collaboration reflects the reality of mutual interdependence and raises issues of common purpose, trust and identification with the community. (We use the collaboration construct in contrast to cooperation as it implies joint activity and shared meaning; not individually contributing components to a task.) Ideally, collaboration in an educational context is founded on communication free of coercion and intimidation while valuing rational argument and discourse. In this regard, problems of understanding need to be raised in open, critical discourse that has the potential for mutual agreement (Habermas in Garrison & Archer, 2000). Collaboration in an educational community has both a social and academic focus; community where open communication is to be nurtured through both cohesive social communication and purposeful academic communication. Educational communities are distinguished by its formal leadership; that is, the academic and social development of the community must be monitored and managed. As we have noted in the previous chapter and will explore subsequently, in the best sense leadership and regulation of learning is a shared responsibility and should be a collaborative process engaged by all members of the educational community. Individual learning cannot be viewed in isolation. Collaborative activity and community building have important influences on each other. Collaboration supports the creation and development of community and community supports the ability to be collaborative (Palloff & Pratt, 2005).

Next we explore collaboration from the inside out; that is, individual cognition and knowledge building processes._

Constructivism and Reflection

As with other foundational topics in this chapter, it is not possible to provide an exhaustive review and discussion of constructivism. One reason is that there is "no single constructivist theory" (Johansson & Gardenfors, 2005, p. 15); constructivism has multiple roots. The essence of constructivism is that the individual is responsible for making sense (creating meaning) of new experiences by building on and integrating previous knowledge and experiences. Perhaps more revealing from our perspective is that the "the general goals of constructivism are for the learner to develop prob-

lem solving and reasoning skills, critical thinking, and self-regulated learning; that is, the ability to engage in independent thought" (Johansson & Gardenfors, 2005, p. 15). As we shall see shortly this is congruent with the concept of inquiry.

At the core of constructivist theory is the work of Piaget. Piaget (1977) began by focusing on the individual but came to recognize the importance of social interaction to recognize and resolve cognitive conflicts. Another important branch of constructivism that is of particular significance here is social constructivism found in the work of Vygotsky (1978). The rich and useful theoretical knowledge base of Vygotsky supports and informs the CoI framework. Consistent with the work of Dewey, thought and social experience can only be separated in the abstract. The key in this view is that learning experiences be carefully designed and socially supported such that learners develop intellectually in a continuous manner. This raises the important role of teaching presence in an educational context – a role and responsibility that must be assumed by all participants in an educational CoI.

Vygotsky laid the foundation for a social constructivist approach to education (Wells, 2000). Consistent with Dewey, the extension of Vygotsky's view is "the notion of learning as a process of inquiry" and the central role of collaborative inquiry in education (Lee & Smagorinsky, 2000, p. 6). Moreover, core to the CoI framework, "In a community of learners, all participants – including those designated as teachers – engage in inquiry (Lee & Smagorinsky, 2000, p. 8). Vygotskian theory applied to education calls for "reconstituting classrooms and schools as communities of inquiry" (Wells, 2000, p. 61). The collaborative and shared processes of a community of inquiry creates Vygotsky's notion of a "zone of proximal development" socially and cognitively through the participation of the members of the community that provides teaching presence in the form of "mediator, negotiator, instigator, or recapitulator" (Kennedy & Kennedy, 2010, p. 11).

Social constructivism incorporates the contextual influences that are a catalyst for learning. The great epistemological advantage of social constructivism is that meaning is precipitated and confirmed through discourse and negotiation. In this regard, there is an expectation (consistent with learning in an educational context) that learning is a process embedded in critical discourse that provides an inherent opportunity to challenge and test understanding (understanding is achieved through shared meaning, negotiation and agreement; with broader agreement collective knowledge is realized). The quality of knowledge construction (meaning and understanding) is dependent on the communication possibilities of the community. This explains why the multiple modes of communication in blended learning designs offer outcome advantages over face-to-face and online alone (Means, Toyama, Murphy, Bakia, & Jones, 2009).

Vygotsky saw the individual and society as mutually interdependent – "both individuals and society are mutually produced and reproduced" (Wells, 2000, p.55). This raises another central construct of Vygotsky which is the role of language and discourse as a means of "sharing meaning making" (Wells, 2000, p.57) and collaboratively constructing knowledge. Discourse in the context of inquiry plays an essential role in constructing meaning and negotiating common understanding. As Petrie (1981) states, the students' internal point of view must be considered if the student is to be brought to the collective understanding of any subject. Thus, constructing knowledge is situated in discourse by way of advancing personal meaning and adding to shared understanding. Learning in an educational context is necessarily collaborative and mediated through discourse (verbal and written) in the context of inquiry.

Consistent with the idea of the inseparability of personal and social experiences, Dewey (1938) argued that through interaction (a key principle of Dewey) these two worlds are unified. It is through interaction where meaning is constructed,

shared and knowledge confirmed. More recently, Stahl (2010) has explored this issue from the perspective of what he calls the science of group interaction and cognition. The idea is to explore "how groups interactionally build knowledge" (p. 25). The theory of group cognition is predicated on the principle that the individual and group are not reducible to the other. Inquiry and problem solving through discourse and co-construction of knowledge has great promise for studying the processes of group learning, co-regulation and metacognition. Certainly the personal and public worlds inherent in the Practical Inquiry model and the collaborative characteristics of the CoI framework have considerable potential for exploring cognition at the group level.

Through this collaborative process of group cognition the idea of societal knowledge arises. Societal knowledge is a social artifact that is an outcome of group cognition and knowledge validation. Group cognition makes possible knowledge building where participants collaboratively construct and extend collective knowledge (Scardemalia & Berieter, 2010). This has been referred to as constructionism, although this is the natural result of a collaborative constructivist approach that resolves the false separation of personal meaning and collective knowledge (shared understanding). In an educational context, both personal meaning and shared understanding (collective knowledge) are artifacts of collaborative inquiry. These issues are explored further in the next chapter.

A community of inquiry is an environment where participants collaboratively construct knowledge through sustained dialogue which makes possible personal meaning making through opportunities to negotiate understanding (cognitive presence). Leadership is essential to precipitate and purposely focus collaborative inquiry (teaching presence) if educational goals are to be achieved. The emotional and interpersonal dimension (social presence) provides the environment where learning can productively be created and sustained. The focus in a CoI is on the individual constructing meaning and collaboratively confirming understanding through critical thinking and discourse. The higher goals are to realize mutual understanding and contribute to societal knowledge in the longer term. Students in an educational context begin by engaging with established social knowledge (disciplinary content) through the interaction with others. This epistemic engagement or interaction with the content, and concurrently with others, enhances the quality of the learning process through critical discourse and negotiation.

Learning communities provide the organization for intellectual challenge and managing cognitive complexity. The integration of the CoI elements (areas of overlap) provides the environment for individuals to go beyond themselves in terms of the depth and breadth of their understanding. Learning communities become self-amplifying through this purposeful and collaborative learning experience. Individuals in such communities are able to grow beyond what is possible in isolation through collaboration and reconstruction. This growth is made possible in large part due to sustained communication and that is enhanced in online and blended learning contexts through combinations of verbal, textual and visual communication (blended discourse). Further discussion of these ideas can be found in the next chapter.

Inquiry

According to Petrie (1981), inquiry is a process leading to the growth of human (collective) knowledge. From this point of view, inquiry inherently focuses on the precepts of community and collaboration. Our interest here is with a constructivist philosophy applicable to an educational context where collaborative communities of learners are purposely engaged. Notwithstanding the close alignment of the CoI framework with social con-

structivism, we prefer to use the term collaborative constructivism that better reflects the collaborative nature of an educational experience. This aligns with the philosophy of Dewey who was clear that constructing personal meaning is a transactional and collaborative effort. Dewey believed that education is the interplay between personal interests and social knowledge (Garrison, 2011). However, Dewey went further by making inquiry central to philosophy and educational practice.

For Dewey, inquiry is the generalization of the scientific process and is consistent with his progressive understanding of education. It is the link between curiosity and deep learning. Inquiry is a process of problem solving based on the scientific method. Inquiry brings unity to thought and action (i.e., reflection on experience). The pursuit of inquiry is dependent upon the development of community. That is, inquiry is socially situated which creates the conditions for the development and sustainability of the community of inquiry approach.

Dewey's (1933) concept of reflective thinking is very much embedded in the inquiry process. As Lipman (2003) states, "the reflective paradigm assumes education to be inquiry" (p. 19). Dewey's goal was to upgrade reflection in the educational environment. He did this by fusing the concepts of community and inquiry. As Lipman (2003) states that, "Dewey had no doubt that what should be happening in the classroom is thinking" (p. 20). He goes on to make the point that, according to Dewey, the great mistake was to confuse the process with the end result of inquiry – "to learn the solutions rather than investigate the problems and engage in inquiry for themselves" (Lipman, 2003, p. 20). It is critically important to appreciate that the CoI theoretical framework is a process model consistent with Dewey's belief in scientific inquiry and the reflective process. The focus on predetermined outcomes does little to engender curiosity, exploration or motivation. Notwithstanding the need not to constrain exploration, there must be purpose and discipline. This balance is, in fact, realized through the collaborative and respectful nature of the CoI.

Lipman (2003) proposed a community of inquiry model that would create the conditions for reflective thinking. Parenthetically, Lipman noted that the phrase community of inquiry was originally coined by C. S. Peirce. In an educational context, communities of inquiry involve questioning, a personal quest for meaning, and a collaborative quest for truth. Some of the features of a community of inquiry are inclusiveness, participation, deliberation/discussion, challenging/questioning, sharing cognition, and modeling (Lipman, 2003). Modeling in an educational community of inquiry is of crucial importance as it introduces the teaching presence construct (leadership and expertise) as an essential shared function (co-inquirer) and something to be nurtured. Teaching presence is not simply an authority figure, although there is likely to be one or more persons with pedagogical and disciplinary expertise that will be expected to provide purposeful leadership at recurring intervals.

Students do not easily and successfully engage in educational inquiry. First, there should be a common interest where the subject is of concern to everyone. As Dewey indicated, there must be the desire – the will to progress through inquiry phases, and forms and techniques to sustain motivation. This reflects the need for social presence to create a shared identity and setting a respectful and trusting climate. However, discourse is a disciplined (reflective and reasoned) form of dialogue or discussion. It is a collaborative process for clarifying and resolving cognitive conflict such as ambiguities and contradictions. Discourse must also be both inclusive and critical (Burbules, 1993) provided through cognitive presence (skeptical, challenging). Setting the emotional climate may well be much less onerous than creating cognitive presence and disciplined inquiry.

Initial resistance to disciplined inquiry is reinforced from a basic human perspective.

Kahneman (2011) argues that individuals tend to rely on fast intuitive thinking based more on feelings (emotion) and previous experience or associations (i.e., automatic, unconscious thought). Unfortunately, however, this is not very reliable. The second type of thinking is rational, slow and effortful. This form of critical thinking produces better decisions/solutions but is much less common as it takes time and effort. We argue here that this is and should be the domain of educational experience and can be facilitated using methods of communication that facilitate reflection. While there is certainly a place for fast-paced spontaneous verbal communication (e.g., to create and sustain interest), we need to explore and understand the benefits of slow written communication (e.g., online discussion forums) for developing critical thinking and deep insights. Education should be an environment to slow down, inquire and reflect upon problems. However, considering that slow rational thinking (i.e., deliberate inquiry) is not the common response for most of us, communities of inquiry can provide the environment and teaching presence to lead, support and model rational higher order learning.

The following quote gives a very good sense of the function of teaching presence in a community of inquiry focused on deliberate and rational inquiry.

...the facilitator triggers the system through raising counterexamples and counter-claims, emphasizing certain elements of the argument, introducing new perspectives or questions when the inquiry seems to have lost direction, or making procedural suggestions – for example moving to a different question that is directly or indirectly related to the concept or problem under inquiry (Kennedy & Kennedy, 2010, p. 10).

In short, a community of inquiry in an educational context is a collaborative process of critical reflection and discourse that is benefited by the teaching presence (facilitation and direction) of an experienced educator and that encourages metacognitive attention to cognitive development (see also chapter two). It is through metacognition and co-regulation that we see the fusion of teaching presence and cognitive presence supported in an environment defined by social presence.

METACOGNITION AND MOTIVATION

Constructivist learning theory necessitates metacognitive awareness in the process of reflective inquiry. Reflective inquiry invites a consideration of how we know, how we learn, and requires being conscious of ourselves as knowers (Lyons, 2010). As Lipman (2003) states, the reflective thinking of inquiry "involves thinking about its procedures at the same time as it involves thinking about its subject matter" (p. 26). Inquiry must be self-corrective thinking and incorporate self-corrective strategies. It is difficult to imagine inquiry (i.e., higher order reflective thinking) without metacognitive knowledge and awareness. This includes not only knowledge of cognition and internal knowledge construction but also monitoring and regulating the inquiry process. Metacognition is intimately connected to engaging consciously in inquiry and making investigations into the problem at hand (Lyons, 2010). Most significantly here, collaboration and discourse play an essential role in metacognitive awareness.

Johansson and Gardenfors (2005) state that in "constructivism, metacognitive awareness also entails a sensitivity to the fact that one's own point of view ... needs to be examined and compared to other perspectives" (p. 16). Collaborative constructivism attempts to make sense of an experience, dilemma or problem in the context of sharing ideas and testing understanding in a community of inquiry. Flavell (1987) states that metacognition is congruent with needing "to communicate, explain, and justify" one's thinking and "these activities clearly require metacognition" (p. 27). Others also believe that metacognition is fa-

cilitated through discourse and collaborative tasks (Brown, 1987; Larkin, 2009). As such, the CoI provides a framework with the potential to study metacognition in a collaborative constructivist educational environment. It provides a coherent context to study the individual and social elements of the construction of personal meaning and co-construction of public knowledge.

With the goal to explore the role of metacognition in a community of inquiry, Akyol and Garrison (2011) proposed and tested a metacognitive construct described in terms of three interdependent dimensions – knowledge, monitoring and regulation of cognition (see Chapter Three). This construct is consistent with much of the literature on metacognition. Knowledge of cognition is an entering metacognitive state that reflects knowledge and motivation associated with the inquiry process. Monitoring of cognition is a form of reflection on action and is associated with assessing the learning process. This includes assessing progression and effort with regard to goals and expectations. Regulation of cognition (reflection in action) "is the enactment and control of the learning process through the employment of strategies to achieve meaningful learning outcomes" (Akyol & Garrison, 2011, p. 184). Each of these dimensions of metacognition has a personal and shared element that constitutes a community of inquiry.

Individual and collaborative perspectives reflect the core dynamic of the Practical Inquiry model and cognitive presence as conceptualized in the CoI framework. It is the process of inquiry that describes the iterative and interdependent nature of the relationship between the individual and social dynamics. From a metacognitive perspective, this includes self-knowledge and public knowledge, self-monitoring and shared monitoring, and self-regulation and co-regulation. It is through discourse (critique, negotiation) within a community of inquiry that personal knowledge, monitoring and regulation are developed over time. In the context of a community of inquiry, individuals are provided the opportunity to assume appropriate degrees of responsibility to monitor and regulate learning while receiving the support and direction of the community. Knowledge, monitoring and regulating of cognition are personal responsibilities that are concurrently distributed within the group. This goes to the heart of a collaborative-constructivist community of inquiry.

Volet, Vauras and Salonen (2009) draw attention to the need to provide an integrative perspective to self and social regulation of learning. While considerable work has been done on self-regulation, they state that:

The identification of social regulation models is not easy because the field is still emerging, messy, and in constant flux. Most models tend to be underdeveloped with limited empirical validation... (p. 218).

We would argue, however, that the metacognition construct in the context of the CoI framework does provide the means to rigorously test models that refuse to dichotomize the individual and social perspectives and, consistent with Dewey, simply see these as two sides of the same coin (different perspectives of the inquiry process). There is also considerable empirical validation of the CoI (Garrison, 2011) that provides a rich environment to study constructs and models such as metacognition and motivation. Moreover, Volet et al. (2009) suggest that special research attention needs to be given to "virtual collaborative learning environments [and] … little is known about the extent to which metacognitive regulation is facilitated, maintained, or alternatively inhibited in such contexts" (p. 223). Again, with its considerable use and validation in online and blended learning contexts, the CoI framework is well positioned for this task.

Metacognition is a complex mix of cognitive and teaching presence elements but is also mediated by social presence and associated motivational influences. Metacognition involves both cognitively and motivationally active participants.

While space does not permit a full exploration of the motivational construct, motivation to engage and persist in a learning experience is a precondition for metacognitive responsibilities. Motivation "reflects perceived value and anticipated success of learning goals at the time learning is initiated" and influences metacognitive effort (Garrison & Archer, 2000, p. 100). Motivation influences engagement in metacognition but motivation is also a consequence of successful metacognition. As Borkowski, Chan, & Muthukrishna (2000) state, an "enjoyment of learning flow[s] from individual strategic events and eventually return to energize strategy selection and monitoring decisions" (p. 8). With regard to the CoI theoretical framework, motivation may be best considered as a learner entering and outcome trait. During the learning process, motivation is manifested as effort (volition) that has a direct impact on the quality of discourse/reflection. Motivational effort is positively enhanced by all three presences consistent with the collaborative experience of a community of inquiry.

CONCLUSION

It is not possible here to do justice to the many theoretical perspectives that have influenced and informed the CoI's theoretical framework. We have attempted to identify and address the central concepts that inform the theoretical foundation and epistemological assumptions of this framework. The core philosophical construct is constructivism as contextualized in a collaborative community of inquiry. Considerable attention was devoted to the relationship between collaborative constructivism and inquiry. Discussion of theoretical issues also necessitated addressing the structural validity of the CoI framework and its constituting elements. More recent conceptual developments such as metacognition and motivation and the nature of their integration in the CoI framework were explored briefly.

In support of the strength and validity of the CoI theoretical framework, it is worth noting that after Jezegou's (2010) rigorous analysis of the framework, she concluded that this critical review "has eliminated our doubts about the model's conceptual solidity and its relevance…that is heuristically stimulating for research on learning" (Conclusion, 2nd paragraph). We hope that the contributions of this chapter will reinforce its theoretical validity and contribute to its practical utility in providing conceptual order and direction to research in e-learning and other higher education contexts. Moreover, we hope this will add to the growing interest and confidence in the CoI as a theoretical framework. We end this discussion with a quote that addresses the potential of communities of inquiry not only for e-learning but all of education.

...the practice of CI [communities of inquiry] represents a pedagogical innovation with implications for whole-system change that may be belied by its apparent methodological simplicity (Kennedy & Kennedy, 2010, p. 13).

It is this great potential and simplicity (i.e., parsimony) that we should strive to maintain as we continue to understand and apply the Community of Inquiry theoretical framework explored in this book.

REFERENCES

Akyol, Z., & Garrison, D. R. (2011). Assessing metacognition in an online community of inquiry. *The Internet and Higher Education, 14*(3), 183–190.

Borkowski, J. G., Chan, L. K. S., & Muthukrishna, N. (2000). A process–oriented model of metacognition: Links between motivation and executive functioning. In Schraw, G., & Impara, J. C. (Eds.), *Issues in the measurement of metacognition.* Lincoln, NE: University of Nebraska-Lincoln.

Brown, A. (1987). Metacognition, executive control, self-regulation and other more mysterious mechanisms. In Weinert, F. E., & Kluwer, R. H. (Eds.), *Metacognition, motivation, and understanding* (pp. 65–116). Hillsdale, NJ: Lawrence Erlbaum Associates.

Burbules, N. (1993). *Dialogue in teaching: Theory and practice.* New York, NY: Teachers College Press.

Dewey, J. (1933). *How we think* (rev. ed.). Boston, MA: D.C. Heath.

Dewey, J. (1938). *Experience and education.* New York, NY: Collier Macmillan.

Flavell, J. H. (1987). Speculations about the nature and development of metacognition. In Weinert, F., & Kluwe, R. (Eds.), *Metacognition, motivation and understanding* (pp. 21–29). Hillsdale, NJ: Erlbaum.

Garrison, D. R. (2011). *E-learning in the 21st century: A framework for research and practice* (2nd ed.). London, UK: Routledge/Taylor and Francis.

Garrison, D. R., & Archer, W. (2000). *A transactional perspective on teaching-learning: A framework for adult and higher education.* Oxford, UK: Pergamon.

Jezegou, A. (2010). Community of inquiry in e-learning: Concerning the Garrison and Anderson model. *Journal of Distance Education, 24*(3).

Johansson, P., & Gardenfors, P. (2005). *Cognition, education, and communication technology.* Mahwah, NJ: Lawrence Erlbaum Associates.

Kahneman, K. (2011). *Thinking, fast and slow*. New York, NY: Farrar, Straus and Giroux.

Kennedy, N. S., & Kennedy, D. (2010). Between chaos and entropy: Community of inquiry from a systems perspective. *Complicity: An International Journal of Complexity and Education, 2*, 1–15.

Larkin, S. (2009). Socially mediated metacognition and learning to write. *Thinking Skills and Creativity, 4*(3), 149–159.

Lee, C. D., & Smagorinsky, P. (2000). Introduction: Constructing meaning through collaborative inquiry. In Lee, C. D., & Smagorinsky, P. (Eds.), *Vygotskian perspectives on literacy research: Constructing meaning through collaborative inquiry* (pp. 1–15). New York, NY: Cambridge University Press.

Lipman, M. (2003). *Thinking in education* (2nd ed.). Cambridge, UK: Cambridge University Press.

Lyons, N. (2010). Reflective inquiry: Foundational issues – A deepening of conscious life. In Lyons, N. (Ed.), *Handbook of reflection and reflective inquiry*. US: Springer.

Means, B., Toyama, Y., Murphy, R., Bakia, M., & Jones, K. (2009). *Evaluation of evidence-based practices in online learning: A meta-analysis and review of online learning studies*. U.S. Department of Education. Retrieved July 29, 2010 from http://www2.ed.gov/rschstat/eval/tech/evidence-based-practices/finalreport.pdf

Palloff, R. M., & Pratt, K. (2005). *Collaborating online: learning together in community*. San Francisco: Jossey-Bass.

Petrie, H. G. (1981). *The dilemma of enquiry and learning*. Chicago, IL: University of Chicago Press.

Piaget, J. (1977). *The development of thought: Equilibration of cognitive structures*. New York, NY: Viking.

Stahl, G. (2010). Group cognition as a foundation for the new science of learning. In Khine, M. S., & Saleh, I. M. (Eds.), *New science of learning: Cognition, computers and collaboration in education*. New York, NY: Springer.

Swan, K., Garrison, D. R., & Richardson, J. (2009). A constructivist approach to online learning: The community of inquiry framework. In Payne, C. R. (Ed.), *Information technology and constructivism in higher education: Progressive learning frameworks* (pp. 43–57). Hershey, PA: IGI Global.

Volet, S., Vauras, M., & Salonen, P. (2009). Self- and social regulation in learning contexts: An integrative perspective. *Educational Psychologist, 44*(4), 215–226.

Vygotsky, L. S. (1978). *Mind in society: The development of higher psychological processes*. Cambridge, MA: Harvard University Press.

Wells, G. (2000). Dialogic inquiry in education: Building on the legacy of Vygotsky. In Lee, C. D., & Smagorinsky, P. (Eds.), *Vygotskian perspectives on literacy research: Constructing meaning through collaborative inquiry* (pp. 51–85). New York, NY: Cambridge University Press.

KEY TERMS AND DEFINITIONS

Community: A group of individuals who are connected and communicate with regard to mutual interests and similar expectations as to process and outcomes.

Community of Inquiry: A learning community where participants collaboratively engage in purposeful critical discourse and reflection (cognitive presence) to construct personal meaning and shared understanding through negotiation.

Constructivism: The individual process of making sense (creating meaning) from new experiences by building on and integrating previous knowledge and experiences; the general goals are to develop critical thinking and metacognitive skills.

Discourse: A collaborative and critical process for clarifying and resolving cognitive conflict through an open and disciplined (reflective and reasoned) form of dialogue or discussion with the potential for mutual agreement.

Inquiry: A process of critical thinking and problem solving based on the generalized scientific method leading to resolution and the growth of personal and collective knowledge.

Metacognition: The confluence of knowledge (entering knowledge), monitoring (reflection on action) and regulation (reflection in action) of cognition.

Motivation: Reflects perceived value and anticipated success of learning goals at the time learning is initiated and influences metacognitive effort.

Chapter 2
Community of Philosophical Inquiry Online and Off:
Retrospectus and Prospectus

David Kennedy
Montclair State University, USA

Nadia S. Kennedy
SUNY Stony Brook, USA

ABSTRACT

This chapter addresses, in psychohistorical, philosophical, and educational terms, the emergence of and prospects for the practice of a specific form of philosophical pedagogy in an online environment. It explores a form of structured group dialogue known as "community of philosophical inquiry," a communal critical thinking discourse that reflects the ongoing transformation of the contemporary information environment into a hybrid zone which combines the literate, the oral, and the imagistic. After a description and analysis of the structure and process of CPI as a complex system, a discussion of the distinctive pedagogical role of a CPI facilitator, and a genealogical look at the post modern information environment, the chapter explores how this "ideal speech situation," which is also a hybrid, is challenged or enhanced through its insertion into the post modern information environment, and how it satisfies the conditions for the communicative ideal of social democracy.

INTRODUCTION

This chapter will address, in psychohistorical, philosophical and educational terms, the emergence of and prospects for the practice of a dialogical pedagogy in an online environment. We will explore a form of structured group dialogue known as "community of inquiry," a form which reflects the transformation, through the virtual collective space created by digital technology, of the contemporary information environment into a hybrid zone that combines the literate, the oral, and the iconic or imagistic. Community of inquiry can be broadly defined as the practice of communal, dialogical interaction centered on the problematization and collaborative reconstruction of philosophical, scientific, moral or aesthetic concepts and the questions in which they are

DOI: 10.4018/978-1-4666-2110-7.ch002

embedded. Because this term has developed many references and connotations over the past half-century, we will, in order to avoid confusion, limit our discussion of the term to what, in Matthew Lipman's and Ann Sharp's original adoption of C.S. Peirce's epistemology, Justus Buchler's metaphysics and John Dewey's logic (Peirce, 1966, 2011; Buchler, 1990; De Marzio, 1997; Dewey, 1916, 1938; Lipman, Sharp & Oscanyan 1980; Lipman, 2003; Sharp, 1987, 1993). Lipman and Sharp understood specifically as community of *philosophical* inquiry, which we will refer to as CPI. We will use the term community of inquiry (CI) to refer to a larger pedagogical category that can be identified by its collaborative, dialogical and constructivist theory of inquiry, but which might take different forms in actual practice and in different disciplines.

There are several advantages to this limitation. Most importantly, it connects directly with the form of group dialogue that has its origins in ancient Greece, most famously in the philosophical practice of Socrates, which represents a benchmark that has even yet to be fully appropriated by Western educational theory and practice. Secondly, philosophical discourse, at least in its more traditional form, has the distinction of operating most visibly according to the epistemological assumptions of critical thinking—that is, through the offering and evaluation of reasons, based on inductive and deductive logical criteria. And finally, philosophical dialogue is unequivocally oriented to personal and collective meaning, as opposed merely to the transmission and/or retention of information. As such it offers an educational form that fully honors Vygotskian social constructivist epistemology and learning theory, and which establishes the conditions both for John Dewey's (1902) "Copernican Revolution" in education and Paulo Freire's (1965) epochal identification of dialogue as a necessary condition for any emancipatory pedagogy, as well as providing a secure place in the curriculum for moral education in the form of ethical inquiry. As a discipline, we may characterize it as the

primary or ur-discourse of education, because it provides a context for the four dimensions of reasoning—formal, informal, interpersonal and philosophical—identified by Cannon and Weinstein (1993) as fundamental to a form of thinking that is both autonomous and dialogical.

The goal of the chapter is, briefly put, to characterize CPI as a discursive form and as a speech community, and to speculate on the consequences of its reproduction in an online environment, through an exploration of the possibilities that virtual and/or blended community of inquiry offers for the growth and development of dialogical educational practice. We will begin by characterizing its systemic distinctives—both phenomenologically as a speech event, and normatively as an educational form vital to authentic social and political democracy; for the first thing to be distinguished in CPI, whether conducted in real or virtual space, is the fundamental political—or we may say, pre-political—aspect of this form of discourse. It represents a clear and compelling alternative to the monological and unilateral discourse that is implicit in transmissional models of pedagogy and curriculum. Simply on the basis of its structure and process, CPI represents a model of a speech community that moves us to problematize and rethink how we as a group perform power, control, and authority, and directly encourages a form of participatory governance and co-creation in small communities like schools. A primary assumption of this chapter is that performing CPI in the altered information environment of virtual space—which is implicitly a global commons--offers a new site for the reconstruction of power in educational settings, and by clear extension, in society as a whole.

A Brief Characterization of CPI

By community of inquiry (CI) we mean any group that makes it its collective task to construct new meaning in a field of knowledge through collaborative, dialogical deliberation. We focus here on philosophical deliberation--the first known example of which is Socrates' group in the Athenian agora—but the term may cover disciplinary inquiry in an academic or research setting, group psychotherapy, or some other. The most basic characteristic of its philosophical form (CPI) is that it is an ongoing, regularly meeting group with a specific deliberative goal of working to reconstruct "common, central and contestable" concepts like truth, justice, friendship, economy, person, education, sex, gender and so forth (Splitter & Sharp, 1995). One main objective of its deliberations is the construction of meaningful arguments, not through transmission, individual reflection or debate, but through what is referred to as building on each other's ideas— that is through distributed thinking in a dialogical context (Kennedy, 1999). The inquiry is understood to advance through reasoning, or the giving of reasons, and each reasoning move represents a reconstruction of the collective argument in the direction of a state of completion which is never more than provisional, and thus final closure is in fact never arrived at (Kennedy, 2004a). The ideal inquiry proceeds through a form of argumentation which, because it is inherently dialogical, is thus by implication a dialectical process, which is to say a process which moves forward through encountering and attempting to resolve tensions or contradictions. The chief pedagogical significance of the constructive process of community of philosophical inquiry is that it operates in the collective zone of proximal development (Vygotsky, 1978), which acts to scaffold concepts, skills and dispositions for each individual. The scaffolding process functions through subprocesses such as clarification, reformulation, summarization, and explanation, as well as through challenge and disagreement.

A CPI group may also be gathered together to investigate common, central and contestable concepts within disciplinary boundaries, like mathematics (e.g. infinity), or history (e.g. progress), or biology (e.g. organism), in which case it may

in fact extend across the curriculum (Kennedy, in press; Kennedy & Kennedy, 2012); or it may be dedicated to an emergent theme structure, whereby one conceptual problematization leads to another; or it may be convened even more non-specifically under the sign of "dialogue." In all cases its members come with the shared intention of undergoing ongoing deliberation together; the expectation that meaning or significance will arise from their conversations that will at least be partially shared by everyone; and that they will experience some sort of reconstruction of belief—or in Lipman's (1992) pragmatic formulation, "self-correction"--through the challenging and testing of each other's assumptions in the common space of dialogue.

Even the most radical forms of CPI—as, for example the non-thematic dialogue groups associated with David Bohm (1990, 1997) or the Society of Friends meeting, in which no one speaks unless inspired by the "inner light"—operate with a set of basic rules of discourse, implicit or explicit, that participants attempt to abide by. And even in the free form Bohmian groups there is one or more leaders—often called "facilitators" (or, in French, "animateurs")--who intervene in order to clarify and coordinate the emergent structure of the argument. That emergent structure is understood to develop through a series of logical and semantic "moves," such as offering and evaluating examples, proposing counter-arguments, exploring implications, classifying and categorizing, summarizing, restating, and so forth. The facilitator's role may be more or less pedagogical, depending on the skills and dispositions of the participants. On the "more" side, the facilitator coaches, models, and intervenes procedurally (e.g. acts to regulate the distribution of turns or speaker length, calls for summarization or location of the argument, supports calls for group response that are unheeded or over-ridden by the next speaker), but remains philosophically self-effacing. On the "less" side, his or her goal is in fact to grow out of his/her special role through the distribution of procedural interventions throughout the group—that is, to promote a system-condition in which all participants, including him or herself, share in regulating the distribution of turns, calling for summarization or restatement, and so on, as well as making propositions, offering alternative hypotheses, offering and evaluating examples, etc.. As such, the regulative ideals of CPI include both distributed intelligence and distributed power. The facilitator's role is to attempt to guarantee—and to teach others to do so—a communicative polity based on Habermas' (1984) notion of an "ideal speech situation," ruled, whether implicitly or explicitly, by a "discourse ethics" for which free assertion and questioning and expression, and the absence of coercion, manipulation, or purely unilateral relations between the group leader and the participants, is understood to be the norm.

CPI as understood here is associated epistemologically with a pragmatic, dialectical understanding of inquiry, and psychologically with George Herbert Mead (1934) and Lev Vygotsky (1978)—the former in the sense that primary meaning arises out of social interaction and is negotiated through language, and that self or subjectivity is an interpersonal construct through and through; the latter in the sense that habits of thought and belief, including the skills and dispositions of critical thinking used in CPI, develop from the mimetic interaction between the *inter*psychic and the *intra*psychic planes, and that CPI is in fact a collectively constructed zone of proximal development, in the sense that the group's zone of actual development is always higher than each member's, and the collective dialogue provides a scaffold for each individual who needs it. More specifically, CPI is associated pedagogically with the educational program Philosophy for Children, and the methodology adopted by its founder, Matthew Lipman and his colleagues (Lipman, et al, 1980; Splitter & Sharp, 1996; Kennedy, 1990, 1994, 2004b, 2010a) that privileges structured communal dialogue as a primary classroom discourse, which it understands as the most fundamental of educational forms in an authentically democratic society. And over the last decade, the work of D. Randy Garrison (2011) and his colleagues has acted to reframe CI theory in the context of three intersecting dimensions—social, cognitive and teaching "presences"—fundamental to a collaborative learning community, and a four-phase "practical inquiry model" based broadly on Dewey's logic of inquiry, and more specifically on his model of reflective thinking (Dewey, 1933). Garrison follows closely on Lipman in construing the CI paradigm as "an essential element of an educational experience when higher-order learning is the desired...outcome," (p. 19), and in seeing the broad goals of CI theory and practice as critical and creative knowledge construction in a collaborative, dialogical context.

CPI as a Complex System

Complexity theory has been steadily gaining recognition over the last half a century as a new way of understanding the organization of systems on all levels—whether organisms, social systems, business organizations, or ecosystems. Contrary to a mechanistic, analytic approach to the study of phenomena, the complexity perspective takes into account all interactions between the components of a system, which it understands as in dynamic interplay.

If we accept the social system theorist Niklas Luhmann's (1995) simple but compelling definition, CPI as a communicative system may be understood as complex, in that it contains more communicative possibilities than can be actualized. On the level of group interaction for example, there are always more themes than can be explored, more questions than can be pursued, and more concepts than the group can take up for inquiry. On the individual level, there are always more possible interventions than one can make. CPI shares many characteristics common to all systems

(Cillier, 1998). For example, its interactions are "rich" in the sense that every interaction influences and is influenced by others. CPI deliberations are nonlinear, in the sense that some interventions are amplified, and have a greater effect than others. Any member of the group can intervene and change the direction of the inquiry with new substantive or procedural suggestion. The inquiry itself can shift direction through a series of non-linear moves, and the conversation can shift between inquiry, reflection on the inquiry, and feedback. The interactive dynamics are constantly changing—whether in levels of participation or levels of clarity of the "argument." This presents a picture very different from the traditional monological, unidirectional model of classroom conversation, in which, when there is interaction, it is between teacher and individual student.

Complexity emerges in the ambiguous, just-barely-in-control interplay between CPI group members, in which the pattern of intervention is recursive—new interventions connect with previous ones and may even appear to repeat them, but their measure of difference opens possibilities for future interventions, thus forming patterns of argument that make of the structure of CPI an emergent constellation of interactions. In fact recursion is a primary characteristic of this form of collective dialogue, demonstrated through members' repetition of utterances, or through paraphrase and summary; recursion is thus associated with redundancy, which assures through repetition that what might not have been well-articulated, or which remains ambiguous, can be communicated again.

Recursion and redundancy are carried by the feedback loops that are endemic characteristics of complex systems. A negative feedback loop has the function of maintaining the system's stability through inhibition and stabilization. For example, a negative loop is initiated when the facilitator or another member rejects an intervention on the grounds that it is not relevant to the current inquiry.

Positive feedback introduces more diversity—for example when a member suggests a new perspective on the issue at hand, thus stimulating reconceptualization. As a whole, the system operates far-from-equilibrium; equilibrium is in fact "enemy" to the system, in that it represents stagnation or actual system-death. As such, the system is fed by a flow of new perspectives, new information, and new meanings. Any stability that is achieved is of a dynamic nature, in a communicative zone that is between chaos (too many disconnected interventions, to the point that meaning-making is impossible) and entropy (no new information at all) (Kennedy & Kennedy, 2010b).

Although it may appear that it is the facilitator who is navigating the direction of the group, unilateral navigation is in fact only possible, if at all, in a closed, controlled system, in which the teacher dictates events and meanings, and inhibits any dynamic emergence. In a collective such as CPI, where each intervention is understood as potentially important, control is distributed throughout the group. Lushyn and Kennedy (2002) identified this as "ambiguous control," since it is never exactly clear how much and to what extent an intervention might affect the course of the inquiry, and group dynamics as well. The facilitator may have more perceived authority to steer the group, but other members—those less constrained by the internalized hierarchy of the traditional model—may exercise their distributed authority from the start, which is welcomed by the facilitator, whose long-term goal is the distribution of power within the system, just as she encourages the emergence of distributed thinking and distributed self-expression.

CPI as a communicative system is always reproducing itself through a self-organizing, or autopoietic process. Along with the production of judgments and arguments and sequences of argumentation, there is the production of ideas—new meanings that coevolve with each individual's thoughts, feelings and expectations. The system is self-balancing, and although there may be crises and breakdowns, the latter represent—potentially anyway—transitions to a new state of dynamic balance. The autopoietic function finds expression in the idiosyncrasies of the group-as-a-whole and the interactions among its member. Notwithstanding its systemic contingency--for in fact it could always be otherwise, and its path is never completely determined—the CI as a communicative system is quite robust, and its emergent structure relatively stable in time and across contexts.

CPI and the Reconstruction of Concepts

CPI exemplifies the primary maxim of complexity theory—that "the system is larger than the sum of its parts" (Laszlo, 1975, p. 69). As such we are not speaking purely metaphorically when we claim that CPI operates as a collective cognitive, affective, and even postural and kinesic ("body language") subject. Gregory Bateson (1989) identified a set of criteria that systems must satisfy in order to be able to function as a *mind*: a) the system is able to recognize and operate on the basis of difference; b) the system must have closed loops along which information about difference and what it produces can be reported; c) most agents in the system are influenced by responses within the system rather than by the original stimulus; and d) the system is self-corrective. All of these criteria are met in a CPI, which thus is able to develop all the processes associated with mind—learning, memory, and decision-making. Another way to describe CPI, then, is as a complex subject.

In a broad sense, it could be said that the mission of a CPI, its task as a working group, is to clarify and to develop concepts. Depending on what one makes of the concept "concept," that might include developing and clarifying feelings as well, for some might argue that every concept is feeling-toned, and vice versa. By "concept" need not be understood something that can be

rendered or examined linguistically, and even in a community of inquiry in which the linguistic is privileged-- as in a CPI--the logic of the argumentation process is seldom predominately linear.

Although it is a complex discursive system, CPI is punctuated by linear incidents—for example when a standard logical entailment unfolds, such as a syllogistic pattern of claims—and guided at least on one level (in its current historical form) by the classical laws of thought (identity, noncontradiction, and the excluded middle). It is dedicated to making propositions or strings of propositions called arguments, which seek to universalize concepts like truth, justice and beauty, self, thinking, animal and so on—that is, to reach a reasoned agreement or disagreement about the necessary and sufficient elements of each concept, and about the criteria through which the concept gets applied, or lived, in the world of objects, persons, and experience. This is often experienced by the participants of a CPI as a process of de- and re-construction of the concept, which has been problematized (rendered problematic) by the very movement to come to a consensus about what it refers to, and what the criteria for applying it in experience are.

When examined intensively by multiple persons in dialogue, each of whom occupies a different place in space and in subjective time, the search for complete agreement must typically settle for a coordination rather than a unification of perspectives. This in fact is probably a safer goal, in that a unified perspective implies either group-think or group dissolution (entropy) once the problem is "solved." But the apparent impossibility of a unification of perspectives, as represented by the ontological disequilibrium guaranteed by the fact of our bodies separated in space and personal time, does not cancel or make less powerful—in fact it possibly makes it more so—the felt teleology of CPI, which is to put back together what, with the attempt to identify and characterize it, has been taken apart. This teleology is double-pronged, in that the deconstruction and reconstruction of the concept is happening both on an individual and a collective level. The implicit understanding of its practitioners is that through reconstruction the concept becomes more salient and more visible in its work in human action and interaction, as well as more commonly construed through the fusion of horizons of the participants. The fact that the process is never completed is in fact a mark of philosophical *praxis*: half-reconstructed, the concept re-enters practice, where it is challenged by context and experience to justify the new understanding of it. It then goes back into dialogue—both inter- and intra-subjective—where the work of reconstruction is taken up yet again.

The overarching educational goal of CPI may be described as constructing another level of awareness—the metacognitive. On the level of the system, this task is operationalized and the goal is pursued through feedback loops. The facilitator, who functions as a mirror in the system, sparingly initiates reflective loops whereby she summarizes, paraphrases, gives a brief recount of an individual intervention or a "status report" on the current state of the system and the inquiry process. Accessing this metacognitive systemic level may be posited as an inherent goal of the group—to become more both reflexive and reflective as a functional whole, which implies a collective identity, a sense of "us" that has some characteristics of "me." This is the work of community. It is both a social and a psychological goal, and, in terms of the work of group deliberation, a cognitive one. The social and psychological goals call for and imply an increased tolerance and appreciation of difference between members, an increased empathy and sympathy, which in turn implies the increased ability to imagine oneself in the position of the other, a disposition to imaginatively inhabit the other's perspectival space. From a cognitive perspective, it is the work of "thinking about thinking"—learning to evaluate reasons, arguments, and interventions in the group with an eye

to improving the functionality and the intensity of meaning overall—that is foregrounded. On a systemic level, the work towards accomplishing this goal is mainly done through the facilitator's engagement in closely maintaining reflective feedback loops. She makes the "thinking about thinking" visible by quick feedback insertions like naming a move ("Tom gave us a counterexample"), or retracing the inquiry ("Now we have two different ideas: Nellie's and Natasha's. Do you agree or disagree with them?")—insertions made in the interest of the system internalizing those reflective moves and beginning to reproduce them. These self-critical skills and dispositions are, on Dewey's (1916) account, basic necessary attributes of the communicative ideal that he calls social democracy, without which authentic political democracy is of doubtful realization.

ASPECTS OF A CHANGING INFORMATION ENVIRONMENT

Given this all-too-brief characterization of the structure and dynamics of CPI, we want to take up the question of how that structure and dynamics may differ or stay the same when transferred from a face-to-face classroom environment to a virtual one. What is perhaps most interesting for analysis is that the virtual environment represents a changed (and still changing) information environment, in which the historical balance between orality, literacy, and the visual or imagistic has been disrupted, and a new distribution of those three informational modes is in the process of emerging.

This new distribution represents, as well as we can determine in this relatively early stage of emergence, a hybrid discourse—a mixing-up of the literate, the oral/aural, and the visual/imagistic. If we examine the traditional associations with each form of communication, we can identify, as the media historian Walter Ong (1982) argues, a "psychodynamic" dimension characteristic of each. On his account, oral discourse as it shaped culture and personality before the invention of the printing press is typically associated with collective presence, immediacy, participation, mimesis, rhetoric (the power of persuasion, or parrhesia, that is, truth-telling), as well as with heightened (relative to the present day) memory and transmission. Oral discourse is also associated with a certain style of temporality: the most characteristic product of the old oral cultures is the evocation of the archetypical, the circular, and the mythic. The "dreamtime" of the Australian aboriginals is a time which, in its infinite repetition, stands still, a timeless sort of time, in which the notion of "progress," "development," constant change, is muted or goes unnoticed. As the time of eternal "now," it is the time of the hero and of the gods, of the creation of the world.

The psychodynamics of literacy, which profoundly shaped the rise of modernity beginning in the 16th century and were triggered by the invention of the printing press and the rapid proliferation of print media, are characterized by distance, separation, displacement, "objectivity," individualism, linear sequence, reversibility, analysis, logic. The world of print is silent, and it removes the reader from the "book of nature"--which is the sole and primary book for oral culture--to the book of the interpretation, analysis, and manipulation of nature. For the psychodynamics of literacy, the cosmos can no longer be grasped through the senses, and understanding is no longer a matter of communal interlocution. Rather than the morphological fields, influences, whole gestalts, fractal relationships or even occult correspondences of the oral cosmos, the literate cosmos is based on the smallest unit of matter that can be identified through analysis, the neutral "building block" out of which the whole world of matter is constructed, like a machine.

The visual or imagistic, which is the third of the modalities that have recently become available in the online information environment in the form of still pictures, video, maps and charts, appears to offer an intensification of visual thinking that follows from the appearance of photography in the mid-19th century, of cinema in the early 20th, and of video in the late 20th. As the printing press did with the written word, technological advance and proliferation of visual media has had the effect of democratizing the language of images, and switched the uses of the image from art towards the documentary and towards self-representation, as in the YouTube video, or the "reality" show, or films utilizing non-actors, or films like Amos Gitai's, (2005) in which the distinction between the real and the fictional is ambiguous. The psychodynamics of the imagistic perhaps represent the greatest challenge to our understanding, and cannot be entered here at any length. But both Guy Debord's *Society of the Spectacle* (1983) and Jean Baudrillard's "Simulacra and Simulation" (1998) offer suggestive analyses; the latter's notion of the "hyperreal" as a world of copies with no original evokes the boundaries of the experience of the virtual image world.

From a psychological perspective, we can explain the phenomenon of hyper-reality as following from the fact that the image has the capacity of being the most deceptive of mediums just because, as an analogue representation, it purports to "tell the truth," and to offer a seamless isomorphism between the thing that is represented and the representation of it. When we hear or read words, which are digital representations, we don't lose sight of the fact that they are signs just because they are so different from what they represent: there is no danger of a confusion between the sign and what it refers to. But when we watch video it is difficult to avoid the implicit assumption that the image and what it represents are the same thing, when in fact they are very different. So we could say that the psychodynamics of the visual involve a kind of hyper-realism in the form of a tendency for what is represented to be "even realer than the real thing," and an inability (or unwillingness) to tell fantasy from reality. As such, it causes a complementary movement, in a shift from the documentary, the descriptive, to the symbolic: life becomes art and visa versa. This tendency is accentuated by the difference in temporality between the visual and both the oral/aural and the literate. The former is static and timeless; even a "moving picture" unfolds outside of time, or in its own time, as in a dream. But we should not ignore the fact that this new representational complexity offers the possibility of developing enhanced visual literacy—the capacity to "read" images with greater sophistication, and to be able to deconstruct images in the sense of recognizing that they represent partial, perspectival glimpses of the reality of what they represent, and that in fact there is no one perspective from which what they represent can be known once and for all—which in turn leads to that epistemological fallibilism that is, arguably, a necessary element of critical thinking.

It is important to note that these three forms of interacting with the world, with other people, and with ideas, have always been present in the armamorium of human sense and meaning. Technologies draw out tendencies and capacities that are already there--although, in what C.S. Peirce (1958) called a "tychistic" universe or "universe of chance" such as ours, that doesn't rule out the possibility of involuntarily creating spaces for psychodynamic tendencies and capacities that do not yet exist. It is also important to remember that none of the characteristics of orality, literacy, or the imagistic are the same characteristics once they enter the world of advanced digital communication. When we consider the psychodynamics of the on-line information environment, we can only speak of a *post*—a post-orality, a post-literacy, and a post imagistic--for the internet offers dramatically different communicative possibilities that emerge from the emergent and mutually transgressive relationship between the three. For example, because of the speed and immediacy of mecha-

nisms for email and "chat," the written word tends to approximate more to speech, with its shortcuts, spelling ellipses and formulaic phrases—and yet it remains the written word, with its inherent capacity for asynchronicity, logical organization, revision, and singularity. For another example, the use of an image—a photo or a video clip—appears to render a written explanation of what it depicts redundant. However, although an image purports to display to the "naked eye" the truth of a thing, it is, as we have pointed out, as much a representation as an oral or written description or account. As such, the use of images in e-discourse introduces an element of ambiguity and indeterminacy that demands critical interpretation, and calls for the skillset most usually represented by critical media studies. And for a third example, the absence of the kinesic and proxemic dimensions of physical presence—body movements, positions, postures, facial expressions, motions, gestures--in online communication, and their unavoidable coherent distortion even when video is present, creates a sort of interpretive vertigo that the interlocutors must use new expressive and hermeneutical skills to master, which may lead to valuable forms of metacognition or higher-order awareness that promote dialogical skills in general.

CPI and the Changing Information Environment

It is at least of historical interest that the two most salient moments of emergence of CPI as a discursive form occurred at corresponding moments of information environment shift and emergence involving the relationship between orality and literacy. The first—the well-known philosophical conversation group convened by Socrates in the public space of the Athenian agora—came at a moment in the history of information environments when writing—literacy in the form of the "scribal" rather than print—was making encroachments on orality. Even as Plato's teacher and mentor

Socrates rails in the *Phaedrus* (Plato, 1961, Section 275) against the new "invention" of writing as eroding memory, decreasing self-reliance, rendering knowledge superficial, distancing the learner from the thing learned, unilateral as opposed to interlocutive, and spreading knowledge among those who will misunderstand or misuse it, his student Plato "records" his words through generating a written document, in which he creates the illusion of transcribing an oral event. Thus already, in CPI's first historical appearance, we encounter a hybrid. Socrates appeared to be speaking extemporaneously—and indeed he was--but the form and performance of his arguments as transcribed by Plato are already fully literate, in the sense of Ong's (1982) characterization of literacy as linear, logical, based upon argument, and both reversible and atemporal, in benefiting from the capacity to go back in the text and reread. So the first glimpse we have of the discursive form of community of inquiry trades on both the oral and the literate. We sense the oral in that the text indicates--as much as a text can indicate an oral event—a collective speech event with agonistic toning, in which the participants are empathetic and participatory, (p. 45) in which there is emphasis on the personalities of the interlocutors, in which a commonly known group of examples (heroes, gods, Homeric characters, etc.) is assumed. But Plato's rendering of the event into text loads it with the marks of literacy: abstract categorization, formal logical reasoning processes, definitions, self-analysis, logical reversibility and so on (p. 55). The fascination of the dialogues of Socrates as rendered by Plato lies in part in this novel combination of the two modes.

If we jump from 370 BCE to 1970 CE, we find Matthew Lipman initiating a similar discursive form as Socrates, and also doing so at another transitional moment in the history of the information environment. This transition leads us, as we have seen, into a realm of hybridity. In the new realm, participants communicate in writing in an orality-tinged situation of interlocution ("chatting," "texting," "posting" or "blogging") on various levels of immediacy or presence, and under the possibility of multiple identities. In a "discussion" board or in email exchanges or blog and wiki exchanges, they engage in a dialogue whose asynchronicity makes it possible for the participants to craft their responses at their leisure, apart from the pressure to respond to face to face interlocution. The net effect is that one does not chat, text, post, or even blog for an abstract audience, for posterity, for "the record," but always for a potentially very real and immediate other, from whom one can very well expect a response; in fact if one does not have a response in this digital space, one has not been successful—the "post" evaporates, or translates into the "cloud" where, paradoxically, no post is ever lost.

Now, even as this new information environment was emerging and taking hold, Lipman's and Sharp's reconstruction of the Socratic model was reintroducing the oral discourse event into the classroom, which, in its Euro-American incarnation anyway, is an educational setting long-characterized by the primacy of the book, and whose very identity may be historically identified with the print revolution of early modernism (Luke, 1989). Community of philosophical inquiry as a speech event restores the common interlocutive space of oral culture—the agora--which, as Foucault (2005) has pointed out in his analysis of ancient Greek and Roman culture—is a space where three kinds of public speech are common, which he calls "rhetoric," "flattery," and *parrhesia* (Gk.) or speech characterized by "frankness, freedom, and openness" (p. 373).

Rhetoric and flattery have their educational forms—whether in debate or the ritual mimesis of patriotic speech or awards ceremonies, or in forms of classroom discourse founded on giving the teacher the "right answer"—but *parrhesia* has typically been reserved for the personal diary, the counselor's couch, or the encounter group. Lipman's CPI is a discourse environment in which personal meaning is expressed in a dialogical rather than a confessional or agonistic environment, thereby opening a space for the formation of a self-narrative that interplays with a group narrative; where one's own thought is generated spontaneously, in oral form, in the context of the thought of others. As such, this reconstruction of the psychodynamics of orality as dialogical rather than agonistic, amounts to a reclamation of the commons, and a return to public discourse. It clears a site for the release and expression of student voice and agency, a return to spontaneous interlocution in a public space, and above all an interlocutive zone for the practice and exercise of *parrhesia*, which may be considered another requirement of the ideal speech situation upon which authentic democracy depends (Vansieleghem, 2012).

What is distinctive about this fully oral event is that it is practiced in Lipman's model as a methodical discourse—a discourse in which argument, logic, entailment, proof, instantiation and syllogism receive specific attention and monitoring—and hence a literate as well as an oral performance. In Socrates' group, this literate structure was provided by Socrates alone, who completely controlled the argument, making of it a disguised monologue. In CPI, it is understood to emerge dialectically as a product of the communal dialogue of the members, which Lipman, taking a phrase from Socrates, refers to as "following the argument where it leads." Members of a CPI take their collaborative inquiry as a text in itself—a text that the group itself is "writing" collaboratively through dialogue, and can simultaneously "read" through metacognitive interlocutive moves such as summarizing, restating, locating the argument ("Where are we?"), evaluating hypotheses and examples, identifying underlying assumptions, and so forth. Several researchers (McCall, 1993 Kennedy, 2006) have demonstrated through transcript analysis that when the spontaneous dialogue of CPI is transcribed and analyzed, one can discern

levels of logical entailment and systemic argument as implicit structural elements in the larger system of the argument. The goal of "live" CPI is to become aware of that larger system even as it is emerging—to "follow it where it leads," making of it simultaneously an oral and a literate event.

Reproducing CPI in a Virtual Environment

Our next task is to identify how CPI as an event and a methodology changes when it is reproduced in the virtual dimension, and to identify both some limitations and some new possibilities that this transposition offers. The alteration of time, space and interactive setting in the virtual dimension, which is the case even when all participants in a CPI conversation are online simultaneously, requires of the facilitator and the group members different strategies and behaviors than in the situation of face-to-face communal dialogue. We will explore a few strategies of initiating, maintaining, and intervening in online dialogue in ways that both promote clear and autonomous thinking in group members, and lead to the emergence, articulation and coordination of the larger structures of argument that are implicit in dialogical discourse.

Because the possible combinations of modalities in an online environment are myriad, we will anchor our exploration in the hypothetical context of a "blended" or "hybrid" environment—a combination of face-to-face and online encounters. Of course this makes for a major difference in the experience of CPI, in that members have the benefit of both an actual, physical presence in a deliberative circle, and the reproduction of that circle in virtual space, leading to a comparative awareness of the communicative possibilities of the two environments, especially if they alternate from meeting to meeting. We will also assume the presence of a technology that makes multiple video conferencing available. The often startling and liberating intimacy that is created by simply re-arranging chairs in a close circle in a classroom cannot—so far anyway—be reproduced online; but advances in video technology promise to create a "simulacrum" of the deliberative circle that may in fact create another sort of intimacy—one that we had not imagined. In the meantime, there may even be unexpected interpretive and communicative advantages to the fragmentation of spatial presence that the current multiple video conference technology creates.

What seems most affected by the shift to virtual space and time in CPI is the role of the facilitator. As we have seen, the goal of the facilitator is to "put herself out of a job" through the distribution of her role throughout the group, and in the face-to-face environment, the inherent logic of this goal and the moves she makes to reach it—modeling and coaching in a process of moving between the substantive and the procedural dimensions of the conversation—is clearly signaled both verbally and gesturally. The practice of introducing feedback loops, through which the recursive and redundant characteristics of the system are given shape and enhanced is, at least as we know it, strongly connected with direct interlocutive presence; to attempt to reproduce that online, even when both sound and picture are present, seems futile.

On the other hand, the work of shaping this just-barely-in-control conversation both by following (e.g. restating, summarizing, connecting concepts and arguments) and leading (e.g. calling for alternative points of view, calling attention to inequalities in participation, identifying contradictions) can be made more effective and systematic just because time is slowed down, giving more opportunity for deliberation and choice of the "next move," and because in the case of a multiple chat context, the space in which and to which the group is present has been rendered completely textual. Here, the CPI speech event and its transcript have merged, are operating simultaneously—a text/speech hybrid. This has implications for what we

have identified as the overarching goal of CPI as the construction of a metacognitive dimension of awareness in which we are thinking about our own thinking.

In communicative system terms, this space in which the speech event is also its transcript presents the possibility for a dramatic reduction of "noise." The gravity and lightness, the color and movement, the depth and ambiguity, the involuntary kinesic coupling and mimesis, the fraught psychological immediacy of physical presence and its affective flows, have been elided from the lived moment through the technological *epoche* or "cut," leaving the group in a radically "mental" space in which undivided attention to the argument is easier to summon. Any given intervention is no longer immediately swept up and appropriated into the recursive and redundant, often chaotic flow of the argument. This represents an enormous potential boost to the metacognitive/reflective dimension in CPI dialogue, in that the "writing" and "reading" of the argument that the group is performing on the screen is virtually simultaneous, but also presents the danger of stagnation through a reduction of spontaneity. The common facilitation technique of asking each participant to identify the move (give an example, make an analogy, connect two arguments, etc.) they are going to make before they speak is even easier to execute in this environment than in the face-to-face, but its overuse can suppress the natural movement of intelligence that the group-as a-whole is exercising, which depends, in fact, not on the elimination of noise, but on maintaining it at an optimal level.

This could be just one example of the unbalancing of the dynamic relation between elements of the system that taking it into virtual space and time represents—one that calls for greater calculation and greater moment-to-moment control by the facilitator in order to rectify than is necessary or desirable in the face-to-face situation. The same increase of facilitator control and even mechanization of the process would apply in the areas of guaranteeing participation by each group member, ordering and regulating turn-taking, locating the argument, and calling for restatement or clarification. This necessary tightening of the facilitator's grip does not, however negate or even hinder her major goal of distributing her role throughout the group. In fact it may enhance it, through providing clearer models of facilitation than are available in the more unruly medium of face-to-face. After modeling a consistent method of organizing the online dialogue for a number of meetings, the facilitator may wish to delegate responsibility for facilitation to each member of the group in turn; in which case the member has a very clear basic protocol to follow, including templates for conversational closure and group self-evaluation. This promises an acceleration of the distribution of the facilitator's role, and an increase in agency on the part of members.

There are more ways than can be explored here in which moving CPI online offers the opportunity to reconstruct the deliberative process in virtual space. A sampling would include: taking advantage of the asynchronous context of the online environment to initiate blogging and wikis about specific concepts, issues, or ongoing discussions; encouraging the use of hypertexting during a given discussion (including during a group text chat), in order to enrich the information base, whether through relevant facts, text, images or videos; constructing mechanisms whereby members can easily hold a vote on immediate issues, like a direction for the conversation to take at a given juncture; alternating between face-to-face meetings, group text chat and group video chat, in order to explore the differences in the semiotic and psychosocial environments that these three modalities offer; and organizing a protocol for private side conversations between pairs or triads during discussions. The latter is an example of a practice that is an irritating distraction during face-to-face group dialogue, but which, in the very different economy of the (in)visible in vir-

tual space, promises to enrich the collaborative environment. All of these techniques represent ways of exploring an information environment that remains in many ways a sort of wilderness, replete both with dangers and with unpredictable new possibilities for communication and for collaborative inquiry.

CONCLUSION

From a psychohistorical perspective, each reigning information environment has been seen to make possible and foster a specific form or style of intelligence, on the assumption that intelligence is a cultural product, an adaptation to a changing environment, and especially to a communications environment. The oral information environment encourages the formulaic, the somatic, the communal—aspects of what Ong (1982, p. 68) calls the "verbomotor"—and the holistic: the ancient theory of correspondences between microcosm and macrocosm that animated ancient sciences such as astrology is the epistemological crown of this form of communication. The advent of print literacy and the book, which make for the solitary activities of reading and writing through which the "psyche is thrown back upon itself" (p. 69) make possible a new analytic intelligence and a new way of seeing the world--a new sense of isolation and separation from the whole that characterizes the modern, Cartesian subject. As oral intelligence is global, holistic, literate intelligence is linear, separative, logical, and results in a radical empiricist epistemology that fosters dramatic technological development, a de-animated, contingent universe, and radical individualism.

As is suggested by the steady rise and development of systems theory beginning in the 20th century, electronic intelligence can be characterized as "complex." It may be simplistic to understand this new, emergent noetic style as a dialectical sublation—the "synthesis" that resolves the contradiction of the "thesis" of orality and the "antithesis" of literacy--but it does provide a useful metaphor for grappling with the implications of the new blend of the oral, the literate and the imagistic that virtual reality embodies, the new form of intelligence that it calls forth, and, correspondingly, the new form of subjectivity that it shapes.

The complex subject is "plugged in," and understands herself as a part of a global system of social assemblages and hybrid networks that are inherently communicative. Because she functions in a complex set of combinatory arrangements of the human and the non-human that makes up the virtual world, she no longer holds to the traditional notions of the social and the natural, the machine and the person, or even the object and the subject (Latour, 2005). Cognitively and affectively, she tends to be decentered, "cool" rather than "hot." Epistemologically, she tends to be non-dogmatic and relativistic, and to favor the horizontal, the rhizomatic over the hierarchical and the arboreal (Deleuze & Guattari, 1980) as a way of understanding and organizing the world.

Relationally, the complex subject mediates between modernist radical individualism and the functional collectivism of the human-machine assemblages of which she is a part. She is "alone-together"—both isolated on her smart phone or her computer and at the same time plugged into the global communicative system, with the agency to carve out her own social and relational niche from the categories offered her by the machinic networks (categories that she has at least the potential to add to or alter). She is part of an intelligent system with no central control, a system based on communication, a system that can be symmetric or asymmetric with real time and space, in which multiplicity and difference drive the formation of new assemblages and networks of assemblages, which in fact make up the electronic commons—a space of common resources, open access, and free interaction--of which she is a part. This makes of her a new sort

of political subject, a subject that Hardt and Negri (2004) have named "multitude," and which, they suggest "makes democracy possible for the first time today," since, in the new information environment, "political sovereignty and the rule of the one, which has always undermined any real notion of democracy, [now] tends to appear not only unnecessary but absolutely impossible" (p. 340). The speed with which information can be shared in virtual space, and the relentless social transparency that the imagistic makes possible through audio-recording and video and image, have already had profound effects on the collective moral imagination, and are powerful weapons in the struggle of the "multitude" to take back the commons from the exploitative privatization and its accompanying corruption that represent a cruel and dangerous element of late capitalist economies and politics.

Community of philosophical inquiry, in the simplicity of its form and the systemic complexity of its process, represents, we have suggested, a ur-discourse not just for education, but for the speech community that is required for the communicative ideal of "social democracy" (Dewey, 1916), without which authentic political democracy is not possible. Mediating as it does between the oral and the literate, CPI is a hybrid form which, in its migration from the Athenian agora to the late 20th century classroom, shows great promise as an exemplary discourse for the electronic commons, both as a vehicle for communal deliberation and as a pedagogy that fosters critical thinking and multiple literacies for the new intelligence emerging in response to a changing information environment, and the new form of subjectivity— which we have called "complex"—that results. Its implementation in online environments can take many forms, as befits the hybridity of the postmodern information environment, with its remarkable combinatory possibilities for balancing the fast and the slow, the real and the hyper-real, the hidden and visible, and its capacity to create mutual presence in a new kind of space. But its fundamental capacity to provide a structure and a process, not just for the internalization of habits of critical thinking, but for authentic democratic practice, remains the same.

REFERENCES

Bateson, G. (1972). *Steps to an ecology of mind.* New York, NY: Ballantine Books.

Baudrillard, J. (1998). Simulacra and simulations. In Poster, M. (Ed.), *Jean Baudrillard: Selected writings* (pp. 166–184). Palo Alto, CA: Stanford University Press.

Bohm, D. (1990). *On dialogue.* Ojai, CA: David Bohm Seminars.

Bohm, D. (1997). *Thought as a system.* New York, NY: Routledge.

Buchler, J. (1990). *Metaphysics of natural complexes* (2nd ed.). Albany, NY: State University of New York Press.

Cannon, D., & Weinstein, M. (1993). Reasoning skills: An overview. In Lipman, M. (Ed.), *Thinking children and education* (pp. 598–604). Dubuque, IA: Kendall Hunt.

Cilliers, P. (1998). *Complexity and postmodernism.* London, UK: Routledge.

De Marzio, D. M. (1997). *Robert Corrington and the Philosophy for Children program: Communities of interpretation and communities of inquiry.* Unpublished masters thesis, Montclair State University, Montclair NJ.

Debord, G. (1983). *Society of the spectacle.* Detroit, MI: Black and Red.

Deleuze, G., & Guattari, F. (1980). *A thousand plateaus: Capitalism and schizophrenia* (Massumi, B., Trans.). Minneapolis, MN: University of Minnesota Press.

Dewey, J. (1916). *Democracy and education.* New York, NY: Free Press.

Dewey, J. (1933). *How we think* (rev. ed.). Boston, MA: D.C. Heath.

Dewey, J. (1938). *Logic: The theory of inquiry.* New York, NY: Holt, Rinehart and Winston.

Dewey, J. (1990). *The school and society & The child and the curriculum.* Chicago, IL: University of Chicago Press. (Original work published 1902)

Foucault, M. (2005). *The hermeneutics of the subject: Lectures at the College de France, 1981-82.* New York, NY: Palgrave Macmillan.

Freire, P. (1965). *Pedagogy of the oppressed.* New York, NY: Seabury.

Garrison, D. R. (2011). *E-learning in the 21st century: A framework for research and practice.* New York, NY: Routledge.

Gitai, A. (2005). *Free zone. Agav Films (France), Agat Films & Cie (France), Golem (Spain), Artémis Productions, Agav Hafakot (Israel), Hammon Hafakot (Israel), Arte France Cinéma.* Belgium: Cinéart.

Habermas, J. (1984). *The theory of communicative action.* Boston, MA: Beacon Press.

Hardt, M., & Negri, A. (2004). *Multitude: War and democracy in the age of empire.* New York, NY: Penguin Books.

Kennedy, D. (1990). Hans-Georg Gadamer's dialectic of dialogue and the epistemology of the community of inquiry. *Analytic Teaching, 11*(1), 43–51.

Kennedy, D. (1993). *Community of inquiry and educational structure. Thinking children and education* (pp. 352–357). Dubuque, IA: Kendall Hunt.

Kennedy, D. (1999). Philosophy for children and the reconstruction of philosophy. *Metaphilosophy, 30*(4), 338–359.

Kennedy, D. (2004a). The role of a facilitator in a community of philosophical inquiry. *Metaphilosophy, 35*(4), 744–765.

Kennedy, D. (2004b). Communal philosophical dialogue and the intersubject. *International Journal for Philosophical Practice, 18*(2), 203–208.

Kennedy, D. (2006). What some second graders say about conflict. In *Changing conceptions of the child from the Renaissance to post-modernity: A philosophy of childhood* (pp. 171–255). Lewiston, NY: The Edwin Mellen Press.

Kennedy, D. (2010a). *Philosophical dialogue with children: Essays on theory and practice*. Lewiston, NY: The Mellen Press.

Kennedy, D. (in press). Rhizomatic curriculum development in community of philosophical inquiry. In Santi, M., & Oliverio, S. (Eds.), *Educating for complex thinking through philosophical inquiry. Models, advances, and proposals for the new millennium*. Napoli, Italy: Liguori.

Kennedy, N., & Kennedy, D. (2010b). Between chaos and entropy: Community of inquiry from a systems perspective. *Complicity: An International Journal of Complexity and Education, 7*(2). http://ejournals.library.ualberta.ca/index.php/complicity/index

Kennedy, N., & Kennedy, D. (2012). Community of philosophical inquiry as a discursive structure, and its role in school curriculum design. In Vansieleghem, N., & Kennedy, D. (Eds.), *Philosophy for children in transition: Problems and prospects* (pp. 97–116). London, UK: Blackwell.

Laszlo, E. (1975). Basic constructs of systems philosophy. In Ruben, B., & Kim, J. (Eds.), *General systems theory and human communication* (pp. 66–77). Rochelle Park, NJ: Hayden Book Company.

Latour, B. (2005). *Reassembling the social*. New York, NY: Oxford University Press.

Lipman, M. (1992). Critical thinking: What can it be? In Oxman, W., Michelli, N. M., & Coia, L. (Eds.), *Critical thinking and learning* (pp. 79–97). Montclair, NJ: Montclair State University.

Lipman, M. (Ed.). (1993). *Thinking children and education*. Dubuque, IA: Kendall Hunt.

Lipman, M. (2003). *Thinking in education* (2nd ed.). Cambridge, UK: Cambridge University Press.

Lipman, M., Sharp, A. M., & Oscanyan, F. S. (1980). *Philosophy in the classroom* (2nd ed.). Philadelphia, PA: Temple University Press.

Luhmann, N. (1995). *Social systems*. Palo Alto, CA: Stanford University Press.

Luke, C. (1989). *Pedagogy, printing, and Protestantism: The discourse on childhood*. Albany, NY: SUNY Press.

Lushyn, P., & Kennedy, D. (2002). Power, manipulation, and control in a community of inquiry. *Analytic Teaching, 23*(2), 103–110.

McCall, C. (1993). Young children generate philosophical ideas. In Lipman, M. (Ed.), *Thinking children and education* (pp. 569–592). Dubuque, IA: Kendall Hunt.

Mead, G. H. (1934). *Mind, self and society*. Chicago, IL: University of Chicago Press.

Ong, W. (1982). *Orality and literacy: The technologizing of the word*. New York, NY: Methuen.

Peirce, C. S. (1958). *Values in a universe of chance* (Weiner, P., Ed.). Garden City, NY: Doubleday Anchor Books.

Peirce, C. S. (1966). The fixation of belief. In Weiner, P. (Ed.), *Selected writings* (pp. 27–40). New York, NY: Dover Publications.

Peirce, C. S. (2011). *The philosophical writings of Peirce (J. Buchler* (New York, N. Y., Ed.). Dover.

Plato,. (1961). Phaedrus. In Hamilton, E., & Cairns, H. (Eds.), *The collected dialogues of Plato* (pp. 475–525). Princeton, NJ: Princeton University Press.

Sharp, A. M. (1987). What is a community of inquiry? *Journal of Moral Education, 16*(1), 37–45.

Sharp, A. M. (1993). The community of inquiry: Education for democracy. In Lipman, M. (Ed.), *Thinking children and education* (pp. 337–345). Dubuque, IA: Kendall-Hunt.

Splitter, L., & Sharp, A. M. (1995). *Teaching for better thinking: The classroom community of inquiry*. Melbourne, Australia: ACER.

Vansieleghem, N. (2012). Philosophy with children as an exercise in parrhesia: An account of a philosophical experiment with children in Cambodia. In Vansieleghem, N., & Kennedy, D. (Eds.), *Philosophy for children in transition: Problems and prospects* (pp. 152–169). London, UK: Blackwell.

Vygotsky, L. (1978). *Mind in society: The development of higher psychological processes*. Cambridge, MA: Harvard University Press.

KEY TERMS AND DEFINITIONS

Collective Zone of Proximal Development: A speech situation in which a discussion group's zone of actual development is higher than each member's, and in which collective dialogue provides a scaffold for each individual who needs it.

Community of Inquiry: The practice of communal, dialogical interaction centered on the problematization and collaborative reconstruction of philosophical, scientific, moral or aesthetic concepts and the questions or problems in which they are embedded.

Community of Philosophical Inquiry: A discussion group with the specific deliberative goal of working to problematize and reconstruct common, central and contestable concepts like truth, justice, friendship, economy, nature, person, and so on, through distributed thinking in a dialogical context.

Complex Subject: A form of subjectivity that understands itself as part of a global system of social assemblages and hybrid human-machine networks that are inherently communicative.

Complex System: A system, whether natural, social, or communicative that is emergent, self-organizing, non-hierarchical, ecological, unpredictable, irreversible and irreducible to its basic constituents. A complex system is comprised of intricate sets of non-linear relationships and feedback loops in a process of constant adaptation—a dynamic interplay between the two limit tendencies of chaos and stagnation.

Distributed Intelligence: The notion that the intelligence is actually or potentially distributed among all the members of a given group with a common task or activity, implying that the whole is greater than the sum of its parts. The term "distribution" can also be applied to power, authority, control, thinking and affect.

Following the Argument Where It Leads: The practice of tracking and responding to the multiple levels of logical entailment, claims and propositions that make up the structural elements in the emergent argumentation-system of a polyvocal, dialogical philosophical conversation.

Ideal Speech Situation: A speech situation ruled, whether implicitly or explicitly, by a discourse ethics for which free assertion and questioning and expression, and the absence of coercion, manipulation, or purely unilateral relations between the group leader and the participants, is understood to be the norm.

Philosophical Praxis: The process whereby a philosophical concept, having been reconstructed through dialogue, re-enters practice, where it is challenged by context and experience to justify the new understanding of it; then goes back into dialogue—both inter- and intra-subjective—where the work of reconstruction is taken up yet again.

Psychodynamics: The characteristic personal and social styles of subjectivity—temporal, perceptual, discursive, narrative, expressive and theoretical--that are present in a collective in any given historical culture. Psychodynamics, on Walter Ong's (1982) account, are profoundly shaped by the information environment. The study of psychodynamics over time is an aspect of the field of psychohistory.

Social Democracy: The practical cultivation of what John Dewey (1916, p. 87) called "a mode of associated living, of conjoint communicated experience" that fosters the values and practices of pluralism and cooperation, with special emphasis on the formation of communities of interest that transcend race, ethnicity, class and national interests and boundaries.

Chapter 3
Metacognitive Development within the Community of Inquiry

Zehra Akyol
Independent Researcher, Canada

ABSTRACT

This chapter focuses on metacognition in relation to learning and cognition and discusses the potential of the Community of Inquiry (CoI) Framework to guide metacognitive development in online and blended learning environments. The commonality between metacognition and the community of inquiry is the interplay between internal knowledge construction and collaborative learning activities. In this regard, the CoI framework provides a model of cognition that operationalizes inquiry with the potential to contextualize and understand metacognition in an online learning environment. The metacognitive construct developed using the CoI framework as a theoretical lens is introduced, and the strategies and activities to support metacognition in a community of inquiry are provided.

INTRODUCTION

Knowing yourself is the beginning of all wisdom.

—Aristotle

Contemporary education aims to put the learner at the center of the learning process by recognizing and valuing the potential of the learner to construct knowledge. However, educational practices do not always reflect intended goals. As Garrison and Archer (2000) noted the incongruence between ideal educational outcomes and actual practices result in students' uncritically assimilating teacher conveyed information rather than assuming responsibility for constructing meaningful and worthwhile knowledge. Certainly there are many contextual and systematic constraints behind this discrepancy. From the learner perspective, the transaction requires a significant role change. Being at the center of the learning process, students must accept increased responsibility for their own learning. The question is whether the students are ready for this transaction and whether the current approaches are really encouraging students to take the responsibility and control of their learning.

DOI: 10.4018/978-1-4666-2110-7.ch003

Taking responsibility for learning is not easy; in fact it can be an extremely challenging process. It requires a student to increase his/her awareness of self as a learner, to understand his/her mental world better. In other words, students need to improve their metacognitive knowledge and skills in order to maximize their potential to construct meaningful and worthwhile knowledge. It is believed and supported by research that the ability to monitor and control learning is crucial both for successful learning and learning how to learn (White, Frederikson & Collins, 2009). This chapter discusses the value of metacognition for learning and explores how a community of inquiry can support and sustain metacognitive development.

What is Metacognition?

Meta as a Greek word literally means "after," "beyond"; in this regard metacognition is a cognition that comes after cognition and also, as Langford (1986) remarks, is presumably related to another cognition. Flavell (1979), one of the pioneers of research on metacognition describes metacognition as consisting of "knowledge or beliefs about what factors or variables act and interact in what ways to affect the course and outcome of cognitive enterprises" (p. 907). Even though there are many different definitions for metacognition, the general consensus is that a definition of metacognition should include: "knowledge of one's knowledge, processes, and cognitive and affective states; and the ability to consciously and deliberately monitor and regulate one's knowledge, processes and cognitive and affective states" (Hacker, 1998, p.11).

In order to better understand metacognition and the relationship between metacognition and cognition, we must begin with an understanding of cognition. According to Langford (1986), cognition is a belief, and a belief about a belief is an example of metacognition; this is called a meta-belief. Langford argues that "whenever a belief is expressed, the person expressing it possesses a corresponding meta-belief, whether it is expressed or not... and whenever a belief could be expressed by its possessor, whether it is expressed or not, a corresponding meta-belief exists" (p.20). Similarly, it could be said that cognition is a precondition for metacognition and creates the content of metacognition. On the other hand, metacognition is vital to cognition. It plays a critical role in various types of cognitive activity such as communication of information, comprehension, memory or problem solving. Metacognition could be considered as the surveillance of cognition since metacognitive processes are internal executive processes that supervise and control cognitive processes (Gourgey, 2001). According to Necka and Orzechowski (2005), cognition refers to regular information processing which is directly responsible for the execution of a cognitive task, whereas "metacognition enables that cognitive processes are executed in the appropriate order and according to some superordinate rules" (p.131). Cognitive strategies enable one to make progress whereas metacognitive strategies enable one to monitor and improve one's progress through evaluating understanding, applying knowledge to new situations (Gourgey, 2001). However, even though the person is in general capable of having meta-beliefs, he may possess a belief without having possessing a corresponding meta-belief. A belief may be true or false; when it is a false belief, "the possessor of meta-beliefs therefore is not only in a good position to assess his beliefs but also has good reasons to do so" (Langford, 1986, p.25).

Another difference between metacognition and cognition is that metacognition is a broad concept relatively independent of subject areas and has broad applications across a number of different settings (e.g., education, law, cognitive psychology). Unlike cognitive skills, metacognitive skills span multiple domains. Schraw (2001) further explains that metacognition is more durable and general than domain specific cognitive skills. Hacker (1998) differentiates metacognitive thinking from other kinds of thinking in that metacognitive thoughts are tied to a person's own internal mental representations of the reality rather than stemming from the person's external reality. Thinking can include what one knows, how it works, and how one feels about it. Flavell (1971), as cited in Hacker 1998), describes metacognitive thoughts as deliberate, planful, intentional, goal-directed, and future-oriented mental behaviors.

The research on metacognition began in the early 1970s mostly focusing on metacognitive development in children. Questions concerning how information is stored in and retrieved from mental structures, how these structures develop with age, and how storage and retrieval are controlled, aroused the attention of many researchers and the answers to these questions enabled the development of Flavell's (1979) model of metacognition and cognitive monitoring (Hacker, 1998). After 1983 a new field of research focusing on metacognition in adults started to grow (Flavell, 2004). Hacker's (1998) review of metacognition research yielded three main categories of research: studies of cognitive monitoring, studies of cognitive regulation, and studies of cognitive monitoring and regulation. The studies in the first category examined people's knowledge and thought processes and how accurately they can monitor their knowledge and processes. Hacker's review indicated that the research from the first category showed several other factors such as the complexity of task (i.e., kind of thought process or knowledge that are being monitored) along with the age factor influencing the cognitive monitoring ability. Studies on the cognitive regulation category examined regulation of one's cognitive processes to cope with changing conditions. The main finding of the studies was that if people are taught metacognitive awareness about the utility and function of a strategy during their learning of it, they are more likely to generalize the strategy to new situations. The third category of research, which examined both monitoring and regulation, focused on organizational and elaboration strat-

egies in memory and how these strategies can be used to improve performance. According to Hacker (1998), the final category of metacognition research has focused on educational applications. Realizing the potential of metacognition to improve teaching and learning experiences, these studies examine ways in which metacognitive theory can be applied to education. The fundamental question these studies were broadly based on is "can instruction of metacognitive processes facilitate learning?" The promise is that metacognitive theory can encourage students to become the agents of their own thinking through improving their awareness and understanding of being self-regulatory organisms (Hacker, 1998).

Today, it is now largely accepted that metacognition is an important ability to develop (Sternberg, 2001), and it has a strong effect on learning and understanding (Schwarts & Perfect, 2004; Hartman, 2001; Maki & McGuire, 2004). Increasing awareness on the importance of metacognition is also expanding the contexts of metacognition research. Though considerable metacognitive research has been conducted in traditional learning environments, recently there is a growing number of studies on metacognition in relation to online learning. Considering that online learning requires enhanced monitoring and regulatory skills, it is crucial to understand the structure and dynamics of metacognition in these text-based online learning settings. For example, in the Weigel, Straughn and Gardner (2010) study, the educators emphasized the cultivation of higher order metacognitive skills for online engagement. They further indicated that students with such skills can better assess the legitimacy of online information and stay focused.

The main challenge of studying metacognition in an online learning environment is that it requires a coherent theoretical framework. This chapter focuses on metacognition in online learning through the lens of the Community of Inquiry (CoI) theoretical framework, which has been validated as a coherent theory to understand the complexities and prescribe the effective conduct of online learning

(Garrison, 2011). The CoI framework encourages the learner to take responsibility for his/her learning and creates conditions (i.e., collaborative-constructivist learning environment) to support and sustain metacognitive development. In fact, the commonality between metacognition and the CoI theoretical framework is the interplay between internal knowledge construction and collaborative learning activities, which will be detailed next. The CoI framework provides a model of cognition that operationalizes inquiry with the potential to contextualize and understand metacognition in an online learning environment. In the following sections the metacognitive construct developed by Akyol and Garrison (2011) will be further explored, elaborating how the elements of the CoI framework support and sustain metacognitive development.

METACOGNITION IN AN ONLINE COMMUNITY OF INQUIRY

The impact of social context on learning has been a study of interest since the recognition and adoption of Vygotsky's perspective on development and paradigmatic shifts in the study of cognition (Lee & Smogorinsky, 2000). Vygotsky (1981), as cited in Wells (2001), argues that all higher mental functions are internalized social relationships. According to Wells (2000), learning is inherently social and takes place through a process of inquiry within a social group. Based upon Vygotskian theory of learning, Wells (2000) describes learning as "a way of referring to transformation that continuously takes places in an individual's identity and ways of participating through his/her engagement in particular instances of social activities with others" (p. 56). In this regard, as Vygotsky claimed, the potential for learning is dependent not only on prior knowledge, the nature of task/ problem, instructional strategies but also the quality of interaction among others (Lee & Smagorinsky, 2000).

The metacognition research has been inevitably influenced by this paradigm and a transition from the early individualistic developmental and cognitive models to the acknowledgment of socially situated metacognition has emerged (Larkin, 2009). There is now a growing recognition of the importance of sharing cognitive experiences (Flavell, 1987; Brown, 1987; Schraw, 2001; Wade & Fauske, 2004; White, Frederiksen & Collins, 2009). As Miell and Miell (1986) point out, people are metacognitive but not only as logical identities but also as social interactants. Therefore, people need to communicate, explain and justify their thinking to self and others; and these activities clearly require metacognition (Flavell, 1987). Similarly, Larkin (2009) suggests that metacognition is facilitated through collaboration.

The CoI theoretical framework reveals the intersection of metacognition and collaboration. As indicated by Akyol and Garrison (2011), the elements of the framework provide the means to operationalize and assess metacognition in online communities of inquiry. While teaching and cognitive presence are essential to understand the structure and dynamics, social presence creates the affective environment for the emergence of shared or social metacognition. Overall, there are three main reasons why the CoI theoretical framework is a promising theory to study social metacognition in online learning environments. First and foremost, learning in a community of inquiry is a reflective and recursive process which both requires and supports metacognitive knowledge and skills. Recursion is the unique property of interpersonal cognition (Miell & Miell, 1986) and, according to Langford (1986), through this possibility, systematic enquiries such as physics and psychology can emerge. White, Frederikson and Collins (2009) also support this idea emphasizing the interplay between metacognition and scientific inquiry. According to the authors, the processes of scientific inquiry - theorizing, questioning and hypothesizing, investigating, and analyzing and synthesizing - are associated with a regulatory process that monitors how well the process is being carried out and whether another process needs to be invoked to deal with any issues that arise.

The process of knowledge development in a CoI is simply a cycle of reflection on ideas till reaching a plausible agreed idea. Progression through the phases of the inquiry is recursive in the sense that the knowledge gained in one phase is used to gather more information in the next higher phase of inquiry. More specifically, it is the cognitive presence in a CoI that represents the cycle of inquiry and creates the means to understand and operationalize metacognition. At the same time, metacognition provides a cognitive map of the inquiry process and the complexities of critical discourse. As Garrison (2011) indicates, for the individual to navigate through the phases of critical inquiry (i.e., triggering event, exploration, integration, and resolution) requires metacognitive awareness. More specifically, to ensure progression through the phases to resolution, it is essential "to understand the inquiry process and what is required at each phase; then to exhibit the skills" (Garrison, 2011, p.50).

On the other hand, knowledge building in a community of inquiry may occur through computer mediated communication, which is usually a discussion board where learners are involved in a reflective writing activity to share, develop and confirm their ideas. In this regard, writing itself is an applied metacognition (Hacker, Keener & Kircher, 2009). Not only generation of thoughts involves monitoring and controlling activities but also transferring the generated thoughts into writing requires monitoring and controlling of the thoughts to ensure they are representing the intended meaning. The monitoring activities are reading, rereading, reflecting and reviewing while the control strategies are editing, drafting, idea generation, word production, translation, diagnosing and revision (Hacker, Keener & Kircher, 2009). Moreover, when students read others' comments,

they also try to understand their thought processes through monitoring activities as well.

Second, teaching presence is essential to describe the regulatory roles and responsibilities of an online student in a community of inquiry (Akyol & Garrison, 2011). In an ideal e-learning environment, students are active participants in the educational enterprise contributing to the solution of emerging problems or difficulties and providing support and assistance to each other throughout the learning process. In a CoI, the responsibilities of teaching presence are shared among all the participants. Through encouraging students to take responsibility for their learning, teaching presence creates the ideal conditions for metacognitive development. That is, students become metacognitively aware and assume the regulatory responsibilities for successfully completing the inquiry process through teaching presence (Akyol & Garrison, 2011). Furthermore, from a structural perspective, the activities in the facilitating discourse and direct instruction category of teaching presence overlap with the regulatory aspect of metacognition. There is a remarkable commonality between the dimensions of teaching presence and those of metacognition in terms of knowledge, monitoring and regulation.

Finally, social presence creates the frame of references for metacognition. The students in a CoI share a context in which each knows the other's frame of reference. Antaki and Lewis (1986) call this as metacognitive world of meaning that allows one to understand what the other says without having to entertain all possible interpretations of what was said. In a CoI, it is the social presence that creates this shared metacognitive world through evolving around a common purpose. Students identify themselves with the group or course of study and communicate purposefully (Garrison 2009). A learning community has shared goals and the achievement of shared goals depends on collaboration (Wells, 2000). Through engagement in collaborative activities, students develop an academic climate in which they all contribute to the critical inquiry and discourse. In such a context, when a belief is expressed, it also becomes available to others; hence not only the possessors of the belief but also other people are put in a position to assess it (Langford, 1986). This creates the possibility of inter-subjective agreement about beliefs which are both shared and known to be shared.

Based on the aforementioned reasons, the metacognitive construct has been developed utilizing the CoI framework in a recent study (Akyol & Garrison, 2011). Applying an iterative process, the researchers explored the behavioral indices of metacognition in an online learning environment. The metacognitive construct has three interdependent dimensions: knowledge of cognition, monitoring of cognition, and regulation of cognition. Metacognition in a community of inquiry is a collaborative process where internal and external conditions are being constantly assessed. Akyol and Garrison (2011) describe metacognition as the set of higher knowledge and skills to monitor and regulate manifest cognitive processes of both self and others.

METACOGNITIVE CONSTRUCT

Based on early definitions of metacognition, it was largely considered that metacognition has two distinct processes – monitoring and control. Similarly, Flavell (1979) argued that metacognition consists of two components – metacognitive knowledge and metacognitive experiences. Knowledge is about the factors (person, task, or strategy) that affect the course and outcome of the cognitive enterprises. Experiences occur during the progress of learning; it is about planning, acting, and evaluating within the progress to achieve learning. Brown (1987) also identifies two types of metacognition: (i) knowledge about cognition, which is knowing what you know and don't know as well as how you learn and (ii) regulation of cognition which includes planning, monitoring,

and regulating your progress. On the other hand, Tobias and Everson (2002) describe metacognition as comprised of three components: the knowledge about metacognition, the ability to monitor one's learning processes, and the meta-ability to control the learning processes.

Unlike most metacognitive models which consider metacognitive knowledge and monitoring (i.e., awareness) as one dimension, the metacognitive construct developed by Akyol and Garrison (2011) realizes the importance of distinguishing these two aspects. As indicated by Pintrich, Wolters and Baxter (2000), metacognitive knowledge is more static and similar to other kinds of knowledge in long-term memory whereas metacognitive monitoring is more "online," "in the moment" and involves students' judgments of their learning during the process of learning. Therefore, knowledge of cognition is considered as a pre-task metacognition while monitoring of cognition is assessment of tasks, understanding, and progress of the inquiry process.

Knowledge of Cognition

Metacognitive knowledge is the explicit knowledge about our own cognitive strengths and weaknesses (Flavell, 1979). Knowledge of cognition (KoC) in a community of inquiry is basically the awareness of self as a learner which is built through the knowledge and motivation associated with the inquiry process, academic discipline and expectancies. Example of KoC would be students' assessment of how they learn best, what they know or do not know about the subject matter, or how they feel with regards to the task or their ability. It is a general aspect of metacognition that can be observed anytime while monitoring and regulation dimensions are more reflective and activity-based metacognitive states (Akyol & Garrison, 2011).

Knowledge of cognition is central to learning effectively and efficiently from instruction (Tobias & Everson, 2002). It is important for students to be able to differentiate what they know or have learned from what they do not know or need to know. Only then can they engage higher levels of metacognitive strategies such as evaluating their learning or employing strategies to improve their learning (Tobias & Everson, 2009). In Akyol and Garrison's (2011) research KoC was observed least in the online discussion and decreased over time. Considering that KoC is an entering metacognitive state and relatively static during the learning process, the authors indicate that monitoring and regulation naturally take place as more dynamic and executive processes while developing shared cognition.

Monitoring of Cognition

Monitoring of cognition (MoC) is the reflective dimension of metacognition. Monitoring refers to one's online awareness of comprehension, understanding and task performance. For instance, periodic self-testing during learning is an example of monitoring activity (Sternberg, 2001). Metacognitive monitoring is comprised of the processes that allow individuals to observe, reflect on or experience his/her own cognitive processes (Schwartz & Perfect, 2004). In a community of inquiry, the monitoring dimension specifically includes assessment of task and understanding progression and effort. In practical terms, monitoring is facilitated by knowledge of practical inquiry and clear expectations of the learning tasks. Through distributed teaching presence students also reflect on each other's contributions while they are engaged in discourse.

Monitoring of cognition is an important ability to judge successfully one's own cognitive processes (Son & Schwartz, 2004). However, the review of Maki and McGuire (2004) reveals that many students including the capable ones with high verbal ability do not always adequately monitor their understanding of text that they have read. Similarly, Son and Schwartz (2004) conclude that metacognitive judgments about learning are intermediate in accuracy; people are not always accurate or sometimes inaccurate.

Regulation of Cognition

Regulation of cognition (RoC) is the interactive aspect of metacognition and refers to a set of activities that help students control their learning. These activities include planning, setting goals, reviewing and applying strategies, as well as taking control of motivation and effort. Schwartz and Perfect (2004) describe these activities as the conscious or non-conscious decisions made based on the output of cognitive processes. Regulation is a collaborative process where internal and external conditions are being constantly assessed. Students are engaged in asking for help or suggesting help to others to reciprocally enhance the learning experience and the realization of intended outcomes. In all three components of metacognition, regulation has a direct impact on cognition and learning. The regulative activity applied by the student may enhance or hinder the learning. Improving human learning could be achieved by improving or altering regulation of cognition (Schwartz & Perfect, 2004). Research also supports the relationship between learning outcomes and regulation of cognition (Sternberg, 2001).

Flavell (1979) argues a close relationship between metacognitive knowledge (i.e., monitoring) and metacognitive experiences (i.e., regulation or control). According to Flavell, metacognitive knowledge can lead and activate metacognitive experiences and metacognitive experiences affect metacognitive knowledge by adding to it, deleting from it, or revising it. In a way, metacognitive experiences are items of metacognitive knowledge that entered consciousness. This relationship has been approved and confirmed by many other researchers as well. Schwartz and Perfect (2004) indicate that control (regulative) processes are revealed by the behavior of a person and is a function of monitoring. Regulation of metacognition is the ability to use the judgments resulted as a function of monitoring of cognition to alter the cognitive behavior. Students who are lacking metacognitive monitoring ability would persist in their applications of inappropriate strategies which, in turn, would result in failure. Therefore, in order for regulation of cognition to impact learning positively, monitoring of cognition should be reinforced. Akyol and Garrison (2011) also provided evidence for the close relationship between monitoring and regulation. In their research it was observed that when students express uncertainty or impasse about their learning (i.e., monitoring), they tend to apply a cognitive strategy to solve the problem or improve their learning (i.e., regulation). The authors indicate that these two aspects of metacognition are inseparable in practice; they are interdependent and interact with each other continuously as learners move imperceptibly between the reflective and experiential world.

In the CoI environment, each presence directly or indirectly contributes to the development of metacognition; however, we see metacognitive activities at the intersections of the CoI elements, especially the intersection of teaching and cognitive presence and the intersection of social and cognitive presence, rather than exclusively within each element. As indicated earlier, social presence creates a focused and purposeful medium or metacognitive world of meaning as named by Antaki and Lewis (1986), in which students can have a direct understanding of what the other says. Teaching presence enables students to become metacognitively aware and assume regulatory skills for each other's learning throughout the inquiry process. Again, through cognitive presence, students have an increased understanding and awareness of the inquiry process which, in turn, helps them improve their regulation of cognition by enabling them to select the appropriate learning strategies corresponding to the level of inquiry. At the intersections, metacognitive activities appear as students openly communicate to support each other's engagement in and progression through the inquiry.

The development of metacognitive construct was an important step to understand the dynamics between metacognition and learning in online collaborative learning. Recently, the research conducted by Shea and his colleagues (in press) also provided evidence of metacognition promoting collaboration and impacting learning (labeled "learning presence"). The intent of these researchers was to articulate a new conceptual element to describe effective learner behavior in fully online courses. However, as emphasized by Garrison (2011), all participants in a CoI reflect varying degrees of each of the three presences; that is, they assume teaching, cognitive and social responsibilities in order to achieve deep and meaningful learning. It is important to stress here that proposing a new presence diverges from the integrity of the CoI framework and the interdependence of its elements, which suggests an individualistic over a collaborative perspective.

Regarding metacognition, a close look at the indicators of "learning presence" shows that they overlap with the indicators of each aspect of the metacognitive construct. However, even though the indicators reflect socially situated metacognitive activities such as "seeking, offering and providing help or information," Shea et al. (in press) emphasize self-regulated learning in their model which focuses on internal processes of learning. Moreover, the authors argue that metacognition is a sub-category of the larger construct of self-regulation. As indicated elsewhere (Akyol & Garrison, 2011), the theoretical construct of metacognition and its relationship to other constructs such as self-regulation and self-efficacy is complex; however, if we are to address collaborative learning, metacognition is shared and collaborative in nature as well. The CoI theoretical framework describes learning as community based and collaborative. Community reflects the context and the purpose in which the academic goals are greatly influenced by societal knowledge and expectations and collaboration reflects the reality of mutual interdependence (see chapter 2).

In this regard, self-regulation could be considered in terms of what the learner brings to the learning environment. As soon as the learner engages in a community of inquiry, it is collaborative metacognition (i.e., co-regulation) that emerges and evolves as core to the learning process. As Hadwin, Järvelä and Miller (2011) indicate, (cited in Torras & Mayordomo, 2011), co-regulation arises through interactions where each participant brings different kinds of self-regulatory challenges and expertise. Recent research has provided evidence of co-regulation or shared metacognition in student-student dialogues as well as teacher-student dialogues (Volet, Summers & Thurman, 2009; Torras & Mayordomo, 2011; Iiskala, Vauras; Lehtinen & Salonen, 2011). It is important to emphasize that the more collaborative the learning is, and the more difficult the task is or the higher level the inquiry is, the more evidence of shared metacognition is found (Akyol & Garrison, 2011; Iskala, et al., 2011). Furthermore, only when the group is engaged in high-level inquiry, rather than merely sharing information, co-regulatory metacognitive activity may lead to the construction of meaningful knowledge and understanding (Volet, Summers & Thurman, 2009). In short, an individualistic view of metacognition or learning is contradictory to the main premise of the CoI theoretical framework. In a collaborative community of inquiry, social regulation cannot be reduced to each community member's individualistic characteristics such as self-regulation (Volet, Vauras & Salonen, 2009).

SUPPORT OF METACOGNITIVE DEVELOPMENT IN A COMMUNITY OF INQUIRY

If the educational change is to be truly inclusive of all the interest involved, the learning context should be restructured as communities of inquiry (Wells, 2000). The learning context influences the development and pursuit of metacognitive skills and knowledge. Therefore, consideration of contextual variables is essential in order to develop valid and reliable measures of metacognition (Borkowski, Chan & Muthukrishna, 2000). The metacognitive construct developed by Akyol and Garrison (2011) reflect specifically the metacognition in an online community of inquiry. Through the effective development of social, cognitive and teaching presence, the CoI framework supports and sustains metacognition in an online learning environment. In this section, the specific strategies and activities to support metacognitive development will be discussed. Teaching presence as the mediating element of CoI that brings together cognitive and social presence in purposeful and synergistic ways (Garrison, 2011) will be used as a framework to explain the strategies. However, before going into the details of these strategies, it is important to mention how metacognition influences the teaching activity itself.

Metacognition in an online community not only applies to learning but also it is important to teaching effectively. Teaching metacognitively enables teachers to reflect on their own teaching such as instructional goals, students' characteristics and needs, content level, teaching strategies and how their teaching will activate and develop students' metacognition (Hartman, 2001). As a result, teaching metacognitively increases instructors' own learning and motivation, and improves their practice. Duffy, Miller, Parson and Meloth (2009) elaborate the complexity of teachers' metacognition. They argue that teachers not only monitor and regulate their own cognitive activity, but also they monitor and regulate students' cognition by promoting content learning, identifying appropriate strategies, making moment-moment decisions to ensure their learning or adjusting individual differences. To do so requires a sufficient level of metacognitive knowledge. Hartman (2001) points out that teachers need to have a repertoire of teaching strategies to allow them to be flexible and shift as the situation requires. This repertoire comprises teachers' metacognitive knowledge which will be improved through their awareness and efforts to apply metacognitive teaching strategies. Increasing teachers' awareness and knowledge about metacognition and the cognitive process is essential for both effective teaching and facilitation of students' learning. The Practical Inquiry model representing the structure and dynamics of the inquiry process could be used for teachers to create a better understanding (i.e., metacognitive awareness) of the collaborative knowledge building process and develop appropriate strategies.

In terms of improving students' metacognition, the consideration should be given to the activities from the early design and organization to the facilitation and direction of instruction. Design and organization aspect of teaching presence provides the structure for the learning experience. For this, teachers must pay attention to metacognitive knowledge of the students when they are establishing the curriculum, defining goals and expectations, structuring learning activities and setting time parameters. More specially, the teachers should be aware of what students know and don't know about the content, what are their weaknesses and strengths as learners, and their repertoire of cognitive strategies. Communicating the goals and expectations and the requirements of the task and content also encourage students to reflect on their metacognitive knowledge. Taking time to discuss the importance of metacognition and its role on learning and cognition would be another important early course activity to enhance student's awareness. If students are convinced that success or failure depends on the effort they make, they realize that they can expect success when they put in the required effort. Beliefs in personal control (i.e., metacognition) over task outcomes can be promoted by convincing them that success is within their control (Borkowski, Chan & Muthukrishna, 2000). Focus on developing strategies for regulation of cognition encourages students to construct knowledge about how, when

and where to use certain strategies to improve their learning (Schraw, 2001). Schraw (2001) therefore, suggests creating a learning environment that promotes mastery rather than focus on performance for metacognitive development. In such environments, students can acquire a broader perspective of strategies and learn the ways to use these strategies to improve their learning, which is especially good for regulation of cognition.

Learning activities should be designed and organized in ways that encourage students to reflect on their own and each other's understanding. Collaborative activities such as pair problem solving encourage students self-monitor, clarify their thinking, and to think about why their strategies are useful (Gourgey, 2001). Teachers should prompt students to collaborate with one another in order to gain deep conceptual understanding (Borkowski et.al., 2000). One important activity that is highly suggested especially for the regulation of cognition is enabling students to lead the discussion (discussed further later). Through sharing the responsibility of instructors, students will be able to take control of their learning, as well as understand and help others' cognitive processes. Finally, learning activities and resources should be designed and organized in a way that enables students to draw on multiple sources of assistance when needed. In this regard, it is also important to create a comfortable and trusting environment through social presence where students can freely question each other's thought processes as well as ask for help without hesitating when they encounter a learning problem.

Extensive practice and reflection are crucial for the development of metacognitive knowledge and skills (Schraw, 2001). A truly collaborative learning environment demands reflection by learners and induces an online awareness of one's cognitive processes, which, in turn, promotes the development of self-regulatory skills. Facilitating discourse and direct instruction categories of teaching presence have more direct impact on the development of metacognitive skills through enabling both reflection and practice. In fact, facilitation activities could be considered as improving monitoring of cognition more while direct instruction could be considered more related to regulation of cognition. Moreover, facilitation and direction may also be observed occurring consecutively and interacting with each other similar to the monitoring and regulation of cognition. For example, when a student identifies self or other's level of understanding or inquiry, he or she can suggest or provide cognitive activities/strategies to help self or other achieve a better understanding or progress to higher phases of the inquiry. Therefore, effective facilitation and direction is important for reinforcing monitoring and regulation of cognition. To do so requires a transactional view of teaching and learning in which responsibility and control issues apply to both teaching and learning. That is, congruent with the educational purpose and the capabilities of the students, roles and responsibilities of teacher are shared between the teacher and students, which is described as distributed teaching presence by Garrison (2011). As indicated earlier, when students are given the opportunity to lead the discussions, they take control of the flow of ideas and knowledge building; they facilitate others' progress by confirming their ideas or providing suggestions when others encounter a problem. Leading the discussions is, therefore, a high level cognitive ability which requires a high level metacognitive ability. In a recent study, it has been found that ample opportunities for metacognitive reflection are important for fostering epistemic agency for knowledge building (Cacciamani, Cesareni, Martini, Ferrini & Fujita, 2011). Such activities could orientate the students towards a deeper exploration of problems and to the formulation of hypotheses. Moreover, seeing the similar evaluative operation carried out by their course peers favors an increase in the evaluative practice of both merging content and strategies during the discussion.

One final note regarding facilitation, and therefore monitoring of cognition, is that early emphasis in the course on metacognition and the shared goals will create a focused academic climate in which students are able to frame each other's cognitive processes. As mentioned earlier, although students have the ability to assess their cognition and make judgments, they may not have accurate judgments about their learning all the time. In such a context, having both the teacher and other students monitor their cognitive level will help them to improve their metacognitive judgments.

Another important strategy is teachers' modeling metacognitive skills. Through verbalizing the thought provoking process, students can develop regulatory capabilities such as monitoring or checking reflection (Borkowski, Chan & Muthukrishna, 2000). They will not only express, defend and question others' ideas but they will also be able to elaborate, clarify and recognize their own and others' thinking processes (Borkowski, Chan & Muthukrishna, 2000). Moreover, when students lead the discourse, they will automatically be modeling metacognitive activities. According to Schraw (2001), students' modeling is better and provides a powerful rationale for these skills within the student's zone of proximal development compared to teachers' modeling.

Finally, one technique that has been found valuable for increasing metacognitive awareness and promoting metacognitive skills is having the students label their discussion postings (Valcke, De wever, Zhu & Deed, 2009; Bai, 2009). In Valcke et al. (2009), students were asked to label their discussion posting using the Bloom's taxonomy. It was found that the labeling strategy both enhanced students' level of cognitive processing and metacognitive regulation in relation to planning, achieving clarity and monitoring. Bai (2009) applied the same approach using the Practical Inquiry model as a guide to facilitate students' critical thinking in online discussion. His research showed that when students have an understanding of the inquiry process, they were able to reach higher levels of cognitive presence in their discussion postings. These findings indicate the strong relationship between monitoring and regulation to progress through the phases of inquiry. The introduction of the Practical Inquiry model early in the course can increase students' awareness of metacognition, which will later enable them to better reflect on their own and other's cognitive presence. This will lead to the development of shared metacognition that contributes to the emergence of advanced cognition.

CONCLUSION

Higher order cognition is closely linked to the processes of cognitive control. As indicated by Necka and Orzechowski (2005), cognitive strategies by themselves are not "intelligent" or "stupid"; rather "they cooperate with other dimensions of individual differences, thus causing the desirable effects" (p. 135), which is broadly known as metacognition. In this chapter, metacognition in an online collaborative environment has been introduced and discussed and the metacognitive construct developed through the lens of the CoI theoretical framework. It has been argued that learning is socially situated and, therefore, involves community and sharing thinking, leading to the development of metacognition (Akyol & Garrison, 2011). As indicated by Cacciamani et al. (2011), metacognition is an important component of advanced epistemic agency which is becoming a common area of practice within the community offering students the possibility of progressively improving their learning strategies.

This chapter discussed the value of metacognition for learning and explores how a community of inquiry can support and sustain metacognitive development. More remains to be learned and explored about metacognition in an online collaborative learning environment. Ongoing research is being conducted to validate the construct quantitatively through the development of metacognition questionnaire and to explore the relationship between metacognition and cognitive presence in an online community of inquiry.

REFERENCES

Akyol, Z., & Garrison, D. R. (2011). Assessing metacognition in an online community of inquiry. *The Internet and Higher Education*, *14*(3), 183–190.

Antaki, C., & Lewis, A. (1986). Mental mirrors. In Antaki, C., & Lewis, A. (Eds.), *Mental mirrors: Metacognition in social knowledge and communication*. London, UK: Sage Publications.

Bai, H. (2009). Facilitating students' critical thinking in online discussion: An instructor's experience. *Journal of Interactive Online Learning*, *8*(2), 156–164.

Borkowski, J. G., Chan, L. K. S., & Muthukrishna, N. (2000). A process–oriented model of metacognition: Links between motivation and executive functioning. In Schraw, G., & Impara, J. C. (Eds.), *Issues in the measurement of metacognition* (pp. 1–42). Lincoln, NE: University of Nebraska-Lincoln.

Brown, A. (1987). Metacognition, executive control, self control, and other mysterious mechanisms. In Weinert, F., & Kluwe, R. (Eds.), *Metacognition, motivation, and understanding* (pp. 65–116). Hillsdale, NJ: Erlbaum.

Cacciamani, S., Cesareni, D., Martini, F., Ferrini, T., & Fujita, N. (2011). Influence of participation, facilitator styles, and metacognitive reflection on knowledge building in online university courses. *Computers & Education*, *58*, 874–884.

Duffy, G. G., Miller, S. D., Parson, S. A., & Meloth, M. (2009). Teachers as metacognitive professionals. In Hacker, D. J., Dunlosky, J., & Graesser, A. C. (Eds.), *Handbook of metacognition in education* (pp. 240–256). Mahwah, NJ: Lawrence Erlbaum.

Flavell, J. H. (1979). Metacognition and cognitive monitoring: A new area of cognitive developmental inquiry. *The American Psychologist, 34*(10), 906–911.

Flavell, J. H. (1987). Speculations about the nature and development of metacognition. In Weinert, F., & Kluwe, R. (Eds.), *Metacognition, motivation and understanding* (pp. 21–29). Hillsdale, NJ: Erlbaum.

Flavell, J. H. (2004). Theory-of-mind development: Retrospect and prospect. *Merrill-Palmer Quarterly, 50*(3), 274–290.

Garrison, D. R. (2009). Communities of inquiry in online learning. In Rogers, P. L. (Eds.), *Encyclopedia of distance learning* (2nd ed., pp. 352–355). Hershey, PA: IGI Global.

Garrison, D. R. (2011). *E-learning in the 21ˢᵗ century: A framework for research and practice* (2nd ed.). London, UK: Routledge/Taylor and Francis.

Garrison, D. R., & Archer, W. (2000). *A transactional perspective on teaching and learning: A framework for adult and higher education.* Oxford, UK: Pergamon.

Gourgey, A. F. (2001). Metacognition in basic skills instruction. In Hartman, H. J. (Ed.), *Metacognition in learning and instruction* (pp. 17–32). Netherlands: Kluwer Academic Publishers.

Hacker, D. J. (1998). Definitions and empirical foundations. In Hacker, D. J., Dunlosky, J., & Graesser, A. C. (Eds.), *Metacognition in educational theory and practice* (pp. 1–23). Mahwah, NJ: Erlbaum.

Hacker, D. J., Keener, M. C., & Kircher, J. C. (2009). Writing is applied metacognition. In Hacker, D. J., Dunlosky, J., & Graesser, A. C. (Eds.), *Handbook of metacognition in education.* New York, NY: Routledge, Taylor & Francis Group.

Hartman, H. J. (2001). Teaching metacognitively. In Hartman, H. J. (Ed.), *Metacognition in learning and instruction: Theory, research and practice* (pp. 149–172). Boston, MA: Kluwer Academic.

Iskala, T., Vauras, M., Lehtinen, E., & Salonen, P. (2011). Socially shared metacognition of dyads of pupils in collaborative mathematical problem-solving processes. *Learning and Instruction, 21,* 379–393.

Langford, G. (1986). The philosophical basis of cognition and metacognition. In Antaki, C., & Lewis, A. (Eds.), *Mental mirrors: Metacognition in social knowledge and communication.* London, UK: Sage Publications.

Larkin, S. (2009). Socially mediated metacognition and learning to write. *Thinking Skills and Creativity, 4*(3), 149–159.

Lee, C. D., & Smogorinsky, P. (2000). Introduction: Constructing meaning through collaborative inquiry. In Lee, C. D., & Smogorinsky, P. (Eds.), *Vygotskian perspectives on literacy research: Constructing meaning through collaborative inquiry* (pp. 1–15). New York, NY: Cambridge University Press.

Maki, R. H., & McGuire, M. J. (2004). Metacognition for text: findings and implications for education. In Perfect, T. J., & Schwartz, B. L. (Eds.), *Applied metacognition* (pp. 39–67). Cambridge, UK: Cambridge University Press.

Miell, D. K., & Miell, D. E. (1986). Recursiveness in interpersonal cognition. In Antaki, C., & Lewis, A. (Eds.), *Mental mirrors: Metacognition in social knowledge and communication.* London, UK: Sage Publications.

Necka, E., & Orzechowski, J. (2005). Higher order cognition and intelligence. In Sternberg, R. J., & Pretz, J. E. (Eds.), *Cognition and intelligence: Identifying mechanisms of the mind.* Cambridge University Press.

Pintrich, P. R., Wolters, C. A., & Baxter, G. P. (2000). Assessing metacognition and self-regulated learning. In Schraw, G., & Impara, J. C. (Eds.), *Issues in the measurement of metacognition.* Lincoln, NE: University of Nebraska-Lincoln.

Schraw, G. (2001). Promoting general metacognitive awareness. In Hartman, H. J. (Ed.), *Metacognition in learning and instruction: Theory, research and practice* (pp. 3–16). Boston, MA: Kluwer.

Schwartz, B. L., & Perfect, T. J. (2004). Introduction: Toward an applied metacognition. In Perfect, T. J., & Schwartz, B. L. (Eds.), *Applied metacognition* (pp. 1–14). Cambridge, UK: Cambridge University Press.

Shea, P., Hayes, S., Smith, S. U., Vickers, J., Bidjerano, T., & Pickett, A. (in press). Learning presence: Additional research on a new conceptual element within the Community of Inquiry (CoI) framework. *The Internet and Higher Education.*

Son, L. K., & Schwartz, B. L. (2002). The relation between metacognitive monitoring and control. In Perfect, T. J., & Schwartz, B. L. (Eds.), *Applied metacognition* (pp. 15–38). Cambridge University Press.

Son, L. K., & Schwartz, B. L. (2004). The relation between metacognitive monitoring and control. In Perfect, T. J., & Schwartz, B. L. (Eds.), *Applied metacognition* (pp. 15–38). Cambridge, UK: Cambridge University Press.

Sternberg, R. (2001). Metacognition, abilities and developing expertise: What makes an expert student? In Hartman, H. J. (Ed.), *Metacognition in learning and instruction* (pp. 247–260). Netherlands: Kluwer Academic Publishers.

Tobias, S., & Everson, H. (2002). *Knowing what you know and what you don't: Further research on metacognitive knowledge monitoring. College Board Report, No. 2002-3.* NY: College Board.

Tobias, S., & Everson, H. T. (2009). The importance of knowing what you know: A knowledge monitoring framework for studying metacognition in education. In Hacker, D. L., Dunlosky, J., & Graesser, A. (Eds.), *Handbook of metacognition in education.* New York, NY: Routledge, Taylor, and Francis.

Torras, M. E., & Mayordomo, R. (2011). Teaching presence and regulation in an electronic portfolio. *Computers in Human Behavior, 27,* 2284–2291.

Valcke, M., De Wever, B., Zhu, C., & Deed, C. (2009). Supporting active cognitive processing in collaborative groups: Potential of Bloom's taxonomy as a labelling tool. *The Internet and Higher Education, 12,* 165–172.

Volet, S., Summers, M., & Thurman, J. (2009a). High-level co-regulation in collaborative learning: How does it emerge and how is it sustained? *Learning and Instruction, 19,* 128e143.

Volet, S., Vauras, M., & Salonen, P. (2009b). Psychological and social nature of self- and co-regulation in learning contexts: An integrative perspective. *Educational Psychologist, 44,* 1–12.

Wade, S. E., & Fauske, J. R. (2004). Dialogue online: Prospective teachers' discourse strategies in computer-mediated discussions. *Reading Research Quarterly, 39*(2), 134–160.

Weigel, M., Straughn, C., & Gardner, H. (2010). New digital media and their potential cognitive impact on youth learning. In Khine, M. S., & Saleh, I. M. (Eds.), *New science of learning: Cognition, computers and collaboration in education* (pp. 2–22). New York, NY: Springer.

Wells, G. (2000). Dialogic inquiry in education: Building on Vygotsky's legacy. In Lee, C. D., & Smagorinsky, P. (Eds.), *Vygotskian perspectives on literacy research: Constructing meaning through collaborative inquiry* (pp. 51–85). New York, NY: Cambridge University Press.

White, B. Y., Frederikson, J. R., & Collins, A. (2009). The interplay of scientific inquiry and metacognition: More than a marriage of convenience. In Hacker, D., Dunlosky, J., & Graesser, A. (Eds.), *Handbook of metacognition in education* (pp. 175–205). New York, NY: Routledge.

KEY TERMS AND DEFINITIONS

Cognitive Presence: The extent to which learners are able to construct and confirm meaning through sustained reflection and discourse.

Community of Inquiry: A group of individuals who collaboratively engage in purposeful critical discourse and reflection to construct personal meaning and confirm mutual understanding.

Knowledge of Cognition (KoC): The awareness of self as a learner which is built through the knowledge and motivation associated with the inquiry process, academic discipline and expectancies.

Metacognition: A set of higher knowledge and skills to monitor and regulate manifest cognitive processes of both self and others.

Monitoring of Cognition (MoC): The reflective dimension of metacognition and refers to one's online awareness of comprehension, understanding and task performance.

Regulation of Cognition (RoC): The interactive aspect of metacognition and refers to a set of activities that help students control their learning.

Social Presence: The ability of participants to identify with the community (e.g., course of study), communicate purposefully in a trusting environment, and develop inter-personal relationships by way of projecting their individual personalities.

Teaching Presence: The design, facilitation, and direction of cognitive and social processes for the purpose of realizing personally meaningful and educationally worthwhile learning outcomes.

Chapter 4
From Distance Education to Communities of Inquiry:
A Review of Historical Developments

Aylin Tekiner Tolu
Bahçeşehir University, Turkey

Linda Shuford Evans
Kennesaw State University, USA

ABSTRACT

The purpose of this chapter is to explain the role and place of the Community of Inquiry (CoI) framework within the history of distance education. The review of the history reveals two important factors for changes in distance education: the effect of leading learning theories of each era and technological advancements. Distance education has moved from a behavioristic, teacher–centered, correspondence study concept, first to an independent learning model, and then to the current student-centered, socio-constructivist and community-based online learning. In this latest era, the post-modernist age, the CoI framework provides online instructors with a functional framework for designing and teaching their courses more effectively. A review of literature as shared in this chapter has also shown CoI to be a robust framework for research.

INTRODUCTION

Online distance education has become an important strategy for higher education institutions. In 2000, Washington State's Higher Education Coordinating board asked the Legislature to pro-vide more funds for online education (Camevale, 2000). Enormous growth in distance education and blended learning is forecasted (Kim & Bonk, 2006). Recently, the 2011 Sloan Survey of Online Learning (Allen & Seaman, 2011) revealed that 6.1 million students were taking at least one online

DOI: 10.4018/978-1-4666-2110-7.ch004

course in the fall 2010 semester. Almost one-third of all students in higher education are enrolled in at least one online course.

Distance learning has been shaped by technological developments especially, Internet and computer mediated communication (CMC) systems and by the shift from instructor-centered to learner-centered approaches (Benjamin, 2003; Palloff & Pratt, 1999). Several researchers have asserted that distance education is entering into a new era that might be termed post-industrial. At the core of this era is collaborative learning and frequent two-way communication (Garrison, 1997, 2000; Peters, 1993). CMC technologies, which can be either synchronous or asynchronous, have a profound impact on the quality of distance learning (Palloff & Pratt, 1999; Wang, 2008). Synchronous communication provides real-time interaction and immediate feedback while asynchronous communication features delayed and generally text-based communication.

A challenge facing distance learners is feeling a sense of isolation and disengagement. Compared to their face-to-face section counterparts, online learners indicated a lower level of sense of community (Rovai & Lucking, 2003). Research also showed that online learners who do not feel a sense of belonging to a class or a connection with class members and the course instructor tend to drop the course or have a low level of satisfaction and learning success (Galusha, 1997; Kubala, 1998; Patton, 2008; Palloff & Pratt, 1999; Rovai & Ponton, 2005). Therefore, creating a community of learners, or in other words, a sense of togetherness in online courses is crucial for students to feel a connection with other learners and instructors for student satisfaction and knowledge acquisition (Dickey, 2004; Ellis, 2001; Ni & Aust, 2008; Palloff & Pratt, 1999; Powers & Mitchell, 1997; Stodel, Thompson, & MacDonald, 2006).

Based on a collaborative and socio-constructivist approach to online education, the Community of Inquiry (CoI) framework not only serves as a framework to study online education, but it can also be used as a guideline to create an effective learning environment where students feel a connection with other learners and the instructor and engage in well-designed collaborative learning activities.

BACKGROUND

Distance Education

Distance learning, or distance education, has been defined in different ways. Distance education is generally used to refer to the pedagogical practice while distance learning is used to refer to student learning. However, they are often used interchangeably including other recent terms such as online learning, e-learning, and web-based instruction. The United States Distance Learning Association (USDLA) provides the following definition for distance education: "The acquisition of knowledge and skills through mediated information and instruction, encompassing all technologies and other forms of learning at a distance." In addition, distance education is defined by Schlosser and Simonson (2002) as "institution-based, formal education where the learning group is separated, and where interactive telecommunications systems are used to connect learners, resources, and instructors" (p. 1). In a more simple way, Keegan (1995) relates distance education to not having an obligation to go to "a fixed place, at a fixed time, to meet a fixed person, in order to be trained" (p. 7). When other definitions are reviewed, it appears that recurring themes in distance education include (a) place referring to physical distance between learner and teacher and it can take place anywhere when necessary hardware/software is available, (b) time (synchronous or asynchronous), (c) path (wide range of paths to reach objectives), and (d) pace (students are flexible in deciding their own pace to some extent).

Distance education has evolved with the technological developments and their impact on instructional technology. The history of distance education is generally categorized according to the media or medium used. For example, Anglin and Morrison (2002) describe the evolution of distance education through five general categories of education delivery modes: correspondence, radio, television, two-way audio/video, and web-based. Using a more broad approach, both Garrison (1985; 1993) and Moore and Kearsley (1995) divide distance education history into three generations. Yet, recently a number of researchers have suggested that a fourth generation (or to some classification, it is the fifth) of distance education has emerged (Garrison & Anderson, 2003; Taylor, 2001; Wang & Sun, 2001).

It should be noted that there is not a linear progression in this order of phases of distance education history. Each new generation improved the quality of two fundamental elements of distance education: subject matter presentation and student-instructor interaction. A proceeding generation does not eliminate the previous generation's systems. Dating back to the 19th century, the first generation is marked by correspondence and independent study. In Europe, in 1833 distance education was carried out through delivery of text-based materials by using postal service, and therefore referred to as correspondence courses. One of the pioneers, Isaac Pitman started a correspondence shorthand course in England in 1840 (Baker, 2006). In 1856, Charles Toussaint and Gustav Langenscheidt began correspondence written language courses for adults throughout Europe, which also set the date for distance foreign language education. Students received content materials in the form of textbook chapters and received self-exercises and worksheets, which made this model a self-learning, self-teaching or home study program (Peters, 2001; Baker, 1999). In the U.S., correspondence courses were first offered in 1890 by the Collier Engineer School of

Mines in Pennsylvania. The course was on mine safety and received so much attention that it turned into the International Correspondence Schools. The world's first college-level correspondence courses were offered in 1892 by the University of Chicago. In the 1930s CBS launched the American School of the Air, which was a biweekly series for elementary and secondary schools. By 1930 there were thirty-nine universities offering correspondence courses in the U.S. Although these correspondence courses lacked student-to-student interaction and frequent and spontaneous interaction between the student and teacher, they set the stage for more sophisticated, effective and complex distance education (Baker, 1999).

The first generation pedagogy for distance education was influenced by behaviorist learning. Based on a positivistic approach, learning was assumed to be objective, and therefore transferrable from 'knower' to the 'learner.' Course teams worked towards simplifying content using graphics and chunking it into sub-parts, and established a kind of relationship between learners and instructor by the use of a didactic tone in the written language. In this generation, distance education brought freedom and educational opportunity to thousands of people with a self-study opportunity.

Referred to as the telecommunications generation by Garrison (1985), the second generation evolved during the middle of the twentieth century when new technologies appeared including radio, television and video broadcasting via satellites. By the late 1940s film became popular, and colleges and universities began developing educational film. In 1950 the Ford Foundation offered grants to develop televised distance education courses (Baker, 2006). Charles Wedemeyer, who is often considered to be the father of American distance education, moved the correspondence study concept to independent learning (Gunawardena, & McIsaac, 2004). Principles of humanism played a role for this conceptual movement. Wedemeyer's pioneering and visionary works made his university, the University of Wisconsin, the largest distance education university in the world at that time. In 1965, the University of Wisconsin launched a statewide telephone-based distance education program for physicians. Four years later, the British Open University was established and became a model to the many other universities worldwide by initializing the structuring program by course teams and founding the instructional technology institute. The British Open University also popularized the use of broadcast television courses at the college level in the 1970s. Although radio added voice and television added both voice and visual media to the learning systems, they still lacked immediate two-way communication. Student-to-student interactions, though not the aim of the system then, were restricted to a group of students who gathered around at a certain place to watch televised courses together. Additionally, it was too expensive and laborious to set up tele-conferences and design and distribute effective materials.

A number of multimedia systems--audio cassettes, videotext, Super-8mm film, video cassettes, telephone, electronic blackboards and computer terminals--were researched and discussed by Bates, a professor at the Open University, in 1977. However, only the cheapest medium, the audio cassettes, were applied largely, which eventually caused a decrease in the number of televised courses (Peters, 2001).

According to Garrison and Anderson (2003), interactive, computer-assisted instruction courses delivered on a CD-ROM or DVD disks are new additions to the second generation distance education. Nonetheless, the production of these materials is expensive and requires highly qualified professionals, so distribution is again problematic. Further, interaction between learners and instructors was again limited to mail and telephone. In this era, the emphasis on self-study (or independent study) continued. Due to high, front-end costs, larger student populations were targeted.

The pedagogy of second generation was under the influence of cognitive learning theory, which "led to the use of advanced organizers, role models, summary reflections and simulated peers to draw the user into a sophisticated media world" (Garrison & Anderson, 2003, p. 37). Audio cassettes and telephone conferences became very popular and significant, especially for distance language education. They enabled teaching and assessment of listening and speaking skills (Wang & Sun, 2001).

The third generation is shaped by the twenty-first century breakthrough improvements in the computer and the Internet technologies. While Taylor (2001) suggests that the difference between asynchronous and synchronous CMC requires a fourth generation, Garrison and Anderson (2003) find this argument too narrow because CMC innovations continue in both asynchronous and synchronous modes.

Although computer technology started in mid-1960s, by the mid-1980s it continued to play only a limited role in educational settings (Wang & Sun, 2001). By the 1990s many schools were still offering distance education via telecourses and video. After the availability of the World Wide Web (WWW) in 1991, distance-learning courses via the web appeared and opened the doors to groundbreaking innovations. In 1993, International University College, founded by Glenn Jones, was launched as a true virtual university offering only online courses and degrees. In the early stages of this period, online distance educators used the web to publicize course content. Through the use of email and other web-based tools, student and teacher interaction as well as interaction among students have increased, leading to more interactive and cost and time-efficient distance learning. Constructivist learning theories have had a profound effect on the third generation distance education systems (Garrison & Anderson, 2003). Learners have become active in constructing and re-constructing knowledge as they participate in collaborative and social learning environments.

At present, distance education is constantly and profoundly impacted by interactive computer mediated communication technologies and the Internet (Sherry, 1996; Wang & Sun, 2001; Garrison & Anderson, 2003). The use of learning management systems (or course management systems) such as Blackboard and Moodle, web-based synchronous systems, social networks, and virtual communities are on the rise and this is why some scholars believe that distance education is embarking on a new generation (Garrison& Anderson, 2003; Taylor, 2001; Wang & Sun, 2001). The fourth generation embraces "the first three major attributes of the Net: information retrieval of vast amounts of content; the interactive capacity of computer mediated communications (CMC); and the processing power of locally distributed processing via computer-assisted programming, usually written in Java" (Garrison & Anderson, 2003, p. 38).

According to Taylor's model, the current generation makes up the fifth one. Based on this model, called an Intelligent Flexible Learning Model, is marked by intelligent functions, intelligent object databases, or in other words automated systems such as automated responses to frequently asked questions and customizable interface of campus portals. Basically, the fifth generation incorporates artificial intelligence with the Web. It stands out to be an integrated system of administrative, student support services and instructional content. CMC carries high importance as it "provides a rich source of thoughtful interactions, which can be structured, tagged and stored in a database and subsequently exploited for tuition purposes on a recurring basis through the application of automated response systems" (Taylor, 2001, p. 5). This makes the system cost effective by enabling the management of a larger learner population which otherwise could not afford high tuition prices. The fifth generation also is likely to be more effective in terms of pedagogical and administrative support services.

Many universities and institutions are yet to implement fourth generation distance education systems. It is obvious that Taylor's fifth generation, automated and advanced systems, will need more years to be adopted widely. The review of distance education through so-called generations highlights the fact that interaction is the vital component of distance education. Garrison and Anderson (2003) highlight that "the type, extent, and integration of various types and modes of interaction is the defining component of each generation" (p. 39).

Further, there appears to be a mapping between learning theories and the use of different types of media and distance education systems in generations. From the 1920s to 1960s, behaviorism was very influential as linear media, such as radio, film, and TV, were being implemented. It was believed that "a wide variety of behaviors can be observed, measured, planned for, and evaluated in ways that are reasonably reliable and valid" (Gustafson, 2002, p. 17). In the 1960s, cognitive science led a shift from behaviorism to cognitivism, from the perspective of information processing. Cognitivism was complemented by a new generation of desktop and personal computing (Whelan, 2005). The influence of cognitivism led to "the use of advance organizers, mnemonic devices, metaphors, chunking into meaningful parts and the careful organization of instructional materials from simple to complex" (Mergel, 1998). Since the mid-1990s, constructivism has become influential. It is accompanied by media and technologies that promote interaction, learner autonomy, knowledge construction, collaboration, scaffolding, and reflection, and offer learners multiple perspectives. Since 1995, new technologies such as the Internet, World Wide Web, microcomputer, interactive video, CD-ROM, and other networked and interactive environments have offered "functionality that goes beyond behaviorist or cognitivist worldviews, and recasts learning as a ubiquitous, experiential, self-driven activity" (Whelan, 2005).

In the present generation, the impact of social learning theories such as sociocultural theory (SCT) on distance learning instructional design and technologies is noteworthy (Gillani, 2000). To engage learners in constructing knowledge, testing their hypotheses, technology is used as a meditational tool to create authentic and meaningful tasks and activities by creating a community of inquiry where learners feel membership. Frequent and quality of interactions between learners and the instructor as well as among learners receive high attention. In addition, assessment involves authentic and challenging practices and focuses on the process rather than the end state.

SCT shifts attention from the instruction as the transmitting knowledge to the instruction as the guidance of socially-based exploration in intellectually rich settings. Computers are used in developing higher-order thinking skills like defining problems, judging, solving, and drawing conclusions as well as information seeking, inquiry, and collaboration. Multimedia/hypermedia and the Internet allow non-linear learning and increased learner autonomy. E-mail and discussion board technology can be an effective knowledge sharing communication tool for asynchronous discussion that promotes both personal and social construction of meaning (Mackinnon, 2004). Similarly, synchronous tools, such as Skype, and Windows Live Messenger, and video conferencing, can promote instant feedback, collaboration, critical thinking, and construction of knowledge. The following is a list of Web 2.0 resources that can be used to enhance collaborative online learning and a CoI development:

- Storage and sharing documents, such as Dropbox and Google docs
- Social networking, such as Twitter, Facebook, Yahoo and Google groups
- Social bookmarking, such as Diigo and Delicious
- Blogs, such as Blogger and Wordpress
- Wikis, such as Wikispaces and Pbworks
- Uploading and using videos, such as YouTube, Glogster, and Teachertube
- Locating and uploading images, such as Flickr, Photobucket, Photopeach, Glogster
- Games and simulations, such as Second life and OpenSim
- Course management systems, such as Moodle and Blackboard. Blackboard (www.coursesites.com), which also includes Elluminate Live, lets instructors create up to five course sites for free.
- Mobile learning (application on cell phones and tablets)
- Web-based recorders such as Pod-O-matic, Chirbit, Voice thread, Voxopop and Voki e-portfolios, such as Mahara and Eduportfolio

This section has traced the history of distance education. To understand and carry out research in distance education, knowing the history and context of distance education is necessary (Gunawardena, & McIsaac, 2004). Each generation is influenced by the leading learning theory of its era and the available media. In the past, research on distance education centered on comparisons of delivery methods, that is comparison of the student success rates in face-to-face courses with that of distance education, which resulted in "no difference phenomenon" (Russell, 1999). Other research topics included media comparison, student attrition rates, the design of instructional materials for mass production, analysis of technologies for delivery of instruction, and the cost effectiveness of programs (Gunawardena, & McIsaac, 2004). The recent research concerns include facilitation and effect of interactions, student satisfaction, learner support systems, learner needs and characteristics, pedagogical use of new technologies, global networking, virtual communities, design and implementation of courses with course management systems, issues of access, social and cultural contexts of distance learning, faculty training, workload and changing roles of online instructors, knowledge construction in mediated learning environment, and online collaborative learning (Sherry, 1996; Gunawardena, & McIsaac, 2004; Harasim, 2001; Rovai, Ponton, & Baker, 2008; Rogers, Berg, Boettcher, Howard, Justice, & Schenk, 2009).

Although early generations emphasized individualized learning with self-study methods, new generations value collaborative and social learning, which recognizes that individual meaning making cannot be separated from social influence as associated with Vygotsky's and Dewey's philosophy of learning. Moreover, with the explosion of information in the Internet age, the sole issue in distance education is not to deliver content to learners anymore, but to teach learners e-learning strategies to manage overwhelming resources and become an effective global learner in culturally diverse learning networks. The current generation enforces a post-modernist and post-industrial approach to distance education (Garrison, 2000).

Interaction as a Core Element in Distance Education

Interaction has been an important concept for learning for decades. John Dewey (1938) considered interaction and the continuity of interaction as two key requirements for an effective learning experience. In distance education, interaction is the core constituent for many models, theories and frameworks (Sherry, 1996; Garrison & Anderson, 2003). Several researchers have argued that distance education is emerging into a new era which might be called postindustrial. At the core of this era are educational transactions based on collaborative learning and frequent two-way communication (Garrison, 1997; Garrison, 2000; Peters, 1993).

In addition, interaction has been the defining element for so-called generations of distance education. During first and second generations of distance education, the original concept of interaction included only learner-instructor interactions. By the third generation, the definition and forms of interaction had expanded. Moore (1989) identified three types of instructional interaction: (a) learner-learner interaction, (b) learner-instructor interaction and (c) learner-content interaction. Hillman, Willis, and Gunawardena (1994) introduced a fourth type of interaction to this model: learner-interface interaction, which takes place between the learner and the technology. In Moore's transactional distance theory, learner-interface interaction pertains to structure, while the first three types fall under the category of dialog, defined as interpersonal interaction. Learner-interface interaction is generally not considered as a separate interaction type, but as a distributed form of interaction taking place in three main types of interaction. Because online distance education utilizes technology for all three types of interactions, learner-interface interaction becomes a part of them (Anderson, 2003). Basically, it refers to the "process of manipulating tools to accomplish a task" (Hillman, Willis & Gunawardena, 1994, p. 34). To elaborate on this process, we can think of a learner's ability to navigate a course site to reach content, take assessments, or use tools to interact with other learners and the instructor.

In 1995, Kearsley made a distinction between real time (synchronous) and delayed time (asynchronous) interaction. This distinction for interactions is important as 'it determines the logistic and "feel" of the distance learning experience' (Gunawardena, & McIsaac, 2004, p. 362).

Asynchronous interaction is mostly text-based. Some examples of asynchronous CMC tools may include listserv, blog, wiki, email, and discussion board. With new improvements on these technologies, users can record their voice or a short video to attach a in their posts (e.g. voice mail in Gmail and Blackboard discussion board).

Kearsley (1995) emphasized that the concept of interaction in distance education is more complicated than it is in a face-to-face learning environment because online interaction has to be distinguished according to content versus teacher versus learner, synchronous versus asynchronous, and according to learner characteristics. Learner differences such as age, personality, and learning styles may interfere with the type and mode of interaction they prefer and feels more comfortable (Gunawardena & McIsaac, 2004).

Asynchronous interaction is the most common type of interaction in distance education as well as the mostly studied in research (Swan, 2002; Stein, Wanstreet,, Glazer, Engle, Harris, Johnston, Simons, & Trinko, 2007; Wang, 2008; Wang & Hsu, 2008). The asynchronous mode affords learners time for flexibility and control. Students have time to reflect on what they read and then respond accordingly, which may augment critical thinking. However, when other students do not participate in a timely manner, or learners do not get immediate feedback, they may get frustrated and lose their motivation (Branon & Essex, 2001).

Synchronous interaction, on the other hand, is immediate. It is especially significant with providing "a sense of excitement and spontaneity that is not present with delayed interaction" (Gunawardena, & McIsaac, 2004, p. 362). Researchers often suggest synchronous communication for promoting social interaction and community building, while asynchronous interaction is used for content delivery and enrichment (Park & Bonk, 2007; Ellis & Romano, 2008; Wang & Newlin, 2002). However, asynchronous and synchronous interaction uses are not limited to these functions. A well-designed course with proper selection of both synchronous and asynchronous interactions is necessary for effective distance education (Branon & Essex, 2001; Wang & Newlin, 2002; Schullo, 2005; Tekiner Tolu, 2010). Advocates of synchronous interactions, "think of asynchronous communication as the 'backbone and muscle' for

course content, while online chats are the 'heart and hustle' of our Web-based classes" (Wang & Newlin, 2002). In a similar way, O'Sullivan (2000) commented that the "synchronous element of courses can be seen as the essence of what it means to 'take a class' or 'be in school'." It is experiencing a greater sense of others' presence that generates a personal connection between instructor and students and among students' (p. 60). Indeed, feelings of isolation from instructor and classmates, which results in a lack of sense of community or belonging to a class is one of the major problems facing distance educators and learners (Rovai & Lucking, 2003; Galusha, 1997; Patton, 2008; Palloff & Pratt, 1999; Rovai & Ponton, 2005). Research revealed that in an online course where only asynchronous communication was used, learners could not feel their classmates as a "real person" and developed a feeling of isolation (Tu & McIsaac, 2002; Branon & Essex, 2001; Stodel, MacDonald & Thompson, 2006).

Online Learning Community

Community and communication share the same Latin root, *communicare*, which means to share and to be in relation with (The International Encyclopedia of Communication). Human nature seeks to communicate and connect with other humans. Sharing, communication, discourse, and community form the basis of all civilizational, scientific, intellectual, cultural, and artistic advances (Harasim, 2002; 2006).

Although its employment for empowering learning in educational settings can be considered recent, community has a long social-theoretical history. Community has been defined and studied in various ways by several disciplines including sociology, psychology, anthropology, political science, education, and instructional technology (Barab, 2003).

Creating and maintaining a community is dynamic, complex and evolving. It is not generally possible to identify launching and dismissal time of a community. Communities undergo constant change and evolution. Members of a community should possess a sense of trust, respect, support and commitment (Tu, 2002; 2004; Palloff & Pratt, 1999).

In the past, "differentiation and membership were relevant factors in the development of community" (Palloff & Pratt, 1999, p. 21). However, the Internet and CMC have shaped the concept of community. Community is not bounded by geography now. Actually, according to Harasim (2006) the Internet is like a community itself. Online communities started with professional development communities in 1986 by OISE Ontario Educators Online Course, and later followed by Global Lab, Lab Net and Star Schools, Educators Network of Ontario in the 90s (Harasim, 2006).

Application of the community concept to online learning can be linked to the paradigmatic shift in education, which reveals transformation in three areas: (a) knowledge transmission to knowledge building, (b) from teacher-centered to learning-centered, and (c) from passive to active learning (Harasim, 2006). In addition, the 21st century has witnessed a socio-economic shift. Virtual learning has dominated the annual growth rate of traditional colleges by four times as it also experienced a 25% rate of yearly increase (2006). Together with these paradigmatic and socio-economic shifts, social learning theories and innovations in technology played a significant role for the growth of interest in online communities of learning. Distance education researchers either designed frameworks for online learning communities or applied the frameworks created for face-to-face (F2F) communities to online learning.

In their comparison of F2F community with online community, Palloff and Pratt (1999) point out that in both community types, members collaboratively negotiate norms. These negotiations become more significant for an online community because they set the foundation of the community. All issues should be discussed openly such as how members will meet, how often, what the goals are, and so on.

The ultimate goal of an online learning community in academic settings is to enhance student learning and satisfaction (Palloff & Pratt, 1999). Learning community "supports and encourages knowledge acquisition...creates a sense of excitement about learning together and renews the passion involved with exploring new realms in education....creates a sense of synergy...supports the intellectual as well as personal growth and development of its members" (Palloff & Pratt, 1999, p. 163). That is why an online learning community is referred as the essence of distance learning (Palloff & Pratt, 1999; 2005).

Researchers provide online instructors with practical guidelines and strategies for building online learning communities. Palloff and Pratt (1999) display a practical and illustrative approach. For them the keys to creation and effective maintenance of an online community of learning cover the following six concepts:

- **Honesty:** Learners should feel a sense of safety and trust. They should know who their classmates are and believe that they will receive honest feedback.
- **Responsiveness:** Collaborative group learning needs to be applied. Interactions among learners and between learners and instructor should be in a timely manner and thorough. The instructor should respond to student needs and concerns.
- **Relevance:** The content and tasks need to be relevant to learners. Seeking and sharing real-life experiences can promote learning.
- **Respect:** Learners need to feel respected as people. Respect can be indicated by welcome messages, self-introductions, immediate and thorough feedback, self and group evaluations by learners, confidentiality among group members, giving consent to group work, and maintaining a code of ethics.

- **Openness:** In an open atmosphere, learners feel free to share their thoughts and feelings without fear of retribution. Openness relates to respect and honesty. Learners who feel respected and a sense of honesty can be open to a learning community.

- **Empowerment:** "A sense of empowerment is both a crucial element and a desired outcome of participation in an online learning community" (p. 162). In a student-centered collaborative learning environment, learners have new roles and responsibilities. They are in control of their learning process as they become experts of their learning, by knowing how to pursue and reconstruct knowledge.

Online learning community frameworks emphasize interaction (CMC), and collaborative and social learning. Tu and Corry (2003), for instance, proposed three major dimensions for online learning communities: instruction, social interaction, and technology. These dimensions need to be maximized consistently to build a community. Tu (2004) emphasizes collaborative group learning to build a learning community in online courses. In the same book, he discusses 21 designs and guidelines to build online learning community. Among these include communication and preparation, team goals, objectives setting, peer support assignments, interactive project presentation, online moderation, online debate, virtual experts, guest moderators, selecting appropriate online communication tools, social collegial, collaborative evaluation and reflections for student learning and collaborative evaluation of teaching. These guidelines and strategies are very valuable to online instructors, not only to build a community of inquiry, but to enhance student learning and satisfaction in general.

COMMUNITY OF INQUIRY (COI)

The Community of Inquiry (CoI) framework was created by Garrison, Anderson, and Archer in 2000 "to provide conceptual order and a tool for the use of computer mediated communication (CMC) and computer conferencing in supporting an educational experience" (p. 87). A community of inquiry is defined as "a cohesive and interactive community of learners whose purpose is to critically analyze, construct, and confirm worthwhile knowledge" (Garrison & Vaughan, 2008, p.9).

The CoI framework combines two critical constructs for learning: community, which explicates social dynamics, social interaction and collaboration to create an environment to support the second construct, inquiry. Inquiry reflects intellectual academic interaction that includes "the process of constructing meaning through personal responsibility and choice" (Garrison & Vaughan, 2008, p. 9). Therefore, an online community of learning differs from other communities due to inquiry. The CoI was derived from extensive analysis and comparison of spoken and text-based CMC, as well as their effects on thinking, research on social-learning, community, social-constructivism, collaborative learning, instructional design, and distance education.

This framework encompasses three overlapping key elements--social presence, cognitive presence, and teacher presence. Deep and meaningful learning in online courses takes place within the community through interaction of these three core elements. The structure of the CoI framework has been confirmed through factor analyses by Garrison, Cleveland-Innes, and Fung (2004), Arbaugh and Hwang (2006), and Arbaugh (2007). The CoI framework proves to be a well-structured model for building an effective learning community (Arbaugh, 2008).

Social Presence

In the CoI framework, social presence is defined as 'the ability of participants in a community of inquiry to project themselves socially and emotionally, as ``real'' people (i.e., their full personality), through the medium of communication being used' (Garrison, Anderson, & Archer, 2000, p. 95). Social presence in this framework differs from Short, et al.'s (1976) static approach. In a CoI, the effect of media by itself is not the most significant factor in shaping the degree of social presence. Instead, the communication context, which includes factors such as motivation, familiarity, skills, commitment, activities, and length of time in using the media, influences the development of social presence. Research identified that social presence can be strongly felt in CMC (Richardson & Swan, 2003; Tu & McIsaac, 2002; Tu, 2004). In text-based CMC, it requires certain strategies and techniques that pertain to those factors in order to enhance immediacy indicators (Rourke, Anderson, Garrison & Archer, 2001; Swan, 2002; 2004).

Social presence includes three progressive categories: open communication, affective expression, and group cohesion. Open communication is related to creating an environment for risk-free expression. For social presence to prosper, learners need to feel free and secure to express themselves openly. They need to engage in reciprocal and respectful exchanges, projecting themselves personally and academically, so that they can "develop personal relationships necessary to commit to, and pursue, intended academic goals and gain a sense of belonging to the community" (Garrison & Vaughan, 2008, p. 19). Interpersonal communication is very important for creating a sense of trust among learners. These are prerequisites for learners to work collaboratively. A community of inquiry is "inherently collaborative" (Garrison & Vaughan, 2008, p. 20). As learners interact and

feel respected, they also should feel responsibility to the community of inquiry.

Affective expression refers to expressing emotions and camaraderie. Once open communication is secured, interpersonal relations can start having emotional expression which in this model is "indicated by the ability and confidence to express feelings related to the educational experience" (Garrison, Anderson, & Archer, 2000). In an online learning environment, it takes a longer time to achieve camaraderie. Humor and self-disclosure are two examples of emotional expression in a community. Humor contributes to social presence. It serves as an invitation to conversation and decreases social distance. Self-disclosure helps learners get to know each other, subsequently establish trust, respect, and support. Self-disclosure involves sharing feelings, experiences, attitudes, and interests. Therefore, in an online course, self-introduction or personal web-pages are very important.

Among the three presences, social presence has been "the most extensively studied, both in online and face-to-face course settings" (Arbaugh, 2007, p. 73). Recent studies on social presence in online learning environments focused on causal or correlational relationships between social presence and student learning and satisfaction in addition to its role in facilitating cognitive presence (Swan, & Shih, 2005; Shea & Bidjerano, 2009; Richardson & Swan, 2000). It has been argued that collaborative learning activities lead to an increase in social presence and online community building (Richardson, & Swan, 2003; Rovai, 2002). Group cohesion and interaction also relates to social presence and learning (Arbaugh, 2005). Though extensively studied, further research is required to better understand how social presence evolves in an online learning community (Garrison & Arbaugh, 2007).

It should be emphasized that social presence without cognitive presence does not lead to an establishment of community of inquiry. However, it is also difficult to develop critical discourse without establishing social presence first (Arbaugh, 2007; Garrison & Arbaugh, 2007; Garrison & Cleveland-Innes, 2005). Garrison and Vaughan (2008) shed light on this:

Establishing social presence is a primary concern at the outset of creating a community of inquiry. Social relationships create a sense of belonging, support freedom of expression, and sustain cohesiveness, but they do not structure and focus academic interests among students. Social interaction is insufficient to sustain a community of inquiry and achieve educational goals...higher levels of learning inevitably require purposeful discourse to collaboratively construct, critically reflect, and confirm understanding. This is what is referred to as cognitive presence (p. 21).

Cognitive Presence

Founded in Dewey's work on reflective thinking and practical inquiry as well as the research on critical thinking and postmodernist paradigm, cognitive presence is defined as the extent to which learners are able to critically reflect, (re)construct, and confirm meaning, through and engaging in reflective and sustained discourse for sharing meaning and confirming understanding (Garrison & Arbaugh, 2007; Ice, Arbaugh, Diaz, Garrison, Richardson, Shea, & Swan, 2007).

Cognitive presence is the central element in "critical thinking, a process and outcome that is frequently presented as the ostensible goal of all higher education" (Garrison & Arbaugh, 2007, p. 89). Cognitive presence is mapped on the cyclical inquiry model of learning, which has two dimensions and four phases. The vertical axis defines the deliberation-action dimension, which refers the recursive nature of inquiry incorporating collaborative activities. The horizontal axis defines the perception-conception dimension, which refers

to the process of meaning construction from experience. While dimensions are abstract processes, the four phases are more like representations of educational experience. These phases of critical thinking are as follows:

1. **Triggering Event:** In this phase, participants recognize a problem, have a sense of puzzlement, or are intrigued by the question or task. They feel motivated to explore content.
2. **Exploration:** Learners utilize a variety of information sources to explore problems, brainstorm ideas, exchange information with others and discuss ambiguities.
3. **Integration:** Here learners participating in learning activities connect ideas and create solutions, and reflect on content.
4. **Resolution:** In this phase, learners describe the ways to test and apply knowledge created; apply ideas, knowledge or solutions to new situations.

Research on community only recently focused on the role of community in formal online courses and its effect on cognitive presence (Garrison & Archer, 2007). Compared to F2F in-class discussions, asynchronous online discussions provide more chance for cognitively rich input because they are open to all learners – students have an equal chance to contribute, and learners have flexible time and resources to process information and construct meaning. In addition, text-based asynchronous communication "reduces the student cognitive load and the need to rely on memory to process large numbers of facts and ideas" (Garrison & Vaughan, 2008, p. 23).

A community of inquiry is found to be less threatening and positively related to perceived learning (Shea, 2006; Shea, Li, & Pickett, 2006; Rovai, 2002). The development of cognitive presence is identified to be the most challenging of the three types of presences (Arbaugh, 2007). Moreover, cultivating higher phases of cognitive presence is quite difficult. Previous research found that most of the time inquiry did not move beyond the information exchange or exploration phases (Garrison et al., 2001; Meyer, 2004). Garrison and Arbaugh (2007) discuss the possible reasons for this challenge and conclude that it is mostly due to teaching presence and group cohesion (social presence) as cognitive presence is strongly related to social presence and the role of teacher. Social presence lays the foundation for critical discourse while teaching presence creates the environment for cognitive presence to develop (Arbaugh, 2007). To proceed along the four phases of cognitive presence, learners need to progress from open communication, to cohesion, and then to personal connections to be able to connect to their group and then participate in collaborative and reflective processes where teacher role is paramount. It has been shown that teaching presence categories had a significant impact on the level of learner engagement in course content in a deep and meaningful manner (Garrison & Cleveland-Innes, 2005). Another study on the effect of task nature revealed that Webquest and debate activities which were well structured led the highest phases of cognitive presence (Kanuka, Liam, & Laflamme, 2007). Even the formulation of questions for discussions influenced student participation (Meyer, 2004). Analyzing the online asynchronous discussions in graduate level educational leadership classes, Meyer (2004) found that only a small percentage of the discussions reached resolution level. To move beyond exploration phase and reach higher levels of thinking, she suggested setting the discussion's agenda, actively moderating the discussion, or modeling how to operate at a higher level and maybe rewarding students. Therefore, sustained development of cognitive presence requires well designed learning tasks, facilitation and direction of inquiry, which brings the discussion to teaching presence.

Teaching Presence

In a CoI, teaching presence is the essential element to bring all elements together to form and sustain the community. Research revealed that teaching presence is a strong predictor of student satisfaction, perceived learning, and sense of community (Akyol & Garrison, 2008; Arbaugh, 2008; Ice, et al., 2007; Shea, Pickett, & Pelz, 2004; Shea, Li, Swan, & Pickett, 2005; Shea & Bidjerano, 2009).

Teaching presence is defined as "the design, facilitation, and direction of cognitive and social processes for the purpose of realizing personally meaningful and educationally worthwhile learning outcomes" (Anderson, Rourke, Garrison, & Archer, 2001, p. 5). Teaching presence begins before the course starts when the instructor plans and designs the course of study, and continues throughout the course with facilitation and direct instruction roles.

Teaching presence encompasses three categories: design and organization, facilitating discourse, and direct instruction. Anderson and colleagues (2001) argue that the process of designing an online course is generally more laborious and time-consuming than planning an equivalent course for F2F teaching. Before the course becomes available to students, the teacher needs to make a thorough planning for the process, evaluation, structure, and interaction aspects of the online course. Because online learning sets new expectations and norms for students, everything needs to be more explicit and transparent. This whole process is conceptualized as the design and organization aspect of teaching presence (Anderson et al., 2001).

Facilitating discourse is described as a critical element to "maintaining interest, motivation and engagement of students in effective learning" (Anderson et al., 2001, p. 7). The teacher facilitates discourse building, and encourages participation by modeling, commenting on posts, identifying areas of agreement and disagreement, keeping the discourse focused on learning objectives, and trying to draw in inactive students.

The final category of teaching presence, direct instruction, refers to teachers providing intellectual and scholarly leadership through in-depth understanding of their subject matter knowledge (Anderson et al., 2001). This role is similar to that of a subject-matter expert. Using subject and pedagogical expertise, the instructor (at least initially) directs learners, provides feedback, and injects knowledge from several resources (Anderson, et al., 2001). Even in a student-centered learning environment, strong leadership is necessary for discussions to stay on track through direct teaching when needed.

Research has highlighted the importance of direct teaching for effective online learning. Students who indicated high levels of effective instructor direct instruction also showed high levels of satisfaction and perceived learning (Tekiner Tolu, 2010; Arbaugh, 2008; Kanuka, Liam, & Laflamme, 2007; Garrison & Cleveland-Innes, 2005; Meyer, 2004; Shea, Pickett, & Pelz, 2004). Elluminate Live is a tool currently used for direct instruction as well as for implementing collaborative and constructivist learning activities and creating a real classroom feel where students could project their own social presence and feel the presence of other members. Students in several studies stated that watching the teacher explain and demonstrate topics was effective for their learning and enhanced the social presence of the instructor (Akyol & Garrison, 2008; Anderson, et al., 2001; Ice, et al., 2007; Kanuka, et al., 2007; Shea & Bidjerano, 2009; Vesely, et al., 2007; Shea et al., 2005).

In conclusion, when used in coordination with asynchronous communication tools such as email, discussion forum and other course management system tools, synchronous interactions have shown to enhance teacher presence and positively contribute to the development of an effective online community of inquiry.

FUTURE RESEARCH DIRECTIONS

Although the CoI framework is moving into its second decade, there is scarce research on its use in online courses integrating synchronous communications (see chapter 6). The majority of the studies analyzed asynchronous discussion board texts, which could only reflect a part of community of inquiry in a course. There is high need for more studies to investigate synchronous interactions and tasks as well as course designs in the light of a CoI framework.

We will continue to be amazed with the new technologies entering into online education. Further research can explore pedagogical applications and results of new multimedia or learning management systems through the lens of the CoI theoretical framework.

CONCLUSION

This chapter reviewed the history of distance education in terms of how it was shaped by learning theories and improvements in technology. The chapter identified the crucial role of the interaction and development of a community of inquiry for effective online learning. Although early generations emphasized individualized learning with self-study methods, new generations value collaborative and social learning, which recognizes that individual meaning-making cannot be separated from social influence as associated with Vygotsky's and Dewey's philosophy of learning. Moreover, with the explosion of information in the Internet age, the sole issue in distance education is no longer simply to deliver content to learners, but to teach learners e-learning strategies to manage overwhelming resources and become effective global learners in culturally diverse learning networks. To overcome new challenges and meet the complex needs, the CoI provides a well-established framework for educators and researchers.

REFERENCES

Akyol, Z., & Garrison, D. R. (2008). The development of a community of inquiry over time in an online course: Understanding the progression and integration of social, cognitive and teaching presence. *Journal of Asynchronous Learning Networks, 12*(3-4), 3–22.

Akyol, Z., Vaughan, N., & Garrison, D. R. (2011). The impact of course duration on the development of a community of inquiry. *Interactive Learning Environments, 19*(3), 231–246.

Allen, E. I., & Seaman, J. (November, 2011). *Going the distance: Online education in the United States, 2011.* Babson Park, MA: Babson Survey Research Group and Quahog Research Group, LLC. Retrieved August 8, 2012, from http://www.onlinelearningsurvey.com/reports/goingthedistance.pdf

Anderson, T. (2003). Getting the mix right again: An updated and theoretical rationale for interaction. *International Review of Research in Open and Distance Learning, 4*(2).

Anderson, T., Rourke, L., Garrison, D. R., & Archer, W. (2001). Assessing teaching presence in a computer conferencing environment. *Journal of Asynchronous Learning Networks, 5*(2).

Anglin, G. J., & Morrison, G. R. (2002). Evaluation and research in distance education: Implications for research. In Vrasidas, C., & Glass, G. V. (Eds.), *Distance education and distributed learning* (pp. 157–180). Greenwich, CT: Information Age Publishing.

Arbaugh, J. B. (2005). Is there an optimal design for on-line MBA courses? *Academy of Management Learning & Education, 4*, 135–149.

Arbaugh, J. B. (2007). An empirical verification of the community of inquiry framework. *Journal of Asynchronous Learning Networks, 11*(1), 73–85.

Arbaugh, J. B. (2008). Does the community of inquiry framework predict outcomes in online MBA courses? *International Review of Research in Open and Distance Learning, 9*(2), 1–21.

Arbaugh, J. B., Cleveland-Innes, M., Diaz, S., Garrison, D. R., Ice, P., Richardson, J., et al. (November 2007). *Community of inquiry framework: Validation & instrument development.* 13th Annual Sloan-C Conference Presentation. Orlando, Florida.

Arbaugh, J. B., & Hwang, A. (2006). Does "teaching presence" exist in online MBA courses? *The Internet and Higher Education, 9*(1), 9–21.

Baker, J. (September 2006). *Baker's guide to Christian distance education.* Retrieved September 17, 2006, from http://www.bakersguide.com/Distance_Education_Timeline/

Barab, S. A. (2003). An introduction to the special issue: Designing for virtual communities in the service of learning. *The Information Society, 19*(3), 197–201.

Benjamin, J. (2003). Interactive online educational experiences: E-volution of graded projects. In Reisman, S., Flores, J. G., & Edge, D. (Eds.), *Electronic learning communities: Current issues and best practices* (pp. 1–26). Greenwich, CT: Information Age Publishing.

Branon, R. F., & Essex, C. (2001). Synchronous and asynchronous communication tools in distance education: A survey of instructors. *TechTrends, 45*, 36–42.

Camevale, D. (2000). New master plan in Washington State calls for more online instruction. *The Chronicle of Higher Education, 46*(22).

Dewey, J. (1938). *Experience and education.* New York, NY: Collier Books.

Dickey, M. D. (2004). The impact of web-logs (blogs) on student perceptions of isolation and alienation in a web-based distance-learning environment. *Open Learning, 19*(3), 279–291.

Ellis, A. (December, 2001). Student-centered collaborative learning via face-to-face and asynchronous online communication: What's the difference? *ASCILITE Conference Proceedings.* Retrieved April 16, 2008, from http://www.ascilite.org.au/conferences/melbourne01/pdf/papers/ellisa.pdf

Ellis, J., & Romano, D. (2008). Synchronous and asynchronous online delivery: How much interaction in e-learning is enough in higher education? In G. Richards (Ed.), *Proceedings of World Conference on E-Learning in Corporate, Government, Healthcare, and Higher Education 2008* (pp. 2615-2620). Chesapeake, VA: AACE.

Galusha, J.M. (1997). Barriers to learning in distance education. *Interpersonal Computing and Technology: An Electronic Journal for the 21st Century, 5*(3/4), 6-14.

Garrison, D. R. (1985). Three generations of technological innovations in distance education. *Distance Education, 6*(2), 235–241.

Garrison, D. R. (1993). Multifunction microcomputer enhanced audio teleconferencing: Moving into the third generation of distance education. In Harry, K., Keegan, D., & Magnus, J. (Eds.), *Distance education: New perspectives* (pp. 200–208). London, UK: Routledge.

Garrison, D. R. (1997). Computer conferencing: The post-industrial age of distance education. *Open Learning, 12*(2), 3–11.

Garrison, D. R., & Anderson, T. (2003). *E-learning in the 21st century: A framework for research and practice.* London, UK: Routledge/Falmer.

Garrison, D. R., Anderson, T., & Archer, W. (2000). Critical inquiry in a text-based environment: Computer conferencing in higher education. *The Internet and Higher Education, 11*(2), 1–14.

Garrison, D. R., Anderson, T., & Archer, W. (2001). Critical thinking, cognitive presence, and computer conferencing in distance education. *American Journal of Distance Education, 15*(1).

Garrison, D. R., & Arbaugh, J. B. (2007). Researching the community of inquiry framework: Review, issues, and future directions. *The Internet and Higher Education, 10*(3), 157–172.

Garrison, D. R., & Archer, W. (2007). A community of inquiry framework for online learning. In Moore, M., & Anderson, W. G. (Eds.), *Handbook of distance education* (2nd ed., pp. 77–88). New York, NY: Lawrence Erlbaum.

Garrison, D. R., & Cleveland-Innes, M. (2005). Facilitating cognitive presence in online learning: Interaction is not enough. *American Journal of Distance Education, 19*(3), 133–148.

Garrison, D. R., Cleveland-Innes, M., & Fung, T. (2004). Student role adjustment in online communities of inquiry: Model and instrument validation. *Journal of Asynchronous Learning Networks, 8*(2), 61-74. Retrieved January 8, 2009, from http://www.sloan-c.org/publications/jaln/v8n2/pdf/v8n2_garrison.pdf

Garrison, D. R., & Vaughan, N. D. (2008). *Blended learning in higher education: Framework, principles and guidelines.* San Francisco, CA: Jossey-Bass.

Garrison, R. (2000). Theoretical challenges for distance education in the 21st century: A shift from structural to transactional issues. *International Review of Research in Open and Distance Learning, 1*(1), 1–17.

Gillani, B. B. (2000). Using the web to create student-centered curriculum. In Cole, R. A. (Ed.), *Issues in web-based pedagogy: A critical primer* (pp. 161–181). Westport, CT: Greenwood press.

Gunawardena, C. N., & McIsaac, M. S. (2004). Distance education. In Jonassen, D. H. (Ed.), *Handbook of research on educational communications and technology* (2nd ed., pp. 355–395). Mahwah, NJ: Lawrence Erlbaum Associates Publishers.

Gustafson, K. L. (2002). What is instructional design. In Reiser, R. A., & Dempsey, J. V. (Eds.), *Trends and issues in instructional design and technology* (pp. 16–25). Upper Saddle River, NJ: Merrill Education/Prentice.

Harasim, L. (2001). Shift happens: Online education as a new paradigm in learning. *The Internet and Higher Education, 3*(1), 41–61.

Harasim, L. (2002). What makes online learning communities successful? The role of collaborative learning in social and intellectual development. In Vrasidas, C., & Glass, G. V. (Eds.), *Distance education and distributed learning. A volume in current perspectives on applied information technologies* (pp. 181–200). Greenwich, CT: Information Age publishing Inc.

Harasim, L. (March, 2006). *Online collaborative learning: The next generation for elearning*. Public Presentation Sao Paulo, Brazil. Retrieved May 16, 2009, from http://www.slideshare.net/aquifolium/linda-harasim-on-online-collaborative-learning

Hillman, D. C., Willis, D. J., & Gunawardena, C. N. (1994). Learner-interface interaction in distance education: An extension of contemporary models and strategies for practitioners. *American Journal of Distance Education, 8*(2), 30–42.

Ice, P., Arbaugh, B., Diaz, S., Garrison, D. R., & Richardson, J. Shea, P., & Swan, K. (2007, November). *Community of inquiry framework: validation and instrument development*. Paper Presented at the 13th Annual Sloan-C International Conference on Online Learning, Orlando, Florida. Received April 10, 2009, from http://communitiesofinquiry.com/files/Sloan%20CoI%20Orlando%202007.pdf

Kanuka, H., Liam, R., & Laflamme, E. (2007). The influence of instructional methods on the quality of online discussion. *British Journal of Educational Technology, 38*(2), 260–271.

Kearsley, G. (1995, May). *The nature and value of interaction in distance learning*. Paper presented at the Third Distance Education Research Symposium, College Park, PA: American Center for the Study of distance Education.

Keegan, D. (1995). *Distance education technology for the new millennium: Compressed video teaching*. ZIFF Papiere. Hagen, Germany: Institute for Research into Distance Education. (Eric Document Reproduction Service No. ED 389 931).

Kim, K. J., & Bonk, C. J. (2006). The future of online teaching and learning in higher education: The survey says. *EDUCAUSE Quarterly, 29*(4), 22–30.

Kubala, T. (1998). Addressing student needs: teaching on the internet. *T.H.E. Journal, 25*(8), 71–74.

LaPointe, D. K., & Gunawardena, C. N. (2004). Developing, testing, and refining a model to understand the relationship between peer interaction and learning outcomes in computer-mediated conferencing. *Distance Education, 25*(1), 83–106.

Mackinnon, G. R. (2004). Computer-mediated communication and science teacher training: Two constructivist examples. *Journal of Technology and Teacher Education, 12*(1), 101–114.

Mandernach, B. J., Gonzales, R. M., & Garrett, A. L. (2006). An examination of online instructor presence via threaded discussion participation. *Journal of Online Learning and Teaching, 2*(4), 248–260.

Mergel, B. (May, 1998). *Instructional design and learning theories.* Retrieved March 13, 2007, from http://www.usask.ca/education/coursework/802papers/mergel/brenda.htm

Meyer, K. A. (2004). Evaluating online discussions: Four different frames of analysis. *Journal of Asynchronous Learning Networks, 8*(2), 101–114.

Moore, M. (1989). Three types of interaction. *American Journal of Distance Education, 3*(2), 1–16.

Moore, M., & Kearsley, G. (1995). *Distance education: A systems view.* California: Wadsworth.

Ni, S., & Aust, R. (2008). Examining teacher verbal immediacy and sense of classroom community in online classes. *International Journal on E-Learning, 7*(3), 477–498.

O'Sullivan, P. B. (2000). Communication technologies in an education environment: Lessons from a historical perspective. In Cole, R. A. (Ed.), *Issues in Web-based pedagogy: A critical primer* (pp. 49–64). Westport, CT: Greenwood Press.

Palloff, R. M., & Pratt, K. (1999). *Building learning communities in cyberspace: Effective strategies for the online classroom.* San Francisco, CL: Jossey-Bass Publishers.

Palloff, R. M., & Pratt, K. (2005). *Collaborating online learning together in community.* San Francisco, CL: Jossey-Bass Publishers.

Park, Y. J., & Bonk, C. (2007). Synchronous learning experiences: distance and residential learners' perspectives in a blended graduate course. *Journal of Interactive Online Learning, 6*(3), 245-264. Retrieved June 22, 2008 from http://www.ncolr.org/jiol/issues/PDF/6.3.6.pdf

Patton, B. A. (2008). Synchronous meetings: A way to put personality in an online class. *Turkish Online Journal of Distance Education, 9*(4). Retrieved January 15, 2009, from http://tojde.anadolu.edu.tr/

Peters, O. (1993). Distance education in a postindustrial society. In Keegan, D. (Ed.), *Theoretical principles of distance education* (pp. 39–58). London, UK: Routledge.

Powers, S. M., & Mitchell, J. (1997). *Student perceptions and performance in a virtual classroom environment.* Paper presented at the Annual Meeting of the American Educational Research Association, Chicago, IL.

Richardson, J., & Swan, K. (2000). How to make the most of online interaction. In J. Bourdeau & R. Heller (Eds.), *Proceedings of World Conference on Educational Multimedia, Hypermedia and Telecommunications* (pp. 1488-1489). Chesapeake, VA: AACE.

Richardson, J. C., & Swan, K. (2003). Examining social presence in online courses in relation to students' perceived learning and satisfaction. *Journal of Asynchronous Learning Networks, 7*(1), 68–88.

Rogers, P., Berg, G. A., Boettcher, J., Howard, C., Justice, L., & Schenk, K. D. (2009). (Eds.), *Encyclopedia of distance learning* (2nd ed.). Hershey, PA: Information Science Reference.

Rourke, L., Anderson, T., Garrison, D. R., & Archer, W. (2001). Methodological issues in the content analysis of computer conference transcripts. *International Journal of Artificial Intelligence in Education, 12*, 8–12.

Rovai, A. P. (2001). Building classroom community at a distance: A case study. *Educational Technology Research and Development, 49*(4), 33–48.

Rovai, A. P. (2002). A preliminary look at structural differences in sense of classroom community between higher education traditional and ALN courses. *Journal of Asynchronous Learning Networks, 6*(1), 41–56.

Rovai, A. P., & Lucking, R. (2003). Sense of community in a higher education television-based distance education program. *Educational Technology Research and Development, 51*(2), 5–16.

Rovai, A. P., & Ponton, M. K. (2005). An examination of sense of classroom community and learning among African American and Caucasian graduate students. *Journal of Asynchronous Learning Networks, 9*(3), 75–90.

Rovai, A. P., Ponton, M. K., & Baker, J. D. (2008). *Distance learning in higher education: A programmatic approach to planning, design, instruction, evaluation, and accreditation.* New York, NY: Teachers College Press.

Russell, T. L. (1999). *No significant difference phenomenon.* Raleigh, NC: North Carolina State University.

Schlosser, L. A., & Simonson, M. (2002). *Distance education: Definition and glossary of terms.* Bloomington, IN: Association for Educational Communications and Technology.

Schullo, S. (2005). *An analysis of pedagogical strategies: Using synchronous Web-based course systems in the online classroom.* Unpublished Doctoral dissertation, University of South Florida, Florida.

Shea, P. (2006). A study of students' sense of learning community in online learning environments. *Journal of Asynchronous Learning Networks, 10*(1).

Shea, P., & Bidjerano, T. (2009). Community of inquiry as a theoretical framework to foster "epistemic engagement" and "cognitive presence" in online education. *Computers & Education, 52*(3), 543–553.

Shea, P., Li, C. S., & Pickett, A. (2006). A study of teaching presence and student sense of learning community in fully online and web-enhanced college courses. *The Internet and Higher Education, 9*(3), 175–190.

Shea, P., Li, C. S., Swan, K., & Pickett, A. (2005). Teaching presence and establishment of community in online environments: A preliminary study. *Journal of Asynchronous Learning Networks, 9*(4).

Shea, P. J., Pickett, A. M., & Pelz, W. E. (2004). Enhancing student satisfaction through faculty development: The importance of teaching presence. In J. Bourne & J. C. Moore (Eds.), *Elements of quality online education: Into the mainstream:* Vol. 5 in the Sloan-C Series (pp. 39-59). Needham, MA: Sloan Center for Online Education.

Sherry, L. (1996). Issues in distance learning. *International Journal of Educational Telecommunications, 1*(4), 337–365.

Short, J., Williams, E., & Christie, B. (1976). *The social psychology of telecommunications.* London, UK: John Wiley & Sons.

Stein, D. S., Wanstreet, C. E., Calvin, J., Overtoom, C., & Wheaton, J. E. (2005). Bridging the transactional distance gap in online learning environments. *American Journal of Distance Education, 19*(2), 105–118.

Stein, D. S., Wanstreet, C. E., Glazer, H. R., Engle, C. L., Harris, R. T., & Johnston, S. M. (2007). Creating shared understanding through chats in a community of inquiry. *The Internet and Higher Education, 10*, 103–115.

Stodel, E. J., MacDonald, C. J., & Thompson, T. L. (2006). Learners' perspectives on what is missing from online learning: Interpretations through the community of inquiry framework. *International Review of Research in Open and Distance Learning, 7*(3), 1–24.

Swan, K. (2002). Building learning communities in online courses: The importance of interaction. *Education Communication and Information, 2*(1), 23–49.

Swan, K. (2004). *Relationships between interactions and learning in online environments.* Retrieved December 21, 2008, from http://www.sloan-c.org/publications/books/interactions.pdf

Swan, K., & Shih, L. F. (2005). On the nature and development of social presence in online course discussions. *Journal of Asynchronous Learning Networks, 9*(3), 115–136.

Taylor, J. C. (2001). Fifth generation distance education. *Higher Education Series, 40.* Received April 10, 2008, from http://www.dest.gov.au/archive/highered/hes/hes40/hes40.pdf

Tekiner Tolu, A. (2010). *An exploration of synchronous communication in an online preservice ESOL course: Community of inquiry perspective.* Unpublished Dissertation, University of South Florida, Tampa, Florida.

Tu, C. (2002). The measurement of social presence in an online learning. *International Journal on E-Learning, 1*(2), 34–45.

Tu, C. (2004). *Twenty-one designs to building an online collaborative learning community.* Westport, CT: Library Unlimited.

Tu, C., & Corry, M. (2003). Building active online interaction via a collaborative learning community. *Computers in the Schools, 20*(3), 51–59.

Tu, C. H., & McIsaac, M. (2002). The relationship of social presence and interaction in online classes. *American Journal of Distance Education, 16*(3), 131–150.

Vesely, P., Bloom, L., & Sherlock, J. (2007). Key elements of building online community: Comparing faculty and student perceptions. *MERLOT Journal of Online Learning and Teaching, 3*(3), 234–246.

Wang, A. Y., & Newlin, M. H. (2002). Integrating technology and pedagogy: Web instruction and seven principles of undergraduate education. *Teaching of Psychology, 29*, 325–330.

Wang, S.-K. (2008). The effects of a synchronous communication tool (Yahoo Messenger) on online learners' sense of community and their multimedia authoring skills. *Journal of Interactive Online Learning, 7*(1), 59–74.

Wang, S. K., & Hsu, H. (2008). Use of the webinar tool (Elluminate) to support training: The effects of webinar-learning implementation from student-trainers' perspective. *Journal of Interactive Online Learning, 7*(3), 175–194.

Wang, Y., & Sun, C. (2001). Internet-based real time language education: Towards a fourth generation distance education. *CALICO Journal, 18*(3), 539–561.

Whelan, R. (2005). *Instructional technology and theory: A look at past, present and future.* Connect: Information Technology at NYU. Retrieved March 13, 2008, from http://www.nyu.edu/its/pubs/connect/spring05/whelan_it_history.html

KEY TERMS AND DEFINITIONS

Asynchronous Communication: Takes place with delayed time. For instance, discussion forums, email, wikis or blogs serve as medium for asynchronous communication.

Cognitive Presence: A component of Community of Inquiry framework and defined as "the extent to which learners are able to construct and confirm meaning through sustained reflection and discourse" (Garrison & Arbough, 2007, p. 161).

Community of Inquiry: A framework for online collaborative learning which highlights that learning occurs within a community through the interaction of three essential elements cognitive presence, social presence, and teaching presence.

Computer-Mediated Communication (CMC): Refers to "the many ways in which computers are used to mediate the transfer of information between individuals.

E-Learning: Refers to learning through electronic networks. It covers a wide range of applications and processes such as, computer-based learning, web-based learning, online learning, virtual classroom, and digital collaboration.

Social Presence: Refers to participants' ability to project their personal characteristics to others as real people in a community of inquiry. Social presence in terms of feeling others social presence refers to the feeling a sense of togetherness, thus feeling free to conduct social interactions.

Synchronous Communication: Refers to real time communication in completely web-based environment through CMC tools such as Instant Messaging (IM) and two-way videoconferences.

Teaching Presence: One of the three elements of Community of Inquiry model. It is defined in terms of designing an online course, facilitating online learning and providing direct instruction when necessary.

Section 2
Design and Implementation

Chapter 5

A Follow-Up Study of the Indicators of Teaching Presence Critical to Students in Online Courses

Kathleen Sheridan
National Louis University, USA

Melissa A. Kelly
National Louis University, USA

David T. Bentz
University of Oregon, USA

ABSTRACT

The purpose of the study presented in this chapter was to examine students' perceptions of the importance of various indicators of teaching presence for their success in online courses. A cross-sectional survey design was used to identify the indicators that students perceived to be most important and to determine whether there were potential differences between graduate students and undergraduate students in terms of the students' perceptions. Although the indicators that students rated as most important were similar for both groups of students, there were statistically significant differences for a few of the indicators. Students' comments suggested additional indicators and provided insights about the importance of dispositions in online courses.

INTRODUCTION

Since the initial conceptualization of the Community of Inquiry (CoI) framework by Garrison, Anderson, and Archer (2000), a host of online education researchers have utilized this framework to explore and explain the dynamics of online learning environments. The CoI framework has provided researchers with a starting point to monitor and track what actually happens within online learning environments and to provide insights on behaviors and processes that deliver a posi-

DOI: 10.4018/978-1-4666-2110-7.ch005

tive online learning environment. As a process model, the CoI has guided processes and defined outcomes of effective environments. The framework also has broader implications, though, and Garrison (2007) and Arbaugh (2007) challenged CoI researchers with providing more practice-based analyses. The present chapter addresses this challenge by examining student perceptions of the importance of various aspects of teaching presence in online courses.

As suggested by the CoI framework, teaching presence can manifest itself in many ways in an online course, including the setup of the course and its delivery. For example, an instructor's presence during setup and development of an online course includes designing and organizing the course. Another example of teaching presence is the instructor's engagement in guiding students' discussions (Garrison, Anderson, & Archer, 2001). While these examples from the CoI framework illuminate aspects of teaching presence in online courses, they do not reveal which aspects are most important for students' success. Research on teaching presence and its relationship with learning experiences suggests which indicators might be valued most by students, but there are few studies that have examined this issue explicitly.

The research presented in this chapter addresses this issue and examines how important various indicators of teaching presence are to students in online courses and which indicators the students perceive as most important for their success. By identifying the relative importance of instructor behaviors for students' perceived success, this research extends the body of literature on teaching presence and can help guide instructors towards behaviors that appear to matter most to students. It also has implications for future modifications of the CoI framework.

BACKGROUND

When Garrison et al. (2000) initially conceptualized the CoI framework, they defined teaching presence as the domain that encourages active discourse and knowledge in the online learning environment. Anderson, Rourke, Garrison and Archer (2001) later codified the three core substructures of teaching presence as direct instruction, facilitating discourse, and instructional design and organization. These substructures were conceived and supported by prior research from Berge (1995), Paulsen (1995), and Mason (1991). Additional research by Shea, Pickett, and Pelz (2003) and Shea, Li, Swan, and Pickett (2005) helped researchers further refine and explore the constructs of teaching presence and classroom community using Rovai's (2002) work. All of these important works, as well as many other recent studies, have helped shape and refine the notion of teaching presence as it relates to the CoI framework and online learning environments.

Research shows that teaching presence plays a key role in students' success in online learning (Bliss & Lawrence, 2009; Garrison & Cleveland-Innes, 2005; Garrison, Cleveland-Innes, & Fung, 2010; Meyer, 2003; Murphy, 2004; Pawan, Paulus, Yalcin, & Chang, 2003; Shea, Pickett, & Pelz, 2003; Swan, 2002; Swan & Shih, 2005; Varnhagen, Wilson, Krupa, Kasprzak, & Hunting, 2005; Vaughan, 2004; Wu & Hiltz, 2004). Likewise, research has indicated that facilitation of discourse and instructional design are of key importance for establishing teaching presence (Mandernach, Gonzales, & Garrett, 2006). Similarly, researchers seem to agree that it is the instructor's responsibility to create a space for social interaction, engage in discourse with the students, provide information and course content, and respond to students in a timely manner (Lowenthal, 2009). Researchers have also found that students in online courses self-reported that their instructor's behavior and actions directly impacted their learning outcomes

(LaPointe & Gunawardena, 2004). However, in a study in which Wise, Chang, Duffy, and del Valle (2004) manipulated the level of social presence that instructors projected to the students, the researchers found that the social presence of the instructor did not have an impact on the students' perceived learning or actual performance in the course but did have an impact on the students' interactions and perceptions of the instructor.

An instructor's online teaching behaviors have also been shown to influence students' sense of cohesion in the online classroom. Shea et al. (2005) found that instructor assistance with student discussions, as well as the quality of the course design, were important for establishing teaching presence in the online environment, and that this presence created a positive relationship that had an impact on students' perceptions of support and inclusiveness. Shea, Li, and Pickett (2006) also reported that as teaching presence increases, a student's sense of community increases as well. Related to this idea, a student's sense of belonging is an aspect of social presence as presented in the CoI framework.

Within the CoI, social presence has three components: affective expression, open communication and group cohesion (Swan, Richardson, Ice, Garrison, Cleveland-Innes, & Arbaugh, 2008). While each component is from the student perspective, the instructor is a key agent in shaping the students' perceptions (Wise et al., 2004). For example, certain actions that the instructor takes or the ways of projecting his or her presence may enhance students' abilities or willingness to express their emotions or make self-disclosures, which are aspects of affective expression. Likewise, the instructor's communication style used in facilitating discourse among the students may influence the students' willingness to engage in open, honest communication with one another. The ways in which the instructor explicitly refers to being part of the group may also enhance students' sense of cohesion and inclusiveness.

The related, interpersonal aspects of teaching and social presence suggest a need to examine these constructs in tandem from students' perspectives. Yet there are few studies that examine whether different aspects of teaching presence vary in terms of their relative importance for students' success in the online environment. There are also few studies that examine the role that education level may play in this importance. In studies that have investigated potential differences in factors associated with success, graduate students and undergraduate students have shown similarities. For example, Holcomb, King and Brown (2004) found that there were "no significant differences between graduate and undergraduate students with regards to the three affective characteristics under study [technology self-efficacy, distance education self-efficacy, and self-regulation measures]" (p. 10). In addition, in a study that examined how education level, gender, age, locus of control, learning style, motivational control, and self-regulated learning components accounted for student success in online courses, only self-regulation was significant in predicting online success (Yukselturk & Bulut, 2007). Concerns about the regression methods used in the study, though, suggest a need to further examine these relationships. Colorado and Eberle (2010) also investigated a potential relationship between self-regulation and demographics among graduate students and "conclude[d] that graduate students have high levels of self-regulated learning characteristics" (p. 9), but that future research involving both undergraduate and graduate students was necessary to confirm their findings.

MAIN FOCUS OF THE CHAPTER

While researchers have used the CoI framework extensively to examine the role of various aspects of presence in student learning and student satisfaction, there are few studies that have explored potential differences among various populations of students enrolled in online courses. Nor have there been many studies that have examined students' perceptions of how important various constructs embedded in teaching presence, social presence, and cognitive presence are for their success in online courses. We address this gap by presenting the results of a study designed to illuminate the importance of various indicators related to teaching presence from the students' perspectives, and we examine potential differences related to the students' education level. Our aims were to answer the following research questions:

1. What are the differences in the importance of various instructor behaviors for graduate and undergraduate students enrolled in online courses?
2. What instructor behaviors do graduate and undergraduate students consider to be the most important for their success in online course?

Methods

To address the research questions, we utilized a cross-sectional survey design. Data collection was conducted online from students enrolled in several online courses offered by the education departments at two large universities in the Midwest (U.S.A.). The questionnaire consisted of three sets of items: 64 close-ended items to measure the importance of various indicators of teaching presence in online courses, 5 open-ended items for students to report which indicators were most important, and a mixture of open- and close-ended items targeting students' experience with online learning and their preferences for various types of learning contexts. The list of indicators of teaching presence was compiled primarily from instruments used to measure teaching presence in online courses, including the CoI framework (Garrison et al., 2000). For example, the indicators FD, FS, and TF (refer to Table 3) were derived from the items

in the direct instruction substructure of teaching presence which target focusing the discussion to help students learn, providing feedback to identify strengths and weaknesses, and providing timely feedback, respectively. For the indicators that were drawn from social presence, the frame of reference shifted from the student to the instructor. For example, indicators such as CC, CI, and CP (refer to Table 3) were written to measure the importance of the instructor taking action to foster open communication. Other literature on the role of teaching presence and community building in online courses, as well as instructor experience, also guided the developed of the indicators. The intent was to present a comprehensive list of typical actions that an instructor would take in setting up, delivering, and monitoring online courses. For each indicator, students were asked to rate its importance on a scale of 1 (not important at all) to 10 (very important). For the open-ended items, students were asked to "write the 5 most important instructor behaviors for your success in an online class."

Results

The conclusions drawn in this chapter are based on data obtained from 245 students who were enrolled in one of two large universities in the Midwest. Based on the demographic data collected, the majority of the participants were enrolled in undergraduate degree programs (n = 181, 73.88%). Most of the other participants were enrolled in graduate degree programs (n = 59, 24.08%). In terms of prior experience with online courses, there was a statistically significant relationship between the number of courses taken (0, 1, 2, 3, or 4 or more) and the level of the degree program (undergraduate, graduate, or other). $\chi^2(df = 8) = 27.41$. As shown in Figure 1, a higher percentage of undergraduate participants (n = 49, 27.07%) had taken four or more prior online classes, as compared to the percentage of graduate participants who had this level of course

Figure 1. Graph of students' prior online course experience by status of degree program

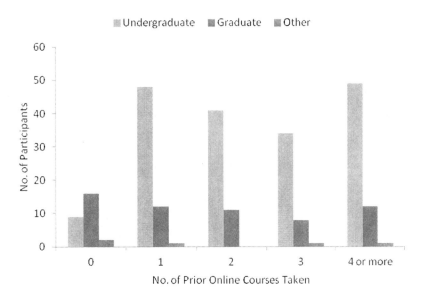

What are the Differences in the Importance of Various Instructor Behaviors for Graduate and Undergraduate Students Enrolled in Online Courses?

experience ($n = 12$, 27.07%). Less than 5% of the undergraduate students had no prior online course experience, but more than quarter of the graduate students ($n = 16$, 27.12%) had not taken any online courses before.

To answer the first research question, we examined the item ratings using two separate units of analysis at the sub-scale and item level. At the sub-scale level, we examined group differences in the summed item ratings for group cohesion, open communication, direct instruction, design and organization, and facilitation. While these constructs align with the substructures of the CoI, it is important to note that they are slightly different in the context of our analyses. For example, group cohesion and open communication represent the importance of the instructor fostering group cohesion and open communication. Direct instruction,

in this context, represents the importance of the instructor focusing the discussion to help students learn, providing feedback to identify strengths and weaknesses, and providing timely feedback. Similarly, design and organization represents the importance of the instructor clearly communicating information such as course topics, goals, instructions, and due dates. Facilitation represents the importance of facilitating discourse among the participants in the course.

Because the distributions of the item ratings did not meet the assumption of normality required for parametric analyses, we used Mann-Whitney U tests to examine the differences in the ratings for the undergraduate students and the graduate students. The results of the tests conducted at the sub-scale level are presented in Table 1. As shown in Table 1, the undergraduate ratings of importance were significantly lower than the graduate ratings for open communication ($U = 6109.0$, $z = 2.05$, $p < .05$), direct instruction ($U = 6504.5$, $z = 2.94$, $p < .05$), and design and organization ($U = 6435.5$, $z = 2.94$, $p < .05$). There were no statistically significant differences between the undergraduate and graduate ratings of group cohesion or facilitation.

Table 1. Results of Mann-Whitney U tests of sub-scale ratings by level of degree level

Presence Construct	Undergraduate				Graduate					
	N	M	SD	Mean Rank	N	M	SD	Mean Rank	U	z
Group Cohesion	169	22.21	7.26	114.15	56	23.70	7.72	131.55	5991.5	1.71
Open Communication	169	22.92	6.94	113.87	56	24.20	8.01	134.83	6109.0	2.05*
Direct Instruction	169	25.23	5.12	110.54	56	26.41	6.07	140.25	6504.5	2.94*
Design and Organization	169	36.17	5.82	112.05	56	36.98	8.14	140.46	6435.5	2.94*
Facilitation	169	47.34	11.26	113.95	56	48.77	12.55	128.27	5728.5	1.40

*$p < .05$.

At the item level, we used the Mann-Whitney U tests to determine whether there were significant differences in the importance of specific indicators between the two groups. As shown in Table 2, there were seven indicators that showed significant differences between the ratings in terms of degree level. For each of these indicators the undergraduate ratings were significantly lower than the graduate ratings.

One of the factors suspected to play a role in the differential importance of various behaviors was prior online course experience. For example, students who had more experience taking online courses might have valued certain instructor actions more or less relative to students who had taken far fewer online courses. Correlation analyses were used to examine this potential relationship between prior online course experience and the importance ratings of a subset of indicators from the survey. The correlations that were statistically significant for either the undergraduate or graduate participants are reported in Table 4.

What Instructor Behaviors do Graduate and Undergraduate Students Consider to be the Most Important for their Success in Online Course?

The 10 indicators that were most important to the students (based on mean item ratings) are listed in Table 5. The items were almost identical for both the undergraduate and graduate students although the relative importance of a few indicators differed. For example, clear communication of course goals was one of the 10 most important indicators for graduate participants ($M = 9.21$, $SD = 2.03$) but was 11th in mean rating for undergraduate participants ($M = 8.91$, $SD = 1.63$). Similarly, receiving feedback on assignments in a timely manner was more important to the graduate participants ($M = 9.29$, $SD = 1.99$) than it was for undergraduate participants ($M = 8.76$, $SD = 1.86$). The two indicators that were in the Top 10 for undergraduate participants but not for graduate participants were providing interesting materials ($M = 9.03$, $SD = 1.56$ for undergraduate participants; $M = 8.81$, $SD = 2.13$ for graduate participants) and providing grading rubrics ($M = 8.92$, $SD = 1.79$ for undergraduate participants, $M = 8.92$, $SD = 2.24$ for graduate participants). As shown in Table 5, there were significant differences between the ratings of importance of various indicators based on the undergraduate or graduate status of the degree program. In all of these cases the undergraduate ratings were significantly lower than the graduate ratings.

The relative importance of several of the indicators was also reflected in the results of a classical content analysis (Leech & Onwuegbuzie, 2007) of the responses submitted for the open-ended items. The purpose of the content analysis was to determine what indicators were

Table 2. Results of Mann-Whitney U tests of item ratings by degree level

Presence Construct / Item ID	Undergraduate				Graduate					
	N	*M*	*SD*	Mean Rank	*N*	*M*	*SD*	Mean Rank	*U*	*z*
Affective Expression										
SB	180	6.96	2.80	131.03	59	7.49	2.78	116.38	5961.00	1.43
Group Cohesion										
CD	180	7.53	2.49	115.36	59	7.93	2.75	131.14	6144.50	1.85
VA	181	7.51	2.48	118.18	59	7.69	2.73	127.63	5760.00	0.09
SC	177	7.25	2.57	114.00	59	7.73	2.75	132.01	6018.50	1.78
Open Communication										
CC	180	7.84	2.35	116.95	59	7.98	2.80	129.31	5858.00	1.22
CP	181	7.71	2.37	116.80	59	7.92	2.81	131.86	6010.00	1.48
CI	179	7.47	2.50	113.32	58	8.05	2.64	136.52	6207.00	2.28*
Direct Instruction										
FD	178	8.11	2.14	116.62	59	8.32	2.21	126.19	5675.50	0.96
FS	178	8.37	2.05	111.49	59	8.98	2.16	141.65	6785.50	3.09*
TF	181	8.76	1.86	114.14	59	9.29	1.99	140.03	6491.50	2.79*
Design and Organization										
CT	180	8.94	1.59	113.42	59	9.22	2.04	140.07	6494.00	2.85*
CG	180	8.91	1.63	113.39	58	9.21	2.03	138.46	6319.50	2.66*
IP	180	9.06	1.49	113.88	59	9.29	2.02	138.66	6411.00	2.71*
CD	181	9.38	1.35	116.48	59	9.41	2.00	132.83	6067.00	2.00*
Facilitation										
AA	179	7.88	2.04	118.69	59	7.83	2.36	121.96	5425.50	0.32
GU	181	8.36	1.92	117.75	59	8.51	2.18	128.95	5838.00	1.11
KE	180	7.94	2.22	115.79	59	8.34	2.29	132.86	6068.50	1.69
KO	180	8.11	2.11	117.09	58	8.31	2.18	126.98	5654.00	0.98
EE	180	8.02	2.16	116.77	59	8.36	2.14	129.86	5891.50	1.30
RC	178	7.06	2.76	115.33	59	7.63	2.57	130.07	5904.00	1.45

most important to the students based on the frequencies of occurrence (i.e., a higher frequency was assumed to indicate greater importance among the students). To compile the results, we initially coded the responses to the open-ended items in a primarily deductive manner based on the codebook developed from the rated items. We created new open codes for any responses that did not match any of the existing codes in the codebook. After completing several coding passes, we began merging codes that reflected similar constructs and refining codes that overlapped. Once we reached consensus on the coding, we engaged in a validation process of checking for and resolving instances of cross coding and code creep (Sheridan & Kelly, 2010). From this final coding pass, frequency data was generated for each code as an indicator of its relative importance, and a subset of the results is presented in Table 6. After elimination of unintelligible responses, there were

Table 3. Partial list of items from the questionnaire administered to students

Item ID	Item
AA	Helps in identifying areas of agreement and disagreement on course topics that helps me to learn
CC	Makes me feel comfortable conversing through the online medium
CD	Makes me feel comfortable disagreeing with other course participants while still maintaining a sense of trust
CD	Clearly communicated important due dates/time frames for learning activities.
CE	Sets clear expectations for discussion participation
CG	Clearly communicated important course goals
CI	Makes me feel comfortable interacting with other course participants
CP	Makes me feel comfortable participating in the course discussions
CR	Makes course requirements clear
CT	Clearly communicates important course topics
EE	Encourages course participants to explore new concepts in a course
EN	Creates a course that is easy to navigate
FD	Helps to focus discussion on relevant issues in a way that helps me to learn
FS	Provides feedback that helps me understand my strengths and weaknesses
FT	Always follows through with promises made to students
GU	Helps in guiding the class towards understanding course topics in a way that helps me clarify my thinking
IM	Provides interesting material
IP	Provides clear instructions on how to participate in course learning activities
KE	Helps to keep course participants engaged and participating in productive dialogue
KO	Helps keep the course participants on task in a way that helps me to learn
PR	Provides grading rubrics for all assignments, projects and discussions
RC	Reinforces the development of a sense of community among course participants
SB	Gives me a sense of belonging in the course
SC	Helps me to develop a sense of collaboration
TF	Provides timely feedback on assignments and projects
UP	Keeps the course calendar updated
VA	Makes me feel that my point of view was acknowledged by other course participants

a total of 1094 responses (809 for the undergraduate students and 261 for the graduate students).

For both graduate and undergraduate students, communication had the highest frequency (19.53% of the responses submitted by undergraduates and 23.37% of the responses submitted by graduate students), as shown in Table 6. This construct represented the instructor communicating with students in a clear and/or timely manner. Examples of responses coded with this construct included

"clear communication with students," "frequent communication," and "prompt responses." Some of the students defined their expectations for timeliness as receiving a response within 24 hours. This response accounted for 4.39% of the total interpretable responses.

Instructor dispositions had the second highest frequency for both undergraduate and graduate students (15.33% of the responses submitted by undergraduates and 13.79% of the responses submitted by graduate students). This construct

Table 4. Spearman correlations between prior online course experience and importance ratings of select items derived from the CoI by degree level (undergraduate or graduate)

Indicator	OC	SB	ON	EE	FD	TF
Online Courses (OC)	--	-.11	-.16*	-.16*	-0.12	.06
Gives me a sense of belonging in the course (SB)	-.27*	--	.64**	.54**	.61**	.30**
Helps keep the course participants on task in a way that helps me to learn (ON)	-.13	.56**	--	.78**	.82**	.38**
Encourages course participants to explore new concepts in a course (EE)	-.14	.48**	.82**	--	.84**	.38**
Helps to focus discussion on relevant issues in a way that helps me to learn (FD)	-.29*	.57**	.76**	.74**	--	.42**
Provides timely feedback on assignments and projects (TF)	.36**	0.12	0.22	.26*	0.24	--

Correlations for the participants enrolled in undergraduate degree programs ($n = 181$) are presented above the diagonal, and correlations for the participants enrolled in graduate degree programs ($n = 59$) are presented below the diagonal.
$*p < .05.$ $**p < .01.$

Table 5. Top 10 indicators with the highest ratings of importance for undergraduate or graduate degree programs

Item	N	M	SD	Mean Rank	N	M	SD	Mean Rank	U	z
CD	181	9.38	1.35	116.48	59	9.41	2.00	132.83	6067.00	2.00*
CE	181	9.03	1.67	115.10	59	9.32	2.01	137.06	6316.50	2.48*
CG[a]	180	8.91	1.63	113.39	58	9.21	2.03	138.46	6319.50	2.66**
CR	181	9.39	1.50	115.56	57	9.46	2.03	132.01	5871.50	2.13*
CT	180	8.94	1.59	113.42	59	9.22	2.04	140.07	6494.00	2.85**
EN	181	9.22	1.48	117.43	59	9.22	2.04	129.93	5896.00	1.40
FT	180	9.11	1.71	119.47	59	9.12	2.02	121.63	5406.00	0.24
IP	180	9.06	1.49	113.88	59	9.29	2.02	138.66	6411.00	2.71**
IM[b]	180	9.03	1.56	119.95	58	8.81	2.13	118.09	5138.50	-.20
PR[b]	181	8.92	1.79	118.86	59	8.92	2.24	125.53	5635.50	0.73
TF[a]	181	8.76	1.86	114.14	59	9.29	1.99	140.03	6491.50	2.79**
UP	181	9.08	1.70	116.19	59	9.25	2.08	133.72	6119.50	1.99*

reflected the instructor's inherent qualities of mind and character and an inclination to act or think in a particular manner. The types of responses that were included in this construct referred to qualities such as being understanding, patient, and/or kind, being helpful, having a sense of humor, being creative and fun, being fair, and being able to deliver good lectures.

The construct that was the third most important differed between the undergraduate and graduate students. For the undergraduate students, accessibility to materials was the construct that had the third highest frequency (13.60% of the responses submitted by undergraduate students). This construct reflected a desire to have access to materials such as good lectures and good textbooks (4.02% of the total responses), PowerPoint presentations,

Table 6. Frequency of responses that students reported as most important for their success in an online class

Rank	Total Students		Undergraduates		Graduates	
	Construct	Freq.[a]	Construct	Freq.[b]	Construct	Freq.[c]
1	Communication	224	Communication	158	Communication	61
2	Instructor disposition	161	Instructor disposition	124	Instructor disposition	36
3	Materials	134	Materials	110	Feedback	33
4	Clarity	128	Clarity	94	Clarity	31
5	Feedback	64	Facilitation	43	Discussion participation	28
6	Facilitation	54	Course structure and navigation	40	Materials	18
7	Discussion participation	51	Availability	36	Facilitation	11
8	Course structure and navigation	49	Feedback	27	Availability Course structure and navigation	**9
9	Availability	46	Understandable	22	Individual reply	6
10	Sends reminders	23	Sends reminders Reviews[d]	20	Sends reminders Knowledgeable[d]	3

high quality and interesting supplemental course materials, instructor videos, guest speakers, and meaningful assignments. Examples of responses that were coded with this construct included "good text book," "have good notes on hand," and "online resources available." This construct was also important for graduate students but accounted for only 6.90% of the total number of responses submitted by this group. For graduate students, feedback was the construct that had the third highest frequency (12.64% of the responses submitted by graduate students). This construct referred to letting students know how they were doing on assignments and in the course and/or providing constructive criticism of their work. Feedback was also relatively important to the undergraduate students, accounting for 3.34% of their responses).

Clarity was the fourth construct that was very important for both undergraduate and graduate students, accounting for 11.62% of the responses submitted by undergraduate students and 11.88% of the responses submitted by graduate students.

This construct represented the desire for the instructor to present course requirements, including due dates and important topics, in a clear, concise manner. Examples of responses that were coded with this construct included "provides clear expectations for the class," "sets clear expectations for discussion participation," and "well outline[d] instructions to assignments."

The construct that was the fifth most important differed between the undergraduate and graduate students. For the undergraduate students, facilitation was the construct that had the fifth highest frequency. This construct reflected a desire to have the instructor guide discussions, help in identifying areas of agreement and disagreement on course topics, keep students engaged in productive dialogue, encourage exploration, summarize students' posts and present material that is challenging (43 responses total, 5.32%). This construct was also important for graduate students but accounted for only 4.21% of the total number of responses submitted by this group. For graduate students, discussion participation was the construct that had the fifth highest frequency (10.73% of the responses submitted by graduate students). Discussion participation involved the desire to have the instructor participate in daily and weekly discussions. This construct was not one of the top responses for undergraduate students.

The sixth most important behavior for undergraduate students was the concept of course structure and navigation. This construct included the desire to have the instructor create a course that was easy to use online, easy to navigate, and where resources were readily accessible (4.94% of the responses submitted by undergraduate students). Examples of responses coded with this construct included "prepared website," "structured well," and "creates a course that is easy to navigate." For graduate students, course structure and navigation was the eighth most important construct (3.45%). The materials construct was the sixth most important construct for this group (accounting for 6.90% of their responses).

The seventh most important instructor behavior for undergraduate students was instructor availability. This construct included the desire to have an instructor that was available and easy to get in touch with by email, phone, or in person. Availability represented 4.44% of the undergraduate responses and only 3.45% of the responses submitted by graduate students, making it eighth in importance for this group. The eighth most important item for undergraduate students was the feedback construct (accounting for 3.34% of the undergraduate responses).

The ninth most frequent construct for undergraduate students was being understandable (accounting for 2.72% of the responses submitted by this group). This construct involved the desire for the instructor to speak in an understandable voice, accent, and dialect. For graduate students, the ninth most frequent construct was individual replies in discussions (2.30% of the responses submitted by graduate students). This construct referred to the student's desire to have the instructor reply to all of their individual posts in discussion sessions.

The tenth most important instructor construct for both graduates and undergraduates was sending reminders (accounting for 1.15% and 2.47% of their responses, respectively). This construct refers to the desire to have the instructor remind students of due dates and other important course information. Both the graduates and undergraduates also had a tied construct that made the Top 10 list. For undergraduates, this construct was reviews (i.e., having the instructor review course content for tests and projects with the students). For graduate students, the tied construct was being knowledgeable, which referred to the desire to have an instructor that is knowledgeable about the course content.

Discussion

The ratings indicated that the aspects of teaching presence that are most important to students relate to making course requirements clear and being responsive to students' needs. These results are consistent with the results obtained by Sheridan and Kelly (2010) in their initial study of students' perceptions. The present results are also consistent with literature that indicates the importance of clarity and communication for student satisfaction in online courses (Durrington, Berryhill, & Swafford, 2006).

Students' responses on the open-ended items in the present study largely affirmed the importance of both the direct instruction and facilitation elements of teaching presence. As reflected by their rank order within the student groups (i.e., all students, undergraduate students, and graduate students), the open-ended responses generally reflected the importance of the following aspects of direct instruction and facilitation: communication, clarity, feedback, facilitation, and discussion participation. These findings are generally consistent with research conducted by Shea et al. (2005) that showed that both components of teaching presence along with students' gender collectively predicted a sense of community among students. The open-ended responses also support the importance of the design component of teaching presence. Two of the top 10 instructor behaviors specifically reflected the students' desires for the instructor to create a well-designed and organized course. Specific instructor behaviors that were important to students included choosing good textbooks and providing online resources, indicating that students wanted their instructors to provide them with quality instructional materials. From both the responses related to course structure and navigation and the item ratings, we found that students highly valued the selection of their instructional materials and the layout, design and navigation of their courses.

Although the intent of the present research was not to determine what indicators of teaching presence might be missing from current models of the construct, the open-ended responses have implications for potentially broadening current conceptions of teaching presence. In particular, students' responses have sparked additional insights into the importance of instructor dispositions. For example, some of the instructor behaviors that we have included in this construct are based on students reporting that it was important to have an instructor who is "understanding," "flexible," and "helpful." The online instructor must be able to compensate for the lack of physical presence by creating an environment in the online classroom that encourages students to be engaged, motivated, validated, and comfortable participating. Thus, the online instructor needs to convey that there is an understanding, kind, empathetic, patient, and creative human being at the other end of the virtual classroom. The breadth of these disposition responses suggest that online instructors should continue to explore and find ways of projecting themselves, their personalities, and teaching styles into the virtual classroom environments. These findings are consistent with previous research on online teaching. For example, White, Roberts, and Brannan (2003) posited that one of the essential components of effective online teaching is creating

a humanizing learning environment. Likewise, Perry and Edwards (2005) found that online instructors who treated learners with respect, provided a positive affirmation, and enhanced the educational experience of the students had a positive impact on their learning. Perry and Edwards also provided an example that describes how online instructors who recognize that students often have competing interests with work, family, and school life can actually reduce stress for students and improve their student's readiness for learning by being flexible and understanding. The current study expands on this notion and suggests a potentially new component to the current conceptualization of teacher presence. Specifically, it highlights the differences between being present and the teacher's presence in the classroom (Sheridan & Kelly, 2010). This distinction may assist instructors who teach courses online to improve their teaching effectiveness, thus creating exceptional learning environments that will enhance student learning.

FUTURE RESEARCH DIRECTIONS

The main purpose of the present study was to examine the relative importance of various indicators of teaching presence based on students' perceptions and determine whether there were differences in these perceptions among graduate students and undergraduate students. The findings indicate that all of the components of teaching presence identified in the CoI framework (design, facilitation and direct instruction) are important to students. Unanticipated findings from the initial study (Sheridan & Kelly, 2010) were replicated in the current study. Students from both studies essentially desire instructors that show humanizing aspects of themselves in the online classroom. These findings lead the authors to posit that the illumination of teacher dispositions as vital instructor behaviors is an important discovery for better understanding the dynamics of online learning environments. Furthermore, we believe that these types of dispositional behaviors strengthen the space between teaching presence and social presence in the CoI framework. We believe that an instructor's disposition (e.g. showing flexibility, being understanding, having a sense of humor, etc.) both enhances direct instruction and facilitation of discourse as well as encourages social presence in the online classroom. Though dispositional behavior may have been implied by the intersection of teaching presence and social presence element within the CoI framework, additional research is needed to definitely establish the role of an instructor's dispositional behaviors in online courses. Future research that examines teaching presence may also warrant a broader conceptualization of the nature of the distinction between an instructor being present and instructor presence (Sheridan & Kelly, 2010). Additional research is also needed to determine how to provide the most effective guidance to online instructors to hone dispositional behaviors in the online classroom.

CONCLUSION

In summary, the present findings indicate that all of the components of teaching presence identified in the CoI framework (design, facilitation and direct instruction) are important to students. The findings also have implications for expanding current conceptions of teaching presence. In particular, replicated findings suggest that the illumination of teacher dispositions as vital instructor behaviors is an important expansion for the current literature on teaching presence.

REFERENCES

Anderson, T., Rourke, L., Garrison, D. R., & Archer, W. (2001). Assessing teaching presence in a computer conferencing context. *Journal of Asynchronous Learning Networks*, 5(2), 1–17.

Arbaugh, J. B. (2007). An empirical verification of the community of inquiry framework. *Journal of Asynchronous Learning Networks*, 11(1), 73–84.

Berge, Z. L. (1995). Facilitating computer conferencing: Recommendations from the field. *Educational Technology Review*, 35, 22–30.

Bliss, C. A., & Lawrence, B. (2009). From posts to patterns: A metric to characterize discussion board activity in online courses. *Journal of Asynchronous Learning Networks*, 13(2), 15–32.

Colorado, J. T., & Eberle, J. (2010). Student demographics and success in online learning environments. *The Emporia State Research Studies*, 46(1), 4–10.

Durrington, V. A., Berryhill, A., & Swafford, J. (2006). Strategies for enhancing student interactivity in an online environment. *College Teaching*, 54(1), 190–193.

Garrison, D. R. (2007). Online community of inquiry review: Social, cognitive, and teaching presence issues. *Journal of Asynchronous Learning Networks*, 11(1), 61–72.

Garrison, D. R., Anderson, T., & Archer, W. (2000). Critical inquiry in a text-based environment: Computer conferencing in higher education. *The Internet and Higher Education*, 2(2-3), 87–105.

Garrison, D. R., Anderson, T., & Archer, W. (2001). Critical thinking, cognitive presence, and computer conferencing in distance education. *American Journal of Distance Education*, 15(1), 7–23.

Garrison, D. R., & Cleveland-Innes, M. (2005). Facilitating cognitive presence in online learning: Interaction is not enough. *American Journal of Distance Education*, 19(3), 133–148.

Garrison, D. R., Cleveland-Innes, M., & Fung, T. S. (2010). Exploring causal relationships among teaching, cognitive and social presence: Student perceptions of the community of inquiry framework. *The Internet and Higher Education, 13*(1-2), 31–36.

Holcomb, L. B., King, F. B., & Brown, S. W. (2004). Student traits and attributes contributing to success in online courses: Evaluation of university online courses. *The Journal of Interactive Online Learning, 2*(3), 1–17.

LaPointe, D., & Gunawardena, C. (2004). Developing, testing and refining of a model to understand the relationship between peer interaction and learning outcomes in computer-mediated conferencing. *Distance Education, 25*(1), 83–106.

Leech, N. L., & Onwuegbuzie, A. J. (2007). An array of qualitative data analysis tools: A call for data analysis triangulation. *School Psychology Quarterly, 22*(4), 557.

Lowenthal, P. R. (2009). Social presence. In Rogers, P., Berg, G., Boettcher, J., Howard, C., Justice, L., & Schenk, K. (Eds.), *Encyclopedia of distance and online learning* (2nd ed., *Vol. 1*, pp. 1900–1906). Hershey, PA: IGI Global.

Mandernach, B. J., Gonzales, R. M., & Garrett, A. L. (2006). An examination of online instructor presence via threaded discussion participation. *Journal of Online Learning and Teaching, 2*(4), 248–260.

Mason, R. (1991). Moderating educational computer conferencing. *Deosnews, 1*(19).

Meyer, K. A. (2004). Evaluating online discussions: Four different frames of analysis. *Journal of Asynchronous Learning Networks, 8*(2), 101–114.

Murphy, E. (2004). An instrument to support thinking critically about critical thinking in online asynchronous discussions. *Australasian Journal of Educational Technology, 20*(3), 295–315.

Paulsen, M. F. (1995). Moderating educational computer conferences. *Computer Mediated Communication and the Online Classroom, 3,* 81–89.

Pawan, F., Paulus, T. M., Yalcin, S., & Chang, C. F. (2003). Online learning: Patterns of engagement and interaction among in-service teachers. *Language Learning & Technology, 7*(3), 119–140.

Perry, B., & Edwards, M. (2005). Exemplary online educators: Creating a community of inquiry. *Turkish Online Journal of Distance Education, 6*(2).

Rhode, J. F. (2008). *Interaction equivalency in self-paced online learning environments: An exploration of learner preferences.* ProQuest.

Rovai, A. P. (2002). Development of an instrument to measure classroom community. *The Internet and Higher Education, 5*(3), 197–211.

Shea, P., Li, C. S., Swan, K., & Pickett, A. (2005). Developing learning community in online asynchronous college courses: The role of teaching presence. *Journal of Asynchronous Learning Networks, 9*(4), 59–82.

Shea, P., Pickett, A., & Li, C. S. (2006). Increasing access to higher education: A study of the diffusion of online teaching among 913 college faculty. *The International Review of Research in Open and Distance Learning, 6*(2). ISSN 1492-3831

Shea, P. J., Pickett, A. M., & Pelz, W. E. (2003). A follow-up investigation of "teaching presence" in the SUNY learning network. *Journal of Asynchronous Learning Networks, 7*(2), 61–80.

Sheridan, K., & Kelly, M. A. (2010). The indicators of instructor presence that are important to students in online courses. *Journal of Online Learning and Teaching, December.*

Swan, K. (2002). Building learning communities in online courses: The importance of interaction. *Education Communication and Information, 2*(1), 23–49.

Swan, K., Richardson, J. C., Ice, P., Garrison, D. R., Cleveland-Innes, M., & Arbaugh, J. B. (2008). Validating a measurement tool of presence in online communities of inquiry. *Od re dak cji*, **88**.

Swan, K., & Shih, L. F. (2005). On the nature and development of social presence in online course discussions. *Journal of Asynchronous Learning Networks*, *9*(3), 115–136.

Varnhagen, S., Wilson, D., Krupa, E., Kasprzak, S., & Hunting, V. (2005). Comparison of student experiences with different online graduate courses in health promotion. *Canadian Journal of Learning and Technology*, *31*(1), 99–117.

Vaughan, N. (2004). Technology in support of faculty learning communities. *New Directions for Teaching and Learning*, (97): 101–109.

White, A., Roberts, V. W., & Brannan, J. (2003). Returning nurses to the workforce: Developing an online refresher course. *Journal of Continuing Education in Nursing*, *34*(2), 59–63.

Wise, A., Chang, J., Duffy, T., & del Valle, R. (2004). The effects of teacher social presence on student satisfaction, engagement, and learning. *Journal of Educational Computing Research*, *31*(3), 247–271.

Wu, D., & Hiltz, S. R. (2004). Predicting learning from asynchronous online discussions. *Journal of Asynchronous Learning Networks*, *8*(2), 139–152.

Yukselturk, E., & Bulut, S. (2007). Predictors for student success in an online course. *Subscription Prices and Ordering Information, 71*.

ADDITIONAL READING

Aggarwal, A. (2000). *Web-based learning and teaching technologies: Opportunities and challenges*. Hershey, PA: IGI Global.

Andersen, J. F. (1979). Teacher immediacy as a predictor of teaching effectiveness. *Communication Yearbook*, *3*, 543–559.

Bates, R., & Khasawneh, S. (2007). Self-efficacy and college students' perceptions and use of online learning systems. *Computers in Human Behavior*, *23*(1), 175–191.

Corbett, A. (2010). Cognitive computer tutors: Solving the two-sigma problem. *User Modeling, 2001*, 137–147.

Garrison, D. R., & Kanuka, H. (2004). Blended learning: Uncovering its transformative potential in higher education. *The Internet and Higher Education*, *7*(2), 95–105.

Iacoboni, M. (2008). *Mirroring people: The new science of how we connect with others*. New York, NY: Farrar Straus & Giroux.

Keysers, C., Kohler, E., Umiltà, M. A., Nanetti, L., Fogassi, L., & Gallese, V. (2003). Audiovisual mirror neurons and action recognition. *Experimental Brain Research*, *153*(4), 628–636.

Kiewra, K. (2005). *Learn how to study and SOAR to success*. Upper Saddle River, NJ: Pearson Education Inc.

Kurtz, G., Sagee, R., & Getz-Lengerman, R. (2003). Alternative online pedagogical models with identical contents: A comparison of two university-level courses. *The Journal of Interactive Online Learning*, *2*(1), 1–7.

Lowenthal, P. R., & Dunlap, J. C. (2010). From pixel on a screen to real person in your students' lives: Establishing social presence using digital storytelling. *The Internet and Higher Education*, *13*(1-2), 70–72.

Mandernach, B. J., Gonzales, R. M., & Garrett, A. L. (2006). An examination of online instructor presence via threaded discussion participation. *Journal of Online Learning and Teaching*, *2*(4), 248–260.

Matthews, D. (1999). The origins of distance education and its use in the United States. *T.H.E. Journal*, *27*(2), 54–66.

Mitchell, T. J. F., Chen, S. Y., & Macredie, R. D. (2005). The relationship between web enjoyment and student perceptions and learning using a web-based tutorial. *Learning, Media and Technology*, *30*(1), 27–40.

O'Reilly, M., & Newton, D. (2002). Interaction online: Above and beyond requirements of assessment. *Australian Journal of Educational Technology*, *18*(1), 57–70.

Olson, T., & Wisher, R. A. (2002). The effectiveness of web-based instruction: An initial inquiry. *International Review of Research in Open and Distance Learning*, *3*(2).

Palloff, R. M., & Pratt, K. (2005). *Collaborating online: Learning together in community*. San Francisco, CA: Jossey-Bass Inc.

Rovai, A. P., & Jordan, H. (2004). Blended learning and sense of community: A comparative analysis with traditional and fully online graduate courses. *International Review of Research in Open and Distance Learning*, *5*(2), 1–17.

Ryan, M., Carlton, K. H., & Ali, N. S. (2004). Reflections on the role of faculty in distance learning and changing pedagogies. *Nursing Education Perspectives*, *25*(2), 73–80.

Sahin, I., & Shelley, M. (2008). Considering students' perceptions: The distance education student satisfaction model. *Journal of Educational Technology & Society*, *11*(3), 216–223.

Snyder, B. (2005). Distance learning, online education, electronic education, electronic learning...call it what you want. *EzineArticles*. Retrieved from http://ezinearticles.com/?Distance-Learning,-Online-Education,-Electronic-Education,-Electronic-Learning...Call-It-What-You-Wa&id=10877

Swann, J. (2010). A dialogic approach to online facilitation. *Australasian Journal of Educational Technology*, *26*(1), 50–62.

Turoff, M. (2006). The change role of faculty and online learning. *Journal of Asynchronous Learning Networks*, *10*(4), 129–138.

Wighting, M. J., Liu, J., & Rovai, A. P. (2008). Distinguishing sense of community and motivation characteristics between online and traditional college students. *Quarterly Review of Distance Education*, *9*(3), 285.

Yildiz, S., & Chang, C. (2003). Case studies of distance students' perceptions of participation and interaction in three asynchronous web-based conferencing classes in the US. *Turkish Online. Journal of Distance Education*, *4*(2).

Young, S. (2006). Student views of effective online teaching in higher education. *American Journal of Distance Education*, *20*(2), 65–77.

KEY TERMS AND DEFINITIONS

Community of Inquiry: A process model conceived by Garrison, Anderson, and Archer in 2000 used to conceptualize the dynamics of online learning environments.

Distance Learning: Learning that occurs either asynchronously or synchronously with an instructor and/or other students who are connected to one another and the digital classroom via electronic communication (such as computer, telephone, satellite etc.).

E-Learning: Any type of electronic teaching and learning that is either self-paced or group-based and synchronous or asynchronous.

Instructor Disposition: Instructor dispositions are the values, ethics, traits and beliefs that mediate the instructor's actions and behaviors towards students.

Online Learning: Teaching and learning that occurs via electronic transmission of knowledge. Typically online learning refers to computer-based learning.

Teaching Presence: The ability of an online educator to project himself/herself into an online learning environment.

Chapter 6
Effective Teaching Practices to Foster Vibrant Communities of Inquiry in Synchronous Online Learning

Annie Saint-Jacques
Université Laval, Canada

ABSTRACT

For the past decade, the Community of Inquiry (CoI) framework has been validated and applied to asynchronous online learning. This chapter proposes to explore its innovative application to synchronous online learning which has to date received little attention in the literature. This chapter reports on effective ways to engage graduate students attending virtual seminars in real time, based on the findings of a qualitative doctoral study that took place in five Francophone and Anglophone North American universities. The crucial role of the faculty member as the facilitator of a rich and ongoing dialogue in the classroom has yet to be identified with, and embraced by faculty, but students are generally satisfied with their virtual graduate seminars.

INTRODUCTION

Research has confirmed the link between the establishment of a sense of community and perceived learning (Garrison & Arbaugh, 2007; Rovai & Jordan, 2004; Shea, Li, & Pickett, 2006). This study aims at examining effective teaching practices in a synchronous online learning environment through the exploration of the virtual graduate seminar. While common in academia, the graduate seminar has not received much attention in the literature in recent years. Therein lays the interest of studying it from a social perspective more aligned to emerging pedagogical considerations derived from recent research. This is the first study examining current educational practices within a virtual graduate seminar.

It is also the first academic study to look into a concrete application of blended online learning design (BOLD) (Power, 2008). This emerging

DOI: 10.4018/978-1-4666-2110-7.ch006

form of online design combines synchronous and asynchronous online learning within a course to leverage the benefits of both modes (see Garrison & Kanuka, 2004). All virtual graduate seminars in this study use this particular approach.

While design considerations are very important in online learning, they need to be supported by strong online learning models. One such model that has received considerable attention over the last decade is the Community of Inquiry framework (Garrison, Anderson, & Archer, 2000). With a focus on critical thinking and collaboration, it "provides a well-structured model and set of guidelines to create effective learning communities in an online learning environment" (Akyol, Vaughan, & Garrison, 2011, p. 232). Consequently, the creation of communities of inquiry in synchronous online environments and effective teaching practices to foster these communities are the focus of this study.

According to Schullo (2005), successful synchronous online teaching strategies include:

- Mini lectures with interactive exercises
- Structured group work and collaborative exercises
- Case study discussions
- Polling and quizzing and student interaction
- Dissemination of electronic content for immediate discussion, feedback, or problem solving
- Reinforcement of ideas, concepts and knowledge
- Question and answer sessions (p. 242)

This study especially highlights the importance of strategies 2, 3 and 6. It also confirmed the results of an earlier study (Stewart, 2008) which for the first time established the link between building social presence and the promotion of learning-centered dialogue in real time.

BACKGROUND

Recent research suggests that sustaining a learning community is a recommended online educational practice (Larramendy-Joerns & Leinhardt, 2006) and that constructivist teaching practices are more appropriate for guiding the design and delivery of online courses in higher education (Bangert, 2010). However, institutions face a number of challenges in implementing an efficient and sustainable online learning experience: student's feeling of isolation (Ludwig-Hardman & Dunlap, 2003; Rovai 2002; Sikora & Carroll, 2002; Slagter van Tryon & Bishop, 2006), high drop-out rates (Angelino, Williams, & Natvig, 2007; Berge & Huang, 2004; Liu, Magjuka, Bonk, & Lee, 2007), faculty dissatisfaction and resistance (Bedford, 2009; Blin & Munro, 2008; Sammons & Ruth, 2007; Shea, Pickett, & Li, 2005), high front-end design costs (Power & Gould-Morven, 2011), and overall administrative issues in relation to the production of quality learning material (Thompson, 2004; Tallent-Runnels, Thomas, Lan, Cooper, Ahern, Shaw, & Liu, 2006).

Faculty members involved in asynchronous online teaching and learning also find it extremely time-consuming (Bolliger & Wasilik, 2009; Cavanaugh, 2005; Lefoe & Hedberg, 2006; Pachnowski & Jurczyk, 2003; Sammons & Ruth, 2007; Shea, Fredericksen, Pickett, & Pelz, 2004; Shea, Pickett, & Li, 2005; Teng & Taveras, 2004; Thompson, 2004; Thompson & MacDonald 2005; and Visser, 2000). This translates into feelings of dissatisfaction and frustration on their part, especially when they have been subjected to institutional pressures (Betts, 1998). Notwithstanding the time factor, faculty members teaching asynchronously also express a sense of disconnection from their students (Osborn, 2009); that connection often being one of the primary reasons why they wanted to teach in the first place.

Yet the biggest challenge in online teaching and learning remains the application of recent research findings based on the promotion of meaningful learning facilitated through careful scaffolding of collaborative learning activities. These findings fully support the importance of learner interaction in online learning effectiveness; in other words, social presence can be seen as a foundation of cognitive presence (Akyol & Garrison, 2011; Arbaugh & Benbunan-Fich, 2006; Garrison & Arbaugh, 2007; Garrison & Cleveland-Innes, 2005; Garrison & Vaughan, 2008; Rovai, 2002; Shea, 2006). The problem is that very few theoretical models exist for online learning, which makes the Community of Inquiry theoretical framework (Garrison, Anderson, & Archer, 2000) all the more interesting. Based on the premise that online learning is a collaborative, constructivist activity, this widely recognized model may guide research and practice in online learning in higher education (Garrison & Arbaugh, 2007).

With the objective of solving some online learning issues, this study is focused on synchronous online learning, described in further detail below. Literature is sparse on current challenges and problems regarding graduate level synchronous online learning, and "scant research has been conducted on variables impacting [it]" (Park & Bonk, 2007). For graduate students, success is tributary of adequate design and organization and direct instruction, but also to the development of "higher-order thought processes through the instructor's active facilitation of discourse" (Kupczynski, Ice, Wiesenmayer, & McCluskey, 2010, p. 33). Park and Bonk (2007) identify "time constraints, lack of reflection, language barriers, tool-related problems, and peers' network connection problems" (p. 245) as challenges of synchronous online learning. Perhaps more importantly, due to time constraints, they report that interactions are marked by task-related issues. Confusion resulting from numerous, simultaneous interactions, the lack of non-verbal communication, and technological glitches are reported in McBrien, Jones and Cheng (2009).

Generally speaking, most of these issues could be addressed by proper design and facilitation,

as research better informs synchronous online learning. There seems to be a strong correlation between learners' rating of their sense of community (and learning experience) and effective teaching presence (Shea, 2006). Consequently, these elements could be considered indicators of a quality learning experience, a notion reinforced by Bangert's (2010) description of teaching presence; that is, " 'methods' that instructors use to create quality online instructional experiences that support and sustain productive communities of inquiry."

The Community of Inquiry Framework

The triadic CoI framework (see Figure 1) is based on the intersection and interdependence of teaching presence, social presence and cognitive presence in an online course (Garrison *et al.*, 2000).

The focus of this chapter is on teaching presence and its three components: 1) design and

Figure 1. The Community of inquiry framework

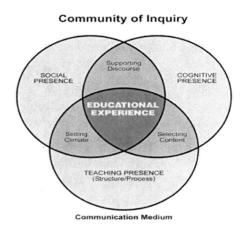

organization; 2) discourse facilitation; and 3) direct instruction (Anderson, Rourke, Garrison, & Archer, 2001), and how it may contribute to successfully bridge the transactional distance between the instructor and online learners (Arbaugh & Hwang, 2006).

The construct of teaching presence can be described as the "methods" that instructors use to create quality online instructional experiences that support and sustain productive communities of inquiry (Bangert, 2010).

Viewed as the "primary catalyst" of social presence and cognitive presence (Kupczynski, Ice, Wiesenmayer, & McCluskey, 2010), teaching presence plays a crucial role in student satisfaction, perceived learning and the development of a sense of belonging (Garrison & Arbaugh, 2007).

Garrison, Anderson and Archer (2000) identified four levels of inquiry corresponding to the increasingly complex phases of cognitive presence in a Community of Inquiry: 1) a triggering event aimed at fostering further inquiry; 2) the exploration of the issue through reflection and discourse; 3) the integration phase where learners construct meaning; and 4) the resolution phase where they can apply and test new knowledge. The ultimate goal of this knowledge-building process is to reach the integration and resolution phases through reflection and meaningful dialogue. Successful design of virtual graduate seminars thus requires careful attention to learning tasks and activities in order to provide students with these opportunities to collaborate toward resolution. These findings are in line with those of Garrison and Cleveland-Innes (2005) as to the need to structure both the course content and participant interactions, as well as those of Akyol, Vaughan and Garrison (2011) pertaining to intentional course design to create a Community of Inquiry.

If proper design is the backbone of collaborative online learning, good facilitation skills and techniques are crucial. "[f]acilitating discourse

during the course is critical to maintaining the interest, motivation and engagement of students in active learning" (Anderson *et al.*, 2001). Effective online dialogue may alleviate communication anxiety among students (Stewart, 2008), and good facilitation skills generate student connectedness in an online environment (Gunawardena, Orteganon-Layne, Carabajal, Frechette, Lindemann, & Jennings, 2006). Additionally, adequate guidance and facilitation will contribute to student achievement of desired resolution outcomes in problem-solving activities (Murphy, 2004).

For its part, direct instruction involves diagnosing misconceptions, providing knowledge from various sources and summarizing the discussion (Garrison & Anderson, 2003). Akyol, Vaughan and Garrison's (2011) research highlights the fact that the use of the term "teaching" instead of 'teacher' allows for the possibility of distributing the responsibilities and roles among participants. While teaching presence closely relates to the faculty member's roles and responsibilities, from a collaborative, constructivist perspective with a focus on social learning, it should be considered "the responsibility of every participant in an online environment" (Stodel, Thompson, & MacDonald, 2006). Indeed, distributed teaching presence may encourage freer discussion and contribute to the professor exercising a less authoritative role (Rourke & Anderson, 2002). Direct instruction also involves focusing the discussion on relevant issues and providing feedback to students.

Finally, an important consideration is the fact that in synchronous online learning, the boundaries between discourse facilitation and direct instruction are very thin, due to increased immediacy, and both are based on the same principles. For clarity purposes, this chapter uses the CoI framework elements as they are traditionally presented.

Blended Online Learning Design

Whereas the CoI framework can guide online learning practices with its focus on socioconstructivist learning, blended online learning design (BOLD) (Power, 2008) can complement it by orienting online learning practices from an instructional design and technology standpoint, with the same socioconstructivist focus. What is blended online learning design? This emerging form of online design combines the immediacy attributes of a synchronous digital learning environment and the reflective attributes of an asynchronous digital learning environment, "resulting in a completely online learning environment" (Power & Vaughan, 2010, p. 22). Virtual classrooms allow learners to "sit" in an online meeting space where the focus is on live teacher-student and student-student interaction (Simonson & Schlosser, 2009). An important online design consideration, Schwier and Balbar (2002) pointed out that "a combination of synchronous and asynchronous experiences seems to be necessary to promote the kind of engagement and depth required in a graduate seminar."

Improved teaching and learning strategies that would provide students with both the convenience of online learning and access to real-time interaction, simulating a face-to-face setting, are needed in today's world (McBrien, Jones, & Cheng, 2009). In parallel, advancement in webconferencing technology has resulted in synchronous teaching and learning becoming more readily available in the classroom (Chen, Ko, Kinshuk, & Lin, 2005). The possibility of providing students with immediate and ongoing feedback (Cogburn & Levinson, 2003), immediate resolution to questions (Carr-Chellman & Duchastel, 2000), and of establishing a strong sense of community (Schwier & Balbar, 2002; Tolu, 2010), are some of the advantages associated with synchronous online learning that faculty should leverage. Faculty members can regain better control of the teaching and learning environment as BOLD "lowers upfront design-related faculty workload" (Power, Vaughan, & Saint-Jacques, 2010). To students, it offers enhanced quality through more engaging and rewarding dialogue (Power & Gould-Morven, 2011).

While this form of online learning does not represent a "one-size-fits-all" solution in any way, it does have the potential to alleviate some of the current online teaching and learning issues, thanks to its immediacy and multimedia features. Recent research findings indicate that synchronous online interaction lessens student feelings of isolation better than asynchronous interaction (Rockinson-Szapkiw, 2009) and contributes to student engagement and satisfaction (Russo & Benson, 2005), while timely reflections occurring on the discussion board provide for more in-depth exploration of topics (Maushak & Ou, 2007).

Indeed, the ties between the CoI framework and BOLD are ties of shared values. Although Leiss (2010) found no significant difference in classroom community based on the use of either the asynchronous or synchronous mode, Tolu (2010) suggested that live class meetings facilitate the manifestation of social, teaching and cognitive presence. This is also evidenced by both Schullo's (2005) case study that highlights the development of social presence as a crucial factor of successful synchronous online learning and Stewart's (2008) findings, which are derived from the synchronous online application of Chickering and Gamson's (1997) seven principles of effective teaching. Consequently, because of the close pedagogical values of both the CoI framework and BOLD, they serve as the theoretical foundation for this chapter.

The Virtual Graduate Seminar

The virtual graduate seminar can be conceptualized as a group discussion with between eight and twenty students usually in attendance (Jaques, 2000, p. 94) and with a teaching method "focused on the acquisition of competences and reflective skills and abilities" (Oberst, Gallifa, Farriols, & Villaregut, 2009).

Overall, the instructor's role is that of an egalitarian participant (Bergquist & Phillips, 1981), guiding students in their exploration of the topic under study and creating a class atmosphere conducive to interaction and collaboration (Neal, 1996). Lecturing is not conducive to interaction (Philips & Powers, 1979), whereas knowledge-building occurs in a social environment and is greatly influenced by mutual interaction (Brown & Duguid, 2000). Figure 2 presents the conceptualization of the virtual graduate seminar.

The analysis of the virtual graduate seminar in synchronous mode sought answers to this research question: Which successful practices can be used to inform guidelines for high quality online learning?

THE RESEARCH METHODOLOGY

Park and Bonk (2007) determined that students appreciate "spontaneous feedback, meaningful interactions, multiple perspectives, and instructors' supports" (p. 245). McBrien, Jones and Cheng's (2009) study confirms earlier findings by Chen and Willits (1999) and Jung (2001) as to "the value of supporting effective forms of interaction between learner-instructor, learner-learner, and learner-content." These authors also reported that varied processes of synchronous online learning

positively impact student involvement. These reasons motivated the study of the virtual graduate seminar as per a blended online learning approach.

Qualitative methods were selected because the virtual graduate seminar is still unexplored territory. "We are in the early stages of understanding and explaining the complexities of online conferencing and educational discourse. The goal is descriptive, not predictive" (Garrison, Cleveland-Innes, Koole, & Kappelman, 2006, p. 4). The graduate seminar itself has not received much attention in the literature since the 1960s. Also, this is the first academic study of an application of blended online learning design. For these reasons, the use of qualitative methods was warranted.

The Context of the Study

The research is based on a multiple-case study (eight cases) conducted in five Francophone and Anglophone North American universities. In all cases, virtual graduate seminars were offered with a blended online learning approach and a socioconstructivist view.

Figure 2. The virtual graduate seminar

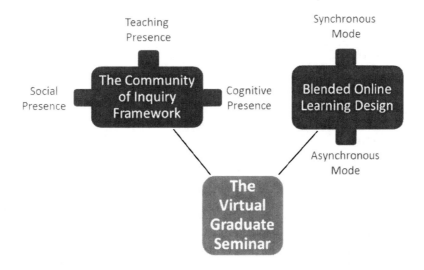

The case study design was selected because it is particularly suitable in a research context where "the focus is on a contemporary phenomenon within a real-life context" (Yin, 2009, p. 2). Additionally, I, as a researcher, had no control over the classroom events given I had observed archived segments of virtual graduate seminars. This study received ethical clearance from my home university Institutional Review Board and from those of the various institutions involved in the research. Table 1 provides a brief overview of the eight cases.

It is worth mentioning that Case 1 was quite different from the other cases in that the class was divided into two groups due to high numbers and the seminars took place every second week for 1.5 hours. Poor quality software seriously impacted on student learning, to the extent that four students admitted they would only watch the recordings and not attend the virtual seminar at all towards the end of the term. The course relied primarily on the asynchronous mode, the virtual seminar being used to give examples from readings and to answer logistics questions, a practice bemoaned by students who wished there would be more synchronous interaction. Interestingly, as they were all from the same geographic area, many teams met face-to-face to attend their online course in small groups and to do the assignments.

In Cases 3 and 5, while the professors embraced a socioconstructivist view, their seminars were more lecture-based than interactive. In Case 3, the

Table 1. A brief overview of research cases

	Faculty Member Experience	**Country, Language**	**Program**	**Students**	**Schedule**
Case 1	Seasoned professional but new professor; new to online teaching; supported by three teaching assistants and an instructional designer	Canada, French	Health Sciences	n=70 68 females 2 males	1.5-hour biweekly graduate seminar
Case 2	Seasoned professor and former instructional designer; expertise in online teaching	Canada, French	Education	n=18 14 females 4 males	3-hour weekly graduate seminar
Case 3	Seasoned professor; first online experience; supported by an instructional designer	Canada, French	Administration	n=12 7 females 5 males	3-hour weekly graduate seminar
Case 4	Two co-teaching lecturers; functional in online teaching	Canada, English	Education	n=8 7 females 1 male	2.5-hour weekly graduate seminar
Case 5	Two seasoned professors; not comfortable with online teaching	Canada, English	Education	n=16 14 females 2 males	2-hour weekly graduate seminar
Case 6	Seasoned professor and former instructional designer; expertise in online teaching; supported by one teaching assistant	United States, English	Education	n=14; 9 females 5 males	3-hour weekly graduate seminar
Case 7	Seasoned professor; functional in online teaching; supported by an instructional designer	Canada, English	Education	n=14 11 females 3 males	3-hour weekly graduate seminar
Case 8	Seasoned professor and former instructional designer; expertise in online teaching	Canada, French	Education	n=18 16 females 2 males	3-hour weekly graduate seminar

interactive component occurred in the breakout rooms where students had a chance to discuss issues and validate their knowledge on a weekly basis. The co-teaching team in Case 5 did not use the breakout rooms because they were not comfortable with the technology.

The Population Samples

Faculty members were selected because of the socioconstructivist orientation they demonstrated in the initial contacts and for their knowledge of the Community of Inquiry framework. By accepting to participate in the study, a professor also consented to a mandatory 45-minute interview and to encourage his or her students to take part in the study as well. When the faculty was supported by teaching assistants or instructional designers, these professionals were also invited to an interview to which they all accepted.

Altogether, ten faculty members participated in the study, and nine[1] were interviewed (six females, three males), as well as 45 graduate students (37 females, eight males), four teaching assistants[2] (three females, one male), and three instructional designers[3] (one female, two males). The 45 students who participated in the interviews and the 50 students who responded to the online surveys all did so on a strictly voluntary basis. Because not all students from every class participated in the study, the student demographics for each case are not precisely known; however, the vast majority of them were employed adults in their thirties and had a focus on lifelong learning for career advancement.

The Data Collection

Data collection took place during the Fall term of 2010 and the Winter term of 2011. Data were collected through *post facto* observation of virtual graduate seminars, interviews with faculty members, graduate students, teaching assistants

and instructional designers, as well as mid-term and post-term online student surveys.

The interview questionnaires consisted of five opinion questions (six in the case of faculty members) and 34 statements adapted from the Community of Inquiry survey instrument (Arbaugh, Clevelland-Innes, Diaz, Garrison, Ice, Richardson, & Swan, 2008; Swan, Richardson, Ice, Garrison, Cleveland-Innes, and Arbaugh, 2008). While the original survey questions were created for asynchronous online learning purposes, they were adapted to the reality of synchronous online learning. Participants were asked to focus on blended online learning design, according to a "synchronous-supported-by-asynchronous" approach.

While the 45-minute interviews (n=61) took place mostly toward the end of the term, observations of one-hour recordings of graduate seminars were carried out about every second week during the term, for a total of five hours of observation per class (40 hours in total). First-hour segments of virtual graduate seminars were observed. The reason for this was the inconsistency in seminar duration. Throughout the semester, both Fall and Winter seminars 3, 5, 7, 9 and 11 were observed for a total of five virtual graduate seminars per course. Each observation followed this sequence: 1) the writing of personal field notes pertaining to literature and more subjective observations; and 2) the use of the criteria grid adapted from the Community of Inquiry survey instrument where I would enter comments under the various rubrics as applicable.

For triangulation purposes, students were also asked to fill out the mid-term online survey and the post-term online survey. Both surveys were inspired by the Community of Inquiry survey instrument, with questions pertaining to interaction, collaboration, engagement and overall satisfaction. I used a 1-5 Likert scale, with 1 being the lowest score and 5 the highest. The first survey focused on the state of the Community of Inquiry at mid-term, the second one, on progress made in terms of interaction and collaboration at the end of the term. I received 82 online surveys (50 mid-term and 32 post-term questionnaires) from 50 students.

The Data Analysis

Using NVivo 9 qualitative data analysis software, interview transcripts and field notes were coded line by line as new concepts emerged. I started with only a handful of nodes pertaining essentially to the Community of Inquiry framework and blended online learning design. I coded the nine faculty interviews first, letting new nodes emerge progressively. This exercise resulted in a total of 130 nodes which were used to thoroughly re-code the nine interviews a second time. Refining the codes and applying them to student, teaching assistant and instructional designer interviews and to the field notes eventually resulted in a total of 192 nodes. At the time of writing, I was still working on the final classification and a possible model of the virtual graduate seminar. The compiling of faculty, student, teaching assistant and instructional designer interview results was completed, as well as the compiling of both student surveys. Results are presented below.

THE STUDY RESULTS

The Faculty and Student Interview Results

Based on faculty and student interviews, Table 2 provides the overall means for each item of the measurement instrument of presence in online communities of inquiry (Swan *et al.*, 2008), with distinct rubrics for teaching presence.

The *Post Facto* Observation Results

In contrast to important course topics, course goals were not always systematically communicated during the various seminars but were provided in writing. In all cases, professors did not always clearly communicate instructions on how to participate in course learning activities. This was problematic in Case 1 due to conflicting guidelines from the professor and three teaching assistants, and in Case 5 due to a lack of technical training among faculty and some students. As for the due dates and timeframes, the professors clearly communicated them but were quite flexible, and this created frustration among students at times.

Identifying areas of agreement and disagreement to help students learn was at times problematic for Faculty 1 due to conflicting information given by four educators, while Faculty 2, 4a, 4b, 5, 6 and 8 did not systematically do this. Keeping course participants engaged and participating in productive dialogue was most problematic for Faculty 1. It was also challenging for Faculty 3, 4a, 4b and 5 mainly because these instructors talked too much, that is, anywhere between 15 and 50 minutes at once. Keeping course participants on task was also an issue in these four classes. When the professor asked a question, it would take some students a few seconds longer to respond and, in some cases, only a few of them would respond. Based on this, it can be inferred that the other students were busy doing something else. Faculty 2, 4, 6, 7 and 8 did make attempts to reinforce the development of a sense of community in the class, which Faculty 5 may not have seen as important due to the fact that students already knew one another well from previous on-campus mandatory courses in their program.

Helping students understand their strengths and weaknesses was a complex task for all professors. Master's students strongly believe in individualized feedback (Ice, Kupczynski, Wiesenmeyer, & Phillips, 2008) and while they literally crave it, written feedback is very time-consuming. Faculty 1 (and her team of assistants), 5 and 7 provided the most extensive feedback, with the latter using criteria grids. Faculty 7 provided ample feedback

Table 2. Overall means for each element of a community of inquiry

	Faculty (n=9)	Students (n=45)
	Mean	Mean
Design and Organization		
1. Clear communication of important course topics	100.0	91.1
2. Clear communication of important course goals	100.0	86.6
3. Clear instructions on how to participate in learning activities	94.4	85.5
4. Clear communication of important due dates/timeframes	94.4	88.9
Discourse Facilitation		
5. Identification of areas of agreement and disagreement	88.9	72.2
6. Guidance towards understanding course topics	100.0	71.1
7. Students engaged and participating	94.4	82.2
8. Students on task	94.4	83.3
9. Encouragement to explore new concepts	94.4	88.9
10. Reinforcement of a sense of community among students	83.3	60.0
Direct Instruction		
11. Discussion focused on relevant issues	100.0	84.4
12. Feedback on strengths and weaknesses	94.4	77.8
13. Feedback offered in a timely fashion	94.4	71.1
Social Presence		
14. Sense of belonging through getting to know students	100.0	60.0
15. Distinct impressions of course participants	88.9	74.4
16. Web-based communication excellent for social interaction	72.2	53.3
17. Feeling comfortable conversing through the online medium	100.0	87.8
18. Feeling comfortable participating in the discussions	77.8	83.3
19. Feeling comfortable interacting with other participants	100.0	85.6
20. Feeling comfortable disagreeing	77.8	77.8
21. Feeling that point of view is acknowledged	72.2	72.2
22. Online discussions helping to develop a sense of collaboration	88.9	60.0
Cognitive Presence		
23. Problems increase interest	88.9	87.8
24. Activities pique curiosity	72.2	80.0
25. Exploration of content-related questions	88.9	90.0
26. Variety of information sources	50.0	72.2
27. Brainstorming to resolve content-related questions	94.4	81.1

continued on following page

Table 2. Continued

	Faculty (n=9)	Students (n=45)
	Mean	Mean
28. Discussions valuable for appreciation of different perspectives	100.0	93.3
29. Combination of new information to answer questions	100.0	90.0
30. Activities helping the construction of explanations/solutions	100.0	94.4
31. Reflection helping the understanding of fundamental concepts	88.9	95.6
32. Students can describe ways to test and apply knowledge	94.4	95.6
33. Students have developed solutions	77.8	81.1
34. Students can apply knowledge	100.0	96.7

on a weekly basis which her students greatly appreciated.

The Student Online Survey Results

Table 3 provides results of the mid-term student survey. Table 4 provides results of the post-term student survey filled out one month after the end of the term. This survey focused on progress achieved toward the end of the term.

DISCUSSION

Where research findings are presented, "F" stands for faculty, "S" for student, "ID" for instructional designer and "TA" for teaching assistant; the first digit designates the case (class), and the last digit designates the student code in the class. All quotations are excerpts from the semi-structured interview transcripts.

Based on the results from interview questions 1 to 4 of the CoI measurement instrument, it stands to reason that design was not a problematic area in this study. However, it can be argued that the scope of design was broader and that many identified issues were directly related to design considerations.

For instance, Faculty 3 (first experience of synchronous online learning) admitted that she did not devote any time to the creation of a community of inquiry. While she was constantly asking students if they had questions or comments and truly cared, she did most of the talking in her seminars, either to ask questions, provide explanations, or give feedback. When a student asked a question, she would immediately respond to it, leading the rest of the class to adopt a very passive attitude. Feedback from her students (interviews and surveys) confirms that interaction was very limited and students did not collaborate.

Most faculty members (83%) thought their actions reinforced the development of a sense of community among course participants while 60% of students agreed. Results from student comments and observations confirm that this is a weaker area, especially in Cases 1 and 3.

When it comes to discourse facilitation, 100% of faculty members thought they were helpful in guiding the class towards understanding course topics in a way that helped students clarify their thinking; 71% of students agreed. This could be due to the fact that subject matter experts are not always able to convey a clear message to non-experts. This also speaks to the need to design virtual graduate seminars with a focus on greater interaction and co-construction of knowledge among students.

As for direct instruction, the provision of feedback was another problematic area. Ninety-

Table 3. Mid-term survey (n=50)

1. Richness of dialogue ranking in the virtual graduate seminar						
1	*2*	*3*	*4*	*5*	*Not known*	*Not applicable*
1	10	**20**	15	4		
2. Frequency of dialogue ranking in the virtual graduate seminar						
1	*2*	*3*	*4*	*5*	*Not known*	*Not applicable*
1	8	16	**21**	4		
3. Student engagement and participation ranking in the virtual graduate seminar						
1	*2*	*3*	*4*	*5*	*Not known*	*Not applicable*
3	5	17	**25**			
4. Respect shown for the diversity of ideas and the possibility to disagree with other students						
1	*2*	*3*	*4*	*5*	*Not known*	*Not applicable*
2	1	9	17	**19**	1	1
5. Interaction ranking in the virtual graduate seminar						
1	*2*	*3*	*4*	*5*	*Not known*	*Not applicable*
2	4	**21**	18	5		
6. Collaboration ranking in the virtual graduate seminar						
1	*2*	*3*	*4*	*5*	*Not known*	*Not applicable*
1	8	17	**18**	4	2	
7. Satisfaction toward the learning experience						
1	*2*	*3*	*4*	*5*	*Not known*	*Not applicable*
2	8	16	**19**	4	1	
8. Efficiency of the virtual graduate seminar as a teaching method						
1	*2*	*3*	*4*	*5*	*Not known*	*Not applicable*
3	6	**17**	**17**	5	2	
9. Extent to which students knew each other prior to the course						
Did not know	*Somewhat knew*	*Knew most*	*Knew one another very well*		*Not known*	*Not applicable*
12	**29**	5	2		2	
10. Perceived sustainability of the Community of Inquiry following the end of the term						
1	*2*	*3*	*4*	*5*	*Not known*	*Not applicable*
9	**19**	9	8	3	2	

four per cent (94%) of faculty felt they provided feedback that helped students understand their strengths and weaknesses; 78% of students agreed. Faculty also thought they provided feedback in a timely fashion (94%) while 71% of students were in agreement. All faculty members (100%) expressed their concerns as the provision of individualized feedback is very time-consuming. This may indicate that practices based on increased peer feedback from the Community of Inquiry could be welcomed by both faculty and students.

The interview results on social presence show that while all professors (100%) believe that getting to know other course participants gives students a sense of belonging in the course, 60% of students agreed. This suggests that the creation of a vibrant community of inquiry, where students feel they belong, requires more than just getting

Table 4. Post-term survey (n=32)

1. Progress ranking: Richness of dialogue at the end of the term

1	2	3	4	5	Not known	Not applicable
	4	15	10	3		

2. Progress ranking: Frequency of dialogue at the end of the term

1	2	3	4	5	Not known	Not applicable
1	4	11	12	3	1	

3. Progress ranking: Student engagement and participation

1	2	3	4	5	Not known	Not applicable
2	4	9	15	2		

4. Progress ranking: Respect shown for the diversity of ideas and the possibility to disagree

1	2	3	4	5	Not known	Not applicable
1		8	15	8		

5. Progress ranking: Interaction at the end of the term

1	2	3	4	5	Not known	Not applicable
1	5	10	14	2		

6. Progress ranking: Collaboration at the end of the term

1	2	3	4	5	Not known	Not applicable
2	5	8	11	6		

7. Progress ranking: Satisfaction toward the learning experience at the end of the term

1	2	3	4	5	Not known	Not applicable
1	2	11	12	6		

8. Progress ranking: Efficiency of the virtual graduate seminar at the end of the term

1	2	3	4	5	Not known	Not applicable
	7	6	12	6	1	

9. Potential of the virtual graduate seminar to sustain a vibrant CoI

1	2	3	4	5	Not known	Not applicable
1	4	9	14	3	1	

10. Perceived sustainability of the Community of Inquiry following the end of the term

1	2	3	4	5	Not known	Not applicable
7	11	7	4	2	1	

to know students. Seventy-two per cent (72%) of faculty considered web-based communication an excellent medium for social interaction as did 53% of students (with only 13% in class 1).

Eighty-nine per cent (89%) of faculty believed online discussions helped students to develop a sense of collaboration; 60% of students agreed. Again, collaboration may require more than just the possibility to interact with peers and this may indicate the need for stronger social presence and interaction. Finally, 98% of students and 100% of faculty members agreed that students could apply the knowledge created in the course to their work or other non-class related activities. Overall, there were no problematic areas with regard to cognitive presence in this study.

Results from the mid-term online survey show that students (n=50) were satisfied or very satisfied with the richness (78%) and frequency of dialogue (78%) in their graduate seminar. Eighty-four per cent (84%) gave a mark of three or higher to student participation and engagement in their seminar, while 90% gave those same marks to respect shown for the diversity of ideas and the possibility to disagree. The vast majority were satisfied with interaction (88%) and collaboration (78%) in their online course. Seventy-eight percent (78%) were satisfied with their learning experience, and the same percentage found the virtual graduate seminar an efficient teaching method.

Results from the post-term online survey show that one month after the end of the online seminar, 88% of students (n=32) gave a mark of three or higher to progress made with regard to the richness of dialogue in the second part of the term. Eighty-one per cent (81%) gave the same mark to progress in the frequency of dialogue, participation and engagement. Students were almost unanimous (97%) as to progress made in terms of respect shown for the diversity of ideas and the possibility to disagree. They saw progress in class interaction (81%) and collaboration (78%). Post-term satisfaction of the learning experience was good to excellent for 90% of students, and 75% found that the virtual graduate seminar was an efficient teaching method. Asked about its potential to sustain a vibrant learning community, 81% thought it was good to excellent.

Interestingly, a majority of students considered that progress was made in all areas of their virtual graduate seminar over the term. Also, it is interesting to note the percentage of student (40%) in both the mid-term and post-term surveys who thought they were likely to stay in touch with peers after the end of the term. It does not appear that their community of inquiry was strong enough to be sustainable after the end of their graduate seminar.

RECOMMENDED SYNCHRONOUS ONLINE TEACHING STRATEGIES

The remainder of this chapter offers recommendations for synchronous online teaching based on research findings. It is divided into two sections. The first one addresses the design and organization component of teaching presence, while the second addresses the "delivery" aspects with discourse facilitation and direct instruction.

Design Solutions Derived from Research Findings

With regard to the design of synchronous online courses, the very first principle derived from this study is the need to scaffold for a Community of Inquiry for its constructive and collaborative nature. Based on student feedback, the following appear to be effective design practices to foster vibrant communities of inquiry in synchronous virtual graduate seminars, as "a greater sense of community is even more important in the online environment" (F6).

Opening the weekly class with a social component seems to please both students and faculty members. This was routinely done in classes 2, 4, 5, 6, 7 and 8, and students did enjoy it, with four noting that they do not always have that opportunity in a face-to-face classroom scenario.

In order to promote the social presence that will foster cognitive presence in the synchronous virtual graduate seminar, faculty can build on a combination of individual, team and group learning activities. According to his students (100% of respondents), F2 uses an effective seminar design. "I really get the feeling that we are working together toward a better understanding instead of having people working on their own" (S2-3).

First, students are required to do weekly readings (individual work). Then, they meet with their teammates – either asynchronously or synchronously as they wish, most of them preferring the latter – to discuss the readings and engage in a problem-solving process where they try to answer their peers' questions and comment on the readings (team work). Subsequently, any unresolved issue translates into a question or comment being posted on the course website. Students read their colleagues' questions and try to answer them. F2 prepares the following synchronous class based on the remaining questions and comments. The actual class time is dedicated to dialogue (group work). Teams take turn in explaining their questions or comments and students engage in collective problem-solving.

Although this is perceived as an effective teaching strategy, three students reported that the format offers no variety and may become boring in the long run. Consequently, it may be a good idea to diversify the seminar activities on a regular basis.

It appears that synchronous online learning may also contribute to a certain extent to the sense of belonging thanks to greater immediacy. According to Leiss (2010), "the feeling of belonging motivates the individual to help meet the needs of others involved within the specified group." Eleven students reported a closeness developing during the virtual graduate seminar. Three students even evoked a sense of loss or mourning following the end of their seminar.

One of the recurrent themes that have emerged during this research is the analogy of what I refer to as the online student "vital space." In a face-to-face classroom, everyone enjoys this vital space that can be conceptualized as the minimum square footage required for people to be able to function as human beings, to breathe, to sit down, to raise their hand, etc. In an online setting, this vital space can be conceptualized as the opportunity for social presence and interaction. Too many students in the virtual classroom or too much talk by the same few people will negatively impact healthy interaction. "With 40 people, well, we sit down, we listen and we wait for someone to ask the question we have, hoping that they will" (S1-16).

In such an environment, the online student does not have the opportunity to express himself or herself, to react to what other people are saying, to ask questions, to help his/her peers. Somehow, this is the equivalent of stripping this person of his/her online presence and empowerment and is counter to socioconstructivist learning principles.

As mentioned previously, students can easily assume a passive attitude and often, they are not used to speaking in the classroom, nor expressing themselves freely. A suggestion to helping students overcome this would be to have an orientation course with some mentors from a previous seminar at the beginning of the semester. This would help them adopt class goals and subsequently remind them of these goals. Explaining the function of a vibrant online community is important to create a frame of reference. By not assuming this critical role, educators do not allow for optimal learner development because students do not have a long tradition of collaborative learning and are not necessarily familiar with the details of it.

Finally, the same holds true for learner-content interaction. At the graduate level, students cannot simply read materials and re-phrase the ideas. Proper design needs to focus on an active learning cycle aimed at problem-solving and new content creation:

In the planning of the material, when you're doing group assignments and you're asking students to present that information, are they just regurgitating all the chapters that everyone was supposed to read for that week, or are they presenting something new, their thoughts and ideas and stimulating a debate, a conversation, more so than just a talking head presentation kind of idea? (ID7).

This section suggested some teaching strategies for improved design and organization in a virtual graduate seminar, with a focus on the creation of a Community of Inquiry as an important support of synchronous online learning. Once a collaborative climate is created through teaching presence, social presence and cognitive presence, students appreciate the dynamics involved and the results achieved.

Yes. I think that again the 14 students (sic), including myself, I'm really impressed by how well we collaborate" (S5-1).

Delivery Solutions Derived from Research Findings

This section covers the discourse facilitation and direct instruction components of teaching presence in a virtual graduate seminar.

It is important to reiterate that discourse facilitation was the most problematic area in this research. Even in more socioconstructivist classes, such as classes 2, 6, 7 and 8, observations show that the professor was often too quick to jump in and provide answers and explanations. These observations are backed by student feedback in Cases 2, 7 and 8.

Engaging students means keeping their interest level high, and authentic learning can promote this type of engagement. In Case 1, 17% of students raised the issue of not being engaged during the seminars (none in the other classes, although engagement was not always rated high), and 13% bemoaned the fact that the examples were not adapted to their reality at all.

With regard to engagement, 40% of students in Case 2, 67% in Case 3 and 25% in Case 5 specifically indicated that synchronous virtual graduate seminars can do a lot for motivation given that students need to come to class prepared to discuss the topics. "We arrive to the seminar with a higher level of preparation, and integration of new knowledge is already well underway" (S2-2). One student even referred to her commitment toward her peers as a "social responsibility." This added benefit was acknowledged by F2, F7 and F8.

F3, F4 and F4-2 reported that students greatly appreciated the "breakout rooms," namely, the

platform feature that allows for private, small-group work within the virtual classroom. Through small-group discussions, students specifically indicated that it is easier to have constructive exchanges (S3-1), participate in group collaborative efforts (S5-2, S6-3), and that they feel more involved (S6-5).

Time is of the essence in synchronous online learning because people need to be active and interact with one another during the valuable live session. In classes 1, 3 and 5, where the professor acted more as "the sage on the stage," 47% of students indicated that they used the online class time to interact with other computer applications and other students (e.g., playing games, chatting, or emailing). The students reasoned that they found it difficult to listen to someone talk for more than fifteen minutes. "There is kind of this side world of our online collaboration that happens a lot on Facebook" (S5-4). Participants generally agreed to this 15-minute maximum limit to their attention span, whether it is the faculty talking or a student presenting.

Visuals do indeed play an important role in student engagement in a synchronous virtual graduate seminar. Twenty-seven per cent (27%) of students indicated that they found it very difficult to stay focused when staring at the same screen for long periods of time:

Something more visually interactive would have been interesting because they didn't have many slides, for sure. [...] We constantly needed to move our mouse or else the monitor would go to sleep ... (S1-12).

When he feels that a lengthier presentation is required, F8 prepares a video clip that will be posted on the course website. This way, students can view it ahead of time, and the real time component of the seminar will remain centered on discussion and student concerns. The synchronous online learning motto should be, "Do not waste precious interactive time; watch ahead of time."

F7 does not hesitate to allow for 15-20 second periods of reflection during her seminars. On one occasion, silence even lasted for 45 seconds before a student shared his thoughts at the microphone. While silence could indicate a problem in synchronous online classes, it should also be considered a support of reflective learning and not be perceived as threatening. Too often, professors ask if there are questions or comments and then wait for five seconds before moving on. Students from Case 1 needed more than five seconds only to click on the microphone and be able to speak. Students do not have time to react when given only a few seconds to think about their question or comment and consider sharing it, but professors consistently allow for four- or five-second pauses before moving forward.

As mentioned earlier, online students expect personalized feedback from their professors. In this study, 23% of students were not satisfied that their professor provided adequate feedback on their strengths and weaknesses; and 29%, that feedback was provided in a timely fashion. From a more socioconstructivist perspective, it would be worth investigating the actual impact of widespread, consistent formative peer feedback in virtual graduate seminars, more suited to a distributed teaching presence where students play a more active role. Again, this raises the question of how to help professors and students adopt new roles in the socioconstructivist classroom (see chapter 16,).

This section addressed discourse facilitation and direct instruction in a graduate virtual seminar. Although all faculty were selected because of their socioconstructivist orientation, from a researcher perspective, I did not find that theirs were socioconstructivist seminars to the extent that they could have been. While they would all encourage group discussion, they assumed a lead role, a role that would sometimes have a negative impact on the desired interaction (especially in Cases 1, 3, 4 and 5) and the democratic orientation sought in their seminar (especially in Cases 2, 7 and 8). Students tend to look up to their professor and will adopt a passive attitude whenever the educator is speaking, out of respect and interest for what is being said. This can result in the professor actually being detrimental to group discussion on a regular basis.

Results here show evidence that students in these groups benefited from constructivist and collaborative learning. But as much as they are willing to, it seems to be very difficult for both faculty members and students to explore and adopt new roles and attitudes in the socioconstructivist classroom. Interestingly, cognitive presence was still very good in all seminars, and post-term satisfaction of the learning experience was good to excellent for the majority of students.

SUMMARY OF EFFECTIVE TEACHING PRACTICES DERIVED FROM THIS RESEARCH

Based on the results of this study, this section provides a summary of effective teaching practices in a virtual graduate seminar designed as a blended online learning environment.

- **Design and Organization**
  - Scaffolding for the establishment of a Community of Inquiry
  - Scaffolding for the integration and resolution phases of cognitive presence
  - Scaffolding for the creation of new content
  - Planning interactive discussion
  - Building on a combination of individual, team and group activities
  - Planning for social components like community circles
  - Focusing on the reinforcement of the sense of belonging to the community

- Planning activities to bring students on par with a socioconstructivist orientation
- **Discourse Facilitation**
  - Creating a safe learning environment
  - Facilitating interaction
  - Being an egalitarian participant
  - Promoting social presence
  - Fostering collaboration
  - Engaging students through authentic learning activities
  - Allowing for silence and reflection pauses
  - Managing time adequately
  - Making good use of visuals
  - Guiding toward resolution
  - Promoting application of knowledge to students' own context
  - Making good use of the various modes and tools
  - Respecting students' virtual vital space
- **Direct Instruction**
  - Focusing discussion on relevant issues
  - Fostering group synergy
  - Ensuring useful feedback
  - Ensuring timely feedback

LIMITATIONS AND FUTURE RESEARCH DIRECTIONS

The research's small sample and the lack of similar studies for comparison purposes represent limitations of this study. This is the first academic research to explore the ties between the Community of Inquiry framework and blended online learning design (BOLD), with the objective of promoting vibrant communities of inquiry in virtual graduate seminars. As such, it may have raised more questions than it answered.

First, while this emergent design approach looks very promising, more empirical research is needed as to the contribution of BOLD to the creation of a Community of Inquiry. Additional qualitative and quantitative data are needed to confirm to what extent the combination of synchronous and asynchronous modes does actually promote effective learning in an online graduate seminar and what the best combination might be.

Second, while the CoI framework has proven well adapted to graduate studies, these communities of inquiry seem to "cease to exist" once the course is over. Several students report a feeling of "mourning" after the end of their virtual graduate seminar and bemoan the fact that all these stimulating connections are suddenly lost. Should a successful Community of Inquiry continue to flourish after the course and, if so, what conditions are required for greater sustainability?

Third, this research has highlighted the fact that faculty members need to embrace a new vision of rich and ongoing discourse facilitation. We need to consider the best ways to help faculty members understand their crucial role as discourse facilitators; how to help them adopt new teaching strategies instead of replicating older, teacher-driven models; and how to help students gain assurance and confidence in socio-constructivist learning models.

Fourth, the whole concept of online student "vital space" has emerged during this research and is definitely worth investigating. For example, in synchronous online learning, how do faculty and students deal with silence? Is it cherished as a reflection pause, welcomed as a learning support, or does it simply contribute to uneasiness or disengagement? Is it threatening because it is perceived as a waste of precious online time? Is it seen as an indicator of technical issues? At the opposite end of the spectrum, what are the consequences of "endless" periods of talk? Do they also contribute to uneasiness or disengagement?

Fifth, the collective reflection on effective practices toward the establishment of vibrant communities of inquiry, including this doctoral study, always points to teaching presence and rightfully so. But there seem to be areas (need for stronger social presence, sense of belonging, interactive discussions, and stimulating feedback) where teaching presence may not always fully respond to student needs. Could faculty or department initiatives, such as thematic interactive online sessions, online informal meetings, electronic newsletters, online workshops and debates, help online students get to know their peers better and provide them with a stronger sense of belonging? Could teaching presence be better conceptualized as a broader pedagogical presence?

CONCLUSION

This chapter has highlighted the fundamental role of faculty members and the positive contribution of blended online learning design in the establishment of engaged communities of inquiry. The faculty role has been scrutinized through the Community of Inquiry framework teaching presence lens. More specifically, strategies pertaining to design and organization, discourse facilitation and direct instruction in a virtual graduate seminar have been emphasized and best practices shared.

Quality online learning indicators are now based on social presence, interaction and a sense of belonging (Rockinson-Szapkiw, 2009). In light of research results emphasizing the vital role of a vibrant Community of Inquiry, the time has come to turn to effective "we(b)-learning" strategies to promote these collaborative communities. I strongly believe that a shift toward a "we-learning" conceptualization may contribute to enhance the student "e-learning" experience.

REFERENCES

Akyol, Z., & Garrison, D. R. (2011). Understanding cognitive presence in an online and blended community of inquiry: Assessing outcomes and processes for deep approaches to learning. *British Journal of Educational Technology, 42*(2), 233–250.

Akyol, Z., Vaughan, N., & Garrison, D. R. (2011). The impact of course duration on the development of a community of inquiry. *Interactive Learning Environments, 19*(3), 231–246.

Anderson, T., Rourke, L., Garrison, D. R., & Archer, W. (2001). Assessing teaching presence in a computer conferencing environment. *Journal of Asynchronous Learning Networks, 5*(2).

Angelino, L. M., Williams, F. K., & Natvig, D. (2007). Strategies to engage online students and reduce attrition rates. *The Journal of Educators Online, 4*(2), 1–14.

Arbaugh, J. B., & Benbunan-Fich, R. (2006). An investigation of epistemological and social dimensions of teaching in online learning environments. *Academy of Management Learning & Education, 5*(4), 435–447.

Arbaugh, J. B., Cleveland-Innes, M., Diaz, S. R., Garrison, D. R., Ice, P., Richardson, J. C., & Swan, K. (2008). Developing a community of inquiry instrument: Testing a measure of the Community of Inquiry framework using a multi-institutional sample. *The Internet and Higher Education, 11*, 133–136.

Arbaugh, J. B., & Hwang, A. (2006). Does "teaching presence" exist in online MBA courses? *The Internet and Higher Education, 9*(1), 9–21.

Bangert, A. W. (2010). Building a validity argument for the community of inquiry survey instrument. *The Internet and Higher Education, 12*, 104–111.

Bedford, L. A. (2009). The professional adjunct: An emerging trend in online instruction. *Online Journal of Distance Learning Administration, 12*(3).

Berge, Z., & Huang, Y. (2004). A model for sustainable student retention: A holistic perspective on the student dropout problem with special attention to e-learning. *DEOSNEWS, 13*(5).

Bergquist, W. H., & Phillips, S. R. (1981). *A handbook for faculty development* (*Vol. 3*). Washington, DC: The Council of Independent Colleges.

Betts, K. S. (1998). Why do faculty participate in distance education? *The Technology Source,* October 1998.

Blin, F., & Munro, M. (2008). Why hasn't technology disrupted academics' teaching practices? Understanding resistance to change through the lens of activity theory. *Computers & Education, 50,* 475–490.

Bolliger, D. U., & Wasilik, O. (2009). An analysis of the history of online graduate-level courses taught by an expert instructor. *MERLOT Journal of Online Learning and Teaching, 5*(1).

Brown, J. S., & Duguid, P. (2000). *The social life of information.* Boston, MA: Harvard Business School Press.

Carr-Chellman, A., & Duchastel, P. (2000). The ideal online course. *British Journal of Educational Technology, 31*(3), 229–241.

Cavanaugh, J. (2005). Teaching online – A time comparison. *Online Journal of Distance Learning Administration, 8*(1).

Chen, N.-S., & Ko, H.-C., Kinshuk, & Lin, T. (2005). A model for synchronous learning using the Internet. *Innovations in Education and Teaching International, 42*(2), 181–194.

Chen, Y.-J., & Willits, F. K. (1999). Dimensions of educational transactions in a videoconferencing learning environment. *American Journal of Distance Education, 13*(1), 45–59.

Chickering, A. W., & Gamson, Z. F. (1987). Seven principles for good practice in undergraduate education. *American Association of Higher Education Bulletin,* 3-7.

Cogburn, D. L., & Levinson, N. (2003). U.S.-Africa virtual collaboration in globalization studies: Success factors for complex, cross-national learning teams. *International Studies Perspectives, 4,* 34–51.

Garrison, D. R., Cleveland- Innes, M., Koole M., & Kappelman, J. (2006). Revisiting methodological issues in transcript analysis: Negotiated coding and reliability. *The Internet and Higher Education, 9,* 1–8.

Garrison, D. R., Anderson, R. T., & Archer, W. (2000). Critical inquiry in a text-based environment: Computer conferencing in higher education. *The Internet and Higher Education, 2*(2-3), 87–105.

Garrison, D. R., & Anderson, T. (2003). *E-learning in the 21st century: A framework for research and practice.* London, UK: Routledge Falmer.

Garrison, D. R., & Arbaugh, J. B. (2007). Researching the community of inquiry framework: Review, issues, and future directions. *The Internet and Higher Education, 10*(3), 157–172.

Garrison, D. R., & Cleveland-Innes, M. (2005). Facilitating cognitive presence in online learning: Interaction is not enough. *American Journal of Distance Education, 19*(3), 133–148.

Garrison, D. R., & Kanuka, H. (2004). Blended learning: Uncovering its transformative potential in higher education. *The Internet and Higher Education, 7,* 95–105.

Garrison, D. R., & Vaughan, N. (2008). *Blended learning in higher education*. San Francisco, CA: Jossey-Bass.

Gunawardena, C. N., Ortegano-Layne, L., Carabajal, K., Frechette, C., Lindemann, K., & Jennings, B. (2006). New model, new strategies: Instructional design for building online wisdom communities. *Distance Education, 27*(2), 217–232.

Ice, P., Kupczynski, L., Wiesenmeyer, R., & Phillips, P. (2008). Student perceptions of the effectiveness of group and individualized feedback in online courses. *First Monday, 13*(11).

Jaques, D. (2000). *Learning in groups*. London, UK: Kogan Page Ltd.

Jung, I. S. (2001). Building a theoretical framework of Web-based instruction in the context of distance education. *British Journal of Educational Technology, 32*(5), 525–534.

Kupczynski, L., Ice, P., Wiesenmayer, R., & McCluskey, F. (2010). Student perceptions of the relationship between indicators of teaching presence and success in online courses. *Journal of Interactive Online Learning, 9*(1).

Larramendy-Joerns, J., & Leinhardt, G. (2006). Going the distance with online education. *Review of Educational Research, 76*(4), 567–605.

Lefoe, G., & Hedberg, J. (2006). Blending on and off campus: A tale of two cities. In Bonk, C., & Graham, C. (Eds.), *Handbook of blended learning environments: Global perspectives, local designs*. San Francisco, CA: Pfeiffer.

Leiss, P. D. (2010). *Does synchronous communication technology influence classroom community? A study on the use of a live Web conferencing system within an online classroom*. Unpublished doctoral dissertation. Capella University, Minneapolis.

Liu, X., Magjuka, R., Bonk, C., & Lee, S. (2007). Does sense of community matter? *Quarterly Review of Distance Education, 8*(1), 9–24.

Ludwig-Hardman, S., & Dunlap, J. C. (2003). Learner support services for online students: Scaffolding for success. *International Review of Research in Open and Distance Learning, 4*(1).

Maushak, N. J., & Ou, C. (2007). Using synchronous communication to facilitate graduate students' online collaboration. *The Quarterly Review of Distance Education, 8*(2), 161–169.

McBrien, J. L., Jones, P., & Cheng, R. (2009). Virtual spaces: Employing a synchronous online classroom to facilitate student engagement in online learning. *International Review of Research in Open and Distance Learning, 10*(3).

Murphy, E. (2004). Identifying and measuring ill-structured problem formulation and resolution in online asynchronous discussions. *Canadian Journal of Learning and Technology, 30*(1), 5–20.

Neal, E. (1996). Leading the seminar: Graduate and undergraduate. *Essays on Teaching Excellence*, a Professional & Organizational Development Network in Higher Education publication. Retrieved September 8, 2009, from http://www.podnetwork.org/publications/essayseries.htm#1995-96

Oberst, U., Gallifa, J., Farriols, N., & Villaregut, A. (2009). Training emotional and social competences in higher education: The seminar methodology. *Higher Education in Europe, 34*, 3–4.

Osborn, D. S. (2009). Wikis, podcasts and more… program policy considerations with online teaching. In Walz, G. R., Bleuer, J. C., & Yep, R. K. (Eds.), *Compelling counselling interventions: VISTAS 2009* (pp. 329–336). Alexandria, VA: American Counselling Association.

Pachnowski, L. M., & Jurczyk, J. P. (2003). Perceptions of faculty on the effect of distance learning technology on faculty preparation time. *Online Journal of Distance Learning Administration, 6*(3).

Park, Y. N., & Bonk, C. J. (2007). Synchronous learning experiences: Distance and residential learners' perspectives in a blended graduate course. *Journal of Interactive Online Learning, 6*(3).

Phillips, H. J., & Powers, R. B. (1979). The college seminar: Participation under instructor-led and student-led discussion groups. *Teaching of Psychology, 6*(2).

Power, M. (2008). The emergence of blended online learning. *Journal of Online Teaching & Learning, 4*(4).

Power, M., & Gould-Morven, A. (2011). Head of gold, feet of clay: The online learning paradox. *International Review of Research in Open and Distance Learning, 12*(2).

Power, M., & Vaughan, N. (2010). Redesigning online learning for graduate seminar delivery. *Journal of Distance Education, 24*(2).

Power, M., Vaughan, N., & Saint-Jacques, A. (2010). *Revisiting the graduate seminar through blended online learning design. American Educational Research Association* (pp. 30–May-4). Denver: Co. April.

Rockinson-Szapkiw, A. G. (2009). *The impact of asynchronous and synchronous instruction and discussion on cognitive presence, social presence, teaching presence and learning.* Unpublished doctoral dissertation, Regent University, Virginia.

Rourke, L., & Anderson, T. (2002). Using peer teams to lead online discussion. *Journal of Interactive Media in Education,* 1.

Rovai, A. P. (2002). Building sense of community at a distance. *International Review of Research in Open and Distance Learning, 3*(1).

Rovai, A. P., & Jordan, H. M. (2004). Blended learning and sense of community: A comparative analysis with traditional and fully online graduate courses. *International Review of Research in Open and Distance Learning, 5*(2).

Russo, T. C., & Benson, S. (2005). Learning with invisible others: Perceptions of online presence and their relationship to cognitive and affective learning. *Journal of Educational Technology & Society, 8*(1), 54–62.

Sammons, M., & Ruth, S. (2007). The invisible professor and the future of virtual faculty. *International Journal of Teaching and Technology, 4*(1).

Schullo, S. J. (2005). *An analysis of pedagogical strategies: Using synchronous Web-based course systems in the online classroom.* Unpublished doctoral dissertation, University of Florida, Florida.

Schwier, R. A., & Balbar, S. (2002). The interplay of content and community in synchronous and asynchronous communication: Virtual communication in a graduate seminar. *Canadian Journal of Learning and Technology, 28*(2).

Shea, P. (2006). A study of students' sense of learning community in online learning environments. *Journal of Asynchronous Learning Networks, 10*(1).

Shea, P., Fredericksen, E., Pickett, A., & Pelz, W. (2004). Faculty development, student satisfaction, and reported learning in the SUNY learning network. In Duffy, T., & Kirkley, J. (Eds.), *Learner-centered theory and practice in distance education* (pp. 343–377). Mahway, NJ: Lawrence Elrbaum Associates.

Shea, P., Li, C. S., & Pickett, A. (2006). A study of teaching presence and student sense of learning community in fully online and web-enhanced college courses. *The Internet and Higher Education, 9*(3), 175–190.

Shea, P., Pickett, A., & Li, C. S. (2005). Increasing access to higher education: A study of the diffusion of online teaching among 913 college faculty. *International Review of Research in Open and Distance Learning, 6*(2).

Sikora, A. C., & Carroll, C. D. (2002). *A profile of participation in distance education: 1999–2000. Postsecondary education descriptive analysis reports (NCES 2003-154). US Department of Education, National Center for Education Statistics.* Washington, DC: US Government Printing Office.

Simonson, M., & Schlosser, C. (2009). We need a plan – An instructional design approach for distance education courses. In Orellana, A., Hudgins, T. L., & Simonson, M. (Eds.), *The perfect online course: Best practices for designing and teaching.* Charlotte, NC: Information Age Publishing Inc.

Slagter van Tryon, P. J., & Bishop, J. M. (2006). Identifying e-mmediacy strategies for Web-based instruction. *Quarterly Review of Distance Education, 7*(1), 49–62.

Stewart, S. (2008). *A study of instructional strategies that promote learning centered synchronous dialogue online.* Unpublished doctoral dissertation, University of South Florida, Florida.

Stodel, E. J., MacDonald, C. J., & Thompson, T. L. (2006). Learners' perspectives on what is missing from online learning: Interpretations through the community of inquiry framework. *International Review of Research in Open and Distance Learning, 7*(3), 1–24.

Swan, K., Richardson, J. C., Ice, P., Garrison, D. R., Cleveland-Innes, M., & Arbaugh, J. B. (2008). Validating a measurement tool of presence in online communities of inquiry. *E-mentor, 2*(24).

Tallent-Runnels, M. K., Thomas, J. A., Lan, W. Y., Cooper, S., Ahern, T. C., Shaw, S. M., & Liu, X. (2006). Teaching courses online: A review of the research. *Review of Educational Research, 76*(1), 93–35.

Teng, T., & Taveras, M. (2004). Combining live video and audio broadcasting, synchronous chat, and asynchronous open forum discussions in distance education. *Journal of Educational Technology Systems, 33*(2), 121–129.

Thompson, M. M. (2004). Faculty self-study research project: Examining the online workload. *Journal of Asynchronous Learning Networks, 8*(3).

Thompson, T. L., & MacDonald, C. J. (2005). Community building, emergent design and expecting the unexpected: Creating a quality eLearning experience. *The Internet and Higher Education, 8*, 233–249.

Tolu, A. T. (2010). *An exploration of synchronous communication in an online preservice ESOL course: Community of inquiry perspective.* Unpublished doctoral dissertation, University of South Florida, Florida.

Visser, J. (2000). Faculty work in developing and teaching web-based distance courses: A case study of time and effort. *American Journal of Distance Education, 14*(3), 21–32.

Yin, R. K. (2009). *Case study research: Design and methods* (4th ed.). Thousand Oaks, CA: Sage Publications, Inc.

ADDITIONAL READING

Chang, S. H., & Smith, R. A. (2008). Effectiveness of personal interaction in a learner-centered paradigm distance education class based on student satisfaction. *Journal of Research on Technology in Education, 40*(4).

Disbrow, L. M. (2008). The overall effect of online audio conferencing in communication courses: What do students really think? *MERLOT Journal of Online Learning and Teaching, 4*(2).

Fejes, A., Johansson, K., & Abrandt Dahlgren, M. (2005). Learning to play the seminar game: Students' initial encounters with a basic working form in higher education. *Teaching in Higher Education, 10*(1).

Garrison, D. R., Cleveland-Innes, M., & Fung, T. S. (2010). Exploring causal relationships among teaching, cognitive and social presence: Student perceptions of the community of inquiry framework. *The Internet and Higher Education, 13*, 31–36.

Georgina, D. A., & Olson, M. R. (2008). Integration of technology in higher education: A review of faculty self-perceptions. *The Internet and Higher Education, 11*, 1–8.

Groen, J., & Li, Q. (2005). Achieving the benefits of blended learning within a fully online learning environment: A focus on synchronous communication. *Educational Technology, 45*(6), 31–37.

Hrastinski, S. (2008). The potential of synchronous communication to enhance participation in online discussions: A case study of two e-learning courses. *Information & Management, 45*, 499–506.

Kienle, A. (2009). Intertwining synchronous and asynchronous communication to support collaborative learning – System design and evaluation. *Education and Information Technologies, 14*(1), 55–79.

Liaw, S. (2004). Considerations for developing constructivist web-based learning. *International Journal of Instructional Media, 31*(3), 309–321.

Lopez, P., & Gallifa, J. (2008). Improving cognitive complexity via seminar methodology in higher education. *Higher Education in Europe, 33*(4).

Ma, W. (2004). *Intellectual gazing: Participatory learning in a graduate seminar.* Unpublished doctoral dissertation, State University of New York at Buffalo.

Ma, W. (2008). Participatory dialogue and participatory learning in a discussion-based graduate seminar. *Journal of Literacy Research, 40*(2), 220–249.

Mitchell, B., & Geva-May, I. (2009). Attitudes affecting online learning implementation in higher education. *Journal of Distance Education, 23*(1).

Ng, K. C. (2007). Replacing face-to-face tutorials by synchronous online technologies: Challenges and pedagogical implications. *International Review of Research in Open and Distance Learning, 8*(1).

Nisbet, S. (1966). A method for advanced seminars. *Universities Quarterly, 20*, 349–355.

Offir, B., Lev, Y., & Bezalel, R. (2008). Surface and deep learning processes in distance education: Synchronous versus asynchronous systems. *Computers & Education, 51*, 1172–1183.

Patton, B. A. (2008). Synchronous meetings: A way to put personality in an online class. *Turkish Online Journal of Distance Education, 9*(4).

Pullen, J. M., & Snow, C. (2007). Integrating synchronous and asynchronous Internet distributed education for maximum effectiveness. *Education and Information Technologies, 12*, 137–148.

Ratkic, A. (2009). Dialogue seminar as a tool in post graduate education. *AI & Society, 23*(1).

Shea, P., & Bidjerano, T. (2009). Community of inquiry as a theoretical framework to foster epistemic engagement and cognitive presence in online education. *Computers & Education, 52*(3), 543–553.

Smyth, R. (2011). Enhancing learner-learner interaction using video communications in higher education: Implications from theorising about a new model. *British Journal of Educational Technology, 42*(1), 113–127.

Vaughan, N. D., & Garrison, R. D. (2006). A blended faculty community of inquiry: Linking leadership, course redesign, and evaluation. *Canadian Journal of University Continuing Education, 32*(2), 67–92.

Wang, S. K., & Hsu, H. (2008). Use of the webinar tool (Elluminate) to support training: The effects of webinar-learning implementation from student-trainers' perspective. *Journal of Interactive Online Learning*, 7(3), 175–194.

Watt, I. (1964). The seminar. *Universities Quarterly*, 18(4), 369–389.

KEY TERMS AND DEFINITIONS

Asynchronous Online Learning: Online learning based on time-independent (and location-independent) learning activities.

Blended Online Learning Design: Synchronous online learning activities supported by asynchronous online learning activities.

Cognitive Presence: Collective meaning negotiation resulting from personal reflection.

Community of Inquiry: Reflection, discussion and validation circle created by the intersection of the teaching presence, the social presence and the cognitive presence.

Distributed Teaching: The sharing of teaching responsibilities among the instructor and students.

Immediacy: In an online setting, immediacy is the foundation of the psychological proximity sought to alleviate feelings of isolation.

Objectivist Model: Also known as the behaviorist model or the instructionist model, it is teacher-driven and evokes the transmission of knowledge as opposed to more socioconstructivist models.

Social Presence: The feeling of proximity people may experience as a result of getting to know their peers.

Socio-Constructivism: Collective knowledge-building taking place in a social environment and strongly influenced by peers.

Synchronous Online Learning: Location-independent online learning activities taking place in real time.

Teaching Presence: The foundation of social and cognitive presence, teaching presence relies heavily on discourse facilitation.

ENDNOTES

[1] Faculty members in Cases 4 and 5 were co-teaching, for a total of 10 faculty members involved in the study, but one professor declined the interview. As a result, a total of nine faculty members were interviewed.

[2] There were three teaching assistants in class 1 due to the high number of students (n=70) and one in class 6.

[3] Faculty 1, 3 and 7 were supported by an instructional designer, whereas Faculty 2, 4, 5, 6 and 8 were not.

Chapter 7
Redesigning Teaching Presence in Order to Enhance Cognitive Presence:
A Longitudinal Analysis

Bart Rienties
University of Surrey, UK

Bas Giesbers
Maastricht University, The Netherlands

Dirk T. Tempelaar
Maastricht University, The Netherlands

Simon Lygo-Baker
University of Surrey, UK

ABSTRACT

Recent findings from research into the Community of Inquiry theoretical framework indicate that teaching presence may encourage critical inquiry, integration of argumentation, and resolution of a task. Using quasi-experimental research, this chapter examines the impact of a redesign of a CMC environment, which by increased instructional design and organisation provided a more explicit scaffolding of the learning phases for learners. It was hypothesised that learners in a redesigned Optima environment would reach higher levels of cognitive presence due to clearer scaffolding. By comparing 4000 contributions to discourse using two content analyses schemes in a longitudinal perspective, the research results reveal that Optima participants contributed less to cognitive presence from the beginning of the course onwards, in particular to integration of argumentation. The main conclusion from this study is that getting the balance of teaching presence right to facilitate learners in the integration and resolution phase is a delicate and complex issue.

DOI: 10.4018/978-1-4666-2110-7.ch007

INTRODUCTION

In Computer-Mediated Communication (CMC), learners have to construct meaning and co-construct knowledge in a blended or entirely online setting. Several researchers (Akyol & Garrison, 2008; Garrison, Anderson, & Archer, 2000; Kirschner, Beers, Boshuizen, & Gijselaers, 2008; Schellens & Valcke, 2005) have found that CMC environments only provide a meaningful and worthwhile learning experience if participants actively contribute to discourse and co-construct knowledge collaboratively. Nonetheless, participation and persisting to contribute to discourse in CMC cannot be taken for granted (Kirschner, et al., 2008; Rienties, Tempelaar, Van den Bossche, Gijselaers, & Segers, 2009). For example, Hammond (2000) argues that a substantial threshold needs to be crossed before learners start to contribute to discussion forums. A mounting body of research has found that learners find it difficult to contribute to online discourse, in particular when integrating various points of argumentation and providing resolutions to a task (Garrison, 2007). That is, establishing a critical mass of interaction whereby learners move beyond the exploration phase of cognitive presence is troublesome (Akyol & Garrison, 2008; Garrison, 2007; Schellens & Valcke, 2005).

The Community of Inquiry framework (Akyol & Garrison, 2008; Garrison, 2007; Garrison, et al., 2000) provides a well-researched theoretical framework to understand how learners and teachers interact and learn together in CMC. In the Community of Inquiry (CoI) framework, a distinction is made between cognitive presence, social presence and teaching presence. Cognitive presence is defined as "the extent to which the participants in any particular configuration of a community of inquiry are able to construct meaning through sustained communication." (Garrison, et al., 2000, p. 89) In other words, the extent learners use and apply critical inquiry in discussions is the key feature of cognitive pres-

ence, as described more elaborately elsewhere in this book (Richardson, Sadaf, & Ertmer, 2012). Social presence is defined as the ability of learners to project their personal characteristics into the community, thereby presenting themselves to the other participants as "real people." A large body of research has found that for learners to critically engage with discourse in CMC settings, they need to create and establish a social learning space (Giesbers, Rienties, Gijselaers, Segers, & Tempelaar, 2009; Goldstein, Leppa, Brockhaus, Bliquez, & Porter, 2012; Rusman, Van Bruggen, Cörvers, Sloep, & Koper, 2009; Van den Bossche, Gijselaers, Segers, & Kirschner, 2006).

The third component of the Community of Inquiry framework, and the primary focus of this chapter, is teaching presence. Anderson, Rourke, Garrison and Archer (2001) distinguish three key roles teachers have that impact upon teaching presence in CMC environments, namely: 1) instructional design and organisation; 2) facilitating discourse; 3) and direct instruction. By designing, structuring, planning, establishing learning goals, process and interaction activities, establishing netiquette, learning outcomes, assessment and evaluation strategies before an online course starts (Anderson, et al., 2001; Biggs & Tang, 2007; Jang, Reeve, & Deci, 2010; Rienties et al., 2011), a teacher can create a powerful learning environment within which learners can learn and interact with their peers and a range of materials. Afterwards, a teacher can either facilitate discourse or provide direct instruction to encourage critical inquiry. According to Anderson et al. (2001, p. 7), "facilitating discourse during the course is critical to maintaining the interest, motivation and engagement of students in active learning". Finally, direct instruction refers to teachers providing intellectual and scholarly leadership and sharing their specific domain-specific expertise with their students.

Although a large number of studies have focussed on cognitive presence and social presence (Garrison, 2007; Garrison & Arbaugh,

2007; Giesbers, et al., 2009; Hughes, Ventura, & Dando, 2007), only limited research has been conducted into understanding how teachers can create and maintain an effective teaching presence (Arbaugh, 2007; De Laat, Lally, Lipponen, & Simons, 2007; Garrison, 2007; Rienties, et al., 2011; Whipp & Lorentz, 2009) that creates conditions for inquiry and quality interactions. In particular, to our knowledge no empirical study on the role of instructional design and organisation has been conducted, whereby (quasi)-experimental research has tested and verified how theory-driven changes in teaching presence influence the CoI. In this study, we aimed to understand how teachers could enhance cognitive presence by clearer instructional design and organisation. Based upon an economics online course that had been designed using principles of Problem-Based Learning (Rienties, et al., 2009; Rienties, Tempelaar, Waterval, Rehm, & Gijselaers, 2006), the course was redesigned in line with the Optima model (Segers, Van den Bossche, & Teunissen, 2003). The Optima (re)design made the scaffolding of the learning phases adopted in PBL more transparent: that is the various (meta)cognitive and social learning processes that learners go through in order to solve problem tasks in economics. In total 82 learners participated in the first design, while 60 learners participated in the Optima (re) design. It was anticipated that with more explicit instructional design and organisation in the form of enhanced scaffolding of the learning phases, over time students in the Optima design would contribute more to cognitive presence and social presence and would maintain a higher quality critical discourse until the end of the course.

BACKGROUND OF THE STUDY: PROVIDING MORE GUIDANCE IN "MINIMUM GUIDED" (E) PROBLEM-BASED LEARNING

Kirschner et al. (2006) suggest that minimal guided instructional approaches, such as Problem-Based Learning (PBL), are less effective and efficient for novice students than guided instructional approaches such as direct instruction. In line with Cognitive Load Theory, Kirschner et al. (2006) argue that problem solving of a complex task only becomes effective when learners are sufficiently experienced. Furthermore, learners may become lost in the task when unable to track their plans and monitor their progress (Quintana et al., 2004). Others have argued however that PBL can provide appropriate scaffolds through face-to-face settings for learners to engage in complex tasks that would otherwise be beyond their current abilities (e.g. Hmelo-Silver, Duncan, & Chinn, 2007; Schmidt, Loyens, Van Gog, & Paas, 2007; Schmidt, Van Der Molen, Te Winkel, & Wijnen, 2009).

In blended and online settings, an increasing number of researchers have found that ICT can provide appropriate scaffolding to reduce the cognitive load for students and facilitate the process management of the task (Quintana, et al., 2004). A large number of researchers have argued that appropriate scaffolding in PBL, and CMC in general, can make disciplinary thinking and strategies explicit (Quintana, et al., 2004), help to structure complex tasks (Weinberger, Reiserer, Ertl, Fischer, & Mandl, 2005), ensure that learners are actively engaged with the learning environment (Beers, Boshuizen, Kirschner, & Gijselaers, 2005), reduce cognitive loads on students (Hmelo-Silver, et al., 2007; Schmidt, et al., 2007), and facilitate the learning processes in small groups (Beers, et al., 2005; Quintana, et al., 2004). For example, previous research in experimental settings (Beers, Boshuizen, Kirschner, & Gijselaers, 2007; Weinberger, et al., 2005) has found that more explicit scaffolding of the cognitive learning process leads to more engagement, discourse and interaction.

In a review of a range of scaffolding designs for ICT, Quintana et al. (2004) developed a scaffolding design framework for inquiry learning for science. It goes beyond the scope of this chapter to elaborate on the entire framework and guidelines for software design. However, given the focus of Community of Inquiry in our context, in particular the process management and articulation and reflection guidelines are relevant. Quintana et al. (2004) recommend that tasks should be structured to a level and complexity in which learners can focus on the most relevant parts of the task. For example, Nadolski et al. (2005) showed that explicit process worksheets to students in law, which provide explicit descriptions on the phases learners should go through when solving a problem, as well as hints or rules of thumb, improved learning task performance. Segers et al. (2003) showed that by providing process worksheets to students in economics learning in PBL, their performance scores increased significantly in comparison to students who used the standard PBL instructional approach. Finally, Quintana et al. (2004) recommend scaffolds that facilitate ongoing articulation and reflection, which can for example, be established by providing reminders and guidance for planning and monitoring. In other words, research from face-to-face and experimental settings indicate that using explicit scaffolds can enhance the cognitive presence of learners.

MEASURING THE IMPACT OF TEACHING PRESENCE ON COGNITIVE AND SOCIAL PRESENCE: A MIXED METHOD APPROACH

Although a decade of research in the Community of Inquiry framework has made a substantial contribution to our understanding of how learners in CMC environments learn, relatively limited research has been conducted in order to determine the actual impact of teaching presence on cognitive presence and social presence (Garrison, 2007). In particular, few studies have used sample sizes above 50 students to investigate the CoI framework (Arbaugh, 2007). Furthermore, most studies using content analyses (e.g. Akyol & Garrison, 2008; Anderson, et al., 2001; Garrison, Anderson, & Archer, 2001) are fairly descriptive and explorative, compare a relatively small amount of discourse, focus on only one or two of the three components of a CoI, and/or conduct analyses over a limited period of time in order to understand how participants are developing cognitive and social presence. Finally, to the best of our knowledge, not a single study has combined the above points with a (quasi)-experimental design based on changing teaching presence in order to measure over time, how cognitive and social presence may be affected.

There are possible explanations for the lack of evidence-based research of the effects of teaching presence on cognitive and social presence. These could be related to practical, methodological, financial and organisational difficulties in using content analysis schemes on a large scale to distil critical inquiry in CMC environments. The aim of content analysis techniques (De Wever, Schellens, Valcke, & Van Keer, 2006; Rourke & Anderson, 2004; Schrire, 2006; Strijbos, Martens, Prins, & Jochems, 2006) is to reveal evidence about learning and knowledge construction within online discussions. According to Garrison et al. (2001), a crucial characteristic that enables a content analysis tool to assess cognitive presence is the use of the model of critical thinking and its ability to reflect on educational practice. However, an increasing number of researchers have argued that content analysis schemes may be too methodologically challenging to be accurately implemented by researchers (Rourke, Anderson, Garrison, & Archer, 2001b; Strijbos, et al., 2006), extremely time consuming, and despite careful methodological efforts, inevitably remain subjective (Lombard,

Snyder-Duch, & Campanella Bracken, 2002; Rourke & Anderson, 2004).

In the CoI framework, separate content analysis schemes have been developed for cognitive presence (Garrison, et al., 2001), social presence (Rourke, Anderson, Garrison, & Archer, 2001a) and teaching presence (Anderson, et al., 2001). In the cognitive presence cycle, students are expected to go through four phases, namely:

1. A triggering event
2. Exploration of the task/problem
3. Integration
4. Resolution

The content analysis scheme of Rourke et al. (2001a) distinguishes three categories in social presence, namely effective expression, open communication and group cohesion. Finally, the teaching presence content analysis scheme of Anderson et al. (2001) distinguishes three categories, namely:

1. Instructional design and organisation
2. Facilitating discourse
3. Direct instruction

Measuring Cognitive Presence and Social Presence Differently

Although the validity of the cognitive presence and social presence coding scheme have been validated by prior research (See Garrison & Arbaugh, 2007 for overview), we opted to choose a different coding scheme for the following four reasons. First of all, most studies conducted in CoI research focus on experienced graduate students (Akyol & Garrison, 2008; Rourke, et al., 2001a) or adult learners (Arbaugh, 2007), while our context was students starting an undergraduate programme. When comparing a range of content analysis schemes, Schellens and Valcke (2005) concluded that the Veerman and Veldhuis-Diermanse (2001) scheme is particularly suited for

analysing knowledge construction among novice undergraduate students. As novice students are less experienced with critical inquiry and critical discourse, less interaction "naturally" takes place at a higher cognitive level (Schellens & Valcke, 2005). Therefore, a content analysis scheme that is more sensitive to distinguishing various phases of cognitive presence was needed, such as the Veerman and Veldhuis-Diermanse (2001) scheme. Second, given that almost 3200 messages needed to be coded by three coders, we looked for an easy-to-use instrument that would allow them to code cognitive and non-cognitive discourse with a single validated instrument. Coders would have to code each of the 3200 student messages twice when using the social presence and cognitive presence content analysis scheme, which would lead to a double work-load and costs.

Third, based upon an initial test with both the Veerman and Veldhuis-Diermanse (2001) and the CoI coding schemes with the three coders and 100 random messages, we found that certain key discourse elements were not identified by the CoI coding scheme. For example, students had to learn to use the CMC environment without specific training in the form of a kick-off setting (see description below). Initially students came across several technical issues for which no specific category in the coding scheme of a CoI existed. Furthermore, a large body of research in PBL and small-group research has found that effective groups and learners do specific (meta-cognitive) planning of how to proceed with the task (Hmelo-Silver, et al., 2007; Schmidt, et al., 2007; Van den Bossche, et al., 2006). Unfortunately, at the time when the coding was conducted, no specific coding category was present in the coding schemes of a CoI to enable this to be captured. However, recent work by Akyol and Garrison (2011) has addressed this by including metacognition in coding activity in CoI.

Fourth, we felt that neither the interactive or cohesive categories of the social presence content analysis scheme of Rourke et al. (2001a) added any additional information that was not already captured by the CMC Polaris system. For example, continuing a thread or quoting from others' messages is automatically visible and captured in Polaris and stored in the database (Rienties, 2010). Furthermore, students had to indicate whether a message was a question or discussion point (as indicated by yellow and blue icons in Figure 1). Finally, by using the thumbs-up or agreement button (similar to the "I like" button in Social Media Sites such as Facebook or Linkedin), students and teachers could express their agreement with other students (see Figure 1). At the same time, the Veerman and Veldhuis-Diermanse (2001) scheme addresses a more rich coding of non-task related discourse and social presence, as specific social and nonsense categories are included. The social category addresses messages that provide social and meta-cognitive support of participants to ongoing cognitive presence. Nonsense messages

are also social messages in nature, however, they are unrelated to the task itself, such as "Who is going to join us for our barbeque after the course has finished" or "I am thrilled that Paul Krugman has won the Nobel Economics prize". Although we disagree with the use of the word nonsense, because building an effective team and social climate requires that students also develop a social learning space, (Van den Bossche, et al., 2006), we have retained the term to retain the wording of the Veerman and Veldhuis-Diermanse (2001) scheme.

Veerman and Veldhuis-Diermanse (2001) make a distinction between non-task related activities:

1. Planning
2. Technical
3. Social
4. Non-sense

Figure 1. Exemplary task 0 of optima model

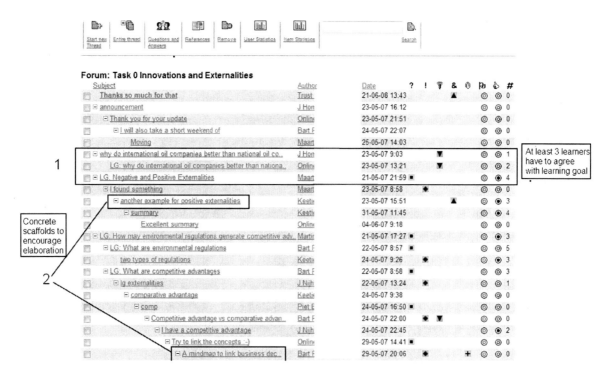

and task-related discourse activities:

5. Facts
6. Experience/opinion
7. Theoretical ideas
8. Explication
9. Evaluation

In the original coding scheme they considered three basic cognitive processing activities, namely new information (facts, experience, theoretical ideas), explication and evaluation. However, Schellens and Valcke (2005) and our own research (Rienties, 2010) found that the three new information categories should be distinguished in separate activities. Furthermore, Schellens and Valcke (2005, p. 961) argue that the five task-

related discourse activities should be ordered in a hierarchical structure, whereby "[c]onsecutive types of communication represent higher levels of knowledge construction". Therefore, we argue that the cognitive presence instrument of Veerman and Veldhuis-Diermanse (2001) is fairly compatible with the cognitive presence scheme of Garrison et al. (2001), as is conceptually illustrated in Table 1.

When students start a new Problem-Based Learning task (Schmidt, et al., 2007), there are several triggers (in PBL language problems) that students can use to start a discussion. After students have identified a particular problem, they are expected to post a so-called learning goal (e.g. why do governments require people to pay taxes?), which is coded as a new idea. The new idea category is similar to the triggering event in Garrison

Table 1. Comparison of the coding scheme of Veerman and Veldhuis-Diermanse (2001) to Community of Inquiry

Veerman and Veldhuis-Diermanse (2001)	Community of Inquiry	Examples from Online Economics Course
Non-task related discourse		
Planning	--	"Shall we first complete Task 1, before we go on with the next one?""
Technical	--	"Does anybody know how to add a graph to my thread?"
Social	Social Presence a) Affective	"I think that a lot of people are very motivated here, which is good"
Nonsense	Social Presence 1. Affective	"Who is going to join us for our barbeque after the course has finished"
Task-related discourse	Cognitive presence	
New fact (that is learners present information that is new in the context of the discussion)	Triggering Event Exploration (If a new solution to learning goal is presented)	"The average rate of inflation in the U.S. for 2004 is 2.7%."
Own experience/opinion	Exploration	"I think that VAT-taxes should be reduced to increase demand".
Theoretical ideas	Exploration	"If we take the Circular Flow Model from the book (Parkin/Bade) you are right, because it only takes households into account".
Explication	Exploration Integration	"There are actually quite a lot of different, more specific market forms, the ones you mentioned are the three big ones (monopoly, oligopoly and perfect competition), but some rare ones exist as well. For example a monopsony exists".
Evaluation	Integration Resolution	

et al. (2001). Afterwards, in PBL students explore potential solutions to the problem by activating their prior knowledge and experience. That is, students try to answer the learning goal based upon their own experience, basic facts, or theoretical knowledge. Afterwards, in the explication phase students weigh the various arguments and discussion points raised and elaborate on the comments of their peers. In other words, this is a type of communication that reflects a further refining and/or elaboration of earlier ideas. Finally, the evaluation phase corresponds to a critical discussion of earlier information or ideas. It goes beyond a simple confirmation or negation and reflects argumentations, reasonings, and justifications and is conceptually similar to the resolution phase. More examples of coded messages can be found elsewhere (Rienties, et al., 2009).

Separating Technical and Social Support in Teaching Presence

Two categories were added to the teaching presence content analysis scheme devised by Anderson et al. (2001), namely technical support and social support. Technical support was originally part of Category 3 (direct instruction), however, other researchers have stressed that an important role of teachers in online settings is to provide this support to ensure that students can effectively learn in a new learning environment (Berge, 1995; Tallent-Runnels et al., 2006). Social support (e.g. providing academic support, further information about student housing in the Netherlands) was added as a separate activity as previous research has highlighted that teachers have an important role in establishing a safe environment (Garrison, 2007; Rusman, et al., 2009; Van den Bossche, et al., 2006), for example by providing pastoral support.

RESEARCH DESIGN

Computer Mediated Communication Environment

The present study took place in an online summer course for prospective Bachelor students of an International Business degree program at an Institute for Higher Education in the Netherlands. The primary aim of this course was to bridge potential gaps in economics knowledge prior to study on a degree program (Rienties, et al., 2006). This online course was delivered over a period of six weeks within which learners were assumed to work for 10-15 hours per week. The participants never met face-to-face before or during the course and therefore had to learn economics using the CMC environment exclusively.

Tasks were constructed to simulate real-world settings but in a semi-structured manner, using a simple-to-complex sequence (Schmidt, et al., 2007), whereby the learners themselves could decide their learning actions and future directions. The learning process within PBL is commonly scaffolded according to the seven-jump method (Schmidt, et al., 2007). That is, problems serve as the context for new learning, whereby learners' prior knowledge is activated (Schmidt, et al., 2009; Segers, et al., 2003). It results in the formulation of learning goals by learners (rather than the tutor), which guide learners to issues that they were unable to solve and therefore requires further investigation (Segers, et al., 2003). Their analysis and resolution result in the acquisition of knowledge and problem-solving skills.

In comparison to a typical application of PBL in face-to-face classroom settings, in e-PBL the phases of the traditional seven jump may be less obvious as learners interact with the materials and discourse with peers at various times during a week and therefore may appear more fragmented. The distinction between the phases, mutual brainstorming, analysing the problem, synthesising and formulation of learning goals in the pre-discussion phase can become blurred in e-PBL, as illustrated in the Appendix. In other words, in e-PBL learners have a large degree of autonomy in the way how, what and when to contribute which may lead to greater fragmentation of the progress being made.

The two settings that are the subject of this study were both based on the principles of e-PBL. The second was a redesign of the first, offering more explicit scaffolding of the various learning process phases, as well as the more explicit articulation and reflection of activities within the various phases aimed at supporting higher levels of knowledge construction. For reasons of clarity, the first setting implemented in the summer of 2006 is referred to as the 'e-PBL design' and the second optimised setting implemented in the summer 2007 is referred to as the 'Optima design'. The CMC environment, tasks, course materials, and assessments were identical in both settings. Both designs included one lead tutor and one back-up tutor and each group was mentored and facilitated several times each day. At the end of each week, the lead tutor made a suggestion of how to proceed with the next task, thereby focusing on process rather than on content. In the e-PBL design, four tutors were responsible for teaching six groups, while in the Optima design two tutors taught five groups. One tutor, who was course conveyor and who was the most experienced tutor in terms of years of teaching economics in PBL, led three groups in the e-PBL design and all five groups in the Optima design. The four other tutors had at least four year experience with Problem Based Learning as a student, as they graduated with a Master degree in economics at this institute.

Discussion Themes and Tasks

Learners participated in a collaborative learning environment using eight discussion forums. There was one cafe-forum where learners could share non-task related information and get to know each other. In addition, there was a "how does PBL work Task 0?" forum, whereby tutors replicated a dis-

cussion to illustrate how e-PBL/Optima worked. The remaining six forums were task-related forums. The first two tasks were introductory and addressed basic terminology to get a feel for the domain. The tasks were designed to relate to the prior knowledge of students, as recommend by Schmidt et al. (2007). The first task focussed on an international student from North-Korea coming to the institute and realising that the way markets function in Western Europe are different, while the second task focussed on explaining a graph of longitudinal Gross Domestic Product growth differences between Europe and the U.S. The following four tasks addressed authentic tasks within micro-economics and macro-economics and became increasingly complex.

Two Cohorts of Learners in Quasi-Experimental Research Setting

Reflection on e-PBL Implementation

Rienties, Giesbers, Tempelaar, Lygo-Baker, Segers and Gijselaers (2012) found that all learners participating in the e-PBL format were satisfied with the overall course and support provided by the tutor. 83% of the learners indicated that the goals of the module were clear; 82% indicated that the internet application was easy to use; 70% were satisfied with the knowledge and skills learned in the module; and 62% were satisfied with the group in which they participated. However, only 43% of the learners indicated that they actively participated in the discussions. During semi-structured interviews conducted two months after the completion of the course with two groups of four learners, respondents indicated that they had found it difficult to understand the structure and scaffolding process of the online course. In particular, they noted they had difficulty understanding the functioning of the e-PBL five jump. Some learners indicated that it was sometimes unclear in which phase of the learning process the discussions were focused. Furthermore, some of the learners complained about the lack of partici-pation by other learners in their group.

Optima Design

Segers et al. (2003) proposed a new seven-jump procedure that consisted of a more explicit scaf-folding based around greater and explanation of the activities learners were expected to perform in order to reach the desired learning outcomes. By providing more explicit scaffolding of the learning phases at the beginning of the module and by providing explicit reminders and guidance to facilitate productive planning, monitoring and articulation, a greater teacher presence was es-tablished. In addition, research in economics and medical education found that the Optima model led to improved learning satisfaction (Chen, Cheng, Weng, Lin, & Tan, 2005) and learning outcomes (Segers, et al., 2003).

In comparison to the e-PBL design, the Op-tima design was adjusted in three ways. First, the five-jump process was extended to a seven-jump process (See Appendix 1 for details). For example, an explicit "Step 4: Elaboration on findings in Step 3" was added to encourage more interac-tion, elaboration and higher cognitive discourse. Learners were encouraged to print out a so-called Optima card, or process overview (i.e. a schematic overview showing the concrete steps in the seven-jump process), and use this card when looking at the discussion forums (Nadolski, et al., 2005).

Secondly, specific scaffolds were given to pro-vide a simple visual overview for learners to show which part of the seven-jump learning process a discussion was positioned. For example, learners could only proceed to the third phase of answering a particular learning goal when at least three (25% of group members) learners agreed (by using a "thumbs-up" button) with the formulation and relevance of the learning goal (LG) as illustrated by number 1 in Figure 1. Only the third learning goal in the marked box 1 (i.e. LG. Negative and Positive Externalities) received at least three

thumbs-ups, thereby the learners did not have to focus on the first two. This provided a visual prompt to show which phase the discussions were in, which provided learners more opportunities to control their learning.

Thirdly, in the Optima design clearer guidelines were given to learners by the teachers over what to do in each of the seven phases in comparison to the e-PBL design. This was introduced to support understanding of the process and how to articulate views (Quintana et al. (2004). For ex-ample, in Step 4 learners were asked to elaborate on their findings by making a mind-map, thereby providing a conceptual overview of the concepts discussed in the task and how they related to each other. Alternatively, learners could question the assumptions of the arguments given before or provide other examples of where they believed the respective theory discussed did not hold, which is illustrated by the two posts marked by number 2 in Figure 1. In this way, more scaffolding was provided to learners on how to proceed within the learning process.

Research Questions and Hypotheses

Based upon on our theoretical framework, we expected that learners in the Optima cohort would reach higher levels of cognitive presence. In line with recommendations of Akyol and Gar-rison (2008), we compared the development of cognitive presence, social presence and teaching presence over time across the two designs in order to enhance our understanding of how the manipulation of teaching presence may influence the learning process.

1. Does providing more explicit scaffolding of the learning phases in CMC lead to more contributions to cognitive presence?
2. To what extent does providing explicit scaffolding lead to higher quality cognitive presence?

3.   To what extent does the scaffolding lead to more social presence?
4.   To what extent does teaching presence change to more facilitating discourse and less instructional design?

METHOD

Participants

Participants were selected based upon their scores on an entry assessment in economics (See Rienties, et al., 2006 for more detail). In total 82 participants were randomly assigned to one of six teams in the e-PBL design, while 60 participants were randomly assigned to one of five teams in the Optima design. The eleven teams had an average of 13.00 members (SD= 2.68, range = 9-17). The average age was 19 years and 48% of the learners were female. No significant differences were found between the two cohorts with respect to prior knowledge, motivation, educational background, age and gender (Rienties, et al., 2012).

Instruments

Content Analysis of Cognitive and Social Presence

Three independent coders (two economists, one educational psychologist), who were blind to the study's purpose and hypotheses, were trained to use the Veerman and Veldhuis-Diermanse (2001) instrument and independently coded all messages. A random sample of 100 messages was used as a test case but the Cronbach alpha was relatively low (0.6). Therefore, an additional meeting with the three coders was established and the divergent results discussed and consensus on the method agreed. The coding took 120-160 hours per coder, who received financial compensation in return. As a unit of analysis, the complete message was chosen as recommended by Schellens and Valcke

(2006). A message was "codeable" when two or more coders used the same category. If this was not the case, the coders discussed to decide whether they could reach agreement on the coding of the message. Learners posted 3186 messages of which 60 (2%) were considered as uncodeable (e.g. no agreement between coders could be reached). The Cronbach alpha (α) for these 3186 messages was 0.903. Most studies have set the minimum α at 0.7 and recommend setting $\alpha > 0.8$. The Cohen's kappa of the coder inter-reliability (coders agreeing with each other) between Coder $1 - 2$, $2 - 3$ and $1 - 3$ was 0.62, 0.63 and 0.61 respectively. De Wever et al. (2006) argue that Cohen's kappa values between 0.4 and 0.75 represent fair to good agreement beyond chance.

Content Analysis of Teaching Presence

171 teacher contributions in three random groups in the e-PBL design were coded by all three coders, with $\alpha= 0.88$ and Cohen's kappa ranged between 0.61-0.78. Given the reliable coding, the remaining three groups of the e-PBL condition were coded by one coder. Two coders coded the 316 messages in the Optima groups, whereby when there was disagreement the third coder independently coded these respective messages, leading to $\alpha=0.88$ and Cohen's kappa= 0.61.

Longitudinal Analysis of Discourse

Students were grouped into a time-slot of their preference that would start between July 1 until August 1. In this way, students were able to combine their summer plans with following the module at a time that suited them. As the 11 groups started at different periods during the summer, the time stamp of the first student message was regarded as the start of the first week. A teacher message was coded as week 0 when it was posted before the first student posted a message online. Given that the lead and back-up teachers moderated the discussions for each group with a varying intensity, we aggregated the responses of both teachers into "a single teacher per group" in order to compare how the teachers facilitated discourse in the eleven groups. As the pace of the groups was (in part) determined by the students, some groups were able to finish the six PBL-tasks within five to six weeks. Other groups worked for a longer time period together, while some groups that completed the tasks continued to use the discussion forums for social talk. In order to provide a common benchmark for our longitudinal analysis, we only used messages that where posted within the first six weeks of the module, leading to 2447 (77%) student messages and 728 (93%) teacher messages (including "week 0" messages).

RESULTS

Static Analysis of Cognitive, Social, and Teaching Presence

On average, in the e-PBL design 20.78 (SD=21.31) messages were contributed per learner, while in the Optima design 13.83 (SD=13.61) messages were contributed per learner during the first six weeks of the module, which is significantly different using an independent sample T-test (F=5.542, t=2.215, p-value=0.03). Using the Veerman and Veldhuis-Diermanse (2001) scheme, 6% of the messages contributed by students were coded as planning, while 4% of the student messages were related to technical issues. In other words, the two added categories to the CoI schemes indicated that in our context planning and technical issues play a role in CMC. Furthermore, 31% of all contributions were to the nonsense category, which illustrated that learners were actively involved in getting to know each other and building a social climate.

Using independent sample T-tests we found some evidence of significant differences in the two designs, as illustrated in Table 2. That is, with respect to social presence, learners in the Optima design contributed significantly more social mes-

sages but less nonsense messages. In addition, in the Optima design there was a lower agreement (thumbs-up) with messages than in the e-PBL design, although statistically insignificant. That is, in the e-PBL condition 48 participants used the agree button at least once, while in the Optima design only 15 participants used the thumbs-up button, but with relatively more intensity. With the exception of social discourse, the direction of the difference was in the opposite direction than we anticipated. The Optima design learners posted fewer non-task related messages and fewer cognitive presence messages, in comparison to the e-PBL design.

On average, teachers in both designs contributed a similar amount of messages per group, namely 68.66 (SD= 17.22) in the e-PBL design and 63.20 (SD= 19.66) in the Optima design. Follow-up content analysis of the five teaching presence categories in Table 3 illustrated similar contributions to teaching presence using a 5% confidence level, which the exception of facilitating discourse. As students in the Optima design were given more explicit scaffolds of what to do in each of the seven learning phases, teachers were able to focus less on facilitating discourse. Furthermore, the addition of technical support and social support to the content analysis scheme of Anderson et al. (2001) seems to have been an important addition to the coding scheme, as 42% of the teaching activities were categorised under these two codings. This helped to reveal that teaching presence was focussed on providing social support in both designs.

Longitudinal Analysis of Cognitive, Social, and Teaching Presence

In Figure 2 the longitudinal developments of cognitive and social presence are illustrated, while in Figure 3 the detailed longitudinal developments of the five categories of cognitive presence are illustrated. In the first week of the module, no significant difference was found between the

Table 2. Comparison of contributions to cognitive and social presence per learner in e-PBL vs. Optima

	e-PBL		Optima		
	M	**SD**	**M**	**SD**	**T-test**
Non-Task Related	9.78	11.99	6.96	6.24	
Category 1: Planning	1.38	1.91	0.83	1.34	
Category 2: Technical	0.85	1.80	0.65	0.95	
Category 3: Social	0.67	1.16	1.80	3.03	3.086***
Category 4: Nonsense	6.88	9.18	3.68	2.71	-2.612*
Agreement with post	12.39	21.79	6.98	22.04	
Cognitive Presence	11.00	13.36	6.87	9.01	-2.075*
Category 5: Facts	3.61	4.29	2.28	4.03	
Category 6: Experience	1.23	2.16	0.83	1.46	
Category 7: Theoretical Ideas	1.60	2.61	1.41	2.22	
Category 8: Explication	4.29	5.63	1.95	2.90	-2.947**
Category 9: Evaluation	0.27	0.52	0.38	0.94	

Independent Sample t-test for e-PBL (n=82) and Optima (n=60)
***Coefficient is significant at the 0.001 level (2-tailed).
**Coefficient is significant at the 0.01 level (2-tailed).
*Coefficient is significant at the 0.05 level (2-tailed).

Table 3. Comparison of contributions to teaching presence in e-PBL vs. Optima

	e-PBL		Optima		
	M	**SD**	**M**	**SD**	**T-test**
Category 1: Instructional Design and Organization	16.33	5.99	12.00	7.52	
Category 2: Facilitating Discourse	10.33	1.75	6.00	2.83	3.120**
Category 3: Direct Instruction	18.33	8.16	17.20	6.38	
Category 4: Technical Support	2.50	1.87	4.20	4.21	
Category 5: Social Support	21.17	9.28	23.80	8.70	

Independent Sample t-test for e-PBL (n=6) and Optima (n=5)
**Coefficient is significant at the 0.01 level (2-tailed).

two designs when looking at cognitive and social presence as a whole. In both cohorts participants were focussed primarily on discourse within the social presence category, as they made efforts to get to know each other during the first week. However, participants in the e-PBL design contributed significantly more experience (F = 16.878, t = 1.972, p-value = 0.05) and explication (F = 46.204, t = 3.121, p-value = 0.00) in comparison to Optima participants. In week 2, the attention shifted more towards work on solving the PBL tasks, as reflected by the increase in cognitive presence in both cohorts. e-PBL participants increased their focus on cognitive presence relatively more than Optima participants, which was marginally significant at 10% level (F = 4.324, t = 1.813, p-value = 0.07), but significant at 1% for explication (F = 11.678, t = 2.647, p-value

Figure 2. Cognitive and social presence development over six weeks of e-PBL vs. optima

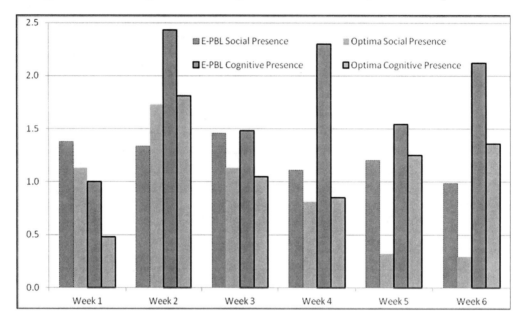

Figure 3. Longitudinal development of cognitive presence per student of e-PBL vs. optima

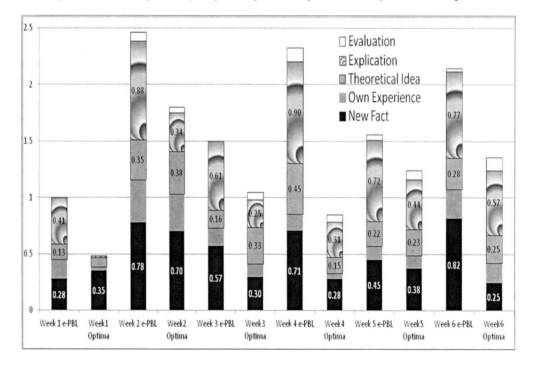

= 0.01). In week 3, both cohorts contributed an almost identical amount of social and cognitive discourse, however e-PBL participants contributed more to explication (F = 20.785, t = 2.472, p-value = 0.02) but marginally less to evaluation (F = 16.013, t = -1.923, p-value = 0.06).

After half the module was finished in week 4, e-PBL participants contributed significantly more to cognitive presence (F = 11.074, t = 3.136, p-value = 0.00) than Optima participants, in particular to new ideas (F = 14.860, t = 2.498, p-value = 0.02) and explication (F = 12.931, t = 2.700, p-value = 0.01). In week 5, e-PBL participants contributed significantly more to social presence (F = 31.199, t = 3.655, p-value = 0.00) but contributed similarly to cognitive presence. Finally, in week 6 there is a noticeable "catch-up activity" from Optima participants with respect to cognitive presence, but with significantly lower contributions to social presence (F = 13.501, t = 2.904, p-value = 0.00) and new ideas (F = 13.090, t = 2.374, p-value = 0.02). In sum, distinguishing the various categories of cognitive presence allowed us to obtain a more in-depth understanding of how participants in the two designs develop critical inquiry and thinking over each of the six weeks. In contrast to our initial expectations, Optima participants with more instructional design and organisation in the form of more explicit scaffolding contributed less to cognitive presence and social presence from the first week onwards. Only in the third week did Optima participants start to actively integrate and elaborate on arguments raised by peers. In four out of six weeks, e-PBL participants were significantly more involved in integrating and elaborating upon the various arguments raised by their peers compared to the Optima participants. We therefore have to conclude that the Optima design leads to less higher quality cognitive discourse.

In Figure 4, the longitudinal developments of the five categories for teaching presence are illustrated. In Week 0, in both conditions a similar amount of contributions, labelled as instructional design and organisation and direct instruction (giving concrete task assignments), are provided. Throughout the course, similar amounts of instructional design messages were posted in the two conditions. Teachers in the e-PBL design appeared to focus more on facilitating discourse from week 2 onwards in comparison to the Optima design. With respect to providing direct instruction, during the first two weeks of the module teachers in the e-PBL condition provided 5.33 direct instruction messages per group, while only 0.40 messages were provided in the Optima condition. Also in weeks 3 and 4 more direct instruction messages were provided in the e-PBL design. In the last two weeks, teachers in the Optima model became more focussed on providing direct instruction, while teachers in the e-PBL design faded their direct instruction, which was significantly different in week 6 (F = 6.292, t = 2.775, p-value = 0.02). With respect to technological support, no substantial differences were found. Finally, teachers in the Optima condition focussed relatively more on providing social support and encouragement during the first four weeks. In the last two weeks the emphasis shifted from social support to direct instruction, which may reflect a need to ensure that the tasks were completed in time.

Although we find only one statistically significantly different contribution to teaching presence, which could be a random error rather than a statistically significant finding, given that there are only 11 groups i.e. teachers to conduct our statistical analysis, we do argue that teachers in two designs established teaching presence in different ways. That is, in the e-PBL design teachers spent more effort establishing direct instruction and explaining how the e-PBL system worked. Over time, the teachers in the e-PBL design focus more on facilitating discourse and towards the end of the course their teaching presence had faded and was very limited. In the Optima design, as the scaffolding of the learning phases was more explicit, the teachers initially focussed less on

Figure 4. Development of teaching presence over six weeks of e-PBL vs. optima

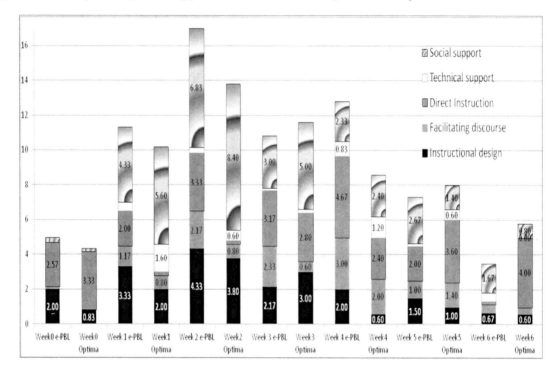

direct instruction and relatively more on providing social support and creating a safe environment. As the participants dropped their contributions in week 4, more specific direct instruction was given in week 5 and 6 to ensure that the goals and tasks were completed. The teaching presence reflects the behaviour found within the two groups of learners and suggests that the teachers were responding to the different student activity prompted by the two different models.

DISCUSSION

In this quasi-experimental study we found that providing more explicit scaffolding of the learning phases in a community of inquiry has a profound impact on learners' behaviour and engagement in terms of cognitive and social presence. An important finding was that in the redesigned learning environment learners contributed less to

higher quality cognitive presence. These results indicate that the more explicit scaffolding of the PBL learning phases primarily had a negative impact on the engagement of participants. That is, while in the e-PBL design learners contributed on average eleven cognitive messages per learner, in the Optima design this reduced to seven messages per learner. A possible explanation for the lower engagement of learners in the Optima design is that the more explicit scaffolding of the Optima seven jump learning process may have narrowed the freedom and autonomy of learners to self-determine their learning actions. However, this result runs contrary to previous research findings. Research in face-to-face settings (Segers, et al., 2003), blended (Chen, et al., 2005; Van der Pol, Admiraal, & Simons, 2006) and experimental settings (Beers, et al., 2005, 2007; Weinberger, et al., 2005) have all previously shown that explicit scaffolding of the learning phases enhances interaction and task performance. In our CMC environment, where learners worked and learned in a collaborative-constructivist learning environment at a distance for a sustained period of time, increased scaffolding reduced discourse.

A second possible explanation for the lower engagement may be found in the fact that learners in the Optima setting had to wait for approval by peers before continuing their learning actions (e.g. discussing a learning goal they were interested). The learning process therefore became more fragmented. In the e-PBL design, learners could (technically) start and complete the learning phases without their peers, that is they could start with a learning goal and provide a set of answers/solutions without receiving approval or feedback from their peers. A drawback of this approach was that learners were not co-constructing knowledge together, which may inhibit the contributions of learners to discourse. The explicit timing in Optima might have negatively influenced the engagement of learners because they were dependent on their peers who they never met apart from online. While Jang et al. (2010) found a strong positive relation between structure and autonomy of teachers and the respective learning environment with behaviour engagement of students during a one-hour face-to-face lesson, perhaps a sustained scaffolding in our online setting may have delayed and/or interfered with the natural flow of interaction of learners. Also Quintana et al. (2004) argue that our understanding of how teachers can effectively fade the scaffolding of the learning phases over time needs more research. A third possible explanation, that needs further exploration, might be that by providing explicit scaffolding and responsibilities of facilitating discourse to students, students might have been overwhelmed by providing both cognitive presence, social presence and (in part) distributed teacher presence to other students. Garrison (2011) indicates that "teaching presence is charged with shaping the appropriate transactional balance and, along with the learners, managing

and monitoring the achievement of worthwhile learning outcomes in a timely manner."

A second important finding was that our static and dynamic (longitudinal) comparison of discourse activities across two designs illustrated the power of using time dimensions in order to enhance our understandings of how learners create and maintain critical inquiry. This was first highlighted by Akyol and Garrison (2008), who conducted a time-series analysis amongst a relatively small group of 16 graduates over a period of nine weeks, but now confirmed in a larger sample using quasi-experimental design. The creation of the Community of Inquiry in our context seemed to be established in the first two weeks of the course. We conducted a thorough, and in the context of Community of Inquiry research, rather unique content analysis of 3200 student messages and 800 teacher messages and afterwards contrasted discourse using a longitudinal time perspective. In the e-PBL design, participants started during the first week to elaborate on and integrate the various argumentations raised by learners within their group. In contrast, Optima participants were primarily focussed on sharing ideas, experience and theoretical ideas, or exploration of the task. Only after three weeks did the Optima participants start to explicate and integrate the various arguments raised. A particularly interesting phenomenon seemed to unfold later in the week 5 and week 6, as Optima participants substantially increased their engagement. To what extent this is a result of the increased teaching presence, in particular direct instruction, from week 4 onwards or whether participants themselves increased their efforts to catch-up before the end of the course is difficult to determine given the causality of relations in the Community of Inquiry. The main conclusion from this study is that getting the balance between facilitating discourse and direct instruction right in a Community of Inquiry to facilitate learners to critically engage is a complex and delicate issue.

Limitations

The results of this study are based on a redesign of an authentic, real environment using quasi-experimental research. A limitation is that we did not measure the interactions between individual and mutual conceptions, emotions and shared regulation among participants (Järvelä, Hurme, & Järvenoja, 2011; Järvelä, Volet, & Järvenoja, 2010; Tempelaar, Niculescu, Rienties, Giesbers, & Gijselaers, 2012). In groups that have more engaged learners, one may expect that more (higher) cognitive discourse activities would be present than other groups. Further research should assess whether group-level effects and dynamic learning processes during discourse of learners also influence behaviour of individual learners in CSCL settings.

FUTURE RESEARCH DIRECTIONS

Future research should investigate how teaching presence can be manipulated in such a way that the key drivers of social interaction, the community of learners, are able to critically engage. We intend to redesign the Optima model so that the progression between stages becomes less restrictive, whereby the first two weeks are explicitly scaffolded to allow all learners to contribute on equal terms, but over time more freedom is given to learners to explore individual learning goals within the task, thereby providing more space for learners to explore alternative solutions. At the same time, we recommend that researchers explore the recent discussions on assigning specific roles to learners (Strijbos & De Laat, 2010), whereby individual learners may be supported to overcome initial resistance in contributing to discourse. In addition, by analysing how learners mutually influence each other in collaborative learning, future research should assess how the type of motivation of one learner (Rienties, et al.,

2009) influences the behaviour of other learners (Järvelä, Järvenoja, & Veermans, 2008).

ACKNOWLEDGMENT

The authors would like to thank Milan Bedlovic for conducting an initial analysis of the Optima redesign in his Master thesis. Furthermore, we would like to thank Wim Gijselaers, Mien Segers and Jan Nijhuis for their input in reshaping the Optima model to our context. Finally, we would like to thank the three independent coders, who have helped to set-up, implement and evaluate the e-PBL and Optima model for a countless amount of hours.

REFERENCES

Akyol, Z., & Garrison, D. R. (2011). Assessing metacognition in an online community of inquiry. *The Internet and Higher Education*, *14*(3), 183–190.

Akyol, Z., & Garrison, R. (2008). The development of a Community of Inquiry over time in an online course: Understanding the progression and integration of social, cognitive and teaching presence. *Journal of Asynchronous Learning Networks*, *12*(3-4), 3–22.

Anderson, T., Rourke, L., Garrison, D., & Archer, W. (2001). Assessing teaching presence in a computer conferencing context. *Journal of Asynchronous Learning Networks*, *5*(2), 1–17.

Arbaugh, J. B. (2007). An empirical verification of the community of inquiry framework. *Journal of Asynchronous Learning Networks*, *11*(1), 73–85.

Beers, P., Boshuizen, H., Kirschner, P. A., & Gijselaers, W. H. (2005). Computer support for knowledge construction in collaborative learning environment. *Computers in Human Behavior*, *21*, 623–643.

Beers, P., Boshuizen, H., Kirschner, P. A., & Gijsclaers, W. H. (2007). The analysis of negotiation of common ground in CSCL. *Learning and Instruction, 17*(4), 427–435.

Berge, Z. L. (1995). Facilitating computer conferencing: Recommendations from the field. *Journal of Educational Technology & Society, 35*(1), 22–30.

Biggs, J., & Tang, C. (2007). *Teaching for quality learning at university* (3rd ed.). Maidenhead, UK: Open University Press.

Chen, L. S., Cheng, Y. M., Weng, S. F., Lin, C. H., & Tan, Y. K. (2005). A computer-based clinical teaching-case system with emulation of time sequence for medical education. *IEICE Transactions on Information and Systems, E88*(5), 816–821.

De Laat, M., Lally, V., Lipponen, L., & Simons, R.-J. (2007). Online teaching in networked learning communities: A multi-method approach to studying the role of the teacher. *Instructional Science, 35*(3), 257–286.

De Wever, B., Schellens, T., Valcke, M., & Van Keer, H. (2006). Content analysis schemes to analyze transcripts of online asynchronous discussion groups: A review. *Computers & Education, 46*(1), 6–28.

Garrison, D. (2007). Online community of inquiry review: Social, cognitive, and teaching presence issues. *Journal of Asynchronous Learning Networks, 11*(1), 61–72.

Garrison, D. (2011). *E-learning in the 21st century: A framework for research and practice* (2nd ed.). London, UK: Routledge/Taylor and Francis.

Garrison, D., Anderson, T., & Archer, W. (2000). Critical inquiry in a text-based environment: Computer conferencing in higher education. *The Internet and Higher Education, 2*(2), 87–105.

Garrison, D., Anderson, T., & Archer, W. (2001). Critical thinking, cognitive presence, and computer conferencing in distance education. *American Journal of Distance Education, 15*(1).

Garrison, D., & Arbaugh, J. B. (2007). Researching the community of inquiry framework: Review, issues, and future directions. *The Internet and Higher Education, 10*(3), 157–172.

Giesbers, B., Rienties, B., Gijselaers, W. H., Segers, M., & Tempelaar, D. T. (2009). Social presence, web-videoconferencing and learning in virtual teams. *Industry and Higher Education, 23*(4), 301–310.

Goldstein, D. S., Leppa, C., Brockhaus, A., Bliquez, R., & Porter, I. (2012). Fostering social presence in a blended learning faculty development institute. In Akyol, Z., & Garrison, D. (Eds.), *Educational communities of inquiry: Theoretical framework, research and practice*. Hershey, PA: IGI Global.

Hammond, M. (2000). Communication within on-line forums: the opportunities, the constraints and the value of a communicative approach. *Computers & Education, 35*(4), 251–262.

Hmelo-Silver, C., Duncan, R. G., & Chinn, C. A. (2007). Scaffolding and achievement in problem-based and inquiry learning: A response to Kirschner, Sweller, and Clark (2006). *Educational Psychologist, 42*(2), 99–107.

Hughes, M., Ventura, S., & Dando, M. (2007). Assessing social presence in online discussion groups: A replication study. *Innovations in Education and Teaching International, 44*(1), 17–29.

Jang, H., Reeve, J., & Deci, E. L. (2010). Engaging students in learning activities: It is not autonomy support or structure but autonomy support and structure. *Journal of Educational Psychology, 102*(3), 588–600.

Järvelä, S., Hurme, T., & Järvenoja, H. (2011). Self-regulation and motivation in computer-supported collaborative learning environments. In Ludvigson, S., Lund, A., Rasmussen, I., & Säljö, R. (Eds.), *Learning across sites: New tools, infrastructure and practices*. New York, NY: Routledge.

Järvelä, S., Järvenoja, H., & Veermans, M. (2008). Understanding the dynamics of motivation in socially shared learning. *International Journal of Educational Research, 47*(2), 122–135.

Järvelä, S., Volet, S., & Järvenoja, H. (2010). Research on motivation in collaborative learning: Moving beyond the cognitive-situative divide and combining individual and social processes. *Educational Psychologist, 45*(1), 15–27.

Kirschner, P. A., Beers, P., Boshuizen, H., & Gijselaers, W. H. (2008). Coercing shared knowledge in collaborative learning environments. *Computers in Human Behavior, 24*(2), 403–420.

Kirschner, P. A., Sweller, J., & Clark, R. E. (2006). Why minimal guidance during instruction does not work: An analysis of the failure of constructivist, discovery, problem-based, experiential, and inquiry-based teaching. *Educational Psychologist, 41*(2), 75–86.

Lombard, M., Snyder-Duch, J., & Campanella Bracken, C. (2002). Content analysis in mass communication: Assessment and reporting of intercoder reliability. *Human Communication Research, 28*(4), 587–604.

Nadolski, R. J., Kirschner, P. A., & Van Merriënboer, J. J. G. (2005). Optimizing the number of steps in learning tasks for complex skills. *The British Journal of Educational Psychology, 75*(2), 223–237.

Quintana, C., Reiser, B. J., Davis, E. A., Krajcik, J., Fretz, E., & Duncan, R. G. (2004). A scaffolding design framework for software to support science inquiry. *Journal of the Learning Sciences, 13*(3), 337–386.

Richardson, J. C., Sadaf, A., & Ertmer, P. G. (2012). Relationship between types of question prompts and critical thinking in online discussions. In Akyol, Z., & Garrison, D. (Eds.), *Educational communities of inquiry: Theoretical framework, research and practice*. Hershey, PA: IGI Global.

Rienties, B. (2010). *Understanding social interaction in computer-supported collaborative learning: The role of motivation on social interaction*. Unpublished manuscript, Maastricht.

Rienties, B., Giesbers, B., Tempelaar, D. T., Lygo-Baker, S., Segers, M., & Gijselaers, W. H. (2012). The role of scaffolding and motivation in CSCL. *Computers & Education. 59*(3), 893-906.

Rienties, B., Kaper, W., Struyven, K., Tempelaar, D. T., Van Gastel, L., & Vrancken, S. (2011). (in press). A review of the role of information communication technology and course design in transitional education practices. *Interactive Learning Environments*. doi:doi:10.1080/10494820.10492010.10542757

Rienties, B., Tempelaar, D. T., Van den Bossche, P., Gijselaers, W. H., & Segers, M. (2009). The role of academic motivation in computer-supported collaborative learning. *Computers in Human Behavior, 25*(6), 1195–1206.

Rienties, B., Tempelaar, D. T., Waterval, D., Rehm, M., & Gijselaers, W. H. (2006). Remedial online teaching on a summer course. *Industry and Higher Education, 20*(5), 327–336.

Rourke, L., & Anderson, T. (2004). Validity in quantitative content analysis. *Educational Technology Research and Development, 52*(1), 5–18.

Rourke, L., Anderson, T., Garrison, D., & Archer, W. (2001a). Assessing social presence in asynchronous text-based computer conferencing. *Journal of Distance Education, 14*(3), 51–70.

Rourke, L., Anderson, T., Garrison, D., & Archer, W. (2001b). Methodological issues in the content analysis of computer conference transcripts. *International Journal of Artificial Intelligence in Education, 12*, 8–22.

Rusman, E., Van Bruggen, J., Cörvers, R., Sloep, P., & Koper, R. (2009). From pattern to practice: Evaluation of a design pattern fostering trust in virtual teams. *Computers in Human Behavior, 25*(5), 1010–1019.

Schellens, T., & Valcke, M. (2005). Collaborative learning in asynchronous discussion groups: What about the impact on cognitive processing? *Computers in Human Behavior, 21*(6), 957–975.

Schellens, T., & Valcke, M. (2006). Fostering knowledge construction in university students through asynchronous discussion groups. *Computers & Education, 46*(4), 349–370.

Schmidt, H. G., Loyens, S. M. M., Van Gog, T., & Paas, F. (2007). Problem-based learning is compatible with human cognitive architecture: Commentary on Kirschner, Sweller, and Clark (2006). *Educational Psychologist, 42*(2), 91–97.

Schmidt, H. G., Van Der Molen, H. T., Te Winkel, W. W. R., & Wijnen, W. H. F. W. (2009). Constructivist, problem-based learning does work: a meta-analysis of curricular comparisons involving a single medical school. *Educational Psychologist, 44*(4), 227–249.

Schrire, S. (2006). Knowledge building in asynchronous discussion groups: Going beyond quantitative analysis. *Computers & Education, 46*(1), 49–70.

Segers, M., Van den Bossche, P., & Teunissen, E. (2003). Evaluating the effects of redesigning a problem-based learning environment. *Studies in Educational Evaluation, 29*, 315–334.

Strijbos, J.-W., & De Laat, M. F. (2010). Developing the role concept for computer-supported collaborative learning: An explorative synthesis. *Computers in Human Behavior, 26*(4), 495–505.

Strijbos, J.-W., Martens, R. L., Prins, F. J., & Jochems, W. M. G. (2006). Content analysis: What are they talking about? *Computers & Education, 46*(1), 29–48.

Tallent-Runnels, M. K., Thomas, J. A., Lan, W. Y., Cooper, S., Ahern, T. C., & Shaw, S. M. (2006). Teaching courses online: A review of the research. *Review of Educational Research, 76*(1), 93–135.

Tempelaar, D. T., Niculescu, A., Rienties, B., Giesbers, B., & Gijselaers, W. H. (2012). How achievement emotions impact students' decisions for online learning, and what precedes those emotions. *The Internet and Higher Education, 15*(3), 161–169. doi:10.1016/j.iheduc.2011.1010.1003

Van den Bossche, P., Gijselaers, W. H., Segers, M., & Kirschner, P. A. (2006). Social and cognitive factors driving teamwork in collaborative learning environments. Team learning beliefs & behaviour. *Small Group Research, 37*, 490–521.

Van der Pol, J., Admiraal, W., & Simons, P. (2006). The affordance of anchored discussion for the collaborative processing of academic texts. *International Journal of Computer-Supported Collaborative Learning, 1*(3), 339–357.

Veerman, A. L., & Veldhuis-Diermanse, E. (2001). Collaborative learning through computer-mediated communication in academic education. In P. Dillenbourg, A. Eurelings, & K. Hakkarainen (Eds.), *European Perspectives on Computer-Supported Collaborative Learning: Proceedings of the 1st European Conference on Computer-Supported Collaborative Learning* (pp. 625-632). Maastricht, The Netherlands: University of Maastricht.

Weinberger, A., Reiserer, M., Ertl, B., Fischer, F., & Mandl, H. (2005). Facilitating collaborative knowledge construction in computer-mediated learning environments with cooperation scripts. In R. Bromme, F. W. Hesse, & H. Spada (Ed.), *Barriers and biases in computer-mediated knowledge communication and how they may be overcome* (5 ed., pp. 15-38). New York, NY: Springer.

Whipp, J., & Lorentz, R. (2009). Cognitive and social help giving in online teaching: An exploratory study. *Educational Technology Research and Development, 57*(2), 169–192.

KEY TERMS AND DEFINITIONS

Community of Inquiry: A conceptual framework consisting of cognitive presence, social presence, teaching presence developed by Garrison et al. (2000) to understand discourse and social interaction in blended and online environments.

Content Analysis: A mixed-method quantitative and qualitative technique to distil critical inquiry in Computer Mediated Communication environments to reveal evidence about learning and knowledge construction within online discussions.

Design-Based Research: A methodological approach that is set in real educational settings, where teachers or researchers redesign the learning environment based upon theoretical foundations (i.e. Community of Inquiry) and principles of design-research. Claims for design-research are essential for identification of educational problems and possible solutions.

Distance Education: A teaching method and technology with the aim of delivering teaching to learners who are not physically present in a traditional educational setting such as a classroom.

Economics: A social science that analyzes the production, distribution, and consumption of goods and services.

Optima Model: An adaptation of the seven-jump Problem Based Learning process by Segers et al. (2003) originally developed by Schmidt (1983) to explicate the required learning activities and outcomes of each of the seven stages.

Scaffolding: A process by which a teacher or a more knowledgeable peer provides assistance that enables learners to succeed in problems that would otherwise be too difficult.

Teacher Presence: The design, facilitation and direction of cognitive and social processes for the purpose of realising personally meaningful and educationally worthwhile learning outcomes.

APPENDIX

Table 4. PBL, e-PBL, and Optima Learning Phases

Traditional PBL 7-Jump	e-PBL 5-Jump	Optima 7-jump
The seven-jump procedure, where 1-5 is pre-discussion and, 6 is self-study and 7 post-discussion. **1. Understand all terms**	**Step 1: Read the task and see if there are any difficult words and check whether somebody else has already defined such words on Polaris** a. If not, state the difficult word in Polaris; b. If yes, see if you agree with the definition of the difficult word and use the "thumbs up" button c. If others have stated difficult words that are not difficult for you, try to explain their meaning to your fellow students.	**Step 1: Read the task and see if there are any difficult words?** a. Check whether somebody else has already defined the difficult word(s) on Polaris. If not, state the difficult word in Polaris by clicking on "start new thread" Click on "start new thread" and start with difficult word in the subject line. For example, 'Nationalisation'. Afterwards, fill in the remaining text boxes so that others can understand why you chose this difficult word. b. Check whether you agree with the definition of the difficult word and use the "thumbs up" button c. If you do not agree with the definition given by others or if a fellow student has stated a difficult word that is not difficult for you, try to explain its meaning to your fellow students.
2. Define the problem	**Step 2: What are the main problems of the task according to you and check if somebody else has already defined these problems on Polaris?** a. If not, state the problem(s) in a question-type form (learning goals). b. If yes, see if you agree with the formulation of the learning goal(s).	**Step 2: What are the main problems of the task?** a. Check if somebody else has already defined these problems on Polaris. If not, state the new problem(s) in a question type form (learning goals). Click on "start new thread" and start with abbreviation LG in the subject line, followed by key terms of your learning goal. For example, 'LG: Why nationalisation OPEC disappointing?'. Afterwards, fill in the remaining text boxes so that others can understand why you chose this problem. For convenience, use for each learning goal a separate new thread. In this way, in the overview everyone can see the main questions raised. b. See if you agree with the formulation of the learning goal(s) and use the "thumbs up" button if you agree with learning goal. c. As soon as 3 or more of your fellow students have agreed with the formulation of the learning goal without that somebody else has rephrased the learning goal, you can proceed to step 3 for this particular learning goal.
3. Analyse the problem -Brainstorm -**Activate prior knowledge** -**Discuss** **4. Synthesise (arrange ideas)** **5. Define learning objectives**	**Step 3: Try to answer one (or more) learning goal(s):** a. By common sense, prior knowledge and/or experience b. Referring to (additional) literature c. Referring to the videos/animated graphs	**Step 3: Try to answer one (or more) learning goal(s) once Step 2c has been completed:** a. Using your prior experience/ knowledge b. By referring to the literature of Bade & Parkin (2006) c. By referring to other sources (internet, videos, graphs, etc)

continued on following page

Table 4. Continued

Traditional PBL 7-Jump	e-PBL 5-Jump	Optima 7-jump
		Step 4: Elaborate on the findings found in Step 3: a. Make a scheme by determining the main points and concepts mentioned at Step 3 MS Powerpoint is a helpful tool to link various ideas, concepts and theories together. For example, the question why nationalisation of OPEC was not as profitable as expected has not one unique answer. There are multiple concepts that explain the failure. By first visualising the main points, important relationships can be distinguished. b. State difficulties in question and answers given thus far At this point of the 7 JUMP, several answers and opinions have been given by yourself and your fellow students. However, most answers make assumptions that can be questioned. For example, your experience about a problem might be different than others, or you have read different articles which say the opposite as mentioned thus far. Bring these different points-of-view into the discussion. c. Give other examples By giving other examples and trying to explain how these different examples relate to the learning goal, important (general) concepts can be identified. For example, the problems faced by OPEC are not unique for OPEC. Dutch beer-brewers were recently accused of forming a cartel. However, the beer-brewers stated that the market was not conducive for cartels. In addition, many problems faced by OPEC are similar to problems faced by governments.
	Step 4: See if you agree with the answers of the learning goals: a. If not, state why you do not agree with the answer. b. If you partly disagree/agree, state what should be added to the answer to receive your complete approval. c. If yes, use the "thumbs up" button. d. If 3 or more students have agreed with the answer (without that anyone has disagreed), the learning goal is answered sufficiently and you can proceed with the remaining learning goals.	**Step 5: Do you agree with the answers of the learning goals?** a. If not, state why you do not agree with the answer. b. If you partly disagree/agree, state what should be added to the answer to receive your complete approval. c. If yes, use the "thumbs up" button. d. If 3 or more students have agreed with the answer (without that anyone has disagreed), the learning goal is answered sufficiently and you can proceed with the remaining learning goals.
		Step 6: Check whether all learning goals and questions are answered: a. If not, go back to step 3
6. Self-Study **7. Report back**	**Step 5: Try to summarize the main points of the entire discussion and see whether all learning goals and questions are answered:** a. If not, go back to step 3 b. If yes, close the discussion by making a short summary and continue with the next task.	**Step 7: Try to summarize the main points of the entire discussion and:** a. Make a short summary of the main points of the entire discussion b. If you partly disagree/agree, state what should be added to the answer to receive your complete approval. c. See if you agree the short summary given by others by using the "thumbs up" button.

Chapter 8
Coaching for Cognitive Presence:
A Model for Enhancing Online Discussions

David S. Stein
Ohio State University, USA

Constance E. Wanstreet
Ohio State University, USA

ABSTRACT

This chapter presents a coaching approach to promote higher-order discussion skills in synchronous chats. Combining the Community of Inquiry framework with elements of the Co-Active Coaching Model has resulted in a guide for coaching interventions and discussion outcomes. The approach separates the discussion process coach's role from that of the course instructor and complements the instructional work of the class. Learners have an opportunity to improve their performance in a voluntary advising relationship that promotes action, learning, and accountability.

INTRODUCTION

Greg: *Do you have enough [to draft the post], Bobby?*
Bobby: *Yeah, enough for a headache.*
Greg: *I was trying to summarize what we had.*
Bobby: *I am going to print this mess out and see.*
Greg: *OK, good luck, Bobby!*

Group discussion is at the heart of inquiry-based courses; and many online courses incorporate

text-based chats to represent a more authentic, real-time form of discussion than asynchronous communication (Curtis, 2004; Davidson-Shivers, Muilenburg, & Tanner, 2001; Hrastinski, 2006). However, as the above chat exchange between discussion summarizer Greg and moderator Bobby illustrates, not all learners have the skills to conduct chats efficiently, integrate ideas, and come to a shared group understanding of the issue under discussion (Wanstreet & Stein, 2011a). Greg and Bobby's exchange illustrates that group members are not sure what learning transpired during the

DOI: 10.4018/978-1-4666-2110-7.ch008

chat. It appears that Bobby has enough content to draft a posting to the entire class, but it is not clear that the group came to a shared understanding or demonstrated other evidence of higher-order learning related to the discussion questions. This resulted, as Bobby noted, in enough content to give him a headache without the aid of summary statements to guide his writing. As instructors, we want to reduce the headaches and help the group avoid a messy discussion experience.

Evidence suggests that learners can be helped to improve their higher-order thinking skills online through coaching (Averweg, 2010; Stein, Wanstreet, Slagle, & Trinko, 2011). This chapter will show how we incorporated the Community of Inquiry framework into a coaching model and provided coaching to an inquiry-based group. It will describe what shortcomings we observed in cognitive presence discussion skills, what we did to promote discussion skill development that fosters higher levels of cognitive presence, and what evidence of improvement we saw in the cognitive presence exhibited by the participants.

DISCUSSION IN COMMUNITIES OF INQUIRY

Academic discussion is not a natural way of conversing for most online learners. While the skills of academic discussion are difficult to learn in a face-to-face setting, the nature of communicating in mediated environments makes discussion a skill that needs practice and guidance from experts in small-group conversations (Wood & Smith, 2005; Hill, 1991). Bridges (1990) posits four essential characteristics for conversation to be called a discussion: learners must interact with one another and direct their messages to the group, listening must be evident in that responses should reflect the content of previous messages and be related to the direction of the talk, the talk is sequential and increasingly builds more complex ideas, and the talk is purposefully directed toward an increased

understanding of the issue. A true discussion must show evidence of assertions, use of evidence to support statements, interaction among the learners toward building an understanding of the issue, use of contradictions to test emerging ideas, and responses that invite participation (Bridges, 1990; Costa, 1990). A lack of knowledge about how to perform in a discussion context might impede the work and the learning of a team. Confusing interactions, conflict, and dysfunctional roles can hinder the quality of the learning experience (Bolton, 1999; Keyton, 1999).

True discussions are critical to the success of inquiry-based learning. In an inquiry-based course, it is the development of a reflective discussion that is under consideration. A reflective discussion is talk that promotes critical and creative thinking in which thoughts and feelings are exchanged among participants for the purpose of attaining a learning objective (Wilen, 1990). Critical thinking is at the heart of cognitive presence, one element of the Community of Inquiry framework, which provides guidance in designing and assessing inquiry-based discussions (Garrison, Anderson, & Archer, 2000).

COACHING IN EDUCATIONAL ENVIRONMENTS

Coaching with the intent of improving individual and team performance is becoming a feature of formal educational environments. Coaching is learner-centered, based on demonstrated needs arising from experiences in the field. Coaching in the educational environment is situated in a particular community of practice's values, actions, and experiences. A coach supports the ongoing efforts of individuals and teams to continually improve their practice and to achieve higher levels of performance (Bolton, 1999; Duncan & Stock, 2010; Tofade, 2010). An academic coach is a master practitioner who bases practice on the research in a particular field of study and who is skilled in the transfer of research-based practices and techniques to a particular learning environment (Sailors & Shanklin, 2010).

Coaching involves a helping skill in working with others. Coaches work with learners to set goals for improvement based on data obtained from listening, observing, reflective discussions, and documents. In an online environment, a coach might lurk in a discussion room watching interactions in the form of text comments; analyze the transcripts from a discussion board or chat room; count posts, including depth and sequencing; and/or work with learners on the feel of the learning space (Baker, Redfield, & Tonkin, 2006).

In an educational coaching environment, the coach does not take on the managerial role of evaluating performance. An academic coach, using metaphors from the life coaching processes, helps individuals attain their own performance goals (Hanley, 2010). It is the responsibility of the learners—those who are coached—to take action on the feedback and insights that arise from the coaching experience. Gill, Kostiw, and Stone (2010) refer to the idea of accountability as the "gradual release of responsibility" (p. 49). Insights derived from the coaching experience shift from the coach to the learner to the group being served. It becomes the responsibility of the individual or the team to embed and sustain the practices gained from the coaching experience.

Chang (2004) suggests that in the online environment, faculty are expected to perform multiple roles, including that of a coach. Yet it is possible and desirable to separate the roles, and other staff can support students as "social connectedness initiators and technical supporters" (Chang, 2004, p. 335). For example, Western Governors University assigns each student a mentor who supports and coaches the student throughout the academic experience. These coaches meet with the students on a weekly basis to provide assistance in setting academic goals, time management, and accessing and navigating learning resources. Weekly meetings are scheduled to discuss progress, identify

problems, and provide guidance (M. Lutz, personal communication, June 15, 2010).

Bolton (1999) suggests that faculty may not have the skills needed to serve as learning coaches and to help students attain higher levels of learning, especially in team environments. She argues that student frustration with team-based learning is a function of structured support and guidance from faculty. She states that faculty are there to teach the content and do not focus on the process of team functioning: "Someone else should be responsible for the process" (p. 235).

Lam (2010) coached students in giving and responding to feedback on English writing assignments. Students were either not skilled or were uncomfortable in providing critical and meaningful comments that would improve the quality of academic work performed by learners. By providing training in the commenting and feedback process in a workshop format, Lam found that teacher support rather than teacher interventions improved the quality and depth of the feedback provided. Context-sensitive and personalized assistance helped students take more initiative in managing their work. Coaching in the process was necessary to building student responsibility and accountability for their learning.

Tofade (2010) has applied the Co-Active Coaching Model (Whitworth, Kimsey-House, Kimsey-House, & Sandahl, 2007) to an academic setting for pharmacy students and new practitioners. The model is designed to generate action and learning, while holding those who are coached accountable for change (Whitworth et al., 2007). The following skills are among those needed for Co-Active Coaching: (1) develop a connection, (2) listen and communicate effectively; (3) keep the end goal in sight, (4) ask powerful or impactful questions, (5) build self-awareness and self-esteem, (6) recognize the whole life, (7) acknowledge efforts and accomplishments, (8) identify limiting beliefs, (9) hold learners accountable, (10) debrief learning, and (11) celebrate accomplishments (Tofade, 2010).

Coaches in academic institutions can be internal to the organization as peer coaches (Baker et al., 2006) or appointed at a district level as master teachers (Gill et al., 2010), or external to the organization as consultants (Kostin & Haeger, 2006). Regardless of the appointment of the coaches, there are tasks common to the process, including developing a professional relationship, using observed data to develop an improvement plan, having meaningful and focused conversations, and engaging in a long-term relationship with the learners (Gill et al., 2010; Kostin & Haeger, 2006). As Baker et al. (2006) discuss, the coach engages in a collaborative relationship in which the coach does not give direct advice but serves as a sounding board for the reflections, insights, and skills that emerge from the conversations about the meaning of the encounters. Coaching as a process is outside the boundaries of daily supervision and depends upon a receptive and voluntary participation. Coaching is grounded in the daily experiences and actions of the coached. To be successful, coaching is based on the practical problems encountered in the situation and continues until self-sufficiency is attained by those coached.

Coaching in academic environments is gaining favor as an approach to achieving higher levels of individual and group performance. The coaching role is provided as a value-added dimension to the daily work performed by the individual. The coach develops a helping rather than an evaluative relationship and works with the individual outside of the daily assignments. The coach provides an opportunity for informal learning. Most important, dialogue and guidance is provided within a specific task-based context. The coach is committed to working with the individual or team on an extended basis. Coaching is not disruptive to the daily work flow but is embedded in the observed performance of those coached.

Coaching is used to improve the quality of the thinking as displayed in a chat room or discussion space. Smith (2008) found in a study of student teachers who were participating in an online course that attempting to quantify the quality of an individual posting was at best difficult and time consuming and that it was not practical to try to provide each student with a grade for a series of content-related posts. Using a rubric to grade a discussion board was seen by the students as subjective given the criteria specified, such as relevance, importance, and critical assessment. We do note that in a study of discussion in a face-to-face environment, graded participation did not decrease participation or increase discomfort with the discussion approach to instruction (Dallimore, Hertenstein, & Platt, 2006).

Academic coaching is provided primarily in a face-to-face mode, while e-coaching is becoming an emerging form for working with professionals at a distance. Boyce and Hernez-Broome (2010) describe e-coaching as having three primary dimensions. Assessment, challenge, and support are tied together through electronic media to create a two-way, as-needed interactive form of performance improvement. A formal definition is provided as "a formal one-on-one relationship between a coach and client in which the client and coach collaborate using technology to asses and understand the client and his or her leadership development needs, to challenge current constraints while exploring new possibilities, and to ensure accountability and support for reaching goals and sustaining development" (p. 141). In an electronic mode, the functions of the coach do not change nor do the expectations for the coaching process. What does change is the timing of the encounters, which might be more convenient in that a just-as-needed approach to receiving information can be developed. A record of the interactions is preserved for later reference and thoughtful comments can be made in an asynchronous manner.

Online universities provide e-coaching for faculty development with the goal of improving online instruction (Dana, Havens, Hochanadel, & Phillips, 2010; Baker et al., 2006). Studies have focused on how learners converse in asynchronous environments (Song & McNary, 2011), and a variety of tools have been adopted for classifying the types of statements that reflect levels of learning and levels of thinking (DeWeaver, Schellens, Valcke, & Van Keer, 2006). Yet few studies have focused on how to provide synchronous online discussion improvement coaching to learners taking a credit course, and few tools have been developed to assist learners in this real-time environment. An emerging body of research suggests that synchronous chats seem to encourage more soliciting of ideas, responses, and information as compared to statements posted only on a discussion board (Stein et al., 2007). If online learning can increase learner self-direction and lead to higher levels of knowledge building, coaching might be able to help learners develop discussion skills adapted to a distance learning environment and develop a pattern of responding that will lead to higher levels of critical and reflective thought. This chapter presents a coaching approach adapted to the distance learning environment with the intent of improving synchronous discussion skills.

In light of the importance of coaching to achieve higher levels of academic performance, we have developed a coaching model that incorporates elements of the Co-Active Coaching Model and the Community of Inquiry framework. Within the CoI framework, learners are encouraged to moderate discussions as a way to build skills in critical thinking and critical reflection and to assume responsibility for individual and group learning. However, Garrison (2011) notes that student moderators should have guidance and support from the instructor to develop skills in content integration as well as moving a group toward resolution. As we considered other coaching models (DeWeaver et al., 2006) and ways of assessing discussion, we found Co-Active Coaching and CoI to be adaptable to identifying coaching tasks that support higher levels of cognitive presence. Our coaching cycle includes observation of chats, analysis of the chat dynamics, and electronic feedback to indicate what learners

have done well and what follow-up work would be required to improve the discussion outcomes. Our model separates the cognitive-performance coach's role from that of the course instructor and is complementary to the instructional work of the class. As acknowledged by Bolton (1999), coaching may not be comfortable for all faculty, especially when evaluation and grading are involved in the relationship. Separating the roles provides the learners with an opportunity to improve performance in a voluntary advising relationship. The coaching process, therefore, is separated from the assessment process.

Discussion Context

Our discussion-based course met in person at the beginning, middle, and end of the course. During the intervening weeks, learners conducted small-group discussions in online text-based chat spaces about issues related to adult learning in the United States. The outcome of the chat discussion was a group posting to the entire class that resolved the weekly issue.

Because multiple chats occurred simultaneously, the amount of time the instructor could be present in any one chat was limited. Therefore, developing discussion facilitation skills was critical to each group's ability to arrive at a resolution during the chat. Shea, Li, and Pickett (2006) report that students prefer directed facilitation from the instructor and may need to be coached in how to organize and facilitate discussions. This is particularly important in courses such as ours that feature learner-led discussions.

Two Types of Coaching

The course under study incorporated two types of coaching: (a) evolutionary, which incorporates reflective dialogue, and (b) functionalist, which is advice-driven (Brockbank, 2008). The instructor provided evolutionary coaching related to course content, and the researcher provided functionalist coaching related to the discussion process. Evolutionary coaching was offered during the group chats, while functionalist coaching was offered 24 hours before each chat. This chapter focuses on the results of the functionalist coaching, which is defined as the facilitation of learning and development by providing encouragement and direction with the purpose of improving learning performance (Bluckert, 2005; Brockbank, 2008; Murphy, Mahoney, Chen, Mendoza-Diaz, & Yang, 2005). Functionalist coaching in this study is task-based and provides deliberative and motivational support to enhance group learning performance (Averweg, 2010; Bluckert, 2005; Longnecker, 2010). While functionalist coaching is a broad concept, it is akin to teaching presence in that teaching presence shapes the transactions among the students and establishes the climate for learning to happen. Through teaching presence, learners become self-regulated and monitor how the exchanges are taking place. The actions are deliberate and serve to motivate and support group learning. Given these definitions, we propose that the indicators of teaching presence can be useful in implementing functionalist coaching.

To close the coaching cycle, feedback was provided within one hour after the chat ended. Feedback is defined as information about the gap between the group's performance and the reference level (Ramprasad, 1983). To be effective, feedback needs to be used by the group in subsequent chats to narrow the gap. Because coaching and feedback were delivered electronically, we have a record of what was said and whether the coaching advice and feedback were used by group members.

FUNCTIONALIST COACHING FRAMEWORK

We have used the Community of Inquiry model in our course design because it provides a framework for analyzing online discussions in terms of teaching presence, social presence, and cognitive presence (Garrison et al., 2000). Teaching presence involves course design and administration, discourse facilitation, and direct instruction. Social presence is the ability of learners to project their personal characteristics to others and coalesce as a group; and cognitive presence is associated with higher-order thinking that results from recognizing problems, exploring suggestions for consideration, integrating concepts, and developing a resolution to the issue under study (Garrison et al., 2000).

In addition to providing a framework with which to assess discussion outcomes, the Community of Inquiry model can serve as a guide for areas in which to provide coaching and subsequent feedback. In terms of the learner-led chats in our course, facilitating discourse in student-moderated sessions represents group responsibility for the conduct of the discussion and shared accountability for the success of the chat outcome (Wanstreet & Stein, 2011b). The teaching presence template describes a structure for building the space for cognitive presence (Anderson, Rourke, Archer, & Garrison, 2001). Coaching in how to facilitate discourse and provide direct instruction as well as to use time efficiently and observe proper netiquette (related to instructional design and organization) may be needed by students who have not experienced a collaborative learning environment.

Our coaching and feedback focused on teaching presence and social presence because they support cognitive presence (Anderson et al., 2001). Before the small-group coaching began, the instructor met in person with the class and provided direct instruction on the importance of setting norms and the roles of the discussants. He encouraged the class to name a moderator and summarizer before each chat. Table 1 shows the instructor's contribution to the discussion process before coaching in the context of small-group chats got under way.

The discussion-skill coaching process began in Week 3 with an observation of a baseline chat. Table 2 shows the categories of teaching and social presence and the type of coaching and

Table 1. Instructor preparation of learners for discussion groups

Week	Mode	Instructional Goal
1	Face-to-face	Role of discussants
2	Face-to-face	Organization of chats

feedback we provided. We based our coaching advice on the literature and on our experience in analyzing chat transcripts for evidence of the kind of dialogue that fosters cognitive presence. For example, group members who reacquaint themselves by sharing details of their personal and academic lives at the beginning of each discussion and orient themselves to the cognitive task by getting organized and stating the issues under study create a climate for group exploration that can lead to higher-order cognitive presence (Stein et al., 2007). Because not all learners have the skills to integrate other viewpoints, synthesize discussion, and reach resolution (Wanstreet & Stein, 2011a), we have provided guidance though coaching. Intermittent coaching in teaching presence helped increase organizational and facilitation skills but did not increase higher-order integration and resolution skills (Stein & Wanstreet, 2008). However, continuous coaching in teaching presence over time increased the level of cognitive presence (Stein et al., 2011). Specifically, in the category of instructional design and organization,

coaching focused on naming a moderator and summarizer for the following week so that undue time was not spent organizing the group each week. In terms of direct instruction, members were coached to summarize the discussion before moving on to the next part of the question so that thoughts could be integrated and synthesized. Regarding facilitating discourse, the group was coached to gain agreement that the response reflects the input of all group members so that all voices and perspectives would be heard.

In terms of social presence, we have found ample evidence of open communication in transcripts we have analyzed; i.e., simple agreement and risk-free expression (Rourke, Anderson, Garrison, & Archer, 1999; Garrison & Arbaugh, 2007) as well as affective expressions of emotion and humor. Therefore, we did not actively coach or provide feedback in those categories. In addition, we examined the transcripts for evidence of cohesive dialogue, such as greetings and use of "we," "our," and "us," which showed the learners working together and coalescing as a group.

Table 2. Community of inquiry elements used in coaching discussion skills

Elements	Categories	Coaching and Feedback
Teaching Presence[a]	Design and organization	Name moderator/summarizer; establish norms
	Facilitating discourse	Gain input from all; check for understanding
	Direct instruction	Present questions, refer to readings, summarize
Social Presence[b]	Open communication	(no direct coaching provided)
	Group cohesion	Use "we," "our," "us"
	Personal/affective	(no direct coaching provided)

[a]Anderson, Rourke, Archer, & Garrison (2001)
[b]Rourke, Anderson, Garrison, & Archer (1999), Garrison & Arbaugh (2007)

Coaching Timeline

As mentioned above, the class under study met in person for the first two weeks of the term. At Week 3, the coach began working with the group of learners randomly chosen for coaching by stating the voluntary nature of the coaching. Group members agreed to participate in coaching provided they could withdraw at any time. The coach analyzed the group's Week 3 chat, which was the initial online discussion, to determine the type of coaching that would be provided for the following week. Coaching began with relatively simple organizational skills, such as naming a moderator. As the course progressed, coaching encompassed more difficult skills, such as checking for understanding and summarizing perspectives. Coaching was provided via e-mail approximately 24 hours in advance of each online chat. Table 3

lists the coaching functions informed by the Co-Active Coaching Model and the coaching activities informed by the CoI framework that were provided each week. To close the coaching cycle, feedback was provided within an hour after the chat ended. Feedback assessed how well the group achieved the goals of the coaching and was also used to inform coaching for the following week's chat.

TEACHING PRESENCE COACHING IN PRACTICE

Coaching followed a progression from simple organizational tasks to more complex instructional tasks as the weeks passed. Organizational tasks included confirming the moderator and summarizer at the beginning of the chat for the current and following week. Because the moderator and

Table 3. Coaching functions and activities by week

Week	Mode	Co-Active Coaching Functions	Coaching Activities
3	Online	Develop a connection before the baseline chat; recognize the whole life; listen	Sent e-mail to group stating the voluntary nature of the coaching and the separation of coaching in discussion skills from the instructor's role. Set expectation that I would respect their time by presenting only a few suggestions each week. "Listened" to the chat by analyzing the group's transcript to inform the initial round of process coaching for Week 4.
4	Online	Communicate in a timely way about group organization and roles; identify limiting beliefs	Encouraged the group to name moderators and summarizers, to follow a convention that signals when their response is complete, and to summarize and check for understanding. Also addressed potential misconceptions about the confidentiality of participation in process coaching.
5	Online	Keep the goal in sight by assessing the efficacy of the process; debrief learning	Reinforced the guidance from Week 4 and added the suggestion to get input on every question.
6	Face-to-face	No coaching (Class met in person and engaged in large-group discussion.)	
7	Online	Build self-awareness; acknowledge efforts	Encouraged group to go beyond unsupported opinion by including examples from the readings and offering reasons why they agree or disagree with a comment; acknowledged moderator's success in facilitating dialogue.
8	Online	Ask impactful questions; hold learners accountable; keep the goal in sight by assessing the efficacy of the process	Questioned the apparent inability to achieve the integration and resolution phases of cognitive presence; offered guidance on how to present the discussion questions and summarize the group members' perspectives.
9	Online	Celebrate accomplishments	Noted the group's improvement in drawing on readings to support their arguments, checking for understanding, and facilitating dialogue.
10	Face-to-face	No coaching because class met in person and engaged in large-group discussion	

summarizer roles rotated among group members, taking time to establish which members would perform those duties reinforced the structure of the weekly meeting. Organizational tasks also included establishing norms to determine the status of individual responses; e.g., typing the word *end* to indicate the completion of a response.

Coaching in Group Organization

Organizational coaching was shared with all groups during the first two weeks of the course when they met in person. In addition, organizational coaching was reinforced before the Week 4 chat in an e-mail sent to the group under study:

Confirm who the moderator and summarizer are at the very beginning of the chat and decide on the next week's moderator and summarizer at that time. You did a nice job of this regarding the moderator [during the baseline chat at Week 3], so keep it going.

Consistently follow a convention that will signal where you are in your response. For example, Bobby and Marcia used ellipses (...) sometimes to signal when they weren't finished. When you are finished, you might try using "end" or some other convention. It cuts down on five people talking at once.

Feedback following the Week 4 chat reinforced what was done well; e.g., "Bobby jumped right in, using ellipses to indicate he was still typing his definition of useful knowledge." Feedback also addressed gaps in role performance:

I can't see that you actually addressed all of the questions, particularly, What is the role of non-formal and informal learning in our culture today? You'll all be moderators at one time or another, so you'll want to make your job easier by getting input on every question. Some people

cut and paste each question from Word into the chat as they move through the discussion.

The final organizational coaching occurred at Week 5. Group members were encouraged to confirm the moderator and summarizer at the beginning of the chat and to identify the following week's moderator and summarizer. The idea of using ellipses to indicate that a response was in progress and *end* to indicate that the response was complete was also reinforced. Feedback for Week 5 acknowledged that the group had successfully completed organizational tasks: "I hope it helps speed up the discussion process that you got your moderators and summarizers set for the next few weeks." For the remainder of the term, it was not necessary to provide coaching or feedback related to the organization of the chats.

Coaching in How to Facilitate Discourse

Ensuring that all group members have the opportunity to provide input on every question is a facilitation task. Facilitating discourse was introduced simply in the coaching for Week 5: "Get input on every question." For the remainder of the term, it was necessary to reinforce coaching in how to facilitate discourse. Guidance included, "Check for everyone's understanding of the summary statement before moving on to the next question" (Week 7) and "Moderator, give everyone a chance to participate in the discussion. By that I mean that if you haven't heard from someone in a while, ask if s/he has anything to add."

Coaching in Direct Instruction

Although process coaching initially focused on the more easily executed organizational tasks, a direct instruction task, summarizing, was introduced at Week 4:

Summarize where you are before moving on to the next question, and check for everyone's understanding.

Summarizing the discussion proved to be a challenge throughout the term. Coaching for Weeks 4, 5, 7, 8, and 9 encouraged the group to "summarize the discussion before moving on to the next question and check that everyone understands the summary." Feedback acknowledged good performance (e.g., "Peter, you provided two good summary statements while managing to contribute to the discussion. This takes a lot of cognitive effort.") or addressed gaps in performance:

I counted about three instances that looked like summary statements, which were supplemented by some of the other group members. It's good that the rest of you expanded on those statements. That should help Jan with the write-up....Going forward, the moderator can signal that it's time to move on or can ask where the group is headed regarding an answer, and then the summarizer can make his/her assessment. (Week 4)

There was no summary for the second question; so remember to provide one if that is your role because when you're the moderator, you'll appreciate it. (Week 7)

A second line of direct instruction coaching and feedback involved encouraging learners to bring in knowledge from other sources, such as the readings, to support their arguments. As was the case with summarizing, drawing on the readings for support proved to be a challenging task in the discussion process. It was not until the final chat of the term that those aspects of direct instruction came together:

It will be helpful for the moderator (and for your own critical thinking ability) if you bring in more specific references from your readings to

supplement your points. A statement that I would classify as exploratory/unsupported opinion (e.g., "Education has been used as a tool of oppression throughout history." Would move up a step on the critical inquiry ladder by having a citation attached to it. (Week 5)

There's still quite a bit of simple agreement; e.g., "I agree with X" without any follow-up as to why. Sometimes simple agreement is good, as in when you agree with the summary, for example. But during the discussion itself, you may have really good reasons for agreeing or disagreeing that could be useful in writing the discussion posting. (Week 7)

I can't tell that the reading came into play at all during your chat tonight....In reading the transcript, I see unsupported statements left and right. That makes it difficult to get to the integration stage, which is necessary before you get to the resolution state as a group. And that makes Bobby's job of drafting the posting very difficult. (Week 8)

Tonight I saw evidence of drawing on the readings and other sources to enhance your chat. I see that you summarized and checked for understanding before moving on to the next question. Thank you. (Week 9)

A content analysis of transcripts from this group that received coaching and another group that did not receive coaching found a change over time for cognitive presence between the groups. The coached group produced a statistically significant higher frequency of cognitive presence than the control group and, with more integrative statements than the control group, had more evidence of higher-order thinking at the end of the term (Stein et al., 2011). The simple organizational tasks involved in teaching presence coaching were easily adopted by group members. More complex instructional tasks, such as facilitating dialogue, integrating readings and other sources of knowledge into the discussion, and summarizing the group's position took repetition over time to have an effect.

FUTURE RESEARCH DIRECTIONS

Sailors and Shanklin (2010), reviewing empirical studies on the effects of coaching, suggest that a coaching approach is effective in promoting greater learning gains among the students taught by elementary school teachers who have been coached as compared to those teachers who have engaged in other forms of professional development or who have not been coached. How coaching might be further applied to the online higher education classroom is a new area for research (Dana et al., 2010).

After reflecting on the coach's actions, we inductively built the Co-Active, CoI Coaching Model and came to understand it from a systems perspective (see Figure 1). Empirically testing how this model works in other discussion settings, with cohort and non-cohort groups, and in a typical adult education program with part-time students would shed light on how well it explains the coaching process and promotes gains in discussion skills. In addition, research into how much coaching is enough to sustain the gains requires more attention as does inquiry into whether the gains in discussion skills transfer to other discussion settings.

Figure 1. The co-active coaching model and the community of inquiry as a combined coaching system

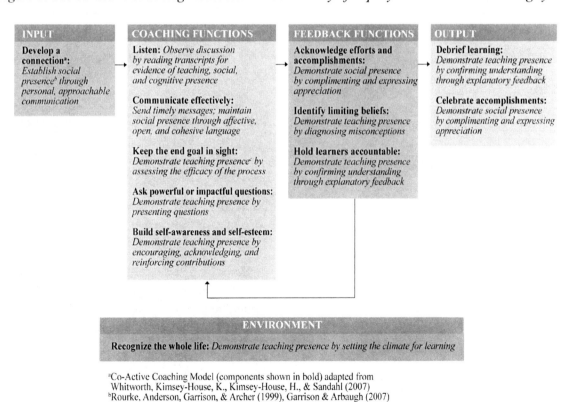

INPUT	COACHING FUNCTIONS	FEEDBACK FUNCTIONS	OUTPUT
Develop a connection[a]: *Establish social presence[b] through personal, approachable communication*	**Listen:** *Observe discussion by reading transcripts for evidence of teaching, social, and cognitive presence* **Communicate effectively:** *Send timely messages; maintain social presence through affective, open, and cohesive language* **Keep the end goal in sight:** *Demonstrate teaching presence[c] by assessing the efficacy of the process* **Ask powerful or impactful questions:** *Demonstrate teaching presence by presenting questions* **Build self-awareness and self-esteem:** *Demonstrate teaching presence by encouraging, acknowledging, and reinforcing contributions*	**Acknowledge efforts and accomplishments:** *Demonstrate social presence by complimenting and expressing appreciation* **Identify limiting beliefs:** *Demonstrate teaching presence by diagnosing misconceptions* **Hold learners accountable:** *Demonstrate teaching presence by confirming understanding through explanatory feedback*	**Debrief learning:** *Demonstrate teaching presence by confirming understanding through explanatory feedback* **Celebrate accomplishments:** *Demonstrate social presence by complimenting and expressing appreciation*

ENVIRONMENT

Recognize the whole life: *Demonstrate teaching presence by setting the climate for learning*

[a]Co-Active Coaching Model (components shown in bold) adapted from Whitworth, Kimsey-House, K., Kimsey-House, H., & Sandahl (2007)
[b]Rourke, Anderson, Garrison, & Archer (1999), Garrison & Arbaugh (2007)
[c]Anderson, Rourke, Archer, & Garrison (2001)

CONCLUSION

Coaching to develop higher-order thinking during online discussions can be conceptualized in terms of a system working over time. The Community of Inquiry framework, in concert with the Co-Active Coaching Model can be used as a way to guide coaching interventions and provide guidance on what actions a coach can take and what discussion outcomes the coach is seeking. The CoI framework helps frame the observations by illustrating how to examine transcripts for evidence of enhanced cognitive presence.

Continuous coaching, even of limited duration, improves cognitive presence discussion skills. However, higher-order thinking skills are more difficult to coach because they take longer to develop. In order to provide a safe place for this skill development, the roles of coach and instructor should be separate.

REFERENCES

Anderson, T., Rourke, L., Archer, W., & Garrison, R. (2001). Assessing teaching presence in computer conferencing transcripts. *Journal of Asynchronous Learning Networks, 5*(2). Retrieved from http://www.aln.org/publications,jaln/v5n2/v5n2_anderson

Averweg, U. R. (2010). Enabling role of an intranet to augment e-coaching. *Industrial and Commercial Training, 42*(1), 47–52.

Baker, J., Redfield, K., & Tonkin, S. (2006). Collaborative coaching and networking for online instructors. *Online Journal of Distance Learning Administration, 9*(4). Retrieved from www.westga.edu/~distance/ojdla/winter94/baker94.htm

Bluckert, P. (2005). The foundations of a psychological approach to executive coaching. *Industrial and Commercial Training, 37*(4), 171–178.

Bolton, M. (1999). The role of coaching in student teams: A just-in-time approach to learning. *Journal of Management Education, 23*(3), 233–250.

Boyce, L. A., & Hernez-Broome, G. (2010). E-coaching: Consideration of leadership coaching in a virtual environment. In Clutterbuck, D., & Hussain, Z. (Eds.), *Virtual coach, virtual mentor* (pp. 139–174). Charlotte, NC: Information Age Publishing.

Bridges, D. (1990). The character of discussion: A focus on students. In Wilen, W. (Ed.), *Teaching and learning through discussion: The theory, research and practice of the discussion method* (pp. 97–112). Springfield, IL: Charles Thomas Publishers.

Brockbank, A. (2008). Is the coaching fit for purpose? A typology of coaching and learning approaches. *Coaching: An International Journal of Theory. Research and Practice, 1*(2), 132–144.

Chang, S. (2004). The roles of mentors in electronic learning environments. *AACE Journal, 12*(3), 331–342.

Costa, A. (1990). Teacher behaviors that promote discussion. In Wilen, W. (Ed.), *Teaching and learning through discussion: The theory, research and practice of the discussion method* (pp. 45–77). Springfield, IL: Charles Thomas Publishers.

Curtis, R. (2004). Analyzing students' conversations in chat room discussion groups. *College Teaching, 52*(4), 143–148.

Dallimore, E., Hertenstein, J., & Platt, M. (2006). Nonvoluntary class participation in graduate discussion courses: Effects of grading and cold calling. *Journal of Management Education, 30*(2), 354–377.

Dana, H., Havens, B., Hochanadel, C., & Phillips, J. (2010). An innovative approach to faculty coaching. *Contemporary Issues in Education Research, 3*(11), 29–34.

Davidson-Shivers, G. V., Muilenburg, L. Y., & Tanner, E. J. (2001). How do students participate in synchronous and asynchronous online discussions? *Journal of Educational Computing Research, 25*(4), 351–366.

DeWeaver, B., Schellens, T., Valcke, M., & Van Keer, H. (2006). Content analysis schemes to analyze transcripts of online asynchronous discussion groups: A review. *Computers & Education, 46*(1), 6–28.

Duncan, H. E., & Stock, M. J. (2010). Mentoring and coaching rural school leaders: What do they need? *Mentoring & Tutoring: Partnership in Learning, 18*(3), 293–311.

Garrison, D. R. (2011). *E-learning in the 21st century: A framework for research and practice* (2nd ed.). London, UK: Routledge/Taylor and Francis.

Garrison, D. R., Anderson, T., & Archer, W. (2000). Critical inquiry in a text-based environment: Computer conferencing in higher education. *The Internet and Higher Education, 2*(2-3), 87–105.

Garrison, D. R., & Arbaugh, J. B. (2007). Researching the community of inquiry framework: Review, issues, and future directions. *The Internet and Higher Education, 19*(3), 157–172.

Gill, J., Kostiw, N., & Stone, S. (2010). Coaching teachers in effective instruction: A Victorian perspective. *Literacy Learning: The Middle Years, 18*(2), 49–53.

Hanley, S. (2010). A sports metaphor in career coaching. *Career Planning and Adult Development Journal, 26*(1), 96–100.

Hill, W. F. (1991). *Learning thru discussion* (2nd ed.). Newbury Park, CA: Sage.

Hrastinski, S. (2006). Introducing an informal synchronous medium in a distance learning course: How is participation affected? *The Internet and Higher Education, 9*(2), 117–131.

Keyton, J. (1999). Analyzing interaction patterns in dysfunctional teams. *Small Group Research, 30*(4), 491–518.

Kostin, M., & Haeger, M. (2006). Coaching schools to sustain improvement. *Education Digest, 71*(9), 29–33.

Lam, R. (2010). A peer review training workshop: Coaching students to give and evaluate peer feedback. *TSEL Canada Journal/Revue TESL du Canada, 27*(2), 114–127.

Longnecker, C. O. (2010). Coaching for better results: Key practices of high performance leaders. *Industrial and Commercial Training, 42*(1), 32–40.

Murphy, K. L., Mahoney, S. E., Chen, C.-Y., Mendoza-Diaz, N. V., & Yang, X. (2005). A constructivist model of mentoring, coaching, and facilitating online discussions. *Distance Education, 26*(3), 341–366.

Ramprasad, A. (1983). On the definition of feedback. *Behavioral Science, 28*, 4–13.

Rourke, L., Anderson, T., Garrison, R., & Archer, W. (1999). Assessing social presence in asynchronous text-based, computer conferencing. *Journal of Distance Education, 14*(2), 50–71.

Sailors, M., & Shanklin, N. L. (2010). Growing evidence to support coaching in literacy and mathematics. *The Elementary School Journal, 111*(1), 1–6.

Shea, P. J., Li, C. S., & Pickett, A. (2006). A study of teaching presence and student sense of learning community in fully online and web-enhanced college courses. *The Internet and Higher Education, 9*(3), 175–190.

Smith, H. (2008). Assessing student contributions to online discussion boards. *Practitioner Research in Higher Education, 2*(1), 22–28.

Song, L., & McNary, S. (2011). Understanding students' online interaction: Analysis of discussion board postings. *Journal of Interactive Online Learning*, *1*(1), 1–13. Retrieved from www.ncolr.org/jiol

Stein, D. S., & Wanstreet, C. E. (2008, August). Effects of coaching on cognitive presence in communities of inquiry. *Proceedings of the 24th Annual Conference on Distance Teaching and Learning*, Madison, WI.

Stein, D. S., Wanstreet, C. E., Glazer, H. R., Engle, C. E., Harris, R. A., & Johnston, S. M. (2007). Creating shared understanding through chats in a community of inquiry. *The Internet and Higher Education*, *10*(2), 103–115.

Stein, D. S., Wanstreet, C. E., Slagle, P., & Trinko, L. A. (2011, August). E-coaching and feedback practices to promote higher order thinking online. *Proceedings of the 27th Annual Conference on Distance Teaching and Learning*, Madison, WI.

Tofade, T. (2010). Coaching younger practitioners and students using components of the co-active coaching model. *American Journal of Pharmaceutical Education*, *74*(3), 51.

Wanstreet, C. E., & Stein, D. S. (2011a). Presence over time in synchronous communities of inquiry. *American Journal of Distance Education*, *25*(3), 1–16.

Wanstreet, C. E., & Stein, D. S. (2011b). Gender and collaborative knowledge building in an online community of inquiry. In Wang, V. C. X. (Ed.), *Encyclopedia of information communication technologies and adult education integration* (pp. 707–722). Hershey, PA: IGI Global.

Whitworth, L., Kimsey-House, K., Kimsey-House, H., & Sandahl, P. (2007). *Co-active coaching: New skills for coaching people toward success in work and life* (2nd ed.). Palo Alto, CA: Davies-Black Publishing.

Wilen, W. (1990). Forms and phases of discussion. In Wilen, W. (Ed.), *Teaching and learning through discussion: The theory, research and practice of the discussion method* (pp. 3–24). Springfield, IL: Charles Thomas Publishers.

Wood, A., & Smith, M. (2005). *Online communication: Linking technology, identity, and culture* (2nd ed.). Mahwah, NJ: Lawrence Erlbaum Associates.

ADDITIONAL READING

Brown, S. W., & Grant, A. M. (2010). From GROW to GROUP: Theoretical issues and a practical model for group coaching in organisations. *Coaching: An International Journal of Theory. Research and Practice*, *3*(1), 30–45.

Collins, A., Brown, J. S., & Holum, A. (1991). Cognitive apprenticeship: Making things visible. *American Educator*, *15*(3), 6–11, 38–46.

Gilbert, K., & Rosinski, P. (2008). Accessing cultural orientations: The online cultural orientations framework assessment as a tool for coaching. *Coaching: An International Journal of Theory. Research and Practice*, *1*(1), 81–92.

Hackman, J. R., & Wageman, R. (2005). A theory of team coaching. *Academy of Management Review*, *30*(2), 269–287.

Hernez-Broome, G., Boyce, L. A., & Whyman, W. (2007). Critical issues of coaching with technology. In L. A. Boyce & G. Hernez-Broome (Eds.), *E-coaching: Supporting leadership coaching with technology*. Symposium conducted at the 22nd Annual Conference of the Society for Industrial and Organizational Psychology, New York, NY.

Longnecker, C. O. (2010). Coaching for better results: Key practices of high performance leaders. *Industrial and Commercial Training*, *42*(1), 32–40.

Thalluri, J., Kokkinn, B., & O'Flaherty, J. (2008). A student coaching scheme for first year university students: Positive learning experiences and individual success in biosciences. *The International Journal of Learning, 15*(9), 135–144.

Tripp, A. (2008). Closing the distance: Success coaching for online education goes mainstream. *Distance Learning, 5*(1), 37–42.

KEY TERMS AND DEFINITIONS

Chat: Text-based tool for conducting synchronous discussions.

Coach: A resource who offers suggestions, observations, and insights to individual teams on an as-needed, just-in-time basis (Bolton, 1999).

Coaching: The facilitation of learning and development by providing encouragement and direction with the purpose of improving learning performance (Bluckert, 2005; Brockbank, 2008; Murphy, Mahoney, Chen, Mendoza-Diaz, & Yang, 2005).

E-Coaching: Coaching delivered electronically.

Evolutionary Coaching: A teaching strategy that incorporates reflective dialogue (Brockbank, 2008).

Functionalist Coaching: An advice-driven teaching strategy (Brockbank, 2008).

Process Coaching: Directives on ways to engage in a text-based chat to promote efficiency in achieving higher-order thinking.

Chapter 9
Strategies and Principles to Develop Cognitive Presence in Online Discussions

Kim A. Hosler
University of Northern Colorado, USA

Bridget D. Arend
University of Denver, USA

ABSTRACT

The chapter is designed to provide online instructors with strategies and techniques for fostering greater cognitive presence in asynchronous online discussion forums. Online discussions, moderated and facilitated by instructors and students, are a staple in online learning environments and provide powerful mechanisms for engaging students in dialogue. However, oftentimes dialogues stall out at the initial inquiry stage, and deeper, critical thinking is neglected. Realizing the foundational nature of discussion forum activities, the authors present ways in which instructors can nurture cognitive presence and foster deeper lines of thinking in online discussions. The chapter outlines the four stages of cognitive presence while offering strategies and question prompts to engender cognitive presence in online discussions. A quick reference guide is included as a discussion aid, suggesting ways to recognize the stages of cognitive presence as well as providing question prompts for engendering greater cognitive presence and critical thinking.

INTRODUCTION

Discussion forums provide a foundational activity for online and blended courses, but many online instructors struggle with the challenges and time commitment of facilitating online discussions, and seek strategies and techniques that foster greater cognitive presence. The concept of cognitive presence emerges from The Community of Inquiry framework. This theoretical framework, originally put forth by Garrison, Anderson, and Archer (2000), offers lenses through which researchers and practitioners can examine various aspects of online and blended teaching and learn-

DOI: 10.4018/978-1-4666-2110-7.ch009

ing, which utilize both face to face instruction as well as online or computer mediated instruction and activities. The original intent of the Community of Inquiry (CoI) framework was to guide the use of online learning environments in support of critical thinking in higher education (Rourke, Anderson, Garrison, & Archer, 2001). A central tenet of this model is that online learners form a community which has the ability to engage collectively in worthwhile and meaningful activities and discourse, in turn creating deeper and more meaningful learning experiences. Garrison, Anderson, and Archer's (2000) model offers three interdependent and overlapping constructs which support and inform online and blended learning practices and pedagogy. Those constructs are social presence, teaching presence, and cognitive presence.

The concept of presence is not new and in the context of blended and online learning environments it generally refers to a sense of being there and available, although the learning environment is virtual. Lombard and Ditton (1997) described presence as the illusion that a mediated experience is not really mediated. Non-mediation according to the authors, provides an "illusion" that the communication medium is not present in a learner's communication environment and that this illusion causes the learner to respond as if the medium or manmade technology was not present (Concept Explication section, para. Presence Explicated). Riva (2009) described presence as a "core neuropsychological phenomenon whose goal is to produce a sense of agency and control" in an environment that supports users and their intentions (p. 159). Online presence in essence refers to one's ability, whether student or instructor, to project a human sensitivity, warmth, and intimacy into an otherwise computer mediated environment, void of the tonal, visual and verbal cues found in the traditional classroom.

Social presence is defined as "... the means by which online participants inhabit virtual spaces and indicate not only their presence in the online environment but also their availability and willingness to engage in the communicative exchanges which constitute learning activity in these environments" (Kehrwald, 2008, p. 94). Garrison et al. (2000) describe social presence as the ability to project oneself as a real person (one's full personality) both socially and emotionally in the online environment. The categories of social presence, as defined by Garrison and Arbaugh (2007) are affective expression, open communication, and group cohesion. Teaching presence as defined by Anderson, Rourke, Garrison, and Archer (2001) is "...the design, facilitation, and direction of cognitive and social processes for the purpose of realizing personally meaningful and educationally worthwhile learning outcomes" (p. 5). Based on this definition, the authors distill three components or elements of teaching presence: instructional design and organization, facilitating discourse, and direct instruction. The third construct of the Community of Inquiry framework is cognitive presence. This chapter explores cognitive presence in detail; what it is, what it offers as a way of critical thinking, and how to engender more of it in the online learning environment.

COGNITIVE PRESENCE

Cognitive presence is defined as "the extent to which learners are able to construct and confirm meaning through sustained reflection and discourse in a critical community of inquiry" (Garrison, Anderson, & Archer, 2001, p. 11). Garrison et al. (2001) elaborated on this definition by stating it is the exploration, construction, resolution, and confirmation of understanding through collaboration and reflection in a community of inquiry. Cognitive presence, grounded in critical thinking (Garrison, et al., 2001; Garrison, Anderson, & Archer, 2004), offers a hierarchical scheme for examining students' thinking processes and ability to achieve richer levels of learning. Kanuka and Garrison (2004) argued that cognitive presence is necessary for higher learning or critical thinking, and according to Shea and Bidjerano (2009), "This focus on critical thinking as a foundation for the model is consistent with current conception of the role of higher education vis-a-vis student learning" (p. 545).

The scheme of cognitive presence, operationalized within the Practical Inquiry Model (Darabi, Arrastia, Nelson, Cornille, & Liang, 2011; Garrison, 2011; Garrison, Anderson, & Archer, 2000) includes four stages: triggering events, exploration, integration, and resolution. Figure 1 illustrates the Practical Inquiry Model as originally conceived by Garrison, et al. (2000).

The triggering event, such as a probing question, problem, event, or dilemma may serve as a vehicle for launching online discussion postings. The triggering event may come from a student or the instructor and should engender a sense of puzzlement and curiosity within the online discussion relative to the content being studied. During the second stage, exploration, students begin to

understand the problem and then move towards a more detailed investigation of relevant information. A contradiction of ideas, personal narratives, unsubstantiated opinions, and descriptions are some of the overt indicators of this stage (Garrison, et al., 2001). Collison, Elbaum, Haavind, and Tinker (2000) referred to this loosely formed, surface type of discussion as "wallowing in the shallows," meaning opportunities for deeper thinking have been missed or ignored (p. 18). Collison et al. (2000) urged movement towards more relevant and deeper course-content related discussions; what they called "reasoned discourse" (p. 18). The third and fourth stages of cognitive presence attempt to move dialogue into the realm of greater examination and critical thinking.

Integration and resolution are the third and fourth stages of cognitive presence respectively. During integration, meaning making takes place; meaning generated from the ideas investigated in the exploration stage. Integration is evident by the application of ideas in terms of how well learners

Figure 1. The practical inquiry model (Reprinted from "Critical Inquiry in a Text-Based Environment: Computer Conferencing in Higher Education," by D.R. Garrison, T. Anderson, and W. Archer, 2000. The Internet and Higher Education, 2, p. 99. Copyright 2000 by Elsevier Science Inc. Reprinted with permission)

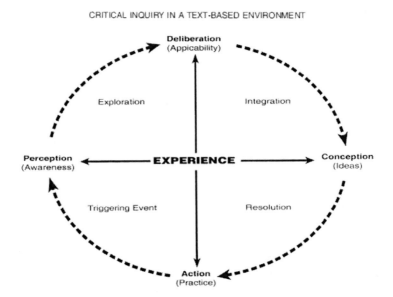

connect to and describe the issue, the problem, or the event under consideration (Garrison, et al., 2001). The last stage of cognitive presence is resolution, representing the most difficult stage to achieve as it involves working out the problem or dilemma by means of direct or vicarious action (Garrison, et al., 2001). Resolution can be achieved through the testing and examination of possible solutions or hypotheses through real-world applications and subsequent observations. Resolution may appear as consensus building within the online learning community based on sound evidence and the absence of conjecture and unsupported opinion.

Although the stages of cognitive presence may not necessarily progress in this order, and have been found to be non-linear (Stein, Wanstreet, Glazer, Engle, Harris, Johnston, Simons, & Trinko, 2007), the objective for instructors is to move the conversation along, fostering deeper levels of thinking, reflection, and critical inquiry in an iterative fashion among the four stages. When asked, most online instructors are quick to point out that managing online discussion forums is a challenging endeavor. They often wonder if they are participating too much and providing too many comments, or if they are not present enough, leaving students to wonder if anyone is paying attention to their postings. Instructors are concerned with the amount of time involved in managing online discussions, and yearn for a guiding strategy in order to make the best use of their limited time. More importantly, many online faculty and instructors struggle with creating meaningful introductory and follow-up discussion questions. There is a need to develop discussion questions that drive to deeper levels of critical thinking and cognitive processing and that foster dialogue which moves beyond the exploration stage of cognitive presence.

Critical Thinking, Metacognition, and Cognitive Presence

Cognitive presence is an unfamiliar concept to some and is often used interchangeably with critical thinking, a broad and ambiguous term in itself. Critical thinking has been conceptualized and defined numerous different ways, and these definitions often differ based on the discipline of origin. Some scholars conceptualize critical thinking as a distinction between lower and higher order thinking. Lower order thinking focuses on memorization or rote learning, such as the knowledge and comprehension levels of Bloom's taxonomy (Bloom, 1956). Higher order thinking skills, such as Bloom's taxonomy of analysis, synthesis, and evaluation levels, are often collapsed under the general term of critical thinking. In a similar way, the conceptualization of learning strategies distinguishes between surface and deep approaches to learning and has similarly broken down student thinking into simple strategies such as rehearsal and repetition, and more complex strategies such as critical thinking. Within the learning strategies taxonomy, critical thinking is defined generally as the extent to which students develop new ways of thinking about course content (McKeachie, Pintrich, Lin, & Smith, 1986).

These represent broad conceptualizations of critical thinking and other researchers have crafted more specific definitions. Scriven and Paul (2008) define critical thinking as "that mode of thinking--about any subject, content, or problem--in which the thinker improves the quality of his or her thinking by skillfully taking charge of the structures inherent in thinking and imposing intellectual standards upon them" (para. 9). Brookfield (1987) defines critical thinking as a process that involves students "in recognizing and researching the assumptions that undergird their thoughts and actions" (p. 17). Moon (2008) defined critical thinking in terms of an activity, involving the assessment of evidence so that one may make a judgment after deep engagement with the subject matter. What many of these more specific definitions of critical thinking have in common is an awareness of one's own thinking, and an ongoing effort to improve one's thinking skills based on intellectual standards.

These definitions show strong overlap with the concept of metacognition. Akyol and Garrison (2011a) defined metacognition in an online learning community as "the set of higher knowledge and skills to monitor and regulate manifest cognitive processes of self and others" (p. 184). They describe three aspects of metacognition; knowledge of cognition, monitoring of cognition, and regulation of cognition. These three aspects support and further clarify the two aspects of awareness and active monitoring of thinking that are inherent in the definitions of critical thinking. Cognitive presence can be viewed as an applied form of critical thinking and metacognition. Cognitive presence, operationalized through the four stages of the Practical Inquiry model, provides a structure upon which to reflect and encourage development of analytical thought. Both critical thinking and metacognition embody the action-reflection axis of the Practical Inquiry model (see Figure 1). It is this intersection, between private reflection and public discourse, where critical inquiry and reflective thought occur.

Encouraging Cognitive Presence

Online interaction and discussion by themselves do not lead to critical thinking or metacognition. Rather, it is a progression of thinking through the four stages of cognitive presence, and the awareness and monitoring of this thinking, that reflects a quality of discourse comparable to critical thinking. Critical thinking is an ongoing process that requires continual support and multiple opportunities for practice (King & Kitchener, 1994; Lynch & Wolcott, 2001). Metacognition also benefits from feedback and practice (Akyol & Garrison, 2011a). Similarly, the cyclical process of cognitive presence involves ongoing reflection and the support of an effective facilitator who provides opportunities to develop awareness of complex problems and to practice drawing conclusions and judgments about them.

Although this chapter focuses on cognitive presence, it is important to note the integrated nature of the three constructs of the Community of Inquiry framework. Cognitive presence occurs in conjunction with social presence and teaching presence, and many aspects of these constructs bear consideration when discussing strategies to encourage cognitive presence. Social presence aspects of creating a supportive online community and ensuring that all students participate are underlying conditions of creating cognitive presence. Several studies have indicated that in order to achieve higher levels of learning and deeper thinking, strong teaching presence is necessary (Garrison & Cleveland-Innes, 2005; Garrison, Cleveland-Innes, & Fung, 2010; Kanuka & Garrison, 2004; Shea & Bidjerano, 2009). However, it appears that teaching presence may be more important than social presence in eliciting higher levels of cognitive presence (Garrison & Cleveland-Innes, 2005). Aspects of teaching presence such as setting discussion guidelines and norms, modeling discussions posts, providing formative feedback about students' participation, and most importantly structuring and guiding discussions contribute to critical and reflective discourse in both online as well as face-to-face communities. Without such guidance, discussions are apt to remain "serial monologues" rather than integrated and collaborative discussions (Chang, Paulus, Pawan, & Yalcin, 2003). The remainder of this chapter is dedicated to providing further details, strategies, examples, and question prompts to help instructors engender and develop students' critical thinking skills; skills evolving through the four stages of cognitive presence; triggering events, exploration, integration, and resolution.

Triggering Events

In order to provide a triggering event that serves as a worthwhile catalyst for discussions, instructors need to consider posing probing questions, or presenting a problem or a dilemma to jump-start a discussion. The nature of this opening problem or question needs to invite curiosity, elicit interest, and encourage differing perspectives. When formulating triggering events, it is incumbent upon faculty and instructors to design engaging questions or role plays, or even foster dissonance and unease (Kanuka & Garrison, 2004) in order to ignite sparks of curiosity signaling initial dialogic engagement. Good questions form the basis of critical inquiry but creating thought provoking and stimulating questions takes time, reflection, and practice. As Walker (2003) wrote, "Questions are only as good as the thought put into them and should go beyond knowledge-level recall" (p. 264). Good questions derived from salient content can trigger thoughtful investigations beginning with queries such as, "why do you think such and such is", or "what would the impact be" or "imagine if" or "what are the consequences" to name a few.

Bender (2003) suggested making questions evaluative, such as "what do you think is more effective" or "which of these options is most efficient" (pp. 69-70). Using questions that support students making comparisons, highlighting contrasts, or making predications (e.g. "what do you think will happen if") can serve to invite students into more meaningful dialogue. The main consideration when forming questions as triggering events is to avoid questions that can be answered simplistically in one or two words or that have one 'right' answer.

Another strategy for engaging students in online discussions initially is to create a scenario or ill-structured problem as a triggering event for which students need to find viable solutions. By providing an intriguing problem, dilemma, or situation, instructors can pique curiosity and evoke a questioning mentality with a story-line, scenario, or background information that results in question generation. For example, in an online introductory instructional design course, students could be presented with a scenario involving a new instructional designer's first assignment on the job. The students could be tasked with providing advice and guidance to this fictitious designer to help her with her first instructional design project. According to Brookfield (2006a) scenario analysis helps place the learner into a situation where he or she is the main character trying "to uncover the implicit and explicit assumptions the actor is operating under, to assess how these assumptions might be checked, and to come up with plausible alternative interpretations of the scenario" (p. 15). It is the presentation of an initial scene that draws the learner in, thereby acting as a trigger to begin further inquiry. As the scenario develops, additional discussion and questioning can encourage students to explore the situation further, looking for ways to integrate what they know with what is occurring in the scenario as well as striving to reach resolution, which in this case would be vicariously testing the guidance offered.

At this point, students may have questions for the characters in the scenario such that these new questions provide additional triggering events leading to other avenues of exploration, integration and potential resolution. Questions such as "why did you do that" or "can you clarify that remark" or "how do you think this guideline will help the designer" all serve as triggering events that can lead to deeper levels of thinking or take the discussion into new directions.

Another triggering event is a well-planned activity such as an online debate regarding a specific topic. Debating is one of many skills attributed to critical thinking (Felton, 2005). For example, the instructor can establish small virtual groups to take opposing views on a content-related topic. According to Felton (2005), debating and questioning combine skills of justification, skepticism, and impartial judgment. He advised that instructors focus on inconclusive and informal arguments when encouraging students to engage in argumentation or debate. Setting up debate teams as a way of initially engaging students in online discussions provides not only a triggering event but also prompts for further questioning which supports movement into deeper stages of cognitive presence. As the debate deepens, it can lead directly to exploration and integration. After all, one can assess an argument's integrity by asking and answering questions (Felton, 2005).

In both of these examples of triggering events, a dilemma-based scenario, or a debate, the instructor can continue to guide and shape the triggering events thereby moving the dialogue into deeper levels of processing, reflection and critical thinking. The trigger, whether it is a question, scenario, or dilemma needs to be structured such that is partially inconclusive and prompts additional questions, curiosity and exploratory inquiry.

Exploration

The next stage in the cognitive presence framework is exploration. Exploration occurs when students begin to understand the nature of the problem and begin to search for relevant information and possible explanations. Students may begin to start brainstorming ideas, and to exchange resources or examples that relate to the topic. Many students will begin sharing their rationale, ideas, and conclusions about the question, or dilemma; but in the exploration stage, these conclusions are primarily based on personal experience or are otherwise unsupported by extensive information. The exploration stage is where students thoroughly examine the question at hand before moving on to more supported explanations. This stage is similar to what Collision et al. (2000) call "sharpening the focus" in online discussions (p. 129).

Most good triggering questions, dilemmas, or scenarios will naturally open the path to exploration, and many students will be able to enter this stage more readily than with other stages. Teach-

ing presence in the exploration stage is concerned with ensuring active and equal participation in the discussions and using facilitation techniques to keep students' energy and effort directed towards exploring the topic. In exploration, the instructor manages the sequence, flow and distribution of the online discussions. Issues of time, frequency of instructor participation, asking the right types of questions, and using the role of facilitator wisely, can push the discussion into deeper forms of exploration.

In the classroom, there has been considerable research about "wait time" between instructor questions and student responses (Duell, 1994; Tobin, 1987). Instructors are often advised to wait at least three seconds after asking a question, and longer for higher level questions, before making further comments. In an asynchronous online discussion, wait time can be seen in terms of days rather than seconds, and this time is conducive to the need for reflection in cognitive presence (Garrison, 2003). A facilitator might want to wait a day or two before responding to a student comment, allowing time for other students to share their ideas and thoughts and setting the precedent that the instructor is not the sole authority figure or the only one with relevant knowledge.

Similarly, the instructor should refrain from responding to every student's post or jumping in to answer every question or thought. In fact, doing so can actually be counterproductive. Students should be allowed time to explore many options before the instructor steps in to assimilate the comments and provide direction. Facilitation that is less frequent but more purposeful has been shown to relate to higher levels of critical thinking (Arend, 2009), setting the stage for integration and resolution. If students become complacent with the instructor jumping in and providing the "right" way of thinking, they lose the need to think about it themselves (Cotton, 1988). Even short confirmatory "I agree" statements can stop the student's thinking process. To address this, it is recommended instructors post general comments to the entire class every so often, referencing student posts, summarizing, and refocusing the discussion (Collison et al, 2000). For example, "Kevin said this…while Sahsa said that. But Maria brings in this other point…it seems there is a common theme of…but we're still looking for reasons why this occurs…what do the rest of you think?"

In the process of supporting an equal and active discussion, the instructor should realize the influence they have in their role. Even though many online classes establish communities of inquiry, the instructor still holds a position of power and their comments in particular need to be supportive of critical inquiry (Brookfield & Preskill, 2005). It is wise for online instructors to take extra steps to make sure their messages are perceived as supportive and not demeaning. In addition, when critical discourse is the goal, instructor facilitation should remain neutral in tone. Comments that indicate the instructor's bias or perspectives, or even comments such as "great point" let the students know what the instructor perceives to be the right way of thinking. Instead, the instructor might comment, "Interesting point, how do you think X would respond" to invite students to think further about the concept. Instructor comments that remain neutral are more supportive of students' critical thinking (Arend, 2009). While it is often necessary to correct misinformation or share an opinion or expertise within a discussion, the instructor should realize that doing so often shuts down the line of questioning.

Another tactic to encourage exploration involves the instructor embodying different "voices" to move the discussion along; voices such as: conceptual facilitator, reflective guide, personal muse, or mediator (Collison et al., 2000). For example, at times it might make sense for the instructor to play the role of personal muse, modeling to students how they might think of everything that has been said so far and how it relates to the question posed. This method of making visible

one's internal dialogue can be a useful way of reinvigorating a discussion that has stalled or is in conflict without confronting any one student individually. For example, an instructor might inject comments or questions such as, "As I read your posts I wonder to myself how they relate back to our opening question. Sometimes I think…but then I also think…, are these compatible ideas? Should I also be considering the impact of…? What do the rest of you think?" Modeling is especially valuable in online discussions and it is suggested that instructors model the appropriate length of discussion posts, as overly lengthy posts feel more like presentations than discussion contributions to students (Chang, et al., 2003).

Although all these aspects of instructor facilitation are important in encouraging exploration, the instructor first and foremost needs to ask questions that incite exploration in students. Exploration question types generally focus on asking for clarification, exploring different sides of an issue, or asking for evidence to move the discussion along towards integration. For example, questions that ask for clarification might include; "can you put that another way," "what's an example of what you're talking about," "can you explain your reasoning," or "student X says this…can anyone explain this in a different way." Questions that ask students to become aware and appreciate different sides of an issue include, "There are various sides to this argument. What would you say if you agreed with X? With Y? With Z?" or ask students to specifically take on a different role or viewpoint. During exploration, the instructor is also trying to move students towards a more supported understanding of their views and will want to inject questions that ask for more evidence, such as, "how do you know that," "what does the author say that supports your argument," "what evidence is there to support this position, idea or claim," or "can someone find an article/website/video clip related to this topic." The instructor can also ask students to consider ideas or perspectives that have not yet emerged, for example, "are there areas of this discussion that need further exploration," or "what voices are we missing."

It may be valuable for discussions to remain in the exploration stage for a while, depending upon the nature of the topic. Several studies indicate that this stage of cognitive presence is where most online discussions remain (Chang, et al., 2003; Garrison & Arbaugh, 2007; Park, 2009). It is unclear if this is by design, or due to lack of instructor facilitation methods, but many instructors desire to take student thinking beyond unsupported brainstorming. At some point, student exploration efforts garner the necessary information and expose a variety of options; therefore the discussion should move into the integration stage.

Integration

The integration stage is a more focused and structured stage of meaning-making that builds on the ideas generated from the exploration stage. In this stage, students and the facilitator begin to probe for deeper understanding as the students cognitive processes move back and forth between reflection and discourse. This stage is similar to what Collision et al. call "deepening the dialogue" (2000, p. 129). Instructors can recognize signs of integration when they see students connect and build on the ideas of others, demonstrate synthesis or convergence in their thoughts and comments, albeit still tentative, and when students begin offering solutions or explanations with supporting rationale or justification.

Although newer studies are showing higher levels of integration in online discussions, (Darabi, et al., 2011; Richardson & Ice, 2010), it was previously noted that many student contributions to online discussions remained in the exploration stage. This could be due to a lack of structure and facilitation focused on integration or resolution. As Meyer (2003) observed, the time and reflection necessary to facilitate integration and reflection is more demanding on instructors than facilitating

the information exchange of the exploration stage. Garrison et al. (2001) concur that integration, "requires active teaching presence to diagnose misconceptions, to provide probing questions, comments, and additional information in an effort to ensure continuing cognitive development, and to model the critical thinking process" (p. 10).

Teaching presence in the integration stage means the online facilitator needs "to clarify and extend the thinking of other people" (Collison et al., 2000, p. 104). In this stage, many different ideas, thoughts, and information play out in discussion, and it's easy for students to become overwhelmed and lose their focus amidst the range of comments. Perhaps the most important part of the facilitator's role in the integration stage is to decide which of the many lines of questioning to pursue. A common mistake is to pursue them all, which only serves to dilute the discussion and cause it to lose focus. Rather, the discussion should stay focused on "manageable content" (Garrison & Cleveland-Innes, 2005). In addition, students may latch on to a chain of thought that is not the most productive, while other times an important comment or question will go largely unrecognized. When this occurs the instructor should encourage students to reflect on the multiple perspectives and assumptions that emerged in exploration and begin to identify tentative solutions. During this stage the instructor starts to move the group towards synthesis by identifying directions within the discussion, refocusing the conversation when needed, and redirecting questions towards solutions.

One of the underlying tenets of inquiry is to understand the thinking process of students. If a discussion is working towards critical and reflective thinking, the facilitator should take time to consider possible misconceptions, fallacies, assumptions, and confusions that are likely to occur (Davis & Davis, 1998). The instructor can use questions or prompts to highlight and challenge these misconceptions, and direct questions towards integration goals. For example, questions in the integration stage might focus on finding relationships or connections, such as "how do these things relate," "is there any connection between what you just said and what X said," or "does your idea challenge or support what we seem to be saying." Other types of questions might focus on finding initial synthesis of ideas, such as "what are one or two important ideas that emerged from this discussion," "where do we seem to have agreement on these issues and what are our areas of disagreement," or "which theory is the most consistent or valuable." Additionally, questions can seek to test tentative solutions, "under what circumstances is this correct," "what might be the likely effect of X," or "how might things have been different if X didn't happen." While clarifying misconceptions and addressing confusion is important to do in both the triggering and exploration stages, it becomes more important now as discussions reach deeper levels of thinking within the integration stage and onwards to resolution.

The benefits of understanding thinking and asking the right questions are not limited to the instructor. Sharing the cognitive presence framework with students and even asking them to self-code their own comments can help their metacognitive awareness and monitoring of their contributions (Chang, et al., 2003). Initial studies indicate that sharing the four stages of cognitive presence with students as a guide for online postings resulted in more instances of integration in the discussion (Bai, 2009), and having students facilitate online discussions enhanced their awareness and regulation of their own thinking (Akyol & Garrison, 2011b).

It has been well studied that students adjust their cognitive thinking processes based on the types of questions posed or the tasks given to them (Eley, 1992; Gibbs, 1993; McKeachie, et al., 1986). In online discussions the type of questions asked influence the level of comments students contribute to discussion (Arnold & Ducate, 2006; Meyer, 2004). Thus simply asking questions that invite integration or structuring assignments with

the task of synthesis or convergence should lead to higher levels of integration.

Resolution

The fourth stage of cognitive presence is resolution. According to Garrison, et al. (2001) this stage entails the resolution of the problem or dilemma by direct or vicarious action. They posited that resolution could be attained by testing the hypothesis, implementing the proposed solution in a practical application, and/or defending the solution offered. Akyol and Garrison (2011a) state that resolution is "where learners collaboratively confirm solutions to the dilemma or problem posed" (p. 186).

However, Rourke and Kanuka (2009) reported finding that resolution is a more challenging and difficult stage to achieve in an online course, while Shea, Hayes, Vickers, Gozza-Cohen, Uzuner, Mehta, Valchova, and Rangan, (2010) believed that using threaded discussions as a way of determining resolution was misguided. Darabi, et al. (2011) found that a scaffolding strategy used in online discussions produced a strong association with the resolution stage and the ability of students to create solutions during this stage. In order to provide scaffolding for students to reach the resolution stage, instructors can lead with questions that probe the "so what" factor (Collison, Elbaum, Haavind, & Tinker, 2000). The "so what" factor gets at responses, solutions, and potential application by asking the learner to examine the "critical relevance and urgency" of their proposed solution (Collison, et al., 2000, p. 145). In this way, pointed questions such as "why do we need to consider this situation," "to whom is this concern of interest," or "were we to know all about this topic, what good would it do" (Collison, et al., 2000, p. 145) help students critically examine their ideas and solutions. Whether these questions are asked towards the end of a discussion thread, after a scenario analysis, or a debate, they promote resolution because students must consider the relevancy and integration of their answers and solutions in a 'why does it matter' defensible context.

In order to work towards resolution, complex strategies may be needed. Darabi et al. (2011) found that strategies which contained more interactive elements and had a task-based orientation to the discussion supported resolution, noting that even providing prompts designed to elicit deeper levels of thinking could not "substitute for the engaging elements required to advance to the resolution stage" (p. 223). These engaging elements or complex strategies include being able to clearly state a position and effectively argue for that position (a debate strategy) while being guided toward consensus by the facilitator (Darabi, et al., 2011). The debate strategy forces students to take a position, examine and explore content relevant to their positions, and then integrate that content into their ensuing argument, all of which exposes them to critical thinking while they problem solve (Darabi, et al., 2011). Additionally, debating as a critical thinking strategy starts with a triggering question or controversy that quickly leads to exploration and integration as the debate unfolds, and concludes with resolution as one side 'wins' the debate based on the quality, credibility, and presentation of the evidence provided.

Brookfield (2006b) offered several questions for wrapping up an online debate, questions that support students' deeper reflection of and critical thinking about the debate strategy. He proposed asking students to address questions such as:

What assumptions about the issue that you hold were clarified / confirmed for you by the debate? Which of your assumptions surprised you during the debate? In other words, were you made aware of assumptions you hold that you didn't know you had? How could you check out these new assumptions? What sources of evidence would you consult? In what ways, if any, were your existing assumptions challenged or changed by the debate? (p. 27)

The questions offered by Brookfield provide a discussion mechanism whereby students can critically think about their learning as a result of the debate and step back to examine their solutions.

Richardson and Ice (2010) also found that students engaged in higher levels of critical thinking (leading into integration and resolution) when instructional strategies like case studies and debates were used, when compared to more common place open ended discussion questions. The authors noted that perhaps achieving resolution is not always a necessary or desired outcome of discussion questions because online discussions may be the beginning of a scaffolding process that leads to deeper levels of thinking, and as such, may offer "evidence of where students' critical thinking levels are at a particular point in time" (Richardson & Ice, 2010, p. 57).

Another component of cognitive presence is "sustained reflection" (Garrison, et al., 2001) which, it can be argued, is an integral part of the resolution stage. Without sustained reflection, the ability to distill a solution or resolve a dilemma becomes stifled. Accordingly, student reflection on course content, activities, and discussions can support deeper thinking about the solutions to problems and dilemmas. Reflection offers opportunities for students to examine critically what they have said and done as well as the viability of their solutions. Through the act of testing their hypothesis, creating a meaningful framework, or finding solutions, students can begin to process their experience at a deeper level and look for ways to defend their solution.

Opportunities for reflection can be provided by evocative discussion questions such as: "Where do you think your answers/ideas/explanations came from," "what do you consider to be the strengths and weaknesses of your solution/approach/response," "how do you think others will respond to your solution/approach/response," or "how are your assumptions about X expressed in the solution/approach/response?" These types of reflective questions support learners stepping outside of themselves to examine their solutions and to critically consider their results in a manner which may provide additional evidence of resolution attainment.

Reflection can also come through individual and personal journal entries, or more transparently through a blog established specifically to debrief the discussion, the activity, or the solutions offered. As Garrison (2003) wrote, "Cognitive presence concerns the process of both reflection and discourse in the initiation, construction and confirmation of meaningful learning outcomes" (p. 4). Without reflection, students do not fully appreciate what they have learned, how far they have come in their learning, and how to apply and use new knowledge gained. Stavredes (2011) offered reflection questions that can help students in their self-directed learning processes and critical thinking. Questions such as "what strategy did I use to ensure I remained on task, what strategy did I use to ensure I was learning, and what knowledge and skills did I use to complete the activity" (Stavredes, 2011, pp. 115-116).

Another strategy for achieving resolution in online courses is outside of the discussion arena; it entails considering work products or artifacts as opportunities to achieve and demonstrate resolution. Work efforts such as case studies, projects, and research papers can provide tangible evidence of resolution (Shea et al., 2010) and therefore should be considered in any discussion of cognitive presence and the resolution stage. Case studies, when aligned with course outcomes, provide learners the opportunity to investigate ill-defined problems reflective of the messy complexities of real-life. Case studies present a problem or a case ranging from simple to complex with varying degrees of background and descriptive information to place the problem in context. The ill-defined or messy problems found in case studies give students the opportunity to work through vague dilemmas, complexity, and issues, providing exposure to settings and contexts they might not otherwise experience. As students work through

a case study, there is ample opportunity to test out possible solutions, discuss alternative resolution scenarios and confirm their understanding. Cases studies provide meaningful vehicles for online students to synthesize and evaluate their answers to pressing problems and to try out various solutions in the safety of a hypothetical situation. As such, the use of case studies encourages analysis, appraisal interpretation and testing solutions, all components of critical thinking and the resolution stage.

Course projects offer another alternative for achieving deeper levels of processing and resolution. Shea et al. (2010) claimed that looking for resolution within discussion postings was perhaps misguided, therefore it is important to consider non-discussion activities as ways of achieving resolution. Project based learning, as explained by The Buck Institute for Education (BIE), allows the learner to experience inquiry as it relates to complex questions, problems and challenges, while still offering students choice and voice in a project (2011). Projects require "critical thinking, problem solving, collaboration, and various forms of communication. Students need to do much more than remember information—they need to use higher-order thinking skills" (Buck Institute for Education, 2011, p. 1). Using projects as an instructional strategy to achieve higher levels of thinking permit students to work together or individually (like case studies), to create a solution to a problem. Project work can integrate desired learning outcomes with the learning students actually achieve and provide measureable evidence of resolution such as when students produce an artifact, apply prior knowledge to the project, or subsequently defend their project as a viable solution to a problem. For example Akyol and Garrison (2011b) found that deep and meaningful learning outcomes were achieved when students were given a course redesign project, where students applied and tested solutions within the project, affirming that structured activities like project and case studies provide for deeper learning.

Depending on the desired outcomes for online discussions, there are effective ways to achieve deeper, critical levels of thinking and hence progression towards resolution. Measured interaction from the instructor, open- ended, probing, and thoughtful questions as well as non-discussion based activities can promote the resolution stage of cognitive presence. The various strategies and question prompts discussed in this section offer guidance towards that end.

GUIDELINES FOR PRACTICE

The Community of Inquiry (CoI) framework was developed when knowledge about online courses was in its infancy. Since then it has become a well-accepted and powerful theoretical framework for understanding the quality of interaction and learning within an online course. As online courses become more common, and technology advances, the CoI framework has remained a valuable lens through which to view online learning. Blended and hybrid courses, perhaps the future of education, will provide new challenges for those researching online learning as instructors will be able to decide between asynchronous and synchronous mediums to achieve various levels of cognitive presence. In the meantime, the Practical Inquiry Model serves as bedrock for cognitive presence and provides a useful means for understanding levels of critical thinking and metacognition in online discussions.

There is still much to learn about effective online discussion facilitation. Much of the literature about discussion facilitation and how to foster deeper levels of thinking in online discussions is theory-based, due to the difficulty in creating experimental studies of something as subjective and sensitive as one's teaching methods and the interpretation of dialogue. This speaks to a need for more qualitative studies about how and why certain facilitation approaches, discussion questions, and online learning activities work in facilitating critical thinking.

In addition, because most online discussions tend to remain in an exploration stage, more practical work about how to use the Community of Inquiry framework to push cognitive presence in both blended and online courses is needed. Determining the thinking levels of student comments in online discussions can be done with time-intensive content analysis and qualitative metrics. However, time-strapped online instructors could benefit from the development of brief, non-intrusive, diagnostic methods for determining levels of cognitive presence within their courses. Such tools could be used by online instructors to modify their facilitation methods and to ask appropriate questions in order to move the discussion towards deeper levels of thinking.

When the stages of cognitive presence are more closely examined, insights into developing effective discussion questions and critical thinking exercises are revealed, providing a practical option for considering students' level of thinking. The authors of this chapter propose using a guide such as the one in the Appendix for this purpose. The guide lists questions prompts and activities developed from the Practical Inquiry Model's four stages which embody cognitive presence.

Within the guide, identifying cues can be used to quickly reveal levels of each of the cognitive presence stages within an online discussion, and to determine where a discussion is focused and where it might be getting stuck. Suggested question prompts are also provided as a means for instructors to move discussions forward. We hope that these prompts will provide momentum to online and classroom discussions and activities as students' progress from the initial triggering event into deeper levels of thinking, critical inquiry and reflection. Understanding and attempting to move discussions through the stages of cognitive presence may lead to greater instances of critical thinking as these stages offer a process which encourages critical thinking.

REFERENCES

Akyol, Z., & Garrison, D. R. (2011a). Assessing metacognition in an online community of inquiry. *The Internet and Higher Education, 14*(3), 183–190. doi:doi:10.1016/j.iheduc.2011.01.005

Akyol, Z., & Garrison, D. R. (2011b). Understanding cognitive presence in an online and blended community of inquiry: Assessing outcomes and processes for deep approaches to learning. *British Journal of Educational Technology, 42*(2), 233–250. doi:doi:10.1111/j.1467-8535.2009.01029.x

Anderson, T., Rourke, L., Garrison, D. R., & Archer, W. (2001). Assessing teaching presence in a computer conferencing context. *Journal of Asynchronous Learning Networks, 5*(2), 1–17.

Arend, B. (2009). Encouraging critical thinking through online threaded discussions. *The Journal of Educators Online, 6*(1), 1–23.

Arnold, N., & Ducate, L. (2006). Future foreign language teachers' social and cognitive collaboration in an online environment. *Language Learning & Technology, 10*(1), 42–66.

Bai, H. (2009). Facilitating students' critical thinking in online discussion: An instructor's experience. *Journal of Interactive Online Learning, 8*(2), 156–164.

Bender, T. (2003). *Discussion-based online teaching to enhance student learning: Theory, practice, assessment.* Sterling, VA: Stylus.

Bloom, B. S. (1956). *Taxonomy of educational objectives, handbook i: The cognitive domain.* New York, NY: David McKay Co.

Brookfield, S. D. (1987). *Developing critical thinkers: Challenging adults to explore alternative ways of thinking and acting.* San Francisco, CA: Jossey-Bass.

Brookfield, S. D. (2006a). *Developing critical thinkers.* Retrieved October 05, 2011, from http://www.stephenbrookfield.com/Dr._Stephen_D._Brookfield/Workshop_Materials_files/Critical_Thinking_materials.pdf

Brookfield, S. D. (2006b). *Discussion as a way of teaching.* Retrieved September 21, 2011, from http://www.stephenbrookfield.com/Dr._Stephen_D._Brookfield/Workshop_Materials.html

Brookfield, S. D., & Preskill, S. (2005). *Discussion as a way of teaching: Tools and techniques for democratic classrooms* (2nd ed.). San Francisco, CA: Jossey-Bass.

Buck Institute for Education. (2011). *What is PBL?* (project based learning) Retrieved October 9, 2011, from http://www.bie.org/about/what_is_pbl

Chang, C., Paulus, T. M., Pawan, F., & Yalcin, S. (2003). Online learning: Patterns of engagement and interaction among in-service teachers. *Language Learning & Technology, 7*(3), 119–140.

Collison, G., Elbaum, B., Haavind, S., & Tinker, R. (2000). *Facilitating online learning: Effective strategies for moderators.* Madison, WI: Atwood Publishing.

Cotton, K. (1988). *Classroom questioning.* School improvement research series close up #5. North West Regional Educational Laboratory. Retrieved October 5, 2011, from the from http://education-northwest.org/webfm_send/569

Darabi, A., Arrastia, M. C., Nelson, D. W., Cornille, T., & Liang, X. (2011). Cognitive presence in asynchronous online learning: A comparison of four discussion strategies. *Journal of Computer Assisted Learning, 27*(3), 216–227. doi:doi:10.1111/j.1365-2729.2010.00392.x

Davis, J. R., & Davis, A. B. (1998). *Effective training strategies.* San Francisco, CA: Berrett-Koehler.

Duell, O. K. (1994). Extended wait time and university student achievement. *American Educational Research Journal, 31*, 397–414.

Eley, M. G. (1992). Differential adoption of study approaches within individual students. *Higher Education, 23*(3), 231–254.

Felton, M. K. (2005). Approaches to argument in critical thinking instruction. *Thinking Classroom, 6*(4), 6-6-13.

Garrison, D. R. (2003). Cognitive presence for effective asynchronous online learning: The role of reflective inquiry, self-direction and metacognition. In Bourne, J., & Moore, J. C. (Eds.), *Elements of quality online education: Practice and direction*. Needham, MA: The Sloan Consortium.

Garrison, D. R. (2011). *E-learning in the 21st century: A framework for research and practice* (2nd ed.). New York, NY: Routledge.

Garrison, D. R., & Anderson, T. (2003). *E–learning in the 21st century: A framework for research and practice*. New York, NY: RoutledgeFalmer.

Garrison, D. R., Anderson, T., & Archer, W. (2000). Critical inquiry in a text-based environment: Computer conferencing in higher education. *The Internet and Higher Education, 2*(2-3), 87–105.

Garrison, D. R., Anderson, T., & Archer, W. (2001). Critical thinking, cognitive presence, and computer conferencing in distance education. *American Journal of Distance Education, 15*(1), 7–23.

Garrison, D. R., Anderson, T., & Archer, W. (2004). *Critical thinking, cognitive presence and computer conferencing in distance education*. Retrieved February 20, 2011, from http://communityofinquiry.com/files/CogPres_Final.pdf

Garrison, D. R., & Arbaugh, J. B. (2007). Researching the community of inquiry framework: Review, issues, and future directions. *The Internet and Higher Education, 10*(3), 157–172.

Garrison, D. R., Arbaugh, J. B., Cleveland-Innes, M., Diaz, S., Ice, P., Richardson, J., et al. (2008). *Community of inquiry framework: Instrument development, validation and application*. Paper presented at the First International Conference of the new Canadian Network for Innovation in Education (CNIE), Banff, Alberta, CA. http://communitiesofinquiry.com/sites/communityofinquiry.com/files/CNIE_CoI_2008_Survey.pdf

Garrison, D. R., & Cleveland-Innes, M. (2005). Facilitating cognitive presence in online learning: Interaction is not enough. *American Journal of Distance Education, 19*(3), 133–148.

Garrison, D. R., Cleveland-Innes, M., & Fung, T. S. (2010). Exploring causal relationships among teaching, cognitive and social presence: Student perceptions of the community of inquiry framework. *The Internet and Higher Education, 13*(1-2), 31–36.

Gibbs, G. (1993). The CNAA improving student learning project. *Research and Development in Higher Education, 14*, 8–19.

Kanuka, H., & Garrison, D. R. (2004). Cognitive presence in online learning. *Journal of Computing in Higher Education, 15*(2), 21–39.

Kehrwald, B. (2008). Understanding social presence in text-based online learning environments. *Distance Education, 29*(1), 89–106.

King, P. M., & Kitchener, K. S. (1994). *Developing reflective judgment: Understanding and promoting intellectual growth and critical thinking in adolescents and adults*. San Francisco, CA: Jossey-Bass.

Lombard, M., & Ditton, T. (1997). At the heart of it all: The concept of presence. *Journal of Computer-Mediated Communication, 3*(2). Retrieved from http://jcmc.indiana.edu/vol3/issue2/lombard.html. doi:doi:10.1111/j.1083-6101.1997.tb00072.x

Lynch, C. L., & Wolcott, S. K. (2001). *Helping your students develop critical thinking skills. (IDEA Paper No. 37).* Manhattan, KS: The IDEA Center.

McKeachie, W. J., Pintrich, P. R., Lin, Y. G., & Smith, D. A. F. (1986). *Teaching and learning in the college classroom: A review of the research literature.* Ann Arbor, MI: University of Michigan.

Meyer, K. A. (2003). Face-to-face versus threaded discussions: The role of time and higher-order thinking. *Journal of Asynchronous Learning Networks, 7*(3), 55–65.

Meyer, K. A. (2004). Evaluating online discussions: Four different frames of analysis. *Journal of Asynchronous Learning Networks, 8*(2), 101–114.

Moon, J. (2008). *Critical thinking: An exploration of theory and practice.* New York, NY: Routledge.

Park, C. L. (2009). Replicating the use of a cognitive presence measurement tool. *Journal of Interactive Online Learning, 8*, 140–155.

Richardson, J. C., & Ice, P. (2010). Investigating students' level of critical thinking across instructional strategies in online discussions. *The Internet and Higher Education, 13*(1/2), 52–59.

Riva, G. (2009). Is presence a technology issue? Some insights from cognitive sciences. *Virtual Reality (Waltham Cross), 13*, 159–169. doi:doi:10.1007/s10055-009-0121-6

Rourke, L., Anderson, T., Garrison, D. R., & Archer, W. (2001). Assessing social presence in asynchronous text-based computer conferencing. *Journal of Distance Education, 14*(3), 51–70.

Rourke, L., & Kanuka, H. (2009). Learning in communities of inquiry: A review of the literature. *Journal of Distance Education, 23*(1), 19–48.

Scriven, M., & Paul, R. (2008). *Defining critical thinking.* Retrieved October 23, 2011, from http://www.criticalthinking.org/aboutCT/define_critical_thinking.cfm

Shea, P., & Bidjerano, T. (2009). Community of inquiry as a theoretical framework to foster "epistemic engagement" and "cognitive presence" in online education. *Computers & Education, 52*(3), 543–553.

Shea, P., Hayes, S., Vickers, J., Gozza-Cohen, M., Uzuner, S., & Mehta, R. (2010). A re-examination of the community of inquiry framework: Social network and content analysis. *The Internet and Higher Education, 13*(1-2), 10–21.

Stavredes, T. (2011). *Effective online teaching: Foundations and strategies for student success.* San Fransicso, CA: Jossey-Bass.

Stein, D. S., Wanstreet, C. E., Glazer, H. R., Engle, C. L., Harris, R. A., & Johnston, S. M. (2007). Creating shared understanding through chats in a community of inquiry. *The Internet and Higher Education, 10*(2), 103–115. doi:doi:10.1016/j.iheduc.2007.02.002

Tobin, K. (1987). The role of wait time in higher cognitive level learning. *Review of Educational Research, 57*(1), 69–95.

Walker, S. E. (2003). Active learning strategies to promote critical thinking. *Journal of Athletic Training, 38*(3), 263–267.

KEY TERMS AND DEFINITION

Asynchronous Discussion: A discussion in which the discussants don't participate simultaneously (in real time).

Cognitive Presence: The extent to which learners are able to construct and confirm meaning through sustained reflection and discourse in a critical community of inquiry.

Critical Thinking: The process of thinking that questions assumptions. It is a way of deciding whether a claim is true, false; sometimes true, or partly true.

Exploration: The inquiry phase which includes understanding the nature of the problem and then searching for relevant information and possible explanation.

Integration: The focused and structured phase of constructing meaning in which decisions are made about integration of ideas and how order can be created parsimoniously.

Resolution: The resolution of the dilemma or problem, whether that is reducing complexity by constructing a meaningful framework or discovering a contextually specific solution.

Triggering Event: The initiation of the inquiry process through a well-thought activity such as a question.

APPENDIX: A GUIDE FOR IDENTIFYING AND ELICITING COGNITIVE PRESENCE (CP)

Table 1. A guide for identifying and eliciting cognitive presence (adapted from practical inquiry descriptors and indicators (Garrison & Anderson, 2003)

CP Phase	Description	Identifying Cues	Question Stems/Strategies
Triggering Event	Activity or question designed to engage, capture student interest, and generate curiosity. May be a dilemma or authentic problems students can relate to.	Sense of puzzlement Realization of a problem or issue Desire to find out more Comment or question that takes the discussion in a new direction	Questions that focus on a problem, issue, dilemma, event, challenge, learning task. May be a controversial statement to open discussion: • What are the pros/cons? • How would you handle this problem/issue/dilemma? • What do you think are the differences (or similarities) between …? • What about the problem/issue/question or dilemma presented surprised you the most? • How would you describe or explain XYZ?
			Probing questions: • Why do you think *person A* said that? • What are your initial thoughts or reactions to *XYZ* ? • Imagine that… • What would you do if …?
Exploration	Students begin to understand the nature of the problem; begin to search for relevant information and possible explanations.	Brainstorming ideas Information exchange Personal narration/opinions Suggestions or unsupported conclusions	Questions that ask for clarification: • Can you put that another way? • What's an example of what you're talking about? • Can you explain your reasoning? • Student X says this. Can anyone explain this in another way?
			Questions that ask students to take on various viewpoints: • What would you say if you agreed with X? With Y? With Z?
			Questions that ask for more evidence: • How do you know that? • What does the author say that supports your argument? • What evidence is there to support this position, idea or claim? • Can someone find an article/website/video clip related to this topic?
			Questions that explore ideas or perspectives that have not yet emerged: • Are there areas of this discussion that need further exploration? • What are we missing?

continued on following page

Table 1. Continued

CP Phase	Description	Identifying Cues	Question Stems/Strategies
Integration	More focused and structured phase of meaning making. Reflective phase marked by critical discourse that shapes understanding. Students and instructor may probe for deeper understanding, correct misconceptions.	• Connecting or building on ideas of others • Synthesis or convergence of information (may be tentative) • Creating solutions or explanations with rationale or justification	Questions that focus on relationships or connections: • How do these ideas relate to each other? • Student X says this but student Y says that. Could these two viewpoints be reconciled?
			Questions that focus on initial synthesis of ideas: • What are one or two important ideas that emerged from this discussion? • Where do we seem to have agreement on these issues, what are our areas of disagreement? • Which theory is the most consistent or valuable?
			Questions seek to test tentative solutions: • Under what circumstances is this correct? • What might be the likely effect of X? • How might things be different if X didn't happen • Does this argument hold up in all circumstances? Where might it break down?

continued on following page

Table 1. Continued

CP Phase	Description	Identifying Cues	Question Stems/Strategies
Resolution	The resolution to the problem or dilemma. Testing and/or application of the solution in a real world context. Can lead to additional triggering events.	• Wrap up • Construction of frameworks or solutions • Testing, applying or defending solutions • Metacognitive awareness	Questions seeking solutions, synthesis, and verification: • Does everyone agree with this conclusion? • What did I learn in *XYZ*? And what will I do with what I learned in *XYZ*? • Where do you think your answers, ideas, or explanations came from?
			Questions that have students appraise their solutions/responses based on evidence: • How to you know this solution, remedy worked? • What evidence do you have to support your evaluations and/or judgments? • What is the value of this? • What assumptions have been confirmed or put into question?
			Questions that ask students to create, present, and defend project work or case studies: • How would you respond to someone who disagrees? • Based on the evidence, what can you deduct from…? • What explanation is most consistent with the data? • Does your solution logically follow from the evidence/data? Online debates, project based assignments, and case studies can be used to move students through all fours stages of cognitive presence.

Chapter 10
An Online Resource to Foster Cognitive Presence

Douglas Archibald
University of Ottawa, Canada

ABSTRACT

This chapter extends the body of research surrounding the Community of Inquiry (CoI) framework and the literature on developing critical thinking in online environments. The findings from a recent multiple site study are discussed. The purpose of the study was to explore the extent to which teaching and social presence and other factors contributed to the development of cognitive presence. The project involved 189 participants in two higher education institutions, enrolled in 10 research methods and educational research courses. The participants used an innovative online resource and participated in online discussion forums to assist them in learning about educational research and developing research proposals. By exploring how participants used this resource, the researcher was able to gain insight into what strategies contributed to improving cognitive presence. Future directions for critical thinking in online environments and strategies for cognitive presence development are discussed.

INTRODUCTION

The impact of Internet technology on critical thinking is of growing interest among researchers. However, there still remains much to explore in terms of how critical thinking can be fostered through online environments for higher education and workplace training groups. This chapter summarizes a recent multiple site study which extends the body of research surrounding the

Community of Inquiry (CoI) framework (Garrison, Anderson, & Archer, 2000) and the literature on developing critical thinking in online environments. The purpose of the study was to explore the extent to which teaching and social presence and other factors contributed to the development of cognitive presence. The intention was to foster opportunities for critical thinking through the design, development, and application of an online learning resource.

DOI: 10.4018/978-1-4666-2110-7.ch010

Essential to this goal was the creation of a learning environment that would enable an online learning community to progressively move to higher levels of critical thinking. There is evidence in the online learning literature that critical thinking skills can be enhanced through the use of a variety of online formats (Duphorne & Gunawardena, 2005; Moore & Marra, 2005). However, other researchers have found that moving an online community of learners to the highest levels of critical thinking is difficult (Garrison, Anderson, & Archer, 2001; Kanuka & Anderson, 1998; Meyer, 2004; Vaughan & Garrison, 2005). The highest levels of critical thinking involve connecting, integrating, and applying new ideas (Garrison, et al., 2000).

The study involved 189 participants from two higher education institutions, enrolled in 10 research methods and educational research courses. The participants used an innovative online resource (Research Design Learning Resource – RDLR; Archibald, 2010) and participated in online discussion forums to assist them in learning about educational research and developing research proposals. By exploring how participants used this resource, the researcher was able to gain insight into what factors fostered the development cognitive presence.

The body of this chapter unfolds with a brief introduction to the CoI framework and cognitive presence. Included is an outline of the literature on critical thinking in educational contexts. This exploration of the literature incorporates a brief discussion on the importance of collaborative learning as an approach to develop cognitive presence. Then, through the lens of teaching presence details of the design principles and strategies the researcher used to design and implement the RDLR will be discussed.

Finally, the conclusion of this chapter will include findings from prior studies that support the findings of the study and strategies for developing cognitive presence. The future research directions section will include recommendations

for promoting cognitive presence in course design and facilitation, as well as some thoughts on the future directions for critical thinking in online environments. By the end of this chapter readers should be able to:

1. Understand why social presence and teaching presence contribute to the development of cognitive presence and critical thinking.
2. Identify strategies to promote critical thinking in online learning environments.

BACKGROUND

Cognitive Presence

Through examination of the relationships between three elements in an online CoI (i.e., teaching, social, and cognitive presence), the researcher was able to gain further insight into whether higher levels of cognitive presence could be reached in an online environment. Specifically, the researcher explored the effects of the design of the online learning resource, direct instruction and facilitation of the discussions (teaching presence) and the extent of the development of the interpersonal relationships among users (social presence) on predicting critical thinking among users (cognitive presence). Furthermore, with regard to the examination of the CoI, the researcher was able determine the ability of social and teaching presence to predict cognitive presence after controlling for several additional variables (i.e., self-directed learning readiness, prior online learning experience, and prior collaborative learning experience).

When designing this study the researcher made an important assumption and that is the concept of cognitive presence in the CoI framework represents the process of critical thinking. The phases of Garrison et al.'s (2000) Practical Inquiry Model were used to assess the critical thinking processes of participants in this research. The model is a four stage cognitive processing model that has been used to assess critical thinking in online discussions (Meyer, 2004). The results and conclusions on critical thinking were drawn from the analysis of the cognitive presence construct of the CoI framework. Therefore, the implications and recommendations the researcher makes about critical thinking are based on Garrison et al.'s (2000) definition of cognitive presence.

A community of inquiry is an extremely valuable, if not essential, context for higher-order learning (Garrison et al., 2001). Eleven years ago, Garrison et al. (2000) published an article describing the CoI framework. At the time, the framework was intended to offer a new theoretical perspective that drew upon earlier research on computer conferencing (Garrison, Anderson, & Archer, 2010). The framework provided an outline of three core elements that were able to describe and measure a collaborative and positive educational experience, namely social presence, cognitive presence, and teaching presence.

Social presence is the ability of learners to project themselves socially and emotionally in an online environment (Gunawardena & Zittle, 1997). Social presence is defined as being an environment in which learners can communicate openly and purposefully, use affective expression, and have the opportunity to develop a sense of group cohesion through collaboration (Garrison & Arbaugh, 2007). However, social presence needs to evolve from establishing social relationships to intellectual focused discussions (Thompson & MacDonald, 2005). Thus social presence provides the foundation for cognitive presence (Garrison & Arbaugh, 2007).

Cognitive presence is the extent to which learners are able to construct and confirm meaning through sustained reflection and discourse in an online discussion forum (Garrison & Arbaugh, 2007) and is grounded in the critical thinking literature (Garrison et al., 2001). Moreover, cognitive presence can be operationalized by a model of critical thinking: the Practical Inquiry Model.

The Practical Inquiry Model is a four-phase process. First, the facilitator (or a learner) presents a thought provoking question or problem of interest to an online discussion that requires inquiry. Learners and facilitator then move to the exploration phase of the model in which they explore the problem or question through critical reflection and discourse. Exploration leads to a phase of integration in which learners integrate or make meaning from the ideas they have explored. The role of the facilitator is very important during this phase, "to probe and diagnose ideas so that learners will move to higher level thinking..." (Garrison & Arbaugh, 2007, p. 161). Integration then leads learners to the last stage of the model: resolution. Resolution represents the highest level of cognitive presence, in which learners apply their new knowledge. Garrison and Cleveland-Innes (2005) found that the structure of an online course design and the leadership provided by the facilitator seemed to have an effect on whether learners are able to engage in a "deep and meaningful approach to learning" (p. 133). Thus, their findings suggested that there is a relationship between cognitive presence and teaching presence.

"Teaching presence is the design, facilitation, and direction of cognitive and social processes for the purpose of realizing personally meaningful and educationally worthwhile learning outcomes" (Garrison & Arbaugh, 2007, p. 163). Direction in this case refers to the instructor's or facilitator's role in guiding the interactions of the learners. Recent research has shown (Garrison & Cleveland-Innes, 2005; Kanuka, Rourke, & Laflamme, 2007) that teaching presence seemed to be significant in determining learners' perceptions of learning, course satisfaction, and sense of belonging to an online community.

The role of cognitive presence is of interest for this chapter. It is based on John Dewey's notion of reflective inquiry (Swan, Garrison, & Richardson, 2009) and can be considered synonymous with the "critical thinking it seeks as an outcome"

(Garrison & Arbaugh, 2007). However, recent empirical research has shown that cognitive presence cannot be studied in isolation of teaching presence and social presence, as all three elements are considered both statistically and conceptually interdependent (Garrison, et al., 2010). Few studies to date have explored the dynamics of online collaborative learning to understand the motivation of learners and critical thinking. Garrison and Arbaugh (2007) hinted that this is an area of future research and it is this gap in our understanding that the researcher wanted to explore. Online learning is a complex phenomenon and among researchers who have used the CoI framework there has been some discrepancy about the interdependence of the elements.

If there is any criticism about the studies using the CoI framework in its earlier years, it is that there has not been an examination of the relative impact each of the three elements has on the others and how that may vary in different educational contexts. Although recent empirical research such as the factor analyses conducted by Arbaugh (2007); Arbaugh and Hwang (2006); Garrison, Cleveland-Innes, and Fung (2004); and Shea and Bidjerano (2009) certainly supports the CoI as a framework of online learning, this work needs to be reinforced by additional study. Until recently, there have been "very few studies that examine the three elements of the framework simultaneously, either quantitatively or qualitatively" (Garrison & Arbaugh, 2007, p. 159). Increasingly studies are exploring the interrelatedness of the framework's elements (Archibald, 2011; Akyol & Garrison, 2011; Akyol, Garrison, & Ozden, 2009). Understanding how teaching presence and social presence relate to cognitive presence was of great interest to me. Moreover, Arbaugh (2007) noted that in addition to examining the relations between the three elements of the framework, other variables such as the characteristics of learners should be studied in concert with them.

Garrison, et al. (2010) noted that cognitive presence should be seen as a "developmental model consistent with the CoI framework as describing the dynamics of a worthwhile educational experience" (p. 6). In other words it should be based on reflective inquiry. Early work on the development of cognitive presence focused entirely on the four phases of the Practical Inquiry Model. The most common method for assessing cognitive presence within a course was to analyse the asynchronous online discussion transcripts using quantitative content analysis (e.g., Garrison et al., 2001; Kanuka et al., 2007; Meyer, 2003; Schrire, 2004). This method involved searching for indicators that represented each of the four phases. However, this approach, developed by Garrison et al., required a number of methodological considerations. Rourke, Anderson, Garrison, and Archer (2001) conducted a review of 16 studies that used content analysis to analyse the transcripts of online discussions. Only three of these studies reported inter-rater reliability figures that indicated the analysis could be replicated by others. In instances where a quantitative framework for transcript analysis is used, the inter-rater reliability needs to be proven.

Determining the unit of analysis in content analysis was another issue (Garrison et al., 2001; Garrison, et al., 2010). Considerations included whether to use a single message, a threaded discussion, or only a single phrase. Garrison and colleagues decided to use "a single message" as the unit (Garrison et al., 2001). A message refers to what an individual participant posts in one thread of a discussion on a single occasion. Lastly, identifying the processes that are involved in each phase of the Practical Inquiry Model needed to be figured out. Being able to identify the level of cognitive presence is another difficult task as the phases are subjective. Therefore, it is difficult to achieve consistency across coders. To help remedy this, a set of descriptors that described the processes within each phase of the model was determined.

In sum, quantitative content analysis was seen as the best way to reliably analyse online discussion transcripts but it had flaws because of the way it was implemented. It is difficult to ensure objectivity in transcript analysis and so researchers need to triangulate the data with other means. Triangulation of data using multiple sources continues to be used in online research studies. Thus, the researcher explored how the RDLR affected cognitive presence by incorporating numerous data collection methods including the CoI framework survey, online discussion transcripts and semi-structured interviews.

Critical Thinking

Critical thinking is a lived activity, not an abstract academic pastime. It is something we all do, though its frequency, and the credibility we grant it, vary from person to person. Our lives are sufficiently complex and perplexing that it would be difficult to escape entirely from feeling that at times the world is not working the way we thought it was supposed to, or that there must be other ways of living (Brookfield, 1987, p. 14).

The concept of critical thinking can probably be traced back to Socrates almost 2,500 years ago (Fasco, 2003; Paul, 1985). Socratic questioning is a technique where the teacher or facilitator asks probing questions that lead learners to understanding and knowledge. Since the time of Socrates, many philosophers and, in more recent times, psychologists have put forth various theories with regard to the process of thinking (Fasco, 2003).

Critical thinking as a modern educational concept can be traced back to Dewey (1933). He used the term "reflective thinking" to describe this concept. Reflective thinking gives learners the opportunity to consciously plan and deepen the meaning of their own experiences. Dewey believed that if a person was not critical of her ideas then she would not be reflective (Garrison, 1991), and deconstructed reflective thought into five phases: suggestions; converting the problem into a question that can be solved; hypothesising; reasoning; and finally testing the hypothesis. Simi-

larly, Brookfield (1995) viewed critical thinking in terms of identifying and challenging assumptions (assumption hunting) and exploring alternative solutions for improved well-being. Brookfield (1987) proposed five similar phases of critical thinking which included, a trigger event, an appraisal, an exploration developing an alternative perspective, and an integration or resolution.

Garrison (1991) considered the process of critical thinking as all-encompassing, involving both problem solving and creative thinking. In fact the processes of problem solving and creative thinking are very similar to critical thinking. Critical thinking has often been associated with problem solving; however, it is more complicated: "critical thinking consists of more skills than are used in the problem-solving approach, and some of these steps include intuitive and creative elements that do not involve any evaluation or justification" (D'Angelo, 1971, p. 19). Viewing critical thinking from a process perspective would include creative elements such as sensing difficulties, finding gaps in information, and being insightful (Garrison, 1991; McPeck, 1981; Perkins, 1986; Sternberg, 1988). Garrison's earlier work on critical thinking involved connecting and making sense of its complexity and influenced his further writing on the subject. Garrison and Archer (2000) suggested that critical thinking results when meaningful learning is realised through a process whereby learners have control and responsibility for their thinking. To demonstrate the critical thinking process, Garrison and Archer developed the Practical Inquiry Model. The following study is an example of how the model has been used in online education to explore critical thinking.

Schrire (2004) conducted a multiple case study involving three online computer conferences or discussion forums, each representing a single case. She wanted to know what patterns of interaction could be found in online discussions, what kinds and levels of critical thinking were present, and how interactions and critical thinking were connected. Each case was studied separately and then cross-case comparisons were made. Her first case represented the full case study in the investigation. The other two cases were partially analyzed in order to answer questions that arose in the study of the first case. She used three models to evaluate critical thinking or cognitive development: Bloom's taxonomy (Bloom, Engelhart, Furst, Hill, & Krathwohl, 1956), the Structure of Observed Learning Outcomes (SOLO) taxonomy (Biggs & Collis, 1982), and the Practical Inquiry Model (Garrison et al., 2001).

Schrire (2004) identified patterns of interaction in all three online discussions, including the following interaction types: instructor-centered, student-centered, synergistic, developing synergism, scattered, and message chains. She also found isolated messages that did not contribute to interaction. The interaction type that indicated collaborative learning processes was the synergistic pattern. Higher order critical thinking skills were demonstrated in two thirds of the messages using all three of models of cognitive development. This percentage is uncharacteristically high compared to other studies that have used content analysis to examine cognition in online transcripts (Garrison et al., 2001; Kanuka et al., 2007). Perhaps this was due to the fact that multiple models, discussions, and coders for analysis were used.

Schrire's (2004) main finding related to the "correspondence found between the type of interaction occurring in asynchronous computer conferencing and the phase of critical thinking. …Synergistic threads showed more advanced phases of critical thinking on the Practical Inquiry Model of cognitive presence than instructor-centered threads" (p. 494). This finding suggests that social constructivist approaches to teaching and learning, such as collaborative learning, may lend themselves to developing critical thinking in an online community of inquiry. It also provides evidence to support the role of social presence as a mediating variable for cognitive presence development.

Collaborative Learning and Adult Education

The roles of peers and the teacher are very important in collaborative learning. O'Donnell (2006) wrote of the role of peers in group learning. She identified that peer learning is an umbrella term that includes collaborative and cooperative learning and other forms of learning in which peers help one another. The concept of peer learning is important in considering the role of social presence in fostering cognitive presence in an online community of inquiry.

Interestingly, O'Donnell (2006) wrote from a social cohesion perspective which relies on "positive interdependence among group members" (p. 783). Interdependence is fostered through group members' concern for one another. Although O'Donnell used examples from an elementary classroom there is certainly a connection between the social cohesion perspective and social presence of the CoI. Social cohesion is considered to be a critical sub-element in social presence (Garrison et al., 2000). In the social cohesion perspective learners work together to solve complex tasks requiring complex cognitive skills (O'Donnell, 2006). Another interesting topic that O'Donnell discussed in this chapter is the importance of quality in discourse. She acknowledged that most learners need support in generating quality discourse. The teacher can support high levels of cognitive activity through providing questions to the learners, which illustrates the role of the teacher in peer learning.

O'Donnell (2006) identified a number of roles that a teacher plays in peer learning: community builder, task developer, teacher as model, coordinator of activities, and evaluator. These roles play a critical role in teaching presence of the CoI framework. The teacher as model is a very important role for example, and sets the stage for social and cognitive presence. The teacher or facilitator provides triggering questions to stimulate critical thinking but also provides feedback to learners.

In the researcher's experience as a classroom teacher and online facilitator this feedback often includes personal stories and references from refereed articles; it becomes a sort of scaffolding. As learners participate further in the discussions the facilitator gradually lets their own support fade as learners look to each other for feedback. The notion of learners providing feedback and support is not new. Bielaczyc and Collins (2006) refer to this sort of scaffolding as creating knowledge-building communities. In knowledge-building communities knowledge is shared by all learners and scaffolds are developed. A community of knowledge building may lead to argumentation (development of arguments that lead to higher order learning) which is an important feature of collaborative learning. "In effective collaborative argumentation learners share a focus on the same issues and negotiate about the meaning of each other's information" (Andriessen, 2006, p. 199).

Technologies that Can Support Collaborative Learning

Web-based technologies can be used to create a rich collaborative learning environment. Technologies are cognitive tools that can help learners engage in meaningful learning alone and with others. The Internet provides immense resources for learners to use when searching for information, solving problems, collaborating with others, and constructing knowledge. Therefore, the Internet is ideal for supporting constructivist and collaborative learning (Huang, 2002; Jonassen, 2000). Technologies should be used as intellectual partners, engagers, and facilitators of thinking and knowledge construction (Jonassen, Peck, & Wilson, 1999). Recently, Norman Vaughan (2010) evaluated a series of courses that were redesigned as blended courses using various Web 2.0 technologies. In one particular course that was redesigned using collaborative activities such as social book marking, led to improved student success and retention

(increased number of students with higher grades and fewer failing or withdrawing from the course).

One of the most common technologies used by educators to promote online collaboration is online asynchronous discussions. There have been numerous studies that have explored asynchronous online discussions in terms of being an effective means of supporting collaborative learning. For example, Richardson and Ice (2010) recently explored three instructional strategies for online discussions, debates, case-based discussions, and open ended discussions all of which promoted collaboration but varied in terms of fostering critical thinking. In another study, Ice, Curtis, Phillips, and Wells (2007) explored the use of audio feedback as opposed to text feedback in asynchronous discussion forums. They found that the use of audio feedback actually gave the learners an increased sense of involvement in the program.

Digital storytelling is another application of technology that can be used as a tool to support collaborative constructivist learning. The creation of digital stories can help learners construct knowledge. It allows for more perspectives and ideas to be shared. "Stories originate in problematic situations; they show the way out of the situations" (McLellan, 2006, p. 28). Her comment stems from learners creating their own digital stories but it can also be applied by watching digital stories as a learning case in which new knowledge is constructed as problems are discussed and solved (Jonassen, 2006). Recently, Lowenthal and Dunlap (2010) explored ways to increase social presence in an online community of inquiry. They started their online courses with an introductory "biography-like" activity designed to allow learners to get to know each other and the facilitators. However, Lowenthal and Dunlap were still not satisfied with how learners perceived them as teachers so they created digital stories "to establish their social presence as instructors" (p. 71). When designing their courses they strived to build in opportunities to engage in authentic activities to establish and encourage social presence. Stories are powerful strategies that help make meaning from experiences and help build connections with prior knowledge (Bruner, 1996; Lowenthal and Dunlap, 2010).

Educators must keep pace with advances in technology in order to be able to provide an ideal learning environment and meet the needs of today's learners (Burbles & Callister, 2000; Jonassen 2000; MacDonald, Stodel, & Farres, 2005; Tham & Werner, 2005). There is a need to improve online education programs through creating authentic learning environments and facilitating relevant learning. In recent years, online collaborative learning has generated interest in higher education and in the workplace as online technologies allow for interaction, socialisation, and collaboration. The Internet can provide learners with the option of working synchronously or asynchronously. Through discussion boards, shared whiteboards, video-conferencing, and chat rooms, learners are able to work collaboratively online to solve problems. The use of technology to facilitate online collaboration to solve authentic problems will improve critical thinking skills and ultimately the online learning experience.

STRATEGIES TO PROMOTE COGNITIVE PRESENCE

Design and Description of the RDLR

The RDLR (Archibald, 2010) was created for the study to help foster the development of critical thinking. Essentially, the RDLR was an interactive online tool to help participants learn about educational research and research design. The RDLR allowed participants to watch videos of researchers talk about the research designs of their recent studies and discuss aspects of the videos that resonated with them with other participants. The RDLR has three major components:

1. A collection of videos where researchers across Canada share their educational research stories
2. An online repository of resources about research design, including scholarly publications of each researcher's work (See Figure 1)
3. An online discussion forum that the researcher facilitated

To improve the participants' understanding of research design, they were asked to select and view 1 of the 14 video stories, each of which was edited into five minute segments. Individual segments covered topics such as research questions, conceptual frameworks, methodology, legitimization or validity, and lessons learned (See Figure 2). After viewing a segment, participants in a small group were invited to respond to several thought-provoking questions in a facilitated online discussion forum, to help guide their ideas for research, make connections with the research stories being viewed, and stimulate discussion amongst participants in the group (See Figure 3). In this way, the RDLR provides learners with the opportunity to collaboratively develop a research proposal and learn about educational research. Examples of thought provoking questions would include, "What practices or polices do you want to change?" and "How could these changes be implemented?"

Methodology

Participants in this study were learners enrolled in one of the following ten research methods courses: (1) a professional development workshop for practicing physicians offered by a professional organization, (2) one of five graduate level courses offered through a Faculty of Education, (3) one of three nursing research methods courses, one at the undergraduate level, one at the graduate level, and one post-graduate, offered at two established

Figure 1. Screen shot of the RDLR presenting the online repository

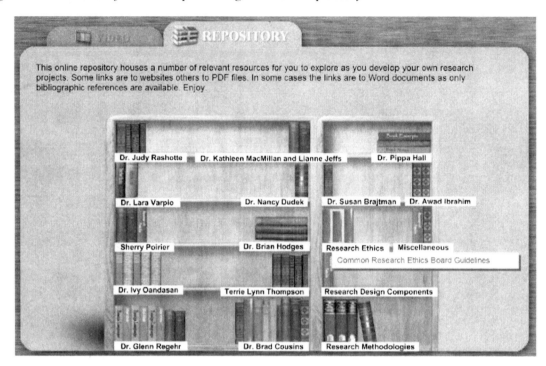

Figure 2. Screen shot of the RDLR presenting the video segments of a research story

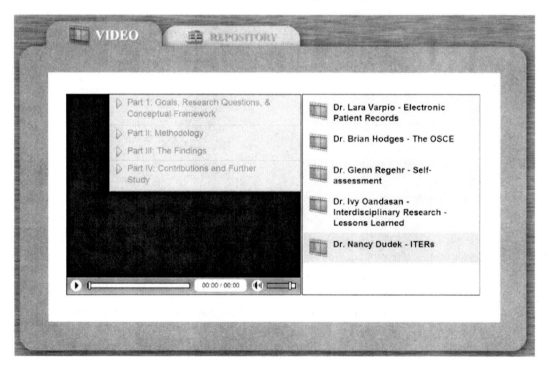

Figure 3. Screen shot of the RDLR presenting a triggering question and link to the discussion forum

Nursing Schools, or (4) an interprofessional community healthcare course. Data was collected from these courses beginning in the Spring of 2008 and culminating in the Spring of 2009. Of the 189 participants, 88% were female, and 72% were less than 36 years of age. Relating to formal online learning experience about 53% of participants had previously taken an online course. Descriptions of the intervention sites, how the RDLR and collaborative activities were used can be found in Appendix A.

The sequential explanatory research design was adopted to guide this study, which is typically used when qualitative data are used to provide more in-depth information about statistically significant or non-significant quantitative results, distinguishing demographic characteristics, or unexpected results. In this design, the researcher first collects and analyses numeric data and then the text data is collected and analysed and connected at the intermediate phase of the study. The rationale for this approach is that the quantitative analysis provides a general understanding of the research problem and the qualitative analysis refines and explains the statistical results in more depth. This design has been discussed extensively in the mixed methods literature (Creswell, 2003; Creswell & Plano Clark, 2010; Rossman & Wilson, 1985; Tashakkori & Teddlie, 1998).

The first (quantitative) phase of the study, involved collecting data using three online surveys, including the Community of Inquiry Survey Instrument (Arbaugh et al., 2008) and analyzing the online discussion transcripts from each research methods course. The goals of the quantitative phase as they pertain to reporting for this chapter included an examination of the relationships between social, teaching, and cognitive presence to gain further insight into whether the use of the RDLR and collaborative online discussions promoted higher phases of critical thinking and an exploration of how participants experienced the development of cognitive presence.

The predictor variables, social and teaching presence, and the dependent variable, cognitive presence were collected through the CoI survey (Arbaugh et al., 2008). The 34 item survey consists of factors that determine each element of the framework. The CoI survey was used as a post evaluation of the RDLR and online discussions. It took participants on average between 5 and 10 minutes to complete. The survey was completed online at the participants' leisure toward the end of the course.

The mean cognitive presence scores were selected as the dependent variable for a regression analysis. Social and teaching presences were treated as independent or indicator variables, as they could predict the development of the cognitive presence.Standard multiple regression was used to determine the extent to which teaching and social presence contributed to the development of cognitive presence; CHAID analysis (an additional multivariate method of analysis) was conducted to shed light on which items of teaching and social presence most influenced the development of cognitive presence, and through conducting hierarchical regression analysis it determined whether the independent variables (social and teaching presences) continued to make a significant contribution to the development of cognitive presence after including the control variables in the regression model. Finally, to explore how participants experienced the development of cognitive presence, a quantitative content analysis was conducted using the online discussion transcripts that resulted from the course activities and postings by the participants and the facilitator (the facilitator of the discussions was also the researcher for this study). The researcher and a colleague with extensive coding experience conducted the analysis to ensure inter-rater reliability. The results of all the analyses were then used to develop an interview protocol and purposefully select participants for the second phase of the study.

The second (qualitative) phase of the study involved text data that were collected from semi-structured interviews. These data helped explain a number of the significant and non-significant results from the first (quantitative) phase of the research. The quantitative results provided an overall, general view of the research problem and the qualitative findings explained the statistical results by allowing the exploration of the participants' learning experiences in more detail.

Quantitative Results

The mean scores of the CoI survey instrument, which was used in this study as a post-test evaluation of the RDLR, and the percentage of positive responses (those participants that indicated they either "agree" or "strongly agree" with the statements of the CoI survey instrument) were used to determine if participants had a positive learning experience using the RDLR. Overall, participants rated teaching presence in a positive light. Participant responses ranged from 50.0-85.2%, compared to only 3.8-18.5% negative responses (those participants that indicated they either "disagree" or "strongly disagree" with the statements of the CoI survey instrument).

Similarly, participants responded favorably to social presence items. Positive responses for the courses ranged from 39.8-69.1%. Negative responses ranged from 3.7-25.9%. Items with high negative responses included: online or web-based communication is an excellent medium for social interaction and online discussion help me to develop a sense of collaboration.

Positive responses for cognitive presence ranged from 44.4-63.9%. Negative responses ranged from 9.3-20.4%. Items with high negative responses included: online discussions were valuable in helping me appreciate different perspectives; I felt motivated to explore content related questions; and I utilized a variety of information sources to explore problems posed in this course.

A standard regression analysis was conducted using the mean scores of the CoI constructs to determine the relationship between teaching presence and social presence with cognitive presence development, through the use of the RDLR. It appeared there was a positive relationship between both social presence and teaching presence with the cognitive presence in the CoI model. Table 1 displays the correlations between the variables, the unstandardized regression coefficients (B), the standardised regression coefficients (β), the semi-partial correlations (sr²), the amount of variability accounted for by the predictor variables (R^2), and the adjusted R^2. The adjusted R^2 value of .69 indicated that almost 70% of the variability in the cognitive presence is predicted by social and teaching presence. Data from Table 1 has been previously published (Archibald, 2010).

Social presence and teaching presence made very strong unique contributions to explaining cognitive presence; both of which were statistically significant (.47 and .45 respectively). The semi-partial correlation coefficients squared (sr²) gave an indication of the relative contribution of each independent variable to the total R^2. In other words it indicated how much total variance in the cognitive presence was uniquely explained by each of social presence and teaching presence

and how much the R^2 would drop if either social presence or teaching presence were not included in the model. It should be noted that the R^2 value includes the unique variance and the shared variance explained by both social and teaching presence. In this model social presence and teaching presence are very strongly correlated (r =.65). Therefore there is a significant amount of shared variance (.45) that is statistically removed when both are included in the regression model. These results are supported with evidence in the literature that effective online learning is a function of the interaction of the three presences, and that social and teaching presence are correlated with cognitive presence (Arbaugh, 2007; Garrison & Arbaugh, 2007; Garrison & Cleveland-Innes, 2005; Garrison, et al., 2010; Shea & Bidjerano, 2009).

A further multivariate analysis was used to unpack the specific items in social and teaching presence that had an effect on cognitive presence development. CHAID analysis produces a regression or decision tree that indicates the most significant breaks in responses to items of the CoI survey instrument that predict responses to another item or construct (Shea & Bidjerano, 2009). The method is a logical next step in determining the extent of the relationships in the CoI framework.

Table 1. Summary of standard regression analysis of social and teaching presences on predicting cognitive presence development in an online community of inquiry

Variable	Cognitive Presence	Social Presence	Teaching Presence	B	β	sr²
Social Presence	.76			.49	.47**	.13
Teaching Presence	.75	.65		.50	.45**	.11
Mean	3.48	3.46	3.80			
Standard Deviation	.67	.64	.59		R^2 = .69ᵃ	
adjusted R^2 = .69						
R = .83**						

**p<.01

ᵃUnique variability = .25; shared variability = .45

The CoI instrument is on a Likert-type scale: 1 (strongly disagree) – 5 (strongly agree)

The standard regression analysis determined there was a positive relationship between cognitive presence, and teaching and social presence. CHAID analysis explores this relationship in more detail as it examines the relationship of individual items which can lead to further insight into the development of cognitive presence. The social teaching presence indicator, "Online discussions help me develop a sense of collaboration" is the highest level item that sorts the respondents on the factor of cognitive presence. Thirty-nine respondents who agreed with this statement reported significantly higher levels of cognitive presence than those who were neutral or disagreed.

Within this high scoring group, the teaching presence item "The instructor helped keep the course participants on task in a way that helped me to learn", respondents reported significantly higher average cognitive presence scores when they also agreed more strongly with this teaching presence item as compared to those who rated the instructor not helping to keep the course participants on task in a way to help their learning. At the third level of categorization, within this high scoring group, respondents who agreed strongly to the social presence item "I felt my point of view was acknowledged by other course participants" were also significantly more likely to report higher cognitive presence scores.

Finally, the online discussions were coded according to the Practical Inquiry Model. Discussions occurred over periods ranging from two weeks to three months depending on the course. Although most of the text messages were considered exploration, many did reach the phase of integration. Unfortunately very few messages reached the highest phase of cognitive presence development. Resolution messages only represented 0-5%. A summary of the distribution of the online transcripts and number of coded messages is presented in Table 2. The column labeled "other" refers to messages that did not relate to cognitive presence. Sites A and F did not have enough discussions to warrant a content analysis.

Qualitative Findings

As mentioned in the methodology section of this chapter, the interview protocol was based on the results of the statistical tests in the first phase of the study with a particular emphasis on the relationship between teaching and social presence with cognitive presence The protocol consisted of thirteen open –ended questions which are presented in Appendix B. The first nine interview questions were intended to get the participants to talk about their overall experience using the RDLR and participating in the discussions as well determine

Table 2. Distribution of messages according to the practical inquiry model categories

Site	No. of Participant Messages	Distribution Over Categories (%)				
		Trigger	Exploration	Integration	Resolution	Other
B	72	10	34	25	0	31
C,D,E	37	16	35	19	3	27
G	116	3	42	40	2	13
H	312	2	41	35	5	17
I	1617	2	52	26	1	19
Total	2154					
Average		6.6	40.8	29.0	2.2	21.4

why teaching and social presences had such an effect on the development of cognitive presence.

The final four questions were not related to quantitative results per se but gave the participants an opportunity to talk about anything that may not have been mentioned previously and could provide insight into cognitive presence. It was through the participants' responses that the researcher was able to gain insight into the strategies they used for developing cognitive presence.

All participants interviewed made some connections with components the RDLR, classmates, and the researcher in relation to promoting cognitive presence. This theme had the most references by far of any of the themes and it helped to explain many significant findings from the first phase of the study (Refer to Table 3). The researcher deconstructed this theme into four subthemes: connections with classmates, connections with the facilitator/researcher, connections to the researchers in the videos, and connections with the repository. Three other themes provided concrete examples for strategies to promote cognitive presence included multiple perspectives, resource design and learning strategies.

There were 45 references to the connections participants made with each other. In many of the interviews, participants commented on how they were able to build on each other's ideas or were enlightened on a particular topic through another's posting. This strategy was one of the most used

and most effective in promoting cognitive presence. One participant commented:

The discussions were great too because it really puts a human perspective and it makes it more personal which is really something that I feel I can connect with. I am not very good at the abstract so I find in discussion it makes it more real for me. I am the kind of person that needs real life examples just speaking in academic terms with abstract vocabulary is sometimes hard for me to grasp but with the discussion I could really ground what I knew (Cathy, site B).

This idea of the discussions making the learning personal and that others had the same questions were echoed by other participants too, "...experiencing the same thing that other people are. I think Ned was really good at reframing what was going on and making that a little more accessible" (Jacob, site B). Participants also enjoyed sharing ideas with each other. This correlates with the exploration phase of cognitive presence and potentially leads to the integration phase. "Yes and she would bounce ideas off me and she was sharing her question and I would share mine" (Libby, site H). Participants appreciated hearing the perspectives of their classmates, me, and the researchers on the videos.

About 40% of the participants interviewed expressed their appreciation for the support and

Table 3. Number of text units by theme*

Theme	Participants	Text Unit Count
Barriers to Cognitive Presence	22 (88%)	61
Learning Preferences	23 (92%)	56
Learning Strategies	12 (48%)	24
Making Connections	24 (96%)	185
Multiple Perspectives	17 (68%)	26
Resource Design	18 (72%)	35
Being a Self-Directed Learner	14 (58%)	24

*a text unit is a sentence or paragraph coded by the researcher to a theme

guidance I provided through the discussions. In particular the triggering questions that were proposed; the role the facilitator played in keeping the discussions moving forward and keeping people on task; and the feedback provided. This is a strategy that facilitators can use in promoting cognitive presence. "I like that you were there at the beginning and not responding to everything that everybody asks. But you are there to give a sense of direction and to stimulate discussion and reflection, that was good" (Wendy, site H). Triggering questions are a key component to cognitive presence as attested to by this participant:

It gave me an idea of how to put together my research question. I find that often when I start a research question it is really too broad, but I guess by looking at the different kinds of discussion questions I can do something like that or change it, giving me examples of what I could do (Cathy, site B).

The feedback that the facilitator provided was very important for participants to feel connected to the discussions and reassurance that they interpreting the information from the video research stories correctly. "I waited for your comments to come back so I knew that I was on the right track" (Annette, site G). Waiting for feedback from me seemed to be a popular strategy as well for many participants. Being confident to move to higher levels of critical thinking is essential and receiving feedback from a facilitator helps foster confidence.

Many of the participants reported they felt a connection with the researchers through the videos. In particular, the videos were able to put a face to the research. One participant commented:

You do feel their passion. It's interesting...they stumble over words, they stutter. When you read a piece of literature its scholarly, its beautifully written, grammatically perfect...It's not the way they talk in real life – they are regular people.

So that was really interesting for me. That was something that really stood out for me. That was very important (Kelly, site H).

Many of the participants noted that the timing between the segments was critical for reflection purposes and was paramount for fostering cognitive presence. "I like the way it progressed, like it sort of went to different sections and you processed that one particular area, take a pause to think about it and then move on to see how it [is] really developed...[otherwise] you wouldn't have had the same response" (Karla, site G). Another participant expressed, "I think I would have lost interest in its entirety because I needed to take a moment and let it all sink in, think about it and take notes" (Ralph, site C).

Furthermore, it was evident from reviewing the transcripts that some participants appreciated the scholarly articles that the researchers had written about their projects, the methodology articles and links. A number of participants commented on how the resources in the repository helped foster cognitive presence, "I was pleasantly surprised at the resources, how they did help me think through" (Jane, site B). Another student commented, "I thought it was good, I really liked the interface with the books. I thought that was smart... I found the lists very helpful. I printed those all off" (Jocelyn, site E). Also, "The repository because there were lots of different perspectives on how to do research and types of research and it provides a really good exemplar at least for me" (Polly, site D).

One resource in the repository was particular helpful in creating critical discourse. This was C-FLO (MacDonald et al., 2005). Participants really connected with one of the researchers in the video section of the resource and identified with her struggles to develop a conceptual framework. For example:

So when I listened to [Tracy], I found it quite helpful because she broke it down into parts and she talked about her feelings about it, including the fact that she felt overwhelmed and that at times she was confused. I think that knowing this made the whole exercise more human and it made me relax a little bit from the internal pressure and demand that I produce is a perfect thing, that I know ahead of time how to do something. She talked about the process of learning and revising, coming back and trying it out. Also there were pictures of her different drafts that she did. You could see a progression from the very initial scratching on the paper to the final product. That was also helpful to have that visual along with the audio that she did (Linda, site B).

It is evident from these testimonies that the use of video is a strategy that course designers and facilitators can use to promote cognitive presence development. The use of video provides alternative perspectives and content that can stimulate critical discourse amongst participants. Resource design, according to the participants interviewed, was an important factor in predicting cognitive presence. It was evident from the results of the CoI survey that teaching presence, of which design and organization are part, significantly contributes to the prediction of cognitive presence. Many participants commented on how logical the RDLR was and that made it easier to learn about research. "...how you organized it was that each individual and what their videos were, you had an index that said introduction, methodology etc. so depending on what I needed to focus on I could actually pick just that" (Linda, site B). Another participant remarked,

It was just having everything around me that I needed and could go to and from my ideas and connect with that information which connected with the information that I was pulling for research to use for my paper. Everything just melted together and was very efficient (Jake, site B).

Thus another strategy participants use is investigation. If the course designer and/or facilitator provide meaningful resources, participants are likely to be more engaged and the potential for cognitive presence development increases.

Interestingly, one of the themes that emerged in the study was actually learning strategies. In the interviews, participants revealed strategies they used to foster critical discourse. Many of the participants described in detail how they transitioned from their personal worlds (reflection) to their shared worlds (online discourse). One participant stated:

I learned them pretty fast and when I was doing the discussion I was curious because I didn't know some of the words of things that the researcher used so I had to go through the online search and find out what they meant. ... I went to the [discussion] groups and they were exactly the same idea I was thinking about but they expressed it in different ways and it was good to hear someone else also thinking the same thing. Also if I was not agreeing with them I would reply and ask why they thought this... (Nadine, site I).

Another student described his approach to the discussions. It was clear that this student was able to build upon the ideas of others which is a critical step in the cognitive presence development process.

I didn't make many comments to other people but here is what I did. I read theirs before I posted mine. ... I wanted to find out what other people were saying and I chose not to respond, I didn't feel the need to. I found it was valuable to read what they were writing. ...I did base what I put down in my discussion after reading what other people wrote; especially I think one other person wrote something about the same video I wrote about. I took theirs and kind of worked off of them in my own discrete way (Ralph, site C).

DISCUSSION

In summary, from this study the researcher determined that participants used a number of strategies to promote cognitive presence. These included building on each other's ideas, sharing ideas, and waiting for feedback from the facilitator or other participants. Furthermore, as the study's facilitator and resource designer, the researcher was able to use strategies to promote cognitive presence such as incorporating video into the resource, providing time for reflection in between video segments, posting scholarly articles for more in depth reading, posing thought provoking triggering questions that were relevant and meaningful, and lastly creating a resource that was logical in design to facilitate exploration.

In terms of contributing to the existing literature many of the findings from this study confirm or extend the work of other educational researchers. For example, results from the standard regression analysis suggest that social presence and teaching presence make strong and statistically significant contributions to explaining cognitive presence and are critical for determining the strategies participants use. Social presence made a very strong unique and significant contribution to explaining cognitive presence ($\beta = .47$). Social and teaching presence accounted for about 69% of the variance in cognitive presence. Moreover, social presence and teaching presence were very strongly correlated ($r = .65$) and therefore contributed to the shared variance (.45) in the model. These results are similar to those of a number of recent studies that have used the CoI survey instrument.

Shea and Bidjerano (2009) found that social and teaching presence accounted for 70% of the variance in cognitive presence among a group of 2159 online participants. Similarly, Garrison, Cleveland-Innes, & Fung (2010) found that perceptions of teaching presence and social presence significantly predicted the perception of cognitive presence. In addition, they found that teaching presence was paramount to maintaining social

and cognitive presence. In both studies social presence significantly and positively contributed to cognitive presence. Thus, social presence is important to cognitive presence.

The relationship between social presence and cognitive presence was also apparent from the qualitative interviews. There were 45 references to the connections participants made with each other that were found in the interview transcripts. Participants commented on how they were able to build on each other's ideas or were enlightened on a particular topic through another's posting. Being able to build on someone else's idea is an indicator of the integration phase of cognitive presence and is a very important strategy indeed.

Of particular interest in this study is that the CHAID analysis showed that participants who agreed that online discussions helped foster a sense of collaboration were more likely to rate their experiences of cognitive presence as high. Moreover, these results suggest that one's perception of working together to answer a common problem in an online discussion is an important predictor for cognitive presence. There is a substantial body of literature indicating that facilitated collaborative learning strategies promote cognitive presence (Garrison & Cleveland Innes, 2005; MacKnight, 2000; Wu & Hiltz, 2004). In order for participants to participate and optimize their learning in a collaborative learning environment they need to have certain skills; for instance being capable, asking the right questions, listening to each other, respecting each other's work and ideas, and building upon each other's ideas (MacKnight, 2000). These skills and strategies need to be supported by the facilitator to ensure that social and cognitive presence are supported and sustained.

The participants who were interviewed made some connections with components of the RDLR, their classmates, and the facilitator that promoted cognitive presence. It was apparent that those participants who were able to make connections with their classmates, the facilitator, and the content of RDLR, had positive learning experiences and were able to explain strategies they used to promote cognitive presence development. The sheer number of references to connections in the interviews (185 out of 411 [45%] references from 96% of the participants) indicated that a sense of connection was vital for cognitive presence and reinforced the relationships among teaching, social, and cognitive presence. In many of the interviews, participants commented on how they were able to build on each other's ideas, were enlightened about a particular topic as a result of reading other postings, and generally enjoyed sharing information. The comments strengthened the argument that social presence supports cognitive presence.

Research on social presence in the 1990s saw social presence as a "one dimensional construct associated with an emotional sense of belonging" (Garrison, et al., 2010). However, this view of social presence has changed and the special role it plays between teaching and cognitive presence has been recognised (Garrison, 2009; Garrison, et al., 2010; Shea & Bidjerano, 2009). The findings from this study are congruent with the notion that social presence is a shared social identity rather a personal identity.

Teaching presence is critical for learner satisfaction, perceived learning, and developing a sense of community (Garrison & Arbaugh, 2007; Garrison & Cleveland-Innes, 2005; Kanuka et al., 2007; Meyer, 2003; Shea, Frederickson, Pickett, & Pelz, 2003). Instructional design and organization is one subscale of teaching presence. Garrison and Arbaugh (2007) noted that developing audio and video, posting lecture notes, and creating a balance of individual and group activities are all part of supporting the course structure that is important for successful online learning. The researchers' video stories and the repository in the RDLR would have contributed to this component of teaching presence and served to build the participants' connections. Indeed, in the interviews, participants made many references to the impact the researcher video stories and associated publications had on

their learning. The participants indicated that the research videos were particularly valuable because they allowed them to "connect the research to the researcher". Participants were able to put a face to the research, which was meaningful to them.

Stories are powerful teaching and learning tools; they help learners make sense of the experience being presented (Bruner, 1996; Lowenthal & Dunlap, 2010; McLellan, 2006).

Recent research has provided evidence that the role of the facilitator in collaborative learning activities is crucial for learners to achieve higher phases of critical thinking:

In this context, interaction must be more structured and systematic. ... It is valuable and even necessary to create a community of inquiry where interaction is seen as communication with the intent to influence thinking in a critical and reflective manner (Garrison & Cleveland-Innes, 2005, p. 134).

It was apparent from the participants interviewed that the researcher's role as facilitator was pivotal in moving the discussions forward. Strategies facilitators can use to promote cognitive presence can include through posing thought provoking questions, answering questions, or suggesting further reading.

Finally participants perceived resource design to be an important strategy or consideration that designers and facilitators can use to promote cognitive presence. Participants indicated the RDLR was convenient to use, easy to navigate, and logically organised. Research using the W(e)Learn Framework (MacDonald, Stodel, Thompson, & Casimiro, 2009) has shown that a well-designed program with well-designed learning activities is critical for cognitive presence and successful learning. According to W(e)Learn, the first step is to consider the structure of the program. These considerations include: pedagogical strategies, interactivity, community, and reusability of the learning resource, among others.

Key to resource design are considerations regarding community and pedagogical strategies. Building community online starts by taking the time to ensure that learners, through thoughtful and well-designed learning activities, get to know each other and have an opportunity to develop a community of practice. Choosing pedagogical strategies is also part of the instructional design process and needs to be considered with building community, "...to maximize collaboration, dialogue, and critical inquiry" (MacDonald et al., 2009, p. 39).

The design process of the RDLR also included online discussion boards. The literature on using this form of asynchronous learning has been well documented (Bliss & Lawrence, 2009; Meyer, 2004). Furthermore, they have been used to facilitate learners' "co-construction of knowledge, engagement of higher order thinking, and...development of critical thinking skills. ...a place where students negotiate meaning of course content and practice skills" (Bliss & Lawrence, p. 16).

In closing, through a greater appreciation of the effects that teaching and social presences have on cognitive presence, designers and facilitators can provide a learning environment conducive to higher levels of thinking. This study provided insight into strategies that influence reflection and critical discourse. Hopefully these suggested strategies will be helpful in creating improved learning experiences.

FUTURE RESEARCH DIRECTIONS

The findings presented in this study offer new opportunities for future research. Furthermore, there remain some unanswered questions that still need to be addressed. The first opportunity has to with exploring technologies in online learning. The CoI survey instrument was useful in assessing the effectiveness of the RDLR. Future research using the CoI survey instrument to explore the utility of other new teaching and learning technologies is warranted. The researcher would add that along with the exploration of new technologies, researchers examine the strategies participants use to foster critical thinking skills and higher order learning. Swan and Ice (2010) cited five studies that are in the process of using the CoI framework to explore cognitive, teaching, and social presence through the use of innovative multimedia tools. We are now in an exciting era of Web 2.0 technologies that need to be explored to determine their effectiveness in formal online education settings.

Collaborative learning is certainly important for sustaining an online community of inquiry and is imperative for developing strategies to promote cognitive presence. Recent research has shown that there is a role adjustment that novice online participants make in order to succeed when learning online. Thus, prior online learning experience may be an important part of how social presence is developed, which in turn affects cognitive presence. However, we need to consider what prior collaborative learning experience and prior online learning experience really mean in terms of sustaining an online community of inquiry.

REFERENCES

Akyol, Z., & Garrison, D. R. (2011). Understanding cognitive presence in an online and blended community of inquiry: Assessing outcomes and processes for deep approaches to learning. *British Journal of Educational Technology, 42*(2), 233–250.

Akyol, Z., Garrison, D. R., & Ozden, M. Y. (2009). Online and blended communities of inquiry: Exploring the developmental and perceptional differences. *International Review of Research in Open and Distance Learning(IRRODL), 10*(6), 65–83.

Andriessen, J. (2006). Collaboration in computer conferencing. In O'Donnell, A. M., Hmelo-Silver, C., & Erkens, G. (Eds.), *Collaborative learning, reasoning and technology* (pp. 197–232). Mahwah, NJ: Erlbaum.

Arbaugh, J. B. (2007). An empirical verification of the community of inquiry framework. *Journal of Asynchronous Learning Networks, 11*(1), 73–85.

Arbaugh, J. B., Cleveland-Innes, M., Diaz, S. R., Garrison, D. R., Ice, P., Richardson, J. C., & Swan, K. P. (2008). Developing a community of inquiry instrument: Testing a measure of the Community of Inquiry framework using a multi-institutional sample. *Internet and Higher Learning, 11*, 133–136.

Arbaugh, J. B., & Hwang, A. (2006). Does "teaching presence" exist in online MBA courses? *The Internet and Higher Education, 9*(1), 9–21.

Archibald, D. (2010). Fostering the development of cognitive presence: Initial findings using the community of inquiry survey instrument. *The Internet and Higher Education, 13*(1-2), 73–74.

Archibald, D. (2011). *Fostering cognitive presence in higher education through the authentic design, delivery, and evaluation of an online learning resource: A mixed methods study.* Unpublished doctoral dissertation, University of Ottawa, Ottawa

Bielaczyc, K., & Collins, A. (2006). Fostering knowledge-creating communities. In O'Donnell, A. M., Hmelo-Silver, C., & Erkens, G. (Eds.), *Collaborative learning, reasoning and technology* (pp. 37–60). Mahwah, NJ: Erlbaum.

Biggs, J. B., & Collis, K. F. (1982). *Evaluating the quality of learning: The SOLO taxonomy.* New York, NY: Academic Press.

Bliss, C. A., & Lawrence, B. (2009). From posts to patterns: A metric to characterize discussion board activity in online courses. *Journal of Asynchronous Learning Networks, 13*(2), 15–32.

Bloom, B. S., Engelhart, M. D., Furst, E. J., Hill, W. H., & Krathwohl, D. R. (1956). *Taxonomy of educational objectives – The classification of educational goals, handbook 1, cognitive domain.* London, UK: Longman Group.

Brookfield, S. D. (1987). *Developing critical thinkers.* San Francisco, CA: Jossey-Bass.

Brookfield, S. D. (1995). *Becoming a critically reflective teacher.* San Francisco, CA: Jossey-Bass.

Bruner, J. (1996). *The culture of education.* Cambridge, MA: Harvard University Press.

Burbles, N., & Callister, T. (2000). Universities in transition: The promise and challenge of new technologies. *Teachers College Record, 102*(2), 271–293.

Creswell, J. W., & Clark, V. L. P. (2011). *Designing and conducting mixed methods research* (2nd ed.). Thousand Oaks, CA: Sage.

D'Angelo, E. (1971). *The teaching of critical thinking.* Amsterdam, The Netherlands: B. R. Gruner N. V.

Dewey, J. (1933). *How we think: A restatement of the relation of reflective thinking to the educative process.* Boston, MA: D. C. Heath.

Duphorne, P., & Gunawardena, C. N. (2005). The effect of three computer conferencing designs on critical thinking skills of nursing students. *American Journal of Distance Education, 19*(1), 37–50.

Fasco, D. Jr., (Ed.). (2003). *Critical thinking and reasoning: Current research, theory, and practice.* Cresskill, NJ: Hampton Press.

Garrison, D. R. (1991). Critical thinking and adult education: A conceptual model for developing critical thinking in adult learners. *International Journal of Lifelong Education, 10*(4), 287–303.

Garrison, D. R. (2009). Communities of inquiry in online learning. In Rogers, P. L. (Ed.), *Encyclopedia of distance learning* (2nd ed., pp. 352–355). Hershey, PA: IGI Global.

Garrison, D. R., Anderson, T., & Archer, W. (2000). Critical inquiry in a text-based environment: Computer conferencing in higher education. *The Internet and Higher Education, 2*(2-3), 87–105.

Garrison, D. R., Anderson, T., & Archer, W. (2001). Critical thinking, cognitive presence, and computer conferencing in distance education. *American Journal of Distance Education, 15*(1), 7–23.

Garrison, D. R., Anderson, T., & Archer, W. (2010). The first decade of the community of inquiry framework: A retrospective. *The Internet and Higher Education, 13*(1-2), 5–9.

Garrison, D. R., & Arbaugh, J. B. (2007). Researching the community of inquiry framework: Review, issues, and future directions. *The Internet and Higher Education, 10*(3), 157–172.

Garrison, D. R., & Archer, W. (2000). *A transactional perspective on teaching and learning: A framework for adult and higher education.* Oxford, UK: Pergamon.

Garrison, D. R., & Cleveland-Innes, M. (2005). Facilitating cognitive presence in online learning: Interaction is not enough. *American Journal of Distance Education, 19*(3), 133–148.

Garrison, D. R., Cleveland-Innes, M., & Fung, T. (2010). Exploring causal relationships among teaching, cognitive and social presence: Student perceptions of the community of inquiry framework. *The Internet and Higher Education, 13*(1-2), 31–36.

Guglielmino, L. M., & Guglielmino, P. J. (1991). *The learner preference assessment.* Organization Design and Development.

Gunawardena, C. N., & Zittle, F. J. (1997). Social presence as a predictor of satisfaction within a computer-mediated conferencing environment. *American Journal of Distance Education, 11*(3), 8–26.

Huang, H. (2002). Toward constructivism for adult learners in online learning environments. *British Journal of Educational Technology, 33*(1), 27–37.

Ice, P., Curtis, R., Phillips, P., & Wells, J. (2007). Using asynchronous audio feedback to enhance teaching presence and students' sense of community. *Journal of Asynchronous Learning Networks, 11*(2), 3-25. Retrieved January 31, 2011, from http://sloanconsortium.org/jaln/v11n2/using-asynchronous-audio-feedback-enhance-teaching-presence-and-students%E2%80%99-sense-community

Jonassen, D. H. (2000). Transforming learning with technology: Beyond modernism and post-modernism or whoever controls the technology creates the reality. *Educational Technology, 40*(2), 21–25.

Jonassen, D. H. (2006). Typology of case-based learning: The content, form, and function of cases. *Educational Technology, 46*(4), 11–15.

Jonassen, D. H., Peck, K. L., & Wilson, B. G. (1999). *Learning with technology: A constructivist perspective.* Columbus, OH: Prentice Hall.

Kanuka, H., & Anderson, T. (1998). Online social interchange, discord, and knowledge construction. *Journal of Distance Education, 13*(1), 57–74.

Kanuka, H., Rourke, L., & Laflamme, E. (2007). The influence of instructional methods on the quality of online discussion. *British Journal of Educational Technology, 38*(2), 260–271.

Lowenthal, P., & Dunlap, J. (2010). From pixel on a screen to real person in you students' lives: Establishing social presence using digital storytelling. *The Internet and Higher Education, 13*(1-2), 70–72.

MacDonald, C. J., Stodel, E. J., & Farres, L. G. (2005). The future of university and organisational learning. In Howard, C. (Eds.), *Encyclopedia of distance learning* (*Vol. II*, pp. 960–968). Hershey, PA: Idea Group.

MacDonald, C. J., Stodel, E. J., Thompson, T.-L., & Casimiro, L. (2009). W(e)Learn: A framework for interprofessional education. *International Journal of Electronic Healthcare, 5*(1), 33–47.

MacKnight, C. B. (2000). Teaching critical thinking through online discussions. *EDUCAUSE Quarterly, 23*, 38–41.

Maxwell, J. A. (2005). *Qualitative research design: An interactive approach* (2nd ed.). Thousand Oaks, CA: Sage.

McLellan, H. (2006). Digital storytelling: Bridging old and new. *Educational Technology, 46*(2), 26–31.

McPeck. J. (1981). *Critical thinking and education.* Oxford, UK: Martin Robertson.

Meyer, K. (2003). Face-to-face versus threaded discussions: The role of time and higher-order thinking. *Journal of Asynchronous Learning Networks, 7*(3), 55–65.

Meyer, K. (2004). Evaluating online discussions: Four different frames of analysis. *Journal of Asynchronous Learning Networks, 8*(2), 101–114.

Moore, J., & Marra, R. (2005). A comparative analysis of online discussion participation protocols. *Journal of Research on Technology in Education, 38*(2), 191–212.

O'Donnell, A. M. (2006). The role of peers and group learning. In Alexander, P., & Winne, P. (Eds.), *Handbook of educational psychology* (2nd ed., pp. 781–802). Mahwah, NJ: Lawrence Erlbaum.

Paul, R. (1985). The critical thinking movement. *National Forum, 65*(1), 2–3.

Perkins, D. (1986). On creativity and thinking skills: A conversation with David Perkins. *Educational Leadership, 43*(8), 12–18.

Roberts, T. S. (2004). Self, peer and group assessment in e-Learning: An introduction. In Roberts, T. S. (Ed.), *Self, peer, and group assessment in e-learning* (pp. 1–16). Hershey, PA: Information Science Publishing.

Rourke, L., Anderson, T., Garrison, D. R., & Archer, W. (2001). Methodological issues in the content analysis of computer conference transcripts. *International Journal of Artificial Intelligence in Education, 12*(1), 8–22.

Schrire, S. (2004). Interaction and cognition in asynchronous computer conferencing. *Instructional Science, 32*, 475–502.

Shea, P., & Bidjerano, T. (2009). Community of inquiry as a theoretical framework to foster "epistemic engagement" and "cognitive presence" in online education. *Computers & Education, 52*, 543–553.

Shea, P., Frederickson, E., Pickett, A., & Peltz, W. (2003). A preliminary investigation of "teaching presence" in the SUNY learning network. In Bourne & C.J. Moore (Eds.), *Elements of quality online education: Practice direction, Vol. 4,* (pp. 279-312). Needham, MA: Sloan Center for Online Education.

Sternberg, R. J. (1988). *The nature of creativity: Contemporary psychological perspectives.* Cambridge: Cambridge University Press.

Swan, K., Garrison, D. R., & Richardson, J. (2009). A constructivist approach to online learning: The community of inquiry framework. In Payne, C. R. (Ed.), *Information technology in and constructivism in higher education: Progressive learning framework*. Hershey, PA: IGI Global.

Swan, K., & Shih, L. (2005). On the nature and development of social presence in online course discussions. *Journal of Asynchronous Learning Networks, 9*(13), 115–136.

Tham, C., & Werner, J. (2005). Designing and evaluating e-learning in higher education: A review and recommendations. *Journal of Leadership & Organizational Studies, 11*(2), 15–24.

Thompson, T.-L., & MacDonald, C. J. (2005). Community building, emergent design and expecting the unexpected: Creating a quality eLearning experience. *The Internet and Higher Education, 8*(3), 233–249.

Uzener, S. (2007). Educationally valuable talk: A new concept for determining the quality of online conversations. *Journal of Online Learning and Teaching, 3*(4), 400–410.

Vaughan, N. D. (2010). Student engagement and Web 2.0: What's the connection? *Education Canada, 50*(2), 52–55.

Vaughan, N. D., & Garrison, D. R. (2005). Creating cognitive presence in a blended faculty development community. *The Internet and Higher Education, 8*, 1–12.

Wu, D., & Hiltz, S. R. (2004). Predicting learning from asynchronous online discussions. *Journal of Asynchronous Learning Networks, 8*(2), 139–152.

KEY TERMS AND DEFINITIONS

Cognitive Presence: In online learning, the extent to which learners are able to construct and confirm meaning through sustained reflection and discourse (Garrison & Arbaugh, 2007). Moreover, cognitive presence focuses on the learner's higher order thinking processes (Garrison et al. 2001).

Collaborative Learning: Distance learners who previously were unable to have much contact with other learners can now take part in discussion forums and group activities. Course management systems such as WebCT and Blackboard Vista incorporate tools for synchronous and asynchronous online communication and learner presentations (Roberts, 2004).

Community of Inquiry Framework (CoI): A conceptual model for online learning that can be used as a research tool or a guide to evaluate programs. Garrison et al. (2000) developed the CoI framework as a means to investigate how computer conference activities could promote critical thinking. The CoI assumes that an effective online learning experience is a result of three essential interdependent elements: teaching presence, social presence, and cognitive presence.

Critical Discourse: In an online discussion, refers to the reflective thinking and collective knowledge building between an individual and a larger group of learners. Uzener (2007) indicates, "that removal of time and space restrictions in such discourse provides better opportunities for reflective thinking that may not be possible in time dependent spoken conversations" (p. 402). Uzener furthers this concept by indicating that, "the sequential and recorded qualities of threaded electronic discourse and its particular demands, such as exactness, coherent organization of thought, clear, and authentic expression, have powerful affordances for collective knowledge building" (p. 402). Meyer (2003), and Swan and Shih (2005) have also contributed to the literature on critical discourse or reflective online discussions.

Critical Thinking: The practice of reflection regarding thought and practice. Learners make connections between their personal and public worlds. Critical thinking is the ability of learners to use creativity, problem solving, intuition, and insight as well as to construct, make sense of and confirm meaning (Garrison & Archer, 2000). Critical thinking is both a process and an outcome. Garrison et al. (2001) acknowledged that as an outcome (e.g., critical inquiry abilities, skills, and dispositions), critical thinking is best understood from an individual perspective through assignments or finished products. The difficulty with assessing critical thinking as an outcome is that it is very complex because it involves creativity and problem solving. As a process, critical thinking can be facilitated by creating an environment conducive to higher order learning. This process can be explored using a tool to assess critical discourse and reflection—the Practical Inquiry Model (Garrison et al.).

Digital Storytelling: Recent technology in media applications has increased the facility of employing stories in online learning programs. Digital storytelling has been shown to promote literacy, collaboration, creativity, and problem-solving (McLellan, 2006). Digital storytelling adds to the resources available to learners for construct-

ing knowledge. It allows for more perspectives and ideas to be shared. "Stories originate in problematic situations; they show the way out of the situations" (McLellan, p. 28). Moreover, the use of digital storytelling and discussion boards can help engage learners in the discussion of stories and sharing of perspectives.

Facilitator: A facilitator of online discussions provides support and guidance to learners. This support can be in the form of asking questions and providing feedback to individual learners. The facilitator's role is to keep the discussion moving in order to assist learners in achieving higher levels of cognitive presence. The facilitator is to "monitor and manage discourse to ensure that it is productive and learners stay engaged" (Garrison, 2009, p. 354).

Instructional Designer: An instructional designer, who approaches learning from a collaborative approach, provides learners opportunities to actively practice what they are learning. In online learning this may include working with subject matter experts to develop content, and adapting instructional materials from traditional face-to-face environments to virtual environments. "Design sets the stage and potential of the learning experience. Design is of particular concern in creating a community of inquiry and collaborative-constructivist learning experiences" (Garrison, 2009, p. 354).

APPENDIX A

Interview Questions

1. What was your overall experience using the resource and participating in the discussions? Please explain.
2. Did the online learning resource help you learn about the research design process? If so, how?
3. How did you see the role of the facilitator? **Probe if necessary:**
   a. Did the facilitator help you with your learning?
   b. Did the facilitator help you reflect upon the videos by asking evocative questions?
   c. Did the facilitator help you think more critically about research?
   d. What could the facilitator have done differently to make your learning experience better?
4. Was the design of the resource conducive to helping you learn more about research? Specifically, did the design of the resource help you reflect and synthesize information? Please explain.
5. How did others in your group affect your learning? **Probe if necessary:**
   a. Did the learners in your group help you explore your ideas?
   b. Were you able to connect or build on anyone else's ideas?
   c. Were you able to apply what you have learned through viewing the videos and participating in the discussions?
6. Did you feel comfortable discussing your ideas with other members of your group? Please explain.
7. Did your prior experience with collaborative learning affect how you participated in the discussions. More specifically, did this prior experience affect how you explored your ideas? Please explain.
8. Did your prior experience of using the Internet make your learning experience easier or more difficult? Do you think your prior Internet experience has helped you become a more critical thinker? Please explain.
9. Do you think being a self-directed learner had any bearing on how you explored and reflected upon the ideas generated from the videos and discussions?

If time allows...

10. What did you like best about the resource?
11. What did you like the least about the resource?
12. How could the learning resource be improved?
13. Did the learning resource help you meet your learning objectives for the course?

APPENDIX B

Intervention Site A (May 2008)

This program was intended for medical educators and teachers who wish to expand the scope of their educational scholarship to include applied research. To benefit from this workshop, participants should have a basic understanding of the principles of educational design and development as well as some practical experience as a teacher, clinical supervisor, or program developer. During the workshop, participants were encouraged to take one of their own educational questions or ideas and translate them into a research proposal. By the end of the day, participants were able to outline the elements of a detailed research proposal including the process involved in articulating a clear research question, the research methodologies most appropriate to answer specific research questions, and an appropriate time line to develop a research proposal and conduct the research.

Interactive large group sessions introduced the basic elements of developing a proposal, and the majority of time was spent in small groups with an expert facilitator, working on the participants' actual projects. During the Medical Education meeting, participants had the opportunity to consider diverse research studies that were presented during both oral and poster sessions. The follow-up session allowed participants' to reconsider their own proposals based on new insights. All participants left with a plan to further develop their own proposals and continue their proposals using the RDLR. Participant recruitment occurred at the end of the workshop which took place on Friday May 2, 2008. The consenting participants were to use the RDLR collaboratively to develop their research proposals. The researcher served as the facilitator of the discussions. The physicians who participated in this workshop and the study were from all regions of the country and many did not know each other before attending the workshop.

Intervention Site B (Fall Semester 2008)

This course prepared learners to consult and use research in education. Among other things, it provided learners with an understanding of how to research topics and read critically, as well as an overview of various types of applied research. The course was designed to meet the special educational needs of working adult learners who wanted to complete their course of study in a stimulating meaningful environment while experiencing the flexibility and convenience of studying anytime and anywhere. Recruitment occurred during the first class which was conducted face-to-face. Participants used the RDLR to develop their several of their assignments which include developing research questions, a conceptual framework and learning about research methods. The researcher served as the facilitator in the discussions. Use of the RDLR and participation in the online discussions was required by the course instructor. Participation in the study was voluntary. The course instructor had no idea who participated in the study and who did not. This course was one of the first courses that M.Ed. students take. Most participants did not know each other.

Intervention Site C (Fall Semester 2008)

This course was a different session of invention site B, conducted face-to-face and had a different course instructor. Recruitment occurred after the course had been in session for about a month. Participants used the RDLR to learn about educational research and possibly help with their assignments. The researcher served as the facilitator in the discussions. Use of the RDLR and participation in the online discussions was not required by the course instructor. Participation in the study was voluntary. The course instructor had no idea of who participated in the study and who did not. This course was one of the first courses that M.Ed. students take. Most participants did not know each other before taking the course.

Intervention Site D (Fall Semester 2008)

This was an introductory educational research course for MA students. Recruitment occurred after the course had been in session for about a month. Participants used the RDLR to learn about educational research and possibly help with their assignments. The researcher served as the facilitator in the discussions. Use of the RDLR and participation in the online discussions was not required by the course instructor. Participation in the study was voluntary. The course instructor had no idea of who participated in the study and who did not. This course was one of the first courses that M.Ed. students take. Most participants did not know each other before taking the course.

Intervention Site E(Fall Semester 2008)

This was a doctoral seminar designed to expose students to a critical study of epistemologies they are encountering in the Ph.D. program. Recruitment occurred after the course had been in session for about two months. Participants used the RDLR to learn about educational research and possibly help with their assignments. The researcher served as the facilitator in the discussions. Use of the RDLR and participation in the online discussions was not required by the course instructor. Participation in the study was voluntary. The course instructor had no idea of who participated in the study and who did not. This course was one of the first courses that Ph.D. students take.

Intervention Site F (Fall Semester 2008)

The trans-disciplinary community health program (TCHP) was designed to train students in health science programs to develop, promote, and deliver a community-based health and wellness program in interdisciplinary teams through the development of onsite projects. Use of the RDLR and participation in the online discussions was not required by the course instructor. Participation in the study was voluntary. The course instructor had no idea of who participated in the study and who did not. As this was an interdisciplinary course participants may have known others in their program.

Interventions Site G (Fall Semester 2008)

This course explored the increasingly complex health problems experienced by the acutely ill patient in the perioperative environment. The registered nurses utilized research, theory and best practice guidelines to develop knowledge in assessing, planning, implementing and evaluating care to this unique population of patients. Increasingly complex situations involving geriatric and paediatric populations, cardiovascular complications, the surgical oncology patient, trauma and shock states are some of the many issues that were explored. Learners were expected to complete a collaborative project that includes developing a case study and simulation scenario that were presented to the class. Participant recruitment occurred during the first class. Two participants were mailed consent forms as they took the course via teleconference. Participants used the RDLR to develop their case study projects and to learn about educational research. The researcher served as the facilitator in the discussions. This course was the final part of the nursing certificate program. The participants would have known each other over the past year. Use of the RDLR and participation in the online discussions was required by the course instructor. Participation in the study was voluntary. The course instructor had no idea of who participated in the study and who did not.

Intervention Site H (Winter Semester, 2009)

The purpose of this course was for students to have the opportunity to learn about the critical appraisal of published research for use in clinical practice and design of future nursing research. Methodological issues related to research problem conceptualization; design selection; sampling; instrument development; data management and analysis. Students had the opportunity to select a problem in their area of specialization and develop a methodological critique of a group of studies or a clinical research proposal. Recruitment occurred during the first class. Participants used the RDLR to develop their several of their assignments. The researcher served as the facilitator in the discussions. Use of the RDLR and participation in the online discussions was required by the course instructor. Participation in the study was voluntary. The course instructor had no idea of who participated in the study and who did not. This was a mandatory in the MSc.N. program. Some participants may have known each other.

Interventions Site I (Winter Semester, 2009)

The purpose of the introductory research course was to give students the opportunity to learn about research methods, and the critical evaluation and appraisal of research in healthcare. Concepts and principles underlying development of studies and criteria for evaluation were applied to studies using various research models. Recruitment occurred during the first class. Participants used the RDLR to develop their several of their assignments. The researcher served as the facilitator in the discussions. Use of the RDLR and participation in the online discussions was required by the course instructor. Participation in the study was voluntary. The course instructor had no idea of who participated in the study and who did not. This was a mandatory second year course in the nursing program. Some participants may have known each.

Intervention Site J (Winter Semester, 2009)

This was a different session of the same course as Sites B and C. It was conducted face-to-face. Recruitment occurred after the course had been in session for one class. Participants used the RDLR to learn about educational research and possibly help with their assignments. The researcher served as the facilitator in the discussions. Use of the RDLR and participation in the online discussions was not required by the course instructor. Participation in the study was voluntary. The course instructor had no idea of who participated in the study and who did not. This course was one of the first courses that M.Ed. students take. Most participants did not know each other before taking the course.

Chapter 11
Relationship between Types of Question Prompts and Critical Thinking in Online Discussions

Jennifer C. Richardson
Purdue University, USA

Ayesha Sadaf
Purdue University, USA

Peggy A. Ertmer
Purdue University, USA

ABSTRACT

This chapter addresses the relationship between types of initial question prompts and the levels of critical thinking demonstrated by students' responses in online discussions. The chapter is framed around a research study involving discussion prompts that were coded and classified using Andrews' typology (1980). Students' responses (n=1132), taken from 27 discussion forums, were coded using the four-stage Practical Inquiry Model (PIM) (Garrison, Anderson & Archer, 2001). Among the nine question types explored, Critical Incident questions were most effective in generating high levels of student thinking. This was followed by Lower Divergent, Shotgun, and Analytical Convergent question responses that mainly resulted in students achieving the Integration phase of the PIM. Moreover, validation of the discussion prompts provides an updated typology that categorizes question prompts based on the verbal structure of online discussions. This chapter provides important implications for instructors who teach online, especially those looking for general guidelines regarding how to structure discussion prompts to elicit high quality student responses.

DOI: 10.4018/978-1-4666-2110-7.ch011

INTRODUCTION

Given the recent rapid growth of online education (Allen & Seaman, 2011), identifying "best practices" for facilitating critical thinking skills and deep learning in online environments has gained considerable interest among researchers and educators (Maurino, 2007; Richardson & Ice, 2010). Although a wide variety of instructional strategies can be used to encourage student learning online, discussion is one of the most commonly used pedagogical methods used in online courses since it has the potential for promoting critical thinking skills (Akyol & Garrison, 2011; Ertmer & Stepich, 2004; Richardson & Ice, 2010; Rourke, Anderson, Garrison, & Archer, 1999; Pena-Shaff & Nicholls, 2004). This chapter examines the relationship of online discussion question prompts and students' critical thinking achieved using different questioning strategies.

While online discussions may potentially be an effective platform for developing critical thinking, researchers believe that posing the right question is crucial to actual knowledge construction (Kanuka & Garrison, 2004; McLoughlin & Mynard, 2009; Richardson & Ice, 2010). According to Wang (2005) questions are the most vital tool for stimulating students' critical thinking and facilitating knowledge construction in online discussions. Yet despite the importance of initial questions, only a handful of studies have explored the role of questions in online discussions, specifically, the role of initial question prompts.

Although the relationship between teachers' questions and the level of students' responses has been established in face-to-face settings (Bloom, 1956; Dillon, 1994; Vogler, 2008), little is known about how this relationship plays out in online settings. With the increasing use of online instruction, it is important to examine the nature and extent of this relationship in the online environment. Andrews (1980) suggested that by helping educators understand how different types of questions can be used to promote different types of student

responses, they can more readily target specific learning outcomes, such as higher-order thinking.

BACKGROUND

The importance of questions as an instructional strategy to facilitate critical thinking is widely acknowledged in the literature, especially advocating the view that higher level questions can support and raise levels of students' thinking (Bloom, 1956; Blanchette, 2010; Chin & Langsford, 2004; Dillon, 1994; Ertmer, Sadaf, & Ertmer 2011). Paul and Elder (2001) defined critical thinking as "the intellectually disciplined process of actively conceptualizing, applying, analyzing, synthesizing, and evaluating information gathered from observation, experience, reflection, reasoning or communication as a guide to belief and action" (p. 371). Encouraging students' critical thinking skills is a common goal of higher education (Arend, 2009). Recent research suggested that online discussions assist students in the development of cognitive skills such as self-reflection, elaboration, and in-depth analysis of learning content (Shaff & Nicholas, 2004). Haavind (2006) emphasized the importance of online discussions for enabling students to explore multiple viewpoints, negotiate meaning, and recognize their own knowledge gaps. Furthermore, online discussions allow students to participate at any time and at their own pace to reflect on issues being discussed. As a result, online discussions can be thoughtful and reflective since students have the time to read others' posts and synthesize their ideas (Maurino, 2007).

Although providing convenience for participation, some studies showed that critical thinking and deep learning are not easily achieved in an online discussion (Garrison, Anderson & Archer, 2001; Hara, Bonk, & Angeli, 1998; Kanuka, 2005). For example, Garrison et al. (2001) found that more than 80% of the 96 posts made in two graduate level courses reflected lower levels of thinking. Similarly, Ertmer et al. (2011) reported very few

(15%) of the 850 online discussion responses that they examined were classified at higher levels of Bloom's taxonomy. McLoughlin and Mynard (2009) examined students' online discussion responses in two different courses and found that 55% of the students' posts ranked at the lower cognitive levels. They concluded that the likely reason for the low levels observed was "due to the nature of the task and the wording of the prompt" (p. 155). As a result, they recommended promoting higher-order thinking in online discussions by carefully constructing initial questions so that students know how to direct their thoughts.

Wang (2005) suggested that asking thoughtful questions can lead to cognitive development and facilitate student construction of their understanding of the content. This is supported by the results of the Ertmer et al. (2011) study, which showed a relationship between the cognitive levels of instructors' questions and the levels of students' discussion responses. That is, higher levels of questions were able to generate responses at higher levels of Bloom's taxonomy, and lower level questions resulted in lower level responses. Similarly, based on the results of her research, Blanchette (2001) concluded that higher cognitive levels of instructor's questions lead to not only greater amounts of interaction, but also higher levels of students' responses.

Recently, researchers have focused their interest on the relationship between structure, or type of question prompt and quality of student responses (Bradley et al., 2008; Ertmer et. al., 2011; Richardson & Ice, 2010). For example, Ertmer et al. (2011) examined the relationship between the types of questions and levels of students' subsequent responses in 19 different discussion forums. Question prompts were classified both by type, as outlined by Andrews (1980), and by levels of critical thinking, as outlined by Bloom (1956). Student responses were coded using Bloom's six levels of cognitive processing. The results of the study showed that among Andrews' question types, Lower Divergent questions (i.e.,

those that required students to analyze information to discover reasons and draw conclusions) were most effective in generating higher levels of student thinking compared to other question types. Moreover, different question prompts differently influenced levels of student responses. However, since the discussions were collected from 10 different courses, representing both undergraduate and graduate courses, it is unclear if extraneous variables (e.g., level and discipline of course, different instructors) influenced these results.

Theoretical Framework

Several content analysis models have been developed specifically to assess the quality of student online postings (Garrison et al., 2001; Gunawardena, 1995; Henri, 1992; Newman, Webb, & Cochrane, 1995), with the Community of Inquiry (CoI) framework (Garrison et al. 2001) being one of the most widely used (Richardson & Ice, 2009; Shea, Hayes, Vickers, Gozza-Cohen, Uzuner, Mehta, Valchova, & Prahalad, 2010). Garrison et al. developed this framework to explain the development and expression of critical thinking in online collaborative environments. The framework assumes that learning occurs within a community through the interaction of three elements of online communication: cognitive presence, social presence, and teaching presence. Relevant to this study, the element of cognitive presence is defined as "the extent to which learners are able to construct and confirm meaning through sustained discourse in the critical community of inquiry" (p.1).

Critical thinking has been defined in many different ways and is usually associated with terms such as inquiry, critical reasoning, problem solving, and cognitive presence (Garrison et al., 2001; Facione, 1990). According to Garrison et al. (2001), critical thinking is both an outcome and a process. As an outcome, it is best understood from an individual perspective—that is, "the acquisition of deep and meaningful understanding as well as content-specific critical inquiry abilities, skills, and dispositions" (p. 3). As a process, it is explained in terms of the sustained group interactions that help students develop higher-order thinking through the iterative process of reflection, discourse, analysis, and synthesis as students go through the phases of inquiry (Akyol & Garrison, 2011). Cognitive presence and critical thinking in the CoI framework reflect the dynamic relationship between personal meaning in learner's private world and group understanding in the shared world which leads to knowledge construction (Garrison et al., 2000). Garrison et al. (2001) emphasize that, "it is important to recognize that cognitive presence focuses on higher-order thinking processes as opposed to individual learning outcomes" (p. 8).

The CoI framework is social constructivist in nature and grounded in the Practical Inquiry Model (PIM) that provides a framework to assess the levels of critical thinking in students' online discussions postings. The PIM includes four phases (Garrison et al., 2001):

1. **Triggering Event:** This phase initiates the inquiry process where learners recognize or identify a problem.
2. **Exploration:** This phase focuses on exploration of the problem as learners exchange information as well as possible explanations.
3. **Integration:** This phase focuses on interpretations/construction of meaning where learners incorporate ideas from the exploration phase to justify hypotheses, connect information from various sources, and evaluate possible solutions to make decisions.
4. **Resolution:** This phase focuses on providing potential solutions where learners implement the proposed solution by means of practical application.

These four phases are not considered discrete, but non linear, as some overlap between phases may occur (Swan, Garrison, & Richardson, 2009). According to Garrison et al. (2001), the PIM fo-

cuses on thinking processes and can be used as a tool to assess critical discourse and higher-order thinking in online discussions.

Purpose

Discussion question prompts are the key to a productive discussion and have the potential to engage students in higher order thinking (Chin & Langsford, 2004). The purpose of this study was to examine the relationship between initial discussion question prompts and the levels of critical thinking represented in students' subsequent responses in online discussions, using the four phases of the PIM. The research questions guiding this study were: What is the relationship between the type of question prompt and students' levels of critical thinking, as represented by their discussion posts? Which initial question prompt types promote the highest levels of critical thinking?

METHODS

Context

This study was designed to examine the relationship between the verbal structure of initial question prompts and the level of students' responses in online discussions. We examined discussion prompts from 10 courses, taught by seven different instructors during five semesters: spring and fall, 2008; and spring, summer, and fall, 2009. Three courses were taught primarily online while seven used online discussions to augment regular class meetings. Courses ranged in size from 9 to 221 students, however in the case of larger classes only a single section was included in the analysis (n=127). The courses included undergraduate to graduate level classes, and represented six disciplines including Educational Technology; Educational Psychology; English Education; Literacy and Language; Speech, Language, and Hearing Sciences, and Veterinary Medicine (see

Table 1). Out of 10 courses, three courses were primarily delivered via Blackboard Vista and seven courses used online discussions as part of a blended approach that supplemented regular course activities. The students in each course engaged in online discussions related to course content during 16-week semesters. In general, students received participation points for the responses posted in the online discussions.

Procedure

Discussion question prompts (n=92) were collected from the 10 courses and were classified into nine question types described in Table 2. While many classification schemes have been used by researchers to categorize questions (Bloom, 1956; Wilen, 1986; Gallagher & Aschner, 1963) this study employed a modified version of Andrews (1980) question typology because it is specifically focused on the impact of the structure of question types on student discussion responses.

To ensure accuracy in the categorization, all 92 questions were classified by two researchers independently and then compared for any differ-

ences. After reviewing each of the classifications, researchers discussed their differences and clarified individual interpretations in order to reach consensus. Eight questions were based on Andrews (1980) and one additional question "Critical Incident" was added to represent another category of question type by the researchers (see Table 2).

Among the 92 discussion question prompts, 70 questions were graduate level and 22 questions were undergraduate level (see Table 3). Overall, among nine question types, PG (n=27) was the most frequently used, followed by FQ (n=16), and BS (n=12); AC (n=4) and FUN (n=4) were the least used question types.

After coming to consensus on the classifications for the 92 discussion prompts (see Table 4), we then selected 27 discussions (3 from each of the final 9 categories) to use for the analysis of students' postings. Question selection with associated discussion was based on the following criteria: questions representing different courses and disciplines, discussions with more interaction (depth) and posts (breadth), and questions that provided the clearest example of the question type.

Table 1. Course and participant details

N	Discipline	Course	Level	Semester	Approach
17	Educational Psychology	Advanced Educational Psychology	Graduate	Fall 09	Blended
9	Educational Technology	Educational Applications of Hypermedia	Graduate	Fall 09	Blended
7	Educational Technology	Educational Technology for Teaching and Learning (1 group of 7, class n=29)	Graduate	Sum 09	Web-based
9	Educational Technology	Foundations of Distance Education	Graduate	Fall 08	Web-based
15	Educational Technology	Introduction to Educational Technology (1 section of 15, class n=221)	Undergrad	Spring 08	Blended
14	Educational Technology	Introduction to Educational Technology (1 section of 14, class n=178)	Undergrad	Fall 08	Blended
21	English Education	Composition for English Teachers	Undergrad	Spring 09	Blended
10	Language and Literacy	English Language Development	Graduate	Fall 09	Blended
12	Speech, Language, & Hearing Sciences	Introduction to Aural Rehabilitation Across the Lifespan (1 section of 12, class n=62)	Undergrad	Spring 09	Blended
13	Veterinary Medicine	Management Topics for Veterinary Technicians	Undergrad	Spring 09	Web-based

Table 2. Types of question prompts (adapted from Andrews, 1980)

	Question Type (abbrev.)	Description
1	Playground (PG)	Questions require the interpretation or analysis of a specific aspect of the material, or "Playground," for discussion. Students are free to discover and interpret the material.
2	Brainstorm (BS)	Questions ask students to generate a number of conceivable ideas, viewpoints, or solutions related to a specified issue. Students are free to generate any or all ideas on the topic.
3	Focal Question (FQ)	Questions relate to a specific issue and require students to make a decision or take a position and justify it. Students are asked to support one of several possible positions.
4	General Invitation (GI)	Questions invite a wide range of responses within a broad topic in an open or unfocused discussion.
5	Lower-Level Divergent (LD)	Questions require students to analyze information to discover reasons, draw conclusions, or make generalizations.
6	Analytic Convergent (AC)	Students are required to examine a relevant material and produce a straightforward conclusion, summarize material, or describe a sequence of steps in a process. Answers require analytical thought but lead to a single correct answer.
7	Shotgun (SG)	Multiple questions that may contain two or more content areas.
8	Funnel (FUN)	Prompt begins with a broad opening question, followed by one or more narrower question, and ending with a very concrete question.
9	Critical Incident (CI)	Questions relate to a scenario or case study students have read; students are typically asked to propose solutions to the issues presented in the scenario/case study.

Table 3. Distribution of questions among 9 question types across course levels

Question Type (abbrev.)	Graduate Level	Undergraduate Level	Total Number of Questions
Playground (PG)	18	9	27
Brainstorm (BS)	11	1	12
Focal Question (FQ)	12	4	16
General Invitation (GI)	7	0	7
Lower- Divergent (LD)	8	2	10
Analytic Convergent (AC)	3	1	4
Shotgun (SG)	6	0	6
Funnel (FUN)	4	0	4
Critical Incident (CI)	1	5	6

Data Analysis

After identifying the 27 discussion prompts (see Appendix for discussion prompts) for coding, researchers independently coded students' postings in four of the discussions using the Practical Inquiry Model (Garrison et al., 2001). Postings (n=1132) were scored at the message level, which varied in length from a sentence to several paragraphs. After coming to consensus on the codes for the responses in these four discussions, each researcher independently coded the remaining 23 discussions. Following this, discussion codes were entered into NVivo, a qualitative analysis software package. Matrix coding queries were then performed in order to examine relationships among specific, selected variables (question type, question level, etc.). (See Figure 1.)

Table 4. Distribution of questions among 9 question types across disciplines

Question Type	Educational Psychology	Educational Technology	Speech, Language & Hearing Sciences	Veterinary Medicine	English Education	Language & Literacy
PG	4	5	1	5	5	7
BS	4	4	1	0	2	1
FQ	4	10	0	1	1	0
GI	2	1	0	0	4	0
LD	3	3	0	1	1	2
AC	0	2	0	0	0	2
SG	2	3	0	0	1	0
FUN	0	2	0	0	2	0
CI	0	3	1	2	0	0
Total	19	33	3	9	16	12

Research Design Validity

Prior to answering the research questions it was necessary to conduct two research design validity checks: one on the sample questions within each of the 9 categories (referred to as validity of discussion prompts and categories) and the other on the courses and participants that made up our sample (referred to as the equivalency of samples analysis). The purpose of these analyses, or validity checks, was to overcome previous limitations in the literature (e.g., Ertmer, Sadaf, & Ertmer, 2011; Ertmer et al., 2011) as well as add to the research base for this study.

Validity of Discussion Prompts and Categories

Prior to determining the relationship between the type of question prompt and students' responses in terms of levels of critical thinking it was first necessary to ensure that the three sample questions for each of the nine categories were comparable and that the coding of the question prompt categories was realistic. Thus, the nine types of questions, with three samples each, and the four levels of critical thinking as measured by the PIM were analyzed. Given the small class sizes for the majority of our observed courses, which resulted in a small "n," a non-parametric approach was utilized. The Kruskal-Wallis technique allowed us to determine if there were any

Figure 1. Data collection and analysis procedures

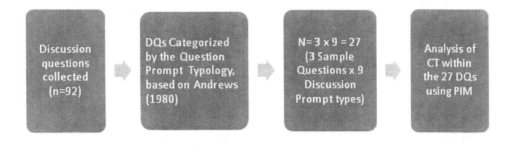

statistically significant differences across the 3 questions analyzed for each of the nine discussion prompt types (see Table 5). The Kruskal-Wallis test evaluates whether the population medians on a dependent variable are the same across all levels of a factor. The test does not make assumptions about normality and is performed on ranked data instead of means (McDonald, 2009).

When a Kruskal-Wallis resulted in a significant difference, the Mann-Whitney technique, which examines unique pairs, was conducted to determine where those differences existed. The Mann-

Table 5. Results for validity of discussion prompts and categories

Question Type	Analysis	Question Codes and Courses*
Playground (PG)	The Kruskal-Wallis indicated that within the Playground (PG) discussion questions there were no statistically significant differences between the questions.	PG1 (VM 246) PG2 (EDCI 560) PG3 (AUS 450)
Brainstorm (BS)	The Kruskal-Wallis indicated that within the Brainstorm (BS) discussion questions there was a statistically significant difference between the questions ($\chi^2(2,n=34)=6.291$, p<.001) with a mean rank of 17.67 for BS1, 16.07 for BS2 and 9.06 for BS3. A Mann-Whitney follow-up determined that the difference was between BS1 and BS2 (p=.001) and BS 1 and BS 3 (p<.001) at the Exploration phase. Additionally, the Mann-Whitney indicated a difference between BS1 and BS2 (p<.001) at the Integration phase.	BS1 (AUS 450) BS2 (EDCI 560) BS3 (EDCI 566)
Focal Question (FQ)	The Kruskal-Wallis indicated that within the Focal Question (FQ) discussion questions there was a statistically significant difference between the questions ($\chi^2(2,n=36)=14.27$, p=.001) with a mean rank of 26.33 for FQ1, 11.30 for FQ2 and 20.06 for FQ3. A Mann-Whitney follow-up determined that the difference was between FQ1 and FQ2 (p=.003) at the Exploration phase.	FQ1 (VM 246) FQ2(EDCI 270) FQ3 (EDCI 566)
General Invitation (GI)	The Kruskal-Wallis indicated that within the General Invitation (GI) discussion questions there was a statistically significant difference between the questions ($\chi^2(2,n=42)=30.458$, p=.001) with a mean rank of 37.50 for GI1, 14.40 for GI2 and 20.00 for GI3. A Mann-Whitney follow-up determined that the difference was between GI1 and GI2 (p<.001) and GI1 and GI3 (p<.001) at the Exploration phase.	GI1 (EDCI 566) GI2 (ENG 391) GI3 (EDCI 391)
Lower-Level Divergent (LD)	The Kruskal-Wallis indicated that within the Lower-Level Divergent (LD) discussion questions there were not any statistically significant differences between the questions.	LD1 (EDCI 566) LD2 (EDCI 591) LD3 (EDCI 566)
Analytic Convergent (AC)	The Kruskal-Wallis indicated that within the Analytic Convergent (AC) discussion questions there was a statistically significant difference between the questions ($\chi^2(2,n=32)=13.30$, p<.001) with a mean rank of 25.35 for AC1, 12.00 for AC2 and 12.88 for AC3. A Mann-Whitney follow-up determined that the difference was between AC1 and AC3 at the Exploration phase (p=.002).	AC1 (EDCI 575) AC2 (EDCI 591) AC3 (EDCI 591)
Shotgun (SG)	The Kruskal-Wallis indicated that within the Shotgun (SG) discussion questions there was a statistically significant difference between the questions ($\chi^2(2,n=42)=23.865$, p<.05) with a mean rank of 22.75 for SG1, 14.00 for SG2 and 35.00 for SG3. A Mann-Whitney follow-up determined that the difference was between SG2 and SG3 (p<.001) and SG1 and SG3 (p=.003) at the Integration phase.	SG1 (EDPS 530) SG2 (ENG 391) SG3 (EDCI 575)
Funnel Question (FUN)	The Kruskal-Wallis indicated that within the Funnel Question (FUN) discussion questions there were not any statistically significant differences between the questions.	FUN1 (EDCI 566) FUN2 (ENG 391) FUN3 (ENG 391)
Critical Incident (CI)	The Kruskal-Wallis indicated that within the Critical Incident (CI) discussion questions there was a statistically significant difference between the questions ($\chi^2(2,n=34)=.924$, p<.001) with a mean rank of 18.33for CI1, 15.64 for CI2 and 19.50 for CI3. A Mann-Whitney follow-up determined that the difference was between CI1 and CI2 (p=.041) at the Exploration phase.	CI1 (VM 246) CI2 (EDCI 270) CI3 (EDCI 575)

*where PG1 =*Playground* sample 1 from the VM 246 course.

Whitney U test, a non-parametric test, can be used in place of an unpaired t-test. It is used to test the null hypothesis that two samples come from the same population (i.e., have the same median) or, alternatively, whether observations in one sample tend to be larger than observations in the other. Although it is a non-parametric test it does assume that the two distributions are similar in shape (Schacht & Aspelmeier, 2005).

In several cases there were statistically significant differences between two of the question samples at one particular level of the PIM. While we acknowledge these differences we also feel that these were inevitable—and as the statistically significant differences were for a particular level and not for a question prompt or a sample discussion question "overall" we do not anticipate these causing major issues. However, in several cases more than one statistically significant difference was found and those results are discussed next.

For the Brainstorm (BS) type of question several statically significant differences were found. For example, students responded differently between sample questions identified as BS1 and BS2 as well as BS1 and BS3 at the Exploration phase (see Figure 2; see Appendix for discussion question prompts). Reviewing the actual discussion question prompts confirmed correct categorizations; however upon further review it may be that the BS1 question asked for a lower level of effort and/or critical thinking as the other two (BS2 and BS3) discussion question prompts asked for students to respond within a more defined scenario. This may indicate a need for the Brainstorm type of question needs to be further refined.

Similarly, there were statistically significant differences between students' responses for the Shotgun (SG) discussion prompts at the Integration phase, specifically between SG3 versus SG1 and SG2 (see Figure 3; see Appendix for discussion question prompts). Again, after reviewing the three sample Shotgun questions they do comply with that category; multiple questions that may contain two or more content areas. However, a difference between the three sample questions that was not previously recognized became apparent. While all three questions asked students to respond to the "why" of a question, SG3 was more limited in scope of potential responses. This

Figure 2. Comparison of brainstorm (BS) question prompt by median values for PIM levels

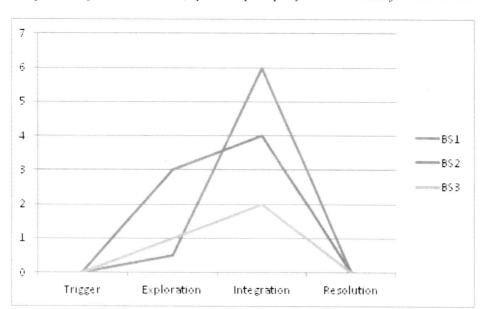

Figure 3. Comparison of shotgun (SG) question prompt by median values for each PIM levels

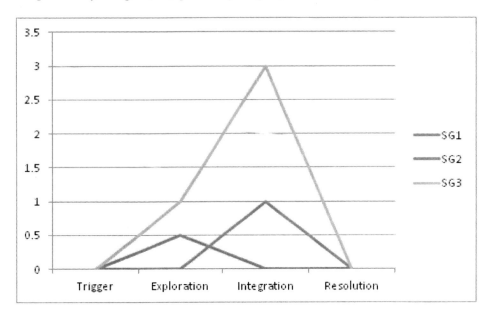

appears to have resulted in the students responding to SG3 to center around the Exploration phase while the SG1 and SG2 student responses centered on the "Integration" phase.

Finally, we would like to address why some of the discussion question prompt cases seem to have a statistically significant difference, with the majority of those differences at the Exploration phase (see Brainstorm, Focal, General Invitation, Analytic Convergent, and Critical Incident). Having reviewed much of the Literature on the PIM in relation to the Community of Inquiry and previously conducted research with the PIM as a measure we consider the overlap between the two phases, which are not linear, to possibly be more difficult to tease apart versus the other phases. For example, the Integration phase is defined as the phase that "focuses on interpretations/construction of meaning where learners incorporate ideas from the exploration phase" (Garrison et al., 2001).

Validity of the Equivalency of Samples

The purpose of this analysis was to demonstrate that although the discussion questions came from a variety of courses (some hybrid, some fully online), content areas, and levels (e.g., undergraduate and graduate) that there were no significant differences among our participants' ability to reach the various levels of critical thinking across our samples.

To demonstrate this hypothesized equivalency we compared the samples by course and by a particular question type category on the four phases of critical thinking (triggering, exploration, integration, and resolution) by (1) examining critical thinking levels by course from within the same program, undergraduate course vs. graduate course level, (2) examining critical thinking across programs/content areas at the same level (either undergraduate or graduate), and (3) examining courses taught by the same instructor (see Table 6). The purpose was to test the null hypothesis, for each comparison, of no significant difference among course participants in their ability to reach the various levels of critical thinking.

Table 6. Mann-Whitney results for validity of equivalency of samples

Question Code or Type	Analysis	Courses
1. Comparisons across course level from within the same program		
Critical Incident (CI)	The two samples did not differ significantly (p<.01) for any of the four levels of critical thinking (Trigger U=36.00, p=.188; Exploration, U=39.00, p=.267; Integration, U=45.00, p=.482; Resolution, U=44.50, p=.441).	EDCI 575 (GR) EDCI 270 (UG)
Focal Question (FQ)	The two samples did not differ significantly (p<.01) for any of the four levels of critical thinking (Trigger U=45.00, p=.194; Exploration, U=45.00, p=.194; Integration, U=49.00, p=.290; Resolution, U=63.00, p=.815.	EDCI 566 (GR) EDCI 270 (UG)
2. Comparisons at the same course level but across programs/content areas		
Playground (PG)	The two sets of participants did not differ significantly (p<.01) for any of the four levels of critical thinking (Trigger U=53.50, p=.291; Exploration, U=62.50, p=.590; Integration, U=72.00, p=1.000; Resolution; U=54.00, p=.319).	VM 246 (UG) AUS 450 (UG)
Focal Question (FQ)	The two sets of participants did not differ significantly (p<.01) for three of the levels of critical thinking (Trigger U=67.50, p=.277; Integration, U=41.00; Resolution, U=84.00, p=.792). A significant difference, however, was found for responses posted at the Exploration level, U=31.50, p=.003. The percent of students' posts for the Exploration phase in VM 246 was 42.65 while the percent for EDCI 270 participants was 33.33.	VM 246 (UG) EDCI 270 (UG)
Analytic Convergent (AC)	The two sets of participants did not differ significantly (p<.01) for three of the four levels of critical thinking (Trigger U=30.00, p=.143; Integration, U=28.00, p=.105; Resolution, U=44.00, p=.684). A significant difference, however, was found for responses posted at the Exploration level, U=10.00; p=.002. The percent of students' posts for the Exploration phase in EDCI 591 was 7.15 while the percent for EDCI 575 was 32.05.	EDCI 591 (GR) EDCI 575 (GR)
3. Comparisons across courses taught by the same instructor		
Lower Divergent (LD)	For this analysis a single course offered in different semesters and utilizing unique question prompts was conducted. The two sets of participants did not differ significantly (p<.01) for any of the four levels of critical thinking (Trigger U=36.00, p=.730; Exploration, U=37.00, p=.796; Integration, U=26.00, p=.222; Resolution, U=36.00, p=.730).	EDCI 566 (GR) EDCI 566 (GR)
Brainstorming (BS)	The two sets of participants did not differ significantly (p<.05) for any of the four levels of critical thinking (Trigger U=27.00, p=.681; Exploration, U=18.50, p=.174; Integration, U=16.00, p=.114; Resolution, U=31.50, p=1.00).	EDCI 560 (GR) EDCI 566 (GR)

1. **Comparisons across course level from within the same program:** The purpose of these analyses was to evaluate the null hypothesis of no significant difference between undergraduate and graduate level course participants' ability to reach the various level of critical thinking as defined by the Practical Inquiry Model (PIM). These analyses demonstrate that the course participants have the same ability, regardless of course level, to post comments at the various levels of critical thinking (triggering, exploration, integration, and resolution).

2. **Comparisons at the same course level across programs/content areas:** Several of the discussion question types were shared by courses at the same level (undergraduate or graduate) but from different content areas. The purpose of these analyses was to evaluate the null hypothesis of no significant difference between the course participants across content areas in terms of their ability to reach the various levels of critical thinking. Results indicated a statistically significant difference within a single phase, Exploration, in two cases, one undergraduate comparison and the other a graduate comparison. However,

differences are likely due to the non-linear nature of the PIM model as previously discussed.

3. **Comparisons across courses taught by the same instructor:** Finally, as the samples allowed, we also conducted analyses for two sets of discussion questions that were part of graduate level courses taught by the same instructor. The purpose of this analysis was to evaluate the null hypothesis of no significant difference among the abilities of participants, enrolled in graduate courses developed and taught by the same instructor, to reach the various levels of critical thinking. The discussion question prompts, all from courses within the Educational technology program, were unique. The finding of no statistically significant differences provides further validation for the categorization of the discussion question prompts as well as the coding of the four levels.

This validity process, aside from allowing for a side-by side comparison across variables (e.g., levels, content areas, instructor, type of discussion questions) provides support for the use of participants from diverse courses in the creation of a sample as well as the categorization of the questions.

RESULTS AND DISCUSSION

Question 1: What is the Relationship between Type of Question Prompt and PIM Phase of Response?

Results based on the PIM analysis (see Figure 4) shows that among the nine question types, responses to Critical Incident (Median=45) and a small number of participants' responses to Playground (Median=4.76), Analytical Convergent (Median=7.14), and Lower Divergent (Median=3.33) achieved the Resolution phase. This was followed by Lower Divergent (Median=73.33),

Figure 4. Comparison of median values of critical thinking levels expressed by students for different question prompts

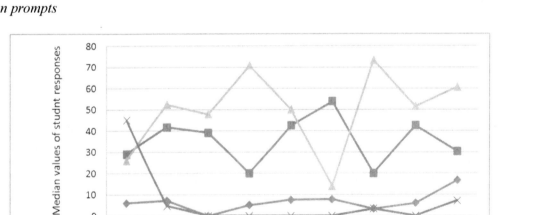

	CI	PG	FUN	SG	BS	GI	LD	FC	AC
Triggering	6	7.23	0	5	7.5	7.69	3.33	5.88	16.67
Exploration	29	41.67	39.13	20	42.5	53.85	20	42.5	30.3
Integration	26	52.38	47.83	70.84	50	14	73.33	51.47	60.61
Resolution	45	4.76	0	0	0	0	3.33	0	7.14

Shotgun (Median=70.84), and Analytical Convergent (Median=60.61) question responses that mainly resulted in students achieving the Integration phase. General invitation (Median=53.85) questions mostly resulted in students achieving the Exploration phase. Although, responses to Analytical Convergent (AC) questions resulted in the greatest number of student responses at the Integration level, a small number of student responses to Analytical Convergent (Median=16.67) questions also resulted at the lowest level of CT and were at the triggering level. This suggests that the nature of the AC questions is one of fluctuation between the phases. The AC, which requires students' provide a single correct answer, may in fact find students moving repeatedly between reflection and discourse during the Integration phase while occasionally returning to the Triggering phase as they refine the issue at hand. This corresponds with Swan, Garrison, & Richardson (2009), who stated that the four phases of the PIM are not considered discrete or linear since students may need to return to a previous phase.

Question 2: Which Question Prompts Promote the Highest Levels of Critical Thinking?

Overall, Critical Incident—which required students to respond to a scenario to create a solution—seemed to be the most influential in generating higher levels of critical thinking compared to other question responses (see Figure 5). This question types facilitated a large number of student responses that reached the Resolution (Median=45) and many at Integration (Median=26) levels of thinking. A review of students' postings revealed that for Critical Incident question prompts, student tended to use their knowledge from the course material and personal experience to create a solution and give examples of how to apply their solutions in a real life situation. Moreover, students justified their solutions with their personal examples and other resources, when asked to clarify any misunderstandings or conceptual conflicts of their peers. This suggest that structuring of questions that require original

Figure 5. Level of students' responses when presented with different types of question prompts

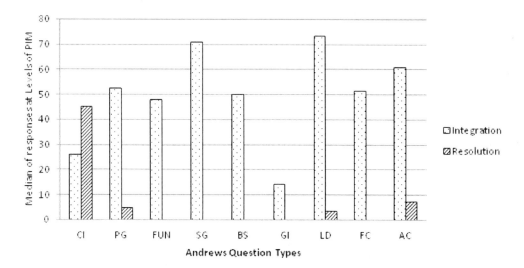

thinking to solve real-world problems and produce a solution can help students to generate a unique response. Moreover, having the ability to provide personal experiences indicates that students were able to relate to the discussions personally, thereby potentially demonstrating that the discussion had real world implications for them in their careers or lives. This aligns with Arnold, Ducate, Lomicka, and Lord's (2009) finding that students' discussions progressed to the synthesis and resolution phase when students were asked to formulate or resolve a problem.

Lower-Divergent, Analytical Convergent and Shotgun question prompts mostly fell into the "Integration phase". For instance, in lower-divergent question responses, students analyzed material to discover reasons to support opinions, and mainly summarize the required material during Analytical-Convergent question responses. In general, these question prompts seemed to facilitate students synthesizing material and connecting relevant ideas from the discussion and describing the issues presented in the discussion. Students also tended to negotiate meaning by producing well-conceived thoughts within their responses as well as agreeing with their peers in order to reach a tentative solution. This finding is aligned with Zsohar & Smith's (2008) conclusion that discussion prompts that incorporate course material, require reflective thinking to go beyond facts, and use judgment to produce knowledge can facilitate higher levels of critical thinking.

Solutions and Recommendations

Although questions are used for many instructional reasons such as focusing attention, promoting recall, and encouraging reflection, using questions to stimulate critical or higher-order thinking is one of the most important goals of education (Gibson, 1999).

Discussion questions are one of the most common and effective strategies for facilitating learning (Clasen & Bonk cited in Limbach & Waugh, 2005), both in online and face-to-face environments; by paying close attention to the questions we ask, we may be able to increase the amount of critical thinking that occurs among our students.

While encouraging higher levels of critical thinking is often the goal of online discussions, every discussion forum has a different objective. Correspondingly, not every discussion question will facilitate or guide learners to achieve the Resolution phase, nor should that be the goal. Instead discussion questions should be designed based on the desired educational objectives. Andrews (1980) suggested that by modifying the types of questions asked, faculty could more readily target the kinds of learning outcomes they wish their students to obtain.

If the goal of online discussion is to facilitate higher levels of critical thinking, then discussion questions that fall within the Critical Incident (CI) types have been shown here to be highly effective. CI questions require original evaluative thinking to create solutions to authentic problems can help students to think in more complex ways to produce a higher level response.

However, when introducing new topics the learning goals generally include the exchange of ideas, providing explanations, and giving suggestions for exploring relevant solutions; in this case Lower Divergent, Shotgun and Analytical Convergent question prompts may be the best strategy. Similarly, instructors can stimulate deeper thinking by omitting recall or memory level questions and using questions that instead require students to describe underlying relationships, to make connections among ideas, to construct meanings, and create or evaluate possible solutions.

Finally, when possible and reasonable allowing for or even asking students to provide personal observations and experiences may also promote responses that are at a higher critical thinking level. In part we suggest this is the case as students then not only see a direct connection or relevance to the discussion question prompt but also because they can transfer what they have previously learned.

CONCLUSION

This study examined the relationships between different types of initial question prompts and the level of students' response, as well as the question prompts that facilitated higher levels of critical thinking. Studies have shown that online discussions can facilitate higher-order thinking (Gilbert & Dabbagh, 2005; Richardson & Ice, 2010), particularly through the use of effective questioning techniques. The results of this study provide evidence of the relationships between different types of initial question prompt and the level of students' subsequent responses.

By collecting and analyzing a number of online discussion questions from across content areas and levels we believe that this research allows us to continue the discussion of designing better discussion question prompts. Moreover, the use of the question prompt typology, based in large part on the work of Andrews (1980), provides for a common language and perspective from which to launch new discussions. Finally, the use of the Practical Inquiry Model, a part of the Community of Inquiry Framework, allowed us understand the nature and levels of critical thinking facilitated by different types of discussion prompts in online discussions.

However, the research process itself has also provided some valuable insights that can be used for future research. For example, by validating the discussion prompts and categories we have provided an updated typology, one congruent with online discussions, that categorizes question prompts based on the verbal structure of online discussions. In the same way, by validating the equivalency of the participants' ability to reach the various levels of critical thinking across diverse courses, we have provided support for the use of participants from diverse courses but equivalent learning environments in the creation of a sample.

The results of this study have important implications for instructors who teach online, especially those looking for general guidelines regarding how to structure discussion prompts to elicit high quality student responses. Because instructors have a lot of control over which questions they ask, and how they structure them, deliberate use of different types/levels of questions may enable them to engender higher quality responses from students. It is our hope that by examining the patterns observed in our results others will be able to modify their own discussion prompts to stimulate higher levels of thinking among their students.

ACKNOWLEDGMENT

The authors of this paper wish to thank Dr. Larisa Olesova and Dr. Yukiko Maeda of Purdue University for their effort and guidance with this work.

The research study presented within this chapter was developed in part under a FIPSE Comprehensive grant, # P116B060421, from the U.S. Department of Education. The contents of this paper do not necessarily represent the policy of the Department of Education, and you should not assume endorsement by the Federal Government.

REFERENCES

Akyol, Z., & Garrison, D. R. (2011). Assessing metacognition in an online community of inquiry. *The Internet and Higher Education, 14*(3), 183–190.

Allen, I., & Seaman, J. (2011). *Going the distance: Online education in the USA 2011*. Wellesley, MA: Babson Survey Research Group.

Andrews, J. (1980). The verbal structure of teacher questions: Its impact on class discussion. *POD Quarterly: Journal of Professional and Organizational Development Network in Higher Education, 2*(3&4), 129–163.

Arend, B. (2009). Encouraging critical thinking in online threaded discussions. *The Journal of Educators Online, 6*(1), 1–23.

Arnold, N., Ducate, L., Lomicka, L., & Lord, G. (2009). Assessing online collaboration among language teachers: A cross-institutional case study. *Journal of Interactive Online Learning, 8*(2), 121–139.

Blanchette, J. (2010). Questions in the online learning environment. *Journal of Distance Education, 16*(2), 37–57.

Bloom, B. (1956). *Taxonomy of educational objectives*. New York, NY: David McKay.

Bradley, M. E., Thom, L. R., Hayes, J., & Hay, C. (2008). Ask and you will receive: How question type influences quantity and quality of online discussions. *British Journal of Educational Technology, 39*, 888–900.

Chin, C., & Langsford, A. (2004). Questioning students in the ways that encourage thinking. *Teaching Science, 5*(50), 16–22.

Dillon, J. T. (1994). The effect of questions in education and other enterprises. *Journal of Curriculum Studies, 14*, 127–152.

Ertmer, P. A., Sadaf, A., & Ertmer, D. (2011a). Student-content interactions in online courses: The role of question prompts in facilitating higher-level engagement with course content. *Journal of Computing in Higher Education*. doi:doi:10.1007/s12528-011-9047-6

Ertmer, P. A., Sadaf, A., & Ertmer, D. (2011b). Designing effective question prompts to facilitate critical thinking in online discussions. *Design Principles and Practices: An International Journal, 5*(4), 1–28.

Ertmer, P. A., & Stepich, D. A. (2004, July). Examining the relationship between higher-order learning and students' perceived sense of community in an online learning environment. *Proceedings of the 10th Australian World Wide Web conference*, Gold Coast, Australia.

Facione, P. (1990). *Executive summary – Critical thinking: A statement of expert consensus for purposes of educational assessment and instruction*. Millbrae, CA: The California Academic Press.

Gallagher, J. J., & Aschner, M. J. (1963). A preliminary report on analyses of classroom interaction. *Merrill-Palmer Quarterly, 9*, 183–194.

Garrison, D. R., Anderson, T., & Archer, W. (2000). Critical inquiry in a text-based environment: Computer conferencing in higher education. *The Internet and Higher Education, 2*(3), 1–19.

Garrison, D. R., Anderson, T., & Archer, W. (2001). Critical thinking, cognitive presence, and computer conferencing in distance education. *American Journal of Distance Education, 15*(1), 7–23.

Gibson, J. (1999). Discussion approach to instruction. In C. M. Reigeluth (Ed.), *Instructional-design theories and models, Vol. III: Building a common knowledge base* (pp. 99-116). New York, NY: Taylor and Francis.

Gilbert, P. K., & Dabbagh, N. (2005). How to structure online discussions for meaningful discourse: A case study. *British Journal of Educational Technology, 36*(1), 5–18.

Gunawardena, C. N. (1995). Social presence theory and implications for interaction and collaborative learning in computer conferences. *International Journal of Educational Telecommunications, 1*(2/3), 147–166.

Haavind, S. (2006). *Key factors of online course design and instructor facilitation that enhance collaborative dialogue among learners.* Paper presented at the annual meeting of the American Educational Research Association, San Francisco, CA.

Hara, N., Bonk, C. J., & Angeli, C. (1998). Content analysis of online discussion in an applied educational psychology course. *Instructional Science, 28*(2), 115–152.

Henri, F. (1992). Computer conferencing and content analysis. In O'Malley, C. (Ed.), *Computer supported collaborative learning.* Heidelberg, Germany: Springer-Verlag.

Kanuka, H. (2005). An exploration into facilitating higher levels of learning in a text-based internet learning environment using diverse instructional strategies. *Journal of Computer-Mediated Communication, 10*(3).

Kanuka, H., & Garrison, D. R. (2004). Cognitive presence in online learning. *Journal of Computing in Higher Education, 15*(2), 30–48.

Limbach, B., & Waugh, W. (Fall, 2005). Questioning the lecture format. *The NEA Higher Education Journal: Thought and Action, 20*(1) 47-56. Retrieved on January 18, 2011, from http://www.nea.org/assets/img/PubThoughtAndAction/TAA_05_05.pdf

Maurino, P. S. (2007). Looking for critical thinking in online threaded discussions. *Journal of Educational Technology Systems, 35*(3), 241–260.

McDonald, J. H. (2009). *Handbook of biological statistics* (2nd ed.). Baltimore, MD: Sparky House Publishing. Retrieved from http://udel.edu/~mcdonald/statintro.html

McLoughlin, D., & Mynard, J. (2009). An analysis of higher order thinking in online discussions. *Innovations in Education and Teaching International, 46*(2), 147–160.

Newman, D. R., Webb, B., & Cochrane, C. (1995). A content analysis method to measure critical thinking in face-to-face and computer supported group learning, interpersonal computing and technology. *An Electronic Journal for the 21st Century, 3*(2), 56-77.

Paul, R., & Elder, L. (2001). *Critical thinking: Tools for talking charge of your learning and your life.* Upper Saddle River, NJ: Prentice Hall.

Pena-Shaff, J. B., & Nicholls, C. (2004). Analyzing student interactions and meaning construction in computer bulletin board discussions. *Computers & Education, 42*(3), 243–265.

Richardson, J. C., & Ice, P. (2010). Investigating students' level of critical thinking across instructional strategies in online discussions. *The Internet and Higher Education, 13*(1-2), 52–59.

Rourke, L., Anderson, T., Garrison, D. R., & Archer, W. (1999). Assessing social presence in asynchronous text-based computer conferencing. *Journal of Distance Education, 14*(2), 50–71.

Schacht, S., & Aspelmeier, J. (2005). *Social and behavioral statistics: A user-friendly approach* (2nd ed.). Boulder, CO: Westview Press.

Shea, P., Hayes, S., Vickers, J., Gozza-Cohen, M., Uzuner, S., & Mehta, R. (2010). A re-examination of the community of inquiry framework: Social network and content analysis. *The Internet and Higher Education, 13*(1-2), 10–21.

Swan, K., Garrison, D. R., & Richardson, J. C. (2009). A constructivist approach to online learning: The Community of Inquiry framework. In Payne, C. R. (Ed.), *Information technology and constructivism in higher education: Progressive learning frameworks* (pp. 43–57). Hershey, PA: IGI Global.

Vogler, K. E. (2008, Summer). Asking good questions. *Educational Leadership, 65*(9). Retrieved from http://www.ascd.org/publications/educational-leadership/summer08/vol65/num09/Asking-Good-Questions.aspx

Wang, C. H. (2005). Questioning skills facilitate online synchronous discussions. *Journal of Computer Assisted Learning, 21*, 303–313.

Wilen, W. (1986). *Questioning skills for teachers* (2nd ed.). Washington, DC: National Education Association.

Zsohar, H., & Smith, J. A. (2008). Transition from the classroom to the Web: Successful strategies for teaching online. *Nursing Education Perspectives, 29*(1), 23–28.

KEY TERMS AND DEFINITIONS

Bloom's Taxonomy: A classification of the different learning objectives that educators set for students.

Cognitive Presence: The extent to which learners are able to construct and confirm meaning through sustained reflection and discourse.

Community of Inquiry: A learning community where participants collaboratively engage in purposeful critical discourse and reflection to construct personal meaning and shared understanding through negotiation.

Critical Thinking: Intellectually disciplined process of actively conceptualizing, applying, analyzing, synthesizing, and evaluating information gathered from observation, experience, reflection, reasoning or communication as a guide to belief and action.

Online Discussion: A form of discussion facilitated by information and communication technologies either synchronous or asynchronous mode.

Practical Inquiry Model: Provides a framework to assess the levels of critical thinking in students' online discussions postings.

Question Prompts: Represent the type of questions that initiate the discussions. They are key to a productive discussion and have the potential to engage students in higher order thinking.

APPENDIX

Table 7. Sample question prompts

Question Prompt Category	Question Prompt	Course	N	Average No. of Responses per Student
AC 1	This is a first-come, first-serve activity. You are each required to choose one learning theory, either from last week's readings, this week's websites, or another source. You are to (1) legitimize the theory by checking into a reputable source (e.g. not just the websites and Wikipedia does not count) and verifying the major principles or components of the learning theory, (2) summarize these components for your peers, and (3) provide us with a scenario where your learning theory would be applicable (e.g. sample activities) to distance learning for this course in particular. In other words, your target audience is your peers and you are coming from the viewpoint of the instructor. Be sure you label your discussion posting with the name of your theory	Foundations of Distance Ed	9	8.66
AC 2	In both articles for this week (Clayton, Barnhardt, & Brisk, 2008; and Ricento, 2005), the authors discuss the complexity and importance of identity for L2 and culturally and linguistically diverse (CLD) learners. On page 32 of *Language, Culture, and Identity*, the authors state that: "Schools are agents of the dominant society and, as such, they reflect the underlying cultural patterns of that society. As long as they reflect the structure and cultural fabric of the dominant society, they can be expected to perpetuate its values, attitudes, and behavior patterns within an implicit framework of assimilation" (Clayton, Barnhardt, & Brisk, 2008). With that being said, how can we as educators and as a society move away from this "framework of assimilation" and increase respect and acceptance of students' diverse identities (including culture and language)? In addition, Ricento ends by stating, "The research approaches and findings presented in this chapter suggest starting points for critical, self-reflective inquiry about how our practices as teachers might better serve the complex interests, desires, and identities of our second and foreign language students around the world" (906).	English Language Dev	10	2.9
	Do you as an educator ever use critical or self-reflective inquiry when considering your own teaching practices? If not, do you believe this could help improve your teaching of diverse groups of students?			
AC 3	What do the changing demographics mean for states like IN? Why do you think these increasing numbers of English Language Learners (ELL) are found in states that did not have significant numbers of ELLs before? Why is it important for us as teachers to know about these changing demographics?	English Language Dev	10	3.3
BS 1	Families of children with hearing loss often turn to the internet for information regarding hearing, hearing loss, intervention practices, and communication modalities (i.e., oral communication, signing systems and ASL). (1) Discuss some of the potential benefits and dangers of relying on internet information for parents. (2) Tell how you would help parents evaluate what they read on-line.	Intro to Aural Rehab across the Lifespan	62/course 12/lab	13.95

continued on following page

Table 7. Continued

Question Prompt Category	Question Prompt	Course	N	Average No. of Responses per Student
BS 2	For this DQ choose either the Internet (ch.10) or Distance Education (ch. 11) to specifically discuss. As an instructor, whether at the K-12, higher education, or business sector, what are the challenges you would face as you move from traditional paper-based instruction to instruction that incorporates the Internet or Distance Education? Be specific and provide some background on the instructional piece you are discussing. (Note: if your particular classroom environment does not seem to afford this type of technology then come from the perspective of you providing instruction to peers, in-service, or you as a learner in a higher education institution	Ed Tech for Teaching and Learning	29/course 7/group	7.57
BS3	Epistemology—one of those terms you will encounter throughout graduate school but may never actually discuss in detail in your courses—until now. The Spiro article talks about epistemic beliefs about the nature of learning and the organization of knowledge (p. 304), the idea that learners, young and old, may hold an unconscious belief about how to organize their knowledge, and this can become tricky once you bring ill-structured lessons into their curriculum or experience. Begin by providing a scenario or observation of such an occurrence in the content area you work in. Next, how would you address their epistemic beliefs and this potential problem with the ideas presented in this week's readings (or other readings)? Support your ideas.	Educational Applications of Hypermedia	9	5.2
CI 1	Students read a brief scenario followed by this question prompt: You are the practice manager at Uptown Animal Hospital. Sean comes to you in tears and describes what has been happening. How would you respond to Sean? Come up with a plan of action for how you might help Sean handle this situation. Be sure to include the possible advantages and disadvantages to implementing your plan.	Management Topics for Vet Technicians	13	3.84
	Describe some things in general that could help this type of "culture of gossip" in a veterinary clinic.			
CI 2	1. Read the following case: Let'simagine that you work for an educational firm that develops learning curriculum for elementary school children. Your company adheres to a verybehavioral/information processing/constructivist [use the one youhave been assigned]oriented viewpoint of learning. A large school district in Texas has come to your company and asked for you to develop a proposal for the development of a science unit of instruction for fifth grade students. Your unit will specifically be focused on "insects." This is a very important potential client for your company and your proposal will be in competition with two other companies.	Introduction to Educational Technology	178/course 14/lab	3.36
	2. Discuss the following: Identify two (or more) key elements based on your theoretical perspective that could be included within the learning materials in order for them to be effective. Explain how and why your elements are associated with your specific theoretical viewpoint. For example, if you are presenting key behavioral elements within your instruction, you might want to explain why reinforcement/rewards would play a critical role.			

continued on following page

Table 7. Continued

Question Prompt Category	Question Prompt	Course	N	Average No. of Responses per Student
Cl3	For the following scenarios you'll be providing instructional design solutions—and there is no one "correct" solution, although there may be "optimal" solutions. To solve your scenario in terms of instructional design you will want to consult your IDA activity sheets and examples. You will work in assigned groups. See week 7 learning module for further instructions.

Scenario 1: A group of 15 US Army personnel, stationed in Afghanistan, would like to work towards their college degree during their down time (as a unit their duties are scheduled so that the group as a whole is never on "down time" all at once. Since they have various backgrounds (all are high school graduates) you have been asked to teach an initial or pilot course for this group, one they can all take that will count as an elective: History and culture of Afghanistan, 1700-present. They are all tentatively to be stationed at this one location for at least the next 4 months. How would you proceed?

Scenario 2: A group of immigrants from Honduras, who are considered highly educated in their own countries (e.g. have bachelor's degrees and specialized training) have been recruited by Butterfly Industries in Middle-of-Nowhere, WY. While the industry skills are the same, they have limited English language skills. Butterfly Industries has asked you, as an expert consultant from Purdue University, to develop a distance course for this group of individuals to help them with the technical language and general language skills to improve their performance but also to help retain them as employees. Moreover, Butterfly Industries is offering to pay the learners to "attend" class Tuesday and Thursday evenings for 10 weeks per session. How would you proceed?

Scenario 3: You have been asked by a local school district to provide 20 of their teachers with a course they can use towards their licensure requirements. The district doesn't have a preference for topics, they want to try "this distance thing", but would like it to be "fun" course so that the teachers that volunteer to enroll will continue to be motivated (by the way, teachers are required to take credits every 5 years to keep their licenses, and the school is not only paying for the college credits but also providing them with a stipend of $250). While you are not certain about your individual leaner's characteristics you can expect a mix across discipline areas. Also, the school district wants you to use the course management system hey have access to, luckily Blackboard since you are also familiar with it. How would you proceed? | Foundations of Distance Ed | 9 | 8.55 |

continued on following page

Table 7. Continued

Question Prompt Category	Question Prompt	Course	N	Average No. of Responses per Student
FQ 1	If you recall back to the first chapter in the Ford book, in her story about Gerald's tires, she talks about Gerald's employees taking a personality test, which is what the Myers Briggs is that Dr. Bill talks about in his power point presentation for this module. Do you think this would be beneficial when hiring new employees where you work? Debate If your last name begins with a letter between A and L – respond to this question from the pro side and explain why you think it would be beneficial to have newly hired employees take a personality test. List specific advantages to administering a personality test to newly hired employees. If your last name begins with a letter between M and Z – respond to this question from the con side and explain why you think it would not be beneficial to have newly hired employees take a personality test. List specific disadvantages to administering a personality test to newly hired employees.	Management Topics for Vet Technicians	13	5.07
FQ 2	**Online Discussion 1: Millennials** Background: At this point in the semester, we have discussed in lecture about learning and the theories of learning. Now we need to go one step further and discuss a very important element in that learning process – the learners. It is important that you think about all of the various types of learners you will potentially encounter; however, for this first online discussion, we will focus on one specific type. For this discussion we need to examine the group of learners known as Millennials (they are also known as the Net Generation or even Generation Y). This is the group that was born sometime between 1978 and 2000. They are a very unique group and one that you probably have some great insights into – most of you are members. Questions to ponder: Will these learners be differently because of their access to these technologies? Do they need to be taught differently? What you need to do: 1. Read these two articles a. Article 1 (Prensky) b. Article 2 (Lang) 2. Discuss the following: *Should the Millennials (or the Digital Natives) be taught differently than how generations of learners of the past were taught?*	Introduction to Educational Technology	221/course 15/lab	2
FQ3	The articles for this week present us with some new and/or alternative ideas to consider as you design your projects. Given these ideas respond to one of the following questions: 1) From the ideas presented in the Koehler, et al. consider your Project 2 concept with a critical eye and try to determine which of the impacts your video will or should include and why, and 2) Select one or two principles from the Clark &Feldon article to discuss in terms of what your beliefs are related to those principles—do you agree or disagree with their principle(s). Remember to support your ideas with the readings and other resources as necessary	Educational Applications of Hypermedia	9	6

continued on following page

Table 7. Continued

Question Prompt Category	Question Prompt	Course	N	Average No. of Responses per Student
FUN 1	**Making Sense of our Multimedia Learning Experiences** Mayer covers some interesting ways to begin to think about how we can think about multimedia learning. For this DQ begin by providing an example of a personal learning experience that involved multimedia, which will also virtually ensure it is a learner-centered approach (include types of multimedia used, context, etc.). Next, look to Mayer's three metaphors for multimedia learning—which fits your experience and why. Continue by including information on the three types of learning outcomes and the two kinds of active learning. Finally, respond to your peers' postings not only with comparisons of these experiences but also possible alternatives to the development of the multimedia experience and/or interpretations of the categories provided by Mayer	Educational Applications of Hypermedia	21/course 10/group	2.2
FUN 2	Hi, class. Here's your prompt for Week 3. You may start a new post or respond to a classmate's post (or both). Reflect on your experiences with writing assignments in middle and high school. What kinds of assignments were they? How did you respond to them? Which of the major composition pedagogies discussed in class did they reflect? Do you think these types of assignments would be effective in your future classes? Why or why not? Field Reflection	Composition for English Teachers	20	1.15
FUN3	Hello, class! This week's topic is argumentative writing/research writing. While we have already discussed argumentative writing somewhat during our discussions last week, we have yet to touch on "the research paper." What do you see as the goal of a high school research paper assignment? Why would a teacher include one in his/her curriculum? What do you think a student should learn as a result of such a project? Can you think of any alternatives to the traditional research paper assignment that could meet these same goals?	Composition for English Teachers	18	1.15
GI 1	Brainstorming and Sharing about Digital Storytelling Activities For this week we are going to take it easy with the DQ. Since we are just starting to think about our Digital Storytelling projects I'd like you to begin by explaining what you plan to do for Project 2. Provide a context and the perspective you'll be taking (e.g. your digital story should include a narrative or "story"). Also, describe how you plan to use your Project 2 for an instructional purpose. Finally, comment and post some ideas on your peers' comments for what they might consider to make their digital story more effective.	Educational Applications of Hypermedia	10	5.33
GI 2	In an effort to broaden our discussions, I'm going to invite you to write about anything of interest to you about the teaching of writing this week. What are you thinking about? Wondering about? What rises to the surface for you when you think about being a writing teacher? If you need some ideas, here are some possible topics: Minute or Muddiest point Papers Creative writing in the English classroom Responding to student writing Grading and rubrics Ideas for your mini-lesson assignment coming up soon--what are you thinking of teaching to us?	Composition for English Teachers	20	.65

continued on following page

Table 7. Continued

Question Prompt Category	Question Prompt	Course	N	Average No. of Responses per Student
GI3	Hello, again! Great job last week on the discussion board. I like that so many of you are responding to each other. Don't forget to go back to Week Seven and rate (using the formal peer review rating scale) the THREE peers underneath your name in the list. Some people don't have any ratings, and some only one. Here's this week's topic. Discuss any of the following topics, linking your comments to class readings and/or discussion. Alternatively, share ideas and ask questions about your upcoming microteaching assignment. Portfolio grading One-on-one conferencing Peer review 21st century writing	Composition for English Teachers	12	1
LD 1	For this DQ each of you have selected a different multimedia principle to serve as the expert for. I've selected a short video from YouTube, "How to eat using chopsticks" http://www.youtube.com/watch?v=5Y9HO-c0dxU For this DQ provide a brief overview of your principle, and make it the subject line for your discussion thread. Next, consider the multimedia video—how is or should your principle be applied? Finally, review other principles that your peers have posted, compare and contrast it with your principle.	Educational Applications of Hypermedia	9	4.66
LD 2	What are at least 2 new concepts, ideas, issues, topics, or terms in the reading for this week? In what ways can you relate these new things to ELLs' cultural identities, language and literacy development, and content area achievement?	English Language Dev (F 09)	10	3.5
LD3	**Digging into Theories Related to Multimedia Learning** There are at least two ways to think about multimedia learning, (1) multimedia learning as information acquisition, and (2) multimedia learning as knowledge construction. Moreover, there are two common ways of presenting multimedia learning: The learner-centered approach says, "How can adapt technology/multimedia to enhance human learning?" The technology-centered approach says, "How can we use the capabilities of the technology in designing multimedia presentations?" I think that these points can serve as a practical framework for thinking about our projects. Given this, where and why (think of the curriculum links/gaps for your learners and the environment) does your project 1 fit within this framework. Refer to the readings as applicable.	Educational Applications of Hypermedia	9	5
PG 1	In the first paragraph of the web article, "Attributes of Good Listening," the author states that, "You cannot be a good leader unless you are a good listener." In 1-2 paragraphs explain in your own words what the author means by this. How are the two (listening and good leader) related? Do you agree or disagree? Explain your reasoning.	Management Topics for Vet Technicians	13	6.46

continued on following page

Table 7. Continued

Question Prompt Category	Question Prompt	Course	N	Average No. of Responses per Student
PG 2	Several of your recent chapters have examined the planning process for integrating technology. Consider a recent example of a technology-enabled lesson you provided or experienced; how does/ would planning for diverse students (gender, ethnicity, SES, special needs, etc.) impact the planning of such a lesson?	Ed Tech for Teaching and Learning	29	7.85
PG 3	Based on your interview of an elderly person with a hearing loss: 1) Share some of the interviewee's concerns and difficult communication situations 2) Give some ideas for dealing with these concerns and difficulties 3) Tell how the interview will impact your professional practice in the future. Be sure to use only the person's initials to protect confidentiality.	Intro to Aural Rehab across the Lifespan (Sp 09)	62/course 12/lab	7.25
SG 1	**Rules for discussion: Answer one question and reply to one other person's response.** 1. Websites such as YouTube and eHow offer "expert videos" that are geared toward the general public, and that can teach anyone how to do anything (anything from baking a cake to flamenco dancing).How do such websites encourage or discourage learning? What are the advantages and/or disadvantages of using such videos or websites to facilitate learning, or as learning tools? 2. In the reading 'Technology to Support Learning' it says "Epistemological authority - teachers possessing knowledge and students receiving knowledge - is redefined, which in turn redefines social authority and personal responsibility." This is in reference to utilizing technology in the classroom. Discuss at least one advantage and one disadvantage to this occurrence. 3. Discuss how the use of intelligent computer programs or tools in the classroom relates to Vygotsky's Zone of Proximal development (ZPD). Give an example that teachers could apply in their classrooms	Advanced Ed Psych	17	1.52
SG 2	Hello, class. I enjoyed reading about your memories of middle and high school writing last week. Don't forget that your experiences are important as you think about how you might teach writing in the future. While you may or may not use assignments you experienced yourself, your memories have helped create your professional teacher identity which affects your pedagogical choices. This week, we are focusing on writing about literature. I would like for you to respond to Chapter 7 in Seven and the related discussions we will have in class this week about writing about literature. Some possibilities for response include reflecting on, why do you think English teachers ask students to write about literature? What should students learn from it? Why do we assign such writing tasks? What kinds of literary responses are the most effective? How do you know when a literary response paper is "good"?	Composition for English Teachers	20	1.2

continued on following page

Table 7. Continued

Question Prompt Category	Question Prompt	Course	N	Average No. of Responses per Student
SG 3	In chapter 3 of the SSAV book the chapter concludes with some myths, I'd like for us to examine. Myth 1: The more interaction there is in a distance education class the better (pg. 82). The section goes on to say that this is a myth according to several studies they cite. Finally, the section says "the forcing of interaction can be as strong a detriment to effective learning as is its absence." The Swan article, on the other hand, tells us that interaction plays a significant role in online learning—what are we to believe? Do we need to find a balance? Or, is it more about what those interactions look like? Are you a proponent of social learning—and believe that students learn from one another as well as instructors? What about student differences, some prefer to learn in communities, others on their own? These are just a few questions to prompt this discussion where you are asked to discuss Myth 1. Also, think beyond the readings to your own experiences or what you would envision in your ideal distance ed. course. Be sure to back up your statements!	Foundations of Distance Learning	9	5.33

Chapter 12
Cooperative and Collaborative Strategies in Blended and Online Learning Environments

Christine E. Nickel
Regent University, USA & Old Dominion University, USA

Richard C. Overbaugh
Old Dominion University, USA

ABSTRACT

This chapter presents the results of a study that investigated the differential effects of cooperative versus collaborative instructional strategies and blended versus fully online delivery methods on various aspects of academic community. Measures include the Community of Inquiry (CoI) Survey instrument, individual and group achievement, student satisfaction with process and product, and their value of community. The treatment was a group-work module in a university foundations-level instructional technology course (n=134). Results suggest that cooperative and collaborative strategies in online and blended environments are equally effective in regard to individual achievement, but that blended cooperative learners perform significantly poorer on group projects. Students were equally satisfied with their groups' process and solution and the group activity did not significantly change students' value of connectedness. Students did not differ according to their perceptions of social presence and cognitive presence, but significant differences were found in perceptions of teaching presence. The course module design highlights the essential elements typical of design strategy based on typical instructional design processes, while using the Community of Inquiry as a theoretical framework that enables "operationalization" of the instructional design process. The design emphasized teaching and cognitive presence but not social presence.

DOI: 10.4018/978-1-4666-2110-7.ch012

INTRODUCTION

The primary purpose of this chapter is to present the results of a study that analyzed and interpreted differences between online and blended students utilizing collaborative or cooperative strategies for a group project. The focus is to explain the impact of a specific instructional strategy designed for and implemented in both blended and fully online formats that emphasized Teaching and Cognitive Presence but not Social Presence in terms of student perceptions of the CoI framework, student satisfaction, course success (individual and group achievement), and value of and preference for collaboration. Because the instructional strategy does not emphasize Social Presence, a unique contribution of the chapter is how students' Community of Inquiry perceptions were differentially affected.

A secondary purpose is to describe the instructional strategy and elucidate on some of the underlying aspects of designing instruction: (a) foundational elements that are typical of instructional design processes and (b) Community of Inquiry as a theoretical framework that enables the "operationalization" of the ID process in a particular teaching/learning situation. We use the word operationalize because most ISD models do not include instructional strategies, forcing the instructional designer to look elsewhere for a theory or model to guide development. We believe this brief section to be relevant because, in higher education settings, faculty often rely on instructional design professionals to convert or construct their courses or course modules without significant awareness of the underlying design elements required.

INSTRUCTIONAL DESIGN

Instructional Systems Design in Context

Course design in higher education has evolved rapidly and significantly over the past 15 years—an evolution commonly attributed at least in part to the adoption of distributed instruction and the attendant need to improve the instructional design capabilities of higher education faculty to ensure reasonable course quality. Clearly, successful instructional design has many facets and layers as epitomized by Reigeluth and Carr-Chelman (2010) but can perhaps be broadly represented by three major domains of (a) the instructional design process, (b) instructional strategies, and (c) theory/epistemology. The latter domain also includes important design or evaluation structures such as the Sloan Pillars of Excellence (Moore, 2002) and the Community of Inquiry Framework (Garrison, Anderson, & Archer, 2000) which have been validated in research literature and are well known to practitioners. Like many complex processes, the domains can be treated discretely but in practice are inextricably linked.

The instructional design process is often considered to be the structured procedural foundation upon which instructional strategies, theory/epistemology, and all related pieces are layered. Perhaps the most well-known is the Systematic Design of Instruction (SDI) by Dick, Carey and Carey (2009), now in its seventh edition. However, even though their SDI process includes critical aspects of instruction, such as learning outcomes, audience analysis, instructional environment analysis and evaluation, guidance on what instructional strategies might be appropriate and how best to deliver them is not provided. ADDIE is also very popular but ADDIE is simply an acronym describing a generic process (Molenda, 2003) that has long been interpreted as desired (Heinich, Molenda, Russell, & Smaldino, 2002; Seals & Glasgow, 1998). In either of these processes designers must "step out" of the process to find and choose a strategy they believe will lead to the most efficacious instruction for a given situation, informed by other factors such as epistemology, best practices theory, and so on, filtered through student profiles and learning environment analyses.

Two texts that integrate instructional design processes with learning strategy and/or other aspects of the design domains are Morrison, Ross, and Kemp's *Designing Effective Instruction* (2007, 2010) and Carr-Chelman's *Instructional Design for Teachers (ID4T)* (2010). The text by Morrison, Ross and Kemp an instructional design text, now in its 6th edition, maintains a focus "on designing instruction in a business setting" (p iii) and includes additional information on domains such as sequencing, instructional strategies, message design, and material/media development. In contrast, *Instructional Design for Teachers (ID4T)* (Carr-Chellman, 2010), is a compact instructional design handbook targeted to k-12 teachers that provides a nine-step model augmented by guidance on pedagogical approaches such as user-design, inquiry learning, and constructivist approaches, and other considerations including meeting standards and media selection.

The somewhat dichotomous interpretation by these two texts of the instructional design process can be aligned with the debatable difference between education and training which, in turn, often evokes a continuum with procedural/behavioristic performance outcomes on one end and higher-order thinking skills/cognitive development on the other. In practice, there are often clear differences in the instructional approach but there is just as often significant overlap resulting in models that appear to address characteristics of both[1]. So what about designing for higher education?

In higher education, the learning environment is largely determined by infrastructure and policy which define aspects of the learning environment such as potential instructional delivery tools, communication media, class sizes and so on. On the other hand, the learners are treated as a fairly homogeneous group, much like the training/business world of the industrial age, and subjected to fairly traditional pedagogy rather than the more learning-centered approaches characteristic of the digital age. Perhaps part of the reason for this is twofold. First, even though instructional design professionals in higher education know how to and can implement information-age designs, they often need to distill their expertise for course design into formulaic approaches that could be considered design templates (much like the appendices to this chapter). A second reason is that the faculty *consumer* of instructional design expertise has limited training in teaching methodology and often prefers an easier approach to packaging his/her course resulting in more a cookie-cutter approach than is desirable.

In the case of the foundations course that served as the treatment in this chapter, a basic design is followed for each of nine modules. Each module begins with an introductory overview, learning outcomes and statement of relevance, followed by reading materials consisting of lead-instructor authored text that includes many links to web-based materials, concluding with a small-group cooperative or collaborative exercise and quiz. The impetus for the research study outlined in this chapter was the need to determine what learning strategy (cooperative or collaborative learning) was most effective with the design of the course and the learning environments. The next section elaborates on cooperative and collaborative learning strategies. A course outline and example module can be found in the appendices to this chapter.

Cooperative and Collaborative Learning as Design Elements

The terms cooperative and collaborative learning have often been used interchangeably in the research literature, perhaps because they both incorporate similar assumptions, including the importance of active learning, small group learning, and the enhancement of social skills through consensus building (Barkley, Cross, & Mayor, 2005; Kirschner, 2001). Yet the instructional strategies differ in some important aspects, specifically in regard to the amount of student control and group structure. The lack of consistent conceptual and operational definitions for cooperative and collaborative learning has made interpretation of some of the research literature problematic (Cuseo, 1992; Dillenbourg, Baker, Blaye, & O'Malley, 1996; Underwood & Underwood, 1999). Adopting the view that cooperative and collaborative learning are similar but separate entities (Bruffee, 1999; Henri & Rigault, 1996; Hooper, 1992) affords more options for investigation, which in turn allow practitioners to apply these principles appropriately.

Roschelle and Teasley (1995) make the following distinction between the terms:

Cooperative work is accomplished by the division of labour among participants, as an activity where each person is responsible for a portion of the problem solving (p. 70).

In contrast, collaborative work involves "the mutual engagement of participants in a coordinated effort to solve the problem together" (p. 70).

Table 1 provides a simple comparison between cooperative and collaborative learning strategies. A more detailed explanation can be found in the paragraphs below.

The Differences between Cooperative and Collaborative Learning

The main differences between cooperative and collaborative learning are characterized by how interaction and control within the activity are structured.

Interaction

While cooperative strategies often emphasize harmony, collaborative groups may just as often experience disagreement (Lipman, 2003). Collaborative and cooperative strategies also differ in that promotive interaction, teamwork skills, and group processing are not emphasized in collaborative learning. The differences stem from the emphases of the strategies. While the focus of cooperative learning is for learners to help one another to be successful in the learning activity and is structured by the instructor to ensure success (Emerson & Mosteller, 2004), collaborative learning focuses on shifting control of learning to students and as-

Table 1. Comparing cooperative and collaborative learning elements

Cooperative Learning	Collaborative Leaning
Theoretical Background: Meaning is constructed by the group via negotiation with peers Group outcome is key Structure is more rigid.	*Theoretical Background:* Meaning is constructed individually via negotiation with peers Individual outcome is key Structure is less rigid.
Structure of Interaction: Tasks are split and accomplished **independently**.	*Structure of Interaction:* Tasks are accomplished together **with little dividing**.
Components[2] Positive Interdependence (Including Positive Role Interdependence) Individual Accountability Group Roles Scaffolded Teamwork Skills Group Processing	*Components* Positive Interdependence Individual Accountability NO Group Roles NO Scaffolded Teamwork Skills NO Group Processing
Expected Outcome The goal is a group created *end product*	*Expected Outcome* The goal is the *construction of knowledge* within a group

sumes that students have the teamwork skills and autonomy necessary to manage their group work (Bruffee, 1999; Millis & Cottell, 1998).

Control

In cooperative strategies, the teacher is still considered the authority and activities are structured to incorporate frequent facilitation from the instructor. In contrast, collaborative approaches give much of the authority for constructing knowledge to the members of student groups, meaning the responsibility for learning shifts from the instructor to the student (Bruffee, 1999) and the less structured design of the group activities reflect that shift.

IMPACT OF THE DESIGN (RESEARCH STUDY)

Purpose of the Study

The purpose of the study was to investigate the impact of using cooperative or collaborative strategies in online and blended learning environments on students' perceptions of teaching presence, social presence and cognitive presence. Additionally, the research investigated the impact of cooperative and collaborative strategies on achievement, satisfaction, and students' value of collaboration. The results serve to inform course designers and instructors on best practices for utilizing these strategies in various learning environments.

Review of Literature

Theoretical Foundations

Cooperative and collaborative learning are based on the concept that humans create meaning within our communities (Shea, 2006) and that these relationships are significant to "welfare, achievement, and mastery" within an educational environ-

ment (Bruffee, 1999, p. 83). Proponents of these instructional strategies also claim that effective instruction goes beyond simple interaction and requires learners to share their experiences in order to negotiate and construct meaning (Garrison, et al., 2000), an act some term "constructive conversation" (Bruffee). Research on collaborative and cooperative learning has been guided by theories of social constructivism and social interdependence (Johnson & Johnson, 1996). The Community of Inquiry framework (Garrison, et al.) has guided much of the current research on critical discourse and collaboration in online learning.

Independent Variables

This study utilized instructional strategy (cooperative and collaborative learning) and course delivery method (online and blended learning environments) as the independent variables.

Instructional Strategy

Cooperative and collaborative learning are some of the most researched forms of student group work and have been established empirically as having a positive effect on numerous student outcome measures, including achievement, satisfaction, and social skill development (Cooper & Mueck, 1990; Cuseo, 1992). While cooperative learning has been well validated in numerous educational contexts, standing "as one of the strongest principles of social and organizational psychology" (Johnson & Johnson, 1994, p. 6), research on cooperative learning is much less common in university and online contexts. Collaborative learning research is more common in higher education settings and has been found to positively impact achievement and satisfaction (Bruffee, 1999).

Method of Delivery (Blended vs. Online)

A plethora of studies have compared traditional face-to-face learning to online learning on variables ranging from achievement, perceptions of learning, student preference, to student satisfaction, faculty satisfaction, sense of community, student retention, and beyond. Research literature has shown online learning to be as effective as face-to-face methods in student achievement (Russell, 2001), while satisfaction results are mixed (Contreras-Castillo, Favela, Perez-Fragoso, & Santamaria-del-Angel, 2004; Piccoli, Ahmad, & Ives, 2001; Priluck, 2004; Rivera, McAlister, & Rice, 2002; Wegner, Holloway, & Garton, 1999). Now that many courses that were originally face-to-face have moved to a blended format (Garrison & Kanuka, 2004) with an expected continual increase in blended courses (Bonk & Graham, 2006), one would presume that many studies would have compared blended and online learning. Yet, few studies have specifically investigated blended courses (Lin, 2008) or compared learning outcomes or satisfaction between students enrolled in blended and online courses (Lim, Morris, & Kupritz, 2007). Few (if any) studies have been conducted that compare online and blended learning environments in regard to cooperative or collaborative instructional strategies. Bourne and Seaman (2005) maintain that research on blended learning is not well defined and that further research on successful pedagogical approaches and best practices are warranted.

Dependent Variables

Achievement

Cooperative vs. Collaborative Learning: Structured cooperative activities featuring role assignments and/or interaction guidelines have been found to beneficially influence achievement (Cavalier, Klein, & Cavalier, 1995; Doymus, 2008; Hall, Rocklin, Dansereau, Skaggs, O'Donnell, Lambiotte, & Young, 1988; Webb & Palincsar, 1996) and attitudes about group learning (Brewer & Klein, 2006). Cooperative learning practitioners suggest that not providing specific guidance, whether in teamwork skills or tasks to perform,

may hinder peer communication (Macdonald, 2003). On the other hand, proponents of collaborative learning strategies put forth that less structure promotes more student control and ownership of the process, which may enhance critical thinking (Brewer & Klein, 2006; Moore, 2005; Schellens, Van Keer, & Valcke, 2005). Yet research results have been inconsistent in regard to the effect of role assignments in group work (Cavalier, et al., 1995; Doymus, 2008; Hall, et al., 1988; Klein & Doran, 1999; Mudrack & Farrell, 1995; Rose, 2002, 2004; Schellens, et al., 2005; Strijbos, Martens, Jochems, & Broers, 2004).

Course Delivery Method: Computer-mediated cooperation and collaboration have the potential to be effective ways to provide flexibility via the time-independent nature of asynchronous communication (McIsaac & Gunawardena, 1996) and to reduce isolation via synchronous and asynchronous communication (Hall, 1997). Collaboration and cooperation have generally been found to be equally effective in online environments and face-to-face environments, yet there are fewer studies that have specifically compared cooperative or collaborative learning outcomes between students enrolled in blended and online courses (Lim, et al., 2007). One study that has compared collaborative learning in online and blended courses found that students in both learning environments achieved high levels of cognitive presence, yet the authors suggest that the conditions provided by the blended course format may have been more suitable for higher-order thinking (Akyol & Garrison, 2011).

Another important issue is whether the structures of the cooperative and collaborative groups will differentially influence group project achievement and individual achievement. Lou et. al (2001) found that cooperative strategies seemed to positively influence group performance and individual achievement, whereas collaborative strategies positively influenced only group performance, suggesting that not all students within collaborative group strategies are equally engaged in the content and able to retain knowledge for post-treatment tests. Recognizing that the current study utilizes a group project assessment and an individual quiz, the findings from Lou et al suggest that further investigation related to cooperative and collaborative structure is needed.

Satisfaction, Value, and Preference for Collaboration

Given that teamwork is becoming more widely used in higher education, a student's value and preference for collaboration is important to investigate. For example, do students generally prefer to work with others and do they see a potential for higher achievement by working with others? Study results are mixed regarding student attitudes of computer-supported cooperative and collaborative learning. Several studies reveal that students were satisfied with their collaborative experience, appreciated the opportunity to collaborate (Brewer, Klein, & Mann, 2003; Dewiyanti, Brand-Gruwel, Jochems, & Broers, 2007; Kitchen & McDougall, 1998) and even found it helpful for their learning (Kim, Liu, & Bonk, 2005). However, several other studies have revealed a student preference for working individually or a denial of the academic benefits of working cooperatively or collaboratively (Hillard, 2006; Kitchen & McDougall, 1998; Klein & Doran, 1999; Uribe, Klein, & Sullivan, 2003). One study revealed that although a majority of students viewed group work positively and thought that it aided them in their work, half of respondents still preferred to work on their own, and nearly 25% saw no value in group work (Oliver & Omari, 2001). Overbaugh and Nickel (2008) found similar results in a study utilizing a similar population of students and the same attitude instrument as the current study. Although face-to-face students valued connectedness and preferred collaboration more than online students, responses were at the "neutral" level of a five-point Likert scale. Furthermore, both face-to-face and online students responded at the neutral point in regard to the potential to achieve more academically

through collaboration. One potential explanation for these results is that convenience and flexibility may be valued over interaction with the instructor and peers by online learners (Fortune, Shifflett, & Sibley, 2006), indicating that students who self-select into an online section of a course are more independent than students who enrolled in a blended learning section (Diaz & Cartnal, 1999).

Another explanation for differences in student attitudes between studies may be due to issues with online cooperative or collaborative learning that may impact preference for or satisfaction with the medium and the process. Students may worry about the amount of time required to make group decisions, students not doing their "fair share" of the work, feelings of isolation from the group, or may feel inhibited about giving constructive criticism (Bonk, Wisher, & Lee, 2004; Graham & Misanchuk, 2004; Gunawardena, Nolla, Wilson, Lopez-Islas, Ramirez-Angel, & Megchun-Alpizar, 2001). While one can speculate that these issues would be alleviated given good course design and practice in a cooperative or collaborative environment, student attitudes before and after a short-term group project may influence achievement and perceptions (Ocker & Yaverbaum, 2001; Williams, Duray, & Reddy, 2006).

Student Satisfaction

Satisfaction is subjective in nature and may be influenced by a variety of environmental and personal factors. As such, student satisfaction is a difficult construct to measure or predict effectively, yet is a crucial factor in evaluating successful programs, courses and activities within higher education institutions.

While much of the literature has focused on comparing student satisfaction in face-to-face and online environments, or face-to-face and computer-mediated environments (which could be blended in nature), few studies have investigated differences in satisfaction between blended learning students and fully online students. While not detailed, Albrecht (2006) stated that an EDU-CAUSE survey found high student satisfaction with blended learning. Leh (2002) reported similar results, although no face-to-face or fully online comparison groups were used. When a blended course is developed, supported and implemented well, researchers have found that a majority of the students will be as satisfied or more satisfied with the blended course as they have with previous face-to-face courses (Harker & Koutsantoni, 2005; Voos, 2003). Challenges to fully online learners, when compared to blended learners, can include perceptions of higher workload and less support (Lim, et al., 2007), possibly due to the lack of social context cues. High levels of interaction and collaboration may be key to highly satisfied students in online and blended courses (So & Brush, 2008).

Looking Deeper into Satisfaction of Learning Activities: While numerous studies have measured student satisfaction in traditional, distance, and online learning, the results are somewhat ambiguous in regards to elements of the learning process that are less satisfying (Thompson & Coovert, 2003). Satisfaction measures often include a variety of questions that investigate everything from satisfaction with the technology, the group members, the discussion, the learning process, and the final project outcome or solution and report them as one score (Thompson & Coovert). If one wants to better understand differences in student satisfaction, using an instrument that further delineates student satisfaction would be most appropriate. For example, a student may be satisfied with the final outcome of a collaborative project, but not the collaboration process, or vice versa (Mejias, 2007). By distinguishing process and outcome satisfaction, inconsistencies in research may be resolved (Mejias). In the case of this study, the goal is to look at student satisfaction in regards to the process of collaborating or cooperating as a group and in terms of the final group solution to the problem.

Process Satisfaction: Process satisfaction "refers to the contentment with the interactions that occur while team members are deriving decisions" (Thompson & Coovert, 2003, p. 138). Studies that have specifically looked at the satisfaction of the interaction process have found that traditional, face-to-face groups tend to be more satisfied with the group interaction process than students who have interacted via the computer (Ocker & Yaverbaum, 1999; Thompson & Coovert; Warkentin et al., 1997), possibly due to familiarity with working in face-to-face groups (Olaniran, 1996), ease of communication (Straus & McGrath, 1994) and lack of lags between member participation (Benbunan-Fich & Hiltz).

Few studies have investigated process satisfaction in blended groups versus completely online groups. One might reason that blended groups are likely to be more satisfied because they have the opportunity to meet face-to-face in class. Yet that conclusion may be highly dependent on how much time members have to converse while in class. Additionally, the amount of time the group has to complete a project is important because satisfaction with the collaboration process has been found to increase over time (Flanagin, Park, & Seibold, 2004; Olaniran, 1996). Process satisfaction may also be influenced by student characteristics and group dynamics (Ocker & Yaverbaum, 2001; Straus & McGrath, 1994) as well as the student's satisfaction in the solution, or "decision confidence" (Olaniran, 1996).

Solution Satisfaction: Solution satisfaction refers to a student's "satisfaction with the solution… that resulted from the collaborative experience" (Ocker & Yaverbaum, 2001, p. 433). Studies have found mixed results when comparing solution satisfaction of face-to-face and asynchronous web-based groups. While several studies found no significant differences in solution satisfaction between face-to-face and web-based groups (Benbunan-Fich & Hiltz, 1999; Fjermestad & Hiltz, 1998; Ocker & Yaverbaum), other studies found that computer-mediated groups were less satisfied with their collaborative outcomes (Thompson & Coovert, 2003; Warkentin, Sayeed, & Hightower, 1997). Contradictory findings may be due the amount of times students have been exposed to asynchronous collaboration (Thompson & Coovert), their general attitude toward collaboration (Ocker & Yaverbaum), or the type of assigned task (Straus & McGrath, 1994). Given mixed results in prior studies and the lack of comparison between blended and online groups, this study will serve to add to the empirical literature.

Student Perceptions of the Community of Inquiry

The Community of Inquiry (CoI) framework identifies three essential elements to a successful higher education experience: cognitive presence, teaching presence, and social presence. This framework of critical thinking and inquiry utilizes the three essential elements as mutual support for assessing asynchronous online interaction (Shea, Fredericksen, Pickett, & Pelz, 2004) and assumes that learning occurs through the interaction of the three essential elements (Rourke, Anderson, Garrison, & Archer, 1999). Ice (2008) suggests that the CoI framework can be used to assess the impact and utility of learning environments and strategies on online interaction. Used as a tool to conceptualize the online learning experience (Garrison & Arbaugh, 2007), each of the three presences is multi-dimensional and is operationally defined in terms of its descriptive categories.

Social Presence: Social presence is interpreted as the ability of learning community members to project their personal characteristics and to connect with others socially and emotionally (Garrison, 2006; Ice, Kupczynski, & Mitchell, 2008) and functions as a support for cognitive presence (Garrison, et al., 2000).

According to Garrison and Arbaugh (2007), social presence can be seen as an evolution from the first category, open communication, where student interaction begins, through the second category, group cohesion, where discourse takes place, and finally to the last step, affective expression, where students feel a sense of camaraderie. Social presence has been found to change significantly over time within a course (Akyol & Garrison, 2008). While social presence is not measured longitudinally in the current study, the duration of the instructional strategies used within the module (in this case, two weeks), is an important element to consider. Differences in social presence between cooperative and collaborative groups may be due to the length of the group activities.

In this study, students' perception of each category helped explain if and how social presence evolved in their group. Perceptions of social presence are linked with student's satisfaction, perceptions of cognitive presence, and perceived learning (Akyol & Garrison, 2008). Therefore, investigating possible differences in social presence perceptions as a function of learning strategy and course delivery mode is vital to identifying best practices for cooperative and collaborative learning.

Cognitive Presence: Cognitive presence is defined as the "extent to which participants in a community of inquiry are able to construct meaning through sustained communication" (Garrison, et al., 2000, p. 89), reflection, and discourse (Ice, et al., 2008), and represents the process of higher-order thinking and learning (Garrison & Anderson, 2003). The other two elements of the CoI framework, teaching presence and social presence, act as vital support for cognitive presence, by facilitating the critical thinking process (Garrison, et al., 2000; Garrison, Cleveland-Innes, & Fung, 2010).

Cognitive presence is operationalized by four phases taken from the practical inquiry model: triggering event, exploration, integration, and resolution (Akyol & Garrison, 2008; Garrison, Anderson, & Archer, 2001). Because cognitive presence has been found to be a significant predictor of student satisfaction, which in turn was a mediator of persistence (Joo, Lim, & Kim, 2011), the comparison of differential student responses in regard to learning strategy or delivery mode is valuable in assessing the effectiveness of the module activity in this study.

Teaching Presence: Teaching presence refers to the design of a course and the facilitation of communication within the course (Garrison, 2006). The teaching presence construct is defined by three components: design and course organization, discourse facilitation, and direct instruction (Shea, Pickett, & Pelz, 2003). Differential results between the groups in this study in regard to any of the three teaching presence components may reveal potential issues in course instructional design or structure, facilitation of student interaction and engagement (Arbaugh, Cleveland-Innes, Diaz, Garrison, Ice, Richardson, Shea, & Swan, 2007a), or providing proper feedback.

According to Murphy (2004), instructor strategies for promoting interaction and critical discourse are essential for students to think and learn critically. In the current study, the lack of direct instructor facilitation in the collaborative group could have affected students' perceptions of cognitive presence and potentially influence achievement.

Teaching presence has been found to influence student perceptions of learning. Therefore, differences in reported teaching presence may influence perceptions of cognitive presence.

Given the complexities of the internal dynamics of each of the three presences, as well as their interdependencies (Akyol & Garrison, 2008) understanding the three presences as they relate to cooperative and collaborative learning, as well as how they relate to blended and online learning, was valuable in terms of evaluating the effectiveness of the instructional strategies and course delivery modes in this study as well as adding to the research literature.

Research Design

Setting and Sample

Participants

This study utilized undergraduate and graduate teacher education students enrolled in a technology integration educational foundations course. The course was designed for students who are at an academic standing of Junior or above. Prior studies using this population have shown the age of students to range from 20 years old to over 50 years of age (Overbaugh, Nickel, & Brown, 2006).

A total of 18 sections of the Instructional Technology and the Classroom course with 254 students enrolled participated. Nine course sections were taught via blended delivery method and nine sections of the course were taught via the online delivery method. The 18 course sections were randomly assigned to the cooperative or collaborative learning strategy. Table 2 articulates the number of students who self-selected into each course format and the number of students assigned to each strategy.

Participants self-selected into blended or online sections of the course, taught by several instructors. Although the course sections are taught by various instructors, the objectives, content and design of the course were the same for each section. Students in the blended sections of the course met three hours per week in "class time", but

Table 2. Descriptive statistics on actual study participants

	Frequency	Percent (%)
Course Format		
Blended	134	52.8%
Online	120	47.2%
Learning Strategy		
Cooperative	134	52.8%
Collaborative	120	47.2%

interacted with classmates and the instructor and submitted assignments via the Blackboard Learning Management System and the LiveText Accreditation Management System

Online students learned completely online, utilizing the asynchronous and synchronous (virtual chat) features of Blackboard and submitting assignments via the LiveText portfolio system. Student participation in the pre-treatment and post-treatment surveys was voluntary and did not affect their grades. Both the online and traditional sections followed the 15-week university calendar, with the blended class meeting for 3 hours weekly. Each section allowed approximately 20 students to enroll.

Independent and dependent variables are listed in Table 3, along with the instruments data instruments used.

Student Perceptions of Group Structure

Groups that were formed to work collaboratively may have adapted to a more cooperative approach, and vice versa. A two-item instrument was created to investigate student perceptions of their group structure. The instrument asked the following questions: (1) Was each of your group members assigned a specific role or task in this activity? and (2) Was your group more likely to work on the whole project together or divide the work up among individual group members? The first ques-

Table 3. Variables and instruments

	Pre-Experimental Data Instruments	Post-Experimental Data Instruments	Research Literature
Independent Variables			
Learning Strategy (cooperative vs. collaborative learning)	n/a	n/a	
Course Delivery Method	n/a	n/a	
Covariates			
Academic Status (undergraduate vs. graduate), gender, age, ethnicity, teaching status, teaching experience, online learning experience	Pre-instructional survey		
Dependent Variables			
Individual achievement individual quiz grade		*Module quiz*	
Group achievement group project grade		Rubric for group project lesson plan	Jonassen (1997)
Student's value of connectedness	Pre-instructional survey	Post-instructional survey	
Student's value of collaborative learning, and	Pre-instructional survey	Post-instructional survey	
Student's recognition of the added achievement potential of collaborative learning	Pre-instructional survey	Post-instructional survey	
Process Satisfaction		Post-instructional survey	Green & Taber (1980); Ocker & Yaverbaum (2001)
Solution Satisfaction		Post-instructional survey	Green & Taber (1980); Ocker & Yaverbaum (2001)
Student Perceptions of Community of Inquiry		Post-instructional survey	Arbaugh, et al., 2008

tion was answered with a yes or no answer. The second question was answered as either "worked on the whole project together" or "divided the work up among members".

Treatment

The course utilized in the study consisted of nine modules that each follow a basic design. In most modules, students apply their new knowledge of instructional technology in projects structured by the 5W/5E[3] (Walters, 2004-2005). An important note is that emphasis was placed on teaching and cognitive presence but not social presence. Even though some modules included the cooperative or collaborative instructional strategies which, of course, require student-to-student interaction, community-building throughout the course was not stressed. The primary reason for this approach was to lower instructor and student workload in the project-based course, particularly because prior research showed that this audience was not receptive to a strategy of high social presence (Overbaugh & Nickel, 2008; Overbaugh, et al., 2006). With regard to the specific module examined in this study, a professional instructional designer redesigned a module that previously presented information on collaborative and cooperative learning at a knowledge level to a design that actually required students to experience cooperative or collaborative learning. Students were required to individually review assigned readings and videos before working in small groups to develop a lesson plan that utilized cooperative learning strategies. The goal of introducing an authentic cooperative or collaborative activity was to facilitate better understanding of the principles behind the strategies as well as promote the use of cooperative strategies in pre-service teachers' future classrooms. A course outline and example module can be found in the appendices of this chapter.

When the students began the module, they were told to complete the assigned readings and videos (stored in Blackboard) within three days. The readings and videos included foundational information on cooperative learning and current examples of cooperative, project-based learning in primary and secondary school classrooms. On the fourth day of the module assignment, students were expected to enter their small group discussion board and chat areas in Blackboard. Group assignments took place prior to the treatment (due to another module that required students to work in groups). Group assignments were generally based on students' availability to meet in the virtual chat room (as required by the previous group activity).

Each group was required to investigate cooperative and project-based learning (utilizing materials provided as well as investigating on their own) and produce a summary lesson plan for a cooperative, project-based lesson. Groups could decide to meet asynchronously, using the discussion board in their small group area, or they could meet synchronously, utilizing the chat function in their small group area. The group was directed to decide how they would meet within one day of entering the small group area. Students were asked to archive all synchronous communication for later analysis.

Each group was given a template to help them create the lesson plan, but was allowed to choose the target audience (age, grade of students) and the subject matter based on identified state Standards of Learning. Students worked on the lesson plan in groups of three or four students using either the cooperative or collaborative learning strategy.

Learning Strategy

Cooperative and collaborative groups were distinguished by the amount of structure provided to and required in the small groups. Cooperative groups were provided with extra instructions that detailed specific roles for group members, scaffolding for promotive interaction and teamwork skills, and group processing (Johnson & Johnson, 1991). Collaborative groups were encouraged to work together to accomplish the assigned tasks, but were not provided with specific member roles or other scaffolding. Both cooperative and collaborative groups were informed that the assignment was complex and needed to be worked on together in order to succeed, thereby emphasizing positive interdependence (Johnson & Johnson) at the same time, students understood that they were individually accountable for the work they did, and that work was reflected in their individual project grade and quiz grade.

Submitting Assignments (Group Projects)

Although students worked in groups, each student was required to turn in their own version of the assignment for grading due to university issues regarding students' digital portfolios and the need for evidence of individual assessments for accreditation requirements. Upon completion of the project, each individual submitted a completed cooperative, project-based lesson plan and was asked to complete the post-experiment survey. All submitted assignments were graded by the researcher.

Individual Quizzes

After submitting the cooperative, project-based lesson plan, each student was instructed to complete a short module quiz. The quiz assessed the student's knowledge retention of the material covered in the course module used in the study. The quiz was created utilizing the Cognitive Process Dimension of the revised version of Bloom's Taxonomy (Krathwohl, 2002) and a blue print. The quiz assessed students' knowledge from a knowledge level through an application level.

Results

Characteristics of the Participants

Of the 389 students enrolled in 22 sections of the course, 91% (n=353) responded to the pre-treatment survey that gathered data about the participants' characteristics and values of connectedness, preference for collaboration, and recognition of the academic potential of collaboration. Data was discarded due to a student's failure in or withdrawal from the course, a student's failure to submit his or her project, or a student's decision to work individually instead of in a group. Results from 4 sections were discarded due to potential conflicts with the study[4]. All of the discarded sections utilized blended delivery method. After discarding participants and course sections due to potential confounding variables, the total number of participants used in the analysis was 254. The number of students enrolled in the blended learning and online course sections and the number of students who utilized the cooperative or collaborative strategies are listed in Table 4.

Student characteristics were evaluated in regard to academic status, gender, ethnicity, teaching status, teaching experience, and online learning experience (see Table 5).

Table 4. Format and strategy

	Frequency	Percent (%)
Course Format		
Blended	134	52.8%
Online	120	47.2%
Learning Strategy		
Cooperative	134	52.8%
Collaborative	120	47.2%

Table 5. Descriptive statistics on characteristics of participants

	Frequency	Percent (%)
Academic Status		
Undergraduate	181	72.1%
Graduate	70	27.6%
Gender		
Male	52	20.5%
Female	202	79.5%
Age		
20 or under	61	24.6%
21 to 25	91	36.7%
26 to 30	29	11.7%
31 to 35	26	10.5%
36 to 40	18	7.3%
41 to 50	18	7.3%
51 or over	5	2%
Ethnicity		
Black, not Hispanic	28	11.3%
Hispanic	9	3.6%
American Indian / Alaskan Native	3	1.2%
Asian, Pacific Islanders	8	3.2%
White, not Hispanic	183	74.1%
Other	10	4%
I choose not to answer this question	6	2.4%
Currently Teaching		
Yes	25	10.1%
No	223	89.9%
Professional Teaching Experience		
Over 2 years teaching full-time in a public or private school	14	7.1%
Less than 2 years full-time teaching experience	10	5.1%
2 or more years teaching part-time in a public or private school	4	2%
2 or more years substitute teaching experience	7	3.6%
Less than 2 years substitute teaching experience	16	8.2%
Teaching in an area other than a public or private school	14	7.1%
No professional teaching experience	117	59.7%
Other	14	7.1%

continued on following page

Table 5. Continued

	Frequency	Percent (%)
Online Experience		
No	110	44.5%
Yes, 1 class	43	17.4%
Yes, 2 classes	19	7.7%%
Yes, 3 or more classes	75	29.5%

Data Analysis

Research Question 1: Achievement

The first research question addressed whether the (collaborative vs. cooperative) and course delivery method (online vs. blended) had a differential effect on individual quiz grades and group project grades. Quiz grades and projects grades were examined separately using a factorial ANCOVA for each. The following covariates were used: age, academic level, online experience, teaching experience, whether the participant was currently teaching, and whether their group followed their assigned learning strategy (actual group structure).

No significant differences were found between course delivery methods and learning strategies in regard to individual quiz grades. A significant interaction was found however, between course delivery method and learning strategy in regard to group project grades (See Figure 1). For course sections delivered through the blended method, group grades were significantly higher for students who utilized the collaborative learning strategy than for students who utilized the cooperative strategy. Online course sections showed generally equivalent group grades for students who utilized the cooperative and collaborative learning strategies. The covariates age and academic level significantly influenced the dependent variable. The findings suggest that for blended course delivery methods in particular, collaborative learning methods resulted in significantly higher group grades than cooperative methods.

Research Question 2: Value of Collaboration

The second research question sought to determine if learning strategy (cooperative vs. collaborative) and course delivery method (online vs. blended) differentially impact students' attitude toward collaboration. The value of collaboration construct is made up of three survey items: (1) students' value of connectedness, (2) students' preference for collaboration, and (3) students' recognition of the potential of collaboration. Before investigating the potential differences between course delivery methods and learning strategy in regard to student attitude toward collaboration as revealed in post-treatment surveys, students' responses from the pre-treatment survey were examined to determine if any differences existed between course delivery methods or learning strategies prior to the treatment. Pre-treatment value of collaboration scores differed significantly between course delivery methods. In each case, students enrolled in the blended course delivery modes responded with higher values of collaboration. The pre-treatment scores were used as covariates when investigating the post-treatment scores.

Figure 1. Estimated marginal means of group project grades

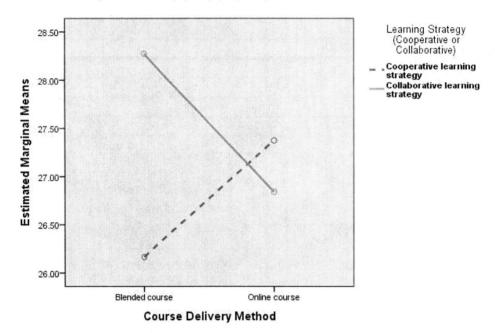

Post-Treatment Value of Collaboration Scores

Results of the MANOVA revealed no significant differences between course delivery methods or learning strategies in regard to students' value of connectedness, preference for collaboration, or recognition of the potential for collaboration.

Research Question 3: Process and Solution Satisfaction

The third research question addressed whether the learning strategy and course delivery method had a differential effect on process satisfaction and solution satisfaction scores. A stepwise MANOVA was performed to determine whether there were significant differences in course delivery method (blended or online) and learning strategy (cooperative and collaborative) for process satisfaction and solution satisfaction scores when accounting for age, academic level, online experience, teaching experience, whether the participant was currently teaching, and whether groups followed their assigned learning strategy. No statistically

significant differences were found between course delivery methods or learning strategies in regard to process satisfaction or solution satisfaction.

Research Question 4: Perception of Teaching, Social, and Cognitive Presence

The fourth research question addressed whether the learning strategy and course delivery method had a differential impact on students' perceptions of teaching presence, social presence and cognitive presence in regard to the project-based group learning activity.

The scores from the three subscales within the CoI Survey instrument, teaching presence, social presence and cognitive presence, were analyzed together using multivariate statistical methods. A stepwise MANOVA was performed to determine whether there were significant differences in course delivery method (blended or online) and learning strategy (cooperative and collaborative) for students' perceptions of teaching presence, social presence and cognitive presence when accounting for students' value of collaboration, process satisfaction, solution satisfaction, age, academic level, online experience, teaching experience, whether the participant was currently teaching, and whether groups followed their assigned learning strategy.

Results of the MANOVA (See Table 6) indicated no statistically significant interaction between the independent variables and no main effect for learning strategy. However, a main effect was found for course delivery method and the covariates post-value of connectedness, post-collaboration potential, process satisfaction, and solution satisfaction were found to significantly affect the dependent variables.

An examination of the Tests of Between-Subjects Effects (Table 7) indicates that the only COI scale that significantly differed between the course delivery methods was teaching presence. The covariate post-value of connectedness significantly affected teaching presence and cognitive presence mean scores. The covariate post-recognition of collaboration significantly affected mean teaching presence and social presence scores. Process satisfaction scores and solution satisfaction scores significantly affected teaching presence, social presence and cognitive presence scores. Online experience significantly affected social presence scores. Additionally, professional teaching experience significantly affected social presence scores.

Table 6. Summary of the MANOVA on the community of inquiry scores by course delivery and learning strategy

	Wilks'Λ	F	Hypothesis df	Error df	p	partial η²
Post-treatment Value of Connectedness	.928	4.558	3	176	.004**	.072
Post-treatment Preference for Collaboration	.966	2.046	3	176	.109	.034
Post-treatment Recognition of Collaboration Potential	.924	4.824	3	176	.003**	.076
Process Satisfaction	.763	18.219	3	176	.000***	.237
Solution Satisfaction	.873	8.511	3	176	.000***	.127
Actual Group Structure	.996	.232	3	176	.874	.004
Age	.990	.604	3	176	.613	.010
Academic Level	.994	.381	3	176	.767	.006
Online Experience	.974	1.596	3	176	.192	.026
Current Teaching Status	.991	.547	3	176	.650	.009
Professional Teaching Experience	.976	1.471	3	176	.224	.024
Course Delivery Method	.932	4.312	3	176	.006**	.068
Learning Strategy	.998	.121	3	176	.356	.018
Course Delivery Method * Learning Strategy	.982	1.087	3	176	.356	.018

***p<.001, **p<.01

Summary of MANOVA on the CoI scores by Course Delivery Method and Learning Strategy, accounting for pre-treatment Value of Collaboration, process satisfaction, solution satisfaction, actual group structure, age, academic level, online experience, teaching status, and teaching experience (n=193)

Table 7. Test of between-subjects for community of inquiry scores by course delivery method and learning strategy (n=193)

	df	F	p	partial η²
Post-Treatment Value of Connectedness				
Teaching Presence	1	5.124	.025*	.028
Social Presence	1	1.076	.301	.006
Cognitive Presence	1	11.860	.001***	.062
Post-Treatment Preference for Collaboration				
Teaching Presence	1	3.262	.073	.018
Social Presence	1	.853	.357	.005
Cognitive Presence	1	.696	.405	.004
Post-Treatment Recognition of Collaboration Potential				
Teaching Presence	1	4.707	.031	.026
Social Presence	1	6.428	.012*	.035
Cognitive Presence	1	1.001	.318	.006
Process Satisfaction				
Teaching Presence	1	18.854	.000***	.096
Social Presence	1	43.639	.000***	.197
Cognitive Presence	1	27.922	.000***	.136
Solution Satisfaction				
Teaching Presence	1	6.119	.014*	.033
Social Presence	1	19.184	.000***	.097
Cognitive Presence	1	17.522	.000***	.090
Actual Group Structure				
Teaching Presence	1	.280	.597	.002
Social Presence	1	.109	.742	.001
Cognitive Presence	1	.067	.796	.000
Age				
Teaching Presence	1	.004	.950	.000
Social Presence	1	1.771	.185	.010
Cognitive Presence	1	.354	.552	.002
Academic Level				
Teaching Presence	1	.114	.736	.001
Social Presence	1	1.147	.286	.006
Cognitive Presence	1	.288	.592	.002
Online Experience				
Teaching Presence	1	.439	.508	.002
Social Presence	1	4.358	.038*	.024
Cognitive Presence	1	.001	.975	.000

continued on following page

Table 7. Continued

	df	F	p	partial η²
Current Teaching Status				
Teaching Presence	1	.317	.574	.002
Social Presence	1	1.055	.306	.006
Cognitive Presence	1	.001	.975	.000
Professional Teaching Experience				
Teaching Presence	1	.007	.936	.000
Social Presence	1	4.279	.040*	.023
Cognitive Presence	1	.355	.552	.002
Course Delivery Method				
Teaching Presence	1	6.091	.015*	.033
Social Presence	1	3.357	.069	.019
Cognitive Presence	1	.355	.552	.002
Learning Strategy				
Teaching Presence	1	.028	.867	.000
Social Presence	1	.031	.861	.000
Cognitive Presence	1	.243	.623	.001
Course Delivery Method * Learning Strategy				
Teaching Presence	1	.449	.504	.003
Social Presence	1	1.393	.239	.008
Cognitive Presence	1	3.141	.078	.017

Teaching Presence Subscales

The Teaching Presence scale consists of three subscales: design and organization, facilitation, and direct instruction. The statistically significant difference in the teaching presence scores between the course delivery methods lead to further investigation of differences according to the subscales. Each subscale was examined utilizing all of the covariates used in the previous ANCOVAs.

Design and Organization

An ANCOVA was used to examine differences between course delivery methods and learning strategies in regard to the teaching presence subscale, design and organization.

Results of the ANCOVA (see Table 8) indicate that an interaction between course delivery and learning strategy occurred. The interaction was significantly affected by the following covariates: process satisfaction and solution satisfaction. The strength of the relationship between the independent variables (course delivery method and learning strategy) and the design and organization subscale was small with the independent variables accounting for 2.7% of the variance of the dependent variable, holding constant the following: post-treatment value of collaboration, process and solution satisfaction, group structure, age, academic level, current teaching status, online experience, and professional teaching experience. Figure 2 illustrates that the interaction is disordinal in nature. More specifically, blended collaborative

Table 8. Summary of ANCOVA on the design and organization subscale by course delivery method and learning strategy

	df	F	p	partial η²
Post-value of connectedness	1	3.124	.079	.017
Post-preference for collaboration	1	2.628	.107	.015
Post-recognition of collaboration potential	1	3.318	.070	.018
Process satisfaction	1	16.947	.000***	.087
Solution Satisfaction	1	5.719	.018*	.031
Actual group structure	1	.040	.842	.000
Age	1	.341	.560	.002
Academic level	1	.014	.907	.000
Online experience	1	.013	.908	.000
Professional teaching experience	1	.003	.959	.000
Current teaching status	1	.047	.828	.000
Course Delivery Method	1	1.291	.257	.007
Learning Strategy	1	.163	.383	.001
Course Delivery Method * Learning Strategy	1	5.002	.027*	.027

Figure 2. Estimated marginal means of teaching presence: design mean

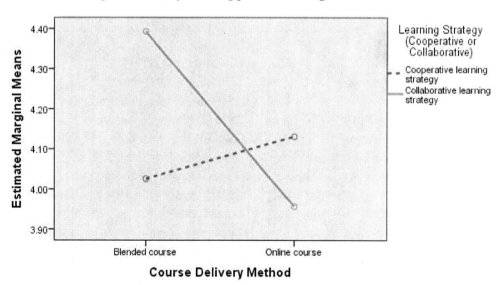

students responded more favorably in regard to the design and organization of the instruction than did blended cooperative students. Conversely, online cooperative students responded more favorably than did online collaborative students.

Facilitation

An ANCOVA was used to examine differences between course delivery methods and learning strategies in regard to the teaching presence subscale, facilitation.

Results of the ANCOVA indicate no significant interaction between the independent variables. Additionally, no significant difference was found between learning strategies. However a main effect was found for course delivery method, $F(1,178)=8.24$, $p<.01$, partial $\eta^2 =.044$. The strength of the relationship between the course delivery method and the facilitation subscale was small with the independent variable accounting for 4.4% of the variance of the dependent variable. The following covariates significantly influenced the dependent variable: post-value of connectedness, post-preference for collaboration, post-recognition of collaboration potential, process satisfaction, and solution satisfaction.

Direct Instruction

An ANCOVA was used to examine differences between course delivery methods and learning strategies in regard to the teaching presence subscale, direct instruction.

Results of the ANCOVA indicate no significant interaction between the independent variables. Additionally, no significant difference was found between learning strategies. However a main effect was found for course delivery method, $F(1,178)=6.23$, $p<.05$, partial $\eta^2 =.034$. The strength of the relationship between the course delivery method and the facilitation subscale was small with the independent variable accounting for 3.4% of the variance of the dependent variable.

The following covariates significantly influenced the dependent variable: post-value of connectedness and process satisfaction.

Review of Findings Individual achievement did not differ according to course delivery method or learning strategy, but a disordinal interaction was found for group project grade, indicating that students in the blended course delivery method performed much more favorably when using the collaborative learning strategy as opposed to the cooperative learning strategy. It is worth noting that no significant difference was found between online cooperative and online collaborative students. Additionally, the online students performed at a similar level to the blended collaborative group (significantly higher than the blended cooperative group). Second, blended students scored higher on pre-treatment value of collaboration items than online students. Once pre-treatment scores were accounted for, post-treatment value of collaboration scores did not differ between course delivery method or learning strategy. Third, no difference was found between course delivery methods or learning strategy for process satisfaction or solution satisfaction. Finally, blended students perceived higher teaching presence than online students. Perceptions of social and cognitive presence did not significantly differ by course delivery method or learning strategy. Teaching presence did not differ according to learning strategy. However an investigation of teaching presence subscales found a disordinal interaction between the independent variables for design and organization, indicating that blended collaborative students responded more favorably than blended cooperative students, while online cooperative students responded more favorably than online collaborative students. The facilitation subscale and the direct instruction subscale significantly differed according to course delivery method, with blended students responding more favorably than online students.

DISCUSSION

Factors Influencing Individual Student Achievement

The first research question addressed whether course delivery method and learning strategy had a differential effect on individual quiz grades and group project grades. Interestingly, there were no differences on quiz grades but both delivery method and learning strategy significantly affected group project grades. More specifically, students enrolled in the blended course delivery method in the cooperative learning groups scored significantly less on the group project than the other three treatment groups. The results are surprising, given that the blended learning environment offers group members the chance to interact face-to-face plus the cooperative learning strategy provides a detailed structure for their group work. One explanation for the lower group project grades is that perhaps the blended cooperative students may have followed a "divide and conquer" strategy (Graham & Misanchuk, 2004) without sufficient ongoing group dialogue or a culminating "meeting of the minds" which contrasts with other studies in which high structured groups had more consistent levels of interaction while low structured groups used more elaboration and critical thinking (Benbunan-Fich, Hiltz, & Turoff, 2002; Brewer & Klein, 2006; Schellens, et al., 2005). Moreover, Cohen (1994) suggests that higher-level learning, like the group project in the present study, may be most effectively achieved in a less structured method (e.g., collaborative) because the instructor-assigned roles in cooperative learning may constrain high-level or elaborative interaction. Support for this argument lies in the lack of difference in the online environment; online students may be naturally inclined to interact with their group whereas the blended students may believe that interaction in the face-to-face meetings may be sufficient, but

in reality is not. Therefore, students in an online course may impose some characteristics of collaborative learning on a cooperative activity.

Factors Influencing Students' Value of Collaboration

When students were asked at the beginning of the course about their (a) value of connectedness with others in their classes, (b) preference for working with others, and (c) recognition for the potential of collaboration to increase academic achievement, those in the blended courses expressed higher values of collaboration than online students and the analyses showed that none of the various treatments caused any change. This might be perceived as disappointing but makes sense because the mean scores for all treatments fell somewhere between neutral and agree, indicating that many students may be somewhat ambivalent toward collaboration (Dziuban, Moskal, Brophy, Shea, & Lorenzo, 2008). Moreover, the nearly three weeks that students engaged in group work may have been insufficient to influence students' perceptions. To further this line of thinking, students' attitudes toward working with others may influence their learning, satisfaction, and perceptions (Ocker & Yaverbaum, 2001; Williams, et al., 2006).

Process Satisfaction and Solution Satisfaction

To dig deeper into student satisfaction, two different aspects were measured: satisfaction with the process of learning by working in a group and satisfaction with the final group outcome. Again, no significant differences were found, which is inconsistent with other studies that found that students engaged in an environment with a face-to-face component tended to be more satisfied with the group process than those who worked exclusively online (Ocker & Yaverbaum, 1999; Thompson & Coovert, 2003; Warkentin, et al.,

1997). Other research found that students in more structured (cooperative) groups perceived higher group efficiency than students in less structured (collaborative) groups (Strijbos, et al., 2004).

More specifically, the lack of differences in process satisfaction found in this study as opposed to other studies may be due to the time allowed for the group work. Flanagin, et al. (2004) noted that satisfaction with the collaboration process can increase over time (in the case of Flanagin et al.'s study, 10 weeks). The project in this study lasted slightly less than three weeks, whereas other studies that found significant differences in process satisfaction between delivery methods used shorter amounts of time (anywhere from two weeks to two hours to 25 minutes) (Ocker & Yaverbaum, 1999; Thompson & Coovert, 2003; Warkentin, et al., 1997). Another explanation for the difference between the results in this study and those of other research may be the amount of computer-mediated interaction required. Several studies that compared online groups with groups that met entirely face-to-face (Olaniran, 1996; Straus & McGrath, 1994; Thompson & Coovert, 2003; Warkentin, et al., 1997; Whitman, Malzahn, Chaparro, Russell, Langrall, & Mohler, 2005). However, in this study, both online and blended groups were required to perform much of their interaction online. Therefore, any differences in process satisfaction between the course delivery methods that may have occurred due to difficulty communicating online and waiting for others to participate may have been negated, because students in all treatments were forced to deal with those communication issues.

The lack of differences in process satisfaction seems to have extended into the lack of differences in solution satisfaction which makes sense particularly because student means in all groups were clustered around four on a five-point scale; students were satisfied with *how* they worked toward a solution and are therefore unlikely to have different perceptions with the outcome itself. This is consistent with some studies that found

no differences in face-to-face and online groups (Benbunan-Fich & Hiltz, 1999; Fjermestad & Hiltz, 1998; Ocker & Yaverbaum, 1999) but not with others (Thompson & Coovert, 2003; Warkentin, et al., 1997). Studies that did find a difference tended to have very short treatment durations. Therefore, the time allocated for the group project was evidently sufficient for the groups to negotiate a solution that left group members satisfied. Additionally, any issues students may have had with the process of group work did not seem to affect their satisfaction with the outcome.

Factors Influencing Student Perceptions of Cognitive Presence, Social Presence, and Teaching Presence

Student perceptions of cognitive presence, social presence and teaching presence were measured utilizing the Community of Inquiry Survey (Arbaugh, et al., 2007a). Each scale was examined separately. While descriptive statistics indicated that blended students' perceptions were higher than online students for each scale, the only statistically significant difference was perceived level of teaching presence by course delivery method only.

Social Presence

The lack of difference between online and blended students' perceived level of social presence is especially surprising given that other research found that students in online courses tend to have poorer perceptions of their discussion quality than students in courses with face-to-face components (Benbunan-Fich & Hiltz, 1999; Whitman, et al., 2005), have to deal with the lack of nonverbal cues (Benbunan-Fich & Hiltz), and often lack "relational intimacy" (Chidambaram, 1996). The lack of significant difference between learning strategies is equally surprising, given that role assignments within group tasks have been found to promote group cohesion (Rose, 2002). However, the findings from this study are consistent with Francescato et al. (2006), who also found no difference in perceptions of social presence when examining collaborative learning in online and face-to-face environments. One reason for the lack of difference between delivery methods or learning strategies may be that students had already worked together briefly in a virtual chat session in their groups prior to the almost three week activity in this study, which may have served as an ice breaker, allowing students to feel more familiar with one another and able to communicate more freely. Thus, social presence may have differed between course delivery methods at the beginning of the course, but that initial, pre-experiment group activity may have been adequate to equalize the level of social presence of students in both delivery methods.

Cognitive Presence

The lack of differences between course delivery methods or learning strategies in regard to student perceptions of cognitive presence is quite interesting. Given that students' individual quiz grades were generally high, the lack of differences is not surprising. However, one might presume that because the blended cooperative students scored lower than all other treatment groups, that a difference in cognitive presence (defined as the extent to which students are able to construct meaning through sustained communication (Garrison, et al., 2000)) might be present. Additionally, because teaching presence often has an impact on cognitive presence (Garrison & Cleveland-Innes, 2005; Garrison, et al., 2010), one might deduce that the differences in teaching presence would impact cognitive presence. The fact that cognitive presence scores did not differ despite the significant differences in group project grades and teaching presence scores raises questions as to what other variables might influence cognitive presence and how closely related the three types

of presence are to each other in this context. The influences on cognitive presence and its relationship with teaching presence and social presence need further study.

Teaching Presence

That blended students perceived a higher teaching presence than online students is not surprising, given that blended students have the advantage of being able to see and interact with their instructor on a weekly basis. However, more interesting results were found when the teaching presence subscales were examined. With regard to the design and organization of the teaching presence subscale, a disordinal interaction between course delivery method and learning strategy was found. More specifically, blended collaborative students responded with higher perceptions than did blended, cooperative students, while in the online environment just the opposite occurred: cooperative students responded with higher perceptions than the collaborative students. The design and organization subscale examines students' perceptions of the instructor's communication of pertinent topics, goals, instruction on participation, and important due dates (Arbaugh, Cleveland-Innes, Diaz, Garrison, Ice, Richardson, Shea, & Swan, 2007b). Therefore, one might expect that online cooperative students, who were provided with a more structured learning strategy, would perceive higher levels of teaching presence for design and organization than online collaborative students. But the difference between the blended cooperative and blended collaborative students is harder to explain. Perhaps the lower design and organization perceptions of the blended cooperative students are somehow connected with their lower group project scores. It could be that the blended cooperative students had a more difficult time following the instructions online because they divided the work amongst themselves and may have worked on the project more as individuals, with only minimal interaction online. Further investigation with content analysis of the group discussion boards and virtual chat areas may be necessary.

Summary of Community of Inquiry Student Survey

The three presences have been found to be interdependent (Akyol & Garrison, 2008) with social presence being a mediating factor between teaching presence and cognitive presence and teaching presence being key to creating and sustaining social presence and cognitive presence (Garrison, et al., 2010). Given these interdependencies, one might question why social presence and cognitive presence did not significantly differ between the treatments when teaching presence did. A likely reason for the difference may be, as Diaz, Swan, Ice & Kupczynski (2010) found, students value teaching presence over the other presences and, to explain their results, posited that students may do so because they view teaching presence as a "necessary condition for the development of social presence" (p. 27). Student perceptions of the importance of teaching presence seem to agree with the findings of Garrison, Cleveland-Innes, and Fung (2010), who further this line of thought by suggesting that teaching presence is "core to establishing and maintaining social and cognitive presence" (p. 35). Moreover, social presence may have been established in the group chat that occurred prior to the experiment in this study. Finally, the lack of difference in cognitive presence in this study shows that students perceived that they were able to learn together no matter the course delivery method or learning strategy; a positive result that affirms the effectiveness of the design of the instructional module.

Summary

Results of this study show that cooperative and collaborative strategies in online and blended environments are equally effective with regard to individual achievement, but that blended cooperative learners perform significantly poorer on group projects and have lower perceptions of teaching presence (in design and organization). Conversely, online cooperative learners had higher perceptions of teacher presence (design and organization) than their online collaborative colleagues.

Despite the differences in group achievement, students were equally satisfied with their groups' process and solution. Blended students value connectedness with classmates, prefer collaboration, and recognize the academic potential of collaboration more than online students at the beginning of the course and the group activity did not significantly change their attitudes. Finally, students did not differ according to their perceptions of social presence and cognitive presence.

A potential conclusion to the findings is that in regard to group achievement, cooperative learning strategies used within a blended environment are less effective than collaborative strategies in blended environments and cooperative or collaborative strategies in online environments. Moreover, blended cooperative groups may desire more teaching presence than blended, collaborative groups, whereas online collaborative groups desire more teaching presence than online cooperative groups.

One might hypothesize that cooperative strategies and, to some extent, online learning favor independent learning while blended learning environments and collaborative strategies are congruent with creating learning communities.

FUTURE RESEARCH RECOMMENDATIONS

Further research is recommended in regard to group project scores in other contexts and the relationship between group project scores and teaching presence scores. This study found that students in the blended, cooperative groups scored significantly lower on group project grades than did the students in the other three treatment groups. This finding was surprising, given that one would suspect that the blended, cooperative treatment may be the most efficient treatment, given the high structure and the students' ability to communicate face-to-face. Therefore, further study is needed, both within the same population and other populations and contexts.

Another interesting finding from this study was that blended cooperative students gave less positive survey responses than blended collaborative students in regard to the teaching presence subscale "design and organization". The design and organization subscale examines students' perceptions of the instructor's communication of pertinent topics, goals, instruction on participation, and important due dates (Arbaugh, et al., 2007b). Given the structure of the cooperative treatment, one might suppose that students in the blended cooperative treatment would respond more favorably than their blended collaborative colleagues in regard to the learning unit's design and organization. This surprising finding, coupled with the difference in group project grades, suggests that the blended cooperative students' perceptions of the learning unit's design and organization may be related to their group project grades. Further study within the same population and other populations is warranted.

The level of interaction within groups may have differed, along with the level of critical thinking reached. While the Community of Inquiry Survey was used to examine differences in regard to the groups' interaction and cognitive presence, the process of constructing meaning and thinking critically (Garrison & Anderson, 2003), the survey relies on student perception and self-report and results may be skewed due to subject effects (McMillan & Schumacher, 2001). Therefore, more in-depth analyses of discussion board and virtual chat content may be necessary to determine how much social presence evolved within groups in each treatment and the level of critical thinking achieved in each group. A useful model for social presence content analysis can be found in articles by Rourke, Anderson, Garrison and Archer (1999). The Practical Inquiry Model (Garrison, Anderson & Archer, 2001; Vaughan & Garrison, 2005) has been widely used for cognitive presence content analysis. A content analysis may provide valuable information to the research literature.

Finally, future studies may be designed to eliminate potential threats to internal and external validity, including differential selection of subjects, diffusion of treatment, and subject effects, population threats and ecological threats (Leedy & Ormrod, 2005; McMillan & Schumacher, 2001).

REFERENCES

Akyol, Z., & Garrison, D. R. (2008). The development of a Community of Inquiry over time in an online course: Understanding the progression and integration of social, cognitive and teaching Presence. *Journal of Asynchronous Learning Networks, 12*(3-4), 3–22.

Akyol, Z., & Garrison, D. R. (2011). Understanding cognitive presence in an online and blended community of inquiry: Assessing outcomes and processes for deep approaches to learning. *British Journal of Educational Technology, 42*(2), 233–250.

Arbaugh, J. B., Cleveland-Innes, M., Diaz, D. P., Garrison, D. R., Ice, P., Richardson, J., Swan, K. (2007a). *Community of Inquiry survey instrument.*

Arbaugh, J. B., Cleveland-Innes, M., Diaz, S., Garrison, D. R., Ice, P., Richardson, J., et al. (2007b). *Community of Inquiry framework: Validation and instrument development.* Paper presented at the 13th Annual Sloan-C Conference.

Barkley, E., Cross, K. P., & Mayor, C. H. (2005). *Collaborative learning techniques: A handbook for college faculty.* San Francisco, CA: Jossey-Bass.

Benbunan-Fich, R., & Hiltz, S. R. (1999). Impacts of asynchronous learning networks on individual and group problem solving: A field experiment. *Group Decision and Negotiation, 8*(5), 409–426.

Benbunan-Fich, R., Hiltz, S. R., & Turoff, M. (2002). A comparative content analysis of face-to-face vs. asynchronous group decision making. *Decision Support Systems, 34,* 457–469.

Bonk, C. J., & Graham, C. R. (2006). *The handbook of blended learning: Global perspectives, local designs* (1st ed.). San Francisco, CA: Pfeiffer.

Bonk, C. J., Wisher, R. A., & Lee, J.-Y. (2004). Moderating learner-centered e-learning: Problems and solutions, benefits and implications. In Roberts, T. S. (Ed.), *Online collaborative learning: Theory and practice* (pp. 54–85). Hershey, PA: Information Science Publishing.

Bourne, K., & Seaman, J. (2005). *Sloan-C special survey report: A look at blended learning.* Needham, MA: The Sloan Consortium.

Brewer, S., & Klein, J. D. (2006). Type of positive interdependence and affiliation motive in an asynchronous, collaborative learning environment. *Educational Technology Research and Development, 54*(4), 331–354.

Brewer, S., Klein, J. D., & Mann, K. E. (2003). Using small group strategies with adult re-entry students. *College Student Journal, 37*(2), 286–297.

Bruffee, K. A. (1999). *Collaborative learning: Higher education, interdependence, and the authority of knowledge* (2nd ed.). Baltimore, MD: Johns Hopkins University Press.

Carr-Chellman, A. A. (2010). *Instructional design for teachers ID4T: Improving classroom practice.* New York, NY: Routledge.

Cavalier, J. C., Klein, J. D., & Cavalier, F. J. (1995). Effects of cooperative learning on performance, attitude, and group behaviors in a technical team environment. *Educational Technology Research and Development, 43*(3), 61–71.

Chidambaram, L. (1996). Relational development in computer-supported groups. *Management Information Systems Quarterly, 20*(2), 143–163.

Clark, R. C., & Mayer, R. E. (2008). *E-learning and the science of instruction: Proven guidelines for consumers and designers of multimedia learning* (2nd ed.). San Francisco, CA: Pfeiffer.

Cohen, E. G. (1994). Restructuring the classroom: Conditions for productive small groups. *Review of Educational Research, 64*(1), 1–35.

Contreras-Castillo, J., Favela, J., Perez-Fragoso, C., & Santamaria-del-Angel, E. (2004). Informal interactions and their implications for online courses. *Computers & Education, 42,* 149–168.

Cooper, J., & Mueck, R. (1990). Student involvement in learning: Cooperative learning and college instruction. *Journal on Excellence in College Teaching, 1,* 68–76.

Cuseo, J. (1992). Collaborative and cooperative learning in higher education: A proposed taxonomy. *Cooperative Learning and College Teaching, 2*(2), 2–4.

Dewiyanti, S., Brand-Gruwel, S., Jochems, W., & Broers, N. J. (2007). Students' experience with collaborative learning in asynchronous Computer-Supported Collaborative Learning environments. *Computers in Human Behavior, 23*(1), 496–514.

Diaz, D. P., & Cartnal, R. B. (1999). Students' learning styles in two classes: Online distance learning and equivalent on-campus. *College Teaching, 47*(4), 130–135.

Diaz, S. R., Swan, K., Ice, P., & Kupczynski, L. (2010). Student ratings of the importance of survey items, multiplicative factor analysis, and the validity of commuity of inquiry survey. *The Internet and Higher Education, 13,* 22–30.

Dick, W., Carey, L., & Carey, J. O. (2009). *The systematic design of instruction* (7th ed.). Upper Saddle River, NJ: Pearson.

Dillenbourg, P., Baker, M., Blaye, A., & O'Malley, C. (1996). The evolution of research on collaborative learning. In Spada, E., & Reiman, P. (Eds.), *Learning in humans and machine: Towards an interdisciplinary learning science* (pp. 189–211). Oxford, UK: Elsevier.

Doymus, K. (2008). Teaching chemical equilibrium with the jigsaw technique. *Research in Science Education, 38*(2), 249–260.

Dziuban, C., Moskal, P., Brophy, J., Shea, P., & Lorenzo, G. (2008). *An underling structure for student satisfaction with asynchronous learning networks*. Paper presented at the 14th Annual Sloan-C International COnference on Online Learning, Orlando, FL.

Emerson, J. D., & Mosteller, F. (2004). Cooperative learning in schools and colleges: II. A review of reviews. In Orey, M., Fitzgerald, M. A., & Branch, R. M. (Eds.), *Educational media and technology yearbook* (*Vol. 29*, pp. 148–170). Westport, CT: Libraries Unlimited.

Fjermestad, J., & Hiltz, S. R. (1998). An assessment of group support systems experimental research: Methodoogy and results. *Journal of Management Information Systems, 15*(3), 7–149.

Flanagin, A. J., Park, H. S., & Seibold, D., R. (2004). Group performance and collaborative technology: A longitudinal and multilevel analysis of information quality, contribution equity, and members' satisfaction in computer-mediated groups. *Communication Monographs, 71*(3), 352–372.

Fortune, M. F., Shifflett, B., & Sibley, R. E. (2006). A Comparison of online (high tech) and traditional (high touch) learning in business communication courses in Silicon Valley. *Journal of Education for Business, 81*(4), 210–214.

Francescato, D., Porcelli, R., Mebane, M., Cuddetta, M., Klobas, J., & Renzi, P. (2006). Evaluation of the efficacy of collaborative learning in face-to-face and computer-supported university contexts. *Computers in Human Behavior, 22,* 163–176.

Garrison, D. R. (2006). Online collaboration principles. *Journal of Asynchronous Learning Networks, 10*(1), 25–33.

Garrison, D. R., & Anderson, T. (2003). *E-learning in the 21st century*. London, UK: Routledge Falmer.

Garrison, D. R., Anderson, T., & Archer, W. (2000). Critical inquiry in a text-based environment: Computer conferencing in higher education. *The Internet and Higher Education, 2*(2-3), 87–105.

Garrison, D. R., Anderson, T., & Archer, W. (2001). Critical thinking, cognitive presence, and computer conferencing in distance education. *American Journal of Distance Education, 15*(1), 7–23.

Garrison, D. R., & Arbaugh, J. B. (2007). Researching the community of inquiry framework: Review, issues, and future directions. *The Internet and Higher Education, 10*(3), 157–172.

Garrison, D. R., & Cleveland-Innes, M. (2005). Facilitating cognitive presence in online learning: Interaction is not enough. *American Journal of Distance Education, 19*(3), 133–148.

Garrison, D. R., Cleveland-Innes, M., & Fung, T. S. (2010). Exploring causal relationships among teaching, cognitive and social presence: Student perceptions of the community of inquiry framework. *The Internet and Higher Education, 13,* 31–36.

Garrison, D. R., & Kanuka, H. (2004). Blended learning: Uncovering its transformative potential in higher education. *The Internet and Higher Education, 7*(2), 95–105.

Graham, C. R., & Misanchuk, M. (2004). Computer-mediated learning groups: Benefits and challenges to using groupwork in online learning environments. In Roberts, T. S. (Ed.), *Online collaborative learning: Theory and practice* (pp. 181–202). Hershey, PA: Information Science Publishing.

Green, S. G., & Taber, T. D. (1980). The effects of three social decision schemes on decision group processes. *Organizational Behavior and Human Performance, 25,* 97–106.

Gunawardena, C. N., Nolla, A. C., Wilson, P. L., Lopez-Islas, J. R., Ramirez-Angel, N., & Megchun-Alpizar, R. M. (2001). A cross-cultural study of group process and development in online conferences. *Distance Education, 22*(1), 85–121.

Hall, D. (1997). Computer mediated communication in post-compulsory teacher education. *Open Learning, 12*(3), 54–57.

Hall, R. H., Rocklin, T. R., Dansereau, D. F., Skaggs, L. P., O'Donnell, A. M., Lambiotte, J. G., & Young, M. D. (1988). The role of individual differences in the cooperative learning of technical material. *Journal of Educational Psychology, 80*(2), 172–178.

Harker, M., & Koutsantoni, D. (2005). Can it be as effective? Distance versus blended learning in a web-based EAP programme. *ReCALL, 17*(1), 197–216.

Heinich, R., Molenda, M., Russell, J. D., & Smaldino, S. E. (2002). *Instructional media and technologies for learning* (7th ed.). Upper Saddle River, NJ: Pearson.

Henri, F., & Rigault, C. R. (1996). Collaborative distance learning and computer conferencing. In Liao, T. T. (Ed.), *Advanced educational technology: Research issues and future potential* (pp. 45–76). Berlin, Germany: Springer-Verlag.

Hillard, A. (2006). *Evaluation of different methods of on-line collaboration/group work forming the coursework assessment in a blended learning module.* Paper presented at the 5th European Conference on e-Learning, University of Winchester, UK.

Hooper, S. (1992). Cooperative learning and computer-based instruction. *Educational Technology Research and Development, 40*(3), 21–38.

Ice, P. (2008). How do we assess the effectiveness of new technologies and learning environments? *Sloan-C View, 7*(2). Retrieved from http://www.sloanconsortium.org/publications/view/v7n2/viewv7n2.htm#Assess

Ice, P., Kupczynski, L., & Mitchell, R. (2008). *Instructional design strategies and the Community of Inquiry framework.* Paper presented at the 14th Annual Sloan-C Conference on Online Learning, Orlando, FL.

Johnson, D. W., & Johnson, R. T. (1991). *Learning together and alone: Cooperative, competitive and individualistic learning* (3rd ed.). Needham Heights, MA: Allyn and Bacon.

Johnson, D. W., & Johnson, R. T. (1996). Cooperation and the use of technology. In Jonassen, D. H. (Ed.), *Handbook of research for educational communications and technology*. New York, NY: Simon & Schuster Macmillan.

Johnson, R. T., & Johnson, D. W. (1994). An overview of cooperative learning. In J. Thousand, A. VIlla & A. Nevin (Eds.), *Creativity and collaborative learning*. Baltimore, MD: Brookes Press.

Jonassen, D. H. (1997). Instructional design model for well-structured and ill-structured problem-solving learning outcomes. *Educational Technology Research and Development*, *45*(1), 65–95.

Joo, Y. J., Lim, K. Y., & Kim, E. K. (2011). Online university students' satisfaction and persistence: Examining perceived level of presence, usefulness and ease of use as predictors in a structural model. *Computers & Education*, *57*, 1654–1664. doi:doi:10.1016/j.compedu.2011.02.008

Kim, K.-J., Liu, S., & Bonk, C. J. (2005). Online MBA students' perceptions of online learning: Benefits, challenges, and suggestions. *The Internet and Higher Education*, *8*(4), 335–344.

Kirschner, P. A. (2001). Using integrated electronic environments for collaborative teaching/learning. *Research Dialogue in Learning and Instruction*, *2*(Supplement 1), 1–9.

Kitchen, D., & McDougall, D. (1998). Collaborative learning on the internet. *Journal of Educational Technology Systems*, *27*(3), 245–258.

Klein, J. D., & Doran, M. S. (1999). Implementing individual and small group learning structures with a computer simulation. *Educational Technology Research and Development*, *47*(1), 97–110.

Krathwohl, D. R. (2002). A revision of Bloom's taxonomy: An overview. *Theory into Practice*, *41*(4), 212–218.

Leedy, P. D., & Ormrod, J. E. (2005). *Pratical research: Planning and design* (8th ed.). Upper Saddle River, NJ: Pearson Prentice Hall.

Leh, A. S. (2002). Action research on hybrid courses and their online communities. *Educational Media International*, *39*(1), 31–38.

Lim, D. H., Morris, M. L., & Kupritz, V. (2007). Online vs. blended learning: Differences in instructional outcomes and learner satisfaction. *Journal of Asynchronous Learning Networks*, *11*(2), 27–42.

Lin, Q. (2008). Student satisfaction in four mixed courses in an elementary teacher education program. *The Internet and Higher Education*, *11*, 53–59.

Lipman, M. (2003). *Thinking in education* (2nd ed.). Cambridge, UK: Cambridge University Press.

Lou, Y., Abrami, P. C., & d'Apollonia, S. (2001). Small group and individual learning with technology: A meta-analysis. *Review of Educational Research*, *71*(3), 449–521.

Macdonald, J. (2003). Assessing online collaborative learning: Process and product. *Computers & Education*, *40*(4), 377–391.

McIsaac, M. S., & Gunawardena, C. N. (1996). Distance education. In Jonassen, D. H. (Ed.), *Handbook of research for educational communication and technology* (pp. 403–437). New York, NY: Simon & Schuster Macmillan.

McMillan, J. H., & Schumacher, S. (2001). *Research in education: A conceptual introduction* (5th ed.). New York, NY: Longman.

Mejias, R. J. (2007). The interaction of process losses, process gains, and meetingsatisfaction within technology-supported environments. *Small Group Research*, *38*(1), 156–194.

Millis, B. J., & Cottell, P. G. (1998). *Cooperative learning for higher education faculty*. Phoenix, AZ: Oryx Press.

Molenda, M. (2003). In search of the elusive AD-DIE model. *Performance Improvement, 42*(5), 34–36. doi:doi:10.1002/pfi.4930420508

Moore, J. C. (2002). *Elements of quality: The Sloan-C framework*. Needham, MA: Sloan Consortium.

Moore, J. C. (2005). Is higher education ready for transformative learning? A question explored in the study of sustainability. *Journal of Transformative Education, 3*, 76–91.

Morrison, G. R., Ross, S. M., & Kemp, J. E. (2007). *Designing effective instruction*. Hoboken, NJ: John Wiley & Sons, Inc.

Morrison, G. R., Ross, S. M., & Kemp, J. E. (2010). *Designing effective instruction* (6th ed.). Hoboken, NJ: John Wiley & Sons, Inc.

Mudrack, P. E., & Farrell, G. M. (1995). An examination of functional role behavior and its consequences for individuals in group settings. *Small Group Research, 26*(4), 542–571.

Murphy, E. (2004). Recognising and promoting collaboration in an online asynchronous discussion. *British Journal of Educational Technology, 35*(4), 421–431.

Ocker, R. J., & Yaverbaum, G. J. (1999). Asynchronous computer-mediated communication versus face-to-face collaboration: Results on student learning, quality and satisfaction. *Group Decision and Negotiation, 8*, 427–440.

Ocker, R. J., & Yaverbaum, G. J. (2001). Collaborative learning environments: Exploring student attitudes and satisfaction in face-to-face and asynchronous computer conferencing settings. *Journal of Interactive Learning Research, 12*(4), 427–448.

Olaniran, B. A. (1996). A model of group satisfaction in computer-mediated communication and face-to-face meetings. *Behaviour & Information Technology, 15*(1), 24–36.

Oliver, R., & Omari, A. (2001). Student responses to collaborating and learning in a web-based environment. *Journal of Computer Assisted Learning, 17*(1), 34–47.

Overbaugh, R., & Nickel, C. (2008). *A comparison of student satisfaction and value of academic community between blended and online sections of a university-level educational foundations course*. Norfolk, VA: Old Dominion University.

Overbaugh, R., Nickel, C., & Brown, H. M. (2006). *Student characteristics in a university-level foundations course: An examination of orientation toward learning and the role of academic community*. Paper presented at the Eastern Educational Research Association Annual Conference, Hilton Head, SC.

Paulus, T. M. (2005). Collaborative and cooperative approaches to online group work: The impact of task type. *Distance Education, 26*(1), 111–125.

Piccoli, G., Ahmad, R., & Ives, B. (2001). Web-based virtual learning environments: A research framework and a preliminary assessment of effectiveness in basic IT training. *Management Information Systems Quarterly, 25*(4), 401–426.

Priluck, R. (2004). Web-assisted courses for business education: An examination of two sections of principles of marketing. *Journal of Marketing Education, 26*(2), 161–173.

Reigeluth, C. M., & Carr-Chellman, A. A. (2010). Understanding instructional theory. In Reigeluth, C. M., & Carr-Chellman, A. A. (Eds.), *Instructional design theory and models* (*Vol. III*). New York, NY: Routledge.

Rivera, J. C., McAlister, M. K., & Rice, M. L. (2002). A comparison of student outcomes & satisfaction between traditional & web based course offerings. *Online Journal of Distance Learning Administration, 5*(3). Retrieved from http://www.westga.edu/~distance/ojdla/fall53/rivera53.html

Romiszowski, A. (1999). The development of physical skills: Instruction in the psychomotor domain. In Reigeluth, C. M. (Ed.), *Instructional design theories and models (Vol. II)*. Mahwah, NJ: Erlbaum.

Roschelle, J., & Teasley, S. (1995). The construction of shared knowledge in collaborative problem solving. In O'Malley, C. (Ed.), *Computer supported collaborative learning* (pp. 69–97). Berlin, Germany: Springer-Verlag.

Rose, M. A. (2002). *Cognitive dialogue, interaction patterns, and perceptions of graduate students in an online conferencing environment under collaborative and cooperative structures.* Doctor of Education Dissertation, Indiana University.

Rose, M. A. (2004). Comparing productive online dialogue in two group styles: Cooperative and collaborative. *American Journal of Distance Education, 18*(2), 73–88.

Rourke, L., Anderson, T., Garrison, D. R., & Archer, W. (1999). Assessing social presence in asynchronous text-based computer conferencing. *Journal of Distance Education, 14*(2), 50–71.

Russell, T. L. (2001). *The no significant difference phenomenon: A comparative research annotated bibliography on technology for distance education.* Montgomery: AL The International Distance Education Certification Center.

Schellens, T., Van Keer, H., & Valcke, M. (2005). The impact of role assignment on knowledge construction in asynchronous discussion groups: A multilevel analysis. *Small Group Research, 36*, 704–745.

Seals, B., & Glasgow, Z. (1998). *Making instructional design decisions* (2nd ed.). Upper Saddle River, NJ: Prentice Hall.

Shea, P. J. (2006). A study of students' sense of learning community in online environments. *Journal of Asynchronous Learning Networks, 10*(1), 35–44.

Shea, P. J., Fredericksen, E. E., Pickett, A. M., & Pelz, W. E. (2004). Faculty development, student satisfaction, and reported learning in the SUNY learning network. In Duffy, T. M., & Kirkley, J. R. (Eds.), *Learner-centered theory and practice in distance education: Cases from higher education* (pp. 343–377). Mahwah, NJ: L. Erlbaum.

Shea, P. J., Pickett, A. M., & Pelz, W. E. (2003). A follow-up investigation of "teaching presence" in the SUNY learning netowrk. *Journal of Asynchronous Learning Networks, 7*(2), 61–80.

Slavin, R. E. (1985). An introduction to cooperative learning research. In Slavin, R. E., Sharan, S., Kagan, S., Lazarowitz, R. H., Webb, C., & Schmuck, R. (Eds.), *Learning to cooperate, cooperating to learn* (pp. 5–15). New York, NY: Plenum Press.

So, H.-J., & Brush, T. A. (2008). Student perceptions of collaborative learning, social presence and satisfaction in a blended learning environment: Relationships and critical factors. *Computers & Education, 51*(1), 318–336.

Straus, S. G., & McGrath, J. E. (1994). Does the medium matter? The interaction of task type and technology on group performance and member reactions. *The Journal of Applied Psychology, 79*(1), 87–97.

Strijbos, J. W., Martens, R. L., Jochems, W. M. G., & Broers, N. J. (2004). The effect of functional roles on group efficiency: Using multilevel modeling and content analysis to investigate computer-supported collaboration in small groups. *Small Group Research, 35*(2), 195–229.

Thompson, L. F., & Coovert, M. D. (2003). Teamwork online: The effects of computer conferencing on perceived confusion, satisfaction and postdiscussion accuracy. *Group Dynamics*, *7*(2), 135–151.

Underwood, J., & Underwood, G. (1999). Task effects on co-operation and collaborative learning with computers. In Littleton, K., & Light, P. (Eds.), *Learning with computers*. London, UK: Routledge.

Uribe, D., Klein, J. D., & Sullivan, H. (2003). The effect of computer-mediated collaborative learning on solving ill-defined problems. *Educational Technology Research and Development*, *51*(1), 5–19.

van Merrienboer, J. J. G., Clark, R. F., & deCroock, M. B. M. (2002). Blueprints for complex learning: The 4C/ID model. *Educational Technology Research and Development*, *50*(2), 39–64.

Vaughan, N., & Garrison, D. R. (2005). Creating cognitive presence in a blended faculty development community. *The Internet and Higher Education*, *8*(1), 1–12.

Vignare, K. (2007). Review of literature - Blended learning: Using ALN to change the classroom: Will it work? In Picciano, A. G., & Dziuban, C. D. (Eds.), *Blended learning: Research perspectives* (pp. 37–63). Needham, MA: Sloan Consortium.

Voos, R. (2003). Blended learning - What is it and where might it take us? *Sloan-C View*, *2*(1), 3–5.

Walters, W. (2004-2005). Infusing technology into any instructional program. *Virginia Society for Technology in Education Journal*, *19*(1), 17-24.

Warkentin, M. E., Sayeed, L., & Hightower, R. (1997). Virtual teams versus face-to-face teams: An exploratory study of a web-based conference system. *Decision Sciences*, *28*(4), 975–996.

Webb, N. M., & Palincsar, A. S. (1996). Group processes in the classroom. In Berliner, D., & Calfee, R. (Eds.), *Handbook of educational psychology* (pp. 841–873). New York, NY: Macmillan.

Wegner, S. B., Holloway, K. C., & Garton, E. M. (1999). The effects of internet-based instruction on student learning. *Journal of Asynchronous Learning Networks*, *3*(2), 98–106.

Whitman, L. E., Malzahn, D. E., Chaparro, B. S., Russell, M., Langrall, R., & Mohler, B. A. (2005). A comparison of group processes, performance, and satisfaction in face-to-face versus computer-mediated engineering student design teams. *Journal of Engineering Education*, *94*(3), 327–333.

Williams, E. A., Duray, R., & Reddy, V. (2006). Teamwork orientation, group cohesiveness, and student learning: A study of the use of teams in online distance education. *Journal of Management Education*, *30*(4), 592–616.

KEY TERMS AND DEFINITIONS

Blended Learning: The planned, pedagogical integration of the strengths of face-to-face learning experiences (verbal and nonverbal communication) with the strengths of online learning (text-based communication and internet resources) (Garrison & Kanuka, 2004; Vaughan & Garrison, 2005; Vignare, 2007). In the course used in this study students enrolled in blended learning classes met in a traditional classroom once or twice a week, but most of the course content and communication was completed via the internet.

Collaborative Learning: Students working in a coordinated effort to solve problems (Roschelle & Teasley, 1995). Collaborative activities are characterized by learners completing the group task and constructing meaning together through dialogue and negotiation (Garrison, et al., 2000; Paulus, 2005). Compared to cooperative learning, collaborative learning is relatively unstructured, neither requiring nor encouraging a division of labor.

Cooperative Learning: Students working together to "attain group goals that cannot be obtained by working alone or competitively" (Johnson, Johnson, & Holubec, 1986). The defining characteristics of cooperative learning are positive role interdependence, meaning that group members take on specific roles and divide the labor accordingly, and scaffolding of teamwork skills and group processing.

Online Learning: Instruction delivered on the computer by way of the Internet (Clark & Mayer, 2008). Online instruction is generally delivered asynchronously but can also be delivered synchronously. In the course used in this study all course content and communication was delivered via the internet.

ENDNOTES

[1]   See, for example, van Merrienboer, Clark and deCroock's (2002) *4C/ID Design for Complex Learning*, Romiszowski's *The Development of Physical Skills: Instruction in the Psychomotor Domain* (1999) which focus on performance outcomes but clearly address cognitive learning.

[2]   More information on the components of cooperative and collaborative learning can be found in Johnson, Johnson, & Holubec, (1986), Slavin (1985), Johnson & Johnson (1991, 1994a) and Johnson, Johnson & Smith (1991, 1998)

[3]   5W/5E is a model that expands upon Who?, What?, Where?, When?, and Why? with Engage, Explore, Explain, Elaborate, & Evaluate

[4]   Data was discarded due to a student's failure in or withdrawal from the course, a student's failure to submit his or her project, or a student's decision to work individually instead of in a group. Of the 389 original participants, 3.9% (n=15) students worked independently and 1.8% (n=7) failed to turn in their project. 6.4% (n=25) withdrew from the course and 8.5% (n=33) failed the course. Additionally, of the 22 course sections, results from 4 sections were discarded due to potential conflicts with the study. One section was discarded because the students and instructor failed to provide the researcher with the student projects for grading. Another section was discarded because the students completed all of their group work in class, instead of online. A third section was discarded because students were allowed to attempt the unit quiz twice. Finally, the fourth section was discarded because the cooperative learning module was offered at a later time in the semester than the rest of the course sections. All of the discarded sections utilized blended delivery method.

APPENDIX A: MODULE OUTLINE

Introduction to the Module

Students in both cooperative and collaborative groups were introduced to the module by way of a video announcement at the beginning of the module. I will explain that I am acting as the instructor for the module and that all questions should come to me. Students understood that they had been assigned to small groups and that they would be working together to create a cooperative, project-based lesson plan for a cooperative learning activity (the target age and subject is the group's choice). All requirements were explained. Additionally, it was explained that this module is part of a research study and that all data gathered will be confidential.

Readings/Videos

Students in both treatments will be responsible for completing the same readings and video viewings and are expected to complete the readings prior to small group discussion. Groups are welcome to conduct further investigation of content online if they wish. All readings, videos, and external links will be available within the Blackboard module. Readings and videos will explain the basic concepts behind cooperative learning and project-based learning and will include examples of cooperative project-based learning for various age groups and subjects.

Group Interaction

(See Table 9.)

Assessments

Acting as the instructor, the researcher will be responsible for grading all cooperative, project-based lesson plan and individual quizzes. The lesson summaries (developed by the small groups but submitted individually) will be assessed via a rubric, which will assess projects based on fulfilling all cooperative and project-based learning elements, logical rationale for choices and integration of technology in the lesson plan.

Individual quizzes will be taken online via Blackboard. Open-ended questions will be graded by the researcher.

Table 9.

Collaborative	Cooperative
Positive Interdependence: Small groups will have the mutual goal of completing the cooperative, project-based lesson plan together (positive goal interdependence). **Positive Identity Interdependence:** Small groups will choose names for themselves	Positive Interdependence: Small groups will have the mutual goal of completing the cooperative, project-based lesson plan together (positive goal interdependence). Positive Identity Interdependence: Small groups will choose names for themselves Positive Role Interdependence: Labor is divided into specific roles
Individual Accountability: Students will understand that peers within the group will evaluate their participation in the group project. If they receive negative peer evaluations due to lack of participation, their grade may be lowered. Additionally, students will understand that they will take an individual quiz at the end of the module – a potential motivation to learn the content.	Individual Accountability: Students will understand that peers within the group will evaluate their participation in the group project. If they receive negative peer evaluations due to lack of participation, their grade may be lowered. Students will be assigned roles within their groups. The success of the group is dependent on their completion of their roles. Additionally, students will understand that they will take an individual quiz at the end of the module – a potential motivation to learn the content.
Group Roles	Leader: Schedules when and how the group will meet (asynchronously or synchronously); helps develop a project schedule and makes sure the group stays on schedule Checker: Checks on group comprehension and checks the grading rubric to make sure the assignment is fully completed Writer/Recorder: Records decisions (makes sure decisions are consensual); edits the final document Prober: Keeps the group from giving superficial answers to questions; encourages the group to explore alternative possibilities
Teamwork Skills	Teamwork Skills: Cooperative groups will be provided with material about how to work effectively in a group. Additionally, the researcher (acting as the instructor) will frequently monitor group discussion to facilitate interaction.
Group Processing	Group Processing: Halfway through the treatment, cooperative groups will be asked to examine how they have been interacting as a group and how they might improve.

APPENDIX B: PROJECT INSTRUCTIONS FOR GROUPS

Instructions for Both Learning Strategy Treatment Groups

Chat or Discussion Board

For this project, you will work together in your group to review what you have read and learned. You will then create an overview of a cooperative lesson.

- Start by following Activity readings below. Do not skip any of the readings, they were all chosen specifically for you.
- Go to your group discussion board (found on the "Groups" button on the left).
- In your discussion board, decide with your group whether you want to use the chat function (synchronous communication) or the discussion board (asynchronous communication) or use both to complete the review of your learning and the project template.
- As a group, discuss the following topics. Do not skip this step – it will help you on your group lesson template as well as on the quiz. All topic readings are found in this project.
  - **Topic 1:** Compare and contrast cooperative and collaborative learning. How are they similar? How do they differ?
  - **Topic 2:** Compare positive interdependence and individual accountability. Why are both necessary for successful effective cooperative learning?
  - **Topic 3:** Discuss examples of way you can integrate technology into Project-Based and Cooperative Learning.
  - **Topic 4:** An integral part of the PBL classroom is the use of probing, thought-provoking, multi-faceted questions that get students to reach high cognitive levels. Give examples of questions or activities that relate to the Remembering, Understanding, Applying and Analyzing levels of Bloom's Taxonomy.
- Once you are finished discussing the questions, work together to follow the next set of instructions (Activity 2) to create an overview of a cooperative lesson based on the project template. Specific instructions on how to complete the group project are below.

Instructions for Students Assigned to the Collaborative Treatment

Group Collaborative Work

In this activity, you will work with your group members (CLICK GROUPS button on the left) to create a summary of a cooperative, project-based lesson. Carefully look over the project template and think about what subject matter you would like to use in the lesson plan prior to meeting with your group (in the "groups section").

Directions for Collaborative Treatment

(See Figure 3.)

Instructions for Students Assigned to the Cooperative Treatment

Group Cooperative Work

In this activity, you will work with your group members (CLICK GROUPS button on left) to create a summary of a cooperative, project-based lesson. Carefully look over the project template and think about what subject matter you would like to use in the lesson plan prior to meeting with your group (in the "groups section").

Before working with your group members, please read the instructions on effective group work) see teamwork document).

Directions for Cooperative Treatment

(See Figure 4.)

Figure 3. Collaborative treatment

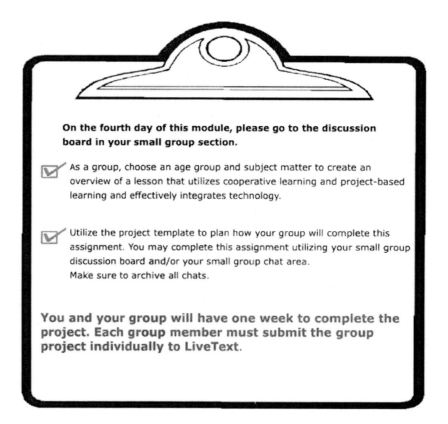

On the fourth day of this module, please go to the discussion board in your small group section.

☑ As a group, choose an age group and subject matter to create an overview of a lesson that utilizes cooperative learning and project-based learning and effectively integrates technology.

☑ Utilize the project template to plan how your group will complete this assignment. You may complete this assignment utilizing your small group discussion board and/or your small group chat area. Make sure to archive all chats.

You and your group will have one week to complete the project. Each group member must submit the group project individually to LiveText.

Figure 4. Cooperative treatment

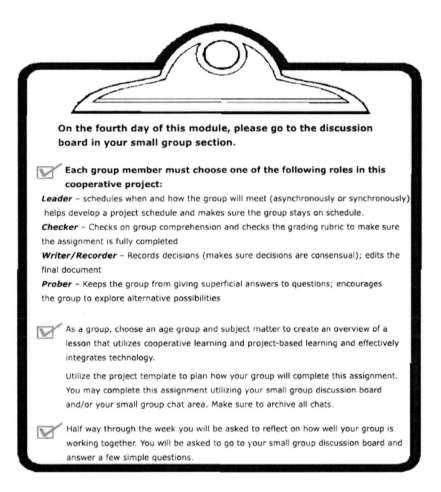

On the fourth day of this module, please go to the discussion board in your small group section.

☑ **Each group member must choose one of the following roles in this cooperative project:**

Leader – schedules when and how the group will meet (asynchronously or synchronously) helps develop a project schedule and makes sure the group stays on schedule.

Checker – Checks on group comprehension and checks the grading rubric to make sure the assignment is fully completed

Writer/Recorder – Records decisions (makes sure decisions are consensual); edits the final document

Prober – Keeps the group from giving superficial answers to questions; encourages the group to explore alternative possibilities

☑ As a group, choose an age group and subject matter to create an overview of a lesson that utilizes cooperative learning and project-based learning and effectively integrates technology.

Utilize the project template to plan how your group will complete this assignment. You may complete this assignment utilizing your small group discussion board and/or your small group chat area. Make sure to archive all chats.

☑ Half way through the week you will be asked to reflect on how well your group is working together. You will be asked to go to your small group discussion board and answer a few simple questions.

Scaffolding Materials (Provided to the Cooperative Treatment Groups)

Teamwork Principles

These Principles are important to cooperating with others effectively. Please read and follow these principles as you work with your group:

- **Positive Interdependence:** Involve people.
  - Ask for ideas, opinions and suggestions
  - Involve people in choices and decisions that affect them
  - Help people to see the 'big picture'
  - Negotiate tasks and procedures
  - Develop team goals together

- **Interactive Learning:** Communicate.
  - Actively listen
  - Find creative ways of sharing information
  - Explain why things are important
  - Keep people informed - encourage people to keep themselves informed
- **Individual Accountability:** Share responsibility.
  - Ensure that each individual is clear about their task/role and their contribution to the team
- **Development of Interpersonal Skills:** Develop teamwork skills.
  - Interpersonal skills
  - Problem-solving, mediation and conflict resolution
  - Effective thinking and decision-making
  - Positive, pro-active style of working
- **Reflection:** Give recognition.
  - Encourage initiative, act on people's ideas
  - Acknowledge contributions and achievements
  - Accent the positives
  - Give constructive feedback
- **Reciprocity:** Build reciprocity.
  - Actively seek to learn from others
  - Take the perspective of other people
  - Give and receive support
  - Develop genuine partnerships with others

Adapted from http://www.ceo.cg.catholic.edu.au/learning/re/tno/strategies/cooperative_learning.htm.

Group Processing

Halfway through the treatment, cooperative groups will be asked to examine how they have been interacting as a group and how they might improve their teamwork. The groups will receive an email notifying them to post to a Group Processing thread within their small group discussion board.

APPENDIX C: LESSON PLAN SUMMARY TEMPLATE

This lesson plan summary template (Table 10) is adapted from the 5W/5E used earlier in the course. Describe what you, as the teacher, need to do to facilitate learning. Include rationale for your decisions (why your choices are appropriate). And be creative! Imagine that the sky is the limit and school budgets and resources are pretty much limitless.

Please type your answers in the right side of the table. Make sure to cover each question in detail, as explained in the project rubric. Make sure to use spell check and that you meet all areas of writing expectations. DELETE the directions when complete.

Table 10. Template

Your Name:	
Names of Other Group Members:	
Lesson Title:	
Subject Area:	
WHO is targeted for this cooperative activity?	
WHAT?	
What is/are the instructional goal(s) of the cooperative activity?	
What technologies are available?	
What technologies would the educator like to use?	
Cooperative Learning	
What kinds of grouping strategies will be used (how many group members? Do members form their own groups or are they assigned?)	
How will positive interdependence be promoted?	
How will individual accountability be promoted?	
List and describe the roles assigned to each group member.	
Describe how the instructor will facilitate teamwork skills and group processing. (How will the teacher teach the group teamwork skills? How will the group examine how well they are working together?)	
WHERE will the lesson be delivered? (classroom, computer lab, other?)	
WHEN will the cooperative activity take place? (warm-up, wrap-up activity, after a particular lesson?	
WHY are your choices for the cooperative activity appropriate?	
HOW will you know that students have learned the subject matter? What kind of assessment will you use?	
Technology Integration	
What type of technology will be integrated into the cooperative lesson?	
Why is the technology appropriate for the lesson?	
WHERE will the technology integration occur? (classroom, computer lab, other?)	
WHY are you using technology integrated into the lesson? (use at least one of the 5 E's: Engage, Explore, Explain, Elaborate, Evaluate)	

APPENDIX D: LESSON PLAN RUBRIC

Table 11. Rubric

	Does not meet criteria	Incomplete (1 pt.)	Partially Proficient (3 pts.)	Proficient (4 pts.)	Exemplary (5 pts.)
Target Audience & Lesson Topic (1, 16%)	Unacceptable performance is evidenced by none of the following criteria met:	Incomplete performance is evidenced by only 1 of the following criteria met:	Partially Proficient performance is evidenced by at least 2 of the following criteria met:	Proficient performance is evidenced by all 3 of the following criteria met:	Exemplary performance is evidenced by all 3 of the following criteria met:
	1. by an explanation of the target audience, including age, grade level, and experience or previous knowledge	1. by an explanation of the target audience, including age, grade level, and experience or previous knowledge	1. by an explanation of the target audience, including age, grade level, and experience or previous knowledge	1. by an explanation of the target audience, including age, grade level, and experience or previous knowledge	1. by a thorough explanation of the target audience, including age, grade level, and experience or previous knowledge
	2. an explanation of the lesson topic, including the goal or purpose of the lesson and the resources used in the lesson	2. an explanation of the lesson topic, including the goal or purpose of the lesson and the resources used in the lesson	2. an explanation of the lesson topic, including the goal or purpose of the lesson and the resources used in the lesson	2. an explanation of the lesson topic, including the goal or purpose of the lesson and the resources used in the lesson	2. a clear explanation of the lesson topic, including the goal or purpose of the lesson and the resources used in the lesson
	3. the assignment posted in the correct location by the assignment date	3. the assignment posted in the correct location by the assignment date	3. the assignment posted in the correct location by the assignment date	3. the assignment posted in the correct location by the assignment date	3. the assignment posted in the correct location by the assignment date
Elements of Cooperative Learning Part I (1, 16%)	Unacceptable performance is evidenced by *none* of the following criteria met:	Incomplete performance is evidenced by *only 1* of the following criteria met:	Partially Proficient performance is evidenced by the following criteria met:	Proficient performance is evidenced by the following criteria met:	Exemplary performance is evidenced by all of the following criteria met:
	1. Positive Interdependence: The learner chose at least one type of positive interdependence to be promoted, gave a detailed explanation of why it is appropriate for the proposed activity and how it will be implemented in the lesson.	**1. Positive Interdependence:** The learner chose at least one type of positive interdependence to be promoted, and stated (with little detail) how it will be implemented in the lesson.	**1. Positive Interdependence:** The learner chose at least one type of positive interdependence to be promoted, and stated *(with little detail)* how it will be implemented in the lesson.	**1. Positive Interdependence:** The learner chose at least one type of positive interdependence to be promoted, gave a *detailed explanation* of why it is appropriate for the proposed activity and how it will be implemented in the lesson.	**1. Positive Interdependence:** The learner chose at least one type of positive interdependence to be promoted, gave a *detailed explanation* of why it is appropriate for the proposed activity and how it will be implemented in the lesson.
	2. Individual Accountability: The learner gave a detailed explanation of how individuals will be held accountable for their own work in the proposed activity.	**2. Individual Accountability:** The learner stated (with little detail) how individuals will be held accountable for their own work in the proposed activity.	**2. Individual Accountability:** The learner stated *(with little detail)* how individuals will be held accountable for their own work in the proposed activity.	**2. Individual Accountability:** The learner stated *(with little detail)* how individuals will be held accountable for their own work in the proposed activity.	**2. Individual Accountability:** The learner gave a *detailed explanation* of how individuals will be held accountable for their own work in the proposed activity.

continued on following page

Table 11. Continued

	Does not meet criteria	Incomplete (1 pt.)	Partially Proficient (3 pts.)	Proficient (4 pts.)	Exemplary (5 pts.)
Elements of Cooperative Learning Part II (1, 16%)	Unacceptable performance is evidenced by *none* of the following criteria met:	Incomplete performance is evidenced by *only 1* of the following criteria met:	Partially proficient performance is evidenced by *at least 2* of the following criteria met:	Proficient performance is evidenced by the following criteria met:	Exemplary performance is evidenced by the following criteria met:
	1. Group Roles: Group roles were created for the proposed activity. Each role was described and rationale for the purpose of each role was given.	**1. Group Roles:** Group roles were created for the proposed activity. Each role was described and rationale for the purpose of each role was given.	**1. Group Roles:** Group roles were created for the proposed activity. Each role was described and rationale for the purpose of each role was given.	**1. Group Roles:** Group roles were created for the proposed activity. Each role was described but the purpose of each role was not rationalized.	**1. Group Roles:** Group roles were created for the proposed activity. Each role was described *and rationale for the purpose of each role was given.*
	2. Teamwork Skills: A detailed explanation of how the teacher will facilitate teamwork skills was provided.	**2. Teamwork Skills:** A detailed explanation of how the teacher will facilitate teamwork skills was provided.	**2. Teamwork Skills:** A detailed explanation of how the teacher will facilitate teamwork skills was provided.	**2. Teamwork Skills:** A brief statement of how the teacher will facilitate teamwork skills was provided.	**2. Teamwork Skills:** A *detailed explanation* of how the teacher will facilitate teamwork skills was provided.
	3. Group Processing: A detailed explanation was given as to how the teacher will facilitate group processing in the proposed activity.	**3. Group Processing:** A detailed explanation was given as to how the teacher will facilitate group processing in the proposed activity.	**3. Group Processing:** A detailed explanation was given as to how the teacher will facilitate group processing in the proposed activity.	**3. Group Processing:** A brief statement was given as to how the teacher will facilitate group processing in the proposed activity.	**3. Group Processing:** A *detailed explanation* was given as to how the teacher will facilitate group processing in the proposed activity.
Cooperative Activity Details (1, 16%)	Unacceptable performance is evidenced by none of the following criteria met:	Incomplete performance is evidenced by only 1 of the following criteria met:	Partially proficient performance is evidenced by 2 of the following criteria met:	Proficient performance is evidenced by 3 of the following criteria met:	Exemplary performance is evidenced by the following criteria met:
	1. An explanation of when the cooperative activity will take place (warm-up, wrap-up activity, after a particular).	1. An explanation of when the cooperative activity will take place (warm-up, wrap-up activity, after a particular lesson).	1. An explanation of when the cooperative activity will take place (warm-up, wrap-up activity, after a particular lesson).	1. An explanation of when the cooperative activity will take place (warm-up, wrap-up activity, after a particular lesson).	1. An explanation of when the cooperative activity will take place (warm-up, wrap-up activity, after a particular lesson).
	2. An explanation of where the cooperative activity will take place (classroom, computer lab, playground, other).	2. An explanation of where the cooperative activity will take place (classroom, computer lab, playground, other).	2. An explanation of where the cooperative activity will take place (classroom, computer lab, playground, other).	2. An explanation of where the cooperative activity will take place (classroom, computer lab, playground, other).	2. An explanation of where the cooperative activity will take place (classroom, computer lab, playground, other).
	3. An explanation of why this choice for a cooperative activity is appropriate (for the age group or topic).	3. An explanation of why this choice for a cooperative activity is appropriate (for the age group or topic).	3. An explanation of why this choice for a cooperative activity is appropriate (for the age group or topic).	3. An explanation of why this choice for a cooperative activity is appropriate (for the age group or topic).	3. An explanation of why this choice for a cooperative activity is appropriate (for the age group or topic).
	4. An explanation of how the instructor will know that the students have learned the subject matter (rubric, quiz, interview, etc.).	4. An explanation of how the instructor will know that the students have learned the subject matter (rubric, quiz, interview, etc.).	4. An explanation of how the instructor will know that the students have learned the subject matter (rubric, quiz, interview, etc.).	4. An explanation of how the instructor will know that the students have learned the subject matter (rubric, quiz, interview, etc.).	4. An explanation of how the instructor will know that the students have learned the subject matter (rubric, quiz, interview, etc.).

continued on following page

Table 11. Continued

	Does not meet criteria	Incomplete (1 pt.)	Partially Proficient (3 pts.)	Proficient (4 pts.)	Exemplary (5 pts.)
Technology Integration (1, 16%)	Unacceptable performance is evidenced by none of the following criteria met:	Incomplete performance is evidenced by only 1 of the following criteria met:	Partially proficient performance is evidenced by 2 of the following criteria met:	Proficient performance is evidenced by 3 of the following criteria met:	Exemplary performance is evidenced by the following criteria met:
	1. A description of what type of technology will be integrated into the cooperative lesson.	1. A description of what type of technology will be integrated into the cooperative lesson.	1. A description of what type of technology will be integrated into the cooperative lesson.	1. A description of what type of technology will be integrated into the cooperative lesson.	1. A description of what type of technology will be integrated into the cooperative lesson.
	2. An explanation of when technology will be integrated into the lesson.	2. An explanation of when technology will be integrated into the lesson.	2. An explanation of when technology will be integrated into the lesson.	2. An explanation of when technology will be integrated into the lesson.	2. An explanation of when technology will be integrated into the lesson.
	3. An explanation where the technology integration will take place.	3. An explanation where the technology integration will take place.	3. An explanation where the technology integration will take place.	3. An explanation where the technology integration will take place.	3. An explanation where the technology integration will take place.
	4. An explanation of why technology is being integrated into the lesson (use at least one of the 5 Es: Engage, Explore, Explain, Elaborate, Evaluate).	4. An explanation of why technology is being integrated into the lesson (use at least one of the 5 Es: Engage, Explore, Explain, Elaborate, Evaluate).	4. An explanation of why technology is being integrated into the lesson (use at least one of the 5 Es: Engage, Explore, Explain, Elaborate, Evaluate).	4. An explanation of why technology is being integrated into the lesson (use at least one of the 5 Es: Engage, Explore, Explain, Elaborate, Evaluate).	4. An explanation of why technology is being integrated into the lesson (use at least one of the 5 Es: Engage, Explore, Explain, Elaborate, Evaluate).
Participation (1, 16%)	Unacceptable performance is evidenced by no knowledge and research evident from provided readings.	Incomplete performance is evidenced by a lack of basic knowledge evident from provided readings.	Partially Proficient performance is evidenced by basic knowledge evident from provided	Proficient performance is evidenced by demonstrating knowledge from provided readings.	Exemplary performance is evidenced by demonstrating *knowledge and research* from provided readings.
	Participant's role is not complete due to lacking in the following areas during the group chat or discussion board activity: content, substance, frequency.	Participant's role is not complete due to lacking in 2 of the following areas during the group chat or discussion board activity: content, substance, or frequency.	Participant's role is not complete due to lacking in 1 of the following areas during the group chat or discussion board activity: content, substance, or frequency.	Participant's role is fulfilled by the following criteria shown in the group chat or discussion board activity: content, substance, and frequency.	Participant's role is fulfilled by the following criteria shown in the group chat or discussion board activity: content, substance, and frequency.

continued on following page

Chapter 13
Let's Enhance Learners' Cultural Discussions:
Developing a Community of Inquiry in a Blended Course

Ana Oskoz
University of Maryland, Baltimore County, USA

ABSTRACT

This chapter reports on a study that examined the construction of a community of inquiry in a blended, foreign language, undergraduate, lower-level course. Students' asynchronous discussions were analyzed by applying the social presence coding scheme developed by Rourke, Anderson, Garrison, and Archer (2001), by Garrison, Anderson, and Archer's (2001) practical inquiry model, and Anderson, Rourke, Garrison, and Archer's (2001) teaching presence code. The results indicate that undergraduate students were able to create an environment that encouraged reflection and meaningful interactions in online discussions. The blended environment, however, promoted different types of social interactions than those previously found in exclusively online discussions, with a lower presence of cohesive and affective indicators. At the cognitive level, this study suggests that while maintaining restrained intervention, a more active instructor presence is needed for entry-level learners to move to a higher level of cognitive activity — one which allows them to integrate concepts and move beyond simple description of concepts and ideas. In terms of teaching presence, the initial instructional design allowed learners to engage in similar interactions to those developed specifically for the online medium; yet, the author also found that the instructor's presence is required for the best educational outcomes.

DOI: 10.4018/978-1-4666-2110-7.ch013

INTRODUCTION

The use of asynchronous computer-mediated communication via particular discussion boards is a popular approach in the foreign language (FL) classroom (e.g. Abrams, 2001, 2003; Bauer, de Benedette, Furstenberg, Levet & Waryn, 2006; Kol & Schcolnik, 2008; Sengupta, 2001; Sotillo, 2000). The discussion board allows students to practice their use of grammatical constructions learned in class (Meskill & Anthony, 2007); to improve their linguistic and syntactic accuracy (Sotillo, 2000); and to develop their skills in academic discourse (Sengupta, 2001; Van Deusen-Scholl, Frei & Dixon, 2005) using appropriate academic vocabulary (Kol & Schcolnik, 2008). The online forums provide "a critical common space in which [to] share and verify hypotheses and points of view, to ask for help deciphering meanings of words and concepts, and to constantly negotiate meanings and interpretations" (Bauer et al., 2006, p. 35); they have been instrumental in enhancing students' reflections on teaching educational practices (Arnold & Ducate, 2006; Arnold, Ducate, Lomicka & Lord, 2005; Celentin, 2007; Pawan, Paulus, Yalcin, & Chang, 2003; Shin, 2008), elaborating course content (Weasenforth, Biesenbach-Lucas, & Meloni, 2002), and enhancing students' cultural reflections (Bauer et. al, 2006; Wildner-Basset, 2005).

The asynchronous and public nature of the discussion board has direct instructional implications for student learning and interactions. The time lag between reading and posting in an online discussion provides "time to recognize connections, understand other's ideas, and develop a detailed response or posting" (Meyers, 2003, p. 60) by giving learners the opportunity to contribute outside material and experiences (Kol & Schcolnik, 2008), link ideas together and make relevant points (Arnold & Ducate, 2006; Kol & Schcolnik, 2008; Newman, Johnson, Cochrane, & Webb, 1996) in a way that is less possible in face-to-face interactions (Sengupta, 2001).

Participating in electronic discussions engages students in explicit, constructive and thoughtful communication (Kol & Schcolnik, 2008), increases accountability (Sengupta, 2001) and enhances critical thinking (Newman et al., 1996; Newman, Webb & Cochrane, 1995).

The use of discussion boards to help learners attain higher levels of cognitive thinking has been widely examined both in online interactions (Arnold & Ducate, 2006; Arnold et al., 2005; Celentin, 2007; Pawan et al., 2003; Shin, 2008) and in blended settings (Akyol & Garrison, 2011; Vaughan & Garrison, 2005). In blended educational contexts, that is, environments that combine both face-to-face and online interactions, "the strengths of each approach are integrated in an appropriate and creative manner" (Vaughan & Garrison, 2005, p. 4). In such an environment, face-to-face interactions offer suitable avenues for initiating new discussions and triggering questions, while the delayed discussion board environment supports reflective dialogue and the integration of ideas (Vaughan & Garrison, 2005). This blended approach is not new in the FL classroom (Abrams, 2001, 2003; Kol & Schcolnik, 2008; Meskill & Anthony, 2007; Sengupta, 1995; Sotillo, 2000; Van Deusen-Scholl et al., 2005). Yet, to understand fully the value of asynchronous online discussions in the blended environment, we need to examine closely how students develop a community of inquiry in a blended setting. Using the theoretical framework for studying communities of inquiry developed by Garrison, Anderson and Archer (2000), this study examined how FL learners developed a community of inquiry using the social presence coding scheme developed by Rourke, Anderson, Garrison, and Archer (2001), the practical inquiry coding developed by Garrison, Anderson, and Archer's (2001), and Anderson, Rourke, Garrison, and Archer's (2001) teaching presence code. This article reports on an in-depth investigation and analysis of students' social and cognitive constructions and teaching presence in a blended environment and discusses the outcomes and implications.

To explore these issues, the following research questions were formulated:

- How do learners project themselves and create a social community (social presence) in the asynchronous exchanges of a blended FL course?
- How do learners construct and confirm meaning through reflection and discourse (cognitive presence) in the asynchronous exchanges of a blended FL course?
- How do learners adopt a teaching presence in the asynchronous exchanges of a blended FL course?

LITERATURE REVIEW

The concept of "community," a theoretical construct drawing increasing attention within academia (Dawson, 2006), has long been considered relevant to achieving high-order thinking (Lipman, 1991). An educational community is a "formally constituted group of individuals whose connection is that of academic purpose and interest who work collaboratively towards intended learning goals and outcomes" (Garrison & Vaughan, 2008, p.17). Garrison and Vaughan point out that academic interest gives purpose and shape to the inquiry process. For Garrison et al. (2000), the three core concepts used in defining a community of inquiry are firstly, cognitive presence, or the extent to which the participants in any community of inquiry are able to construct meaning through sustained communication (Garrison et al., 2001); next, social presence, or "the ability of participants to identify with the community (e.g., course of study), communicate purposefully in a trusting environment, and develop inter-personal relationships by way of projecting their individual personalities (Garrison, 2009, p. 352); and thirdly, teaching presence, or the design and integration

of the cognitive social processes involved in a community of inquiry for educational purposes (Garrison et al., 2000). It is the integration of the three presences that creates a successful learning environment (Garrison et al., 2001).

The Practical Inquiry model developed by Garrison et al. (2001) reflects four phases of critical thinking and cognitive presence. The triggering event, the first phase, begins with the presentation of an issue, dilemma or problem. In the second phase, exploration, the learners shift between the private and reflective world of the individual and social exploration. In the third phase, integration, learners construct meaning from the ideas generated in the exploratory phase. In the fourth phase, resolution, learners arrive at a resolution of the issue in question by means of direct or vicarious action. While it could be considered that cognitive presence is the desired educational goal, cognitive presence "is more easily sustained when a significant degree of social presence has been established" (Garrison et al., 2000, p. 13). Social presence is, in turn, divided into three main categories — affective, interactive, and cohesive — which are subdivided into a series of indicators. The presence of behaviors included in the indicators under the affective, interactive and cohesive categories may facilitate the success of the cognitive process (Garrison et al., 2000). However, while student interaction might enhance cognitive presence (Rovai, 2002), interaction by itself does not always equate to higher levels of cognitive presence. Teacher presence, finally, is composed of three components: instructional design and organization (the planning involved before the starting of the course); facilitating discourse (the critical discussions required to achieve the course goals); and direct instruction (the intellectual input provided by the instructor). It establishes the "appropriate social and cognitive presence[s] and, ultimately, the establishment of a critical community of inquiry" (Garrison et al., 2000, p. 96). Teaching presence, therefore, "bring[s] together social and cognitive presence in an effective and efficient manner", making it the binding element in creating a community of inquiry (Garrison & Vaughan, 2008, p. 24). There is ample research that has examined the nature of cognitive presences (Akyol & Garrison, 2011; Arnold & Ducate, 2006; Celentin, 2007; Kanuka, Rourke, & Laflamme, 2008; Pawan et al., 2003; Shin, 2008; Vaughan & Garrison, 2005); social presences (Arnold & Ducate, 2006; Arnold et al., 2005; Lomicka & Lord, 2007; Rogers & Lea, 2005; Shin, 2008); and teaching presences (Arbaugh & Hwang 2006; Shea, Li, & Pickett, 2006; Stacey, 2002) in student online interactions.

With regard to social presence, several studies have presented evidence to reject the possibly intuitive notion that the text-based online environment cannot provide an atmosphere that supports social presence (Arnold & Ducate, 2006; Arnold et al., 2005; Lomicka & Lord, 2007; Nippard & Murphy, 2007; Rogers & Lea, 2005; Rourke et al., 2001; Shin, 2008). Differences in types and numbers of indicators of social presence (Arnold et al., 2005; Lomicka & Lord, 2007; Rourke et al., 2001; Shin, 2008) might well be explained by the task's effect on student interactions (Arnold et al., 2005). As Anderson and Garrison (1998) suggested, "for meaningful interactions to occur between learner and content, the learner must actively engage [with] the content materials" (p. 106). According to Arnold et al., (2005), tasks that require learners to share their personal and even vulnerable experiences lead to higher levels of affective indicators than those tasks in which students answer specific questions. In contrast, tasks that require discussion are conducive to higher levels of agreement and reference to specific content of the discussion. Social presence, however, tends to decline across tasks (Rourke et al., 2001) unless friendships are formed (Arnold et al., 2005). For a successful working relationship, the construction of a social community in the online groups seems to be crucial during the first weeks; after this initial period, the community is assumed to be intact and self-sustaining, resulting, there-

fore, in lower levels of social indicators (Arnold et al., 2005; Lomicka & Lord, 2007; Molinari, 2004). To enhance learners' collaboration and to minimize reliance on instructor intervention, Shin, (2008), Vandergrift (2002), and Wu (2003) suggested the instructor should adopt a "restrained presence" and refrain from commenting during discussions —thus encouraging learners to find and voice their own opinions. The instructor facilitates collaboration and interaction by designing structured interactions that require reflection on the discussion itself, and by assigning roles to learners in the group discussion (Wu, 2003). Learners' social presence, therefore, is only possible with a clearly designed task that inherently promotes communication.

Previous studies examining cognitive presence have generally found that students tend to linger most in the exploratory phase, where they are exploring the topic and providing personal opinions, and least in the resolution phase, when they are testing solutions (Akyol & Garrison, 2011; Akyol, Garrison, & Ozden, 2009; Arnold & Ducate, 2006; Celentin, 2007; Garrison et al., 2001; Kanuka et al., 2008; Meyer, 2003; Newman et al., 1995; Newman et al., 1996; Pawan et al., 2003; Shin, 2008). Apart from a few exceptions (Pawan et al., 2003), most studies show that students exhibit a higher presence in the integration phase than in the trigger phase (Arnold & Ducate, 2006; Celentin, 2007; Garrison et al., 2001; Kanuka et al., 2008; Pawan et al., 2003; Shin, 2008). When comparing exclusively online to blended courses, Akyol and Garrison (2011) and Akyol et al., (2009) found that blended courses showed higher levels of integration than exclusively online courses, perhaps because they allowed learners to start their discussions off face to face. Yet, in both online and blended environments, reaching higher levels of cognitive presence has been associated with teaching presence: this is demonstrated by factors such as clearly outlining participation requirements, activity design, content selection, pedagogical targets, and evaluation criteria (Akyol & Garrison,

2011; Arnold & Ducate, 2006; Celentin, 2007; Nippard & Murphy, 2007; Pawan et al., 2003). Yet, despite the relevance of teaching presence for the full integration of social and cognitive presence elements in the online environment, it is not possible to assign one presence more relevance than another because, as Garrison and Cleveland-Innes (2004) suggested, "satisfaction and success result when all three elements are integrated harmoniously in a way that supports critical discourse and reflection" (p. 31). In the light of this statement, it is relevant to explore the extent to which the interplay of these presences creates a successful learning environment in a blended FL classroom.

METHODOLOGY

The following section provides an outline of the research project design and a detailed description of the chronology of data collection. There is also a description of the data analysis, using an adapted version of Garrison et al.'s (2000) Community of Inquiry framework, which was used to determine the nature and extent of social and cognitive presence in learner discussions.

Background Information

The objective of this study was to examine how learners built a community of inquiry as they discussed cultural topics in an asynchronous online environment. Although the process was applied in both face-to-face and online interactions (see the Procedure section), this article focuses mainly on students' online interactions.

Participants and Setting

The course under study was a one third-semester Spanish class from a mid-sized Atlantic-coast university, consisting of 20 students. For the discussion board activity, students were divided randomly by the instructor into five groups of four, to enable all participants to have their voices heard in the cultural discussions. Following Arnold and Ducate's (2006) suggestions, each group had a leader, who was in charge of starting, maintaining, and wrapping up the cultural discussion, and three members who answered the leader's posts and the member postings of their group. The role of leader rotated around all group participants, so that each student had the experience of being leader for one discussion board and being a regular member for three discussion boards. When taking the role of leader, students acted as moderators, performing, in that way, a significant part of the teaching presence role (Anderson et al., 2001). The teacher adopted a "restrained presence" (Vandergrift, 2002; Wu, 2003), limiting her participation to the face-to-face interactions in the classroom. Although the instructor did not participate in the online discussion, she provided the triggering prompt and discussed the cultural topic with the students at the beginning and at the end of the online interaction in the face-to-face classroom. During the online conversation, the instructor also read the prompts and highlighted some of their content to the class, either to encourage further participation or to ask learners to strengthen the content of their own comments and reflections.

Tasks

As part of the blended instructional model, students participated in four in-class or online discussions about certain cultural topics (i.e., bargaining, advertising, the elderly, and urban vs. suburban lifestyles) related to various chapters of the course textbook. While book activities were discussed in class, and all leaders answered to the same instructor-initiated prompt, students' cultural discussions tended to go in different directions according to the information they gathered while searching the Internet, journals, or other sources.

As with the studies of Bauer et al., (2006), Ducate and Lomicka (2005), and O'Dowd (2006), the students' first language (L1) was used for the cultural discussions in this classroom. Although it might seem counter-productive to use the L1 in an FL language class, using the L1 avoids the risk that a group of individuals may dominate due to higher proficiency level in the FL. It also enables students to express their views fully and in detail, to formulate questions and hypotheses clearly, and to provide complex, nuanced information, since they are not restricted by limited linguistic ability (Bauer et al., 2006, p. 35). This could also be defended from a socio-cultural perspective: as other researchers have noted: "If learners can use the L2 as a primary means of social communication, the fact that they need to rely on their L1 for mental regulation should not be a cause of concern" (Antón, Di Camilla, & Lantolf, 2003, p. 278). Therefore, (1) following Bauer et al., (2006) and O'Dowd (2006), (2) taking into account that the L1 has a role in L2 learning as a psychological mediating tool (Antón et al., 2003), and (3) considering that the students

in the present study were taking an intermediate/low course in Spanish, it was predicted that using the L1 would enhance discovery, reflection and integration of ideas in the discussion boards. The in-class cultural activities in which the instructor was involved, however, were conducted in the students' L2, thus maintaining a linguistic balance in the cultural discussions.

Procedure

For each task the entire process took about three weeks (see Figure 1). At the beginning of each chapter, the instructor and students had an initial discussion related to the cultural topic in the face-to-face class. Shortly afterwards, the instructor posted a prompt, based on that topic, to continue the conversation. The leader of each group answered the initial prompt and expanded the scope and depth of the discussion by seeking out additional information from other sources. The leader then asked questions that would elicit a critical and thoughtful response to extend the discussion. Group members researched, posted, described, and elaborated with additional information. They also asked further questions to keep

Figure 1. Schedule and activities of discussion board postings

Week	Activities involved
Week 1	Instructor and students start a discussion regarding the cultural topic. After class, instructor uploads prompt to blackboard. Group leader answers to prompt providing (1) personal opinion, (2) information retrieved from external sources, (3) analysis of the information, and (4) questions to promote the conversation.
Weeks 2-3	Group members answer to leader and to another class member providing (1) personal opinion, (2) information retrieved from external sources, (3) analysis of the information, and (4) questions to promote the conversation.
Week 3	Group leader summarizes findings from the entire group. Instructor and students discuss findings in the classroom.

the conversation going. At the end of the chapter, teacher and students discussed the asynchronous online comments and findings in the face-to-face classroom. To provide learners with clear timelines, the starting and closing points of the online discussions were marked in the students' syllabus. In addition, students also had a calendar that specified the dates by when (1) the leader had to initiate the conversation, (2) all the group members had to complete the conversation, and (3) when the leader had to post the online discussion summary.

Data Analysis

The electronic postings made during the semester constituted the data for the study; these were subjected to qualitative content analysis using an adapted version of Rourke et al.'s. (2001) social presence framework — affective, interactive, and cohesive categories — (see Figure 2). Several modifications were made to this framework. First, in the affective category, the indicator of humor was eliminated, because there were no instances of humor in students' interactions. The indicator of emotions was divided into two indicators, one for conventional expressions of emotion and the other for unconventional expressions using emoticons or capital letters. Second, within the interactive category, the indicator of continuing a thread was eliminated because students used the same message in answer to different group members. The reply function, therefore, did not signal students addressing their content to one specific person. Following Arnold et al. (2005), the indicator of appreciation/complimenting was sub-divided into two indicators, each with a different function. "Appreciation" referred to students acknowledging the finding of interesting sources or the starting of a conversation. "Complimenting" referred to students praising the content of others. There were three additional indicators regarding students' interactions with the task; these were: inquiring (i.e., students asking each other how

to find sources of information), directing a topic (i.e., students guiding each other on how to approach the task), and guiding participation (i.e. students asked to share their findings with the rest of the group).

Cognitive presence was analyzed using the practical inquiry framework (Garrison et al., 2001), i.e., triggering event, exploration, integration, and resolution categories (see Figure 3).

Teaching presence was analyzed using Anderson et al.'s (2001) framework, i.e., design and organization, facilitating discourse, and direct instruction (See Figure 4). For teaching presence, Anderson et al. (2001) suggested using the message as a unit because a complete message can be assigned to a unit, making this a relatively faster and more reliable method. In this study, however, to obtain a fuller understanding of which aspects of teaching presence appeared in the learners' discussions, the researcher opted to use the speech segment. Resembling cognitive presence, the speech segment often corresponded to paragraphs. Several modifications were made to the three categories of teaching presence. First, in the instructional design and organization category, the indicators of "setting curriculum," "designing methods" and "establishing netiquette" were eliminated because there were no instances of them in students' interactions. This might be because the instructor's guidelines (pre-set in the curriculum), had already grouped the students, identified a leader for each discussion, and established the parameters regarding the expectations for the discussion board interactions. Second, in the facilitating discourse category, the "areas of agreement /disagreement" indicator was eliminated because it was considered to be a repetition of "social presence"; the indicator "assessing the efficacy of the process" was also eliminated because there were no instances of it. Third, in the direct instruction category, the indicators "Confirm understanding through assessment and explanatory feedback," "diagnose misconceptions" and "respond to technical questions" were also

Figure 2. Categories, indicators, and examples of social presence

Category	Indicator	Definition	Example
Affective	Expressions of emotions	Conventional expressions of emotion	"One thing that surprised me was how aggressive the sellers were"
	Emphasis/emoticons	Unconventional expressions of emotions, includes repetitious punctuation, conspicuous capitalization, emoticons	"I plan to post again, so stay posted ☺"
	Self-disclosure / Vulnerability	Presents details outside of the class, or expresses vulnerability	"I know the second article wasn't the best, but I think the first article is great and discusses our topic."
Interactive	Quoting from another's message	Using software features to quote another's entire message or cut and paste selections	"With regard to your comment 'In addition of explaining channel choices'..."
	Referring explicitly to others' messages	Direct references to contents of others' posts.	"perhaps what Penny meant by a bumpy ride."
	Asking questions	Students ask each other	"Or, do you think that the 85% of people who currently live with their children will stay this way?"
	Complimenting	Complimenting others or contents of others' messages.	"I think that everyone touched on several ideas with relation to haggling that brought us some very interesting questions."
	Expressing appreciation	Expressing appreciation for work of others	"Thank you to our group leader Ismael for starting us off."
	Agreement	Expressing agreement with content of others' messages	"However, I must agree with July."
	Inquiring	Asking group members to find other sources of information	"Can you find any information on the family relationships that may cause the elderly to live with their children or on their own?"
	Supporting/guiding information	Providing students with guidance regarding routes to take	"Look at it from both perspectives"
	Inviting participation	Asking students to share their ideas and findings with the group	"If anyone has any further comments or findings, please let me know."
Cohesive	Vocatives	Addressing or referring to a participant by name or "you"	"I enjoyed reading your posts, July and Darrel."
	Inclusive pronouns	Addressing the group as *we, us, our group*	"... because we all considered Spanish customs more casual when it came to advertising."
	Phatics, salutations	Communication that serves purely social function: greetings, closures	"Hello all"

eliminated. The indicator of "inject knowledge from diverse sources" was split into "inject knowledge from sources such as Internet, other classes, journals" and "inject knowledge from personal experience." We decided this because learners were encouraged to include their personal experiences in their conversations as a lead-in to their own research about the topic.

Following the model of Arnold and Ducate (2006), and given that students addressed sev-eral topics in a single posting, the unit of analysis was the speech segment, which is defined as "the smallest unit of delivery, linked to a single theme, directed at the same interlocutor" (Henri & Rigault, 1996, p. 62). When examining social presence, Rourke et al., (2001) and Lomicka and Lord (2007) pointed out that boundaries are not always clear when analyzing different units. Therefore, the following statement "perhaps what Penny meant by bumpy ride" was coded as "referring explic-

Figure 3. Categories and examples of cognitive presence

Categories	Description	Example
Trigger	State of dissonance/feeling of unease resulting from an experience, asking questions, sense of puzzlement	"Do you think that the elderly in Spain choose to live on their own, or because of raising problems in health care they have no choice but to live in their own homes and get help if necessary?"
Exploration	Search for information/ knowledge/alternatives that might help make sense of the situation/ problem; search for clarification; information exchange, discussion of ambiguities	"I found an interesting article about Dolce and Gabbana pulling all their advertising in Spain."
Integration	Integrating information into a concept/idea; looking for insights/ gaining some understanding of acquired information/knowledge; Connecting ideas, creating solutions	"It is hard to tell, but.... this shows that while right now Spain's poverty rate is relatively low, money is a factor in the reason why many elderly people have not left their children".
Resolution	Application of idea/concept; Vicariously Apply New Ideas, critically assess solutions	After reading a couple of articles on the subject, I think that the retirement age is going to have to be raised, not just in Spanish nations, but all over Europe and the United States as well".

itly to another's message" (interactive), and "referring to a participant by name" (cohesive). When examining cognitive presence, in practice, the speech segment often corresponded to paragraphs, since this is how people tend to organize written communication (McKenzie & Murphy, 2000). The researcher and a second coder independently analyzed all students' entries in the first discussion board for social presence, cognitive presence and teaching presence, reaching an inter-rater reliability of.92. After this first analysis of an early session, the researcher independently analyzed the three other discussion boards.

RESULTS

The transcripts of the four discussion boards were subjected to qualitative and quantitative analysis. Students produced the largest amount of output during the third discussion, with a total of 11,118 words, while the fourth discussion had the lowest number of words, with 6,243 words (see Figure 5). Overall, students produced the largest number of posts in the first discussion (37 posts) and this decreased considerably in the fourth discussion (20 posts).

With regard to social presence, there were 599 instances representing its categories and indicators (see Figure 6). Overall, the most frequent social category found in the data was interactive (62.27%), followed by the cohesive (26.21%) and

Figure 4. Categories, indicators, and examples of teaching presence

Category	Indicator	Description	Example
Instructional design and organization	Establishing time parameters	Negotiating time lines for group activities and student project work.	"I will probably try to wrap it up sometime around 10:00pm. So, please, post before if you can."
	Utilizing medium effectively	Providing guidelines and tips to make effective use of the medium.	"Ok, keep on looking for sources to cite to try to keep on the conversation moving."
Facilitating discourse	Seeking to reach consensus/ understanding	Articulating consensus and shared understanding.	"I think that in our discussion we acknowledged that some advertisements achieve a certain beauty through the use of the human figure and other artistic elements."
	Encouraging, acknowledging or reinforcing students' contributions	Acknowledging their classmates' participation in the course by replying in a positive, encouraging manner to other students' submissions.	"I looked at the website about subliminal messages. That is very interesting."
	Setting climate for learning	Encouraging their classmates to explore concepts in the course ("think out load").	"Remember to pitch in with your own new topics that you would like to discuss so we can get some good ideas flowing"
	Drawing in participants, prompting discussion	Helping each other to keep engage and participating in productive dialogue.	"Do you have any other thoughts or ideas about this?"
Direct instruction	Present content/questions	Presenting content or questions that helped students to learn.	"Advertising is a form of art. If you think about Pablo Picasso or Diego Velazquez, do you think they made their art for advertising purposes"
	Focus the discussion on specific issues	Revisiting topics in the discussion that assisted learners to learn.	"The government is setting an overall precedent for the way in which women are portrayed in advertising".... "It seems that the government is trying to be more conservative and.... It will lead to some interesting developments regarding censorship and what is shown to public".
	Summarize	Develop and explicitly delineating the context in which knowledge growth has taken place.	"Tony, you bring up the idea that some buyers.... Jane, I think that your friends who bargain ...."
	Inject knowledge from different sources (websites, other classes, etc.)	Providing information from a variety of sources that assisted each other to learn.	"The article outlined the basics of haggling."

Figure 5. Number of words and posts on the discussion boards

	DB1	DB2	DB3	DB4	Total
Words	9,978	10,090	11,118	6,243	37,429
Posts	37	31	31	20	119
Range posts	4-10	4-9	4-10	3-5	

Figure 6. Percentages of the categories of social presence in each discussion board and across discussion boards

Category	Indicator	DB1	DB2	DB3	DB4	Sub Total	Total
Affective	Emotion / Feeling	9	0	1	4	14	
	Emphasis/ emoticons	1	6	1	2	9	
	Self-disclosure / Vulnerability	12	2	8	5	27	
		22 (10.4%)	8 (4.44%)	10 (7.57%)	11 (14.2%)		51 8.51%
Interactive	Direct quote	1	2	0	0	3	
	Referring to another's message	80	81	54	25	240	
	Asking questions	20	11	13	11	55	
	Complimenting	9	5	2	1	17	
	Appreciation	4	0	0	0	4	
	Agreement	11	9	4	3	27	
	Encouragement	3	2	4	2	11	
	Directing a comment	4	3	7	6	20	
	Inviting participation	2	9	1	2	14	
		134 (63.80%)	122 (67.77%)	85 (64.39%)	50 (64.93%)		391 62.27%
Cohesive	Vocatives, names	30	34	26	10	100	
	Use of inclusive pronouns	21	8	4	2	35	
	Phatics, salutations	3	8	7	4	22	
		54 (25.71%)	50 (27.77%)	37 (28.03%)	16 (20.77%)		157 26.21%
Total		210 (35.05%)	180 (30.05%)	132 (22.03%)	77 (12.85%)		599

the affective (8.51%) categories. When examining the amount of social presence in each discussion board, the data showed a descending trend in the percentages of social presence; discussion board 1 presented 35.05% of the instances, discussion board 2, 30.05%, and discussion board 3, 22.03% of the overall amount of instances. The last discussion board dropped to 12.85%.

Regarding cognitive presence, there were 493 instances, representing the four cognitive categories (see Figure 7). The most common cognitive category occurring in the data was exploration (57.81%), followed by integration (23.73%), trigger (16.83%), and only rarely by resolution (1.62%). Looking at the results by discussion board, the discussion that presented the highest

Figure 7. Percentages of the phases of cognitive presence in each discussion board and across discussion boards

Categories	DB1 bargaining	DB2 advertising	DB3 the elderly	DB4 urban/suburban	Total
Trigger	18(13.63%)	30(21.42%)	18(12.41%)	17(22.36%)	83(16.83%)
Exploration	77(58.33%)	80(47.14%)	81(55.86%)	47(61.84%)	285(57.81%)
Integration	33(25%)	30(21.42%)	42(28.97%)	12(15.78%)	117(23.73%)
Resolution	4(3.03%)	0(0%)	4(2.75%)	0(0%)	8(1.62%)
Total	132(26.77%)	140(28.40%)	145(29.41%)	76(15.42%)	493 (100%)

incidence of cognitive presence was the third discussion board, with 145 instances, followed closely by the second discussion board, with 140 instances, and the first discussion board, with 132 instances; the fourth discussion board presented the lowest amount of cognitive presence, with 76 instances.

In terms of teaching presence, there were a total of 490 instances representing the different categories and indicators for this aspect (see Figure 8). Overall, the most frequent teaching category mentioned was direct instruction (60%), followed by facilitating discourse (37.55%) and instructional design and organization (2.45%). Regarding the extent of teaching presence, the data showed that the four discussion boards showed similar percentages; discussion board 1 presented 23.92% of the instances, discussion board 2, 32.65%, discussion board 3, 36.92%, and discussion board 4, 14.08% of the overall numbers of instances.

The dataset was then assessed further by treating each discussion board as the unit of analysis, giving a sample size of $N = 4$. The frequencies of each type of interaction were then assessed across the four discussion boards. Descriptive statistics are presented in Figure 9.

The researcher first addressed the extent to which there is a relation between social, cognitive,

and teaching presence. Figure 10 presents Spearman rank correlations (the nonparametric alternative to the Pearson correlation) between all pairs of interactions. Social and cognitive presence in general (total scores) were only correlated $\rho = .20$, $p > .05$. Social and teaching presence were slightly higher at $\rho = .40$, $p > .05$. Finally, cognitive and teaching presence were correlated quite highly at $\rho = .80$, $p > .05$. No correlations were significant because of the very small sample size ($N = 4$). The cognitive, social, and teaching presence factors showed a wide range of correlations, some even negative. Finally, the correlations between factors within cognitive presence, social presence, or teaching presence tended to show the highest correlations. A few showed perfect correlations, $\rho = 1.00$, which is possible, since Spearman correlations are based on ranks. If the ranks are in the same order for each type of factor, then the variables will be perfectly correlated. No correlations other than the perfect ones reached statistical significance, due to the small sample size.

The first research question asked whether learners project themselves and create a social community (social presence) in the asynchronous exchanges within a blended FL course. The researcher was also interested in knowing whether one social presence category appeared more than the other two. For the first part of this question,

Figure 8. Percentages of the categories of teaching presence in each discussion board and across discussion boards

Category	Indicator	DB1	DB2	DB3	DB4	SbTotal	Total
Instructional design/organiz	Establishing time parameters	1	1	2	0	4	
	Utilizing medium effectively	0	0	6	2	8	
		1 (0.85%)	1 (0.63%)	8 (5.56%)	2 (2.90%)		12 (2.45%)
Facilitating discourse	Seeking consensus /understanding	6	20	5	0	28	
	Encourag/acknowled students contributions	20	29	28	12	89	
	Setting climate for learning	2	6	1	2	11	
	Drawing in participants, prompting discussion	15	15	16	10	56	
		40 (34.19%)	70 (43.75%)	50 (34.72%)	24 (34.78%)		184 (37.55%)
Direct instruction	Present content	6	25	21	8	60	
	Focus discussion on specific issues	9	25	11	9	54	
	Summarize discussion	5	2	2	1	10	
	Inject knowledge from articles, internet, etc.)	29	33	39	16	117	
	Inject knowledge from personal experiences	27	4	13	9	53	
		76 (64.96%)	89 (55.63%)	86 (59.72%)	43 (62.32%)		294 (60.00%)
		117 (23.88%)	160 (32.65%)	144 (29.39%)	69 (14.08%)		490

the reader is referred back to Figure 6 for the frequencies of the different social factors across the discussion boards and to Figure 9 for the summary statistics. In order to determine statistically whether some categories of social presence were appearing more often than others, the Friedman test, the nonparametric alternative to a repeated measure analysis of variance (ANOVA), was used. Figure 11 shows the mean ranks and the chi-square statistic for the Friedman test.

The Friedman test results were significant (X^2 (2) = 8.00, p <.05) indicating that the factors of social presence do not appear with the same frequency in the online discussions. The Friedman

test does not allow for specific post-hoc tests to pinpoint where these differences lie; therefore, the Wilcoxon Sum Rank Test was used to compare pairs of interactions for differences. The Wilcoxon Sum Rank Test did not flag any of the differences as significant (i.e., p <.05), but all were found to be close to significant (all ps =.07): Interactive appeared closer to significant than cohesive and affective, and cohesive appeared closer to significant than affective.

The second research question asked how learners construct and confirm meaning through reflection and discourse (cognitive presence) in asynchronous exchanges within a blended FL

Figure 9. Descriptive statistics for types of interactions across discussion boards (N=4)

Interaction type	Median	M	SD	Range
Cognitive presence total	136.00	123.25	31.95	76 – 145
Trigger	18.00	20.75	6.18	17 – 30
Exploration	78.50	71.25	16.26	47 – 81
Integration	31.50	29.25	12.58	12 – 42
Resolution	2.00	2.00	2.31	0 – 4
Social presence total	156.00	149.75	58.17	77 – 210
Affective total	10.50	12.75	6.29	8 – 22
Humor	0.00	0.00	0.00	0 – 0
Emotion/feeling	2.50	3.50	4.04	0 – 9
Emphasis	1.50	2.25	1.89	1 – 5
Emoticons	0.00	0.25	0.50	0 – 1
Self-disclosure/ Vulnerability	6.50	6.75	4.27	2 – 12
Interactive total	103.50	97.75	38.06	50 – 134
Direct quote	0.50	0.75	0.96	0 – 2
Referring to other's message	67.00	60.00	26.47	25 – 81
Asking questions	12.00	13.75	4.27	11 – 20
Complimenting	3.50	4.25	3.59	1 – 9
Appreciation	0.00	1.00	2.00	0 – 4
Encouragement	2.50	2.75	0.96	2 – 4
Agreement	6.50	6.75	3.86	3 – 11
Directing a comment	5.00	5.00	1.87	3 – 7
Inviting participation	2.00	3.50	3.70	1 – 9
Cohesive total	43.50	39.25	17.11	16 – 54
Vocatives	9.50	8.75	4.99	2 – 14
Names	16.50	16.25	6.55	8 – 24
Inclusive pronouns	6.00	8.75	8.54	2 – 21
Phatics, salutations	5.50	5.50	2.38	3 – 8
Teaching presence total	130.00	122.25	38.30	70 – 159
Instructional design/organization total	1.50	3.00	3.37	1 – 8
Establishing time parameters	1.00	1.00	0.82	0 – 2
Utilizing medium effectively	1.00	2.00	2.83	0 – 6
Facilitating discourse total	46.00	47.75	21.06	24 – 75
Seeking consensus /understanding	5.00	8.75	11.12	0 – 25
Encourage/	24.00	22.25	7.93	12 – 29

course; that is, to what extent is cognitive presence appearing in the students' online interactions. The researcher was also interested in whether one cognitive presence category appeared more than the other three. For the first part of this question, the reader is referred back to Figure 7 for the frequencies of the different cognitive factors across the discussion boards, and to Figure 9 for the summary statistics. In order to determine statistically whether some factors of cognitive presence were appearing more often than others, the Friedman

Figure 10. Spearman correlations between types of interactions (N=4)

	1. Cog	2. Trig	3. Exp	4. Int	5. Res	6. Soc	7. Aff	8. Int	9. Coh	10. Tea	11. Ins	12. Dis
1. Cognitive	--											
2. Trigger	.63	--										
3. Exploration	1.00	.63	--									
4. Integration	.80	.32	.80	--								
5. Resolution	.45	.00	.45	.89	--							
6. Social	.20	.63	.20	.40	.45	--						
7. Affective	-.60	-.63	-.60	.00	.45	.20	--					
8. Interactive	.20	.63	.20	.40	.45	1.00	.20	--				
9. Cohesive	.20	.63	.20	.40	.45	1.00	.20	1.00	--			
10. Teaching	.80	.95	.80	.40	.00	.40	-.80	.40	.40	--		
11. Instruct	.32	-.50	.32	.32	.24	-.74	-.10	-.74	-.74	-.21	--	
12. Discourse	.80	.95	.80	.40	.00	.40	-.80	.40	.40	1.00	-.21	--
13. Direct	.95	.83	.95	.63	.24	.32	-.74	.32	.32	.95	.06	.95

Note. Because of the small sample size ($N = 4$), no correlations were statistically

Figure 11. Friedman tests for types across interactions for social presence (N=4)

Interaction	Mean rank	$X^2(df)$
Social presence		
Affective	1.00	8.00(2)*
Interactive	3.00	
Cohesive	2.00	

*p < .05.

test was used. Figure 12 shows the mean ranks and the chi-square statistic for the Friedman test.

The Friedman test results were significant (X^2 (3) = 11.15, p <.05) indicating that the factors of cognitive presence do not appear with the same frequency in the online discussions. The Wilcoxon Sum Rank Test did not flag any of the differences as significant (p <.05), but several were found to be close to significant (all ps =.07): Exploration appeared closer to significant than Trigger, Integration, and Resolution; and Resolution appeared less close to significant than Trigger, Exploration, and Integration. Integration and Trigger were seen in roughly equal frequencies (p >.07).

The third research question asked how learners adopt a teaching presence in the asynchronous exchanges of a blended FL course; that is, to what extent is teaching presence a feature of learners' online interactions. The researcher was also interested in whether one teaching presence category appeared more than the other two. For the first part of this question, the reader is referred back to Figure 8 for the frequencies of the different cognitive factors across the discussion boards and to Figure 9 for the summary statistics. In order to determine statistically whether some factors of teaching presence were appearing more often than others, the Friedman test was used. Figure 13

shows the mean ranks and the chi-square statistic for the Friedman test.

The Friedman test was significant, X^2 (2) = 8.00, p <.05, indicating that the various aspects of teaching presence do not appear with the same frequency in the online discussions. The Wilcoxon Sum Rank Test was used to compare pairs of interactions for differences. The Wilcoxon Sum Rank Test did not flag any of the differences as significant (i.e., p <.05), but all were found to be closer to significant (all ps =.07): Direct instruction appeared closer to significant than instructional design/organization and facilitating discourse, and facilitating discourse appeared (marginally) more significant than instructional design/organization.

The researcher was also interested in knowing whether there was a significant difference in the levels of social, cognitive and teaching presences across the discussion boards. The Friedman test was used to determine statistically whether some discussion boards encouraged more cognitive or social presence than others. Figure 14 shows the mean ranks and the chi-square statistic for the Friedman tests for social presence (top), cognitive presence (medium) and teaching presence (bottom) across tasks.

The Friedman test results for social presence were significant, X^2 (3) = 10.82, p <.05, indicating

Figure 12. Friedman tests across types of interactions for cognitive presence (N=4)

Interaction	Mean rank	X^2 (df)
Cognitive presence		
Trigger	2.38	11.15(3)*
Exploration	4.00	
Integration	2.63	
Resolution	1.00	

*p < .05.

Figure 13. Friedman tests across types of interactions for teaching presence (N=4)

Interaction	Mean rank	$X^2(df)$
Teaching presence		
Instructional design/organization	1.00	8.00(2)*
Facilitating discourse	3.00	
Direct instruction	2.00	

*$p < .05$.

that the discussion boards showed varying levels of social presence in the online discussions. The Wilcoxon Sum Rank Test, used to compare pairs of interactions for differences, did not flag any of the differences as significant (i.e., $p < .05$), but two were found to be close to significant (all ps =.07): DB1 had more social presence than DB4; DB3 had more social presence than DB4. Regarding cognitive presence, the Friedman test results were close to significant (X^2 (3) = 7.70, p =.053), indicating that the discussion boards showed varying levels of cognitive presence. The Wilcoxon Sum Rank Test indicated that DB3 had more cognitive presence than DB1 (p=.014); DB1 had more cognitive presence than DB4 (p=.004); DB2 had more cognitive presence than DB4 (p =.016) and DB3 had more cognitive presence than DB4 (p=.021). In terms of teaching presence, the Friedman test result was close to significant, X^2(3) = 7.29, p =.063, indicating that the different discussion boards showed various levels of teaching presence in the online discussions. The Wilcoxon Sum Rank Test indicated that there were a few significant or close to significant differences among databases. Specifically, DB2 had more teaching presence than DB4 (p =.029), and DB3 had more teaching presence than DB4 (p =.013). DB1 had almost more significance teaching presence than DB4 (p =.052).

DISCUSSION

The aim of this study was to understand the extent to which learners in a blended FL undergraduate course projected themselves and created a social community while constructing and confirming meaning through reflection and discourse in electronic asynchronous exchanges. This study examined social, cognitive and teaching presence following Garrison et al.'s (2000) social presence construct, Practical Inquiry model and teaching presence. The results of the study were significant, indicating that students did engage in social interactions that promoted cognitive presence.

With regard to social presence, as with previous studies in both online and blended environments, interactive was the most common category (Akyol et al., 2009; Arnold et al. 2005; Lomicka & Lord, 2007; Shin, 2008), although only close to significantly higher than cohesive and affective, accounting for more than 60% of the instances of social presence. As in the study of Lomicka and Lord (2007), the most common indicator referred to content, which was followed by asking questions, and showing agreement. These indicators illustrate not only students' awareness of the collaborative nature of the discussion but also the tightness of a task design that encouraged learners to incorporate each others' comments, to

Figure 14. Friedman test across discussion boards for cognitive, social, and teaching

Interactions	Mean rank	$X^2(df)$
Social presence		
DB1	3.03	10.82(3)*
DB2	2.81	
DB3	2.36	
DB4	1.81	
Cognitive presence		
DB1	2.75	7.70(3)+
DB2	2.63	
DB3	3.50	
DB4	1.13	
Teaching presence		
DB1	2.45	7.29(3)++
DB2	3.00	
DB3	2.86	
DB4	1.68	

++$p = .063$. +$p = .053$. *$p < .05$.

continue conversation threads, to acknowledge the topic initiator, to agree or disagree with other group members, and to provide further informed insights that supported those of their partners.

The interactive category was followed by cohesive, first, and affective, second, in results that were similar to Akyol et al.'s (2009) results in a blended environment. Students mainly used vocatives and frequently addressed each other by name, a natural move given that one post was used to answer the comments of different group members. Writing specific names added a sense of cohesiveness that would not have occurred had the students only reflected on previous com-

ments without referring to the author. However, the use of salutations, whose primary function is to strengthen the sense of community, was less frequent than in other studies (Lomicka & Lord, 2007). Salutations might seem superfluous when students see each other in a class where they have already created that sense of community. Echoing So and Brush (2008), it seems that in a blended environment students do not feel a strong need to comply with social norms and engage in certain aspects of the social interaction usually required in online interaction, because they have already had the opportunity to socialize in the classroom.

The affective category was the least apparent type of social presence, confirming Akyol et al.'s (2009) results. There were instances of vulnerability and conventional forms of expression, such as Julia's (pseudonym) expression of frustration when she said: "I posted a few days ago and I haven't heard anything [back]". However, the use of unconventional expressions of emotion, such as capitalization, punctuation or emoticons, which compensate for the lack of body language, facial expression, and vocal intonation normally available in face-to-face interactions, was almost nonexistent. While the use of these graphic forms might arise naturally in exclusively online environments, the blended class allows students to express their emotions verbally in the classroom. The characteristic that blended environments bring to the asynchronous discussions might be even more evident if we consider the nonexistence of humor — an indicator seen in previous studies (Arnold et al., 2005; Lomicka & Lord, 2007; Shin, 2008). The high interactivity found with other indicators, such as expressing agreement or referring to another's comments, implies good relationships among the participants. These results suggest that in a blended course, students view the discussion board as an integral tool necessary to complete an assignment. While students still make effective use of other social indicators that enhance interaction and communication, they do not need to employ humor or other social indicators to build the affective aspects of a community because these have already been established in their classroom interactions.

Although there were no significant differences in social presence across tasks, the descriptive table indicates a decreasing number of social instances across discussion boards. Two reasons might explain this decrease. First, as suggested by Rourke et al., (2001), Lomicka and Lord (2007) and Molinari (2004), the first weeks of interaction are crucial in the groups' development of a social community, after which point it is assumed to be intact and self-sustaining. Second, as noted by Arnold and Ducate (2006), the task guidelines and assessment tool provided students with clear expectations for the tasks. The (slightly) increased number of cognitive instances (except in the last discussion board) suggest that while the guidelines provided students with a clearer understanding of what was expected from them in terms of content, these guidelines might have also hindered the social interaction among participants. For example, in the first discussion board there were four instances in which students appreciated another's comments or efforts at the beginning of the semester, but by the second discussion board, when students knew each other better, due to their classroom interaction, they stopped using those virtual signs of appreciation. In addition, by the second discussion board, students had already received a grade and would have reviewed task expectations with the instructor. It is likely that students focused on those aspects that would reflect directly on their grade and neglected other social indicators, such as complimenting each other on their work.

Regarding cognitive presence, the results of the study indicate that there were close to significant differences in the presence of the four phases of cognitive presence. Yet, the results of this study resemble more those of exclusively online interactions (Arnold & Ducate, 2006; Garrison et al., 2001; Kanuka et al., 2007; Meyer, 2003; Newman et al., 1996; Newman et al., 1995; Pawan et al., 2003; Shin, 2008) than the results from blended environments (Akyol et al., 2009; Akyol & Garrison, 2011). Out of all the categories, exploration was the most common cognitive category evident in the data. In addition to sharing their insights and personal opinions with regard to the topic in hand, learners also referred to their sources, often providing links and excerpts describing what they found, but still lacking the skill to make connections between their findings and the topic. Meyer (2003) and Vaughan and Garrison (2005) suggested that brainstorming activities and other activities associated with exploration might be better suited to the face-to-face environment. In the case of this study, the exploration phase took place at two different times. The initial face-to-face interaction allowed students to become familiar with the topic. At that time, the instructor introduced the topic and, in her role of content expert, further guided the learners in how to explore the different topics effectively in their online interactions. The task design as developed by the instructor, therefore, conditioned students' interactions in the online discussions. Also, as Kanuka et al., (2007) have suggested, although exploration is not critical thinking *per se*, brainstorming and exploration form an antecedent to higher levels of understanding: this is therefore a relevant and important phase in the learning process.

In contrast to Akyol et al.'s (2009) and Akyol and Garrison's (2011) studies of blended interactions, the second most common category was integration (23.73%) which rated significantly higher than resolution. In the integration phase, students built upon other students' comments and supported their own insights and responses with information they had found. Although the frequency of responses in the integration phase was higher than those reported by Celentin (2007), Garrison at al., (2001), Pawan et al., (2003), and Shin (2008), it was less than reported in studies by Arnold and Ducate (2006) and Shin (2008). The latter two were studies that, similarly to this one, provided specific guidelines for the assignment. However, in contrast to Arnold and Ducate's (2006) study, participants in our study were undergraduate students and they might have needed more guidance to discuss the cultural topics. Following the model of Vandergrift (2002) and Wu (2003), the instructor adopted a restrained presence, participating only in the face-to-face interactions. The low level of teacher presence, which potentially allows each group to create its own space of discovery (Arnold & Ducate, 2006), together with the lower cognitive maturity of learners, might have restricted the students' ability to reach higher levels of cognitive activity. Although students researched and presented information that would have allowed them to make substantiated conclusions, they often lingered in the description stage without providing any deeper analysis. Therefore, the suggestion that the "instructor must take an active role to assist, or guide, the discussions" (Kanuka & Garrison, 2004, p. 29), to achieve higher levels of cognitive activity in online discourse, must be taken into consideration in the design of undergraduate, blended lower-level courses.

The category of trigger was seen more frequently in this study than in previous ones (Celentin, 2007; Garrison et al., 2001). In this category the instructor, in the role of moderator, acts to frame or trigger the issue of discussion. This study showed an even higher percentage of this category than that of Arnold and Ducate (2006), in which (1) the role of the instructor, as in this study, had a low presence, and (2) the students had been assigned specific roles. In our study, the instructions and assessment guidelines given to the students stated explicitly that asking questions to keep the discussion alive was an important component of the activity. Thus, although group leaders were responsible for starting, maintaining and wrapping up the conversation, all group members could influence the direction of the discussion. The higher percentage of triggers indicates that students did assume the responsibility of maintaining and directing the conversation.

Finally, the category of resolution appeared the least, a result that supports previous findings in both online and blended studies (Akyol et al., 2009; Akyol & Garrison, 2011; Arnold & Ducate, 2006; Garrison et al., 2001; Meyer, 2003; Shin, 2008). Garrison et al., (2001) had already suggested that computer-based conferencing might not be conducive to attaining the resolution phase. Furthermore, they pointed out that introductory courses or tasks without a clear goal might not support students to achieve higher levels of critical inquiry. Even Akyol and Garrison's (2011) learners, who completed tasks that moved students through the different phases of practical inquiry, indicated that resolution occurred in individual final projects rather than in online discussions. In our study, the cultural tasks set did not guide learners to reach the resolution phase. There were rare occasions when learners came close to this goal; for example, students hypothesized about current public health practices in Spain compared with the US system and, after reading about the treatment of the elderly in Spain and the costs of health care (even before the current economic turmoil), Dylan commented: "…the retirement age is going to have to be raised, not just in Spain, but all over Europe and in the United States as well." Despite the potential of this insight to move the discussion forward, the overall results confirm the difficulty of achieving resolution in online interactions. However, these results do suggest that discussion board tasks might well allow students to gain insights into and understanding of cultural information, and to connect and integrate ideas.

The development of a community of inquiry in a blended environment with low levels of teacher interaction implies a redefinition of the role of the learner, who, as required by the tasks guidelines, was responsible for actions such providing content, including sources, acknowledging other group members' contributions, and even prompting others to participate in the discussion. Here we would like to note two factors that need to be taken into account. First, Anderson et al. (2001) proposed the message as the unit of analysis. In this study, however, the researcher preferred to use the speech segment in her exploration of how teacher presence featured in learners' interactions. This change of unit of analysis might explain why our results differ in some ways from those of previous studies. Second, this study focused on how learners adopt the role of the instructor, and not on how the instructor establishes teaching presence in online interactions, as it has been studied in previous research (e.g. Gorsky & Blau, 2009). We therefore hope that our study results might provide a complementary view by focus-

ing on teaching presence in online interactions conducted exclusively by learners.

Analysis of our results indicates that there were significant differences in the instances of the three identified categories of teaching presence. Direct instruction was the most frequently occurring category, in contrast to two other blended studies: Vaughan and Garrison (2006), which reported more instances of facilitating discourse related to social presence (Anderson et al., 2001); and partially differing from the study of Akyol et al. (2009), which reported equal percentages of instances in both the categories of facilitating discourse and direct instruction. Vaughan and Garrison (2006) suggested that, because their participants started to teach each other through the establishment of open and trusting relationships, there was a connection between direct instruction and the social presence category of group cohesion. While the results of the current study could suggest that learners were more concerned with the content of their message than with establishing a cohesive group, it is also possible that because learners already saw each other several times a week their need to demonstrate strong cohesion was lower than for Vaughan and Garrison's participants, who belonged to different departments. Another explanation might be that, owing to the restrained presence of the instructor, learners overcompensated for the instructor figure by providing information either from external sources, personal experience or by focusing on specific points. In terms of the frequency of indicators, the results of this study differ from Kamin et al.'s (2006) study of online environments. Their study found that the instructor tended to summarize and provide feedback, and spent less time presenting content; however, we found that, probably because of the nature of the task guidelines, indicators related to content were the most common ones. In fact, injecting knowledge from sources was the most frequent indicator, followed by including personal experiences and other content. As with the findings of Shin (2008), learners seemed to have difficulty in summarizing their own interactions at the end of the discussion. Although it was a task requirement, and completed by all the groups for the first task, learners were inclined to ignore it in later tasks. It is possible that summarizing is considered a task traditionally conducted by the instructor or, because the topic was finally discussed in the class, learners did not see a need to complete it in the discussion board. Learners, therefore, focused on those aspects that helped them move the conversation forward and that kept the discussion relevant.

The second most common category was facilitating discourse; this reflects the findings of Kamin et al. (2006) in their study of an online environment, but contrasts with Akyol et al.'s (2009) and Vaughan and Garrison's (2006) findings in blended environments. The discrepancy might again be due to the task guidelines, which asked students to draw other participants into their conversation — one of the indicators for this category. Our results, however, did confirm Vaughan and Garrison's findings regarding the diminishing instances of this category. While the category of facilitating discourse increased from the first to the second discussion, its presence had started to decrease by the last two tasks. As already mentioned, Anderson et al. (2001) suggested that this category overlaps with many of the behaviors identified in the model of social presence. It seems that there was higher correlation between the categories of facilitating discourse and cognitive presence (in particular with the phases of trigger and exploration) than when discussion follows direct instruction. This might be because, although learners did acknowledge each other's work, draw each other in for participation, and even seek consensus, they were more interested in triggering questions and integrating ideas than in acknowledging other group members' contributions. With regard to the indicators, as found by Shin (2008), the most common category was encouraging/acknowledging students' contributions, followed by drawing in participants. In contrast

to Shin, however, our learners did seek to reach a consensus, especially in the art task that seemed closest to their hearts. In terms of establishing a climate for learning, those instances in which learners attempted to encourage their classmates to explore concepts in the course ("think out loud"), were less frequent in the data, but still present when learners wanted to encourage group members' participation: "Remember to pitch in with your own new topics that you would like to discuss so we can get some good ideas flowing." As with the summarizing indicator in the direct instruction category, learners might think that establishing a climate for learning and suggesting to classmates what directions to take in their thinking processes might be more the instructor's responsibility rather than their own.

Finally, different from Kamin et al. (2006), but similar to Akyol et al. (2009), and Vaughan and Garrison (2006), instructional design and organization was the least common category recorded in learners' interactions. Anderson et al. (2001) have previously suggested that this category tends to be missing from online discussions because much of the task design and organization happens before the class starts. For example, in this study the course instructor had set the curriculum, designed the task, divided the participants' roles, established clear parameters for online participation and talked about netiquette ahead of the task. However, unlike Vaughan and Garrison, the indicators for this category (establishing parameters of time and utilizing the medium effectively) did appear in the online discussions (except for the last one). Notwithstanding the zero participation of the instructor during the online discussions, learners were able to recreate what Shea et al. (2010) called an "instructional equilibrium". Once learners knew what was expected from them, they filled in the instructor's role and took up the responsibility of successfully completing the online discussion. When learners realized that their group members were not performing to the expectations required from the assignment, such as in task 3 (the elderly), learners also established additional time parameters to ensure the task was completed: "Please, let me know by tomorrow morning" and suggested strategies to utilize the medium effectively and to advance their conversations: "I strongly suggest to everyone to go to this particular article for a more informed discussion." Therefore, although the category of instructional design and organization is viewed mainly as the instructor's domain, learners can step up to it when necessary to complete the task successfully.

The tasks completed in the discussion boards, related to the topics of advertising and the elderly, allowed learners to engage with the content actively and meaningfully (Anderson & Garrison, 1998) mostly because of personal or academic interest. Learners also gained a sense of ownership over the content and drew each other in more consistently once they understood the online discussion process. The topic of advertising, although it did not show any examples of resolution, produced a lively discussion led by several visual media and women's studies majors, who, in addition to offering their personal opinions, were able to incorporate content material from their other classes. The more emotive topic of the elderly, despite some grumbling about the difficulty of finding information, ("Please cite any sources that you can find because trust me, they are a lot harder to find then the past couple of [discussion boards] that we have done"), produced the highest cognitive presence of the four discussions, and also the highest number of instances in the exploration and integration categories. In both these tasks, learners pursued specific topics, such as a Dolce & Gabanna advertisements, that motivated them to discuss social perceptions of art. All the tasks were significantly higher in cognitive presence than the last discussion board (urban vs. suburban living). This finding, however, must be read with caution given that, overall, students' participation dropped considerably for the last discussion board. In addition to the fatigue students might feel at the end of the semester, many students re-

ported constant problems with the university's IT system. Some students retyped their interactions, but others, faced with data loss, abandoned the task, which explains the low participation levels reflected in the data.

CONCLUSION

The purpose of this study was to examine the extent to which learners projected themselves and created a social community while constructing and confirming meaning through reflection and discourse in asynchronous exchanges within a blended FL course. The results of the study indicate that students created an environment that encouraged reflection and meaningful interactions in online discussions. With this data, it is now possible to answer the two research questions that prompted this study.

The first research question sought to examine how learners project themselves and create a social community in the asynchronous exchanges of a blended FL course. While the three categories of social presence were evident in online interactions, the types of indicators we looked for were somewhat different from those found in exclusively online environments. Some indicators common to both environments are: referring to each others' messages, asking questions, and addressing another person by name. Other indicators, such as humor, unconventional forms of expression, and salutations were either nonexistent or rarely used. As mentioned earlier, these types of affective and cohesive indicators might be less necessary in a classroom environment in which students have already created a community. The second question asked how a practical community of inquiry could be established in a blended environment. As with previous studies in the online environment, but unlike blended environment studies, we found that exploration was the most common cognitive category in students' posts, followed by integration, trigger, and lastly, resolution. The results of the study underscored the difficulty in achieving the resolution phase in the discussion boards, and highlighted the role of the instructor, particularly in asynchronous discussions involving lower-level FL learners. At the undergraduate level at least, rather than allowing students to create their own space independently, a more visible instructor presence seems to be required for learners to reach higher levels of cognitive activity. The third research question sought to examine to what extent learners adopt a teaching presence in the asynchronous exchanges of a blended FL course. The results of the study, although slightly different from previous studies in blended environments, suggest that, provided the course instructor settles the curriculum, designs a task with clear parameters, and provides specific guidelines regarding effective use of the online medium, learners will indeed start to adopt the role of the instructor and create a socially interactive community that achieves high levels of cognitive activity. However, the learner might not feel adequate to conduct certain processes — such as confirm understanding through assessment and explanatory feedback, or assess the efficacy of the process — that have traditionally been associated with the instructor. Overall, teaching presence, albeit distributed between instructor and learners, was strong, and brought together "social and cognitive presence in an effective and efficient manner" (Garrison & Vaughan, 2008).

This study aimed to further our knowledge of how to create a community of inquiry in an online environment, this time in a FL undergraduate blended course. Yet, there are several limitations which may affect the generalizability of this study; the low number of subjects, technological problems, and the units of measurement selected. Increasing the sample size (1) would permit fur-

ther statistical analysis of the data and (2) might reveal different trends in student interactions. In addition, although the Garrison et al.'s (2000) model used in this study provided a useful way of gauging the effectiveness of the discussion board, we could collect additional data by using other frameworks.

It would also be of great interest to survey learners (Arbaugh et al., 2006; Shea et al., 2006) to assess the influence of teaching presence and their perceptions of the cognitive and social presences achieved in the context of cultural discussions with a blended cohort of learners. In addition, examining and comparing patterns of interaction and task engagement among groups could provide better understanding of which interactions allow some groups to achieve higher levels of cognitive development. It would also be of interest to examine and compare learners' social, cognitive, and teaching presence in face-to-face vs. asynchronous online interactions. Yet, despite the study's limitations, our results highlight the potential of the electronic discussion board to create a community of inquiry in a blended environment. The benefits of research into online learning is clear: If we are to improve students' ability to transform information into concepts and ideas, to transform knowledge into understanding, and to connect ideas and create solutions, it is essential to embrace the possibilities of the blended classroom environment and to capitalize on the strengths that face-to-face and online interactions jointly bring to the instructional process.

REFERENCES

Abrams, Z. (2001). Computer-mediated communication and group journals: Expanding the repertoire of participant roles. *System, 29,* 489–503.

Abrams, Z. (2003). The effect of synchronous and asynchronous CMC on oral performance in German. *Modern Language Journal, 87*(2), 157–167.

Akyol, Z., & Garrison, R. (2011). Understanding cognitive presence in an online and blended community of inquiry: Assessing outcomes and processes for deep approaches to learning. *British Journal of Educational Technology, 42*(2), 233–250.

Akyol, Z., Garrison, R., & Ozden, Y. (2009). Online and blended communities of inquiry: Exploring the developmental and perceptional differences. *International Review of Research in Open and Distance Learning, 10*(6). Retrieved from http://www.irrodl.org/index.php/irrodl/article/view/765/1436

Anderson, T., & Garrison, D. R. (1998). Learning in a networked world: New roles and responsibilities. In Gibson, C. (Ed.), *Distance learners in higher education* (pp. 97–112). Madison, WI: Atwood Publishing.

Anderson, T., Rourke, L., Garrison, D. R., & Archer, W. (2001). Assessing teaching presence in computer conferencing context. *Journal of Asynchronous Learning Networks, 5*(2), 1–17.

Antón, M., DiCamilla, F., & Lantolf, J. (2003). Sociocultural theory and the acquisition of Spanish as a second language. In Lafford, B., & Salaberry, R. (Eds.), *Spanish second language acquisition. State of the science* (pp. 262–284). Washington, DC: Georgetown University Press.

Arbaugh, J., & Hwang, A. (2006). Does "teaching presence" exist in online MBA courses? *The Internet and Higher Education, 9,* 9–21.

Arnold, N., & Ducate, L. (2006). Future language teachers' social and cognitive collaboration in an online environment. *Language Learning & Technology, 10*(1), 42–66.

Arnold, N., Ducate, L., Lomicka, L., & Lord, G. (2005). Using computer-mediated communication to establish social and supportive environments in teacher education. *CALICO Journal, 22,* 537–566.

Bauer, B., de Benedette, L., Furstenberg, G., Levet, S., & Waryn, S. (2006). The Cultura Project. In Belz, J. A., & Thorne, S. L. (Eds.), *Internet-mediated intercultural FL education* (pp. 31–62). Boston, MA: Heinle & Heinle.

Celentin, P. (2007). Online education: Analysis of interaction and knowledge building patterns among foreign language teachers. *Journal of Distance Education, 21*(3), 39–58.

Dawson, S. (2006). Online forum discussion interactions as an indicator of student community. *Australasian Journal of Educational Technology, 22*(4), 495–510. Retrieved from http://www.ascilite.org.au/ajet/ajet22/ajet22.html

Ducate, N., & Lomicka, L. (2005). Exploring the Blogosphere: Use of web logs in the foreign language classroom. *FL Annals, 38*(3), 410–421.

Garrison, D. R. (2009). Communities of inquiry in online learning: Social, teaching and cognitive presence. In Howard, C. (Eds.), *Encyclopedia of distance and online learning* (pp. 352–355). Hershey, PA: IGI Global.

Garrison, D. R., Anderson, T., & Archer, W. (2000). Critical inquiry in a text based-environment: Computer conferencing in higher education. *The Internet and Higher Education, 2*(2-3), 87–105.

Garrison, D. R., Anderson, T., & Archer, W. (2001). Critical thinking, cognitive presence and computer conferencing in distance education. *American Journal of Distance Education, 15*(1), 7–23.

Garrison, D. R., & Cleveland-Innes, M. (2004). Critical factors in student satisfaction and success: Facilitating student role adjustment in online communities of inquiry. In Bourne, J., & Moore, J. (Eds.), *Elements of quality online education: Into the mainstream* (pp. 29–38). Needham, MA: Sloan-C.

Garrison, D. R., & Vaughan, N. (2008). *Blended learning in higher education: Framework, principles and guidelines*. San Francisco, CA: Jossey-Bass.

Gorsky, P., & Blau, I. (2009). Online teaching effectiveness: A tale of two instructors. *International Review of Research in Open and Distance Learning, 10*(3), 1–27.

Henri, F., & Rigault, C. R. (1996). Collaborative distance learning and computer conferencing. In Liao, T. (Ed.), *Advanced educational technology: Research issues and future potential* (pp. 45–76). Berlin, Germany: Springer Verlag.

Kamin, C. O'Sullivan, P., Deterding, R., Younger, M., & Wade, T. (2006). A case study of teaching presence in virtual problem-based learning groups. *Medical Teacher, 28*(5), 425–428.

Kanuka, H., & Garrison, D. R. (2004). Cognitive presence in online learning. *Journal of Computing in Higher Education, 15*(2), 21–39.

Kanuka, H., Rourke, L., & Laflamme, E. (2007). The influence of instructional methods on the quality of online discussion. *British Journal of Educational Technology, 38*(2), 260–271.

Kol, S., & Schcolnik, M. (2008). Asynchronous forums in EAP: Assessment issues. *Language Learning & Technology, 12*(2), 49–70. Retrieved from http://llt.msu.edu/vol12num2/kolschcolnik. pdf

Lipman, M. (1991). *Thinking in education*. New York, NY: Cambridge University Press.

Lomicka, L., & Lord, G. (2007). Social presence in virtual communities of foreign language (FL) teachers. *System, 35*, 208–228.

McKenzie, W., & Murphy, D. (2000). "I hope this goes somewhere": Evaluation of an online discussion group. *Australian Journal of Educational Technology, 16*(3), 239–257. Retrieved from http://www.ascilite.org.au/ajet/ajet16/mckenzie. html

Meskill, C., & Anthony, N. (2007). Form-focused CMC: What language learners say. *CALICO Journal, 25*(1), 69–90. Retrieved from https:// www.calico.org/html/article_677.pdf

Meyer, K. A. (2003). Face-to-face versus threaded discussions: The role of time and higher-order thinking. *Journal of Asynchronous Learning Networks, 7*(3), 55–65. Retrieved from http://www. aln.org/publications/jaln/v7n3/pdf/v7n3_meyer. pdf

Meyer, K. A. (2004). Evaluating online discussions: Four different frames of analysis. *Journal of Asynchronous Learning Networks, 8*(2), 101–114. Retrieved from http://www.aln.org/publications/ jaln/v8n2/pdf/v8n2_meyer.pdf

Molinari, D. L. (2004). The role of social comments in problem-solving groups in an online class. *American Journal of Distance Education, 18*(2), 89–101.

Newman, D. R., Johnson, C., Cochrane, C., & Webb, B. (1996). An experiment in group learning technology: Evaluating critical thinking in face-to-face and computer-supported seminars. *Interpersonal Computing and Technology: An Electronic Journal for the 21st Century, 4*(1), 57–74. Retrieved from http://www.helsinki.fi/ science/optek/1996/ n1/newman.txt

Newman, D. R., Webb, B., & Cochrane, C. (1995). A content analysis method to measure critical thinking in face-to-face and computer supported group learning. *Interpersonal Computing and Technology: An Electronic Journal for the 21st Century, 3*(2), 56–77. Retrieved from http://www.helsinki.fi/science/optek/1995/n2/newman.txt

Nippard, E., & Murphy, E. (2007). Social presence in the web-based synchronous secondary classroom. *Canadian Journal of Learning and Technology, 33*(1). Retrieved from http://www.cjlt.ca/content/vol33.1/nippard.html

O'Dowd, R. (2006). The use of videoconferencing and e-mail as mediators of intercultural student ethnography. In Belz, J., & Thorne, S. (Eds.), *Internet-mediated intercultural FL education* (pp. 86–120). Boston, MA: Thomson Heinle.

Pawan, F., Paulus, T. M., Yalcin, S., & Chang, C.-F. (2003). Online learning: Patterns of engagement and interaction among in-service teachers. *Language Learning & Technology, 7*(3), 119–140. Retrieved from http://llt.msu.edu/vol7num3/pawan/

Rogers, P., & Lea, M. (2005). Social presence in distributed group environments: The role of social identity. *Behaviour & Information Technology, 24*(2), 151–158.

Rourke, L., Anderson, T., Garrison, R. D., & Archer, W. (2001). Assessing social presence in asynchronous text-based computer conferencing. *Journal of Distance Education, 14*(2). Retrieved from http://cade.athabascau.ca/vol14.2/rourke_et_al.html

Rovai, A. P. (2002). Sense of community, perceived cognitive learning, and persistence in asynchronous learning networks. *The Internet and Higher Education, 5*(4), 319–332.

Sengupta, S. (2001). Exchanging ideas with peers in network-based classrooms: An aid or a pain? *Language Learning & Technology, 5*(1), 103–134. Retrieved from http://llt.msu.edu/vol5num1/sengupta/

Shea, P., Li, C., & Picket, A. (2006). A study of teaching presence and student sense of learning community in fully online and web-enhanced courses. *The Internet and Higher Education, 9*, 175–190.

Shin, J. K. (2008). *Building an effective community of inquiry for EFL professionals in an asynchronous online discussion board* (Unpublished doctoral dissertation). University of Maryland, Baltimore County, Maryland.

So, H.-J., & Brush, T. A. (2008). Student perceptions of collaborative learning, social presence and satisfaction in a blended learning environment: Relationships and critical factors. *Computers & Education, 51*(1), 318–336.

Sotillo, S. (2000). Discourse functions and syntactic complexity in synchronous and asynchronous communication. *Language Learning & Technology, 4*(1), 82–119.

Stacey, E. (2002). Social presence online: Networking learners at a distance. *Education and Information Technologies, 7*(4), 287–294.

Van Deusen-Scholl, N., Frei, C., & Dixon, E. (2005). Co constructing learning: The dynamic nature of foreign language pedagogy in a CMC environment. *CALICO Journal, 22*(3), 657–678.

Vandergrift, K. E. (2002). The anatomy of a distance education course: A case study analysis. *Journal of Asynchronous Learning Networks, 6*(1), 76–90.

Vaughan, N., & Garrison, D. R. (2005). Creating cognitive presence in a blended faculty development community. *The Internet and Higher Education, 8*, 1–12.

Vaughan, N., & Garrison, D. R. (2006). How blended learning can support a faculty development community of inquiry. *Journal of Asynchronous Learning Networks, 10*(4), 139–152.

Weasenforth, D., Biesenbach-Lucas, S., & Meloni, C. (2002). Realizing constructivist objectives through collaborative technologies: Threaded discussions. *Language Learning & Technology, 6*(3), 58–86. Retrieved from http://llt.msu.edu/vol6num3/weasenforth/

Wildner-Bassett, M. E. (2005). CMC as written conversation: A critical social-constructivist view of multiple identities and cultural positioning in the L2/C2 classroom. *CALICO Journal, 22*(3), 635–656.

Wu, A. (2003). Supporting electronic discourse: Principles of design from a social constructivist perspective. *Journal of Interactive Learning Research, 14*(2), 167–184.

KEY TERMS AND DEFINITIONS

Cognitive Presence: The extent to which the participants in any community of inquiry are able to construct meaning through sustained communication (Garrison Anderson, & Archer, 2001).

Discussion Boards: Critical common spaces in which [to] share and verify hypotheses and points of view, to ask for help deciphering meanings of words and concepts, and to constantly negotiate meanings and interpretations (Bauer, de Benedette, Furstenberg, Levet, & Waryn, 2006, p. 26)

Educational Community: A "formally constituted group of individuals whose connection is that of academic purpose and interest who work collaboratively towards intended learning goals and outcomes" (Garrison & Vaughan, 2008, p.17).

L1: The first language of the speaker/learner.

L2: The second language of the speaker/learner.

Social Presence: The ability of participants to identify with the community, communicate purposefully in a trusting environment, and develop inter-personal relationships by way of projecting their individual personalities (Garrison, 2009, p. 352).

Teacher "Restrained Presence": A faculty role that balances restraint and presence to let students find and voice their opinions in the online environment (Vandergrift, 2002).

Teaching Presence: The design and integration of the cognitive social processes involved in a community of inquiry for educational purposes (Garrison, Anderson, & Archer, 2000).

Chapter 14
Application of CoI to Design CSCL for EFL Online Asynchronous Discussion

Yoshiko Goda
Kumamoto University, Japan

Masanori Yamada
Kanazawa University, Japan

ABSTRACT

This chapter provides suggestions on how to apply the Community of Inquiry (CoI) framework to design computer-supported collaborative learning (CSCL) for English as foreign language (EFL) learning. Online asynchronous discussion was the focus. A case study (five discussion activities with 42 students at a university in Japan) was used to investigate the relationships between a CoI and (1) EFL learners' participation level, (2) their satisfaction with online discussion, (3) their perceived contributions to the discussion groups, (4) English proficiency as a foreign language, and (5) their interactions during the discussion. Suggestions were developed based on the study results: (1) students must be supported to establish open communication of social presence (SP) for productive participation, (2) teaching presence (TP) and cognitive presence (CP) indicated students' satisfaction, (3) the design and organization of TP and the open communication of SP should be considered for student contributions to a learning community, (4) The CSCL activities may provide opportunities to practice English for all level students, and (5) students need help to establish SP first and then shift their focus to academic purposes. The results and discussion lead to the importance of the careful design of CSCL, including problem identification for assigned activities.

DOI: 10.4018/978-1-4666-2110-7.ch014

INTRODUCTION

Computer-supported collaborative learning (CSCL) has been used to help learners acquire higher-level cognitive thinking skills and adopt constructivist, social-cognitive, and situated-leaning theories. In English as a Foreign Language (EFL) learning settings, the use of CSCL has increased, because it gives learners more opportunities to apply and practice what they have learned. CSCL allows students to express their ideas and communicate with others. Students should use a foreign language to express ideas and communicate with others in CSCL programs, which could lead to a unique Community of Inquiry (CoI).

Students with beginning or intermediate level of EFL require more time to express their ideas in English since they have to search proper words in the targeted language and to monitor and evaluate their results consulting with newly learned rules and grammar. In order to acquire higher level language proficiency, both quantitative and qualitative language practices are necessary. Asynchronous discussion could provide a better learning setting for such learners with limited EFL. They could take time to think and monitor their comments as well as to read and comprehend other members' comments and opinions.

This chapter discusses the application of the CoI framework used to design asynchronous on-line discussion for EFL learners, illustrating the case study at a university in Japan. The course of the case study was designed as a blended learning, weekly face-to-face self-paced learning with computer and self-study activities outside of the classroom. Collaborative learning generally demands more time for learning activities and the asynchronous discussions were conducted outside of the classroom to increase students' self learning time to ensure their quantitative practice. Five discussion activities were held in the course. The discussion for a topic lasted two weeks and in the middle, students came to the classroom and stud-

ied the CALL materials individually. There was no time allocated for the group discussion in the classroom, although the instructor gave students overall feedback on the on-going discussions for about 10 minutes at the end of the class.

The course was designed and implemented based on the Collaborative Problem Solving (CPS) approach (Nelson, 1999) in the instructional design (ID) and the Teaching and Learning Guideline for CoI (Garrison, 2011). The CPS approach consists of two categories, (a) comprehensive guideline and (b) process activities. Its comprehensive guideline defines the major role of teachers, the activities of learners, and the process activities to provide detailed procedures of collaborative learning with strategies that both teachers and learners can use. The CoI guideline indicates specific actions of teachers according to the plan (design and organization) and implementation (facilitation, and direct instruction) phases. Both CPS and CoI embrace collaborative-constructivist approaches, but CPS does not consider online context, especially asynchronous communication although it provides steps for the collaborative learning procedure. CoI integrates online learning features and the teachers' roles in an asynchronous learning environment. The rationales for employing both CPS and CoI are as follows. CPS was useful to design the activity process of each discussion and the integration of the discussion activities and other types of instructions because it contained the information of conditions for using CPS and four types of comprehensive guidelines; instructor-implemented methods, learner-implemented methods, instructor- and learner-implemented methods, and interactive methods. However, implementation and interactions focus on the face-to-face setting. The steps suggested in CPS and CoI are similar, but the CoI framework provides guideline and strategies to integrate online communication into learning. Combinations of three presences; teaching presence, social presence, and cognitive presence in the CoI framework gave directions what to consider and how to implement for asynchronous collaborative learning activities.

In order to support discourse outside of the classroom, integration of social presence (SP) and cognitive presence (CP) of CoI was a concern. In-class feedback from the instructor was carefully provided to foster students focus and resolve issues with the interaction between teaching presence (TP) and CP. As to direct instruction of TP, tendencies of mistakes related to the grammar or wordings and misconception due to culture differences should also be pointed out in EFL setting, which may be unique for a foreign language learning context.

One of the salient characteristics for Japanese EFL learners is that most students are afraid of making mistakes and try to be perfect when they use and even practice English. This may be one of the obstacles for successful CSCL in an EFL setting in Japan. To solve this problem, collaborative climate needs to be established. The CoI framework indicates that social presence (SP) and teaching presence (TP) help establish climate. When CSCL is designed for EFL learners, the indication between SP and TP could be considered to increase desirable openness of the community climate.

The purpose of this research is to investigate factors affecting CSCL design and implementation for EFL learners. The CoI framework was utilized for the research investigation besides the course design and implementation. Five factors will be examined with the CoI framework. The research questions are as follows: (1) What element(s) of CoI affect EFL learners' participation level?, (2) What element(s) of CoI affect learners' satisfaction with online discussion?, (3) What element(s) of CoI affect learners' perceived contributions to the discussion groups?, (4) Does English proficiency as a foreign language have any relationship with the CoI?, and (5) What element(s) of CoI affect the learners' interactions during the discussion?

This chapter consists of three parts: (1) a literature review on the practice and impacts of CSCL on EFL learning; (2) a case study that explores the relationships among CoI and EFL learner participation level, learner satisfaction, and how CoI and EFL contribute to a community; and (3) the implications to CSCL design for EFL learners based on the CoI framework.

BACKGROUND

CSCL and Language Learning

Due to the current pedagogical paradigm shift to constructivism, social constructivism, and situated learning, the importance of interaction and collaboration are strongly emphasized for effective and meaningful learning, encouraging the research and practice of computer-mediated communication (CMC) for CSCL.

CSCL is an interactive learning environment based on the socio-constructive learning perspective. One of the key issues concerns how active and continuous interaction should be established in CMC (Barnes, 2008). In particular, interpersonal communication should be promoted to establish an active virtual learning community using social media. Collaborative learning, with high interaction among learners in both computer-based and face-to-face situations, can lead to high performance in socio-emotional development (eg., increased personal satisfaction) (Benbunan-Fich, Hiltz, & Harasim, 2005). The background and the importance of CSCL interactions will be briefly discussed first, and current issues related to the social presence concept will be described.

CSCL Design for Language Learning

CSCL promotes cognitive change through group interaction and activities (King, 2007). Digiano, Goldman and Chorost (2008) state that information and communications technology (ICT) applications can be the center of effective learning environments for distributed, interactive, collaborative and constructive learning, and learning assessment. The recent trend of using CMC tools (such as social media) for CSCL provides learners with opportunities to solicit and share knowledge while developing common ground with their peers and teachers (Rennie & Morrison, 2007).

Active interactions are essential for successful CSCL. Therefore, quality social interactions require a group atmosphere where individuals share experiences and knowledge (Reneland-Forsman & Ahlbäck, 2007). One common issue in CSCL concerns how to support learners' social interactions. CMC is often used for language learning as the platform of CSCL. CMC is effective for the promotion of language learning through a high degree of interaction such as the production of target language utterance (Furstenberg, 1987). There are several reasons for the positive effects of CMC on language learning: the reduction of anxiety about utterance (Kelm, 1992); the ease of revision in the learner's utterances before posting in the discussion (Lee, 2002); and the promotion of social interaction which promotes the negotiation of word meanings where learners ask others for the meaning of words (Smith, 2002; Morris, 2005). These findings are related to Second Language Acquisition (SLA) theory.

Long (1981, 1989) indicated that social interaction promoted communication and language acquisition through the active negotiation of meanings. Comprehensive input and output play an important role in communicative language learning. Comprehensive input implies written or spoken information given in a language that the learner can comprehend (Krashen, 1985). In SLA, communication skills, in particular, are acquired through communication among participants. One example is the interaction between learners and teachers (Long, 1981). Interaction refers to meaningful communication that enables the understanding of, and stimulates the production

of, comprehensive input. When people face a problem, such as a misunderstanding, they resolve the problem before continuing communication (Clark, 1994). For example, when learners cannot understand their interlocutor's utterance, they may ask that it be repeated, or the interlocutor may modify or paraphrase the statement to facilitate understanding. Comprehensive output refers to learning activities, such as uttering, repeating, or writing, where students receive comprehensive input through interaction (Swain, 1995). Swain (1995) claimed that output has three functions: to identify the gap between what the learner can and cannot express; to hypothesize about testing, such as the trial-and-error method; and to perform metalinguistic functions, such as reflective learning.

The CSCL design for language learning has been discussed since the middle of 1990's, with the advancement and use of the Internet (Chapelle, 2001). In particular, researchers have been discussing asynchronous (ACMC) and synchronous (SCMC) CMC, which play a primary role in language acquisition. In ACMC, students learn the target language by self-pacing and reflection (Hiltz & Goldman, 2005). These students consider ideas and utterances, which raises their grammatical consciousness (Lamy & Hampel, 2007). However, self-pacing can become an obstacle in facilitating effective language learning through ACMC communication. Weller and Mason (2000) pointed out that ACMC reduces the pressure to reply to the interlocutors, forcing them to wait, sometimes a long time for the student's reply. ACMC may weaken the effect of social interaction in communicative language learning.

The effect of SCMC on the second language learning was also reported. SCMC is similar to face-to-face communication but it promotes more equal utterance than face-to-face communication (Chun, 1994), promotes active social interaction between learners (Smith, 2002), and allows learners to use various communication strategies (Lee, 2002). One disadvantage of SCMC is that high-proficiency learners tend to participate in discussions, which leads to more pressure for low-proficiency learners (Lamy & Hampel, 2007). Yamada (2009) focused on the communication media in SCMC, and he investigated the effect of communication media on psychological factors and performances in communicative English learning. Yamada compared four types of SCMC: videoconferencing, audio conferencing, text chat with images, and plain text chat. He found that any media that allows the use of social cues creates positive psychological effects, such as the learning to communicate in English, and these psychological factors promote learning performance, including the number of speech and self-corrections where learners correct their grammatical errors by themselves. Text communication promotes the confidence in grammatical accuracy and then increases the amount of self-correction (Yamada, 2009).

Abrams (2003) reported interesting findings when comparing ACMC with SCMC from the viewpoint of utterance. The results revealed that language learners using SCMC outperform those who use ACMC, and those who did not use CMC at all in communicative language learning(control group), in terms of the amount of speech in face-to-face discussion.

RELATIONSHIPS AMONG COI AND EFL LEARNING: METHODOLOGY

In this section, the relationships among three presences (social, cognitive, and teaching) of the Community of Inquiry (CoI) framework and EFL online discussion will be explored, based on a case study held at a university in Japan. This CoI will be investigated in relation to (1) EFL learners' participation level, (2) learners' satisfaction with online discussion, (3) learners' perceived contributions to the discussion groups, (4) English proficiency as a foreign language, and (5) the learners' interactions during the discussion.

Participants

Forty-two freshmen at Kumamoto University participated in the research (Male: 39, Female: 3), who were majoring in science. These students had minimal computer skills and knowledge, such as keyboard typing, required for participation in the study.

Course Descriptions and Activity Design

The case study was used during a Computer Assisted Language Learning (CALL) course, which was a mandatory two-credit course for the freshmen at the university. The course was delivered in a blended manner, where face-to-face and online communications were both required. It had 15 face-to-face classes, and online activities were utilized outside of the classroom to enhance the face-to-face learning materials that were used. The five online discussion activities are illustrated in Table 1.

As mentioned before, the course was designed and implemented based on the Collaborative Problem Solving (CPS) approach (Nelson, 1999) in the instructional design (ID) and the Teaching and Learning Guideline for CoI (Garrison, 2011). CPS was utilized to design the overall course procedures and evaluation and CoI was employed to design how the technology was integrated into learning activities considering the interactions among contents, an instructor, and students.

The integration of social presence (SP) and cognitive presence (CP) of CoI were concerned to support students' discourse. The instructor gave feedback and directions to help students focus and resolve issues considering the interaction between TP and CP. The feedback included ones related to the grammatical, lexical, semantic, and cultural mistakes. To establish the online collaborative climate, the interaction between SP and TP were taken into account. Both CPS and CoI embrace

Table 1. Discussion topics and descriptions

Discussion	Topic	Problem
1	Your Ideal House	What is your ideal house? Please share your ideas with the group members
2	Items to Carry During Earthquakes	What should we bring with us when another earthquake hits us? First, have your group list as many items you feel are necessary for your survival as you can. Then, choose three of the most important items from your discussion.
3	Factors to Activate Group Discussion	What is important to make a discussion group into an active learning community? Based on your experiences of Group Discussion 1 and 2, please identify what type of factors and determine the three most important factors in your group.
4	Nuclear Power Plants	What do you think of the nuclear plants in Japan? Discuss the topic "The Japanese Government should abolish nuclear power plants." Please find evidence to support your opinions using the Internet or other resources, and share the information with your group members. Please choose a position on the topic as a result of the discussion in your group.
5	Foreign Country to Live	Suppose we have to move to a country outside of Japan. If you had to live in another country for 10 years, which country would your group choose to live in? Choose one country, and identify your reasons for choosing that country at the end of today's discussion.

constructivist perspectives. The constructivist perspective states that authentic inquiry, a divergent view, and collaboration promote student learning. Those perspectives were considered when course materials and activities were designed. For example, in the face-to-face class, Voice of America (www.voiceofamerica.com) was used to create listening and reading materials to provide students with authentic contexts. In the Second Language Acquisition (SLA) theory, written and spoken materials in a targeted language were also viewed to increase comprehensive inputs (Krashen, 1985) for quality interactions. As discussed in the literature review section, interaction enables the understandings and stimulates the production of comprehensive input.

The discussion activities were selected at the design phase of the instructional design, whose essential elements include analysis, design, development, implementation, and evaluation phases, because these activities could provide not only collaborative learning, but opportunities of comprehensive output in SLA (Swain, 1995). The five discussion topics in Table 1 related to the news topics were selected by the instructor who considered the students' interests and familiarity in order to motivate the students, gather their attention, and relate their previous knowledge and/or experiences to the topic (Keller, 2010).

The instructor did not basically join the group discussions. As the CoI framework suggests, the instructor tried to give clear instructions on the learning topics, course goals, activities, and time frames before the discussion activities. Facilitations to deepen the discussion were conducted in the classroom in the middle of the two-week discussions. The instructor encouraged students' open arguments and interactions and supported them to focus on the topic. She also tried to correct common mistakes and expressions in EFL. All through the discussion activities, the instructor made efforts to let students engage the activities emphasizing the importance of each student as a community member.

The bulletin board system (BBS) of the learning management system (LMS), Blackboard, was adopted for the discussion activities. All students were required to participate in all of the activities. There were four to six members in each group and the group memberships were randomly determined for each topic. In face-to-face classes, learning activities were mainly done individually, while between the regular face-to-face classes, students worked in groups. Each discussion lasted two weeks and in the middle of the two weeks, one face-to-face class was inserted to provide facilitation from the instructor.

Instruments

The Col survey (Swan, Richardson, Garrison, Cleveland-Innes,, & Arbaugh, 2008) and a researcher-developed questionnaire were conducted at the end of the semester. Students' Col level, learner participation level, satisfaction and contributions to the asynchronous discussion activities, and English proficiency were measured. The Col survey consists of 34-five-point Likert scales. The internal consistencies were reported with Cronbach's alpha as 0.94 for Teaching Presence (TP), 0.91 for Social Presence (SP), and 0.95 for Cognitive Presence (CP) (Swan et al., 2008).

To determine the participation level, the total number of student comments was counted to identify how active each student was during the asynchronous discussion for the primary quantitative analysis. The students' comments were qualitatively focused to investigate the quality of the interaction.

The questionnaire was used to collect students' satisfaction ratings and their perception about their own contribution to the community. Student satisfaction ratings were gathered using a 4-point Likert scale, with "1" meaning not satisfied at all and "4" meaning very satisfied. The contribution rate was an average percentage of each student's perspective contribution to the community (i.e., group), while assuming that the total effort of all members in a group was 100%.

Students' English abilities were measured with a standardized test, TOEIC® IP (Institutional Program), developed and provided by Educational Testing Service (ETS). There were two parts to the test, listening and reading, and its final score ranges from 10 to 990. TOEIC-IP scores are not official, but they are as reliable as the original TOEIC scores. The TOEIC-IP score was employed partially for the final grading of the course. Taking TOEIC-IP was an essential requirement for course credit and all registered students should have taken the test one month prior to the end of the semester. The students' total scores were utilized to analyze the relationship between English ability and Col presences.

The interactions and Col relationship were evaluated and students' comments of the discussion activities were encoded with the indicators of Col (Garrison, 2011). The instructor provided most of the feedback and intervention when she met students in the classroom. The SP and CP of the Col were used to focus on asynchronous communication in this research. There were three categories with 12 indicators for SP, and four categories with four indicators for CP that were adopted for coding. To increase credibility, the authors discussed the inconsistent codings and came to agreement for all comments. Garrison, Cleveland-Innes, Koole, and Kappelman (2006) noted the importance of the unit of analysis for the coding of a Col. For many years in the twentieth century, researchers used the sentence as a unit of analysis (Harre, 2001). Sentences were employed as a unit of analysis, because the comments indicated more information. However, the level of detail made encoding procedures more complicated and interpretation much more difficult.

Data Analyses

There were two major analyses required for the research purposes. MANOVA was utilized as the primary statistical procedure for the first four research purposes related to students' Col level: participation level, satisfaction, contributions to the asynchronous discussion activities, and English proficiency. The MANOVA analysis allows researchers to test the simultaneous differences

Table 2. Discussion comments, sentence, and word counts

Discussion	Comments	Sentences	Words	Sentences/Comment	Words/Sentence
1	107	178	635	1.66	3.57
2	200	297	1806	1.49	6.08
3	81	118	957	1.46	8.11
4	6	14	182	2.33	13.00
5	151	315	2138	2.09	6.79
Total	**545**	**922**	**5718**	**1.69**	**6.20**

among groups of multiple variables (Cohen, Cohen, West, & Aiken, 2003). MANOVA also controls the inflation of experiment-wise Type I and Type II errors. The independent variable (IV) was the CoI level, and the dependent variables (DV) were the number of discussion comments, the students' satisfaction, the students' contribution, and TOEIC. To consider students' characteristics, the score of three presences (teaching, social, and cognitive) were categorized into three level, High >= 3.5, 3.5 < Medium < 2.5, and Low < 2.5. The combination patterns were used for the primary data analysis. There were 27 (3*3*3) patterns available, because there were three levels for the three presences. Once the overall MANOVA was found to be significant, then the IV and each DV would be tested individually. To get more detailed information about the relationships between the CoI level and DVs, the correlation matrices were discussed.

Each ratio of the sentences of students' comments after coding based on the indicators for the SP and CP is provided. Although all three elements of CoI support students' discourse in an integrated fashion, the instructor did not join the discussions and just gave the directions and overall comments in the classroom. TP is removed for the data analysis in this study. Thus, SP and CP are used to investigate the quality of the students' interactions in this research.

RESULTS

Descriptive Statistics

The descriptive statistics of the discussion comment numbers and satisfaction and contribution variables are shown in Table 2 and Table 3 respectively. The discussion topics 1, 2, and 5 show a larger number of comments; however, the word-sentence ratio for topic 4 was 13.00, which was the highest of the five topics. Table 3 reports the average of discussion contribution was 35.49%, which indicates that students averaged slightly higher than one-third of the whole group contribution in terms of their perceived contribution to the discussion activities. The average TOEIC score is 449.88 with the range of 315 to 620.

The results of the descriptive statistics for TP, SP, and CP from the CoI survey are provided in Table 4. As Table 4 shows, TP of the students was relatively high with the grand mean from all three categories of TP at 3.98. The category of "design

Table 3. Descriptive statistics results for the dependent variables of discussion satisfaction, contribution, and TOEIC

	N	Min	Max	M	SD
Discussion Satisfaction	42	2.00	4.00	2.95	0.58
Discussion Contribution	42	0.00	75.00	35.49	21.73
TOEIC	42	315.00	620.00	449.88	70.98

Table 4. Descriptive statistics for CoI three presences

CoI		Question	m	sd
Teaching Presence	TP1: Design & Organization	1. The instructor clearly communicated important course topics.	4.21	0.90
		2. The instructor clearly communicated important course goals.	4.38	0.58
		3. The instructor provided clear instructions on how to participate in course learning activities.	4.45	0.59
		4. The instructor clearly communicated important due dates/times frames for learning activities.	4.45	0.74
	TP2: Facilitation	5. The instructor was helpful in identifying areas of agreement and disagreement on course topics that helped me learn.	3.69	0.84
		6. The instructor was helpful in guiding the class towards understanding course topics in a way that helped me clarify my thinking.	4.07	0.81
		7. The instructor helped to keep course participants engaged and participating in a productive dialogue.	4.02	1.02
		8. The instructor helped keep the course participants on task in a way that helped me learn.	3.90	0.82
		9. The instructor encouraged course participants to explore new concepts in this course.	3.45	0.97
		10. The instructor's actions reinforced the development of a sense of community among course participants.	4.24	0.73
	TP3: Direct Instruction	11. The instructor helped to focus discussion on relevant issues in a way that helped me to learn.	4.14	0.93
		12. The instructor provided feedback that helped me understand my strengths and weaknesses.	3.38	1.06
		13. The instructor provided feedback in a timely fashion.	3.64	0.98
Social Presence	SP1: Affective Expression	14. Getting to know other course participants gave me a sense of belonging in the course.	3.83	1.08
		15. I was able to form distant impressions of some course participants.	3.67	1.14
		16. Online or Web-based communication is an excellent medium for social interaction.	3.98	1.07
	SP2: Open Communication	17. I felt comfortable conversing through the online medium.	3.64	1.27
		18. I felt comfortable participating in the course discussions.	3.79	1.09
		19. I felt comfortable interacting with other course participants.	3.86	1.07
	SP3: Group Cohesion	20. I felt comfortable disagreeing with other course participants while still maintaining a sense of trust.	3.31	1.14
		21. I felt that my point of view was acknowledged by other course participants.	3.88	0.80
		22. Online discussions helped me to develop a sense of collaboration.	3.60	0.89
Cognitive Presence	CP1: Triggering Event	23. The problems posed increased my interest in course issues.	3.86	0.75
		24. The course activities piqued my curiosity.	3.79	0.90
		25. I felt motivated to explore content related questions.	3.52	0.86
	CP2: Exploration	26. I utilized a variety of information sources to explore problems posed in this course.	2.93	1.22
		27. Brainstorming and finding relevant information helped me resolve content related questions.	3.31	1.02
		28. Online discussions help me to develop a sense of collaboration.	4.26	0.73
	CP3: Integration	29. Combining new information helped me construct explanations/solutions.	3.71	0.81
		30. Learning activities helped me construct explanations/solutions.	4.02	0.64
		31. Reflection on course content and discussions helped me understand fundamental concepts in this class.	3.98	0.78
	CP4: Resolution	32. I can describe ways to test and apply the knowledge created in this course.	3.26	1.01
		33. I have developed solutions to course problems that can be applied in practice.	3.19	1.09
		34. I can apply the knowledge created in this course to my work or other non-class related activities.	3.67	0.87

Table 5. Descriptive statistics results of seven types of CoI ([a]TP: Teaching Presence, SP: Social Presence, CP: Cognitive Presence. [b]H: The average is equal to or greater than 3.5, M: The average is less than 3.5 and equal to or greater than 2.5. L: The average is less than 2.5)

Dependent Variable	Community of Inquiry[a]			*m*	*sd*	n
	TP	SP	CP			
Discussion Comment Number	H[b]	H	H	14.37	4.19	19
	H	H	L	14.43	3.15	7
	H	L	H	9.60	4.04	5
	H	L	M	17.00	.	1
	H	L	L	7.50	6.86	4
	L	H	L	11.00	1.41	2
	L	L	L	7.75	4.99	4
			Total	12.43	4.96	42
Discussion Satisfaction	H	H	H	3.00	0.67	19
	H	H	L	3.00	0.58	7
	H	L	H	3.20	0.45	5
	H	L	M	2.00	.	1
	H	L	L	3.00	0.00	4
	L	H	L	2.50	0.71	2
	L	L	L	2.75	0.50	4
			Total	2.95	0.58	42
Discussion Contribution	H	H	H	34.25	22.79	19
	H	H	L	46.71	16.40	7
	H	L	H	43.60	26.96	5
	H	L	M	20.00	.	1
	H	L	L	30.00	24.49	4
	L	H	L	42.50	3.54	2
	L	L	L	17.50	15.00	4
			Total	35.49	21.72	42
TOEIC Score	H	H	H	440.79	69.65	19
	H	H	L	470.71	75.47	7
	H	L	H	483.00	44.94	5
	H	L	M	315.00	.	1
	H	L	L	400.00	55.53	4
	L	H	L	470.00	98.99	2
	L	L	L	488.75	65.49	4
			Total	449.88	70.98	42

and organization" scored highest among the three ($M = 4.38$) and the "direct instruction" scored lowest ($M = 3.72$). Question items 3 and 4 marked highest with $M = 4.45$. Most students thought that the instructor provided adequate details about how to participate in the research and what the due dates/time frames were for the course's learning activities.

SP scored slightly lower than the TP with the grand mean of 3.73. There were three categories, affective expression, open communication, and group cohesion, in the SP statistics. The highest average was the "affective expression" ($M = 3.84$), followed by "open communication" ($M = 3.76$). Survey item 16, "Online or web-based communication is an excellent medium for social interaction" had the highest mean at $M = 3.98$. The high mean implies that most students have positive impressions of CMC.

The grand mean for CP was 3.61 and this was the lowest among three presences of CoI. The highest average was survey item 28 ($M = 4.26$), while the lowest was item 26 ($M = 2.95$). From these results, students might appreciate the diverse perspectives achieved through the asynchronous online discussion, but they might regret that they did not use various information sources for the discussion problems.

The seven types with the combination of the three levels for three presences are summarized in Table 5. Forty-two students were categorized into seven types. There were 19 students (45.24%) with high TP, high SP, and high CP levels (H-H-H), and only four students (9.52%) had all low levels (L-L-L). Only one student had a high TP, low SP, and medium CP (H-L-M). The highest number of discussions posted by one student was 17, and this student had a high TP, low SP, and

medium CP. The lowest average comment number was 7.5, and both students had high TP, low SP and low CP on their CoI.

The average of the discussion satisfaction was 2.95, and most students chose between 3 and 4 for their satisfaction levels. The H-L-M student and the students with low TP averaged less than 3 in the satisfaction level. As to the discussion contribution, the L-L-L students averaged the lowest at 17.5%. The highest contribution of 46.71% was claimed by the H-H-L type.

When the CoI types and TOEIC were compared, the H-L-M student scored the lowest at 315 on the TOEIC. Other types averaged over 400. The interesting thing is that TOEIC average score of the L-L-L type was the highest at 488.75.

Student CoI Types and Dependent Variables

The results of ANOVA were statistically significant (Wilks' *Lamda* = .355, $F(24, 113) = 1.63$, $p < .05$). This implies that when all dependent variables are considered simultaneously, the CoI types had a significant correlation. Table 6 illustrates the significance that was found in the discussion comment number and the CoI types as the results of ANOVA. However, the Tukey's HSD, one of the ad-hoc analyses for ANOVA, did not show significance between any groups. The possible reason might be that very few cases in several types made the analysis difficult. For

Table 6. ANOVA results

Dependent Variables	SS	df	MS	F	p	R²	Adjusted R²
Discussion Comment #	377.80	6.00	62.97	2.98	0.02	0.34	0.22
Discussion Satisfaction	1.86	6.00	0.31	0.90	0.51	0.13	−0.02
Discussion Contribution	2993.43	6.00	498.91	1.07	0.40	0.16	0.01
TOEIC	45091.07	6.00	7515.18	1.63	0.17	0.22	0.08

Table 7. Correlation matrix of CoI and dependent variables (* p < .05, ** p < .01)

		Discussion Comment Number	Discussion Satisfaction	Discussion Contribution	TOEIC
Community of Inquiry	Teaching Presence (TP)	.195	.347*	.247	−.056
	Social Presence (SP)	.483**	.287	.222	−.101
	Cognitive Presence (CP)	.120	.313*	.206	−.047
Teaching Presence (TP)	Design & Organization	.232	.346*	.424**	.091
	Facilitation	.136	.324*	.177	−.048
	Direct Instruction	.177	.237	.117	−.160
Social Presence (SP)	Affective Expression	.363*	.172	−.016	−.254
	Open Communication	.436**	.269	.350*	.033
	Group Cohesion	.357*	.229	.148	−.046
Cognitive Presence (CP)	Triggering Event	.200	.307*	.285	−.022
	Exploration	.227	.281	.185	−.047
	Integration	−.010	.264	.143	−.178
	Resolution	−.006	.213	.091	.050

example, there was only one case for the H-L-M type. The Fisher's LSD, which was said to be less rigorous in the statistical test, was conducted just for our reference. When alpha was set to .05, the H-H-H type had significant differences from the H-L-M, H-L-L, and L-L-L, and the H-H-L was significantly different from the H-L-L and L-L-L. The results suggest that there were different tendencies concerning the number of discussion comments between the higher and the lower CoI types. When students perceived teaching and social presence at high levels, then, they might produce more comments compared to other combinations.

THREE PRESENCES OF COI AND DEPENDENT VARIABLES

So far, student characteristics were focused on examining the relationships between the CoI and the dependent variables. Next, each presence of the CoI framework are explored. Table 7 provides the correlation matrix of the CoI and the targeted dependent variables. From the perspectives of the presences, the SP and the discussion comment number have a significant relationship ($r = .483$, $p < .01$), and the TP and CP have significant relationships with the satisfaction variable (TP: $r = .347$, SP: $r = .313$, $p < .05$). No significant correlation was observed between any of the presences and TOEIC. Through a comparison of the subcategories of each presence (teaching, social and cognitive) and the DVs, the category, design, and organization, it is evident that TP has a significant correlation with satisfaction and contribution, and its facilitation category is significantly related to satisfaction. The "affective expression" ($r = .363$), "open communication" ($r = .436$), and "group cohesion" ($r = .357$) categories in SP relate to the comment number significantly. The open communication also shows significance in its relationship to the contribution ($r = .350$). In CP, only the triggering event category was significant in its correlation with satisfaction.

The further analysis was conducted to explore which items specifically are related to the dependent variables. When the focus is on the discussion comment number, the CoI survey item 19, "I felt comfortable interacting with other course participants," has the strongest positive correlation, and it is statistically significant ($r = .47$, $p < .01$). The survey items 14: "Getting to know other course participants gave me a sense of belonging in the course," 18: "I felt comfortable participating in the course discussions," 22: "Online discussions help me to develop a sense of collaboration," and 23: "Problems posed increased my interest in course issues," are also significantly related to the number of comments. Except for item 23, all are SP items.

With regard to satisfaction, survey item 2: "The instructor clearly communicated important course goals," is significantly related ($r = .42$, $p < .01$). Item 3: "The instructor provided clear instructions on how to participate in course learning activities," item 4 "The instructor clearly communicated important due dates/time frames for learning activities," and item 10: "Instructor actions reinforced the development of a sense of community among course participants" of TP, along with item 16: "Online or web-based communication is an excellent medium for social interaction" of SP, and item 25: "I felt motivated to explore content related questions" of CP have a significant relationship with satisfaction.

The dependent variables, the satisfaction, and the contribution are significantly related to each other with $r = .45$. CP is significantly correlated with TP survey item 2: "The instructor clearly communicated important course goals," SP items 18 "I felt comfortable participating in the course discussions" and 19: "I felt comfortable interacting with other course participants," and CP items 23: "Problems posed increased my interest in course issues," and item 30: "Learning activities helped me construct explanations/solutions." TOEIC is significantly correlated (negatively) with survey item 15: "I was able to form distinct impressions of some course participants" ($r = -.34$, $p < .05$).

Students' Interactions and Social/Cognitive Presences

The results of the relationship between student interactions during asynchronous discussion and the CoI's SP and CP are presented in order to test the fifth research purpose, which is to investigate the learners' interactions during the discussion in terms of the CoI. Each sentence of the students' comments during the discussion was coded according to the CoI's SP and CP indicators and the

Table 8. Percentage of indicators for social presence against total number of sentences

| | Social Presence | | | | | | | | | | | |
| | Interpersonal Communication | | | Open Communication | | | | | | Cohesive Communication | | |
Discussion	Affective expression	Self-disclosure	Use of humor	Continuing thread	Quoting from others' messages	Referring explicitly to others' messages	Asking questions	Complimenting/ expressing appreciation	Expressing agreement	Vocatives	Addressing or refers to the group using inclusive pronouns	Phatics, salutations
1	12.70%	12.17%	2.65%	6.88%	0.00%	0.53%	6.88%	7.94%	13.23%	1.06%	1.59%	1.59%
2	22.40%	6.49%	6.49%	0.00%	1.62%	3.90%	7.79%	3.90%	15.58%	0.97%	14.61%	3.90%
3	3.20%	2.40%	0.80%	0.00%	0.00%	0.80%	3.20%	9.60%	22.40%	0.00%	16.00%	0.80%
4	0.00%	5.56%	0.00%	0.00%	0.00%	0.00%	5.56%	0.00%	5.56%	0.00%	16.67%	0.00%
5	10.66%	8.78%	2.51%	0.00%	0.00%	0.31%	5.02%	7.52%	7.52%	0.00%	0.94%	2.82%

Table 9. Percentage of indicators for cognitive presence against total number of sentences

Discussion	Cognitive Presence			
	Triggering Event	Exploration	Integration	Revolution
	Evocative (inductive)	Inquisitive (divergent)	Tentative (convergent)	Committed (deductive)
1	7.94%	66.14%	3.17%	0.00%
2	8.44%	49.03%	8.77%	0.00%
3	4.00%	60.00%	0.00%	0.00%
4	5.56%	88.89%	0.00%	0.00%
5	5.33%	70.53%	0.94%	0.00%

percentages of each indicator for the total number of sentences is 100% as reported in Table 8 and Table 9 respectively.

The affective expression indicator is defined as "conventional expressions of emotion, or unconventional expressions of emotion, including repetitious punctuation, conspicuous capitalization, and emoticons," according to Garrison (2011, p. 38). This indicator was counted when a sentence implied respect and welcome with informal expression, such as emoticons and capitalization. In Discussions 1, 2, and 5, the indicator of "affective expression" in interpersonal communication of SP illustrates a relatively higher percentage, more than 10%. In Discussions 1, 2, and 3, the indicator of "expressing agreement" in "open communication" of SP shows more than 10%. In the "cohesive communication" category, where cohesive communication means addressing the group using inclusive pronouns, such as we, us, our, the group shows around 15% of all of the sentences written for the discussions 2, 3, and 4.

The SP indicator ratio to number of sentences seems to differ according to the discussion problems. On the other hand, the CP indicator count seems stable, regardless of the discussion problems. The indicator "exploration" offers higher percentages for the total number of the sentences. Unfortunately, there were no sentences coded into the "committed" indicator.

DISCUSSION

This section will discuss the characteristics necessary for designing CSCL for EFL learners based on the results of the case study. The discussion will be organized according to the five research purposes.

Suggestions on CSCL Design for EFL Learning

An asynchronous discussion setting of CSCL is beneficial for EFL learners because it gives students more opportunities to use and practice English. In this context, it is essential to reveal methods to increase students' expressions during the discussion. The results in Table 5 and ANOVA suggest that higher CoI levels might have a positive relationship with the number of student comments in the discussions. The higher CoI, especially of TP and SP a student has, the more s/he may post comments during the discussion. The results of the participation level and CoI in Table 7 illustrate that social presence is a key element for students' producing more statements. In addition to encouraging students to form affective expression and group cohesion in a learning community, the establishment of open communication is crucial. When students perceived high-level of TP and SP, it may also increase the number of postings to the discussion.

The results in Table 7 show that the discussion satisfaction is significantly correlated with TP and CP. The design, organization, and facilitation categories have stronger positive relationship with the satisfaction. This implies that when the learning context is well-designed and the students perceived clear instruction of the course goals and learning activities, the students tend to be satisfied with the design and organization. When the students felt that their instructor helps form a sense of community, they were satisfied with the asynchronous discussion. This supports the results of Garrison and Cleveland-Innes (2005), who emphasized structure and leadership for higher-order learning. The structure indicates design and leadership refers to the facilitation of the study and the direct instruction category in the Col survey.

Col survey item 25 in the "triggering event" category of CP is also significantly related to student satisfaction. This implies that when students felt motivated to explore the related content, they showed higher satisfaction. When students are interested in a discussion topic and eager to seek more information, they might feel more satisfied after the discussion.

Table 7 does not show a significant relationship between the satisfaction and SP, but the individual variable correlation matrix in Table 8 shows the significance between Col survey item 16 in SP and satisfaction, which indicates a positive attitude toward and acceptance of technology as a social communication tool. To increase student satisfaction with the online discussions, helping them create positive attitudes toward web-based communication might be considered when the CSCL is designed.

As a member of the learning community, contributions of each member are important factors for the enlivenment of the community. The community of inquiry benefits tremendously from diversity and the perspectives of the members. How to extract contributions of the community members is one of the most significant issues in learning-community studies. Overall scores of the Col presences, TP, SP and CP, have no relationship with the contribution in Table 7. However, when viewing the individual survey items, item 2 in TP and item 19 in SP have a relatively higher relationship with contribution. This may imply that some subcategories of each presence independently relates to contribution. In such a case, the design and organization in TP and the open communication in SP should be important in increasing the students' perceptions of their contributions to the community. In other words, when we design CSCL for students' high contributions, it seems influential to set clear course or activity goals and prepare a comfortable learning environment for their interactions.

Students in the case study have been learning English as a foreign language. Language proficiency was thought to play a critical role in an asynchronous discussion before this research was conducted. However, based on the results, TOEIC was not related to the Col or any other dependent variables. Therefore, other factors must be more influential than English proficiency on students' learning activities, satisfaction, and contribution. The effects of the learning activities were not the focus of the research. If the learning outcomes and learning process are the focus in the future, language proficiency might have an effect on the results. To achieve higher levels of EFL proficiency, further advancement of EFL practice will be reached. More complicated and ill-structured problem may be prepared, which should require bigger vocabulary size and fluency of language use. In such a case, language proficiency may affect the quality of interactions and educational experiences resulted in Col.

The sentences of the students' comments are analyzed in terms of the SP and CP. Focus on the SP, at the beginning of the learning activities (i.e., Discussion 1), where self-disclosure marks are 12.1%, while in other discussions less than 10% of sentences show this indicator. This result is consistent with the previous research. According to Brown (2001), SP becomes transparent as the focus shifts to academic purposes and activities.

The ratio of the "affective expression" in the interpersonal expression and the "expressing agreement" in open communication might change according to discussion topics. As shown in Table 1, discussion topics 1, 2, and 5 seem to obtain students' interests. This issue may be related to survey item 23 "Problems posed increased my interest in course issues," although the item is included in "triggering event" in the CP. Item 23 has significant correlation with the comment number, satisfaction, and the contribution. Setting proper problems appears to be essential when designing a productive learning environment for EFL learners if the researcher wants to increase student comments. SP, including the "affective expression" indicator, has a direct effect on climate and open communication.

The "expressing agreement" indicator is included in the open communication category of the SP. Garrison (2011) claims that expressing agreement "reveals engagement in the process of critical reflection and discourse" (p.39). Open communication plays an important role in a reflective e-learning community of inquiry. According to Table 9, discussions 4 and 5 might not give students many opportunities for reflection and insight.

From the perspective of CP, the nature of the discussion problems that did not require the student's application, test, or defense, had no count on the "committed" indicator. Most discussion problems asked students to brainstorm their own ideas and then find an answer as a group. These answers were matched to the indicators "triggering event (evocative)" and "exploration (inquisitive)." Only a few groups in Discussion 1, 2, and 5 reached an agreement at the end of the discussion. This lack of agreement explains why the "integration (tentative)" ratio is smaller.

The discussion problem might directly affect the students' comments and interactions. When "affective expression" in SP increases too much, the research illustrates that more irrelevant expressions, which are not directly related to the discussion topics, may increase; and meaningful interactions in CP directly related to the discussion topic may decrease. If this is the case, it is important to maintain an appropriate level of SP for meaningful interactions in CP. This result is similar to the relationship between anxiety, performance, and effective classroom climate. A small amount of anxiety may improve performance (Shipman & Shipman, 1985), which is often called "facilitating anxiety." An open and positive classroom atmosphere is fundamental for quality interactions to lead to learning; but a little businesslike atmosphere should also be kept for effective learning and the accomplishment of the learning goals (Davis & Thomas, 1989).

According to our observation, once students established open communication in SP, then they start to concentrate on the discussion topics. The SP and CP indicator ratio to the number of sentences provided by the students might not simply shift over time, which slightly disagrees with Swan (2003) who suggests that shifts of SP over time in online discussion will occur. The result emphasizes the importance of encouraging students to maintain an appropriate level of SP and focus on academic purposes as Brown (2001) suggests. To help students focus on academics, instructors prepare authentic and slightly challenging topics that will require higher content knowledge and cognitive skills.

Limitation of the Study and Future Research Implications

There are several limitations of the study. First, more case studies with a variety of settings should be investigated. Garrison and Arbaugh (2007) point out that more empirical evidence is needed to validate the CoI framework for online learning. EFL learning is affected by culture, mother tongue, societies, etc. A community of inquiry should be examined among not only Japanese but other nationalities. Settings among mixed nationalities and international settings should be considered to reveal greater support of CSCL for EFL learning. A longitudinal study, where observations occur over a certain period of time, is also required. Longitudinal studies could provide us with significant information on how students learn and acquire their language skills.

Blended learning was employed in this study. Most of the facilitations and direct instructions were conducted during the face-to-face classes. Other settings, such as a full online course and other types of blended learning, should be examined in future research.

As to quality interactions, SP and CP were the focus of this study. TP should be also included in the future research. Strategies of discourse analysis should be reconsidered in the future also. In this research, each sentence was coded and used as a unit of analysis. The validity of using sentences as the unit of analysis should be discussed further. Compared to the indicators of SP for coding, those of CP are rough, and it may be difficult to obtain detailed information on student interactions.

Discourse analysis is emerging from different academic disciplines, including linguistics, cognitive psychology, and social psychology and so on. The definitions of discourse fall into the three main categories, (1) anything beyond the sentence, (2) language use, and (3) a broader range of social practice, according to Schiffrin, Tannen, and Hamilton (2001). Lee (2002) compared accuracy and fluency of intermediate EFL students in synchronous and asynchronous CSCL. She suggested that synchronous and asynchronous CMC would affect EFL learners' negotiation strategies. For further investigation of the interactions and communication during learning activities, the perspectives of discourse analysis can be applied for both EFL learning and collaborative learning considering CMC types.

CONCLUSION

Garrison (2011) states that design and organization, facilitating discourse and direct instruction in TP supports setting climate and monitoring and regulating learning that is incorporated with SP and CP. The SP and CP interdependence could also affect the quality of interactions, and all three presences together produce worthwhile educational experiences in the CoI framework. Based on the case study described and discussed in this chapter, the following is a summary of suggestions to apply the CoI to design CSCL, especially with regard to asynchronous discussion for EFL learning.

- Support open communication to increase the number of student comments during a discussion, which is the preferred participation level in CSCL.
- Evaluate TP and CP during design and implementation to encourage student satisfaction with the asynchronous discussion.
- Consider the design and organization of TP and open communication of SP to gain student contributions.
- Use CSCL activities to help students at all proficiency levels to practice English, because CSCL may not depend too highly on students' EFL proficiency.
- Help students establish SP first and then shift their focus to academic topics to increase the quality of student interactions during the learning activities.

The careful design of a learning community, including appropriate problem setting, seems to be the most important when we apply the CoI framework to CSCL for EFL learners. In order to create effective and attractive of learning activities, perspectives of instructional design could be merged into the CoI framework.

This course was designed and implemented based on the Collaborative Problem Solving (CPS) approach (Nelson, 1999) in the instructional design (ID) and Teaching and Learning Guideline in the CoI (Garrison, 2011). The CPS approach consists of two categories, (a) comprehensive guideline and (b) process activities. The comprehensive guideline defines the major role of teachers, the activities of learners, and the process activities to provide detailed procedures of collaborative learning with strategies that both teachers and learners can use. The CoI guideline indicates specific actions of teachers according to the plan (design and organization) and implementation (facilitation, and direct instruction) phases. The social presence and cognitive presence of the CoI seem convenient and useful for teachers to plan and implement collaborative learning, considering the important factors affecting online learning. To design CSCL, combinations of those two approaches, instructional design and CoI, could empower higher-order learning through collaboration in a learning community where the CPS is used to form the structure of collaborative learning and CoI uses online communication for quality interactions. Instructional design theories have provided useful guidelines, especially in terms of direct instructions and motivation design in structural formal learning settings. CoI has been developed for learning community and provided meaningful guidelines for online communications. For effective and interesting CSCL, it may be beneficial to integrate pre-existing approaches for traditional face-to-face instructions and newer approaches of changing pedagogical and technological theories for learning. In order to improve education and learning with technology, further research is required to address the study's limitations.

This chapter discussed the application of the CoI framework used to design asynchronous online discussion for EFL learners. The asynchronous online discussion setting is particularly effective for EFL learners because it provides sufficient time for learners to read other contributor's comments, think about those comments, and write their thoughts. The discussion could add useful information such as practical usage of the CoI framework for researchers who seek to determine the validity of the CoI framework. Furthermore, this research could be a useful tool for practitioners to use when they design and implement collaborative learning environments for non-native English speakers.

REFERENCES

Abrams, Z. I. (2003). The effect of synchronous and asynchronous CMC on oral performance in German. *Modern Language Journal*, *87*(2), 157–167. doi:10.1111/1540-4781.00184

Barnes, S. B. (2008). Understanding social media from the media ecological perspective. In Konijn, E. A., Utz, S., Tanis, M., & Barnes, S. B. (Eds.), *Mediated interpersonal communication* (pp. 14–33). New York, NY: Routledge.

Benbunan-Fich, R., Hiltz, S. R., & Harasim, L. (2005). The online interaction learning model: An integrated theoretical framework for learning networks. In Hiltz, S. R., & Goldman, R. (Eds.), *Learning together online - Research on asynchronous learning networks* (pp. 19–37). Mahwah, NJ: Lawrence Erlbaum Associates.

Brown, R. E. (2001). The process of community-building in distance learning classes. *The Internet and Higher Education*, *5*(2), 18–35.

Chapelle, C. A. (2001). *Computer applications in second language acquisition – Foundations for teaching, testing and research*. Cambridge, UK: Cambridge University Press.

Chun, D. (1994). Using computer-assisted class discussion to facilitate the acquisition of interactive competence. In Swaffar, J., Romano, S., Arens, K., & Markley, P. (Eds.), *Language learning online: Theory and practice in the ESL and L2 computer classroom* (pp. 57–80). Austin, TX: Labyrinth Publications.

Clark, H. H. (1994). Managing problems in speaking. *Speech Communication, 15,* 243–250. doi:10.1016/0167-6393(94)90075-2

Cohen, J., Cohen, P., West, S., & Aiken, L. (2003). *Applied multiple regression/correlation analysis for the behavioral sciences* (3rd ed.). Hillsdale, NJ: Lawrence Erlbaum Associates.

Davis, G. A., & Thomas, M. A. (1989). *Effective schools and effective teachers.* Needham Heights, MA: Allyn & Bacon.

Digiano, C., Goldman, S., & Chorost, M. (2008). *Educating learning technology designers.* New York, NY: Routledge.

Furstenberg, G. (1987). Teaching with technology: What is at stake? *ADFL Bulletin, 28*(3), 21–25.

Garrison, D. R. (2011). *E-learning in the 21st century: A framework for research and practice.* New York, NY: Routledge.

Garrison, D. R., & Arbaugh, J. B. (2007). Researching the community of inquiry framework: Review, issues, and future directions. *The Internet and Higher Education, 10*(3), 157–172. doi:10.1016/j.iheduc.2007.04.001

Garrison, D. R., & Cleveland-Innes, M. (2005). Facilitating cognitive presence in online learning: Interaction is not enough. *American Journal of Distance Education, 19*(3), 133–148. doi:10.1207/s15389286ajde1903_2

Garrison, D. R., Cleveland-Innes, M., Koole, M., & Kappelman, J. (2006). Revisting methodological issues in the analysis of transcripts: Negotiated coding and reliability. *The Internet and Higher Education, 9*(1), 1–8. doi:10.1016/j.iheduc.2005.11.001

Harre, R. (2001). The discursive turn in social psychology. In Schiffrin, D., Tannen, D., & Hamilton, H. E. (Eds.), *The handbook of discourse analysis.* Malden, MA: Blackwell Publishing.

Hiltz, S. R., & Goldman, R. (2005). What are asynchronous learning networks? In Hiltz, S. R., & Goldman, R. (Eds.), *Learning together online: Research on asynchronous learning networks* (pp. 3–18). Mahwah, NJ: Lawrence Erlbaum Associates.

Keller, J. M. (2010). *Motivational design for learning and performance: The ARCS model approach.* New York, NY: Springer. doi:10.1007/978-1-4419-1250-3

Kelm, O. (1992). The use of synchronous computer networks in second language instruction: A preliminary report. *Foreign Language Annals, 25*(5), 441–454. doi:10.1111/j.1944-9720.1992.tb01127.x

King, A. (2007). Scripting collaborative learning processes: A cognitive perspective. In Fischer, F., Koller, I., Mandl, H., & Haake, J. M. (Eds.), *Scripting computer-supported collaborative learning – Cognitive, computational and educational perspectives.* New York, NY: Shpringer. doi:10.1007/978-0-387-36949-5_2

Krashen, S. (1985). *The input hypothesis: Issues and implications.* London, UK: Longman.

Lamy, M.-N., & Hampel, R. (2007). *Online communication in language learning and teaching.* Hampshire, UK: Pagrave Macmillan. doi:10.1057/9780230592681

Lee, L. (2002). Synchronous online exchanges: A study of modification devices on non-native discourse. *System, 30,* 275–288. doi:10.1016/S0346-251X(02)00015-5

Long, M. (1981). Input, interaction, and second language acquisition. *Annals of the New York Academy of Sciences, 379,* 259–279. doi:10.1111/j.1749-6632.1981.tb42014.x

Long, M. (1989). Task, group, and task-group interactions. *University of Hawaii's Working Papers in ESL, 8*(2), 1-26.

Morris, F. (2005). Child-to-child interaction and corrective feedback in a computer mediated L2 class. *Language Learning & Technology, 9*(1), 29–45.

Nelson, L. M. (1999). Collaborative problem solving. In Reigeluth, C. M. (Ed.), *Instructional-design theories and models, II.* Mahwah, NJ: Lawrence Erlbaum Associates.

Reneland-Forsman, L., & Ahlbäck, T. (2007). Collaboration as quality interaction in web-based learning. *Journal Advanced Technology for Learning, 4*, 30–35.

Rennie, F., & Morrison, T. (2007). *E-learning and social networking handbook: Resources for higher education.* New York, NY: Routledge.

Schiffrin, D., Tannen, D., & Hamilton, H. E. (Eds.). (2001). *The handbook of discourse analysis.* Malden, MA: Blackwell Publishing.

Shipman, S., & Shipman, V. C. (1985). Cognitive styles: Some conceptual, methodological, and applied issues. In Gordon, E. W. (Ed.), *Review of research in education* (*Vol. 12*). Washington, DC: American Educational Research Association. doi:10.2307/1167151

Smith, B. (2002). The use of communication strategies in computer-mediated communication. *System, 31*, 29–53. doi:10.1016/S0346-251X(02)00072-6

Swain, M. (1995). Three functions of output in second language learning. In Cook, G., & Seidhofer, B. (Eds.), *Principle and practice in applied linguistics* (pp. 125–144). Oxford, UK: Oxford University Press.

Swan, K. (2003). Developing social presence in online discussions. In Naidu, S. (Ed.), *Learning and teaching with technology: Principles and practices* (pp. 147–164). London, UK: Kogan Page.

Swan, K., Shea, P., Richardson, J., Ice, P., Garrison, D. R., Cleveland-Innes, M., & Arbaugh, J. B. (2008). Validating a measurement tool of presence in online communities of inquiry. *E-Mentor, 2*(24), 1–12.

Weller, M., & Mason, R. (2000). Evaluating an open university web course: Issues and innovations. In Asensio, M., Foster, J., Hodgson, V., & McConnell, D. (Eds.), *Networked learning 2000: Innovative approaches to lifelong learning and higher education through the internet* (pp. 361–368).

Yamada, M. (2009). The role of social presence in learner-centered communicative language learning using synchronous computer-mediated communication: Experimental study. *Computers & Education, 52*(4), 820–833. doi:10.1016/j.compedu.2008.12.007

ADDITIONAL READING

Arnold, N., & Ducate, L. (2006). Future foreign language teachers' social and cognitive collaboration in an online environment. *Language Learning & Technology, 10*(1), 42–66.

Arnold, N., Ducate, L., Lomicka, L., & Lord, G. (2005). Using computer-mediated communication to establish social and supportive environments in teacher Education. *CALICO Journal, 22*(3), 537–566.

Cooke-Plagwitz, J. (2008). New directions in CALL: An objective introduction to Second Life. *CALICO Journal, 25*(3), 547–557.

Derks, D., Fischer, A. H., & Bos, A. E. R. (2008). The role of emotion in computer-mediated communication: A review. *Computers in Human Behavior, 24*, 766–785. doi:10.1016/j.chb.2007.04.004

Develotte, C., Guichon, N., & Vincent, C. (2010). The use of the webcam for teaching a foreign language in a desktop videoconferencing environment. *ReCALL, 22*(3), 293–312. doi:10.1017/S0958344010000170

Fernandez-Garcia, M., & Martinez-Arbelaiz, A. (2002). Negotiation of meaning in nonnative speaker-nonnative speaker synchronous discussions. *CALICO Journal, 19*(2), 279–294.

Gass, S., Mackey, A., & Pica, T. (1998). The role of input and interaction in second language acquisition. *Modern Language Journal, 82*(3), 299–305. doi:10.1111/j.1540-4781.1998.tb01206.x

Gass, S. M., & Varonis, E. M. (1989). Incorporated repairs in nonnative discourse. In Eisenstein, M. (Ed.), *The dynamic interlanguage: Empirical studies in Second language variation* (pp. 71–86). New York, NY: Plenum Press.

Jepson, K. (2005). Conversations – and negotiated interaction – in text and voice chat rooms. *Language Learning & Technology, 9*(3), 79–98.

Ko, C.-J. (2012). A case study of language learners' social presence in synchronous CMC. *ReCALL, 24*(1), 66–84. doi:10.1017/S0958344011000292

Lee, L. (2005). Using web-based instruction to promote active learning: Learners' perspectives. *CALICO Journal, 23*(1), 139–156.

Levy, M., & Stockwell, G. (2006). *CALL dimensions: Options & issues in computer assisted language learning*. Mahwah, NJ: Lawrence Erlbaum Associates.

Lomicka, L., & Lord, G. (2007). Social presence in virtual communities of foreign language (FL) teachers. *System, 35*, 208–228. doi:10.1016/j.system.2006.11.002

O'Dowd, R. (2005). Negotiating sociocultural and institutional contexts: The case of Spanish-American telecollaboration. *Language and Intercultural Communication, 5*(1), 40–57. doi:10.1080/14708470508668882

Salaberry, R. M. (2000). Pedagogical design of computer mediated communication tasks: Learning objectives and technological capabilities. *Modern Language Journal, 84*(1), 28–37. doi:10.1111/0026-7902.00050

Savignon, S. J., & Roithmeier, W. (2004). Computer-mediated communication; Texts and strategies. *CALICO Journal, 21*(2), 265–290.

Smith, B. (2003). Computer-mediated negotiated interaction: An expanded model. *Modern Language Journal, 87*(1), 38–57. doi:10.1111/1540-4781.00177

Van Lier, L. (1996). *Interaction in the language curriculum: Awareness, autonomy, and authenticity*. London, UK: Longman.

Warchauer, M. (1997). Computer-mediated collaborative learning: Theory and practice. *Modern Language Journal, 81*(4), 471–481.

Warschauer, M. (1996). Comparing face-to-face and electronic discussion in the second language classroom. *CALICO Journal, 13*(2-3), 7–26.

Weng, P.-D., Chou, T.-C., & Wu, T.-C. (2011). An interactive synchronous e-learning system for corporate knowledge management: Lessons learned from saveCom. *Communications in Computer and Information Science, 217*(4), 279–287. doi:10.1007/978-3-642-23339-5_51

Yamada, M., & Akahori, K. (2007). Social presence in synchronous CMC-based language learning - How does it affect the productive performance and consciousness of learning objectives? *Computer Assisted Language Learning, 20*(1), 37–65. doi:10.1080/09588220601118503

Yamada, M., & Goda, Y. (2012). Application of social presence principles to CSCL design for quality interactions. In Jia, J. (Ed.), *Educational stages and interactive learning: From kindergarden to workplace training* (pp. 31–48). Hershey, PA: IGI Global. doi:10.4018/978-1-4666-0137-6.ch003

Yamada, M., & Kitamura, S. (2011). The role of social presence in interactive learning with social software. In White, B., King, I., & Tsang, P. (Eds.), *Social media tools and platforms in learning environments: Present and future* (pp. 325–335). Springer. doi:10.1007/978-3-642-20392-3_19

Yang, Y.-F. (2011). Engaging students in an online situated language learning environment. *Computer Assisted Language Learning*, *24*(2), 181–198. doi:10.1080/09588221.2010.538700

Zähner, C., Fauverge, A., & Wong, J. (2000). Task-based language learning via audiovisual networks: The LEVERAGE project. In Warschauer, M., & Kern, R. (Eds.), *Network-based language teaching: Concepts and practice* (pp. 186–203). Cambridge, UK: Cambridge University Press.

KEY TERMS AND DEFINITIONS

Community of Inquiry (COI): Community which teachers and learners interact in text-based online communication.

Computer Assisted Language Learning (CALL): Technology- use for enhancing language learning.

Computer-Mediated Communication (CMC): Communication using communication tools such as e-mail, BBS, chat.

Computer Supported Collaborative Learning (CSCL): Learning promoted by interactions and communication mediated electronic tools including both synchronous (e.g., video-conferencing, chat) and asynchronous systems (e.g., bbs, mailing list).

English as a Foreign Language (EFL): English viewed from non-native English speakers.

Instructional Design: Systematic design of instruction to increase its effectiveness, efficiency, and attraction. It usually includes five elements and steps: analysis, design, development, implementation, and evaluation.

Social Media: Communication media for social interaction, which promotes interpersonal communication.

Chapter 15
The Case for the Community of Inquiry (CoI) Influencing Student Retention

Katrina Meyer
University of Memphis, USA

ABSTRACT

This chapter reviews the research on the CoI framework and student retention and relates the CoI framework to existing retention theories developed for the pre-Internet world and for online learning. The ability of the CoI framework to improve student retention is discussed as well as the relative impact the framework may have on retention, given other influences on retention as captured by several retention theories. A theoretical link between the CoI framework and retention is proposed, through the intermediary of student learning.

INTRODUCTION

As earning a college degree becomes ever more essential to positive life outcomes for students, student success will become more important for society. Students, parents, government funders, businesses, and higher education institutions want students to enroll and stay enrolled through graduation. Unfortunately, higher education budgets face further constraints at the same time as the public wants the educational process to be more efficient, both on the part of students using higher education resources but also on the part of

higher education institutions providing services that help students enroll, learn necessary skills and knowledge, and graduate.

This is why increased attention has been placed on the retention (usually captured by the rate that first-year students return for their sophomore year) or persistence (from fall term to fall term and on to graduation) of students in college, be they in face-to-face or online programs. The problem, as it has been characterized in the press, has been lower rates of retention in online programs that have raised concern about the quality of online programs. The proposal to be explored in this

DOI: 10.4018/978-1-4666-2110-7.ch015

chapter is whether the Community of Inquiry (CoI) framework for online learning can deliver improved retention rates at a time when both students and higher education institutions need to be more efficient with constrained personal and institutional resources.

BACKGROUND

The Retention Problem

The data on retention of online programs is, however, neither clear nor consistent. Jenkins (2011), citing "countless studies," claimed success rates in online courses "of only 50 percent – as opposed to 70-to-75 percent for comparable face-to-face classes" (Jenkins, 2011, ¶3). Unfortunately, such claims as this one are common in the popular literature, and show neither online learning nor face-to-face courses in a particularly good light and may be inaccurate as well. A recent email exchange on a listserv devoted to distance and online learning about online retention rates elicited more detailed responses from representatives of several institutions. The California Community Colleges and Broward College had online retention rates that were 7% below face-to-face retention rates and Montgomery College had a retention rate for online and blended courses that was 4% lower than for face-to-face courses. Both Athabasca University and the North Dakota University System found that 85% of undergraduate students finished their online courses. On the other hand, the University of Memphis has experienced the opposite phenomenon: Online courses have pass rates above, and failure and withdrawal rates below, students in on-campus courses. These figures present a situation where retention data for online courses is not as bad as some may think, and may be improving as experience with designing and delivering online courses is gained.

The CoI Framework

The Community of Inquiry (CoI) framework posits three "presences" – social, teaching, and cognitive – which, when combined, create an effective learning community in the online course. Social presence focuses on the ability of students to project their personalities during course discussions, communicate clearly and well, create trust among course participants, and develop interpersonal relationships with others in the course. Teaching presence stresses the design, facilitation, and direction of the course's activities, projects, and/or discussion, be it by the instructor or others. Cognitive presence focuses on the process of practical reflection, including the development or construction of meaning through a four-stage process (triggering question, exploration, integration, and resolution). When the three presences overlap, students can benefit from a cohesive educational experience that creates community and engenders learning.

THE EVIDENCE FOR COI'S INFLUENCE ON STUDENT RETENTION

Introduction

This section tackles two issues. First, what is the evidence that the CoI impacts student retention, and second, what processes might explain this impact? While the CoI framework was not developed to tackle the problem of student retention, researchers immediately investigated whether online coursework purposefully designed to create the behaviors within each of the three presences encouraged learning to occur. As this research developed further, attention began to be paid to the framework's effect on student retention. Research on the CoI framework has found both separate influences for each presence as well as combinations of presences on retention.

Social Presence

The evidence that achieving social presence in an online class has an impact on student retention comes from several studies. In a survey of over 28,000 students at the American Public University System, Boston, Diaz, Gibson, Ice, Richardson, and Swan (2009) found that 21 of the 34 CoI items were statistically significant predictors of retention, and eight of these 21 items were for elements of social presence, nine were for cognitive presence, and four for teaching presence. A total of 20.2% of the variance in student re-enrollment was accounted for by two social presence indicators ("Online or web-based communication is an excellent medium for social interaction" and "I was able to form distinct impressions of some course participants") and 88% of the social presence items were significant predictors of student retention. Positive findings for the role of social presence in student retention have also been found by Liu, Gomez, and Yen (2009).

The relationship of social presence to retention may be a complicated one. In Diaz, Swan, Ice, and Kupczynski (2010), students rated the importance of each CoI survey item and produced the lowest mean score for social presence items (m=3.52) when teaching presence items were rated highest (m=4.05). This may capture students' perception that social presence is not as important as what teachers are expected to do. Or perhaps students are more influenced by social presence than they suspect, or the influence is largely unconscious. It may be that the role played by social presence on retention is also hidden by students' perceptions of what ought to matter in their decision to stay or leave school.

Another way that social presence may impact retention is through learning. Picciano (2002) found positive significant relationships between students' assessment of interaction and participation and their learning in the course. Russo and Benson (2005) found significant correlations between students' perceptions of other students in the course and satisfaction with their own learning. After redesigning courses to incorporate more collaborative learning requiring interaction with others, Vaughan (2010) found that the retention rate climbed to 100% in the redesigned courses. For these students, a successful learning experience – aided by social presence – may contribute to the decision to stay enrolled. These studies seem to support the role of social presence in the decision to stay in college, perhaps mediated by the student's learning.

This connection – from social presence through learning to retention – is supported by the decision of Garrison (2011) to reconceptualize social presence to be more learning centered. Rather than being non-learning-related interactions, social presence is comprised of more purposeful or learning-related interactions. This change aligns social presence more closely with course learning outcomes which confirms the importance of interactions that are focused on learning that Picciano (2002) found.

Teaching Presence

Let us now return attention to the research on teaching presence in the CoI framework. The Boston et al. (2009) study (as mentioned earlier) found four of its 17 significant indicators of retention to be from teaching presence, or one-third of all teaching presence items on the CoI survey. Meyer, Bruwelheide, and Poulin (2006) surveyed adult students in a certificate program that had 97% retention and asked them to evaluate how valuable 23 items from the CoI framework were in influencing their decision to stay enrolled. All three of the teaching presence constructs were valued highly based on a five-point Likert scale: Instructional design and organization (m=4.63), facilitate discourse (m=4.56), and direct instruction (m=4.50). All of these means were higher than other items related to online learning (e.g., convenience), Tinto's (1987) model of student attrition, and other retention models (to be discussed in a later section).

Other studies focus on the role of teaching presence on student learning, which may strengthen the influence of teaching presence on retention. In a study of course-level disenrollment investigated through the lens of the CoI, Ice, Gibson, Boston, and Becher (2011) found that effective "instructional design and organization" (an element of teaching presence) was a significant predictor of student satisfaction but "facilitation of discourse and cognitive integration" (also teaching presence) was a negative predictor of satisfaction. This intriguing inconsistency may be a reflection of individual instructor activities or have another explanation. In an investigation of instructional design (one of the main elements of teaching presence), Kupczynski, David, Ice, and Callejo (2008) found no significant relationship between elements of instructional design and organization and student learning. What is interesting is that when asked what factors contributed to their success, 20.9% of the factors were in instructional design and organization, but 37.1% of the factors contributed to a lack of success. These results, and perhaps the Ice et al. (2011) results as well, may mean that students who learn see elements of instructional design as having a modest role to play but instructional design gets more of the blame if they do not learn as well as they ought. This finding may be similar to that of Diaz, Swan, Ice, and Kupczynski (2010) above, which found that students minimized the role of social presence in their learning as well. These studies may capture a human need to attribute one's success more to one's own efforts than the situation or context.

Cognitive Presence

The third "presence," cognitive presence, captures the thinking process that students go through to solve problems, from a "triggering question," to exploration, integration, and resolution. It is known as "practical inquiry" and it depends upon becoming aware of a problem (triggering question), deliberating on its aspects (exploration), developing ideas about the problem (integration), and moving to action (resolution). In the only study that looked at cognitive presence and student retention of over 27,000 students, Boston et al. (2009) found that nine factors that comprise cognitive presence were significant indicators (these were 75% of all the cognitive presence items) of retention. In terms of student satisfaction, Ice et al. (2011) found that the triggering event phase of cognitive presence was a significant predictor of student satisfaction. Perhaps the other phases (exploration, integration, resolution) are more influential for learning, but are harder or more demanding to do and thus less likely to be credited by students as satisfying.

Prior studies have investigated the role of cognitive presence in online discussions (Meyer, 2004, 2003) as well as other online strategies for student interaction, such as debates, case studies, and open-ended discussions (Richardson & Ice, 2010). While students preferred the open-ended discussions, a greater percentage of students reached the integration stage in case-based discussions (78%) and debates (77%) than open-ended discussions (60%). Shea and Bidjerano (2009) also found that achieving higher-order thinking required that instructors help students gain comfort and understanding of what critical thinking entailed. Such studies argue for a more structured approach to online communications rather than "hoping for the best" or relying on students' interest in thinking more critically.

What is more intriguing, however, is the role that social and teacher presence may have on cognitive presence. Archibald (2010) found that teaching and social presence explained 69% of the variance in cognitive presence even after controlling for a variety of prior experiences with online learning and collaborative learning as well as learning readiness. This makes sense and is supported by Rodriguez, Plax, and Kearney (1996), who found that teacher presence influenced cognitive learning which may capture the ability of teachers and students to go beyond passive knowledge acquisition (such as in a lecture) and make learning more active and based on interactions with others, which of course includes teachers. These three studies (Archibald, 2010; Rodriguez et al., 1996; Shea & Bidjerano, 2009) recognize the way the CoI framework captures an interaction between and among the presences, achieving a mutually-supportive learning experience.

Because the CoI framework was developed in part based on Dewey's (1910) problem-solving process, called by Dewey "reflective thinking," it has a solid basis in subsequent learning theory and instructional methods based on his work. Dewey proposed that reflective thinking followed a pattern that began with a problem, proceeded to analysis, then suggested solutions, reflected on the solutions and weighed their advantages and disadvantages, and then selected the best solution. This has been described as the "discussional pattern or the steps in the discussional process" [Dewey, 1910, p. 16]. This process not only encourages learning, but it can also bring joy and satisfaction to the individual who is using one's intellectual abilities to think, reason, and solve problems. This is more than preparing for a career, but a preparation for thinking critically about all of life's challenges.

And although many earlier studies that look into the CoI or cognitive presence do not address retention *per se*, perhaps a logical connection between learning, cognitive presence, and student retention can be safely hypothesized. If effective online communications bring students to higher levels of cognitive function (say, the integration and resolution stages of cognitive presence), the learning Dewey identified as reflective thinking can also encourage the academic integration that the retention theories (to be discussed in the next section) proposed by Tinto (1987) and Bean and Metzner (1985), would impact retention. These connections bear further exploration and, of course, more detailed research.

COI AND RETENTION THEORIES

Tinto's Theory of Academic Departure

Perhaps the most prominent theory of retention is that of Vincent Tinto (1987, 1999). It was developed prior to the explosion of online learning, and therefore applying this theory to online courses is cause for caution. However, we need to evaluate pre-Internet theories for their reasonable application to this modern learning form. It may be that the phenomenon of retention in the online world is not very different from the face-to-face world, or it may be different, and certainly such comparisons need to be studied. In the meantime, we must rely on the retention theories that are most prominent despite their development prior to online learning.

Tinto (1987, 1998) developed and tested a theory of student departure that has been studied, affirmed, and adjusted by numerous researchers (Astin, 1984; Nora, 1987; Pascarella & Terenzini, 1980; Terenzini & Pascarella, 1997). It is based on two processes of integration into the college or university: academic integration and social integration. Academic integration is affected by the student's academic performance and his/her interactions with faculty and staff, and social integration is affected by the student's involvement with extracurricular activities and peer-group interactions. One can see that these influences – especially the interaction with peers – may have a close corollary in social presence, but are not a perfect fit between the CoI framework and Tinto's (1987) theory. CoI stresses interaction within the online course, while Tinto appears to stress peer interactions more broadly, or those that occur in many other college contexts (e.g., student clubs, social events). So we cannot claim the two – social presence in the CoI and social integration in Tinto -- are exactly the same, but neither do they capture wholly different concepts.

It is important to note that Tinto's (1987) theory includes other variables that are important, such as "pre-entry attributes" (family background, skills and abilities, and prior schooling) and "goals and commitments" (intentions), and the latter do change during college. The full model is reproduced in Figure 1.

As a result of research on this model, Tinto (1998) concluded that "involvement matters" (p. 167). The more involvement students achieve in the academic and social realms, the more likely they are to persist. And the more they see "those interactions as positive and themselves as integrated into the institution" (1998, p. 167], the more likely they will persist in their college studies. However, integration is less important for students at two-year colleges, who – perhaps because these students are more likely to be adults and/or working -- may find their validation and

social lives elsewhere (Rendon, 1994; Terenzini, Rendon, Upcraft, Millar, Allison, Gregg & Jalomo, 1994). Thus, the Tinto Model has been found to be especially helpful in explaining departure of traditional-age students and especially those at four-year colleges, but has been less effective in explaining the departure of adult students, those at two-year colleges, or perhaps online students who may be adults and/or located at a distance from the campus. Another advantage of the Tinto model, however, is in its stressing that institutions can affect student integration. Its widespread use has been partially responsible for the creation of learning communities and Freshman Interest Groups (FIGs) at colleges and universities.

While Tinto (1987) stressed the importance of students' academic integration into the institution, primarily through interactions with faculty and staff, one can detect a possible connection

Figure 1. Tinto's (1994) model of institutional departure

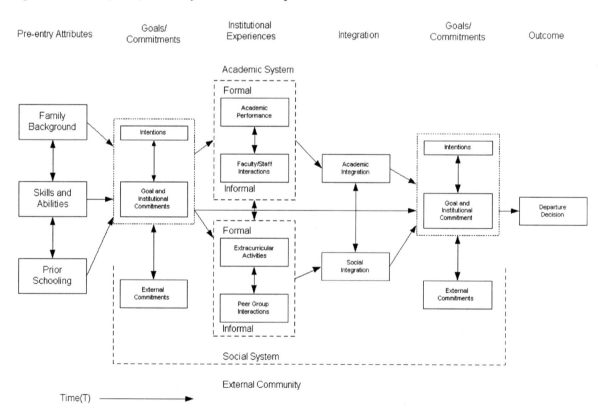

to teaching presence, which relies in part on the interaction with faculty designed into the course through instructional design choices and organization of the online course. As noted earlier, the two concepts – teaching presence in CoI and academic integration in Tinto – are not exactly the same, but they include some similar behaviors in each concept.

The Tinto model may not be completely appropriate for explaining the retention of students in online programs. However, given that this model can be characterized as the original if not most widely accepted model for attrition, any examination of online student retention must include it. Another important point to consider is how or where the CoI framework fits into Tinto's model; in short, CoI seems to fit into Tinto's "academic system." This insight leads to two possible conclusions; first, that the influence of CoI on retention is only a small part of the larger retention model and second, its influence is through maximizing the academic experience of students enrolled in online courses. Both of these insights will be taken up again in discussions of other retention theories.

Bean and Metzner's Retention Theory

Perhaps the theory of student attrition (i.e., dropping out of college) developed by Bean and Metzner (1985) and Metzner and Bean (1987) can be usefully applied to understanding student retention in online classes. Bean and Metzner studied nontraditional student attrition, including adults and part-time students. While not all online students are nontraditional, many online students are, so applying this retention theory to online and distance education may be somewhat more fruitful for this discussion. It is also important to remember that Bean and Metzner's theory was developed many years prior to online learning and may not be perfectly applicable to online learning in ways that have not been studied.

Bean and Metzner's (1985) model (see Figure 2) contrasts with Tinto's (1987) and describes a student who is less influenced by social integration with his or her peers at the institution and places greater influence on the utility of the education being received, as well as greater influence on encouragement from friends, employers, and family. However, academic integration (Tinto's concept) – meaning success in learning and interaction with faculty and staff – is perhaps even more influential for these students. In any case, these are modifications to Tinto's theory that make imminent sense: adults are more likely to be pursuing post-secondary education to train for a new job or to gain sufficient skills for professional advancement. They are perhaps more focused on achieving their goals (e.g., finishing the program, gaining the skills needed), and learning is therefore more important than the social aspects of college. Their friendships are already in place through their jobs, neighborhoods, and families, and these friendships matter in terms of providing encouragement for enrolling and sticking with their college coursework. These insights were confirmed by Grosset (1991), whose study of community college students found that social integration was more important to younger students (17-24) than older students (25+), study skills (essential to academic success) were the most important predictor of attrition for older students, and cognitive and personal development as well as goal commitment was important for persistence for all groups.

The model also places greater emphasis on external factors, such as the availability of finances to pay for college as well as work and family obligations (which will be taken up in a later section). In any case, "perceptions of utility" (a Bean and Metzner term) in the online course or program would make a difference to the adult online student and would likely impact the ability of the CoI-designed course to encourage greater student retention. One might expect that the Bean and Metzner (1985) model will be more

Figure 2. Bean and Metzner's (1985) theory of student attrition

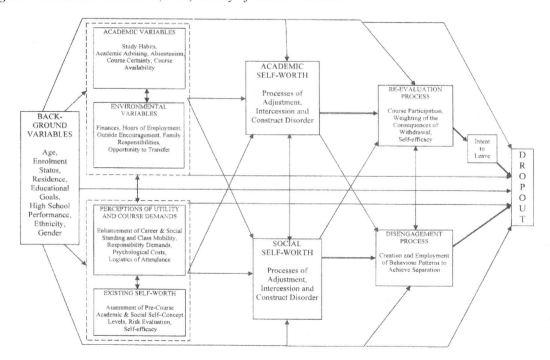

influential in explaining the behavior of the students in online programs, who tend to include more adults or more individuals with instrumental aims for enrolling in an online course (such as earning credit to complete a program or enrolling in a course that is offered in a convenient format). This expectation must be borne out by further research but makes sense based on the findings of Meyer et al. (2006), which focused on the near-perfect retention of adults enrolled in an online professional certification program. Terezini et al. (1994) also chronicled differences in college involvement among diverse types of students from different types of schools (liberal arts, community college, large university). Perhaps the student – and his age or her career needs; her ethnicity or his college type – play a bigger role than currently recognized in determining retention and the relative importance of teaching or other presences.

Much like Tinto's (1987) model, the CoI fits within only a subpart of the Bean and Metzner (1985) model. In short, one can see the CoI affect-

ing the variables labeled as "perceptions of utility and course demands," although CoI is clearly more than these concepts. Again, this relationship of the CoI to Bean and Metzner's model leads to two insights; first, that the influence of CoI on retention is only a small part of the larger retention model and second, its influence is through maximizing the academic experience of students enrolled in online courses.

Other Models and Influences on Retention

Berge and Huang (2004) summarized the influences on retention including sociological influences (including social forces), organizational influences (including policies, organizational characteristics, and administrative processes), economic influences (including cost and cost-benefit analyses), and psychological influences (including a range of personal and psychological characteristics). One can see elements of these four types of influences in Tinto's (1987) and

Bean and Metzner's (1985) models of retention. However, the final model proposed by Berge and Huang (2004) presents only three types of variables: personal, institutional, and circumstantial. This combination of variables makes the model context-sensitive, and allows institutions to take the delivery method (e.g., online coursework) and the design of online courses into consideration as they develop approaches aimed to improve student retention. The model is not so different from those of Tinto or Bean and Metzner, but has the advantage of being developed with online learning in mind. However, while it acknowledges the full range of influences mentioned earlier, it focuses on those elements that institutions can control (e.g., the design of online coursework) and places less emphasis on external influences like the role of finances and work obligations.

Rovai (2003) also developed a retention model that combined the more relevant portions of the models of Tinto (1987) and Bean and Metzner (1985) for the online student. The final model (Figure 3) does not incorporate all elements of the Berge and Huang (2004) model, but does add the need for appropriate learning skills for the online mode, such as computer literacy, information literacy, and time management. Muse (2003) confirmed the importance of these skills when he studied community college students who dropped out of web-based courses. The reason most often given was the student's inability to get access to or install the learning materials. This seems an obvious external factor and stresses the importance of knowing students' capability for online instruction and not assuming that all students are technology literate when they enroll. In another study of community college students, Doherty (2006) found that lack of time management skills and procrastination were primary reasons for failing or dropping out of a web-based course. Not surprisingly, Holder (2007) found that persisters in distance learning programs scored higher on time and study management skills as well as self-efficacy. In another study of 354 online students,

Morris, Finnegan and Wu (2005) investigated computer logs and the frequency and duration of student participation in the learning management system. Approximately 31% of the variance in completion rates was derived from the student participation measures. These studies confirm that students bear responsibility for their own success or completion of a course, be it through a serious pursuit of learning and practicing time management skills or logging into the course and participating in its activities.

But Rovai (2003) also notes the importance of pedagogical choices of instructors and student learning styles in his model. This area – of pedagogical choices -- is likely where the CoI framework might fit best were a comprehensive model be attempted. If this is true, then it places the role of CoI in student retention into a much larger context (as was true for the CoI and Tinto's and Bean and Metzner's models), one which assigns to CoI an influence but also recognizes a range of other influences captured in the larger models. Put simply, CoI may influence student retention because it is an important academic experience that influences student retention. Although this may seem untoward to suggest, perhaps the Tinto and Bean and Metzner models might be revised to add an influence for the design of the online course and its influence on student retention.

External Factors

It is fair at this stage to pose a question: To what extent could CoI influence student retention? Or perhaps the more comprehensive question to answer first is, what are the other external influences on retention?

As Bean and Metzner (1985) proposed and Rovai (2003) included in his model, external factors can and do influence the student's ability to stay enrolled in college. These external factors include finances, work responsibilities, transfer credits, and life crises. The research on retention

Figure 3. Rovai's (2003) model of persistence in online programs

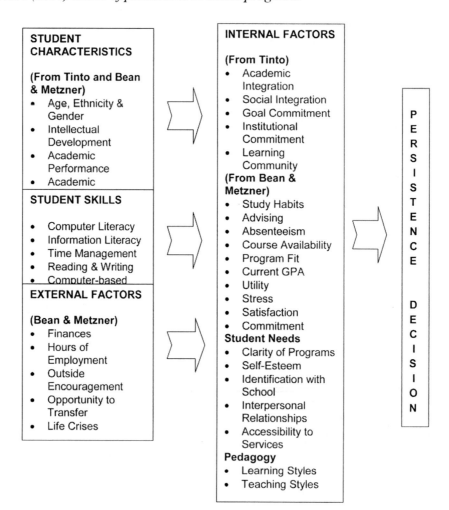

confirms the importance of these, especially in regards to online students.

The ability of students to transfer credits into a program, enroll in more than one course per term, and accumulate credits toward a degree has been found to decrease student dropout rates (Boston, Ice & Gibson, 2011; Boston & Ice, 2011). This relationship may be simply explained, as a student accrues (or transfers in) credits, he or she becomes more committed to finishing the degree and finishing becomes more conceivable or within one's grasp. Or as Boston (2010) concludes, a student who takes only one or two courses per

year will need approximately 10 years to finish, and "a 10-year commitment may be easier to walk away from in the early stages than after a substantial amount of credits have been earned" (para. 9). In fact, 40.3% of students at an online university who dropped out (Boston, 2010) did so after taking only two courses and 65.3% who dropped out took four or fewer classes. So students with fewer course credits earned are the most likely to drop out, which certainly justifies focusing institutional attention on those students (be they freshman, transfers, and other types of students) who are enrolled for the first time.

Also, grades do matter and the experience of getting a D or F grade or withdrawing from a class also impacts the decision to drop out (Boston & Ice, 2011; Boston, et al., 2011). This is the same concept that is included in "institutional experiences" in Tinto's model (Figure 1) and "internal factors" in Bean and Metzner (Figure 2), so there appears to be a solid theoretical foundation for saying that success matters, and doing well in class helps the student not only be able to, but want to, continue his or her education.

The individuals who administer online and distance programs have been aware of the problems that students express, from feeling disconnected to the course and other students to being inconsistent or undisciplined in their involvement with the class. A number of "engagement" techniques have been proposed to offset these problems, from having faculty call the student at home to their providing clearer instructions and breaking the class into smaller groups for discussion in the hope that students will connect with each other. However, in a study where half the students received the faculty's extra effort and the other half did not, these engagement strategies had little or no impact on dropout rates (Leeds, Campbell, Ali, Brawley & Crisp, in press). Does this imply that these techniques never work or that they cannot overcome other contributors to student attrition? This is a problem with research that focuses on some influences on retention without incorporating all or most of the influences outlined in prior models. Studying one tactic for improving retention in isolation will likely produce incomplete understanding of what is going on. In any case, the Leeds et al. (in press) findings are different from those of Sweet (1986) who found that distance education students did respond to direct telephone contact from the faculty and other students and these contacts helped them continue in their studies. Clearly, further research needs to expand on our understanding of the effectiveness of various engagement strategies, but perhaps these strategies are not effective for some students who face work demands, for example, or are effective when combined with other factors, such as a well-designed course or a strong personal or professional commitment or need to finishing the course. A more comprehensive approach is needed to this research on engagement strategies.

What perhaps is made clear from this review of external factors is that institutions and students cannot ignore that many non-traditional students, especially many online students, have other obligations and demands on their time, from full-time jobs to families to the inevitable crises that occur in life. These obligations necessarily take time and attention away from schoolwork and lessen the likelihood that students earn the grades they need to continue and to enroll in more than a course per term. And since, given the economic hard times both institutions and students are experiencing, there may be little that institutions can do about this.

COI AND LEARNING: THE INFLUENCE ON RETENTION

The larger issue is whether online learning, designed with the Community of Inquiry framework in mind, can offset both the external influences discussed above as well as other kinds of influences that contribute to a student's decision to leave a course or program. If the CoI can influence students in this situation, it will be to make the learning experience more involving and the learning more productive thereby encouraging engagement and the joy of learning on the part of the student. Ample evidence exists from the research literature on the CoI that the framework, and the elements that comprise it, do influence learning outcomes. Swan, Matthews, Bogle, Boles, and Day (in press) found evidence that a CoI-designed course did improve student learning outcomes. Reviews of CoI research by Garrison and Arbaugh (2007) and Garrison (2007; 2011) prove that the framework can and does improve the likelihood that learning will occur. What is argued here is that there is a link between the CoI framework to learning and from learning to retention. That link is not unique, of course, but is based on several retention models, such as Tinto's "academic integration" and Bean and Metzner's "utility" and Rovai's "pedagogical" choices. It requires further study to establish if learning is the moderating or connecting variable in the CoI-to-retention relationship as proposed in Figure 4.

The conceptual model in Figure 4 recognizes that the CoI is perhaps one influence on retention, but neither the only nor perhaps even the strongest influence. The external factors (such as being employed full time or having family obligations, financial need, appropriate technical equipment, family support and encouragement), academic factors (such as pedagogical choices, course demands and design, perception of utility), social factors (such as peer or teacher interaction, involvement in campus groups or events), and other factors (such as time and management skills, life crises, progress toward a degree) all may play a role in influencing the student's decision to stay in college. How these various factors interact with each other or interact with the CoI will need to be investigated and the unique contributions of

each factor determined. It will also be necessary to investigate whether these influences are different for different students. Ultimately, these several factors may also influence how well the CoI-designed course can influence learning as well. The model in Figure 4 is an attempt to look at retention in online courses in a more comprehensive manner and will likely lead to specific insights that are more helpful to an institution desirous of changing its policies or practices to encourage more students to stay enrolled in their online studies.

If learning is the intermediary between the CoI and retention as is argued here, it will likely operate through one of several mechanisms. For example, a student may decide that if the learning experience is good enough, he may sleep a little less or find time to study before or after work or during weekends and evenings. Or the learning brings satisfaction to the student and she may rearrange other obligations and work harder to learn as much as she can. However, we need to recognize that while a course may be designed with the CoI in mind, a student's other obligations may take precedence over enrollment and this may be the best decision for them at the time. In other words, the CoI is no more a "magic bullet"

Figure 4. Proposed model connecting COI, learning, and retention

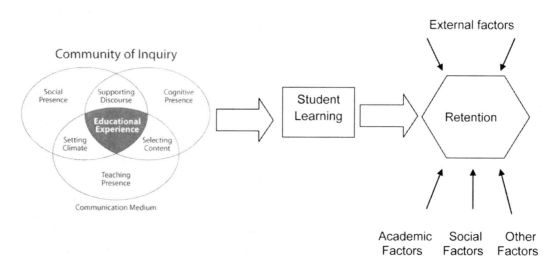

in the search for a solution to student retention than other solutions that have been promoted.

SOLUTIONS AND RECOMMENDATIONS

This fairly extensive discussion of the CoI framework and student retention theories can conclude with some tentative recommendations. First, under the category of "do no harm," online courses should continue to be designed using the best of what is known about how to encourage student learning in online courses. Clearly, the CoI framework is such an approach, as are such best practices in online course design as Quality Matters (http://www.qmprogram.org). As higher education institutions, we owe students the best we can deliver in the online setting.

Second, if the retention theories of Tinto (1987) and Bean and Metzner (1985) are helpful in placing the CoI into a larger theoretical context, the CoI can be used to improve online student retention. The principles of "academic integration" and "utility" can be maximized by using the CoI to design courses that require active student learning, consistent and challenging involvement with the content, and efforts to connect what is learned with the student's current and future professional or practical needs. The CoI can engage students with faculty and other students and challenge students to expand their thinking while tackling their online assignments or discussions. For younger, more traditional-aged online students, the issues may be planning for and developing tools that help them learn how to learn online and to develop self-discipline in their study habits.

Third, the argument so far has been that the CoI framework could be one of the influences on retention, but perhaps it cannot overcome the influence of external factors. Even were we as institutions and faculty to do everything we can to design courses that involve and connect students, students will drop out as a result of facing one of

life's challenges. And adult, online students face challenges to their study, from paying rising fees to finding time to study to handling multiple and pressing demands. Excellent online programs may continue to experience some student attrition simply because one student may lose a job, or his parent becomes ill, or her child needs greater attention. These life events happen to students and will continue to happen in the future.

FUTURE RESEARCH DIRECTIONS

This chapter has identified several research needs, including measuring the separate or unique impact of CoI-designed courses on student retention. Does a CoI course offset external factors such as a job loss or mitigate other student qualities such as poor study skills or lack of self-discipline? In other words, what is its impact relative to other factors that we know influence a student's decision to leave college? Furthermore, does a CoI-designed course interact or mediate other factors? Does achievement or experience of student learning overcome work or family issues? Given the current economic conditions that plague so many families and governments, finding answers to whether CoI-designed courses can overcome or offset discouraging external factors is urgently needed.

We certainly need to continue to measure retention when online courses are designed using CoI and we can explore if one or more presences or elements within each presence are more influential on the decision to stay than another. And we may need to study if there is a residual amount of student attrition that is normal and to be expected. Another area for study is the differences between online and face-to-face students, or the lack of differences, and how these qualities affect student retention in the two settings. Finally, does online learning need a theory of retention of its own or can Tinto (1987) or Bean and Metzner (1985) be modified to better capture the decision to stay enrolled on the part of online students?

CONCLUSION

Given the number of influences on students, perhaps retention will always be a problem for higher education. We may never experience perfect retention, and expecting complete retention of every student may be unreasonable. That does not mean we should not try to both recruit students with the potential to benefit from higher education, but keep them through their studies. That includes designing online courses with an eye to fully implementing the CoI framework and evaluating the courses, the intricacies of the learning process, and student learning in the online setting to consistently improve our courses and processes over time. We need to find out whether and to what extent the CoI-designed course can offset the external influences that affect student retention.

However, the retention problem may also be the result of various policies not under the control of institutions and their staff. Governments and families want to maximize access to higher education to ensure that all who benefit, can. And yet to ensure the success of all who enroll may not be likely. The role of competing policies (of increasing access versus ensuring success) cannot be ignored as they contribute to retention problems. This does not mean that institutions do not have a moral responsibility to do their best to achieve student success, but retention problems may be an artifact of being in an open society that values access to a known societal good. However, no one would argue that only those who are guaranteed to succeed should be admitted to higher education.

Despite these philosophical and policy quandaries, the research as it stands today confirms that the CoI framework can and does influence student retention. This chapter has argued that the CoI may do this by ensuring student learning which in turn impacts the student's decision to stay enrolled, and that several retention theories support this assumption. By placing the CoI frame-work within various retention theories, we can conclude that designing online courses using the CoI framework will be one way to improving, but not eliminating, problems with student retention.

REFERENCES

Archibald, D. (2010). Fostering the development of cognitive presence: Initial findings using the community of inquiry survey instrument. *The Internet and Higher Education, 13*, 73–74. doi:10.1016/j.iheduc.2009.10.001

Astin, A. (1984). Student involvement: A developmental theory for higher education. *Journal of College Student Personnel, 25*(3), 297–308.

Bean, J. P., & Metzner, B. S. (1985). A conceptual model of nontraditional undergraduate student attrition. *Review of Educational Research, 55*(4), 485–540.

Berge, Z. L., & Huang, Y. (2004). A model of sustainable student retention: A holistic perspective on the student dropout problem with special attention to e-learning. *DEOSNEWS, 13*(5). Retrieved from http://www.ed.psu.edu/acsde/deos/deosnews/deosnews13_5.pdf

Boston, W. (2010). *Online student retention*. Retrieved from http://wallyboston.com/2010/10/21/online-student-retention

Boston, W., & Ice, P. (2011). Assessing retention in online learning: An administrative perspective. *Online Journal of Distance Learning Administration, 14*(2).

Boston, W., Ice, P., Díaz, S. R., Richardson, J., Gibson, A. M., & Swan, K. (2009). An exploration of the relationship between indicators of the community of inquiry framework and retention in online programs. *Journal of Asynchronous Learning Networks, 13*(3), 67–76.

Boston, W., Ice, P., & Gibson, A. M. (2011). Comprehensive assessment of student retention in online learning environments. *Online Journal of Distance Learning Administration, 14*(1).

Dewey, J. (1910). *How we think.* Boston, MA: D. C. Heath & Co. doi:10.1037/10903-000

Díaz, S. R., Swan, K., Ice, P., & Kupczynski, L. (2010). Student ratings of the importance of survey items, multiplicative factor analysis, and the validity of the community of inquiry survey. *The Internet and Higher Education, 13*, 22–30. doi:10.1016/j.iheduc.2009.11.004

Doherty, W. (2006). An analysis of multiple factors affecting retention in web-based community college courses. *The Internet and Higher Education, 9*, 245–255. doi:10.1016/j.iheduc.2006.08.004

Garrison, D. R. (2007). Online community of inquiry review: Social, cognitive, and teaching presence issues. *Journal of Asynchronous Learning Networks, 11*(1). Retrieved from http://sloanconsortium.org/sites/default/files/v11n1_8garrison.pdf

Garrison, D. R. (2011). *E-learning in the 21st century: A framework for research and practice* (2nd ed.). London, UK: Routledge/Taylor and Francis.

Garrison, D. R., & Arbaugh, J. B. (2007). Researching the community of inquiry framework: Review, issues, and future directions. *The Internet and Higher Education, 10*, 157–172. doi:10.1016/j.iheduc.2007.04.001

Grosset, J. M. (1991). Patterns of integration, commitment, and student characteristics and retention among younger and older students. *Research in Higher Education, 32*(2), 159–178. doi:10.1007/BF00974435

Holder, B. (2007). An investigation of hope, academics, environment, and motivation as predictors of persistence in higher education online programs. *The Internet and Higher Education, 10*, 245–260. doi:10.1016/j.iheduc.2007.08.002

Ice, P., Gibson, A., Boston, W., & Becher, D. (2011). An exploration of differences between community of inquiry indicators in low and high disenrollment online courses. *Journal of Asynchronous Learning Networks, 15*(2), 44–69.

Jenkins, R. (2011, May 22). Why are so many students still failing online? *The Chronicle of Higher Education.*

Kupczynski, L., Davis, R., Ice, P., & Callejo, D. (2008). Assessing the impact of instructional design and organization on student achievement in online courses. *International Journal of Instructional Technology and Distance Learning, 5*(1). Retrieved from http://itdl.org/Journal/Jan_08/article01.htm

Leeds, E., Campbell, S., Ali, R., Brawley, D., & Crisp, J. (in press). The impact of student retention strategies: An empirical study. *International Journal of Management in Education.*

Liu, S., Gomez, J., & Yen, C. (2009). Community college online course retention and final grade: Predictability of social presence. *Journal of Interactive Online Learning, 8*(2), 165–182.

Metzner, B. S., & Bean, J. P. (1987). The estimation of a conceptual model of nontraditional undergraduate student attrition. *Research in Higher Education, 27*(1), 15–38. doi:10.1007/BF00992303

Meyer, K. A. (2003, Fall). Face-to-face versus threaded discussions: The role of time and higher-order thinking. *Journal of Asynchronous Learning Networks, 7*(3). Retrieved from http://www.aln.org/publications/jaln/v7n3/pdf/v7n3_meyer.pdf

Meyer, K. A. (2004, April). Evaluating online discussions: Four different frames of analysis. *Journal of Asynchronous Learning Networks, 8*(2). Retrieved from http://www.aln.org/publications/jaln/v8n2/pdf/v8n2_meyer.pdf

Meyer, K. A., Bruwelheide, J., & Poulin, R. (2006). Why they stayed: Near-perfect retention in an online certification program in library media. *Journal of Asynchronous Learning Networks, 10*(4), 99–115.

Morris, L. V., Finnegan, C., & Wu, S. (2005). Tracking student behavior, persistence and achievement in online courses. *The Internet and Higher Education, 8*, 221–231. doi:10.1016/j.iheduc.2005.06.009

Muse, H. E. Jr. (2003). The web-based community college student: An examination of factors that lead to success and risk. *The Internet and Higher Education, 6*, 241–261. doi:10.1016/S1096-7516(03)00044-7

Nora, A. (1987). Determinants of retention among Chicano college students. *Research in Higher Education, 26*(1), 31–59. doi:10.1007/BF00991932

Pascarella, E. T., & Terenzini, P. (1980). Predicting persistence and voluntary dropout decisions from a theoretical model. *The Journal of Higher Education, 51*(1), 60–75. doi:10.2307/1981125

Picciano, A. G. (2002). Beyond student perceptions: Issues of interaction, presence, and performance in an online course. *Journal of Asynchronous Learning Networks, 6*(1), 21–40.

Rendon, L. (1994). Validating culturally diverse students: Toward a new model of learning and student development. *Innovative Higher Education, 9*(1), 33–52. doi:10.1007/BF01191156

Richardson, J. C., & Ice, P. (2010). Investigating students' level of critical thinking across instructional strategies in online discussions. *The Internet and Higher Education, 13*, 52–59. doi:10.1016/j.iheduc.2009.10.009

Rodriguez, J., Plax, T. G., & Kearney, P. (1996). Clarifying the relationship between teacher nonverbal immediacy and student cognitive learning: Affective learning as the central causal mediator. *Communication Education, 45*, 293–305. doi:10.1080/03634529609379059

Rovai, A. P. (2003). In search of higher persistence rates in distance education online programs. *The Internet and Higher Education, 6*, 1–16. doi:10.1016/S1096-7516(02)00158-6

Russo, T., & Benson, S. (2005). Learning with invisible others: Perceptions of online presence and their relationship to cognitive and affective learning. *Journal of Educational Technology & Society, 8*(1), 54–62.

Shea, P., & Bidjerano, T. (2009). Community of inquiry as a theoretical framework to foster "epistemic engagement" and "cognitive presence" in online education. *Computers & Education, 52*(3), 543–553. doi:10.1016/j.compedu.2008.10.007

Swan, K., Matthews, D., Bogle, L., Boles, E., & Day, S. (in press). Linking online course design and implementation to learning outcomes: A design experiment. *The Internet and Higher Education.*

Sweet, R. (1986). Student dropout in distance education: An application of Tinto's model. *Distance Education, 7*(2), 201–213. doi:10.1080/0158791860070204

Terenzini, P., Rendon, L. I., Upcraft, M. L., Millar, S. B., Allison, K. W., Gregg, P. L., & Jalomo, R. (1994). The transition to college: Diverse students, diverse stories. *Research in Higher Education, 35*(1), 57–73. doi:10.1007/BF02496662

Terenzini, P. T., & Pascarella, E. T. (1997). Voluntary freshman attrition and patterns of social and academic integration in a university: A test of a conceptual model. *Research in Higher Education, 6*(1), 25–43. doi:10.1007/BF00992014

Tinto, V. (1987). *Leaving college: Rethinking the causes and cures of student attrition*. Chicago, IL: University of Chicago Press.

Tinto, V. (1998). Colleges as communities: Taking research on student persistence seriously. *Review of Higher Education, 21*(2), 167–177.

Vaughan, N. D. (2010). A blended community of inquiry approach: Linking student engagement and course redesign. *The Internet and Higher Education, 13,* 60–65. doi:10.1016/j.iheduc.2009.10.007

KEY TERMS AND DEFINITIONS

Cognitive Presence: The process of practical reflection, including the development or construction of meaning through a four-stage process (triggering question, exploration, integration, and resolution).

Persistence: The re-enrollment of a student from year to year to graduation.

Retention: The re-enrollment of a student from fall to fall term or fall to spring term.

Social Presence: The ability of students to project their personalities during course discussions, communicate clearly and well, create trust among course participants, and develop interpersonal relationships with others in the course.

Teaching Presence: The design, facilitation, and direction of the course's activities, projects, and/or discussion, be it by the instructor or others.

Chapter 16
Community of Inquiry Framework, Digital Technologies, and Student Assessment in Higher Education

Norman Vaughan
Mount Royal University, Canada

ABSTRACT

A number of educational researchers have stated that assessment drives learning in higher education (Biggs, 1998; Hedberg & Corrent-Agostinho, 1999; Marton & Saljo, 1984: Ramsden, 2003; Thistlethwaite, 2006). Entwistle (2000) indicates that the design of the assessment activity and the associated feedback can influence the type of learning that takes place in a course or program. For example, standardized tests with minimal feedback can lead to memorization and a surface approach to learning while collaborative group projects can encourage dialogue, richer forms of feedback, and deeper modes of learning. The purpose of this chapter is to demonstrate through a research study how the Community of Inquiry framework and digital technologies can be used to support a triad-approach to student assessment in higher education. This approach consisted of integrating self-reflection, peer feedback, and teacher assessment practices in a pre-service teacher education program at a Canadian University.

INTRODUCTION

The Community of Inquiry (CoI) theoretical framework (Garrison, 2011) has been instrumental in helping researchers and practitioners appreciate the core elements of collaborative learning and what it takes to create and sustain collaborative communities. The CoI is a generic framework that directs attention to the process of constructing and confirming deep understanding. The three main elements of the CoI framework are social presence, cognitive presence, and teaching presence. Each of these elements and their overlap must be considered in the design and delivery of

DOI: 10.4018/978-1-4666-2110-7.ch016

collaborative learning assessment activities and outcomes. Social presence is defined as the ability of participants to identify with the interests of the community (e.g., the course of study), communicate purposefully in a trusting environment, and develop inter-personal relationships by way of participants projecting their individual personalities. The CoI framework is about deep and meaningful learning experiences operationalized through cognitive presence. Cognitive presence is defined in terms of the Practical Inquiry model. Practical inquiry represents phases (problem, exploration, integration, and resolution) of a collaborative-constructive educational experience. The final element, teaching presence, provides the leadership that focuses and sustains a productive collaborative community. Teaching presence is responsible for the design, facilitation and direction of the educational experience (Figure 1).

There has been a shift in the way teachers and researchers think about student learning in higher education, over the last two decades. Instead of characterizing learning as an acquisition process based on teacher transmission, it is now more commonly conceptualized as a process of students actively constructing their own knowledge and skills (Barr & Tagg, 1995; DeCorte, 1996). Stu-

Figure 1. Community of inquiry framework

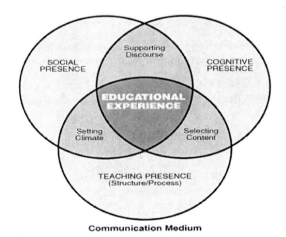

dents interact with subject concepts, transforming and discussing them with others, in order to internalize meaning and make connections with what they already know. Terms like 'learning-centered', which have entered the vocabulary of higher education, are one reflection of this new way of thinking. Even though there is disagreement over the precise definition of a learning-centered approach, the core assumptions are "active engagement in learning and learner responsibility for the management of learning" (Lea, Stephenson & Troy, 2003, p.323).

Despite this shift in conceptions of teaching and learning, a parallel shift in relation to assessment and feedback has been slower to emerge. In higher education, the assessment process is still largely controlled by and seen as the responsibility of teachers; and feedback is still generally conceptualized as a transmission process, even though some educational researchers have challenged this viewpoint (Sadler, 1998; Boud, 2000; Yorke, 2003). Teachers 'transmit' feedback messages to students about what is right and wrong in their academic course work, about its strengths and weaknesses, and students use this information to make subsequent improvements.

There are a number of problems with this transmission view of assessment and feedback. Firstly, if the assessment process is exclusively in the hands of teachers, then it is difficult to see how students can become empowered and develop the self-regulation skills needed to prepare them for learning outside higher education institutions and throughout life (Boud, 2000). Secondly, there is an assumption that when teachers transmit feedback information to students these messages are easily decoded and translated into action. Yet, there is strong evidence that feedback messages are often complex and difficult to decipher, and that students require opportunities to actively construct an understanding of them (e.g., through discussion) before they can be used to regulate performance (Ivanic, Clark & Rimmershaw, 2000; Higgins, Hartley & Skelton, 2001). Thirdly, viewing feedback as a cognitive process involving only transfer of information ignores the way feedback interacts with motivation and beliefs. Research shows that feedback both regulates and is regulated by motivational beliefs. For example, external feedback has been shown to influence how students feel about themselves (positively or negatively), and what and how they learn (Dweck, 1999). Fourthly, as a result of this transmission view of assessment, the workload of teachers in higher education increases year by year as student numbers and class sizes become larger. One way of addressing this issue is to re-examine the nature of assessment feedback, and who provides it (e.g., self, peer, and teacher), in relation to its effectiveness in supporting learning processes.

Self-Assessment

Alverno College (2006) defines self-assessment feedback as "the ability of students to observe, analyze, and judge their own performances on the basis of criteria and to determine how they can improve it" (p.1). Akyol and Garrison (2011) have recently demonstrated how this notion of self-regulated learning or metacognition "in a community of inquiry is a collaborative process where internal and external conditions are being constantly assessed" (p. 184). In addition, they have described three dimensions of metacognition, which involve the knowledge, monitoring, and regulation of cognition (see Chapter 3). The knowledge of cognition refers to awareness of self as a learner and includes entering knowledge and motivation associated with the inquiry process, academic discipline, and expectancies. The monitoring of the cognition dimension implies the awareness and willingness to reflect upon the learning process. And, the regulation of metacognition focuses on the action dimension of the learning experience. It involves the employment of strategies to achieve meaningful learning outcomes.

Two major criticisms of self-assessment in higher education are that students do not possess the necessary skills and experience to properly assess themselves, and thus, this form of assessment is unreliable and simply leads to grade inflation (Rust, 2002). Conversely, others suggest that self-assessment is a key process for helping students to reflect, understand, and take action and responsibility for their learning (Brown, 2004).

Peer Assessment

The Foundation Coalition (2002) indicates that "peer assessment allows students to assess other students (their peers) in a course. Peer assessment can also provide data that might be used in assigning individual grades for team assignments" (p.1). The French moralist and essayist Joubert (1842) is attributed with the quote "to teach is to learn twice" and in an effective community of inquiry all participants are both learners and teachers. The term "teaching" rather than "teacher" presence implies that everyone in the community is responsible for providing input on the design, facilitation and direction of the teaching process.

A number of concerns have been raised about this assessment approach including students' lack of confidence in the process, their ability to provide meaningful feedback, and pressure from peers to provide positive feedback and grades (Langan & Wheater, 2003). These issues are countered by those who emphasize that peer assessment provides students with richer and more authentic opportunities to learn from their peers (e.g., view and critique each other's work) as well as potentially reducing teacher workload (Boud, 2007).

Teacher Assessment

Teacher assessment practices in higher education are often limited to high-stakes summative assessment activities such as mid-term and final examinations (Boud, 2000). The role of a teacher in a community of inquiry is to provide ongoing and meaningful assessment feedback in order to help students develop the necessary metacognitive skills and strategies to take responsibility for their learning.

Thus, teachers in a community of inquiry place a greater emphasis on formative assessment practices (Alberta Assessment Consortium, 2002; American Association of Higher Education, 1996; Gibbs, 2006; Gibbs & Simpson 2004 and Gorsky, Caspi & Trumper, 2006). Pask's (1976) Conversation Theory of Learning suggests that learning takes place through our intrapersonal (inner voice) and interpersonal (external voice with others) conversations and that assessment feedback helps shape and regulate this dialogue in higher education courses. Nicol and Macfarlane-Dick (2006) have developed seven principles of good assessment feedback based on the work of Pask:

1. Helps clarify what good performance is (goals, criteria, standards)
2. Facilitates the development of self-assessment and reflection in learning
3. Delivers high quality information to students about their learning
4. Encourages teacher and peer dialogue around learning
5. Encourages positive motivational beliefs and self esteem
6. Provides opportunities to close the gap between current and desired performance
7. Provides information to teachers that can be used to help shape teaching

The CoI combined with the use of collaborative digital technologies such as blogs, wikis, and other social networking applications in higher education can provide an opportunity to reinforce these principles of good assessment feedback. The term Web 2.0 was coined by O'Reilly in 2005 to describe the trend in the use of World Wide Web technology

to enhance creativity, information sharing, and, most notably, collaboration among users. Brown and Adler (2008) add that the capabilities of these Web 2.0 tools have "shifted attention from access to information toward access to people" (p. 18). Through the use of a research study this chapter will illustrate how the CoI and digital technologies can be used to create meaningful assessment activities for students in higher education.

METHODS OF INVESTIGATION

An action research (Stringer, 2007) approach was utilized to investigate how the CoI and digital technologies could support student assessment in higher education. Gilmore, Krantz and Ramirez (1986) define such a framework as:

Action research...aims to contribute both to the practical concerns of people in an immediate problematic situation and to further the goals of social science simultaneously. Thus, there is a dual commitment in action research to study a system and concurrently to collaborate with members of the system in changing it in what is together regarded as a desirable direction. Accomplishing this twin goal requires the active collaboration of researcher and client, and thus it stresses the importance of co-learning as a primary aspect of the research process (p.161).

This approach consisted of quantitative (pre- and post-course online surveys) and qualitative (online journal entries and post-course student interviews) research methods to collect and analyze data from students enrolled in a pre-service teacher education course entitled, Current and Emerging Pedagogical Technologies. This is a second year course where students explore and investigate the potential for integrating digital technologies into their future teaching practice.

Data Collection

Data was collected by an undergraduate student research assistant (USRA) during the fall 2009 semester. The USRA invited all students enrolled in the course to be part of this research project and a total of 22 students participated in this study (96% response rate). The project received institutional ethics approval and the students signed an informed consent form. The consent form offered the participants confidentiality and the ability to withdraw from the study at any time.

The data collection process began with a pre-course online survey. The purpose of this survey was to identify students' initial perceptions about the value of self-reflection, peer feedback, and teacher assessment based on previous course experiences. The survey consisted of a mixture of Likert-scale and open-ended questions and the second version of the *Free Assessment Survey Tool* (http://toofast.ca) was used to administer an online version of the survey.

Throughout the semester the student participants were also asked to complete an online journal entry after each major assessment activity (total of 5 assignments). These journal entries asked students to explain how they made use of self-reflection, peer review, and teacher assessment feedback to improve each of the course assignments (n=22, 96% response rate). The *Mahara ePortfolio system* (http://mahara.org) was used to facilitate this online journaling process.

At the end of the fall 2009 semester, the students were asked to complete a post-course online survey about their perceptions of self-reflection, peer feedback, and teacher assessment based on their course experience (n=18, 78% response rate). This survey consisted of identical questions from the pre-course survey.

Finally, the students were invited to participate in a 30 minute post-course interview with the USRA to discuss the course assessment practices as well as the preliminary survey and journal findings. Four students volunteered to be interviewed

and these interviews were digitally recorded and transcribed by the USRA.

Data Analysis

A constant comparative approach was used to identify patterns, themes, and categories of analysis that "emerge out of the data rather than being imposed on them prior to data collection and analysis" (Patton, 1990, p. 390). The pre- and post-course online survey along with the journal data were exported into *MS Excel* for statistical and thematic analysis by the USRA and the course instructor. Comparisons were made between students' pre- and post-course survey responses. This data was correlated with the students' journal responses throughout the semester. At the end of the fall 2009 semester, a preliminary report was compiled and emailed to each of the student participants who were then invited to participate in a post-course interview to discuss the initial study findings. These interviews were digitally recorded and transcribed.

FINDINGS

The findings from this research study are highlighted with regards to student comments about how a CoI approach and digital technologies could support self, peer, and teacher assessment practices and activities.

Self-Assessment

The pre-course survey results indicated that students had a wide range of perceptions regarding the value of self-assessment feedback. One student indicated "I don't find it too important to me. I see by my grades how I am doing instead of evaluating myself" (Survey Participant 11) while another stated "I would rather get feedback from a teacher or a peer" (Survey Participant 6). A number of students commented that they did not have much previous experience with self-assessment activities and thus, "I can sometimes have a hard time recognizing where I can improve when I'm self evaluating" (Survey Participant 17).

During the course, students used digital technologies to support several self-assessment activities such as *Audacity* (http://audacity.sourceforge.net/) for self-assessment narrations of project artifacts (e.g., digital stories created in *MS Photostory* (http://www.windowsphotostory.com/), *Google Blogger* (http://www.blogger.com/home) for online journaling, and *Google Sites* (https://sites.google.com/) for the creation of an ePortfolio. The students who participated in this study were asked to rate the value of self-assessment feedback before and after the course. The results are displayed in Table 1.

These results suggest that some students had a higher perception regarding the value of self-assessment at the end of the course but approximately one-third of the students were still ambivalent about the use of this type of assessment feedback. These findings were confirmed in the post-course interviews when students were asked to describe how they used self-assessment feedback to improve their course work. One student stated that assessment was the responsibility of the course instructor and "Personally I didn't feel I needed to do it...I don't really value my opinion on assignments once I've finished them" (Interview Participant 3). Conversely, another student described how self-assessment activities helped her internalize her learning "I could see how I did things, what worked and what didn't. I could also see my goals and if I really got to where I wanted

Table 1. Students' perceptions of the value of self-assessment feedback

	High/Very High	Medium	Low/Very Low
Before course	41%	45%	14%
After course	59%	35%	6%

to be" (Interview Participant 1). This comment was echoed by Interview Participant 4 who indicated "When I started to analyze and critique my own work I started seeing areas for improvement. I always want to give myself a good self evaluation so I made changes or modified certain parts of the assignment to feel comfortable about giving myself a fair but good evaluation."

Peer Assessment

The student participants expressed a number of concerns about peer assessment activities based on their previous course experiences in the pre-course survey. These issues ranged from frustration, confusion, and academic loafing to intimidation with the process. For example, one student stated that "It was frustrating because it didn't really mean anything. The teacher re-marked the assignment anyways..." (Survey Participant 15). Another student was confused by the peer assessment process as "I didn't know if their feedback would be right or wrong" (Survey Participant 21). Several students commented about academic loafing "I feel sometimes my classmates may not be paying attention and just give marks based on the hope that people will grade them lightly" (Survey Participant 5) and how the fear of intimidation limits the quality and honesty of the peer assessment "Students are always intimidated when evaluating their peers in fear of giving them a bad mark" (Survey Participant 11).

Digital technologies were used in the course to support a variety of peer assessment activities. These activities included using *Google Docs* (www.docs.google.com/) for peer review of student lesson plans. The group tools in the *Blackboard Learning Management System* (http://www.blackboard.com/) to provide peer review of project artifacts (e.g., digital stories created in *MS Photostory* - http://www.windowsphotostory.com/). And, *Wikispaces* (http://www.wikispaces.com/) for the co-construction and peer editing of online discussion summaries and class notes.

The students were also asked to rate the value of peer-assessment feedback before and after the course (Table 2).

Before the course, less than twenty percent of the students had a high perception of the value of peer assessment feedback; whereas, after the course, a very slight majority of students had a more positive perception of this form of assessment feedback. These results were tempered by the post-course interview results. One student indicated "I can see how it would be useful but I found that my peers either gave me wrong feedback, like telling me to do it one way when clearly the assignment said to do it another way, or just told me something I already knew and was working on" (Interview Participant 1). Another student described how she used peer-assessment feedback "as a guide-line for my work. It was nice to have someone review my work in the middle of the process because it let me know that I was on the right track" (Interview Participant 4). And Interview Participant 2 stated that "Any time we are able to have more eyes on something to add suggestions, it is worthwhile to take advantage of it".

Teacher Assessment

In the pre-course survey, students indicated they received a range of assessment feedback from their instructors, which was usually summative in nature. One student stated that "It all depends on the teacher" (Survey Participant 3) while another complained that "No one tells me anything and since I don't have the same teachers for each

course, I don't really know how to improve my course work" (Survey Participant 21). Several students stressed "that it is important to be able to adapt to requirements that others set for you" (Survey Participant 14).

Interactive technologies were used by the course teacher primarily to provide students with formative assessment feedback. For example, the teacher gave initial assessment comments and grades on all assignments in digital format (e.g., student lesson plans in *Google Docs*, digital stories in *MS Photostory*, WebQuests in *QuestGarden* - http://questgarden.com/). Students then had the opportunity to revise their assignments based on this feedback and resubmit final versions to their ePortfolios (e.g., *Google Sites*) for summative assessment. It appears that this emphasis on formative feedback impacted students' perceptions regarding the value of teacher assessment (Table 3).

These survey results indicate that almost all of the students involved in this study had a much higher perception of teacher assessment, after the course. In the post-course interviews, the students explained how they used the teacher's formative assessment comments to improve their course work. "The feedback allowed me to re-examine how I did something and then go back to review and make changes where necessary" (Interview Participant 2). For several students, this was the first time they had received formative feedback from a teacher and one student commented that "...having an instructor give you a first mark, and then being able to go back and revise was really helpful in improving my work" (Interview Par-

Table 2. Students' perceptions of the value of peer assessment feedback

	High/Very High	Medium	Low/Very Low
Before course	19%	62%	19%
After course	53%	23.5%	23.5%

Table 3. Students' perceptions of the value of teacher assessment feedback

	High/Very High	Medium	Low/Very Low
Before course	64%	36%	0%
After course	94%	6%	0%

ticipant 1). Another student emphasized how he "really liked the formative feedback from the instructor because it allows you to improve on similar assignments you might have to do again in the same class or maybe another course – sort of like a building block approach to learning" (Interview Participant 4).

DISCUSSION AND RECOMMENDATIONS

The student participants in this research study provided recommendations for how a CoI approach and digital technologies could be used to design meaningful self, peer, and teacher assessment activities in their online journal assignment postings and the post-study interviews.

Self-Assessment

With regards to self-assessment practices, the students provided specific recommendations for how digital technologies could be used for grading rubrics and online journaling in higher education courses.

Rubrics

The Teaching, Learning, and Technology (TLT) Group (2011) define a rubric as "an explicit set of criteria used for assessing a particular type of work or performance. A rubric usually also includes levels of potential achievement for each criterion, and sometimes also includes work or performance samples that typify each of those levels" (n.p.). The participants in this study indicated that rubrics can be useful for clarifying assignment and assessment expectations only when students are actively involved in their co-construction. In the post-study interviews, one participant stated that without student involvement rubrics "can become simple check-lists, a way to make sure that you've covered everything the teacher wants for the as-

signment rather than what you really wanted to do and learn" (Interview Participant 3). Unfortunately, this comment suggests that without student involvement rubrics have the potential to support a surface rather than a deep approach to learning.

In terms of recommendations, the students suggested that several types of digital technologies could be used to support the co-construction of assessment rubrics. These included applications such as *Rubistar* (http://rubistar.4teachers.org/index.php), *Teachnology* (http://www.teach-nology.com/web_tools/rubrics/), and *Google Docs* (www.docs.google.com/). The students in this study preferred using *Google Docs* based on the simplicity and their familiarity with this tool. An example of a co-constructed assessment rubric for a lesson plan assignment is illustrated in Figure 2.

The study participants also recommended that students should have the opportunity to practice applying the co-constructed rubric to previous completed course work and that students should have the ability to add one unique grading component or criteria (e.g., creativity).

In addition, digital technologies can be used to provide a variety of options for students to self-assess themselves. For example, students can use *Audacity* (http://audacity.sourceforge.net/), an open-source audio tool, to create self-assessment narrations of how they achieved the various learning outcomes outlined in the rubric. The use of self-assessment audio feedback can be of powerful way for students to internalize their learning (Ice, Curtis, Phillips & Wells, 2007).

Online Journals

Students in professional programs such as Teacher Education and Nursing are often required to maintain either a course or program journal. Online blogging tools such as *WordPress* (http://wordpress.org/) and *Google's Blogger* (www.blogger.com/) are commonly being used to support this type of self-assessment activity.

Figure 2. Assessment rubric for a lesson plan assignment (http://tinyurl.com/lessonplanrubric)

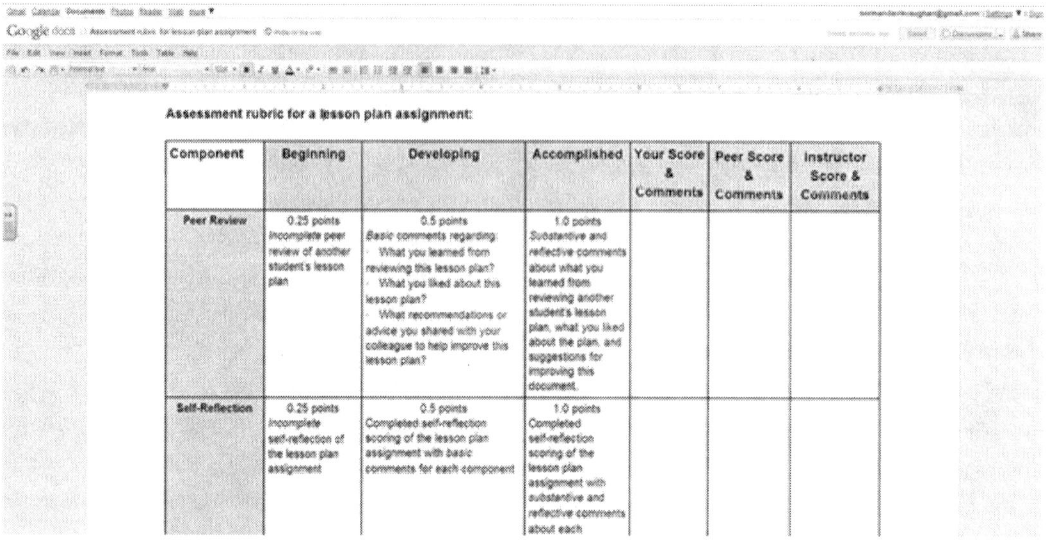

Assessment rubric for a lesson plan assignment:

Component	Beginning	Developing	Accomplished	Your Score & Comments	Peer Score & Comments	Instructor Score & Comments
Peer Review	0.25 points *Incomplete peer review of another student's lesson plan*	0.5 points *Basic comments regarding:* · What you learned from reviewing this lesson plan? · What you liked about this lesson plan? · What recommendations or advice you shared with your colleague to help improve this lesson plan?	1.0 points *Substantive and reflective comments* about what you learned from reviewing another student's lesson plan, what you liked about the plan, and suggestions for improving this document.			
Self-Reflection	0.25 points *Incomplete* self-reflection of the lesson plan assignment	0.5 points Completed self-reflection scoring of the lesson plan assignment with *basic* comments for each component	1.0 points Completed self-reflection scoring of the lesson plan assignment with substantive and reflective comments about each			

Students in this study indicated online journals can be useful for self-reflection but that too often they can become a "boring and repetitive activity when I am simply being asked to reply to a set of teacher directed questions. Usually, I just post what I think the teacher wants to hear not what I'm really thinking" (Interview Participant 2). Again, without student involvement, this type of self-assessment activity can reinforce a surface rather than a deep approach to learning.

The study participants strongly recommended that students should have much greater control over their online journal postings. They suggested that there should be more opportunities for "freedom of expression rather than conforming to a teacher set structure" (Interview Participant 1). The students involved in this study proposed that their online journal assignment should be focused on processed-orientated postings that led to a final product such as an end of the semester self-reflection paper. And, that this paper could be assessed using a co-constructed rubric in *Google Docs*.

Peer Assessment

The student participants suggested a variety of ways that peer assessment activities could be enhanced through the use of digital technologies in the post-study surveys and interviews. They indicated the biggest barrier to completing this type of peer activity, outside of class, was finding a common time and place to meet. The students suggested that digital technologies could potentially be used to overcome this challenge. For example, the group areas in learning management systems such as *Blackboard* could be used to communicate and share documents about the peer assessment process for individual and group projects. These group areas usually consist of asynchronous (e.g., email and discussion board) and synchronous (e.g., chat) communication tools along with a file exchange function.

The students also indicated that during the course they had been impressed with how easy it was to provide peer review feedback on written assignment by sharing *Google Docs* (Figure 3). This application allowed them to control who had commenting and editing privileges for their documents.

Figure 3. Peer review of a writing assignment in Google Docs

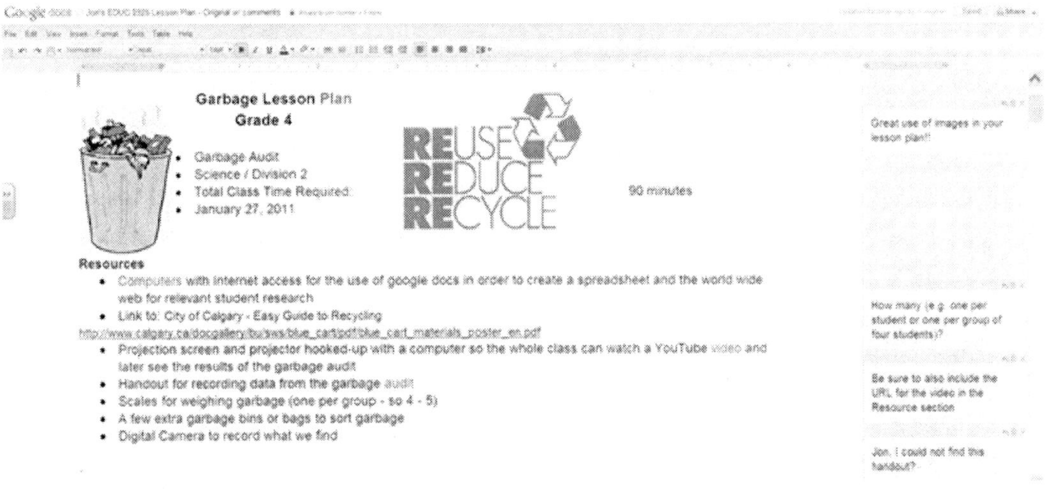

In addition, online journal applications such as *Blogger* could be used to provide peer review feedback on individual project work and wiki tools such as *Wikispaces (*http://www.wikispaces.com/*)*). The history files of a wiki summary clearly demonstrate the contribution and critique that was made by each member of the group.

A number of students involved in this study were also taking an introductory Biology course. They commented on how the teacher in this course was using the University of California at Los Angeles' *Calibrated Peer Review* (http://cpr.molsci.ucla.edu/) tool to teach them how to provide constructive feedback to their peers on the laboratory manuscript assignments for the course. The Biology teacher also used personal response systems (e.g., clickers) for study group quizzes and discussion prompts. Crouch and Mazur (2001) describe how clickers can be used to support a form of peer instruction. The process begins with the teacher posing a question or problem. The students initially work individually toward a solution and 'vote' on what they believe is the correct answer by selecting the desired numbered or lettered response on their clicker. The results are then projected for the entire class to view. For a good question, there is usually a broad range of responses. Students are then required to compare and discuss their solutions with the person next to them in the classroom in order to come to a consensus. Another 'vote' is taken but this time only one response or clicker per group can be utilized. In most circumstances, the range of responses decreases and usually centers around the correct answer. As an alternative to this process, this Biology teacher also had groups of students generate the quiz questions in advance of the classroom session.

While the student participants appreciated the ability of a CoI approach and digital technologies to provide increased flexibility and communication opportunities to complete peer assessment activities, outside of the classroom, they had several concerns. First, a number of students expressed concern about their lack of experience with peer assessment in the post-study interviews. They strongly recommended that teachers should "provide guidance and a class orientation on how to give each other meaningful feedback" (Interview Participant 4). Another student suggested that there should be "opportunities for oral and written feedback" (Interview Participant 2). He thought that digital technologies were being used primarily to provide written peer feedback and that in a true community of inquiry students should also be learning how to provide oral feedback to each other. This comment was echoed by a student who suggested that teachers should "provide class time to begin and conclude peer assessment activities" (Interview Participant 1). She believed that this combination of face-to-face and online interaction would help to build trust and accountability for the peer assessment process.

Teacher Assessment

In terms of teacher assessment, the student participants provided several suggestions about how digital technologies could be used to support these practices. The first idea was to have teachers use collaborative writing tools such as *Google Docs* to provide formative assessment feedback at checkpoints or milestones for individual or group projects. This would allow students to receive teacher feedback throughout the process of constructing the project rather than just focusing on summative assessment feedback for the final product.

The students also encouraged teachers to take a portfolio approach to assessment. This would involve students receiving a second chance or opportunity for summative assessment on their course assignments. For example, students would initially submit and receive teacher assessment for each of the required course assignments. Throughout the semester, students would have the opportunity to revise these assignments, based on the initial teacher feedback, and then post them to their course or program portfolios for final summative assessment by the teacher. There are a range of e-Portfolio tools that can support this process ranging from the *LiveText* (https://www.livetext.com/) commercial application to the free *Google Sites* (http://sites.google.com/) tool.

In addition, digital technologies can be used to support external expert assessment opportuni-

ties. For example, students can publically share critiques of academic articles by using blogging tools such as *WordPress* and *Blogger*. The authors' of these articles can then be invited to post comments about these critiques to the students' blogs. External experts can also provide assessment feedback on individual or group presentations through the use of web-based video technologies. These types of presentations can be video recorded and either streamed live (e.g., *Livestream* - http://www.livestream.com/) or posted to a video sharing site such as *YouTube* (http://www.youtube.com/). The external experts can then provide assessment feedback in either synchronous (e.g., real-time audio) or asynchronous formats (e.g., online discussion forums) to the students. Figure 4 illustrates a video recording of an individual student presentation that has been posted to *YouTube*.

Besides providing ideas on how the CoI and digital technologies could be used to support teacher assessment activities, the student participants in the interview sessions also had three recommendations for faculty members. The first recommendation was that teachers should "focus on providing students with ongoing formative assessment feedback rather than on just summative midterm and final examination comments" (Interview Participant 2). The second was that teachers should strive to "provide oral feedback in addition to their written assessment feedback. For example, teachers could request that students meet with them during office hour sessions to orally debrief about assignments" (Interview Participant 4). Finally, Interview Participant 3 emphasized "Let us provide instructors with more feedback on their assignments and teaching practice throughout the semester, not just at the end" and he recommended Angelo and Cross' (1993) book on *Classroom assessment techniques: A handbook for college teachers* to facilitate this process.

Figure 4. Example of a video recording of student presentation posted to YouTube

CONCLUSION

The pre-service teacher education students who participated in this research study were also asked to describe how they combined the use of self, peer, and teacher assessment feedback to improve their course work. One student commented that "I used the self-reflection for checking my work and making sure I had everything I needed. I used peer-review for a different perspective on my work and I used instructor feedback to understand how I could improve my work" (Interview Participant 4). Another student stated that "Self reflection showed me what I liked about my work and what needed to be improved, peer feedback gave comments on what could be done better and then instructor feedback gave ideas on how the assignment could be fixed up to get a better mark" (Interview Participant 2).

In addition, there were numerous comments in the student online journals about how a community of inquiry approach and digital technologies helped them integrate these three forms of assessment into a triad approach (Figure 5).

For example, students were using rubrics, blogs, and online quizzes to provide themselves with self-reflection and feedback on their course assignments. Students received further feedback on their course work from their peers through the use of digital technologies such wikis and clickers. Finally, teachers and in some cases external experts reviewed students' ePortfolios and used video technologies to observe student performance, diagnose student misconceptions, and provide additional formative assessment feedback.

In conclusion, the research study presented in this chapter has demonstrated that self, peer,

Figure 5. Using a community of inquiry and digital technologies to support a triad approach to assessment

and teacher assessment activities in a community of inquiry should be an integrated process rather than a series of isolated events in order to help students develop their own metacognitive skills and strategies.

REFERENCES

Akyol, Z., & Garrison, D. R. (2011). Assessing metacognition in an online community of inquiry. *The Internet and Higher Education, 14*(3), 183–190. doi:10.1016/j.iheduc.2011.01.005

Alberta Assessment Consortium. (2002). *About classroom assessment*. Retrieved from http://www.aac.ab.ca/final2002.doc

Alverno College. (2001). *Assessment essentials: Definition of terms*. Retrieved from http://depts.alverno.edu/saal/terms.html

American Association of Higher Education and Accreditation. (1996). *Nine principles of good practice for assessing student learning*. Retrieved from http://www.niu.edu/assessment/Manual/media/9Principles.pdf

Angelo, T. A., & Cross, K. P. (1993). *A handbook of classroom assessment techniques for college teachers*. San Francisco, CA: Jossey-Bass.

Barr, R. B., & Tagg, J. (1995). A new paradigm for undergraduate education. *Change, 27*(6), 13–25. Retrieved from http://critical.tamucc.edu/~blalock/readings/tch2learn.htm

Biggs, J. (1998). Assumptions underlying new approaches to assessment. In Stimson, P., & Morris, P. (Eds.), *Curriculum and assessment in Hong Kong: Two components, one system* (pp. 351–384). Hong Kong: Open University of Hong Kong Press.

Boud, D. J. (2000). Sustainable assessment: rethinking assessment for the learning society. *Studies in Continuing Education, 22*(2), 151–167. Retrieved from http://www.education.uts.edu.au/ostaff/staff/publications/db_28_sce_00.pdf doi:10.1080/713695728

Boud, D. J. (2007). *Rethinking assessment for higher education: Learning for the longer term*. London, UK: Routledge.

Brown, J. S., & Adler, R. P. (2008). Minds on fire: Open education, the long tail, and learning 2.0. *EDUCAUSE Review, 43*(1), 17–32.

Brown, S. (2004). Assessment for learning. *Learning and Teaching in Higher Education, 1*(1), 81-89. Retrieved from http://www2.glos.ac.uk/offload/tli/lets/lathe/issue1/articles/brown.pdf

Creswell, J. W. (1997). *Qualitative inquiry and research design: Choosing among five traditions*. Thousand Oaks, CA: Sage.

Crouch, C. H., & Mazur, E. (2001). Peer instruction: Ten years of experience and results. *American Journal of Physics, 69*(9), 970–977. doi:10.1119/1.1374249

DeCorte, E. (1996). New perspectives on learning and teaching in higher education. In Burgen, A. (Ed.), *Goals and purposes of higher education in the 21st century*. London, UK: Jessica Kingsley.

Dweck, C. (1999). *Self-theories: Their role in motivation, personality and development*. Philadelphia, PA: Psychology Press.

Entwistle, N. J. (2000). Approaches to studying and levels of understanding: The influences of teaching and assessment. In Smart, J. C. (Ed.), *Higher education: Handbook of theory and research* (*Vol. XV*, pp. 156–218). New York, NY: Agathon Press.

Foundation Coalition. (2002). *Peer assessment and peer evaluation*. Retrieved from http://www. foundationcoalition.org/publications/brochures/2002peer_assessment.pdf

Garrison, D. R. (2011). *E-learning in the 21st century: A framework for research and practice* (2nd ed.). London, UK: Routledge/Falmer.

Gibbs, G. (2006). How assessment frames student learning. In Bryan, C., & Clegg, K. (Eds.), *Innovative assessment in higher education* (pp. 23–36). London, UK: Routledge.

Gibbs, G., & Simpson, C. (2004). Conditions under which assessment supports students' learning? *Learning and Teaching in Higher Education, 1*, 3–31.

Gilmore, T., Krantz, J., & Ramirez, R. (1986). Action based modes of inquiry and the host-researcher relationship. *Consultation, 5*(3), 161.

Gorsky, P., Caspi, A., & Trumper, R. (2006). Campus-based university students' use of dialogue. *Studies in Higher Education, 31*(1), 71–87. Retrieved from http://old.oranim.ac.il/Docs/CSHE_A_139217. pdf doi:10.1080/03075070500392342

Hedberg, J., & Corrent-Agostinho, S. (1999). Creating a postgraduate virtual community: Assessment drives learning. In B. Collis & R. Oliver (Eds.), *Proceedings of World Conference on Educational Multimedia, Hypermedia and Telecommunications.* (pp. 1093-1098). AACE: Chesapeake, VA. Retrieved from http://www. editlib.org/p/7040

Higgins, R., Hartley, P., & Skelton, A. (2001). Getting the message across: The problem of communicating assessment feedback. *Teaching in Higher Education, 6*(2), 269–274. doi:10.1080/13562510120045230

Ice, P., Curtis, R., Phillips, P., & Wells, J. (2007). Using asynchronous audio feedback to enhance teaching presence and students' sense of community. *Journal of Asynchronous Learning Networks, 11*(2), 3–25.

Ivanic, R., Clark, R., & Rimmershaw, R. (2000). What am I supposed to make of this? The messages conveyed to students by tutors' written comments. In Lea, M. R., & Stierer, B. (Eds.), *Student writing in higher education: New contexts*. Buckingham, UK: Open University Press.

Joubert, J. (1842). *Pensees*. Retrieved from http://www.doyletics.com/art/notebook.htm

Langan, M. A., & Wheater, C. P. (2003). Can students assess students effectively? Some insights into peer-assessment. *Learning and Teaching in Action, 2*(1). Retrieved from http://www.celt.mmu.ac.uk/ltia/issue4/langanwheater.pdf

Lea, S. J., Stephenson, D., & Troy, J. (2003). Higher education students' attitudes to student centred learning: Beyond 'educational bulimia'. *Studies in Higher Education, 28*(3), 321–334. doi:10.1080/03075070309293

Marton, F., & Saljo, R. (1984). Approaches to learning. In Marton, F., Hounsell, D., & Entwistle, N. (Eds.), *The experience of learning*. Edinburgh, UK: Scottish Academic Press.

Nicol, D. J., & Macfarlane-Dick, D. (2006). Formative assessment and self-regulated learning: A model and seven principles of good feedback practice. *Studies in Higher Education, 31*(2), 199–218. doi:10.1080/03075070600572090

O'Reilly, T. (2005). What is web 2.0? *O'Reilly Network*. Retrieved from http://oreilly.com/web2/archive/what-is-web-20.html

Pask, G. (1976). *Conversation theory: Applications in education and epistemology*. Amsterdam, The Netherlands: Elsevier.

Patton, M. Q. (1990). *Qualitative evaluation and research methods* (2nd ed.). Newbury Park, CA: Sage Publications.

Ramsden, P. (2003). *Learning to teach in higher education* (2nd ed.). London, UK: Routledge.

Rust, C. (2002). The impact of assessment on student learning: How can the research literature practically help to inform the development of departmental assessment strategies and learner-centred assessment practices? *Active Learning in Higher Education, 3*(2), 145–158. doi:10.1177/1469787402003002004

Sadler, D. R. (1998). Formative assessment: revisiting the territory. *Assessment in Education, 5*(1), 77–84. doi:10.1080/0969595980050104

Stringer, E. T. (2007). *Action research* (3rd ed.). London, UK: Sage Publications.

Teaching, L., & the Technology (TLT) Group. (2011). *Rubrics: Definition, tools, examples, references*. Retrieved from http://www.tltgroup.org/resources/flashlight/rubrics.htm

Thistlethwaite, J. (2006). More thoughts on `assessment drives learning'. *Medical Education, 40*(11), 1149–1150. doi:10.1111/j.1365-2929.2006.02638.x

Yorke, M. (2003). Formative assessment in higher education: moves towards theory and the enhancement of pedagogic practice. *Higher Education, 45*(4), 477–501. doi:10.1023/A:1023967026413

KEY TERMS AND DEFINITIONS

Classroom Assessment Techniques: Simple, non-graded, anonymous, in-class activities (e.g. surveys, one minute papers) that give both the teacher and the students useful feedback about improving the teaching-learning process.

Digital Technologies: Devices and applications which have the ability to store, process and transmit information through the use of electronic or optical pulses that represent binary digits or bits (0 and 1).

ePortfolio: A purposeful collection of digital information and artifacts that demonstrates student development or provides evidence of specific learning outcomes, skills and competencies.

Metacognition: The awareness and ability to monitor and regulate one's learning.

Peer Assessment: Students assessing the work of their peers.

Rubric: An assessment tool used to clearly communicate the expectations of an assignment, project, or performance. The criteria and standards of the rubric are aligned with the learning outcomes for the activity.

Self-Assessment: A self-reflective process of assessing our own knowledge, skills, and attitudes.

Teacher Assessment: Teachers assessing the academic work of their students.

Section 3
Administrative Issues and Organizational Support

Chapter 17
Pedagogical Counseling Program Development through an Adapted Community of Inquiry Framework

María Fernanda Aldana-Vargas
Universidad de los Andes, Colombia

Albert Gras-Martí
Universidad de los Andes, Colombia

Juny Montoya
Universidad de los Andes, Colombia

Luz Adriana Osorio
Universidad de los Andes, Colombia

ABSTRACT

This chapter describes an institutional Pedagogical Counseling program-assessment and systematizing initiative in terms of an adapted Community of Inquiry framework. An inquiry through pedagogical-counseling experience-exchange process was set up to analyze, assess and potentiate ongoing support activities by the staff members of the Center for Research and Development in Education (CIFE) in counseling projects of undergraduate and postgraduate programs. Garrison, Anderson, and Archer's (2000) Community of Inquiry framework has been adapted to the authors' pedagogical counseling process in order to conceptualize CIFE staff's review exercise. The process includes ample opportunities to discuss and reflect on key counseling design questions, explore counseling programs from a pedagogical perspective and implement and evaluate new tutoring designs. This chapter describes the inquiry process and the lessons learned from the implementation of the pedagogical counseling inquiry exercise.

DOI: 10.4018/978-1-4666-2110-7.ch017

INTRODUCTION

CIFE, the Center for Research and Development in Education of the University of los Andes, is responsible for promoting innovation, pedagogical expertise and research in education both within and outside the Campus. After more than 10 years of experience and a great number of successful Pedagogical Counseling (PC) projects carried out with University lecturers in various undergraduate and graduate programs, where a number of education innovation projects were developed, implemented and evaluated, the need was felt to pause and make a collective reflection exercise as a Center. For this purpose, we set up an inquiry exercise to analyze and discuss the various experiences in PC accumulated by the diversity of CIFE's pedagogical experts that orient the design and implementation of pedagogical innovations in close interaction with the lecturers. We wished to make explicit all the practical and tacit knowledge of the community's members, as well as organize, describe, categorize and systematize the ample spectrum of practical approaches to PC that have been developed in our Center.

The purpose of this chapter is to describe an institutional initiative intended to address the diversity of teacher accompanying experiences conducted by CIFE staff members and to outline improved practices for future PC projects, in particular to find common aspects and cross-project fertilization possibilities. The aim is to extract knowledge and know-how from an essentially non-formalized and non-structured large set of cases. The exercise took the form of an engaged and collaborative approach of the CIFE staff, with a focus on the *rendezvous* of a variety of practices and an evaluation of the PC program. This meta-analysis exercise is called Inquiry through Pedagogical-Counseling Experience-Exchange (ITPCEE). The pedagogical approach used to frame the program is inquiry-based learning from

and with colleagues, specifically a Community of Inquiry (CoI). As we shall see, the CoI framework was crucial to framing the PC experiences and shaping the role of the various players within the overall exercise, as well as providing a route map for the future of the PC program.

In the next section we shall describe CIFE's standard approach to PC. In the following next section, we shall describe the background and the objectives of the review, assessment, systematizing and future-planning exercise. Then, we shall outline the CoI framework as originally formulated by Garrison et al. (2000), and describe how we have adapted this framework to our project. The method used the data and the relevant details of the ITPCEE process relevant to our PC review exercise, will be described and discussed later. Finally, summary of the main conclusions and the new perspectives opened up along the process are provided.

CIFE'S PEDAGOGICAL COUNSELING

CIFE is an example of a University Educational Development Center or Center of Teaching Excellence, offering guidance and multiple resources for Teacher Professional Development (Perry & Smart, 2007). The Center has experience in various programs for counseling of University lectures, with the objective of improving the educational quality of the undergraduate and postgraduate programs that the University offers. The PC process aims to generate an authentic and profound dialogue about specific and contextualized innovations in teaching practices, with a view to identifying counseling elements and strategies that may lead to improvements in that particular teaching and learning process. In many cases the Laboratory of Investigation and Development on Informatics and Education (LIDIE), a branch of

Figure 1. Schematics of PC projects undertaken by CIFE. Groups of CIFE staff members (teams A, B, C...) participate in one or several PC projects (PC1, PC2...). The PCs have different sizes and objectives, and the target may involve individual University lecturers, a group of lecturers or even a whole University program. Elements like the quality assurance and the development of technological needs, embrace every project.

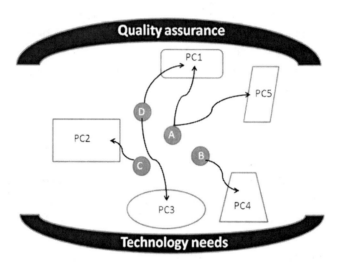

CIFE, has included in the strategies of PC the generation of learning environments supported by Information and Communication Technologies.

We outline in Figure 1 the schematics of standard PC processes undertaken by CIFE. One or various CIFE teams (A, B, C, etc.) attend each PC process (PC1, PC2, etc.). In all CIFE PC projects, the accompanying process is done via a collaborative work and with the participation of teams of professionals of a variety of disciplines such as pedagogy, systems engineering, psychology, graphic design and so on. Sometimes, but not often, a CIFE staff with expertise in the lecturer's discipline as well as in pedagogy is also present in the accompanying team.

After more than a decade of research and development about classroom innovations under CIFE guidance we feel that the quality of the pedagogical accompanying process is determinant in the process of designing and implementing an educational innovation initiative. Furthermore,

the CIFE program satisfies one of the basic requirements (Garrison, 2004) for a major effort in improving teaching and learning processes in our University to be effective, namely, a strong institutional leadership. And also, our experience in PC is aligned with the ingredients for course redesign efforts to be sustainable as described by Garrison and Kanuka (2004). Here we transcribe these requirements, slightly edited to fit our project:

- **Creation of Clear Institutional Direction and Policy:** This is attested by the wide experience in PC in our University under the auspices of CIFE.
- **Establishment of a Single Point of Support, Quality Assurance, and Project Management:** Since the establishment of the CIFE unit in our University ten years ago as a research and development unit in education, an interdisciplinary team as-

sures the evaluation and the quality of the PC programs that are undertaken by the Center.

- **Creation of an Innovation Program:** Providing support and incentives to faculty and departments to initiate teaching and learning innovation processes, this is a basic element of CIFE's program is the development of Virtual Learning Environments (AVAs, or *ambientes virtuales de aprendizaje*, in Spanish). The PC programs range from individual lecturer's needs, to all the subjects of a semester and even to a full University program.

- **Investment in Establishing a Reliable and Accessible Technology Infrastructure:** Whenever relevant, the technological aspects of a CIFE PC program are dealt with by the corresponding LIDIE teams in CIFE. Furthermore, the University has a strong technology-access program with resources and technical support readily available to all members. This support is provided by the DTI (Information Technologies Directorate, or *Dirección de Tecnologías de Información*) and the use of a Blackboard®-based University platform.

- **Strategic Selection of Prototype Projects:** We are in the midst of the process of creating a Web portal (http://conexiones.uniandes.edu.co) where, apart from many teaching and networking resources for University lecturers, a selection of good teaching and learning projects will be made available to the whole Campus and worldwide.

- **Development of Formal Counseling Design Support:** Made available through a structures process, this is one of the main objectives of the present ITPCEE exercise via the CoI framework.

- **Systematic Evaluation of Satisfaction and Success of the Innovative Teaching and Learning Redesign:** As mentioned above, Figure 1, the evaluation element of any PC project is an essential ingredient of our efforts.

- **Creation of a Task Group:** This effort addresses issues, challenges, and opportunities as well as communicates and recommends new directions to the university or community. It is the core of CIFE's mission within the University.

The objectives above are present in CIFE's continued efforts, and require constant reevaluation. Just as the University of Calgary in a different context (Vaughan & Garrison, 2006a, p.70), the University of los Andes: "systematically addressed these requirements. Once policy was developed, awareness raised, and resource commitment achieved, the challenge was to create an instructional support system that could sustain" the redesign process of teaching and learning innovation projects via PC. The meta-analysis of the PC processes provided by the ITPCEE exercise described in this paper is seen by staff as an opportunity to evaluate and eventually redesign and conceptualize how we approach teachers' coaching in PC in ways that realize increased effectiveness, convenience, and efficiency. At the heart of the ITPCEE process is the goal to engage CIFE staff in critical discourse and reflection, from which new knowledge should emerge. For that purpose, staff took responsibility to construct meaning from past experiences and confirm general potentialities through active participation in the inquiry process.

The setting up of a CoI for its evaluation and redesign efforts are described next.

OBJECTIVES OF THE INQUIRY PROCESS

The objectives of this experience-exchange and inquiry exercise were a consequence of the situation as perceived by the CIFE PC teams. Specifically, and in spite of the wide experience in a multitude of counseling projects that CIFE has accumulated over the years, several issues were detected:

- Little systematization existed of the experience on pedagogical counseling.
- Knowledge transfer and documentation of the different strategies that had been implemented by the groups of experts were non-existent or not well documented.
- Little use was made by new members of CIFE of the practical and tacit knowledge about PC that had been developed in the past.
- No systematic online interaction mechanism had been provided so far for CIFE members.
- An urgent need existed to optimize efforts and design lines of action for the future of the counseling programs.

These issues were particularly pressing because the CIFE staff has tripled in size over the years and the turn-over rate of the many graduate assistants that collaborate with the staff is also large on a yearly basis. For this reason, we decided to set up an ITPCEE exercise and, as we shall argue immediately, to analyze its evolution with a convenient adaptation of the CoI framework.

When a decision was made to review and assess the CIFE practices and experiences over the years, several possibilities for the format of this exercise were considered. The process could perhaps take the form of a progress report or of a decennial showcase book. However, we wished to spend time and efforts in a deeper and more long-lasting and fruitful exercise; for that purpose, we needed a theoretical guideline because, in the words of

Akyol (2009): "Research done without reference to theory runs the risk of collecting questionable data based on capricious thinking". A review of the literature on process review options yielded the following four main results:

1. Setting up a task force effort
2. Starting up a Community of Practice (Wenger, 1998)
3. Starting up a Learning Community (Bielaczyc & Collins, 1999)
4. Designing an analytical framework similar to the CoI framework (Garrison et al., 2000)

The first option, setting up a task force, was readily discarded because our review and planning exercise was not intended to conclude within a fixed deadline or with a well-defined product as a result. As for the second and third options, even though we think that the Community of Practice theoretical framework is a sound and valuable tool to deal with teams involved in PC practices like those we are dealing with, we believe that as a starting point we needed to create, firstly, the conditions for such a community to develop. In fact, although CIFE staff is quite used to collaborate and to team-work, especially within multidisciplinary teams as described above, there was no experience of working as an all-encompassing community; so, the possibility of developing a Learning Community or a Community of Practice are eventually options for the future.

On the other hand, although Communities of Practice and Communities of Inquiry both share many complementary features (Friedman, 2001) we argue that setting up a PC Community of Inquiry exercise is more appropriate for our actual research and development goals. However, the experience described in this paper may well become the initial step towards developing a Community of Practice, even a Virtual one, in the sense of Galvis Panqueva and Leal Fonseca (2006)[1]: "Virtual communities of practice may be an effective mechanism to favor processes of permanent actualization and improvement of the professional activity of teachers" and, then, the familiarity with CoI frameworks will be invaluable (Friedman, 2001).

For all these reasons we decided to explore the applicability of the CoI framework as an appropriate theoretical standpoint from which to try to conceptualize the extensive review of CIFE PC practices which had just started in our Center. We are aware that the CoI framework has been originally designed to address the important problem of student learning outcomes in blended and online settings. However, we feel that this framework is potentially applicable in other "learning settings", where the activities that led to those learning results were not formally defined beforehand and these activities took place over a long period of time and involving rather disparate teaching and learning situations, as in our PC projects. In fact, a similar application of the CoI framework was published by Vaughan and Garrison (2006b) in the analysis of a blended-course redesign process.

So, for the purpose to enrich our practice of PC, the adapted CoI framework may be a convenient tool to conceptualize the aforementioned process because, according to Arbaugh, Cleveland-Innes, Diaz, Garrison, Ice, Richardson, & Swan (2008), "The importance of a community of inquiry is that, while the objective of critical reflection is intellectual autonomy, in reality, critical reflection is thoroughly social and communal." As pedagogical consultants we share both relative autonomy of action and common challenges, and via exchange and formalization of past experiences within the context of a CoI we may learn from each other as well as generate innovative protocols for the larger-scale projects and more resource-efficient procedures for future PC projects. Furthermore, according to Dewey (1933), "...community means meaningful association, association based on *common interest* and endeavor. The essence of community is *communication*..." (cited by Morgan & Metni, 2006). Our CoI fits this description since the various teams working in CIFE share both common interests and endeavor in accompanying innovative teaching experiences with University lecturers in different disciplines. Furthermore, the various features spelled out by Arbaugh et al. (2008) are easily identified in our CoI, namely the question that drives the community, the small-group working setting, which includes critical discourse in a rather multi-disciplinary environment that "incorporates *research methods* such as information gathering and synthesis of ideas". Accordingly, we shall also use the following three categories in analyzing our PC CoI analysis: social presence, cognitive presence and teaching presence (Garrison, 2007). All these features associated with CoI will be discussed at length in this chapter in relation to our ITPCEE exercise.

In conclusion, full analysis of CIFE's PC review and systematization exercise will be made in terms of CoI theoretical framework, and the logical framework approach will be used as a background for analysis. In the following section first we shall outline the basic elements of the CoI framework and then we shall extend and adapt this framework to our project.

ADAPTATION OF THE COI FRAMEWORK

We take the CoI as a process model and as a useful guide to analyze our systematizing effort. While the CoI framework has been shown to be predictive of student perceived learning and satisfaction with online learning (Arbaugh, 2008), we are using this theoretical framework to analyze the evolution and the outcomes of our inquiry exercise. Also other authors have extended the CoI framework out of their originally intended field of application. For instance, McKlin, Harmon, Evans, & Jone (2001) used the cognitive portion of the framework as a coding scheme to test the results of previous studies of a neural networking process. Also, Vaughan (2004) has adapted and applied the CoI framework to a faculty development context.

As mentioned above, the ground for the CoI framework was laid by Garrison et al. (2000) in terms of three presences: cognitive, social and teaching presences. According to Akyol (2009): "Cognitive presence, as operationalized through the Practical Inquiry model, is a process that is consistent with the transactional nature of the CoI framework. (...) Cognitive presence can be both a student activity or a prescription, (that is) it describes potentially learning activities as well as prescriptions for deep and meaningful learning. (p.125).

Furthermore, (Akyol, 2009), "cognitive presence includes:

- Searching for relevant information
- Connecting and integrating information
- Actively confirming the understanding in a collaborative and reflective learning process" (p.125)

All the activities mentioned above are present in our ITPCEE exercise, with the role of the "student" being taken by the individual PC team members and "student activity or prescription" being the PC suggestions for the design of particular learning environments. Furthermore, according to Swan, Shea, Richardson, Ice, Garrison, Cleveland-Innes and Arbaugh (2008), "cognitive presence may be the least researched and understood of the three presences, yet it is cognitive presence that goes for the heart of a CoI" (p. 4). The development of the cognitive presence construct by Garrison et al. (2000) is grounded in the critical thinking literature and operationalized by the Practical Inquiry model (Garrison et al, 2001). Similar to Vaughan (2004) we shall adapt and apply the CoI framework to a faculty development context in which case the cognitive presence becomes an inquiry process into counseling practice (Vaughan & Garrison, 2006b). The ability of the community to support and sustain this inquiry forms the social presence. The opportunities for blended (face to face and online exchanges) support are encapsulated

within the pedagogical (or teaching) presence. The intersection of the three presences gives rise eventually to the learning or educational experience or, in our case, to insights on the PC process.

Two levels of analysis of CIFE's efforts are possible: one can investigate individual PC processes (micro-level of analysis) or one can look at the overall systematizing exercise where we analyze all PC processes that we have participated in over the years (macro-level of analysis). In both cases one may use adequate adaptations of the CoI framework. We shall comment briefly on the two levels, although for reasons of space in this chapter we shall only address the macro-level of analysis.

At the micro-level of analysis we have a large number of individual PC experiences. The social and cognitive presences are also basic elements of our individual PC projects. Social presence is conveyed via the interdisciplinary teams that design, implement and evaluate the PC process, in conjunction with the lecturers involved. Cognitive presence in our case is a dynamic state of awareness where various interdisciplinary backgrounds (from the team members) strive to produce the optimal PC experience. Here, the "teaching presence" is the more fundamental aspect of our work and, in fact, teaching presence is the triggering factor in the process. In our adapted model we interpret this teaching presence as the teaching project that the lecturers wish to improve or innovate upon.

A few words on the social presence are in order. Of course, in every PC project there are regular meetings where all project participants discuss, plan and evaluate the various stages of the project. However, the social presence of a PC project is maximized when the CIFE pedagogical expert also holds informal discussions with the lecturers involved in the project (Becerra Labra, Gras-Martí, Hernández Hernández, Montoya Vargas, Osorio Gómez, & Sancho Vinuesa, 2012). This social interaction in informal meetings (let us say at coffee breaks after a lecture, and after having observed the implementation of a given set of suggestions in the lecture hall, for instance) helps creating confidence and opportunities for discussion of pedagogical initiatives that contribute to the success of the PC project.

Figure 2 shows the adapted CoI that one may use for the analysis of individual PC processes. The cognitive presence is embodied in the interdisciplinary expertise of the individual PC teams. The selection of particular strategies to address a specific counseling problem, with the collaboration of the accompanied teacher (teaching presence) leads to a formal and informal exchange of suggestions and procedures that are successful in the right collaboration climate. The connection between the social and the cognitive presences is conveyed by the appropriate discourse that supports the PC process. These three presences are focalized in the particular educational experience. Elements of this social presence are common with the macro-level of analysis to be discussed next.

At the macro-level of analysis conducted via the ITPCEE process we address the whole set of individual counseling process. The adapted CoI framework that we have used in our analysis of this inquiry process can be schematically represented as in Figure 3. The cognitive presence in

Figure 3 is now embodied in the explicit expertise and, more importantly, in the tacit expertise that has accumulated the CIFE staff in PC processes. The social presence is a fundamental part of the exercise, since it is the first occasion that these exchanges take place as a Center since it was established. And the pedagogical presence is framed by the basic principles that guide all CIFE's PC processes. This part is more explicit and commonly shared among the staff than the cognitive presence. Connecting these three presences are actions like supporting discourse (based on basic readings previous to each meeting and seminars given by experts external to CIFE), strategy selection (a process that takes place after individual PC experiences have been discussed) and setting agendas for the following sets of meetings. All this contributes to the reflection on counseling practice, a reflection that aims at systematization and laying the grounds for proactivity and innovation for future PC experiences.

So, in essence, the three presences, linked by the corresponding activities, lead in the micro-level of analysis to the design of learning environments, Figure 2, and to the reflection about counseling practice in the macro-level of analysis,

Figure 2. Adaptation of the CoI framework for the micro-level of analysis of PC (single PC experiences) (Adapted from Garrison, Anderson & Archer, 2000)

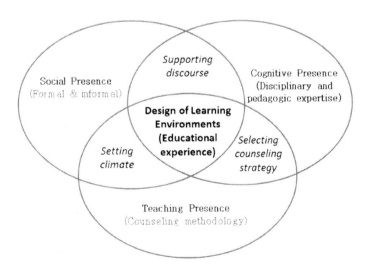

Figure 3. Adaptation of the CoI framework for the macro-level of analysis of the ITPCEE process (overall PC experiences) (Adapted from Garrison, Anderson & Archer, 2000)

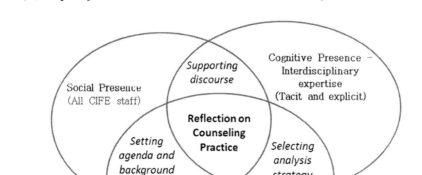

Figure 3. For a more detailed analysis of the inquiry process (ITPCEE) we need, though, to modify the Practical Inquiry model.

Within the cognitive-presence sphere Garrison, Anderson and Archer (2001) developed the standard Practical Inquiry model as a more detailed process description. The original Practical Inquiry model is defined by two axes, a vertical axis reflecting the integration of thought and action and a horizontal axis reflecting the interface of deliberation and practice. This interface is integrated by the perception or awareness of experience in the conception of ideas. This "experience cycle" that leads to cognitive development, with the necessary aid of teaching and social presence, is furthermore made explicit in the Practical Inquiry model via a four phase sequence, labeled as follows: triggering event, exploration, integration and resolution. For more details of this process model see Garrison et al. (2000, 2001).

In line with the adapted CoI framework sketched in Figures 2 and 3, and for the analysis of the ITPCEE effort, we have adapted the Practical Inquiry model as shown in Figure 4. As in the original Practical Inquiry model, the vertical axis reflects the integration of thought and action,

as well as the collaborative nature of individual teams' efforts and social interaction during the exercise. The model integrates discussion and reflection episodes which are conducted in a manner that will be described in the next section. These processes take place over a several week period. The horizontal axis represents the interface of the deliberation on individual PC experiences and the synthesis and distillation of the whole set of experiences. The extremes of the horizontal axis are episodes of conception and common process awareness. As indicated by the model proposed by Garrison et al. (2000), these extremes are also the points of insight and understanding. Overall, Figure 4 contains procedures or actions outside the circle, and the products obtained from these are pictured inside the circle.

As indicated in Figure 4, the inquiry process model can be divided in four distinct phases for analytic purposes: exploration, comparative analysis, distillation and renewed practices. However, these phases often occur in practice in a combination of ways. For instance, the comparative analysis may lead directly to a set of renewed procedures. And the exploration of past experiences taking place after several sessions of Prac-

Figure 4. Modified practical inquiry model (Adapted from Garrison, Anderson & Archer, 2001)

tical Inquiry have occurred, may lead directly to a distillation that encompasses all the episodes under scrutiny. At any rate, the basic theoretical elements of the adapted Practical Inquiry model are, of course, deliberation, conception, basic practices and agreed procedures, as indicated by the ends of the two crossing axes, Figure 4. Furthermore, the cycle of the Practical Inquiry model need not always be circulated in the same direction, as the inquiry process progresses.

Next, the basic inquiry model will be applied to the CIFE's PC program inquiry process.

INQUIRY THROUGH PEDAGOGICAL COUNSELING EXPERIENCE EXCHANGE (ITPCEE)

First we shall describe the startup and initial phases of the inquiry process. Then we shall describe the categories that we have designed in order to analyze the whole experience and we shall discuss these categories in terms of our particular inquiry process: ITPCEE.

Setting up the Inquiry Process

CIFE teams conducting PC with lecturers in various disciplines have developed over time a number of strategies for their professional practice. For this reason, CIFE decided to set up a space for collective reflection and interchange of counseling knowledge and experiences which may lead to enriching the practice. The field of PC is a recognized area of research and development since the 90s, and deals with the analysis of educational counseling at University level for academic development (Perry & Smart, 2007). We work within a constructivist setting (Lueddeke, 1999) and action research methods in education are given priority in our community, especially in the formal and non-formal, as well as traditional and online educational settings that are part of the PC projects. Furthermore, Elliot's (1990) analysis of the relationship between an external research agent and the lecturer directly relates to our work (see Comparative Analysis).

The ITPCEE process was set up as a series of face to face meetings interspersed with online exchanges. The initial purpose of the exercise was formulated as follows: *To start a dialogue about the pedagogical practices of CIFE staff that take part in Pedagogical Counseling to lecturers, in various disciplines and different educational levels. To share our strategies to the initial questions about our pedagogical work, given in Table 1.* These categories emerge from the questions that were set up at the initial stages of the inquiry process. Before starting this space of exchange we explored which topics of PC could be of common interest and could represent an opportunity to strengthen the counselors' practice in two ways: in the development of each PC exercise and in the construction of a collective knowledge based on the experiences of the various teams.

The inquiry process evolves around initial questions for each session that is reformulated in more precise terms as the experience evolves. Although various theoretical sources are used in the inquiry, the main source for reflection is the practitioners own counseling experience. We shall describe the various 'moments' through which CIFE staff has evolved in the ITPCEE and the types of interactions that occurred among them, in terms of a CoI along the lines expressed by Garrison, Anderson, & Archer, (2010). The three main moments in the community development process, the initial moment, the moment of topic exploration, and the moment of methodological exploration, will be analyzed in the Exploration section.

The meetings' focus is on the particular approaches that are applied in overcoming the daily challenges that one encounters in the counseling process. This leads us to concentrate in our past practices and to reflect upon them. Initially, two phases for the community development were planned: a series of exploratory sessions, followed by a series of regular and formal meetings. Periodic meetings were planned for eight months, and a follow up will be based on online interaction. About 22 members of CIFE were invited to the face to face working sessions; 60-80% members attended each session regularly. Cloud computing resources and communication tools have been employed to support the community via online exchange and storage of information. In particular a virtual space is shared among the members where all the papers for discussion are stored, as well as the presentations and documents containing the diagnosis and conclusions of each working session.

The starting points for discussions were various documents about the pedagogical principles of CIFE. During the first phase, various team members exposed their counseling experiences. The objective of the first series of meetings was to recognize the various avenues that are followed by the CIFE groups in order to identify the initial needs and topics that are addressed when a counseling project is started.

Each presentation was followed by group work and a discussion of the main issues brought out

Table 1. Initial questions and categories for the ITPCEE inquiry process with the objective of carrying out research and to learn (collectively) about the practice of PC

Questions	Categories
How are we thinking about the pedagogical aspects in the counseling processes that we perform both within and outside the University? How do we conceptualize / understand the pedagogical counseling process? Must this process be different according to the different disciplines attended? What characterizes the PC practice in CIFE's pedagogical model?	How is the pedagogical element understood? How is the PC understood? How is disciplinary knowledge integrated in the counseling process? (That is, what is its relation with the place CIFE occupies in the organizational structure of the University?). What characterizes the PC practice?

by the presentation and concluded with a socialization of the discussions and proposals of each group as well as a suggestion for the topic to be dealt with in the following meeting. The outcomes of these activities were always posted in the CoI digital space. About midterm in the calendar of meetings an online survey was administered, in order to acknowledge the current interests of the team members as well as a means of collecting suggestions for the contents of the second phase of the development of the CoI.

The group work on each session's starting questions was based on two kinds of information: a practical component arising from the PC of each participant and a conceptual component, related to program evaluation and teacher formation. Apart from agreeing on the topic for each session, the methodological principles were agreed upon also, and whenever appropriate one of the teams presented their own view and experience. This served as a generating topic that led later on to a space of refection with the participants organized in small cross teams (i.e., teams that had as few overlapping members from ordinary PC teams as possible). Different forms of participation were sought after, in order to favor reflexive analysis among all members of staff involved in the ITPCEE.

Elements for the Analysis of the Inquiry Process

As we have described, the focus of the ITPCEE exercise is on the connection between CIFE's staff counseling practice and the accompanied teachers' course redesign. This project is part of the professional development program for faculty that wishes to improve their teaching and their students' learning. The CoI framework was used to guide the inquiry via the ITPCEE process. The framework is based on a collaborative constructivist perspective of education, the integration of "personal reconstruction of experience and social collaboration" (Garrison & Archer, 2000, p.11).

Table 2 shows how we have also adapted the CoI framework to our own project. The three basic spheres or presences of the CoI framework are categorized in various phases, and an indicator for each of these phases has been provided. In the following we shall comment briefly on the table contents, as applied to the ITPCEE process.

Cognitive Presence

According to Vaughan (2010) "cognitive presence is the element in the CoI framework that is most basic to success in higher education." Cognitive presence is evident in our ITPCEE exercise in the interdisciplinary expertise that CIFE members bring to each individual PC project, and the ability of the group to reflect upon our past PC experiences in search for meaningful practices to illuminate the future. Together with social and teaching presence, they facilitate the emergence of new perspectives on the PC practice. Cognitive presence means (Garrison & Anderson, 2003) "facilitating the analysis, construction, and confirmation of meaning and understanding in a community of learners through sustained discourse and reflection" (p. 55). This is one of the objectives of the ITPCEE project, where 'meaning' and 'understanding' refers to the PC process as practiced by various CIFE teams.

The CoI framework developed by Garrison et al. (2000) offers new possibilities of comprehension of the dynamics of the ITPCEE. Apart from reaching new knowledge or learning about PC in each moment of the process, one also achieves the implementation of a collective inquiry process that can be recognized as a form of cognitive presence, in which the proposed categories can be found: exploration, confrontation, synthesis and distillation. The activities that are proper of cognitive presence, as appointed by Akyol (2009), can be found in the ITPCEE through the following kinds of exercises:

Table 2. Community of inquiry for ITPCEE process — Categories and indicators for the macro-level of analysis of the inquiry process. The categories of the Cognitive Presence sphere are taken from Figure 4. (Adapted from Vaughan and Garrison, 2006a)

Sphere	Description	Category/Phase	Indicators
Cognitive Presence – Interdisciplinary Expertise (Tacit / Explicit)	The extent to which CIFE faculty are able to construct and conduct PC through sustained reflection, discourse, and application in a specific learning environment.	Exploration	Setting up the stage with the accompanied lecturer and defining key questions or issues for investigation
		Comparative Analysis	Exchanging perspectives and information about PC processes with CIFE colleagues, and making explicit tacit assumptions and procedures
		Distillation	Extracting ideas and procedures from individual PC project developments
		Renewed Practices	Forming new ideas related with innovative teaching practice
Social Presence (All CIFE staff)	The ability of faculty in the ITPCEE process meetings and exercises to project themselves socially and emotionally with past real experiences and with their full personalities. Faculty learn best from each other.	Establishing Individual PC Experiences	Expressing emotions and results from the individual experiences
		Open Communication	Detailed expression and introspection on PC experiences
		Group Cohesion	Fostering collaboration and inter-team fertilization
Pedagogical Presence (Structure / Process)	The design, facilitation, and direction of the inquiry and community processes for the purpose of realizing person-ally meaningful and educationally worthwhile learning outcomes for faculty in an environment that carefully integrates face-to-face and online sessions and activities.	Organizing and design-ing the PC development program	Setting various PC objectives and methods
		Facilitating discourse in the community	Stimulating and sustaining the sharing of personal experiences and insights
		Extracting direct instruction for faculty participants, from past experiences	Modeling and focusing discussion, activities, and ITPCEE project construction

- Searching for relevant information: the relevant information is identified from the reflection on the own practice, by iden-tifying the challenges and questionings that emerge from this practice in PC that is in agreement with CIFE's pedagogical principles.
- Connecting and integrating information: the meetings are conducted as peer learn-ing exercises, with a foundation both in practical and theoretical knowledge.
- Starting from the topics that were decided as theme axes, actively confirming the un-derstanding in a collaborative and reflec-tive learning process in which a personal and a collective inquiry process occurs, oriented to identifying and analyzing the learning outcomes from each one of the shared experiences.

As mentioned in previous section, the original Practical Inquiry model developed by Garrison et al. (2000) to guide the analysis of cognitive pres-ence in blended educational experiences contained four categories: triggering event, exploration, integration, and application/resolution. We have modified them to exploration, confrontation, synthesis and distillation, in order to describe and analyze the inquiry process in our ITPCEE project, Figure 4 and Table 2. Let us comment upon them in detail.

Exploration

Along the process one may identify the elements that configure the exploration. We initially recognize the questionings that each participant brings as a result of their personal experience; then a group discussion allows us to identify those aspects that the group considers are essential for PC practice, and which have to be analyzed and understood for collective analysis and for strengthening of individual teams' practice.

Comprehension and analysis of the experiences are the initial steps of the inquiry process. Peer experiences help in illustrating and understanding the ways that the group has been addressing these nodal questions. Although each experience contributes in itself some element to the practice, it also offers input for a comparative analysis that allows the recognition of different perspectives about the aspects under scrutiny.

The ITPCEE process started with the 'exploration' of a specific PC case. In spite of the fact that CIFE has a 'culture' for PC, usually most of CIFE staff is unaware of specific PC past procedures for the large variety of situations that have demanded CIFE's pedagogical assistance in the past. The presentation of a specific case is an opportunity to make explicit the team's implicit and explicit assumptions about PC. This is called tacit and explicit knowledge in other contexts (Benner, 1984; Dreyfus & Dreyfus, 1986). Lots of questions arise about the PC case that is presented in a given session as well as concerning each staff's past experiences with PC projects.

First Meeting: Initial Moment

The first question that we addressed was the role and challenges played by disciplinary knowledge in a PC process. This question invited reconsidering the function of a University center for lecturer's professional development like CIFE, and how to approach this function from the different faculties. Since this is a relatively new service in Universities, the definition of its tasks and identity is a relevant topic for study.

Various views emerged about the possibilities of a PC offered from a specific disciplinary expertise or from a more multidisciplinary formation centered around "general" aspects of teaching and learning. The need was also put forward to clarify the role that PC fulfills in the pedagogical experts' experience and, in that respect, what should the counselor's role be in the educational experience that it is accompanying.

The discussion, based upon the analysis of theoretical sources and various PC experiences, led to new questionings and renewed comprehension. We decided, then, to address in parallel various aspects of the counseling process, namely, purpose, scope, topics involved and the necessary methodology to conduct it. The importance to address the counseling process from a research perspective was recognized, that is, to understand it as a practice that requires systematization, understanding and input coming from research.

Here are some of the questions that arose in the process:

- What kind of (pedagogical?) knowledge do the lecturers have, and what is the knowledge that we expect them to develop from our counseling and professional development program?
- How do lecturers learn how to teach?
- How is it taught in the specific lecturer's area?
- What kind of knowledge is proper of teaching as a profession?
- What kind of abilities, knowledge and practices must the PC teams acquire in order to effectively accompany the lecturers and to instruct them in a program of professional development for the teaching of specific subject areas?

Moment of Theme Exploration

In response to the purposes of this CoI we analyzed the diagnostic stage as the initial moment of every PC process. With this aim, the participants analyzed their own experience with the following question as a reference guide: How can we identify the necessity or the opportunity of an intervention, in which the PC will focus?

These activities led to the recognition that the counseling practice is a complex endeavor, and many questions arose in terms of the scope, emphasis and methodology of the intervention. In order to achieve a better comprehension of these aspects we referred to the diversity of theoretical standpoints from which staff members oriented their pedagogical practices. Particular attention received the methodology of action research and the logical framework approach for the analysis and evaluation of the pedagogical needs of a specific lecturer or a specific learning situation.

As more and more experiences were systematized and discussed, the evidences arose for a variety of approaches, knowledge, capabilities, or tools developed, that enriched the participants' theoretical and practical toolset, and also demanded a deeper study. As a result, four central topics

for reflection emerged related to the diagnosis, which allowed for an integral view of the counseling process. These topics are displayed in Figure 5. From these four reflection axes it is possible to strengthen the counseling practice and, at the same time, to allow for the particular aspects in the intervention of each one of the projects. The central consensus was to develop counseling in agreement with CIFE's pedagogical principles, which are based upon "critical thinking, participation and reflection". As indicated in Figure 5, a first synthesis was achieved, including a consensus about procedures and conceptions.

Moment of Methodological Exploration

Each time an experience was socialized, new perspectives were introduced that were, in turn, analyzed from the evolving perspectives. The topics or axial aspects considered regularly were the pedagogical principles (reflexive, critical and participative) and the research perspective; they both contributed to making explicit the assumptions underlying the implementation of the counseling process.

Therefore, the research process itself became a new theme axis which was addressed in two

Figure 5. Clockwise from the top left, central topics in the initiation of a PC process

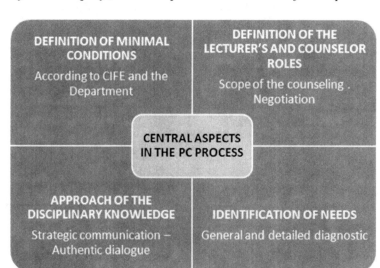

directions: as a methodology for counseling and as a means to construct knowledge about the PC (counseling as an object of study). In the first direction, we analyzed experiences based on action research, a methodology which is consistent with the principles that were outlined above. On the other hand, by taking counseling as an object of study allowed us to approach the complexity that this practice represents and at the same time to look deeply into common interests that may translate into collective learning. In fact, by undertaking the counseling process as a research practice one puts forward new objectives in the educational experience, both for the lecturer under counseling and for the team, since the aim is not just to solve an educational need but the counseling process becomes a new possibility to build knowledge in a collaborative manner with both actors involved, lecturer and counseling team.

The process as described so far can be visualized as a progressive spiral-like analysis in which every comprehension stage leads to new questionings which, upon discussion and elaboration, offer a new level of comprehension about the initial topics of the ITPCEE, Figure 6.

Comparative Analysis

The second category of the adapted practical inquiry model in Figure 4 and Table 2 is 'comparative analysis, a process based upon 'confrontation,' that is, searching for a clarification of the PC process conducted by various teams and by each staff member's experience in these teams. The confrontation phase of the ITPCEE process

consists of a series of presentations and reflections that allows CIFE staff to become immersed in a sort of meta-PC analysis in their own right. This process was initiated eight months ago and is still ongoing.

Early in the ITPCEE project, the CIFE staff was introduced to the CoI framework as an aid for reflection about their own PC experience and to address the second stage, 'comparative analysis.' In the reflection that follows each PC case that is presented in a regular meeting, staff members split up in various working subgroups that address one or several of general questions that the presentation has prompted. In this manner, CIFE members take a community or team approach toward the analysis of the PC processes. An effort is made so that staff who have collaborated in teams in past PC experiences, do not coincide in the subgroups that are formed.

Each regular session concludes with a socialization of the conclusions reached by each working group and a summary of the session is posted to an electronic discussion and reference board. This specific website was prepared for the ITPCEE exercise. The discussion forum serves as a reference and consulting space for future meetings in the series, as well as a place for all staff members to stay updated (usually an average 70% staff attends a particular meeting).

As a provisional outcome of the comparative analysis process participants are asked to provide basic knowledge about the general aspects of a PC project that should be common to all PC, Figure 7. This knowledge is conceptualized in terms of general and disciplinary specific strategies and the

Figure 6. Evolving nature and stages in the ITPCEE process in the authors' CoI

- o Counseling as a research activity.
- o Orientation from the pedagogical principles of CIFE.
- o Needs, roles, disciplinary knowledge, boundary conditions.

Figure 7. Fundamental aspects of the PC process

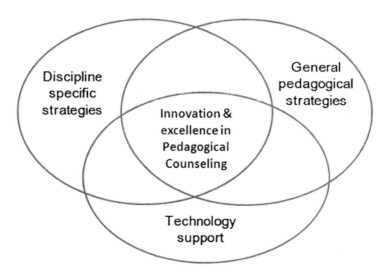

necessary technological support for innovation. The aim is to provide excellence in particular PC processes.

Often, the comparative analysis phase is enhanced by inviting external experts to address some of the controversial or relevant issues that show up during the exploration activities. These experts usually introduce foreign models and reflections that are useful for CIFE's staff, especially with regards to the two phases mentioned so far, and the next phase, distillation.

The socialization of experiences shows evidence of the diversity of practices that different teams share when performing PC. This diversity is due to a number of factors: proximity in the disciplinary areas of the lecturers and the PC experts, the counselor's expertise, the commitment or interest shown by the lecturers, the independence or autonomy that the lecturers display in course redesigns, etc. All this diversity is appreciated as an opportunity to deepen into the comprehension of the topics under study.

Distillation

The next category of the adapted practical inquiry model is distillation and synthesis, which in the original Garrison et al. (2000) model was called 'integration'. In the ITPCEE project it is a difficult process to extract the more relevant assumptions, suggestions and procedure from various PC experiences, so that they may become a relevant and useful ingredient in one's future PC project. However, this is the most useful outcome of the ITPCEE process from the point of view of the individual CIFE staff members. The last category, renewed practices, that we shall discuss later, belongs more to CIFE as an institution, not to its individual staff members.

The dynamics of the community includes opportunities for synthesis of the aspects under study and the opportunities to achieve a validation of the consensus that may be reached. In this manner, learning constructed from the experiences of various teams is spelled out after the collective perspective is imprinted upon them. As a result of the synthesis of experiences one may achieve:

- Orienting a counseling process from the pedagogical principles of CIFE, giving new meanings to the experience and possibly suggesting different ways of addressing the various PC components; it suggests a redefinition of the roles of the accompanied lecturer and the counselor, especially regarding the commitment of both lecturer and counselor.
- A counseling process based upon research represents a methodological approach that brings new elements to the knowledge about the counseling practice and at the same time favors the professional development of the lecturer undergoing PC.

In the process of distillation and synthesis, each staff member's approach to PC has to be enriched with the development of a coherent and refreshed approach to PC, which makes use of the conclusions reached in the exploration and discussions stages that have been held. The refined PC model has to be put into practice, though, and new problems and viewpoints will have to be considered then, which will lead to further synthesis efforts, in an ever-expanding PC process development. In fact, the always changing educational environment, both at individual course level and at the broad University level, assures a need for continuous synthesis and reformulation of PC exercises. This makes the CoI effort a valid and lasting framework for CIFE staff professional development (Perry & Smart, 2007) and a place for growth in creativity.

Often, the synthesis effort requires more than one regular staff meeting during the ITPCEE exercise, and individual team meetings are conducted outside of the regular meetings. The communication among these team meetings is conducted both face to face and online, via the group website.

As an example of the distillation process we may show an interesting way to analyze single PC processes from the perspective of the educational roles assumed by the consultant, that is, the

function that CIFE staff members hold in each particular process. Following Champion, Kiel, & McLendon (1990) a two-dimensional consulting role grid may be drawn taking into account the consultant responsibility for project results, and the consultant responsibility for clients' growth. The intensity of the intervention roles (low, moderate, high) may also be depicted in the grid. In Figure 8 we have adapted this consulting role grid to the analysis of CIFE's PC efforts. The horizontal axis indicates the intensity of the consultant's responsibility for project results, and the vertical axis gives a measure of the consultant's responsibility for the accompanied lecturers' growth. As an example, three specific itineraries are shown, corresponding to three particular micro-processes. In case I, a direct change of role from a reflective observer to a coach and, later on, a partner is described. This is a situation where both the project results and the professional development of the participants are maximized. In case II, the emphasis is on professional development, which increases from a hands-on expert role to a counselor, via a facilitators' intermediate phase. The low intervention line of Figure 8 is not crossed in this case. And in case III an increase in the level of quality results is achieved as well as a more sophisticated role of the pedagogical expert as a modeler. A high level of intervention is needed in this case.

This topic of the role of PC intervention, as well as more specific results of the ITPCEE process in terms of the counseling practices will be presented elsewhere.

Renewed Practices

One expects that the knowledge built in this process is incorporated in the development of the new projects, as new comprehensions are achieved of the components that configure the PC, as long as collective work spaces are available, both for the development of projects and for the collective reflection about the counseling practice. The new knowledge becomes part of the renewed

Figure 8. Three sample itineraries (I, II and III) in a project results versus professional development map. Each axis has a qualitative scale from low to high achievement. The dotted cross line marks the boundary between low intervention (below the line) and high intervention (above the line). (Based on Champion et al., 1990)

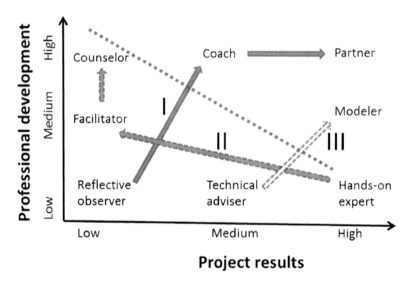

reference frame from which further projects will be designed and developed.

The fourth category of the practical inquiry model, renewed practices, is the more difficult phase for CIFE as an institution, because it demands planning and implementing essential knowledge coming from a great many and varied individual PC projects, so that a general set up for CIFE projects can be defined.

As mentioned in CIFE's Pedagogical Counseling section, the fact that these general basic procedures and assumptions applicable to any PC project were not explicitly stated in the past although they were shared by CIFE staff as implicit or tacit knowledge, made this overall ITPCEE exercise so necessary, interesting and useful for our center. In the words of Garrison and Anderson (2003), referring to their own fourth category, application/ resolution: "the results from this phase often raise further questions and issues, triggering new cycles of inquiry, and, thereby, encouraging continuous learning" (p. 60). The distillation phase of the

ITPCEE project is a mid-term objective, since a layout of general and all-encompassing rules of procedure can only be formulated after many past PC's experiences are exposed and analyzed, and each staff member has appropriated the valuable output for her or his own practice. This is more truthful in PC endeavors because a 10 year-plus experience in PC has shown that each project presents itself with very specific pedagogical and technological problems.

An essential aspect of all PC programs involves the evaluation of the implementation of the program, in order to determine its effectiveness from the point of view of the lecturers involved as well as the lecturer's students. Furthermore, internal and general CIFE evaluation procedures have to be developed for individual projects. The evaluation stage involves then the various ingredients of the PC process: accompanying procedures, lecturer's implementation, technological tools developed eventually, and students' receptions of these innovations.

Social Presence

Garrison (2009) defines social presence as "the ability of participants to identify with the community, communicate purposefully in a trusting environment, and develop inter-personal relationships by way of projecting their individual personalities." Social presence becomes a major challenge in virtual and blended environments. However, most of the ITPCEE process has been carried out during regular staff meetings which can be described as being perceived by CIFE faculty participating in a familiar and safe environment. The process has been characterized also by an eagerness to learn from each other. Participants report to have adapted several strategies presented by other members during our sessions and discussions. This feature makes this process a perfect opportunity for a faculty development program based on peer teaching and learning.

The social presence construct developed by Garrison et al. (2000) contains three categories with corresponding indicators for social presence: emotional expression, open communication and group cohesion. In order to describe and analyze the ITPCEE process we have modified them in Table 2, Establishing individual experiences, Open communication, and Group cohesion.

Establishing individual experiences is the starting point and the basis for the whole ITPCEE process, in an environment that increases the possibility of faculty in the meetings and exercises to project themselves socially and emotionally with past real experiences and with their full personalities. All this happens in an atmosphere of open communication, that is, with a detailed expression and introspection on PC experiences. Participants trust their peers enough to be able to assess their past experiences weighting their strengths and weaknesses and to present their right choices as well as their mistakes during their counseling projects. And finally, group cohesion was essential to fostering collaboration and cross-team fertilization. During the process the possibility emerged of conforming new inquiry groups aimed to answer the different questions that have come out during the sessions. This action opened the possibility to interact with different members of the Center with whom we had not worked before. This cross-team fertilization allows seeing new perspectives on the issues studied and have evolved into new inquiry groups sharing research and writing interest about counseling in higher education. The results of the process will be seen in several forthcoming publications.

Pedagogical Presence

Anderson, Rourke, Garrison, & Archer (2001) define teaching presence as "the design, facilitation, and direction of cognitive and social processes for the purpose of realizing personally meaningful and educationally worthwhile learning outcomes" (p. #). For the purposes of the ITPCEE project we have defined pedagogical presence as the design, facilitation, and direction of the inquiry and community processes for the purpose of realizing personally meaningful and educationally worthwhile learning outcomes for faculty in an environment that carefully integrates face-to-face and online sessions and activities. The teaching presence construct developed by Garrison et al. (2000) contains three categories in which they group the indicators for teaching presence: instructional management, building understanding and direct instruction. In order to describe and analyze the inquiry process in the ITPCEE we have modified them to organizing and designing the PC development program, facilitating discourse in the community, and extracting direct instruction for faculty participants from past experiences.

Organizing and designing the PC development program was an essential target of the whole exercise. From the beginning, the ITPCEE aimed to fostering professional development among CIFE staff taking advantage of a supportive collegiate environment that allows us to explore new methods. Being part of the group in charge of organizing the sessions gave direction to the group activities by planning session objectives around key questions and issues suggested by our counseling practices over the years. From the first session we also worked on the application of CIFE pedagogical principles: criticism, participation and reflection. These principles not only guided the planning and development of our activities but also gave direction to the inquiry itself by constantly considering questions like: what does it mean to develop pedagogical counseling guided by those principles?

Facilitating discourse in the community means stimulating and sustaining the sharing of personal experiences and insights. As we explained before, each session began with the socialization of previous counseling experiences by individual members of the team. This part of the session has proved to be of great significance for all the participants as they can relate their own personal experiences to those exposed, and discuss and integrate new insights into their own counseling practices.

And thirdly, extracting direct instruction for faculty participants, from past experiences was achieved by modeling and focusing discussion, activities, and ITPCEE project construction. "We never educate directly, but indirectly by means of the environment" (Dewey, 1916, p. 78). The very form of these sessions replicates the features of the learning environments we seek to promote when supporting faculty professional development of teaching practices: Inquiry based and problem oriented, peer teaching and learning, collaborative learning, authentic performance, intrinsic motivation and formative evaluation. All these features went without saying during the sessions of the project but we were all aware of their happening.

CONCLUSION AND FUTURE RESEARCH DIRECTIONS

The objectives of the PC inquiry exercise were fulfilled as we have discussed in detail in this chapter. From the point of view of the CoI theoretical framework one may ask what have we gained in the ITPCEE exercise by modeling it with the adapted CoI framework and Practical Inquiry model? The CoI framework is a rich and powerful tool for analyzing the practice of our group. The process of applying a CoI framework for the analysis of the development and structuring of shared experiences in a given field of practice may be of use to develop similar procedures in academic communities.

Although the first phase of development of the CIFE unit has been the result of individual lecturers or individual University programs approaching CIFE with a pedagogical consulting request, in a second phase starting after the ITPCEE exercise described in this paper the University aims at a more structured and widespread action that affects lecturers in every University department. In this new environment, the experience and fresh conceptualization of PC practices achieved by means of the approach outlined in this work will be of the utmost significance, and will clear the way for the emergence of renewed and more powerful intervention schemes.

In this new environment we shall keep an eye open to the possibility of designing an even more sophisticated analytical tool, based upon the modified CoI framework as developed in this work, that will accompany the application of PC principles to larger-scale projects.

REFERENCES

Akyol, Z. (2009). *Examining teaching presence, social presence, cognitive presence, satisfaction and learning in online and blended course contexts.* Doctoral dissertation, Middle East Technical University, 2009.

Akyol, Z., Arbaugh, J. B., Cleveland-Innes, M., Garrison, D. R., Ice, P., Richardson, J. C., Swan, K. (2003). A response to the review of the community of inquiry framework. *Journal of Distance Education / Revue de l'Éducation à Distance, 23*(2) 123-136.

Anderson, T., Rourke, L., Garrison, D. R., & Archer, W. (2001). Assessing teaching presence in a computer conferencing context. *Journal of Asynchronous Learning Networks, 5*(2), 1–17.

Arbaugh, J. B. (2008). Does the community of inquiry framework predict outcomes in online MBA courses? *International Review of Research in Open and Distance Learning, 9,* 1–21.

Arbaugh, J. B., Cleveland-Innes, M., Diaz, S. R., Garrison, D. R., Ice, P., Richardson, J. C., & Swan, K. P. (2008). Developing a community of inquiry instrument: Testing a measure of the Community of Inquiry framework using a multi-institutional sample. *The Internet and Higher Education, 11*(3-4), 133–136. doi:10.1016/j.iheduc.2008.06.003

Becerra Labra, C., Gras-Martí, A., Hernández Hernández, C., Montoya Vargas, J., Osorio Gómez, L. A., & Sancho Vinuesa, T. (2012). (accepted). Renovación de la Enseñanza Universitaria Basada en Evidencias (REUBE): Una metodología de acción flexible. *Perfiles Educativos.*

Benner, P. (1984). *From novice to expert: Excellence and power in clinical nursing practice.* Menlo Park, CA: Addison-Wesley. doi:10.1097/00000446-198412000-00025

Bielaczyc, K., & Collins, A. (1999). Learning communities: A reconceptualization of educational practice. In Reigeluth, C. M. (Ed.), *Instructional design theories and models* (*Vol. II,* pp. 30, 269–292). Mahwah, NJ: Lawrence Erlbaum Associates.

Champion, D. P., Kiel, D. H., & McLendon, J. A. (1990). Choosing a consulting role. *Training and Development Journal, 44*(2), 66–69.

Dewey, J. (1933). *How we think.* Boston, MA: D.C. Heath.

Dreyfus, H. L., & Dreyfus, S. E. (1986). *Mind over Machine: the power of human intuition and expertise in the age of the computer.* Oxford, UK: Basil Blackwell.

Elliot, J. (1990). Teachers as researchers: Implications for supervision and for teacher education. *Teaching and Teacher Education, 6*(1), 1–26. doi:10.1016/0742-051X(90)90004-O

Friedman, V. (2001). Creating communities of inquiry in communities of practice. In Reason, P., & Bradbury, H. (Eds.), *Handbook of action research. Participative inquiry and practice.* London, UK: Sage.

Galvis Panqueva, Á. H., & Leal Fonseca, D. E. (2006). Aprendiendo en comunidad: más allá de aprender y trabajar en compañía. *Eduweb. Revista de Tecnología de Información y Comunicación en Educación, 1,* 9–32.

Garrison, D. R. (2004). Transformative leadership and e-learning. In K. Matheos & T. Carey (Eds.), *Advances and challenges in eLearning at Canadian research universities* (pp. 46–54). CHERD Occasional Papers in Higher Education, 12, University of Manitoba.

Garrison, D. R. (2007). Online community of inquiry review: Social, cognitive and teaching presence issues. *Journal of Asynchronous Learning Networks, 11*(1), 61–72.

Garrison, D. R., & Anderson, T. (2003). *E-learning in the 21st century: A framework for research and practice.* New York, NY: Routledge. doi:10.4324/9780203166093

Garrison, D. R., Anderson, T., & Archer, W. (2000). Critical inquiry in a text-based environment: Computer conferencing in higher education. *The Internet and Higher Education, 2*(2-3), 87–105. doi:10.1016/S1096-7516(00)00016-6

Garrison, D. R., Anderson, T., & Archer, W. (2001). Critical thinking, cognitive presence and computer conferencing in distance education. *American Journal of Distance Education, 15*(1), 7–23. doi:10.1080/08923640109527071

Garrison, D. R., Anderson, T., & Archer, W. (2010). The first decade of the community of inquiry framework: A retrospective. *The Internet and Higher Education, 13*, 5–9. doi:10.1016/j.iheduc.2009.10.003

Garrison, D. R., & Archer, W. (2000). *A transactional perspective on teaching and learning. A framework for adult and higher education.* Oxford, UK: Pergamon.

Garrison, D. R., & Kanuka, H. (2004). Blended learning: Uncovering its transformative potential in higher education. *The Internet and Higher Education, 7*(2), 95–105. doi:10.1016/j.iheduc.2004.02.001

Lueddeke, G. R. (1999). Toward a constructivist framework for guiding change and innovation in higher education. *The Journal of Higher Education, 70*(3), 235–260. doi:10.2307/2649196

McKlin, T., Harmon, S. W., Evans, W., & Jones, M. G. (2001). Cognitive presence in web based learning: A content analysis of students' online discussions. *American Journal of Distance Education, 15*(1), 7–23.

Morgan, C., & Metni, E. (2006). *United beyond our diversity, a global panorama - Tiles of unity.* Presented at The role of Information Communications Technology (ICT) in Bridge Building and Social Inclusion. University of Ulster, Northern Ireland. Retrieved December 2, 2010 from http://www.socsci.ulster.ac.uk./education/ict_conf/abstract/morgan.html

Perry, R. P., & Smart, J. C. (2007). *Scholarship of teaching and learning in higher education.* New York, NY: Springer. doi:10.1007/1-4020-5742-3

Swan, K., Shea, P., Richardson, J., Ice, P., Garrison, D. R., Cleveland-Innes, M., & Arbaugh, J. B. (2008). Validating a measurement tool of presence in online communities of inquiry. *E-Mentor, 2*(24), 1-12. Retrieved June 23, 2010, from http://www.e-mentor.edu.pl/e_index.php?numer=24&all

Vaughan, N., & Garrison, D. R. (2006b). How blended learning can support a faculty development community of inquiry. *Journal of Asynchronous Learning Networks, 10*(4), 139–152.

Vaughan, N. D. (2004). Technology in support of faculty learning communities. In Cox, M. D., & Richlin, L. (Eds.), *Building faculty learning communities: New directions for teaching and learning, No. 97* (pp. 101–109). San Francisco, CA: Jossey-Bass. doi:10.1002/tl.137

Vaughan, N. D. (2010). A blended community of inquiry approach: Linking student engagement and course redesign. *The Internet and Higher Education, 13*(1-2), 60–65. doi:10.1016/j.iheduc.2009.10.007

Vaughan, N. D., & Garrison, D. R. (2006a). A blended faculty community of inquiry: Linking leadership, course redesign and evaluation. *Canadian Journal of University Continuing Education, 32*(2), 67-92. Retrieved May 12, 2010, from http://www.extension.usask.ca/cjuce/articles/v32pdf/3223.pdf

Wenger, E. (1998). *Communities of practice: Learning, meaning, and identity*. New York, NY: Cambridge University Press.

KEY TERMS AND DEFINITIONS

Disciplinary vs. Pedagogical Knowledge: Expertise that has to converge in an approach to improve the Teaching and Learning process of a given subject matter by means of a Pedagogical Counseling process.

Inquiry Through Pedagogical-Counseling Experience Exchange (ITPCEE): A process set up to analyze, assess and potentiate ongoing support activities by the staff members of the Center for Research and Development in Education (CIFE) in counseling projects of undergraduate and postgraduate programs.

Pedagogical Counseling: A process whereby a pedagogical expert accompanies a teacher in order to analyze specific teaching and learning scenarios, and from an evaluation of his/her current practices, he/she suggests and helps implement ways to try and improve them.

Pedagogical Principles: The basic approach to the design of an adequate teaching and learning scenario, which involves reflexive, critical and participative activities.

Teaching and Learning Process: The combination of materials, methodologies, attitudes, evaluation plans, etc., that a teacher develops in order to help his/her students to learn a given subject material.

Tutoring Design: The plan, materials, methodologies, etc., that the pedagogical counselor designs and implements in collaboration with a teacher.

ENDNOTE

[1]   (Our translation).

Chapter 18
Fostering Social Presence in a Blended Learning Faculty Development Institute

David S. Goldstein
University of Washington Bothell, USA

Carol Leppa
University of Washington Bothell, USA

Andreas Brockhaus
University of Washington Bothell, USA

Rebecca Bliquez
University of Washington Bothell, USA

Ian Porter
University of Washington Bothell, USA

ABSTRACT

To help faculty develop well-designed blended courses, the Community of Inquiry (CoI) framework (Garrison, Anderson & Archer, 2000) was used to design and deliver a ten-week Hybrid Course Development Institute (HCDI) for faculty members from a variety of disciplines. The faculty experienced a blended format and developed courses based on the three components of the CoI framework: cognitive presence, teaching presence, and social presence, the last of which is particularly challenging to achieve. This chapter provides an overview of the HCDI structure, content, and assessment, and suggests ways to foster social presence in and beyond a blended learning institute for faculty members.

DOI: 10.4018/978-1-4666-2110-7.ch018

INTRODUCTION

In this chapter, we aim to describe how we used the Community of Inquiry framework (Garrison, Anderson & Archer, 2000) to undergird a ten-week Hybrid Course Development Institute at the University of Washington Bothell, focusing most keenly on social presence. The social presence construct, and the CoI framework in general, proved to be remarkably successful linchpins for faculty members learning to design blended learning courses from the ground up. We describe in detail the HCDI, explain how social presence operates on three levels in our conception of blended learning on our campus, and present the methods and results of assessing the Institute among the faculty members who participated and among the students enrolled in those teachers' blended-learning courses. We conclude by providing some additional lessons we learned from our first HCDI.

HYBRID COURSE DEVELOPMENT INSTITUTE

The UW Bothell Hybrid Course Development Institute (HCDI) was created in response to increased individual faculty interest in blended teaching and learning, demonstrated efficacy of well-designed blended learning courses (Means B, Toyama Y, Murphy R, Bakia M, Jones K, 2010; Sorg, 2002), popularity of blended courses with students, a need for coordinated faculty development in blended teaching, the opportunity for external funding to support the pilot project for the Nursing Program, and matching internal funding to extend this project to the campus. We received funding from a Promise of Nursing for Washington, Nursing School Grant Program administered by the Foundation of the National Student Nurses' Association in July 2010 to work on increased student access to nursing education. We created a 10-week faculty development course that was delivered in a blended format during Autumn Quarter 2010.

Six Nursing faculty members participated in and completed this blended course; each focused on either the development of a new course, or the revision of a current course into a blended format combining face-to-face and online content. For the HCDI, a blended course was defined as having between 30% and 70% of student coursework online (adapted from Sloan Consortium, 2010). In addition to the Nursing faculty, the UW Bothell Teaching and Learning Center sponsored an additional five faculty members from other academic programs on campus who also completed the HCDI. This cross-program mix of faculty was greatly appreciated by all faculty participants as they formed relationships and partnerships within and across program boundaries on our campus.

We based the HCDI on the Community of Inquiry (CoI) framework developed by Garrison et al. (2000) because, as Shea and Bidjerano (2009) note, "faculty can benefit from understanding, emphasizing, and integrating the components of the model to guide the development of online [and, we would add, blended] courses" (551). The Community of Inquiry (CoI) framework has been used widely as a model for structured learning. In an educational context, a community of inquiry is "a group of individuals who collaboratively engage in purposeful critical discourse and reflection to construct personal meaning and confirm mutual understanding" (Garrison, 2011, p. 15). The strength of this framework lies in its articulation of three interrelated concepts: cognitive presence, teaching presence, and social presence. In their well-known Venn diagram, Garrison and Vaughan (2008) show that any two of the elements in the trio interact with one another, while the intersection of all three components results in the holistic educational experience. We designed the HCDI to demonstrate the main elements of the CoI: Cognitive Presence, Teaching Presence, and Social Presence. The faculty participants received a copy of the Garrison and Vaughan (2008) book as a text for the HCDI and we both modeled the

CoI elements, and required the participants to use the CoI in the design of their blended courses.

The HCDI was designed to give the faculty the "student experience" of a blended course, meaning we conducted the HCDI itself as a blended "course" that met three times in person during the 10-week Autumn Quarter. For the other weeks, the faculty participants worked online with various assignments and deadlines to meet. They worked independently and in groups as they analyzed and designed their blended courses and activities. We have found that the majority of faculty members do not have formal training in pedagogy and have learned how to teach in a "guild" model—first as an apprentice/student (emulating favorite professors/teaching practices they have had when they were students and/or avoiding those practices they disliked), and then as a practitioner/professional. The majority of our faculty members have never taken a blended course so it was important that they gain the student perspective or complete their "apprentice" phase in blended teaching and learning as they learned the content of how to teach in this mode.

Our central learning goal was that participants would create a peer-reviewed, new or redeveloped course syllabus for a blended learning format. Other learning goals included developing effective course and assessment strategies for the blended model, the development of at least one online learning object, and enhanced experience with Web 2.0 tools such as wikis and blogs.

We started the Institute online since we recognized the difficulty of scheduling a meeting during the first week of classes. Initial activities included participants completing the pre-Institute survey (teaching presence), doing some readings in Garrison and Vaughan on blended learning (cognitive presence) and posting a personal introduction in an online discussion board (social presence). For each assignment and activity, we connected back to the CoI framework to illustrate how an activity would promote social, cognitive, or teaching presence, noting that social presence

and teaching presence are known to affect cognitive presence—the actual learning of the concepts (Garrison, Cleveland-Innes, & Fung, 2010) and that, in academic settings, social presence "cannot be artificially separated from the purposeful nature of educational communication (i.e., cognitive and teaching presence)" (Garrison, 2007, p. 65). Moreover, Ke (2010) finds that adult learners who report a stronger sense of community tend to be more satisfied with their learning experience. Other online activities included working on writing good discussion questions, discussing the benefits and challenges of blended learning, sharing learning objects, posting drafts of syllabi, and sharing resources. In addition to the class-wide discussion forums, each participant also had an individual discussion forum to aid in peer review exercises.

Keeping with our effort to model effective blended learning practice, we used the three face-to-face sessions to focus on activities that involve rapid verbal and visual exchanges such as mini-presentations with questions and answers, and brainstorming activities that typically work better in a face-to-face environment (Garrison & Vaughan, 2008). Our presentations were typically 20 minutes or shorter and focused on introducing topics such as the research on blended learning and the CoI framework. Small group and community activities were also valuable as faculty members talked about their online activities in the Institute, brainstormed how to handle workload challenges, and shared examples of activities that worked well in enhancing student learning among other topics.

One of the things we had not anticipated was how important the three face-to-face meetings became for participants to succeed in the Institute. Missing the second meeting proved to be quite detrimental for one faculty member who struggled to catch up and who felt less connected with the group. This issue was discussed at the last meeting, and it served to emphasize the importance of social presence as a key element for student success—one that often gets taken for granted or neglected.

The face-to-face sessions also provided in-class time for working on activities such as completing a hybrid learning planning worksheet (Table 1) and peer reviewing each other's draft syllabi. The worksheet provided a blueprint for developing a blended course syllabus and was helpful for participants to carefully think through what worked best online and what worked best face-to-face and the links between the formats. To be effective, the online and face-to-face portions of a class have to interconnect (Garrison & Vaughan, 2008). To that end, we concluded each face-to-face session with a preview of coming online activities, while we worked toward each face-to-face session during the online portions of the HCDI.

Because we offered netbooks as an incentive for participating in the HCDI, we also spent some time during the face-to-face session troubleshooting hardware and software issues. In hindsight, this used up valuable time that could have been better spent working on pedagogical issues and is one of the reasons that the next Institute offered honoraria rather than a computer.

We also made a wide variety of materials available online for participants to peruse if they were interested. We provided links to learning object repositories such as the Multimedia Educational Resource for Learning and Online Teaching (MERLOT, http://www.merlot.org), TED (http://www.ted.com), the Nursing Education and Technology (NEAT, http://webcls.utmb.edu/neat), Flickr (http://www.flickr.com), and Creative Commons (http://creativecommons.org), and posted a variety of blended teaching resources such as rubrics, copyright advice, best practices, and examples.

HCDI PARTICIPANTS' EVALUATION

We had two primary goals for the evaluation of the HCDI. The first was to assess our faculty participants' experience with the Institute structure and material covered (i.e. did the HCDI support a successful redesign process for their blended courses?). Faculty participants in the HCDI were surveyed at the beginning of the quarter-long Institute, at the midpoint of the Institute, and after the Institute was completed.

In order to assess the technology/web tool learning needs of the faculty, participants were asked to rate their level of experience with the following tools: Online Educational Repositories, Creative Commons, Podcasting Software, Narrated PowerPoint presentations, and Blackboard discussion boards. As a pre-assessment of their experience and comfort with various pedagogies, participants were asked to identify their level of expertise in course development and delivery as listed in Table 2.

The comparison data from the pre- and post-surveys indicate an improvement in the faculty participants' self-identified expertise with blended course pedagogy and experience using peda-

Table 1. Hybrid learning planning worksheet sample content

Worksheet			
Weekly Modules (assuming 30% to 50% of regular class time online)	What class activities will be face to face? How much time do you estimate each activity will take?	What class activities will be online? How much time do you estimate each activity will take?	1. How do these activities address your learning goals? 2. How do the F2F and online activities relate to and support each other? 3. How do the activities represent teaching, cognitive and/or social presence? How does this balance in the course?
Week 1 (Week 2, etc.)			

Table 2. Pre- and post-HCDI participant pedagogy expertise survey results

Self-Rated Expertise in:	Pre-Institute Mean (SD)	Post-Institute Mean (SD)
Developing/delivering a hybrid course	3.0 (1.4)	4.0 (1.3)
Assessing student learning in online work	3.0 (1.5)	3.7 (1.1)
Supporting student social presence online	3.0 (1.5)	3.8 (1.0)
Clearly expressing the course expectations for student learning objectives in a hybrid course	3.1 (1.5)	4.1 (1.2)
Clearly expressing the course expectations for student behavior in a hybrid course	3.0 (1.4)	4.2 (1.1)
Identifying what learning activities work best online	2.9 (1.3)	4.1 (0.5)
Identifying what learning activities work best in person	5.0 (1.0)	5.0 (0.8)
Creating effective online activities	2.9 (1.2)	3.7 (0.7)
Creating effective in person activities	5.2 (1.1)	5.5 (0.5)

1=no experience; 2=very low; 3=low; 4=medium; 5=high; 6=very high

gogically useful Web tools and resources. In nearly every category in which we asked faculty to identify their level of experience or expertise, the increase in mean response from the pre-survey to the post-survey was statistically significant, as determined by the Wilcoxon Ranked Sum Test. Only in their level of experience with Blackboard discussion boards and in their level of expertise with identifying what learning activities work best in person did the participants not indicate a statistically significant enhancement across the surveys.

When asked an open-ended question regarding the major benefits of the HCDI in the post-survey, one faculty participant responded that she was "able to really think through and practice the process of developing a hybrid course," and another participant remarked on no longer "find[ing] it so daunting anymore to develop and teach a true hybrid course."

Interestingly, there were cases where faculty actually downgraded their self-identified expertise with a particular teaching method or tool in

the post-survey as compared to the pre-survey. For example, one faculty member downgraded her levels of expertise in "supporting student social presence online," "expressing the course expectations for student learning objectives in a hybrid course," "expressing the course expectations for student behavior in a hybrid course," and "identifying what learning activities work best online." Rather than indicating a failure on the part of the Institute or the individual faculty member, these data suggest that one of the benefits of the process of designing a blended course is the ability to rethink ingrained teaching practices. Thinking "outside of the classroom," if you will, forces faculty members to return to the classroom and see it anew and perhaps recognize their need for further development.

STUDENTS' EVALUATION

Our second HCDI evaluation goal was to assess satisfaction of students enrolled in participants'

Table 3. Student satisfaction with blended format (selected questions)

Question: Compared to other non-hybrid courses, how would you rate...	Increase or No Difference	Decrease
Amount of interactions with other students	73%	27%
Amount of interaction with instructor	65%	35%
Quality of interaction with other students	80%	20%
Quality of interaction with instructor	78%	22%
	Agree/Strongly Agree	Unsure/Disagree
Would you take another hybrid course?	82%	18%

redesigned blended courses so as to inform the planning process for future Institutes and the ongoing development of blended courses at UW Bothell. A blended course student feedback survey was adapted from Garrison and Vaughan (2008) and administered to students in the re-designed courses taught following the completion of the HCDI as part of their general course evaluations. Using a five-point scale, students were asked to rate the amount and quality of interaction experienced with both their instructor and other students in the course as well as the likelihood of taking another blended course in future. One of the HCDI faculty participants also administered a midpoint satisfaction survey to students in her class and their narrative comments have been considered as part of our findings.

Data collected spanned a total of eight blended classes with approximately 150 total responses. It is important to note that most data collected were purely quantitative so drawing conclusions beyond what is statistically significant is difficult. However, some qualitative data were available from the midpoint satisfaction survey mentioned above, and in the form of handwritten notes on the student feedback survey.

Student evaluation responses indicate that between 65% and 81% of students saw an enhancement or, at the least, no difference in the quality and quantity of interaction with their peers and instructors in the blended format course. Table 3 shows that 80% of students also reported that they would take another blended course in future.

Qualitative data, while limited, indicated that scheduling flexibility and convenience for commuting and working students were important considerations for participation in blended courses. Sample student feedback included the following:

- Reasonable workload; ratio of class meetings to online sessions works.
- Online [blended] option allowed me to take this class.
- I was very anxious about a hybrid class at first. I am a person who needs constant feedback and in this class I am able to get constant feedback.
- Face to face meetings keep me well connected.
- The class works great for me because I live [on an island] and decreasing my travel to and from the mainland allows me more time to concentrate on homework and family.
- I thought it would be challenging and hard not to be in class every week but everything is explained very well and is well organized.
- I was a little apprehensive at first about taking a hybrid course (my first one) but everything has been very straight-forward and beyond organized. The BB site is updated in a timely manner and instructions are more than easy to follow.

- I really like the hybrid option, which there isn't too much of with UWB.
- I think we should offer more hybrid [for working students].
- Able to do it at my convenience and pace.

ADDITIONAL LESSONS LEARNED

We anticipate that the Hybrid Course Development Institute will remain a key element in preparing faculty members to develop well-designed blended courses, giving us the opportunity to revise and improve the Institute based on empirical and anecdotal data from each iteration. For subsequent Institutes, we will use the CoI survey (http://communitiesofinquiry.com/methodology), a well-validated instrument for CoI-based activities. We look forward to capitalizing on what we have learned, summarized below, from the first Institute.

Universality of Good Course Design

The HCDI functioned as a time and space for participants to rethink their teaching methods and practices in general as much as it functioned to teach them the unique aspects of blended course design. The Institute's facilitators and participants discovered that most of the best practices in blended course design apply to the design of any course, regardless of mode.

Need for Appropriate Faculty Incentives

We provided a netbook computer for each participant as an incentive for participation. Now that netbooks are losing ground to tablets such as the iPad, which many of our faculty members already own, we will take a different approach to providing incentives for participation. Following a practice used at Pepperdine University, we hope to provide a staged, monetary incentive, involving $500 in academic-related spending credit for completing the HCDI, followed by an additional award of $500 after both the first and third offerings of the revised blended course (total $1500 possible) to ensure a sustained return on our investment.

The Structured "Student Experience" for Faculty Participants

In this faculty institute and in others led by some of the authors (Leppa, Brockhaus & Planchon-Wolf, 2005), we have discovered that putting faculty participants into the position of students is invaluable. In this case, faculty participants appreciated experiencing a blended course from the student perspective, complete with the ten-week time frame, individual and group assignments, and deadlines and reminders and struggling to fit the work into already full schedules. We feel that this format has been crucial to the Institute's successful outcomes. In future Institutes, we hope to incorporate empirically validated principles of adult learning and experiential learning in the opening session of HCDI.

Web 2.0 Content and Contributions

We had an initial goal of having faculty explore Web 2.0 sites and materials and to create materials to share on the web in one of the sites designed for this (e.g. MERLOT [http://www.merlot.org/]). This goal was too much for this first HCDI. Faculty participants required more time to focus on the structural elements of their blended course design and spent time carefully thinking through what material to put online and how. The result was better-developed blended courses based on solid evaluation of the elements of the CoI framework. When an Institute participant changed elements of a course for a blended format, the change was driven by CoI principles, which is a complex task unto itself without having to consider multiple technologies. Web 2.0 content and contributions would be a better focus for a more advanced HCDI in the future.

THREE LEVELS OF SOCIAL PRESENCE

While designing and running the HCDI, we were repeatedly reminded of how much faculty members typically concentrate on the selection of course content, which, in the CoI framework, resides at the intersection of cognitive presence (learners' construction and confirmation of meaning [Garrison, Anderson, & Archer, 2001]) and teaching presence (how the facilitator designs and conducts the enterprise to achieve learning outcomes [Anderson, Rourke, Garrison, & Archer, 2001]).

Most faculty members, in fact, instinctively comprehend cognitive presence and teaching presence. They understand the influence that the atmosphere they foster in the classroom, the manner in which they conduct themselves with their students, and the assignments and activities they design—the course content—powerfully influence what students learn. They typically pay less attention, though, to social presence, which is the degree of participants' identification as members of a community and of developing meaningful relationships by communicating with one another in a trustworthy environment (Garrison, 2009). Social presence supports discourse among group members. The intersection of social presence with teaching presence sets the climate for learning. Both of these intersections—group membership support and climate for learning—are intangible aspects of the classroom. Teachers and students know when they are not present, but these are often overshadowed or ignored in favor of cognitive presence and teaching presence—the teachers' "comfort zone." Moreover, faculty members participating in the HCDI, especially those from science and technology fields, sometimes suspect that focusing on social presence will take time away from cognitive presence. In a blended learning course, social presence requires even greater consideration because the tacit social interaction in face-to-face classroom settings is significantly

reduced when much of the course takes place online. Affect, however, is one of three main categories of social presence, in addition to cohesive and interactive. Partly because emotion tends to be underprivileged and underemphasized in higher education (Goldstein, 2010), many faculty members pay scant attention to the importance of students' feelings of inclusion and connection. This oversight can be exacerbated by the online aspects of blended courses because instructors are likely to believe that, to whatever extent they do attend to students' feelings of camaraderie and connection, those elements are best achieved in the classroom. Therefore, online work can be seen as inherently impersonal. Moreover, instructors likely have greater difficulty ascertaining students' feelings in the online environment, even if they are inclined to be concerned. We found it highly worthwhile, then, to focus most intently on social presence in the HCDI while helping faculty members learn how to foster a community of inquiry in a blended learning format. Social presence has become not only a key theme in the HCDI, but in also UW Bothell's blended learning faculty development initiatives. Indeed, we find that the concept of social presence carries value on multiple levels, in multiple valences, from the micro level to the macro.

Micro Level: Individual Courses

We understood at the outset that providing guidance regarding the conceptualization of and approach to social presence would be crucial to the successful design and implementation of our Institute participants' blended learning courses. Because online discussions typically serve as cornerstones of the online portion of blended courses, we naturally spent a lot of time building participants' expertise in best practices. We sought to call their attention to the affective as well as cognitive aspects of their students' postings.

For example, Delfino and Manca (2007) offer one approach to ascertaining the emotional state of online discussion board participants. They found that their own students, most of whom were experiencing an online learning environment for the first time, used figurative language to navigate new problems associated with a new learning mode and unfamiliar technology. Metaphors and analogies allowed the students to fit new material into previously understood and comfortable territory. More importantly, though, the students also used figurative language to convert new, individual understandings into knowledge shared by their classmates; such language is "the elective means with which to explicate and conceptualize tacit knowledge into knowledge shared among the group" (p. 2208). Instructors can thereby assess their students' sense of social presence partly by paying particular attention to the analogies and metaphors that students use in the online discussion boards in blended courses, an approach we are incorporating into the second HCDI. For example, one faculty participant described his students' fruitless and shallow comments as a discussion board "cul-de-sac." That geographic metaphor enabled his peers to visualize an intellectual "dead end," so that this participant's figurative language which helped him conceptualize a problem also helped the other participants affectively as well as intellectually connect with him.

Having students sometimes lead online discussions in teams, rather than relying exclusively on oneself as the instructor to initiate and maintain online discussions, can help establish social presence in the online environment. Rourke and Anderson (2002) describe assigning groups of four students—in this case, graduate students in a course on managing communications networks—to take turns facilitating computer-based conferences among class members. They found statistically improved satisfaction and learning compared to exclusively instructor-led discussions. Most salient to their findings is that the students perceived the best conferences to be responsive, interesting, and structured, characteristics they found more often in peer-led confer-

ences than in instructor-led conferences. Rourke and Anderson note that these key characteristics are not intrinsic to student-led conferences, but the fact that those conferences were led by teams of four facilitated the achievement of the three aspects of teaching presence that they identified as crucial for this particular type of technically-oriented course (instructional design, facilitating discourse, and direct instruction). This approach simultaneously enhanced social presence in the course, such as the students' recognition of the value of their teammates.

Of course, online discussion boards are not the only venue for social presence outside of the classroom. Sharing feelings of triumph or frustration in the face-to-face sessions visibly deepened the interrelationships among the participants. Rogers and Lea (2005), however, note that social presence can be fostered beyond face-to-face or online communication. They find that a sense of inclusion can stem from a group's shared social identity. They note, in fact, that this phenomenon can be exploited to foster social presence even among remote, distributed group members, such as in a fully online course. Thus, in a blended learning course, social presence can be augmented by focusing on the shared identity of the group. We suggest some ways of doing this in the next subsection.

Middle Level: HCDI

While the faculty members collaboratively learn how to foster social presence in their individual courses (micro-level), they also experience the development of social presence in the Institute itself. Our attempt to foster a community of inquiry in the HCDI thus represents a middle level of social presence. In the first iteration of the HCDI, though, we experienced less success on this level, having to acknowledge that we did not always practice what we preached regarding best practices in blended learning courses.

A faculty development "class" raises issues beyond those in a typical blended learning course. Unlike students in a two- or four-year college or university, our faculty members intend to work together on our campus indefinitely. It is especially important to us, therefore, to attend to social presence in a context that is broader and longer in range than we might usually aim for in a blended course for students. Particularly given our campus's goal of 20% of our courses mounted in a blended format by 2015, we are keenly interested in developing a productive, inviting community of inquiry focused on blended learning, and our HCDI participants, past and present, are naturally instrumental to achieving such a climate. We found that this intention is quite challenging to realize.

After the end of the Autumn 2010 schedule of activities, we planned for an on-going online discussion among participants as they launched their revised courses and ran into problems or discovered new ideas. This did not happen. Any questions from faculty were directed to the HCDI leaders and the open discussion board remained empty. In contrast, we held one in-person, post-Institute meeting which was well-attended (8 of the 11 participants) and had a lively discussion of trials and successes. Without the structure and the defined purpose of the original 10-week course, the learning community dissipated. The participants no longer had a shared purpose so the participation dwindled and then ceased altogether as other priorities took their attention. If we desire an on-going learning community for blended course teachers on our campus, we need to craft a clear, explicit purpose.

To accomplish this goal in the second HCDI, we structured the online discussion board with more opportunities for peer-to-peer interaction—crucial for deepening critical thinking among students (Barber, 2011) and therefore among faculty members designing exercises for students—and built such conversation into weekly assignments for the participants. Even with these extra opportunities for interaction, participants in our second Institute advocated for even more relevant peer interactions, leading us to create pairings or small groups related around interests and disciplines. These groups were then used for peer review for the last four weeks of the Institute.

We also have made on-going conversations beyond the Autumn 2011 Institute an explicit expectation from the outset. We hope to leverage the participants' learning by fostering a community of inquiry that supports these early adopters in sharing expertise with faculty colleagues who have not participated in an HCDI. This sustained community of inquiry is modeled in part upon the successful teaching circles which for years have been coordinated by our campus's Teaching and Learning Center. Comprising small groups of faculty members, typically from different academic programs and disciplines, these teaching circles spend a year researching, studying, discussing, and disseminating ideas about specific aspects of teaching and learning (e.g., alternative assessment methods, best practices for small-group work, etc.). Although potentially larger, with more than 20 HCDI alumni, the blended learning community of inquiry will serve a similar purpose: to support one another and non-HCDI colleagues in providing the best blended learning opportunities possible for our students. By providing a safe environment for sharing affective responses as well as ideas, this community of inquiry is more likely to achieve its goals (Akyol & Garrison, 2008), particularly given our campus's emphasis on interdisciplinary, applied knowledge rather than "pure" disciplinarity (Arbaugh, Bangert, & Cleveland-Innes, 2010).

Also, following Rogers and Lea (2005), who point out the importance of group identity for social adhesion, we can publicize the cohort beyond the HCDI itself, emphasizing the "specialness" of the group's identity in other venues of campus life such as faculty retreats. Even naming the group (e.g., "HCDI Cohort 2" or "the 2011-12 HCDI Cohort") or referring to the participants as Hybrid Learning Fellows, can enhance social presence in the Institute. Swan and Shih (2005) found correlations between students' perception of a high level of social presence and their engagement with online discussions; we note the mutual reinforcement of social presence and online participation.

The HCDI's focus on social presence in blended formats had a spill-over effect, forcing faculty to perhaps for the first time think about how they foster social presence in the face-to-face classroom, as well as online. Some do so quite well, but struggle to describe it clearly. The CoI framework helps with this. Other faculty members have little regard for what they consider to be a social waste of time, without regard to its consequences for teaching and learning. For them, the CoI framework helps highlight the ways in which social presence augments rather than detracts from the cognitive presence and teaching presence in their courses. An interesting result of our first HCDI was that several participants rated themselves higher in fostering social presence in the classroom on the pre-assessment and lower on the post-assessment, when they had learned what social presence entails in the CoI framework, showing not a decline in capability but an increase in understanding of multifaceted social presence.

Macro Level: Campus

Our institution has set a goal of offering at least 20% of our courses in a blended format within four years—an ambitious goal given our current benchmark of approximately 5% of courses being blended. Blended learning is squarely consonant with our campus priorities. Building social presence in a campus-wide blended learning community of inquiry will be crucial as we strive to fully institutionalize blended learning.

In our year-long campus-wide discussions that resulted in our 21st Century Campus Initiative (University of Washington Bothell, 2008)—our collective statement of values, vision, and priorities guiding our work at least for the next decade—we identified seven key areas that resonate with our mission: student-centered[ness], growth,

resourcefulness, diversity, community, innovation, and sustainability. Remarkably, all seven themes pertain to blended learning.

First and foremost, our faculty members and administrators understand that student learning in well-designed blended courses can surpass that in fully face-to-face or fully online courses, which aligns with our commitment to remaining deeply student-centered. We strive to keep student learning as the principal consideration in each decision we make. Not only do we intend to expand our offerings of the proven blended mode of learning, but we also have committed resources to ensuring that the blended courses are crafted as thoughtfully and effectively as possible; hence, the HCDI. Also, because more than 90% of our students commute to campus, they value the scheduling flexibility that the blended format affords; they can commute to campus once a week rather than twice. This extra flexibility could come at a cost of fewer social connections among students, already an area of concern for a commuting campus. Emphasizing social presence in blended courses can help students maintain campus connections on multiple levels.

The University of Washington Bothell is the fastest-growing four-year campus in Washington State. Since 2003, our student body has grown 160%, to about 3,300 full-time equivalent (FTE) students, without any increase in office or classroom space. Although fully-online courses might accommodate our growth even more than would blended learning courses, the latter is much closer to our tradition of fostering strong relationships between students and faculty members. Because most of our classes meet twice a week (Monday and Wednesday or Tuesday and Thursday), we can pair blended courses to double the capacity of each classroom (i.e., one blended course uses a classroom on a Monday with the rest of the work elsewhere, including online, while another course works uses the classroom on Wednesday and works outside the classroom for the rest of the week). This approach also exemplifies the themes of innovation and resourcefulness.

Blended learning courses also help us achieve our diversity goals. As a campus of the University of Washington dedicated to serving a region nearly 40,000 square miles west of the Cascade Mountains, we strive to provide access to traditionally underrepresented populations, first-generation students, and students from rural as well as urban areas. The convenience of reduced in-class hours coupled with the support found with an on-campus, in-class component make blended learning attractive to many students who otherwise might feel alienated. Less commuting also reduces the campus's carbon footprint, enabling greater progress toward our sustainability goals.

Recognizing the potential of blended learning in achieving campus goals, the campus-wide Technology Advisory Committee (TAC), comprising faculty, staff, and students, charged a Hybrid Learning Subcommittee in 2010 to develop a campus roadmap for blended learning (Tippens, Brockhaus, Chan, Estes, Fletcher, Fukuda, Goldstein, Hiebert, McKittrick, Rhoades & Wille, 2011). In its report, the Subcommittee outlined key elements for the campus to become a leader in national conversations about blended learning:

- Offer at least 20% of all courses in blended format
- Provide each student the opportunity to take at least one blended course while attending UW Bothell
- Articulating internally and externally the value of blended learning
- Explicitly tying blended learning to other campus-wide initiatives
- Coordinate blended learning to achieve the greatest benefits to the campus

- Attract, hire, and reward faculty and staff members for expanding and improving blended learning
- Commit resources for several years for the growth of blended learning
- Offer at least five degrees or program options in a blended format (Brockhaus, Leppa, Bliquez, Goldstein, & Porter, 2011)

The Subcommittee members recognized that none of these tactics were worthwhile without ensuring the quality of the blended courses themselves. They note, "Because teaching online [including in a blended format] requires a significant change in teaching methodology (Hartman, Dziuban & Brophy-Ellison, 2007; Blignaut & Trollip, 2003), faculty development is absolutely essential to creating effective online [and blended] coursework (Ashley-Fridie, 2008; Blignaut, et al., 2003; Moore, Moore & Fowler, 2005)" (Brockhaus, et al., 2011, 11-12). Indeed, an emphasis on social presence can constitute a significant change of the traditional higher education model of instruction at UW Bothell and lead to enhanced student learning outcomes, hence, its emphasis in the HCDI. This focus on faculty development takes its form most significantly in the Hybrid Course Development Institute, based largely from previous faculty development institutes on teaching with technology (Goldstein, Tippens, Behler, Brockhaus, Collins, Erdley, Fletcher, Goldberg, Leadley, Leppa, Resnick, Turgut & Van Galen, 2009). Moreover, the HCDI serves as a cornerstone in building social presence among faculty, staff, and students pursuing blended learning excellence.

CONCLUSION: SOCIAL PRESENCE IN AN ONGOING COMMUNITY OF INQUIRY

In analyzing the assessment data from our HCDI participants and from their students in blended learning courses, we have been struck by the significance of social presence. The students often noted how their success stemmed from feeling "well-connected." The faculty members in HCDI experienced a strong camaraderie, even with cohort members from academic programs other than their own—relationships fostered by intentional pairing for peer feedback assignments—as evidenced by constant encouragement in face-to-face sessions and online and a great deal of joking and laughing. On the macro level, a campus-wide community of inquiry studying, discussing, implementing, assessing and revising blended learning courses has proved to be more challenging, but it is clear to us that concentrating on social presence will be crucial for our success. Although each element of the CoI framework is essential, we are convinced that faculty members come to cognitive presence and teaching presence a bit more naturally; for blended learning courses and curricula, especially, social presence demands careful, sustained consideration.

ACKNOWLEDGMENT

Support from the Promise of Nursing for Washington, Nursing School Grant Program administered by the Foundation of the National Student Nurses' Association, and from the Teaching and Learning Center and the Office of Academic Affairs, University of Washington Bothell, is gratefully acknowledged. We wish to thank Amber Parsons for statistical analysis assistance.

REFERENCES

Akyol, Z., & Garrison, D. R. (2008). The development of a community of inquiry over time in an online course: Understanding the progression and integration of social, cognitive and teaching presence. *Journal of Asynchronous Learning Networks*, *12*(2-3), 3–23.

Anderson, T., Rourke, L., Garrison, D. R., & Archer, W. (2001). Assessing teaching presence in a computer conference environment. *Journal of Asynchronous Learning Networks*, *5*(2).

Arbaugh, J. B., Bangert, A., & Cleveland-Innes, M. (2010). Subject matter effects and the Community of Inquiry (CoI) framework: An exploratory study. *The Internet and Higher Education*, *13*, 37–44. doi:10.1016/j.iheduc.2009.10.006

Ashlie-Fridie, B. (2008). Take the fear out: Motivating faculty to design online courses. In K. McFerrin, et al. (Eds.), *Proceedings of Society for Information Technology & Teacher Education International Conference 2008*, (pp. 1325-1330). Chesapeake, VA: AACE.

Barber, T. C. (2011). The online crit: The community of inquiry meets design education. *Journal of Distance Education*, *25*(1). Retrieved from http://www.jofde.ca/index.php/jde/article/view/723/1189

Blignaut, S., & Trollip, S. (2003). A taxonomy for faculty participation in asynchronous online discussions. In D. Lassner & C. McNaught (Eds.), *Proceedings of World Conference on Educational Multimedia, Hypermedia and Telecommunications 2003*, (pp. 2043-2050).

Brockhaus, A., Leppa, C., Bliquez, R., Goldstein, D., & Porter, I. (2011). *Technology Advisory Committee Hybrid Learning Subcommittee draft report, June 2011*. Retrieved November 20, 2011, from http://www.uwb.edu/getattachment/it/tac/tacdocs/TAC-hybrid-learning-report-2011.pdf

Delfino, M., & Manca, S. (2007). The expression of social presence through the use of figurative language in a web-based learning environment. *Computers in Human Behavior, 23,* 2190–2211. doi:10.1016/j.chb.2006.03.001

Garrison, D. R. (2007). Online community of inquiry review: Social, cognitive, and teaching presence issues. *Journal of Asynchronous Learning Networks, 11*(1).

Garrison, D. R. (2009). Communities of inquiry in online learning. In Rogers, P. L., Berg, G. A., Boettcher, J. V., Howard, C., Justice, L., & Schenk, K. D. (Eds.), *Encyclopedia of distance learning* (2nd ed., pp. 352–355). Hershey, PA: IGI Global. doi:10.4018/978-1-60566-198-8.ch052

Garrison, D. R., Anderson, T., & Archer, W. (2000). Critical inquiry in a text-based environment: Computer conferencing in higher education. *The Internet and Higher Education, 2*(2-3), 87–105. doi:10.1016/S1096-7516(00)00016-6

Garrison, D. R., Cleveland-Innes, M., & Fung, T. S. (2010). Exploring causal relationships among teaching, cognitive and social presence: Student perceptions of the community of inquiry framework. *The Internet and Higher Education, 13,* 31–36. doi:10.1016/j.iheduc.2009.10.002

Garrison, D. R., & Vaughan, N. D. (2008). *Blended learning in higher education: Framework, principles, and guidelines.* San Francisco, CA: Jossey-Bass.

Goldstein, D., Tippens, B., Behler, C., Brockhaus, A., Collins, P., Erdley, B., & Van Galen, J. (2009). *Technology and Teaching Innovation Task Force final report: May 28, 2009.* University of Washington Bothell.

Goldstein, D. S. (2010). Once more, with feeling: Whole people and partial lessons. *National Teaching and Learning Forum, 20*(1), 5–7.

Hartman, J., Dziuban, C., & Brophy-Ellison, J. (2007). Faculty 2.0. *EDUCAUSE Review, 42*(5), 62–77.

Ke, F. (2010). Examining online teaching, cognitive, and social presence for adult students. *Computers & Education, 55,* 808–820. doi:10.1016/j.compedu.2010.03.013

Leppa, C., Brockhaus, A., & Planchon-Wolf, J. (2005). Developing online teaching and learning resources that engage faculty. In G. Richards (Ed.), *Proceedings of World Conference on E-Learning in Corporate, Government, Healthcare, and Higher Education,* (pp. 866-871). Chesapeake, VA: AACE.

Means, B., Toyama, Y., Murphy, R., Bakia, M., & Jones, K. (2010). *Evaluation of evidence-based practices in online learning.* Washington, DC: U.S. Department of Education. Retrieved November 10, 2011, from http://www2.ed.gov/rschstat/eval/tech/evidence-based-practices/finalreport.pdf.

Moore, A., Moore, J., & Fowler, S. (2005). Faculty development for the net generation. In D. Oblinger & J. Oblinger (Eds.), *Educating the Net generation,* (pp. 11.1-11.15). Retrieved November 20, 2011, from http://www.educause.edu/educatingthenetgen

Rogers, P., & Lea, M. (2005). Social presence in distributed group environments: The role of social identity. *Behaviour & Information Technology, 24*(2), 151–158. doi:10.1080/01449290410001723472

Rourke, L., & Anderson, T. (2002). Using peer teams to lead online discussions. *Journal of Interactive Media in Education, 1,* 1–21.

Shea, P., & Bidjerano, T. (2009). Community of inquiry as a theoretical framework to foster epistemic engagement and cognitive presence in online education. *Computers & Education, 52,* 543–553. doi:10.1016/j.compedu.2008.10.007

Sloan Consortium. (2010). *Blended/hybrid courses*. Retrieved November 20, 2011, from http://commons.sloanconsortium.org/discussion/blendedhybrid-courses

Sorg, S. E. (2002). *Blended learning: Experiences at the University of Central Florida*. PowerPoint presentation. Retrieved August 14, 2011, from http://commons.ucalgary.ca/~lcportal/documents/sorg/Blended%20Learning%20U%20of%20Calgary%2012-04-02.htm

Swan, K., & Shih, L. F. (2005). On the nature and development of social presence in online course discussions. *Journal of Asynchronous Learning Networks, 9*(3), 115–136.

Tippens, B., Brockhaus, A., Chan, E., Estes, R., Fletcher, B., Fukuda, M., Goldstein, Hiebert, McKittrick, Rhoades & Wille, L. (2011). *University of Washington Bothell Technology Advisory Committee FY11 annual report*. Retrieved November 20, 2011, from http://www.uwb.edu/getattachment/it/tac/tacdocs/FY11-Annual-Report.pdf

University of Washington Bothell. (2008). *21st century campus initiative*. Retrieved November 11, 2011, from http://www.uwb.edu/getattachment/21stcentury/21cci-c.pdf

KEY TERMS AND DEFINITIONS

Blended Learning: A mode of instruction in which a significant portion of learning takes place outside the classroom—usually but not necessarily online—replacing some in-class time.

CoI Survey: An instrument for assessing the effectiveness of activities based on the Community of Inquiry Framework.

Community of Inquiry: "A group of individuals who collaboratively engage in purposeful critical discourse and reflection to construct personal meaning and confirm mutual understanding" (Garrison, 2011, p. 15).

Faculty Development: The process of helping faculty members learn more for the improvement of student learning.

Faculty Institute: A sustained initiative in which faculty members develop projects with experts and peers, in contrast to one-time workshops.

Social Presence: The degree of participants' identification as members of a community and of developing meaningful relationships by communicating with one another in a trustworthy environment.

Web 2.0: A term loosely describing a second generation of World Wide Web content in which users themselves provide a significant portion of a web site's content.

Chapter 19
Teaching in an Online Community of Inquiry:
Faculty Role Adjustment in the New Higher Education

Martha Cleveland-Innes
Athabasca University, Canada

ABSTRACT

Regardless of education delivery mode – face-to-face, online, distance, or some combination through blended learning – teaching (and learning) is changing. Online learning, whether synchronous or asynchronous, offers a range of instructional practices previously unavailable in either distance or face-to-face higher education. A principled approach to teaching allows faculty to stay on track of teaching requirements, regardless of delivery mode. These principles may support new teaching practices, but, if adopted, will also change the way the role of faculty is configured and executed in the higher education context.

INTRODUCTION

Good teaching cannot be reduced to technique; good teaching comes from the identity and integrity of the teacher (Palmer, 1998).

A community of inquiry is a distinct personal and public search for deep learning, meaning and understanding. In online community, new roles are necessitated by the nature of the communication which compels students to assume greater responsibility for, and control over, their learning. Given this enhanced communication; "each form of transport not only carries, but translates and transforms the sender, the receiver and the message" (McLuhan, 1995, p. 90). In addition to onlinedness (Hughes, 2004), a collaborative learning community necessitates the adoption of personal responsibility and shared control. This goes to the heart of an online learning community; a significant shift from the transmission of information in the lecture hall and the passive role of

DOI: 10.4018/978-1-4666-2110-7.ch019

students. Note the dual change in responsibility and role for both teachers and students; they move both to inquiry-based teaching and learning *and* to virtual environments with unique perceptions, actions and interactions. It is this exponential difference in online communities of inquiry that shapes the new role for faculty teaching online – we come back to this notion often in the following discussion.

The role change required to integrate new teaching technology into the role of faculty is unequivocally linked to the pedagogical requirements embedded in creating a community of inquiry – online, face-to-face or both. The perceived space, and transition process, available to move new teaching strategies into the current role of faculty in higher education rests on one hand with faculty themselves and in the other in the context in which faculty work. This chapter considers both.

The Importance of a Community of Inquiry in the New Higher Education

In spite of increasing offerings of online learning experiences in post-secondary education (Allen & Seaman, 2010), clarity about the most appropriate role for teachers to play an in this new learning environment is still under discussion (Cleveland-Innes, Garrison & Kinsel, 2008; Cleveland-Innes, Sangra-Morer & Garrison, 2008; Cleveland-Innes & Garrison, 2009). While new technologies are often expected to make work easier, they also involve the development of new competencies (Birch, 2001).

Online teaching and learning involves the use of the Internet for interaction and collaborative engagement previously unavailable to teachers and students. What changes are required to the role of faculty member to allow engagement in online teaching? Any effective teacher must be true to the learning objectives of the subject-matter at hand while attending to the multitude of characteristics students bring to the experience. Effective

teachers bridge content and student needs through appropriate student engagement; a tactic as old as education itself. The role of effective teacher in online and blended learning environments is newer and more complex. Even more complex are the implications of adopting the new teaching requirements into the current role of faculty. Realistic expectations of the role of faculty and how much, and how fast, changes may be made in teaching are required. All the teaching development and technology training in the world will not realize significant quantities of teaching change, even for the most motivated to do so, until the context changes to support and reward teaching in ways that it has not in the past and, in addition, support the increased requirements for teaching activity using new technology.

A transition to an institution–wide commitment to inquiry-based teaching and learning model would serve to create a context to support a new teaching role for faculty, and guide the adjustment to this new model. This model of learning is not unique to online learning, but has been suggested for traditional face-to-face learning environments, where faculty both explain the process of scholarly inquiry and engage students in the process of scholarly inquiry (Donald, 2002; Lipman, 2003). Inquiry-based teaching and learning uses inquiry strategy to involve students in the active exploration of content, problems, and questions on a particular topic. This active engagement can foster motivation (Artino, 2009; 2010) and develop higher order thinking and deep, meaningful learning. Theory developed to explicate inquiry-based practice in an online community of inquiry (Garrison, Anderson & Archer, 2001) is the most researched model for online, inquiry-based teaching and learning (Arbaugh, Cleveland-Innes, Diaz, Garrison, Ice, Richardson, Shea & Swan, 2008). Identified in over seven-hundred scholarly articles on the topic of online learning, this model, explained in detailed earlier in this book, describes the critical elements of an online community of inquiry: social, cognitive and teaching presence.

It is essential to note that the development of community is not the center point of a community of inquiry. Rather, community emerges through the development of social presence and sound facilitation of inquiry-based practices. This excellence in facilitation, one component of teaching presence, will come from a process of assessing individual learner needs, supporting those needs with the many facets of the learning environment and managing the complex dynamic between instructor, student, and content through interaction.

TEACHING PRESENCE

Support for Teaching in Communities of Inquiry

Teaching presence is defined as "the design, facilitation and direction of cognitive and social processes for the purpose of realizing personally meaningful and educationally worthwhile learning outcomes" (Anderson, Rourke, Garrison & Archer, 2001). The key role of teaching presence in establishing and sustaining a successful community of inquiry is well documented (Akyol & Garrison, 2008; Arbaugh, 2008; Garrison, Cleveland-Innes & Fung, 2009; Shea, Li, Swan & Pickett, 2005). This concept, in an intricate dynamic with the other elements of the community of inquiry conceptual framework, offers new ways of thinking about the role of teacher and the role of student.

Online inquiry-based learning provides a virtual universe of possibilities and required professional choices for the teacher. Ironically, teaching presence is enhanced when participants are required to assume greater self-responsibility and direction. The power of influence of teaching presence is only now beginning to be identified and well-articulated (Garrison, Cleveland-Innes & Fung, 2009; Cleveland-Innes, Sangra-Morer & Garrison, 2008).

In the first instance, teachers must make the elements of the community of inquiry explicit and foster a collaborative, comfortable environment of interaction; all participate and all are engaged as equal and valuable members of the group. In addition, participants must be comfortable contributing to the discourse while having the confidence to respectfully challenge ideas.

Critical to the role of teacher in the fostering of teaching presence is allowing and supporting individual responsibility and the teaching of others. This notion of shared leadership in the inquiry-based community requires that participants take some responsibility for fostering social, cognitive and teaching presence among all the other members of the community. The faculty member in the role of teacher can enable or restrain such action; the theory suggests the former. Hence, the use of the term teaching presence rather than teacher presence – the term identifies the requirement of an inquiry-based engagement of all participants, by all participants. The new role for the teacher is, therefore, less central and dominating.

This is not to diminish the requirement for direct instruction, and facilitation of such a dynamic. The teacher must be prepared to identify the design and requirements, clarify expectations, engage and facilitate interaction and critical discourse, assess understanding and diagnose and correct misconceptions.

These aspects of teaching presence which foster a community of inquiry are interchangeable in face-to-face, blended and online environments. Moving online and teaching in an inquiry-based model are significant role adjustments for faculty and students. Virtual environments involve communication and community foreign, or non-native, for both teacher and students. In other words, both require new ways of engaging, interacting, learning and contributing. This dual complexity adds another element to the role change for faculty teaching in an online community of inquiry – support for students making the adjustment. Simply adding opportunities for virtual interaction and collaboration will not ensure that students will adjust to an inquiry-based process or the virtual online experience; support and scaffolding, not only for the content and course objectives themselves but for the new role of online, inquiry-based student, is necessary for the teacher. This is a tall order for faculty adjusting to the same changes.

Without this adjustment, the opportunity to enhance deep and meaningful learning is diminished. However, this notion of shared responsibility and growth in teaching presence, while constituting new and multiple roles and responsibilities, allows for mutual support as well. Varying degrees of responsibility for teacher and student allow each to monitor and regulate the dynamics of the learning community. A community of inquiry then, given the culture of shared academic goals and processes, adds complexity while at the same time providing increased support for the changes that are necessary.

Thus, online learning communities demand and support role adjustment. As a new social role, the pathway to competence will occur over time for students and faculty as the role becomes prevalent and normalized. In this early stage, online communities will contribute to the socialization process for those engaging in this new role. The result is a new role and a new identity for faculty and students; teachers and learners. While the adoption and enactment of social roles is a standard, commonplace element of everyday experience, becoming an online teacher and learner has unique characteristics. For most moving online, role models demonstrating the required and expected activities are not present until one is already engaged in an online experience.

CHANGING ROLES FOR FACULTY

Understanding Role and Role Change

'Role' is used here as a sociological construct, defined as a collection of behavioral requirements associated with a certain social position in a group, organization or society (Kendall, Murray & Linden, 2000). At its most general level, role expectations are dictated by the social structure. Individuals who engage in the role are guided, through a process of socialization, to appropriate role performance. Socialization is the "process by which people learn the characteristics of their group...(and) the attitudes, values and actions thought appropriate for them" (Kanwar & Swenson, 2000, p. 397).

At the theoretical level, role change must be understood as a rudimentary social process that occurs repeatedly in any social group. Normally part of the social sub-text, this process entails individuals continually testing behaviors until they settle into a pattern of individual behavior for which they most often receive a favorable response. This behavioral pattern then becomes their role repertoire and the basis for individual role identity. Role change for faculty (at the level of institutional structure) and role identity adjustment (at the level of the individual faculty engaged in a new ways of teaching) may be facilitated through deliberate intervention by those in positions of influence.

Role change is an iterative process of exchange and change between individuals interacting as part of a structured social environment. Role change occurs in the form of continually shifting role expectations and requirements. The role exists *sui generis* as a generalized set of requirements. In the case of complex roles (such as faculty member), the generalized role can be difficult to pinpoint, as it continually shifts. This is particularly true for developing roles such as the role of online teacher, for in many ways we are 'making it up' as we go.

Under different conditions where long-standing roles exist, individuals engage in 'role-taking' behavior, where observation and mimicry of role models allow those new to the role to 'practice' appropriate role behaviors. 'Role making' occurs as individuals construct aspects of the role with their own individual meanings and satisfying behaviors attached. This occurs under social conditions where such individual autonomy is allowed; such is usually the case for faculty. It also occurs where role models are not readily available, and construction of the role is required (Blau & Goodman 1995).

Findings from a recent study of faculty teaching online (Cleveland-Innes & Garrison, 2009) give a picture of the integral adjustment as both teachers and learners become 'present' in an online community of inquiry. Evidence here affirms Garrison & Cleveland-Innes' (2005) premise that "teaching presence must be available, either from the facilitator or the other learners, in order to transition from social to cognitive presence." (p. 16). Without adequate support from the instructor, student role adjustment occurs without clear reference to expectations. This lack creates a situation that fails to sustain interest and engagement. Previous evidence demonstrated that learners without guidance operate remotely: "without instructor's explicit guidance and 'teaching presence,' students were found to engage primarily in 'serial monologues'" (Pawan, et al., 2003, p. 119). Teaching presence supports sustained and beneficial academic interaction, movement within the presences of online inquiry-based community and points of reference and direction regarding new role expectations – expectations that relate to 'onlinedness' and inquiry-based processes.

Facilitation

Faculty identified the facilitation of interaction as a central means to relieve initial anxieties and to create group cohesion. As stated earlier in this book (Garrison, 2012), "collaboration in an educational context is founded on communication free of coercion and intimidation while valuing rational argument and discourse." Through supported, open communication, students learn they are not alone in their anxiety and that other students as well as the teacher can offer valuable insights. By sharing opinions and experiences, students become familiar with each other, develop mutual bonds and a sense of belonging and safety, all leading to increases in motivation to learn. Group dynamics will differ across sections and courses: one group may develop a strong learning community characterized by rigorous discourse, while another may never gel and interactions may be limited. In cases of intense cohesion, groups can take on a life of their own, requiring little effort on the part of the teacher. Conversely, when cohesion is weak, encouraging students to interact is "kind of like dragging a sled over gravel…it's really hard work" (research participant).

Student-student interaction serves to broaden understanding of subject matter and role expectations. As different backgrounds and experiences are used to interpret course content, students have the opportunity to consider matters from multiple perspectives. They may re-examine previously held interpretations and perspectives in light of new information. "The experience they brought was extremely valuable and without that [student interactions] the course would simply not have been of the same value" (research participant).

The differences between face-to-face and online interactions were interpreted as having both benefits and drawbacks. Information presented face-to-face can be immediately clarified in response to non-verbal cues that may indicate students' interest (or lack of), confusion or emotional reactions. These cues are absent or more subtle online; it requires more vigilance on the part of online instructors, who must deliberately engage students to determine benefit from additional resources, or if they are struggling with concepts or emotionally reacting to content. Online text-based discourse allows learners to revisit and reflect on discussions and produce more in-depth analyses. By keeping conferences open after discussions have moved on to other areas allows students to revisit older lessons in light of their subsequent learning, assisting them to make connections and see larger themes. Online interactions were also considered to be preferable to face-to-face because students have more opportunity to participate. While "discussion bullies" may prevent others from speaking up in class, text-based formats allow everyone to express themselves, and to have more control over the timing and placement of their comments: "this was his opportunity to… have his voice heard where he wants it heard, when he wants it heard" (research participant).

Direct Instruction

Instructors saw themselves as active participants in the learning process rather than experts transmitting knowledge to their students. "Because I'm part and parcel of the discussion board as well, um, I am responding to individual uh, comments… and I'm also expecting students to take me on as well… and, and I've told them, you know, do not hesitate in challenging me…if I write something that is completely out to lunch, you know, as far as you're concerned, let's, let's get it on and discuss that. Because that's, that's part of the learning curve too" (research participant).

This refers to direct instruction, the shaping of perspective and debate of knowledge claims. However, much of the exchange between instructor and student in an inquiry-based, online environment is for the purposes of facilitating discourse. Timing and quantity are key. Comments must be delivered at an appropriate time in order to facilitate

dialogue. "I try to avoid jumping into a discussion too soon. Because some students will, rightly or wrongly view me as the voice of authority. And I want to let them have their own, let them have their voices heard first before I jump in and completely derail it or ruin somebody else's thunder if you will" This is different than responses to questions or assessment processes. Here, teacher immediacy is paramount (Swan, 2002).

Findings from this study suggested that 'role-taking' described above is evident. Instructors' suggest their messages are carefully crafted to avoid misinterpretations and that they model appropriate online behavior such as regular participation, friendly, supportive reactions and keeping the course on track. Questions are used to initiate discussions, stimulate additional dialogue and foster deeper processing. Debates may occasionally drift from their intended themes and require refocusing. Student participation is encouraged and their subsequent efforts are acknowledged. Instructors share how course concepts have affected their professional practice and encourage students to apply content to experiences. Additional resources are offered to allow individual interests to be pursued.

In summary, findings indicate that

- Online environments foster inquiry-based learning.
- Students and instructors are changing to operate effectively in such environments.
- Instructors are aware of, and supportive of, the student adjustment.

Less evident were notions about the changes instructors had to make for themselves, and how instructors were aware of, and supported in, their adjustment to online teaching. The higher education context and how this impacts the change to inquiry-based and online teaching and learning is discussed below.

TEACHING AND THE NEW HIGHER EDUCATION

According to Keller (2008), changes in many things including technology "constitutes [sic] the most consequential set of changes in society since the late nineteenth century, when the nation went from a largely domestic, rural, agrarian mode of living to an industrial, international, and urban economy" (Preface xi). Consequently, for higher education, "this set of circumstances is going to force all academic enterprises to rethink their place and purpose not just in philosophical terms but in very pragmatic ways as well." (Beaudoin, 2003, p. 520). These philosophical and pragmatic changes also affect teaching practice and the role of teacher.

It is unrealistic to expect higher education faculty to have sound, current, content expertise, a productive research program, an active service commitment and be expert online teachers. The biggest lie in the academy is that the role of faculty, and its rewards and responsibilities, is made up of a seemingly balanced set of activities around teaching, research and service (Atkinson, 2000). With some variation across type of institution, research is the most valued work and most notably rewarded. While this reality has not changed, "classroom teaching and course materials (have become) more sophisticated and complex in ways that translate into new forms of faculty work... such new forms are not replacing old ones, but instead are layered on top of them, making for more work." (Rhoades, 2000, p, 38). It is time to clarify this reality and consider how, if at all, changes in teaching are, or may be, integrated into the role of faculty member.

It is within this traditional higher education context that change is available for faculty who wish to use current Internet technology to enhance learning (Cleveland-Innes & Garrison, 2010). At the same time, higher education institutions which are "notorious resisters to change" (Garrison & Kanuka, 2004, p. 102) struggle to remain competitive in an increasingly marketized context in which they must compete for institutional resources (Zepke, 2007). Complicating matters is the push for academic capitalism and the use of business models in higher education. Rhoades (2006) argues that higher education systems are out of balance as a result of non-profit higher education choosing to model itself after private enterprise. Rhoades proposes these effects are not without consequence and asserts there is a lack of evidence that educational entrepreneurialism is viable. Among the outcomes of choosing academic capitalism and the new economy, he identifies new modes of producing research, teaching and service as well as conceptions of curriculum as a commodity and of faculty as knowledge workers. He offers that higher education can "rebalanced" through organized and careful re-examination of its options and choices. Rhoades concludes by advocating for social entrepreneurialism, a path that will allow higher education to achieve it social mandate while exercising its entrepreneurial spirit.

This social agenda supports improvements in education access and quality learning experiences afforded by online education delivery. However, the transition won't occur successfully without concomitant adjustments in the role of faculty and the context in which faculty operate. The academy's resistance the change is well documented; "critics of higher education lament that technology has changed, the economy has changed, families have changed, religious values have changed, race relations have changed ... (yet) colleges and universities have remained relatively unchanged" (Keller 2008, p. 4). Systematic development processes with support and leadership to transform will move individuals and institutional structures in new directions (Cleveland-Innes, 2009; Latchem & Hanna, 2001; McGuinness 2005). Existing organizational realities must give way to new structures and new pedagogical models as technology, new roles and current socioeconomic trends become part of higher education.

A principled approach to teaching with technology has been suggested by Cleveland-Innes and Garrison (2012). These principles suggest the necessary underpinnings for instructional design and delivery choices made in the new higher education, delivered face-to-face, online or a blend of both.

1. Encourage collaborative, reciprocal and cooperative contact among students and between students and faculty.
2. Design learning activities for high engagement and active learning.
3. Model and expect self-direction, responsibility and timeliness.
4. Encourage and support access to, and consideration of, multiple forms of information.
5. Communicate clear objectives and high expectations.
6. Respect competencies and diverse ways of learning.
7. Foster open communication, affective expression and group cohesion.
8. Facilitate and reward inquiry that includes critical reflection, respectful debate and movement toward resolution.
9. Design for, encourage, and support the use of web-based collaborative learning applications.
10. Ensure assessment is congruent with intended processes and outcomes. (page 232).

These principles illuminate the increasing complexity that is now part of teaching. We consider this complexity a major catalyst in the move towards inquiry based learning. Traditional delivery, usually lecture-based, provides multiple opportunities to enhance delivery (videos, power point, handouts, etc.) but functions as a transmission model. The faculty role is one of course designer and presenter of information. If we contrast this conventional teaching to distance education, with mass production of self-directed learning materials is accompanied by a distant and

directive teaching role. In this role, the teacher is no longer the designer or the deliverer, but the mediator and examiner of learning. These two teaching roles are, in contrast to the collaborative nature of online and blended learning environments, relatively simple. The new role of teacher must include much of what has come before, and must include the integration of multiple delivery modes and facilitation of learners constructively making sense of it all – including a wealth of resources they can, with guidance, find themselves.

Even before the imposition of new technology, both excellent teaching and excellent research records were difficult to achieve. Fairweather's (2002) research suggests that new ways of teaching will make it more difficult for faculty to be exemplars of research and teaching. This study examines the myth of the "complete faculty member" – that is one who can sustain high levels of productivity in both research and teaching at the same time. Data from the 1992–93 National Survey of Postsecondary Faculty provided a representative sample of 29,764 part-time and full-time faculty in 962 American research universities, doctoral-granting universities, comprehensive colleges and universities and liberal arts colleges. For the purpose of that study, Fairweather identified faculty as highly productive researchers if refereed publications exceeded the median for program and institutional type over a two year period. Faculty members identified as highly productive teachers were those above the median in student classroom contact hours. In the first instance, 22% of faculty in 4-year institutions met both criteria. However, adding collaborative instruction to the teaching criterion reduced the percentage of highly productive researchers and teachers to about 6%.

This time consuming collaborative instruction is central to the benefits of online, inquiry-based, teaching and learning. The individualization of communications, and the role of instructor as a facilitator of student participation and learning, add to instructor workload when teaching online

(Davidson-Shivers, 2009). A central advantage of online delivery is the opportunity to better engage learners in more active and collaborative educational experiences. Tomei (2004) proposes that online student expectations for on-demand, continuous feedback necessitates smaller class sizes relative to those in traditional classroom instruction. This is one option available to compensate for the imposition of time online teaching will impose. For Tomei, the 40-40-20 formula for allocating faculty time (40 percent teaching, 40 percent research, and 20 percent service) suggested by the American Association of University Professors (AAUP) is unrealistic for faculty teaching in an online environment.

It is unrealistic to assume that emerging Internet technologies, online courses and inquiry-based learning will transform teaching practices in higher education within the current context shaping faculty roles. According to Saint-Jacques (2012) the "crucial role of the faculty member as the facilitator of a rich and ongoing dialogue in the classroom has yet to be identified with, and embraced by faculty" (p. x.). It may be necessary to reconfigure and redefine conceptions of research and scholarship for the online environment and the unique needs of its faculty (Yick, Patrick & Costin, 2005).

CONCLUSION

Regardless of education delivery mode – face-to-face, online, distance or some combination through blended learning – teaching (and learning) in higher education is changing. It is critical that we consider how major social change is and should influence teaching and learning, but we must also ask how the existence of online and blended teaching and learning is changing the role of face-to-face teacher. Online and blended

teaching and learning offers a range of pedagogical practices previously unavailable in either distance or face-to-face higher education. Online inquiry-based learning can be conceived of as the new education, where issues such as interaction and dialogue are introduced back into the model. But broader than interaction and dialogue, the new teaching model, online and otherwise, involves "adopting a set of assumptions and practices congruent with the ideal of a community of inquiry found in the mainstream of higher education" (Garrison & Cleveland-Innes, 2010, p.19). In the role of teacher as bricoleur, one takes what they need from multiple sources to craft sound practice. Rather than recipes and best practices, we see teaching in the new higher education as constructed and crafted, based on content, student needs and the available technologies.

REFERENCES

Allen, I. E., & Seaman, J. (2010). *Learning on demand: Online education in the United States, 2009*. (Research Report No. 7). Retrieved from http://www.sloanc.org/publications/survey/pdf/learningondemand.pdf

Anderson, T., Rourke, L., Garrison, D. R., & Archer, W. (2001). Assessing teaching presence in a computer conferencing context. *Journal of Asynchronous Learning Networks, 5*(2). Retrieved from http://www.aln.org/publications/jaln/v5n2/v5n2_anderson.asp

Arbaugh, J. B. (2008). Does the community of inquiry framework predict outcomes in online MBA courses? *International Review of Research in Open and Distance Learning, 9*, 1–21.

Arbaugh, J. B., Cleveland-Innes, M., Diaz, S., Garrison, D. R., Ice, P., & Richardson, J. C. (2009). Developing a community of inquiry instrument: testing a measure of the Community of Inquiry framework using a multi-institutional sample. *The Internet and Higher Education, 11*, 133–136. doi:10.1016/j.iheduc.2008.06.003

Artino, A. R. Jr. (2009). Think, feel, act: Motivational and emotional influences on military students' online academic success. *Journal of Computing in Higher Education, 21*, 146–166. doi:10.1007/s12528-009-9020-9

Artino, A. R. Jr. (2010). Online or face-to-face learning? exploring the personal factors that predict students' choice of instructional format. *The Internet and Higher Education, 13*(4), 272–276. doi:10.1016/j.iheduc.2010.07.005

Atkinson, M. P. (2001). The scholarship of teaching and learning: Reconceptualizing scholarship and transforming the academy. *Social Forces, 79*(4), 1217–1229. doi:10.1353/sof.2001.0029

Blau, J. R., & Goodman, N. (Eds.). (1995). *Social role s & social institutions*. New Brunswick, NJ: Transaction Publishers.

Cleveland-Innes, M. (2009). New directions for higher education: Challenges, opportunities and outcomes. In U. Ehlers & D. Schneckenberg (Eds.), *Changing cultures in higher education*. New York: Springer International.

Cleveland-Innes, M., & Garrison, D. R. (2009). The role of learner in an online community of inquiry: Instructor support for first time online learners. In Karacapilidis, N. (Ed.), *Solutions and innovations in web-based technologies for augmented learning: Improved platforms, tools and applications* (pp. 167–184). Hershey, PA: IGI Global. doi:10.4018/978-1-60566-238-1.ch001

Cleveland-Innes, M., & Garrison, D. R. (2012). Higher education and post-industrial society: New ideas about teaching, learning, and technology. In Moller, L., & Huett, J. (Eds.), *The next generation of distance education: Unconstrained learning* (pp. 221–248). New York, NY: Springer. doi:10.1007/978-1-4614-1785-9_15

Cleveland-Innes, M., Sangra-Morer, A., & Garrison, R. (2008). *The art of teaching in an online community of inquiry: The online teacher as bricoleur.* Paper published in the 5th European Distance Education Network Research Workshop, Paris, France.

Davidson-Shivers, G. V. (2009). Frequency and types of instructor-interactions in online instruction. *Journal of Interactive Online Learning, 8*(1). Retrieved September 28, 2010, from www.ncolr.org/jiol/issues/PDF/8.1.2.pdf

Donald, J. (2002). *Learning to think: Disciplinary perspectives*. San Francisco, CA: Jossey-Bass Publishers.

Fairweather, J. S. (2002). The mythologies of faculty productivity: Implications for institutional policy and decision making. *The Journal of Higher Education, 73*(1). Retrieved September 23, 2010 from http://202.198.141.77/upload/soft/0000/73.1fairweather02%5B1%5D.pdf

Garrison, D. R., & Kanuka, H. (2004). Blended learning: Uncovering its transformative potential in higher education. *The Internet and Higher Education, 7*(2), 95-105. doi:10.1016/j.iheduc.2004.02.001

Garrison, D. R. (2013). Theoretical Foundations and Epistemological Insights of the Community of Inquiry. In Akyol, Z., & Garrison, D. R. (Eds.), *Educational communities of inquiry: Theoretical framework, research and practice* (p. 1-11). Hershey, PA: IGI Global.

Garrison, D. R., Anderson, T., & Archer, W. (2001). Critical thinking, cognitive presence, and computer conferencing in distance education. *American Journal of Distance Education, 15*(1), 7–23. doi:10.1080/08923640109527071

Garrison, D. R., & Cleveland-Innes, M. (2010). Conclusion. In Cleveland-Innes, M. F., & Garrison, D. R. (Eds.), *An introduction to distance education: Understanding teaching and learning in a new era* (pp. 137–164). New York, NY: Routledge.

Garrison, D. R., Cleveland-Innes, M., & Fung, T. (2009). Exploring causal relationships among cognitive, social and teaching presence: Student perceptions of the community of inquiry framework. *The Internet and Higher Education.* doi:doi:10.1016/j.iheduc.2009.10.002

Gudea, S. R. (2008). *Expectations and demands in online teaching: Practical experiences.* Hershey, PA: IGI Global. doi:10.4018/978-1-59904-747-8

Hughes, J. (2004). Supporting the online learner. In Anderson, T., & Elloumi, F. (Eds.), *Theory and practice of online learning.* Canada: Athabasca University.

Kanwar, M., & Swenson, D. (2000). *Canadian sociology.* Iowa: Kendall/Hunt Publishing Company.

Keller, G. (2008). *Higher education and the new society.* Baltimore Johns Hopkins University Press.

Kendall, D., Murray, J., & Linden, R. (2010). *Sociology in our times* (2nd ed.). Ontario, Canada: Canadian Cataloguing in Publication.

Latchem, C. and Hanna, D.E . (2001). Lessons for the future. Latchem, C. and Hanna, D.E., Eds. *Leadership for 21st century learning: Global perspectives from educational perspectives,* pp. 235-240. Sterling, VA: Stylus Publishing.

Lipman, M. (2003). *Thinking in education* (2nd ed.). Cambridge, UK: Cambridge University Press. doi:10.1017/CBO9780511840272

Maxwell, J. A. (2005). *Qualitative research design. An interactive approach* (2nd ed.). New York, NY: Sage Publications.

McQuinness, A.C. (2005). The states and higher education. In Altbach, et al., Eds., *American higher education in the 21st century* (pp. 198-225). Baltimore: John Hopkins University Press.

McLuhan, M. (1995). *Understanding media: The extensions of man.* Cambridge, MA: The MIT Press.

Palmer, P. (1998). *The courage to teach: Exploring the inner landscape of a teacher's life.* San Francisco, CA: Jossey-Bass.

Rhoades, G. (2006). The higher education we choose: A question of balance. *The Review of Higher Education, 29*(3), 381–404. Project MUSE database. doi:10.1353/rhe.2006.0015

Rhoades, G., & Maitland, C. (2004). Bargaining workload and workforce on the high tech campus. *The NEA 2004 Almanac of Higher Education* (pp. 75-81). Retrieved from http://www.nea.org/assets/img/PubAlmanac/ALM_04_06.pdf

Saint-Jacques, A. (2012). Effective teaching practices to foster vibrant communities of inquiry in synchronous online learning. In Akyol, Z., & Garrison, D. R. (Eds.), *Educational communities of inquiry: Theoretical framework, research and practice* (p. xx). Hershey, PA: IGI Global.

Shea, P., Li, C. S., Swan, K., & Pickett, A. (2005). Developing learning community in online asynchronous college courses: The role of teaching presence. *Journal of Asynchronous Learning Networks*, *9*(4), 59–82.

Swan, K. (2002). Immediacy, social presence, and asynchronous discussion. In Bourne, J., & Moore, J. C. (Eds.), *Elements of quality online education* (*Vol. 3*, pp. 157–172). Needham, MA: Sloan Center for Online Education.

Tomei, L. (2004). The impact of online teaching on faculty load: Computing the ideal class size for online courses. *International Journal of Instructional Technology & Distance Learning*, *1*(1). Retrieved from http://www.itdl.org/journal/Jan_04/article04.htm

Yick, A., Patrick, P., & Costin, A. (2005). Navigating distance and traditional higher education: Online faculty experiences. *International Review of Research in Open and Distance Learning*, *6*(2). Retrieved from http://www.irrodl.org/index.php/irrodl/article/view/235

Zepke, N. (2007). Leadership, power and activity systems in a higher education context: Will distributive leadership serve in an accountability driven world? *International Journal of Leadership in Education: Theory and Practice*, *10*(3), 301-314.

KEY TERMS AND DEFINITIONS

Bricoleur: One who uses the material at hand to create something of their own conception; a handyman or woman; a "do-it-yourself"-er.

Community of Inquiry: A group of learners who review, reflection on, analyze and resolve information, particularly that which addresses complex problems.

Deep Learning: Learning which involves high intellectual engagement, thoughtful accommodation and serious assimilation, all leading to meaningful transformation on the part of the learner.

Direct Instruction: Supportive action explicitly identifying what must be learned.

Facilitation: Supportive action making something done easier or more readily accomplished.

Faculty Role: A complex set of socially defined actions and activities which are expected and required of one in a position called faculty.

Higher Education: Education beyond the secondary level, usually involving abstract thought and advanced logical reasoning.

Teaching Presence: The use of planning, facilitation and instruction activities on the part of a leader in an instructional activities; the extent to which instructional activity can be identified and ascribed to one individual in a learning group.

Chapter 20

Pedagogical Requirements in a University–Context Characterized by Online and Blended Courses:
Results from a Study Undertaken through Fifteen Canadian Universities

Dodzi J.-A. Amemado
University of Montreal, Canada

ABSTRACT

This research was undertaken in fifteen Canadian universities, using interviews of higher education teaching center managers and IT specialists, all of them having university-teaching backgrounds. The study concerned the ramifications to teaching requirements as university education shifts into the digital era. The research was predicated upon the Community of Inquiry (CoI) framework (Garrison, Anderson, & Archer, 2000). In the light of this theoretical framework, the results demonstrated the importance of the elements of the framework: teaching presence, cognitive presence, and social presence. Interestingly, in the responses collected, the frequency of some indicators over others, such as information exchange, discussion, and collaboration, led to the conclusion that some categories, such as group cohesion, should be given a greater consideration in the CoI framework and, therefore, should be given more weight toward the pedagogical requirements for online/blended teaching and learning.

DOI: 10.4018/978-1-4666-2110-7.ch020

INTRODUCTION

Information and communication technologies (ICT), precisely the Internet, have become a significant component that cannot be ignored in any university education setting today (Allen & Seaman, 2004; 2007). In the first part of this research (Amemado, 2010), it appeared that conventional universities are in a pronounced period of change, with higher education institutions evolving rapidly into partly or completely online postsecondary programs. As revealed, the most current changes include blended learning courses, bimodal universities, virtual universities, universities using diverse models and universities operating with artificial intelligence (Amemado, 2010).

Taking the idea of institutional change a step further, this research aimed at exploring teaching and learning implications for the current technologically-modified university environment. The main research question was: "What are the pedagogical requirements for the particular context of evolution of conventional universities under the influence of ICT?"

The research objectives were to identify more indicators for a teaching and learning context consistent with technology integration. In other words, the study aimed at finding other indicators and the most referenced by the participants. Finally, the research makes suggestions for strategic planning for online and blended learning to provide an easy transition.

BACKGROUND: LITERATURE REVIEW AND THEORETICAL FRAMEWORK

Literature Review

The literature review around pedagogy in higher education covers a variety of elements, ranging from teaching conditions to ICT integration models. Herron (1998) mentioned seven conditions for successful teaching in an Internet-based environment, consisting among others:

- Identifying resources for both students and professors
- Facilitating course management
- Sharing information with the university community
- Web-surf efficiency

As for Lieblein (2000), some of these conditions are new pedagogical approaches, the suitability of the working environment and the choice of pedagogical tools. Other research mentioned the importance to adapt methods according to synchronous or asynchronous work styles (Dringus, 2000; Dringus & Scigliano, 2000, Palloff & Pratt, 2001). These pedagogical warnings and prerequisites led Guri-Rosenblit (2001) to focus on the concept of teaching models as a key to online teaching success. As per Grabe and Christopherson (2005), the primary interest of the Internet is its role as a communication system and research tool. More and more research focuses on work modalities that should ultimately guide the choice of appropriate teaching and learning models and the use of these technological tools (Ahern, Thomas, Tallent-Runnels, Lan, Cooper, Lu & Cyrus, 2006; Finegold & Cooke, 2006; John & Sutherland, 2005; Thompson & MacDonald, 2005; Henri, 2001; Privateer, 1999).

One of the main ideas that follow from this literature review is an advocacy for new working modalities to create a new culture for university pedagogy aligned with online teaching and learning environments. Echoing this major idea, John and Sutherland (2005) mentioned that quality in teaching and learning is the result of three elements: the culture of the community, the pedagogy and the technology used. But the culture of the community is most important, as it favors the appropriate pedagogy (John & Sutherland, 2005), adding that the technology is mainly a learning tool. Moore, Fowler and Watson (2007), Stewart

(2004), Dawson (2006) and Rovai (2004) share the same idea that pedagogical approaches should consider learning as a social and interactive activity and be based on the sense of community between learners and their collaboration.

In fact, several elements constitute the pedagogical dimension of the advent of information and communication technology (ICT) in higher education, such as the quality of ICT integration models, appropriate working methods, adequacy of pedagogical approaches, availability of online learning resources, course management, communication modes between professors and students, etc. Overall, the literature around these pedagogical requirements proves the urgency of a new academic culture built upon collaboration. This finding, following from the literature review, led to the choice of the Community of Inquiry Framework of Garrison, Anderson & Archer (2000) as the theoretical perspective of this research.

Compared to other theoretical frameworks in the field of ICT used to teach in higher education, the CoI proves to be a better choice. For instance, the Theory-Based Design Framework for E-Learning by Dabbagh (2005) is commonly referenced. This framework integrates teaching strategies (collaboration, articulation, reflection, role-playing, exploration, problem resolution), appropriate learning technologies (synchronous and asynchronous communication), pedagogical constructs (open and flexible learning, etc.). However, the Theory-Based Design Framework for E-Learning doesn't give the entire space to intrinsically pedagogical elements covering just two of the three elements of the framework, whereas the CoI in its three dimensions treats elements strictly pedagogical. There is also the TSL model (teaching-studying-learning) by Uljens (1997) that also applies to network education in higher

education. If its strong asset is the very pedagogy-centered approach, the CoI framework remains more detailed with regard to the items included in the framework. Another appreciable model is the CSALT networked learning model (Goodyear, 2001). It has been designed for network collaboration with reference to university teaching and distinguishes the tasks pertaining to the professor from the learner's activities, while focusing on the organizational context and teaching strategies (collaborative learning). However, when it comes to clarity and organization of the categories and indicators, the CoI framework again appears to be a better choice. Another framework is the Conversational Framework by Laurillard (2002). Although known for its focus on learning experiences, the Conversational Framework seems rather more fitted to small groups working in network. This aspect, as a criticism of the Conversational Framework, is also shared by Goodyear (2001).

Apart from these points of comparison, the CoI framework has been used and tested in entirely online learning contexts, as well as in blended environments. Therefore, another reason why this framework was chosen is that it applies to online settings as well as to blended learning environments that are the current trend in North American higher education institutions, and in the universities selected for this research. As highlighted by its authors, the CoI framework, with its emphasis on critical thinking and collaboration, provides a well-structured model and a set of guidelines to create effective learning communities in online and blended learning environments (Garrison & Anderson, 2003; Garrison & Vaughan, 2008; Akyol, Garrison & Ozden, 2009).

In that way, and for all these reasons based on comparison with other different models, the CoI framework can be considered to best suit the objective and the research question of this study.

THEORETICAL FRAMEWORK: THE COMMUNITY OF INQUIRY FRAMEWORK

A main idea of the Community of Inquiry (CoI) framework (Garrison, Anderson & Archer, 2000), is the urgency of a new culture of work based on collaboration between participants in an online teaching and learning environment. The CoI framework has three components or elements that are: social presence, teaching presence and cognitive presence. As shown in Figure 1, each element consists of categories that are characterized by their indicators. The operationalization of the three elements, especially the "cognitive presence," is based upon the work of Dewey (1933) on reflective thinking and inquiry, where inquiry is viewed as a practical endeavor (Cleveland-Innes, Garrison & Kinsel, 2007). Indicators such as information exchange, sense of puzzlement, connecting ideas, application of new ideas, risk-free expression, encouragement to collaboration, focusing on discussion and sharing personal meaning are all necessary ingredients to facilitate and improve the learning and teaching environment.

Social presence has been defined by Garrison (2009) as "the ability of participants to identify with the community (e.g., course of study), communicate purposefully in a trusting environment, and develop inter-personal relationships by way

Figure 1. Framework

Community of Inquiry

ELEMENTS	CATEGORIES	INDICATORS (examples only)
Social Presence	Open Communication Group Cohesion Affective Expression	Risk-free expression Encourage collaboration Emoticons
Cognitive Presence	Triggering Event Exploration Integration Resolution	Sense of puzzlement Information exchange Connecting ideas Apply new ideas
Teaching Presence	Design & Organization Facilitating Discourse Direct Instruction	Setting curriculum & methods Sharing personal meaning Focusing discussion

of projecting their individual personalities." Social presence is viewed as a primary prerequisite to collaboration and critical discourse. As explained by Akyol, Garrison and Ozden (2009) and Garrison and Anderson (2003), social presence facilitates the achievement of cognitive objectives by instigating, sustaining, and supporting critical thinking in a community of learners. Social presence is composed of three categories: affective expression, open communication and group cohesion. Affective responses are the expression of emotions, humor, and self-disclosure that support interpersonal relationships. Open and purposeful communication occurs through recognition, encouragement of reflective participation, and interaction. Cohesion and group identification are achieved by addressing participants by name, using salutations, and using inclusive pronouns, such as *we* and *our* (Garrison & Anderson, 2003; Akyol, Garrison & Ozden, 2009).

As for the cognitive presence, it's defined by Garrison, Anderson & Archer (2000) as "the extent to which the participants in any particular configuration of a community of inquiry are able to construct meaning through sustained communication". Cognitive presence is composed of four categories: triggering event, exploration of possible facts, integration of elements of solution and resolution. As explained by Garrison and Anderson (2003), the first phase is the initiation of the inquiry process through a problem or dilemma; the exploration phase is the process of understanding the nature of a problem then searching for relevant information and possible explanations; the integration phase involves a focused and structured construction of meaning; and finally the resolution phase of a problem is attained by constructing a meaningful framework or by discovering specific solutions. The indicators pertaining to each of these four categories are: sense of puzzlement, information exchange, connecting ideas, and apply new ideas (Garrison & Anderson, 2003).

The third and last element of the model is teaching presence. As pointed out by Anderson, Rourke, Garrison and Archer (2001), teaching presence is considered to be "the design, facilitation and direction of cognitive and social processes for the purpose of realizing personally meaningful and educationally worthwhile learning outcomes". Subsequently, Garrison and Anderson (2003) came to give teaching presence a regulatory and mediating role, in the sense that it conveys "all the elements of a community of inquiry together in a balanced and functional relationship congruent with the intended outcomes and the needs and capabilities of the learners". Three categories relate to teaching presence: design and organization; facilitating discourse; and, direct instruction. Some of their indicators are respectively setting curriculum and methods, sharing personal meaning and focusing discussion. From the work of Garrison and Anderson (2003), the first category, design and organization, is the macro-level structure of the learning experience. The second category, facilitating discourse, is critical to maintaining students' interest, motivation and engagement. As for the third category, direct instruction is associated with more specific content issues such as diagnosing misconceptions, injecting knowledge from diverse sources, or summarizing the discussion.

The CoI framework has been tested and confirmed through many research studies during the last ten years of its existence (Akyol, Garrison & Ozden, 2009). Among the pedagogical models related to online teaching and collaboration, the CoI framework is the one to have attracted more attention from researchers (Garrison & Arbaugh, 2007).

This study has been undertaken with specialists involved in online and blended teaching and learning, and unlike previous research studies, it has revealed the primacy of some categories over others in the CoI framework. For example, the results of this study have widely highlighted the importance of "group cohesion" and "role adjustment" for an online community of inquiry.

METHODOLOGICAL FRAMEWORK

This study intended to explore the pedagogical requirements necessary to get the most of teaching and learning activities, in a university context highly influenced by online technologies changing the higher education landscape into blended courses, bimodality institutions, open and distance education.

Fifteen Canadian universities[1] were selected on the basis of their use and integration of information and communication technologies (ICT) for teaching and learning as indicated on their websites. All provide distance-based learning programs in addition to face-to-face courses that could sometimes be blended courses.

The 24 interviewees (at least one and at most two per university) who participated in the research were experts in the integration of ICT within conventional universities as well as having substantial experience in teaching, researching and overseeing university teaching centres. The study used interviews (face-to-face, by telephone and by e-mail) as indicated in Table 1.

The respondents were identified through a selection method known as "sampling by contrasted cascade," consisting of choosing research participants by reference from previous interviewees. As Van der Maren (1996) explained, this method of sampling has the advantage of revealing in detail the scattering effects revealing range of divergences (Van der Maren, 1996).

In terms of the participants' characteristics, as mentioned earlier, they were either directors of teaching and learning centers, with a background in teaching and technology use/integration, or specialists in university teaching. Most were current university professors working with teaching centers on technology integration in university teaching and learning. The respondents had an average of 18 years experience in the field of teaching with technologies. Twelve with 20 to 30 years experience in the field of university teaching and ICT integration. Six participants had 13 years experience, four possessed 11 years experience, and two had nine years experience.

The data was collected through interviews. Face-to-face and telephone interviews lasted on average 30 minutes. All responses obtained through interviews were transcribed and then subjected to a qualitative content analysis that was also applied to written responses obtained through e-mail.

The main question asked of participants was: "What are the pedagogical requirements necessary to get the most of teaching and learning activities, in a university context highly influenced by online technologies changing the higher education landscape into blended courses, bimodality institutions and open and distance education?" In the course of the interviews, subsidiary-questions pertaining to the CoI framework categories were also asked.

Strategies Used to Ensure Reliability

Apart from the selection method (the sampling technique known as "contrasted cascade") that helped in ensuring the transferability of the study, member check and triangulation were used to

Table 1. Interviews

	Face-to-Face Interviews	Telephone Interviews	Responses Received by Email	Total Number of Interviews
Interviewees	9	6	9	24

ensure reliability of the data and the study. For the member check process, a one-page text summarizing the essence of each interview was sent to the respondents. This was the process for the data collected through both telephone and face-to-face interviews. Comments were then received from the interviewees and used to validate the accuracy of their ideas and main conclusions.

Triangulation was also used as another strategy to minimize distortion in the study, with the data being validated through two cross-examination processes. First, it was confronted with the information available on the participating universities' websites. During execution, a convergence was noted between what was said by participants, data regarding distance education, and the degree to which technologies are integrated into the participating universities.

The second cross-examination process was undertaken while analyzing the data collected. All of the responses received from the three different sources (telephone, face-to-face and e-mail) were indiscriminately coded, processed and analyzed. All three sources were given equal consideration to minimize any possible effect on the data.

Data Analysis

Without dissociating the transcribed data from text-based responses received through e-mail, all the material was categorized on the basis of their commonality and resemblance to similar descriptions and definitions. Mixed coding was used to set a fixed number of rubrics (in this case, the three elements of the CoI framework) and envision an open set of categories and indicators refined during the course of the analysis. A mixed coding is more appropriate to the methodological requirements of exploratory research (Van der Maren, 1996).

Therefore, guided by the CoI theoretical framework, the data were coded in three groups (rubrics) corresponding to the three presences (cognitive, social and teaching). In a practical way, the categories mentioned in the framework

were used as a starting point. Then, as the analysis proceeded, equivalent keywords used by the interviewees were retained to replace some of the initial categories (taken from the model) to create other new sub-categories. In that way, as a requirement of the mixed coding, new lexical items (in terms of indicators) were added when new units of meaning appeared during the coding and analysis process. As well, when required, reformulation took into consideration the lexicon used by the participants.

The above description, based on seven coding phases and using the content analysis recommended by Van der Maren (1996), is detailed in part in Table 2.

FINDINGS/RESULTS

After the coding process, and especially following the categorization of similar or identical considerations expressed by the interviewees, it was easier to understand the pedagogical implications of the evolution of conventional universities in the era of ICT use and integration. The coding shed light on three groups of pedagogical implications that parallel the three elements of the CoI framework. First, reference was made to the "content of the exchanges between professors and students" and "knowledge building" (2.1.). Secondly, extensive mention was made of the importance of "developing efficient and simplified pedagogical materials," "choosing tools that are germane to pedagogical needs," "referring to constructivist approaches," "constantly searching for a balance between face-to-face and online teaching" and the benefits of "interaction and collaborative work enabled by some advanced new technologies" (2.2.). Thirdly, the respondents named some indicators pertaining to "group cohesion" in order to ensure social presence in online working environments (2.3.). As it appears, these three categories successively refer to cognitive, teaching and social presences.

Table 2. Content analysis

Coding Phases	Coding the Data Collected
Phase One: Temporary list of the rubrics (key topics or indicators) about which indications will be sought throughout the text data.	A temporary list of the three rubrics: • **Cognitive presence:** information exchange, apply new ideas, connecting ideas, sense of problem resolution, etc. • **Social presence:** open communication, group cohesion, encourage collaboration, affective expression, etc. • **Teaching presence:** organizing teaching and methods, discussion, initiate subjects of discussion, focusing on discussion and sharing of personal reflections, etc.
Phase Two: Rereading the data raised/collected in order to recall the context of the production of the information.	All the transcripts along with the text responses received by e-mail have been reread in extenso, before undertaking the coding.
Phase Three: To have the respondents confirm (validate) the essence of what they said.	An e-mail has been sent to each respondent with a one-page synthesis of the main ideas expressed by them, in order to obtain their confirmation.
Phase Four: Examining the data in order to emerge the units of analysis and identify the keys of the categories contained in the text.	All the indications referring to categories and indicators pertaining to the three elements (cognitive, social and teaching presences) have been identified and categorized.
Phase Five: Extracting significant excerpts that will be coded. Then assembling all paragraphs corresponding to a rubric under the same title.	A limited but exhaustive number of the significant excerpts from the verbatim have been retained and categorized according to the categories and indicators of the CoI framework.
Phase Six: Identify meaningful segments (keywords or clauses), from the reading of the units of meaning and significant excerpts. These segments constitute the codes.	After eliminating the repetitions, these codes were retained: • References and excerpts relating to teaching in online and hybrid environments (Teaching presence). • Strategic and theoretical references to problem resolution, information exchange, etc. (Cognitive presence). • Units referring to actors' roles and to group cohesion, etc. (Social presence).
Phase Seven: Final list of the coding.	A final retention of the segments, based on their frequency of occurrence, was made. The segments were classified under each of the codes identified in phase six. They came from the analysis of all the units of analysis. These are presented and discussed in the results and findings.

Learning Issues

The results under of this category parallel "cognitive presence". Garrison, Anderson and Archer (2001) defined cognitive presence as "the extent to which the participants in any particular configuration of a community of inquiry are able to construct meaning through sustained communication". For operational purpose, cognitive presence is composed of four categories: triggering event, exploration of possible facts, integration of elements of solution, and resolution. Table 3 shows the findings, including the indicators mentioned by the respondents and their frequency.

More than half of the participants (54%) reported that online working contexts should rely on methods that favor communication and the search for information.

The excerpt below summarizes the overall view of the other dozen interviewees whose reflections related to "Cognitive presence":

ICT should become a tool (...) to facilitate the communication between the professor and the student, but I think that at a more profound impact level, between students. Also, the search for information, we all now function by Internet search (...). Written text-based productions remain very important (Interviewee X1, from University Y9).

Table 3. Findings

Categories of Cognitive Presence	Indicators Mentioned by the Respondents	Frequencies
Triggering Event	Problem-based learning	25%
Exploration	Internet searches Discover-based learning Learning by searching	54%
Integration	Constructing a work that has a sense Written production Communication between professors/students and students/students	62.5%
Resolution	Problem resolution Concrete knowledge acquisition through activities Knowledge acquisition through collaboration	75%

This participant, as with the other statements in this category, is advocating for working models that enable the search for information, the communication between professors and students, and between students, as well as highlighting the importance of written productions, searching via the Internet, and building a meaningful work. Representative of the other participants' views, the above-quoted mentions almost all the indicators stated under cognitive presence in the CoI framework.

In another excerpt that echoes reflections from about fifteen respondents, online working should refer to learner-centered theories such as research-based learning, problem solving, learning by discovering, problem-based learning, as well as constructivist and behaviorist approaches, with the objective to acquire concrete knowledge:

Problem-based learning, discovery learning, inquiry-based learning—any theory that is student centered and constructivist. Behaviorist theories can and do still apply to ICT use where the goal is the acquisition of concrete knowledge (Interviewee X1, from University Y11).

In the same order of ideas, another respondent referred to socio-constructivist learning theories, such as communal constructivism, as being the most appropriate for an online working context.

The respondent made the precision that the objectives of such a working model are knowledge acquisition through collaboration and interaction with other learners:

I think social constructivist learning theories lend themselves particularly well to the integration of ICT, specifically, communal constructivism. Characteristics of that model include: knowledge acquisition through collaboration and interaction with other learners, learning with and for others, opportunity to contribute to a communal knowledge base for the benefit of existing and new learners (Holmes & Gardner, 2006 – E-learning: Concepts and Practice) (Interviewee X2, from University Y11).

The main indicators brought out by the participants in the study are: knowledge acquisition through collaboration, interaction between learners, research-based learning, problem resolution and discovery learning, information search, communication between professors and students, communication between students, written productions, Internet search and building a meaningful work. Most are identical to the indicators associated with the cognitive presence in the Community of Inquiry framework, which are information exchange, applying new ideas, sense of puzzlement and connecting ideas.

Table 4. Findings and frequency

Categories of Teaching Presence	Indicators Mentioned by the Respondents	Frequencies
Design & Organization	Instructor's preparation Changes in teaching modality and philosophy Organization and access to the course materials, simplified and efficient teaching materials Increased collaboration	75%
Facilitating Discourse	Constructivist and communal constructivist approaches to maintain students' commitment Face-to-face and online environment for a deeper student commitment	62.5%
Direct Instruction	Exchanges, discussions, More interactive discussions for a more collaborative work Fora, emails, other tools	54%

Teaching Issues

This part of the results aligns with "teaching presence" in the CoI framework. As mentioned earlier, teaching presence is defined as "the design, facilitation and direction of cognitive and social processes for the purpose of realizing personally meaningful and educationally worthwhile learning outcomes" (Anderson, Rourke, Garrison & Archer, 2001). Later, Garrison and Anderson (2003) considered teaching presence as having a regulatory and mediating role in the sense that it conveys "all the elements of a community of inquiry together in a balanced and functional relationship congruent with the intended outcomes and the needs and capabilities of the learners". Its three categories are design and organization, facilitating discourse and direct instruction.

Table 4 summarizes the findings by the indicators that emerged from the participants' interviews and inputs, as well the frequency in which the indicators were mentioned.

In the research findings relating to teaching presence in the CoI framework, interviewees refer to "organizing teaching and methods," "discussion," "initiating topics of discussion," "focusing on discussion" and "sharing personal reflections."

The respondents pointed out the potential of ICT to facilitate a teaching setting convenient to learning. Furthermore, they stressed the impor-

tance of the necessary arrangements to bring up to date such a technologically-influenced teaching environment. In the excerpt below, one of the respondents makes mention of three areas where ICT already have an effect:

Such technologies are already having a profound effect on teaching, but often not in the ways that people might think. Three areas: Instructor preparation. Because faculty must post materials and plan activities throughout the term. Increased on-line collaboration. Distribution and access to course materials (Interviewee X1, University Y6).

Other respondents noticed the impact of the online teaching context on the teaching relationship. This view is shared by over a third of respondents. The excerpt below is an illustration of these views:

(...) It's not so much in the teaching itself that I see much difference. It's in the relationship between the professor and the student. Whatsoever via the fora, the e-mail or other tools, that relationship has changed (Interviewee X1, University Y4).

In summary, the interviewees express that a change is underway in teaching, especially at the levels of teacher preparation, online collaboration through forums, access to the course materials, teaching and learning flexibility, as well as possible change in university teaching.

Furthermore, over three-quarters of the respondents made much of the development of a teaching context specific to ICT use supported by new effective and simplified pedagogical materials. This consideration is reflected in the following excerpt:

One of the key elements to teaching, it's the time that university professors will spend to develop their pedagogical material. Develop new effective and simplified pedagogical materials (Interviewee X1, University Y1).

While highlighting the importance of an organized teaching setting, the respondents emphasize that the choice of technologies be consistently made in accordance with pedagogical approaches and needs:

Technologies must be fully fastened to or perfectly integrated in pedagogical approaches, and it seemed to me that where the shoe often pinches is that the tools are adopted without having that perfect synchronization (...) tools are selected that don't quite meet pedagogical needs (Interviewee X1, University Y5).

As anticipated consequences to a good teaching setting, a respondent, whose view is also held by several other interviewees, cites a reduction in dropout rate and in the feeling of isolation especially in distance education. Constructivist and communal constructivist approaches are referred to as an asset in fighting dropout and isolation:

I believe ICT will/do generally improve overall teaching and learning in higher education provided their implementation is grounded a theoretical framework that supports their use (i.e., socio constructivism, communal constructivism). Furthermore, these technologies designed around the appropriate framework hold the potential to

overcome attrition rates and feelings of isolation, particularly in distance learning (Interviewee X2, University Y11).

Interviewees pointed out the necessity to review teaching methods to promote exchanges and discussions between professors and students. The challenge of finding a balance between face-to-face and online environments remains even if ICT have the potential to make the group work effective. Face-to-face will enable more discussions and a richer involvement on the part of the students. The excerpt below is greatly shared by the respondents:

The greatest benefit requires professors to modify their teaching philosophy and modality to embrace the new possibilities opened by the use of ICT (...) Faculty are wise to embrace an approach that involves more active and collaborative learning. Certain activities that were formerly done in the classroom can be moved on-line thereby allowing face-to-face class time to have more discussion and richer student engagement. However face-to-face is still the preferred mode so the challenge is one of finding a balance between online and f2f (Interviewee X1, University Y7).

As discussions have been deemed to be so important to these teaching settings, this interviewee is in agreement with more than half of the respondents by pointing out that ICT are tools which can help change the nature of the discussions by making them more interactive. Therefore, it relies on the role-players (faculty and students) to make the most of that potential to the benefit of their exchanges:

It [technology] helps in information gathering, more interactive referencing, for people looking for reference sites in the class, in theory lab of wireless, a change in the nature of discussion in the class, much more interactive but perhaps much more relevant, and I would say the final thing is it will probably help to make students work collaboratively (Interviewee X2, University Y2).

In substance, the pedagogical factors that go hand in hand with ICT use to achieve a teaching context favorable to learning are: the development of effective and simplified pedagogical materials; the choice of tools that are in phase with pedagogical needs; the recourse to constructivist approaches; the search for a balance between face-to-face and online teaching-environment; and, the interaction and the collaborative work made easier by some current or new technologies.

Other Pedagogical and Administrative Issues

Due to the social component of the findings classified under this section, such as group cohesion, collaboration, communication and mainly participants' roles in a community of learning, this part aligns with "social presence". In the CoI framework, under the social presence dimension, three categories are mentioned:

1. **Open Communication:** With a referred indicator as risk-free expression
2. **Group Cohesion:** Encourage collaboration as an example of indicator
3. **Affective Expression:** Emoticons are referred to as a type of indicator of that third category.

Social presence has been defined by Garrison (2009) as "the ability of participants to identify with the community (e.g., course of study), communicate purposefully in a trusting environment, and develop inter-personal relationships by way of projecting their individual personalities." Concerning its place in the teaching philosophy of online and blended environments, social presence is viewed as an essential preliminary step

to collaborating and critical discourse. Based on earlier research, Garrison and Anderson (2003) acknowledged that social presence facilitates achieving cognitive objectives by instigating, sustaining, and supporting critical thinking in a community of learners.

Table 5 summarizes the research findings in accordance with the indicators mentioned by the respondents and frequencies.

Under social presence, the category most referred to by interviewees was group cohesion (62%). It was also the category most detailed in the comments given by respondents. In line with group cohesion, half of the interviewees (50%) mentioned open communication as an essential component to collaboration. The importance of group cohesion, along with its implications such as role distribution, emerged as the main finding in this research.

The large reference to indicators classifiable under group cohesion could be indicative of that category's significance to social presence in online and blended teaching contexts. And as highlighted by the respondents, participant awareness of their specific roles in the process can be considered as a prerequisite for a group to be cohesive. Otherwise a real social presence couldn't be ensured for members in any given community.

The respondents have thereby pointed to the different parts professors, students and administrators should take in the community of inquiry, to ensure group cohesion, and collaboration.

Expected Administrative Skills in Teaching Activities to Ensure Group Cohesion

From the general point of view of almost all interviewees, the academic work of university teaching will need more administrative skills and support than simply teaching, in a university

Table 5. Findings in according with indicators

Categories of Social Presence	Indicators Mentioned by the Respondents	Frequencies
Open Communication	Mentoring approaches Management theories Reflective, collaborative, and efficient learners' participation	50%
Group Cohesion	**Teachers:** Facilitating learning, discerning knowledge and their sources, especially with the advent of the web 2.0 medias Moderating online courses Doing research **Students:** Active partners, more responsible and contributors to knowledge creation and content construction **Administrators & Technology Specialists:** Helping professors and students	62.5%
Affective Expression		0%

context where working online and e-learning are taking up space.

The following excerpt is revealing of that overview:

Universities will need more and more administrators for e-learning. More managers, directors and ICT specialists. Universities have to meet agencies' needs coming to universities for professional programs (MBA, etc.). (...) Universities have to compete, so they have to offer many training and studies opportunities. (...) In short, more management and less academic for universities in the coming years (Interviewee X1, University Y3).

In the same vein, another interviewee expressed that mentoring approaches, resting on management theories, will be called for:

I believe it's going to be less teaching from the front of the class, and the work will be, perhaps I guess, more a management, corporate stream, organization stream, [inaudible] management theories. It will be a mentor approach (Interviewee X2, University Y2).

The next point of view follows and specifies that professors must see themselves in the role of learning facilitators that get students involved:

Faculties have to see their role as facilitators of learning, as creating an environment for learning to occur. They need to focus on student success and less on filtering out the "weak" students. Faculty need a greater comfort and facility with technology and have to find ways to bridge between research and teaching to keep the students engaged (Interviewee X1, University Y7).

The same idea, shared by nearly two-thirds of the interviewees, is delivered by this participant who points out that professors will act more and more as facilitators:

Teachers will act as facilitators, gatekeepers and teachers but the process will most likely be formalized in an ICT setting (Interviewee X2, University Y3).

The same proportion of respondents think that another new characteristic of the professor role will consist of discerning the source of students' contribution to the knowledge content:

With the implementation of ICT, particularly Web 2.0 technologies, in teaching and learning, the instructor's role shifts from knowledge deliverer to that of discerner of knowledge, recognizing students as full and active partners and contributors to knowledge creation and content construction.

Students will take more responsibility for their own learning and that of the community which the learning occurs (Interviewee X2, University Y11).

As to course development, more than half of the respondents consider that it will fall less and less under the responsibility of professors and more to other professionals:

Certainly I think we're going to see situations where courses are going to be designed by more others than by just teachers. They will probably work together with other kind of experts to assist in developing their courses. The courses tend to become more and more public as they go online. (...). When they go to online environment and therefore more people are involving in designing courses (Interviewee X1, University Y8).

Another consideration from a participant makes an exhaustive synthesis of the comments shared by the majority of the interviewees. According to this view, there will be more part-time professors who will take charge of moderating online courses (designed by full-time professors in concert with part-time professors), while full-time professors will devote most of their time to research:

I suspect there will be a shift to more sessional faculty moderating online courses that full-time faculty either design by themselves or in conjunction with the sessionals. Full-time faculty will then focus more on research (Interviewee X1, University, Y11).

Finally, according to more than sixty percent of the interviewees, administrators will need to provide more flexibility to the institution as well as help to professors and students:

Administrators have to provide more flexibility in the institution and be less policy-bound. They have to ensure that the systems are there to sup-port both the faculty and students. These systems include the behind-the-scenes IT infrastructure as well as professional development and student success centers (Interviewee X1, University, Y7).

In summary, and in line with the anticipated changes to teaching roles in a university-context largely subject to ICT integration, academic work will henceforth be in need of more administrators and other groups of professionals such as part-time professors who will take responsibility for moderating online courses. This anticipated administrative infusion may not be seen as a good thing and might seem controversial. But clearly, teaching will become more a facilitation of learning and professors will be called upon to discern students' knowledge contribution and their sources. In such a learning context, mentoring approaches, resting upon management theories, would be necessary.

Students' Role

At an overall proportion of 62.5%, interviewees are of the view that students will be more efficient learners through collaboration and participation than in the past. The following excerpt is an example of what participants said in that regard:

Students have to become more participatory, reflective, and collaborative to be effective learners. We now know this as a result of research in the field of education. ICT helps this shift. The Web 2.0 notion that blurs the distinction between the producer of media and the consumer of media parallels this shift. In the past, the teachers produced and the students consumed. Now this is turned on its head, the students are producers and consumers (Interviewee X1, University Y7).

In the same vein, another participant added that students will be more involved by taking charge of their own learning:

Students, I think, are going to be more involved more monitoring their learning more than that was in the past. The technologies really facilitate that (Interviewee X1, University Y8).

According to one of the interviewees, a teaching centre expert, students have to be considered as contributors to the knowledge creation and to the content construction processes:

With the implementation of ICT, particularly Web 2.0 technologies, in teaching and learning, the instructor's role shifts from knowledge deliverer to that of discerner of knowledge, recognizing students as full and active partners and contributors to knowledge creation and content construction. Students will take more responsibility for their own learning and that of the community which the learning occurs (Interviewee X2, University Y11).

In brief, and in terms of new roles, in order to ensure group cohesion and collaboration in conventional university settings under the changing effect of online work and e-learning, universities will need more administrators and more ICT specialists to offer support to professors and students. As well, other experts will likely emerge to develop courses.

In addition to becoming facilitators, professors will also face the challenge of discerning the reliability of knowledge sources available on the Web.

Students will become both producers and consumers of knowledge through a greater participation and collaboration enabled by the ICT. In this way, they will be more involved to guide their own learning.

As open communication and group cohesion are recommended in the CoI framework, the more the participants will adapt to the aforementioned changes, the more open the communication and cohesive the group will become in blended and online teaching and learning environments. See Figure 2 for a histogram of the results.

DISCUSSION AND A PROPOSED CONTRIBUTION TO THE COI FRAMEWORK

This discussion part of the research findings draws a parallel between the pedagogical requirements of the CoI framework and the results that emerged through the study; and between the research results and the current scientific literature, especially regarding collaborative knowledge building. The second point of discussion is a proposed contribution to the CoI framework regarding the question of participant roles in the new teaching context as it arises from the findings, which reflects recent literature on the CoI framework. The third point of this section is concerning the adequacy of the CoI framework to blended courses.

In terms of the pedagogical requirements identified by the respondents, the elements of reference (knowledge acquisition through collaboration, interaction between learners, research-based learning, problem-based learning, discovery-based learning, information search, communication between professors and students, and between students themselves, written productions, etc.) are in agreement with the three presences, their categories and indicators. The study also revealed the importance of ensuring social, teaching and cognitive presences in online and blended working environments.

However, some indicators identified by the participants, such as information exchange, discussion and collaboration, proved to be congruent or relevant to either of the three presences. In this respect, the CoI framework possesses some interchangeable indicators between its three elements. In that, the dividing barrier between them proves to be permeable. While not a criticism, this is an informed comment on the internal flexibility of the CoI framework.

The research results on the benefits of collaboration align with some recent literature. In a study undertaken by Shea and Bidjerano (2009),

Figure 2. Histogram of the results

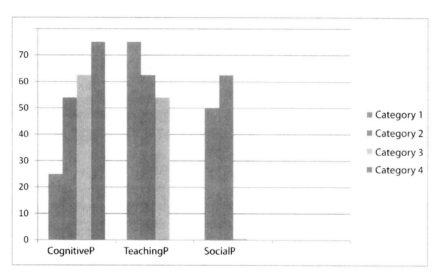

Cognitive Presence (Cognitive P):
(From left to right): Category 1 = Triggering event; Category 2 = Exploration; Category 3 = Integration; Category 4 = Resolution.

Teaching Presence (Teaching P):
(From left to right): Category 1 = Design & Organization; Category 2 = Facilitating Discourse; Category 3 = Direct Instruction.

Social Presence (Social P):
(From left to right): Category 1 = Open Communication; Category 2 = Group Cohesion; Category 3 = Affective Expression.

learner's role as collaborative knowledge constructors was found to be more articulated and extended through a community of research. Along the same lines, other studies emphasized the need of building learning communities in order to increase students' participation and promote learning within online and blended learning environments (Rovai, 2002; Palloff & Pratt, 2005; Barab, Kling, & Gray, 2004; Conrad, 2005; Colachico, 2007). Also, Lipponen (2002) and Stahl (2000) highlighted that collaborative construction of knowledge is pre-eminently a social process (social presence) in which participants co-construct knowledge by means of social interactions. According to this view, shared by these two researchers, collaborative reflection helps present one's views to peers

with the intent of having a different perspective. Referring to collaborative activities in online and blended environments, Lin, Hmelo, Kinzer and Secules (1999) observed that social reflexive discourse has three advantages: a) a greater interaction between participants; b) a more motivating reflection; and, c) ideas and thoughts become artifacts and objects for subsequent reflections. These points are broadly similar to the results from this research. Another corroborating research is the one done by Yukawa (2006) regarding online collective learning. Yukawa's study underlined the potential of collaborative reflection as a crucial process in group learning. Yukawa (2006) also analyzes how a group of participants builds knowledge and how group activities supported by online technologies can be designed to reinforce problem-based learning, as recommended by Cohen and Nycz (2006) and Duffy and Kirkley (2004). Group participation/collaboration is also emphasized in terms of group cognition (Stahl, 2006), contribution theory (Clark & Brennan, 1999 quoted by Stahl, 2006), and intersubjective comprehension (Yukawa, 2006).

In summary, the respondents shared and confirmed what emerged from the scientific literature regarding efficient teaching and learning with the integration of new technologies. There is strong agreement on the recourse to the new pedagogical approaches, such as communal constructivism (Tangney, FitzGibbon, Savage, Meehan & Holmes, 2001), based on knowledge acquisition through collaboration, interaction and learning with others. The urgency for a new university culture where students take an active part is also considered critical as it previously appeared in the works of Ahern, Thomas, Tallent-Runnels, Lan, Cooper, Lu and Cyrus (2006); Finegold and Cooke (2006); John and Sutherland (2005); Thompson and MacDonald (2005); Henri (2001); and, Privateer (1999).

The second point of this discussion is a proposed contribution to the CoI framework. In light of the results obtained, some categories within the CoI framework deserve greater consideration compared to others, given their regular mention in the respondents' comments. The group cohesion category was referred to by 62.5% of the respondents while affective expression was not mentioned at all. Similarly, some indicators such as participant roles are worth being explicitly mentioned in the CoI framework under the category of group cohesion of social presence, given their unanimously suggested importance by the respondents.

Concerning this role adjustment, the respondents' views once again reflect the very recent literature on the CoI framework. The latest works by the model's authors, especially two recent papers (Cleveland-Innes & Garrison, 2010;

Cleveland-Innes, Garrison & Kinsell, 2007), are indicative of the question of role adjustment to ensure group cohesion and collaboration in a changing conventional university setting under the increasing effect of e-learning and online work in general. Regarding students, Cleveland-Innes and Garrison (2010) mentioned the results of research that students experiencing online learning for the first time also experience an adjustment in the learner's role. The adjustment was noticed at five levels:

1. Modes of interaction
2. Self-identity
3. Instructor role
4. Course design
5. Technology use

In the same research, instructors from two open and distance learning programs were interviewed and confirmed the role adjustment in the five areas identified by the students. As shown in the present research, this role adjustment should be understood in light of the specific requirements of the learner's role in an online community intended to learning, researching, contributing and collaborating with peers. Equally, when Cleveland-Innes and Garrison (2010) stated that these adjustments constitute challenges for online learning that have to be facilitated and supported, it could be another reason to explicitly mention participants' roles or role adjustment in the CoI framework.

Differences between activities in an online environment, compared to face-to-face context, explain the changes in roles of the participants, especially students. Cleveland-Innes and Garrison (2010), referring to Knuttila (2002), point out that the concept of role relates to expected and generally accepted ways of behaving, acting and interacting. However, as Cleveland-Innes and Garrison (2010) made the distinction, unlike the adoption and playing of social roles, becoming an online learner has a unique characteristic. For many students, it's only when they are engaged in an online course that they learn and experience the required and expected activities (Garrison & Cleveland-Innes, 2003). In the same way that the respondents in this research have called attention to changes in roles as a critical component to deal with the new learning environment of online and blended courses, Cleveland-Innes and Garrison (2010) recognized in their study that new roles are necessary in an online community due to the nature of the communication that requires students to take greater responsibility and control over their learning (Cleveland-Innes & Garrison, 2010). Combined with participants' responses, this constitutes the reason why a review of the CoI framework seems necessary to reflect participant roles as an indicator under the category of group cohesion of the social presence. Classifying this role construct under social presence, doesn't mean that the changes in roles only occur in activities reflecting social presence. Previous studies (Cleveland-Innes, Garrison & Kinsell, 2007), as well as the current one, all bring about changes in roles in cognitive presence (verbal and spontaneous communication is replaced by text-based communication that becomes the primary reflection tool); and in teaching presence (different ways of course design and role adjustment for professors). However, the reality of role playing appears more of a social construct that is linked to group cohesion.

Also, as pointed out earlier, not only role adjustment but other indicators mentioned by the participants such as information exchange, discussion and collaboration, relate to either of the three presences. In this regard, role adjustment is another example that the CoI framework possesses some interchangeable indicators among its three elements, leading to the conclusion that the barrier separating the three presences is permeable.

Finally, while this study was undertaken in conventional universities delivering online programs and blended learning courses, the results are in line with earlier findings in which the CoI framework was used as a theoretical framework.

This proves that despite the differences between online and blended contexts, the CoI framework is applicable to both blended and online learning environments. As indicated by Garrison and Kanuka (2004), the blended learning environment is particularly effective in supporting a community of inquiry.

Strategic Planning for Online and Blended Learning to Provide Easy Transition

The study, regarding strategic planning for online and blended learning to provide easy transition, identified lessons at three levels: material or technological, theoretical and administrative.

Technology

According to the experts who participated in this research, key elements to an easy transition to online teaching are:

- The development and use of new, efficient and simplified pedagogical tools. Some suggest that professors spend more time developing their pedagogical materials, as simplified tools ease the adaptation process. Such a view also reflects Rogers' (1995) suggestions on the ways to attain success in innovation, especially the importance for the tools to offer a low degree of complexity.
- The importance of communication and information search tools. As well, the technologies used in a blended context should really help in specific ways such as information gathering and interactive referencing that will effect change in the nature of discussion in the class and wireless labs. This change would make discussion much more interactive, perhaps more relevant, and help students work collaboratively.

• Moving on-line certain activities, formerly done in the classroom, thereby allowing face-to-face class time to involve more discussion and a richer student engagement. This is with regard to the online versus classroom activities. For example, the participants pointed out that ICT can allow for more effective group work and support a variety of formative assessment, even if face-to-face interaction proves to be the preferred mode. This leads to the critical challenge identified by interviewees: finding the right balance between online and face-to-face.

Theory

On the theoretical side, some considerations were identified favoring the transition to online learning.

Problem-based learning, discovery learning, inquiry-based learning and constructivist theories in general, as well as any student-centered theory, were regularly cited by the experts to provide ICT with the goal of acquisition of concrete and communal knowledge. They considered the metaphor of student as an "empty vessel" and teaching as the act of "delivering content" as a dated and ineffective model and encouraged faculty to embrace an approach that involves a more active and collaborative teaching approach.

Also, the crucial role of the faculty was highlighted by the participants. Not only do faculty facilitate vertical communication between students and themselves, as well as horizontal communication between students, but faculty is also expected to regularly reflect on the learning objectives to organize the new environment in line with the constant re-imaging of those objectives.

Administration

At an administrative level, the interviewees suggested methods to face the new organizational challenges related to online and blended learning environments. The main point mentioned was how to manage the academic workload at the institution level. The experts were unanimous to state that:

• The administrative support must increase with the advent of online and blended learning. "Universities will need more and more administrators for e-learning... more management and less academics in coming years", one explained. Another expert stated that "it's going to be less teaching, and the work will be more a management, corporate stream, organization stream, with management theories" and concluded that "it will be a mentor approach". Such anticipated changes in the academic workload again lead to new interactions between professors and students.

• The ICT setting is a keystone in terms of strategies. As one of the respondents mentioned, "teachers will act as facilitators, gatekeepers and teachers but the process will most likely be formalized in an ICT setting." Other types of experts will certainly assist teachers in developing courses as they become more and more accessible online. And as indicated by a significant number of the respondents, more sessional faculty will likely be moderating online courses with full-time faculty, either designing courses by themselves or in conjunction with sessionals. Full-time faculty will then have more time to focus on research.

• Administrative systems should be put in place to support both faculty and students, IT infrastructure as well as professional development and student success centers. Especially with the trend and changes related to universities providing online and blended courses.

419

RECOMMENDATIONS AND FUTURE RESEARCH DIRECTIONS

In terms of recommendations, many points emerged that can be summarized in the following five:

- The importance of role adjustment, highly mentioned by the respondents, is worth being explicitly indicated in the CoI framework under the category of group cohesion of the social presence element.
- Conventional universities need a specific faculty or department to establish the appropriate technologies and ICT integration models.
- Universities must consider organizing regular best practices sessions for their professors working in online and blended learning environments.
- For future research perspectives, more research has to be undertaken regarding the appropriate ratio of face-to-face / distance learning with respect to the specific learning objectives at stake.
- Finally, as the students' responsibility to take charge of their learning is growing, with the advent of ICT integration in university education, further research on the CoI framework may be needed to allocate a specific space to students in the community of inquiry.

CONCLUSION

This study revealed the importance of collaborative knowledge construction, problem-based learning, discovery-based learning and the relevancy of constructivist approaches, for teaching, learning and cooperating in an online and blended environment. These findings back results from previous research undertaken by Shea and

Bidjerano (2009), Akyol, Garrison and Ozden (2009), McCombs and Miller (2007), Yukawa (2006), Cohen and Nycz (2006), Stahl (2006), Palloff and Pratt (2005), Duffy and Kirkley (2004), and Lin, Hmelo, Kinzer and Secules (1999).

As well, this research highlighted the primary need for role adjustment when it comes to collaborating in an online and blended context for teaching and learning in higher education. This is consistent with recent research findings made by Cleveland-Innes and Garrison (2010) and Cleveland-Innes, Garrison and Kinsell (2007).

Also, the study has confirmed the adequacy of the CoI framework, not only within an online environment, but also with blended environments. This again echoes some recent research undertaken by Garrison and Anderson (2003), Garrison and Vaughan (2008), Akyol, Garrison and Ozden (2009), and Garrison and Kanuka (2004).

Furthermore, the finding that proves to be of particular interest to the CoI framework, as well as to the field of technology integration in teaching and learning, is the preeminence of social-related factors such as group cohesion which is facilitated and reinforced by appropriate role models played by all participants in any online intellectual activity, especially teaching and learning in a university context.

REFERENCES

Ahern, T. C., Thomas, J. A., Tallent-Runnels, M. K., Lan, W. Y., Cooper, S., Lu, X., & Cyrus, J. (2006). The effect of social grounding on collaboration in a computer-mediated small group discussion. *The Internet and Higher Education, 9*, 37–46. doi:10.1016/j.iheduc.2005.09.008

Akyol, Z., Garrison, D. R., & Ozden, M. Y. (2009). Online and blended communities of inquiry: Exploring the developmental and perceptual differences. *International Review of Research in Open and Distance Learning, 10*(6), 65–83.

Allen, I., & Seaman, J. (2007). *Online Nation: Five years of growth in online learning.* Needham, MA: Sloan Consortium.

Allen, I. E., & Seaman, J. (2004). *Entering the mainstream: The quality and extent of online education in the United States, 2003 and 2004.* Needham, MA: Sloan-C.

Amemado, D. (2010a). University models with high-growth probability, under ICT integration, during the next decade in North America. In J. Sanchez & K. Zhang (Eds.), *Proceedings of World Conference on E-Learning in Corporate, Government, Healthcare, and Higher Education 2010* (pp. 1309-1313). Chesapeake, VA: AACE.

Amemado, D. (2010b). *Changements et évolution des universités conventionnelles sous l'influence des technologies de l'information et de la communication (TIC): Le cas du contexte universitaire nord-américain.* Unpublished doctoral dissertation, University of Montreal, Canada.

Anderson, T., Rourke, L., Garrison, D. R., & Archer, W. (2001). Assessing teaching presence in computer conferencing context. *Journal of Asynchronous Learning Networks, 5*(2), 1–17.

Barab, S. A., Kling, R., & Gray, J. H. (2004). Introduction. In Barab, S. A., Kling, R., & Gray, J. H. (Eds.), *Designing for virtual communities in the service of l earning* (pp. 3–15). New York, NY: Cambridge University Press. doi:10.1017/CBO9780511805080.005

Cleveland-Innes, M., & Garrison, D. R. (2010). The role of learner in an online community of inquiry: Instructor support for first-time online learners. In Karacapilidis, N. (Ed.), *Web-based learning solutions for communities of practice: Developing virtual environments for social and pedagogical advancements* (pp. 167–184). Hershey, PA: IGI Global.

Cleveland-Innes, M., Garrison, D. R., & Kinsel, E. (2007). Role adjustment for learners in an online community of inquiry: Identifying the challenges of incoming online learners. *International Journal of Web-Based Learning and Teaching Technologies, 2*(1), 1–16. doi:10.4018/jwltt.2007010101

Cohen, E. B., & Nycz, M. (2006). Learning objects: An informing science perspective. *Interdisciplinary Journal of Knowledge and Learning Objects, 2,* 23–34.

Colachico, D. (2007). Developing a sense of community in an online environment. *International Journal of Learning, 14*(1), 161–165.

Conrad, D. (2005). Building and maintaining community in cohort-based online learning. *Journal of Distance Education, 20*(1), 1–21.

Dabbagh, N. (2005). Pedagogical models for e-learning: A theory-based design framework. *International Journal of Technology in Teaching and Learning, 1*(1), 25–44.

Dawson, S. (2006). A study of the relationship between student communication interaction and sense of community. *The Internet and Higher Education, 9*(3), 153–162. doi:10.1016/j.iheduc.2006.06.007

Dewey, J. (1933). *How we think* (rev. ed.). Boston, MA: D.C. Heath.

Dringus, L. P. (2000). Towards active online learning: A dramatic shift in perspective for learners. *The Internet and Higher Education, 2*(4), 189–195. doi:10.1016/S1096-7516(00)00023-3

Dringus, L. P., & Scigliano, J. A. (2000). From early to current developments in online learning at Nova Southeastern University: Reflections on historical milestones. *The Internet and Higher Education, 3*(1-2), 23–40. doi:10.1016/S1096-7516(00)00031-2

Duffy, T. M., & Kirkley, J. R. (Eds.). (2004). *Learner-centered theory and practice in distance education: Cases from Higher Education*. Mahwah, NJ: Lawrence Erlbaum.

Finegold, A. R. D., & Cooke, L. (2006). Exploring the attitudes, experiences and dynamics of interaction in online groups. *The Internet and Higher Education, 9*(3), 201–215. doi:10.1016/j.iheduc.2006.06.003

Garrison, D. R. (2009). Communities of inquiry in online learning: Social, teaching and cognitive presence. In Howard, C. (Eds.), *Encyclopedia of distance and online learning* (2nd ed., pp. 352–355). Hershey, PA: IGI Global. doi:10.4018/978-1-60566-198-8.ch052

Garrison, D. R., & Anderson, T. (2003). *E-learning in the 21st century: A framework for research and practice*. London, UK: Routledge/Falmer. doi:10.4324/9780203166093

Garrison, D. R., Anderson, T., & Archer, W. (2000). Critical inquiry in a text-based environment: computer conferencing in higher education. *The Internet and Higher Education, 2*(2-3), 87–105. doi:10.1016/S1096-7516(00)00016-6

Garrison, D. R., Anderson, T., & Archer, W. (2001). Critical thinking, cognitive presence, and computer conferencing in distance education. *American Journal of Distance Education, 15*(1), 7–23. doi:10.1080/08923640109527071

Garrison, D. R., & Arbaugh, J. B. (2007). Researching the community of inquiry framework: Review, issues, and future directions. *The Internet and Higher Education, 10*(3), 157–172. doi:10.1016/j.iheduc.2007.04.001

Garrison, D. R., & Cleveland-Innes, M. (2003). Critical factors in student satisfaction and success: Facilitating student role adjustment in online communities of inquiry. In Bourne, J., & Moore, J. (Eds.), *Elements of quality online education: Into the mainstream* (pp. 29–38). Needham, MA: Sloan-C.

Garrison, D. R., & Kanuka, H. (2004). Blended learning: Uncovering its transformative potential in higher education. *The Internet and Higher Education, 7*(2), 95–105. doi:10.1016/j.iheduc.2004.02.001

Garrison, D. R., & Vaughan, N. (2008). *Blended learning in higher education*. San Francisco, CA: Jossey-Bass.

Goodyear, P. (2001). *Effective networked learning in higher education: notes and guidelines*. Networked Learning in Higher Education Project (JCALT), Centre for Studies in Advanced Learning Technology, University of Lancaster. Retrieved February 24, 2010, from http://www.csalt.lancs.ac.uk/jisc/guidelines_final.doc

Grabe, M., & Christopherson, K. (2005). Evaluating the advantages and disadvantages of providing lecture notes: The role of Internet technology as a delivery system and research tool. *The Internet and Higher Education, 8*(4), 291–298. doi:10.1016/j.iheduc.2005.09.002

Guri-Rosenblit, S. (2001). Virtual universities: Current models and future trends. *Higher Education in Europe, 26*(4), 487–499. doi:10.1080/03797720220141807

Henri, F. (2001). Des cours sur le web à l'université. In T. Karsenti & L. Larose (Eds.), *Les TIC...au cœur des pédagogies universitaires* (117-143). Québec, Canada: Presses de l'Université du Québec.

Herron, T. L. (1998). Teaching with the Internet. *The Internet and Higher Education, 1*(3), 217–222. doi:10.1016/S1096-7516(99)80168-7

John, P., & Sutherland, R. (2005). Affordance, opportunity and the pedagogical implications of ICT. *Educational Review, 57*(4), 405–415. doi:10.1080/00131910500278256

Knuttila, M. (2002). *Introducing sociology: A critical perspective.* Don Mills, Canada: Oxford University Press.

Laurillard, D. (2002). *Rethinking university teaching. A conversational framework for the effective use of learning technologies.* London, UK: Routledge. doi:10.4324/9780203304846

Lieblein, E. (2000). Critical factors for successful delivery of online programs. *The Internet and Higher Education, 3*(3), 161–174. doi:10.1016/S1096-7516(01)00036-7

Lin, X., Hmelo, C., Kinzer, K., & Secules, T. J. (1999). Designing technology to support reflection. *Educational Technology Research and Development, 47*(3), 43–62. doi:10.1007/BF02299633

Lipponen, L. (2002). *Exploring foundations for computer-supported collaborative learning.* Paper presented at the 4th Computer Support for Collaborative Learning: Foundations for a CSCL Community, (CSCL-2002), Boulder, Colorado.

McCombs, B. L., & Miller, L. (2007). *Learner-centered classroom practices and assessments: Maximizing student motivation, learning, and achievement.* Thousand Oaks, CA: Corwin Press.

Moore, A. H., Fowler, S. B., & Watson, C. E. (2007). Active learning and technology: Designing Change for faculty, students, and institutions. *EDUCAUSE Review, 42*(5), 43–60.

Palloff, R., & Pratt, K. (2001). *Lessons from the cyberspace classroom: The realities of online teaching.* San Francisco, CA: Jossey-Bass.

Palloff, R. M., & Pratt, K. (2005). *Collaborating online: Learning together in community.* San Francisco, CA: Jossey-Bass.

Privateer, P. M. (1999). Academic technology and the future of higher education. *The Journal of Higher Education, 70*(1), 60–79. doi:10.2307/2649118

Rogers, E. M. (1995). *Diffusion of innovations* (4th ed.). New York, NY: Free Press.

Rovai, A. P. (2002). Sense of community, perceived cognitive learning, and persistence in asynchronous learning networks. *The Internet and Higher Education, 5*(4), 319–332. doi:10.1016/S1096-7516(02)00130-6

Rovai, A. P. (2004). A constructivist approach to online college learning. *The Internet and Higher Education, 7*(2), 79–93. doi:10.1016/j.iheduc.2003.10.002

Shea, P., & Bidjerano, T. (2009). Community of inquiry as a theoretical framework to foster "epistemic engagement" and "cognitive presence" in online education. *Computers & Education, 52*(3), 543–553. doi:10.1016/j.compedu.2008.10.007

Stahl, G. (2000c). *A model of collaborative knowledge-building.* Paper presented at the Fourth International Conference of the Learning Sciences (ICLS 2000), Ann Arbor, MI.

Stahl, G. (2006). *Group cognition: Computer support for building collaborative knowledge.* Cambridge, MA: MIT Press.

Stewart, B. L. (2004). Online learning: a strategy for social responsibility in educational access. *The Internet and Higher Education, 7*(4), 299–310. doi:10.1016/j.iheduc.2004.09.003

Tangney, B., FitzGibbon, A., Savage, T., Meehan, S., & Holmes, B. (2001). Communal constructivism: Students constructing learning for as well as with others. In J. Price et al. (Eds.), *Proceedings of Society for Information Technology & Teacher Education International Conference 2001* (pp. 3114-3119). Chesapeake, VA: AACE.

Thompson, T. L., & MacDonald, C. J. (2005). Community building, emergent design and expecting the unexpected: Creating a quality eLearning experience. *The Internet and Higher Education, 8*(3), 233–249. doi:10.1016/j.iheduc.2005.06.004

Uljens, M. (1997). *School didactics and learning.* Hove, UK: Psychology Press. doi:10.4324/9780203304778

Van der Maren, J.-M. (1996). *Méthodes de recherche pour l'Education* (2nd ed.). Montréal, Canada: Presses de l'Université de Montréal.

Yukawa, J. (2006). Co-reflection in online learning: Collaborative critical thinking as narrative. *International Journal of Computer-Supported Collaborative Learning, 1*(2), 203–228. doi:10.1007/s11412-006-8994-9

ADDITIONAL READING

Baran, E., Correia, A. P., & Thompson, A. (2011). Paths to exemplary online teaching: A look at teacher roles, competencies and exemplary online teaching. In T. Bastiaens & M. Ebner (Eds.), *Proceedings of World Conference on Educational Multimedia, Hypermedia and Telecommunications 2011* (pp. 2853-2860). Chesapeake, VA: AACE.

Bates, A., & Sangrà, A. (2011). *Managing technology in higher education: Strategies for transforming teaching and learning.* San Francisco, CA: Jossey-Bass/John Wiley & Co.

Benson, R., & Brack, C. (2009). Developing the scholarship of teaching: What is the role of e-teaching and learning? *Teaching in Higher Education, 14*(1), 71–80. doi:10.1080/13562510802602590

Blankson, J., & Kyei-Blankson, L. (2008). Nontraditional students' perception of a blended course: Integrating synchronous online discussion and face-to-face instruction. *Journal of Interactive Learning Research, 3*(19), 421–438.

Cartelli, A. (2006). *Teaching in the knowledge society – New skills and instruments for teachers.* Hershey, PA: Information Science Publishing. doi:10.4018/978-1-59140-953-3

Chew, E. (2008). Book review: Blended learning tools for teaching and training (B. Allan, Ed.). *Educational Technology & Society, 11*(2), 344-347.

Collison, G., Elbaum, B., Haavind, S., & Tinker, R. (2000). *Facilitating online learning: Effective strategies for moderators.* Madison, WI: Atwood Publishing.

Delfino, M., & Persico, D. (2007). Online or face to face? Experimenting with different techniques in teacher training. *Journal of Computer Assisted Learning, 23*(5), 351–365. doi:10.1111/j.1365-2729.2007.00220.x

Devonshire, E. (2006). Re-purposing an online role play activity: Exploring the institutional and pedagogical challenges. In L. Markauskaite, P. Goodyear, & P. Reimann (Eds.), *Proceedings of the 23rd Annual Conference of the Australasian Society for Computers in Learning in Tertiary Education: Who's Learning? Whose Technology?* (pp. 205–208). Sydney, Australia: Sydney University Press.

Dziuban, C., Moskal, P., Brophy, J., & Shea, P. (2007). Technology-enhanced education and millennial students in higher education. *Metropolitan Universities, 18*(3), 75–90.

Ellis, R. A., Goodyear, P., Prosser, M., & O'Hara, A. (2006). How and what university students learn trough online and face to face discussion: Conceptions, intentions and approaches. *Journal of Computer Assisted Learning, 22*(4), 244–256. doi:10.1111/j.1365-2729.2006.00173.x

Goodyear, P., Salmon, G., Spector, J., Steeples, C., & Tickner, S. (2001). Competences for online teaching. *Educational Technology Research and Development*, 49(1), 65–72. doi:10.1007/BF02504508

Jeffcoat Bartley, S., & Golek, J. H. (2004). Evaluating the cost effectiveness of online and face-to-face instruction. *Journal of Educational Technology & Society*, 7(4), 167–175.

Kim, J. (2009). Development of social presence scale. In T. Bastiaens, et al. (Eds.), *Proceedings of World Conference on E-Learning in Corporate, Government, Healthcare, and Higher Education 2009* (pp. 446-451). Chesapeake, VA: AACE.

Lockyer, L., & Bennett, S. (2006). Understanding roles within technology supported teaching and learning: Implications for staff, academic units, and institutions. In O'Donoghue, J. (Ed.), *Technology supported learning and teaching - A staff perspective* (pp. 210–223). London, UK: Idea Group. doi:10.4018/978-1-59140-962-5.ch014

Mazzolini, M., & Maddison, S. (2006). The role of the online instructor as a guide on the side. In O'Donoghue, J. (Ed.), *Technology supported learning and teaching- A staff perspective* (pp. 224–241). London, UK: Idea Group. doi:10.4018/978-1-59140-962-5.ch015

Miller, C., Hokanson, B., & Hooper, S. (2009). Role-based design: Rethinking innovation and creativity in instructional design. In T. Bastiaens et al. (Eds.), *Proceedings of World Conference on E-Learning in Corporate, Government, Healthcare, and Higher Education 2009* (pp. 1804-1811). Chesapeake, VA: AACE.

Salmon, G. (2004). *E-moderating: The key to teaching and learning online* (2nd ed.). London, UK: Routledge Falmer.

Salmon, G. (2005). Flying not flapping: A strategic framework for e-learning and pedagogical innovation in higher education institutions. *Alt-J. Research in Learning Technologies*, 13(3), 201–218. doi:10.1080/09687760500376439

Shaw, K. (2001). Designing online learning opportunities, orchestrating experiences and managing learning. In Stephenson, J. (Ed.), *Teaching and learning online: Pedagogies for new technologies* (pp. 53–66). Sterling, VA: Stylus.

Shea, P. (2011). Learning presence in the community of inquiry model: Towards a theory of online learner self- and co-regulation. In T. Bastiaens & M. Ebner (Eds.), *Proceedings of World Conference on Educational Multimedia, Hypermedia and Telecommunications 2011* (pp. 2556-2565). Chesapeake, VA: AACE.

Shea, P., & Bidjerano, T. (2011). Understanding distinctions in learning in hybrid, and online environments: An empirical investigation of the Community of Inquiry Framework. *Journal of Interactive Learning Environments*, 1-16. DOI: 10.1080/10494820.2011.584320

Shea, P., Hayes, S., Uzner, S., Vickers, J., Wilde, J., Gozza-Cohen, M., & Jian, S. (accepted for publication). Learning presence: A new conceptual element within the Community of Inquiry (CoI) framework. *The Internet and Higher Education*.

Shea, P., Li, C. S., & Pickett, A. (2006). A study of "teaching presence" and student sense of learning community in fully online and web-enhanced college courses. *The Internet and Higher Education*, 9(3), 175–191. doi:10.1016/j.iheduc.2006.06.005

Singh, G., O'Donoghue, J., & Worton, H. (2005). A study into the effects of elearning on higher education. *Journal of University Teaching and Learning Practice*, 2(2), 13–24.

Stromso, H. I., Grottumt, P., & Lycke, K. H. (2007). Content and processes in problem based learning: A comparison of a computer mediated and face to face communication. *Journal of Computer Assisted Learning, 23*(3), 271–282. doi:10.1111/j.1365-2729.2007.00221.x

Swan, K., Shea, P., Fredericksen, E., Pickett, A., Pelz, W., & Maher, G. (2000). Building knowledge building communities: Consistency, contact and communication in the virtual classroom. *Journal of Educational Computing Research, 23*(4), 359–383.

Volman, M. (2005). A variety of roles for a new type of teacher educational technology and the teaching profession. *Teaching and Teacher Education, 21*(1), 15–31. doi:10.1016/j.tate.2004.11.003

Wise, A., Saghafian, M., & Padmanabhan, P. (2009). Comparing the functions of different assigned student roles in online conversations. In T. Bastiaens, et al., (Eds.), *Proceedings of World Conference on E-Learning in Corporate, Government, Healthcare, and Higher Education 2009* (pp. 2034-2042). Chesapeake, VA: AACE.

Wuensch, K., Aziz, S., Ozan, E., Kishore, M., & Tabrizi, M. H. (2008). Pedagogical characteristics of online and face-to-face classes. *International Journal on E-Learning, 3*(7), 523–532.

KEY TERMS AND DEFINITIONS

Blended Courses: The term "blended courses" or "hybrid courses" is used to define a teaching program where some courses are taught in a face-to-face setting, in the presence of the students, while other courses are taught online, at distance. Sometimes, in a single course, some activities are done in a face-to-face context and other activities are undertaken online. This approach is also called "blended" or "hybrid courses". The academic institution providing blended courses is often referred to as a "bimodal" institution.

Changes in Roles: The concept of changes in roles relates to students and professors activities, adaptation and different ways of interacting in the new academic context of online and blended courses. These roles differ in how to interact and collaborate in a conventional face-to-face context, but prove to be very important for cohesion and success in group activities.

Collaboration: In a university learning context, when students and professors work together on a specific subject, all of them share a common goal. To attain this shared-knowledge common goal, they have to collaborate or build together. The work of building together in an organized way, or collaboration, to attain the common goal.

Conventional University Setting: This designates face-to-face, classroom courses, with little use or no use of Internet technologies to teach, learn and interact.

Group Cohesion: In a community of learning where many learning activities are shared by members (for instance, professors and students), the concept of group cohesion points to how every member considers his/her activities in relation to collaboration with other members. This sense of community and team work generates a shared understanding amongst all who participate in the group activities. This coordinated teamwork and smooth cooperation between all the participants creates group cohesion.

Higher Education: Post-secondary level teaching and learning that occurs mainly in universities, colleges and institutes. The term also refers to the community of professors and students, the higher academic institution itself, as well as to the courses and education provided in these high-level learning and teaching institutions.

ICT Integration: Integration, as opposed to simply using ICT, refers to how to work, teach, or learn with information and communication technologies (ICT). In fact, while ICT is used, integrating them supposes an underlying consideration of theoretical and epistemological orientations to create and acquire knowledge.

New University Culture: The new university environment, that integrates more and more Internet and flexible technologies for teaching and learning, makes it easier for students and professors to work collaboratively as a real community. The term "new University culture" therefore refers to this new academic context, in which teaching theories and methods based on collaboration can be easily aligned with a technology-based environment, in which students take an active part.

Online Courses: Also referred to as e-learning. Online courses by definition are courses that are exclusively taught online and where students are involved in a distance learning experience. This distance education experience can be either synchronous or asynchronous.

Pedagogical Requirements: This term alludes to appropriate theoretical approaches in line with a specific teaching and learning environment. In this case, online and ICT-based setting for teaching and learning in higher education is the context

in question, where there is a need for appropriate theoretical approaches ranging from the use of technologies to the interaction between students and professors.

ENDNOTE

[1] There were fifteen Canadian universities that participated in the research. From Ontario were Carleton University (Ottawa), Lakehead University (Thunder Bay), University of Guelf (Guelf), University of Ontario Institute of Technology (Oshawa), University of Ottawa (Ottawa), Queens University (Kingston), Ryerson University (Toronto), University of Waterloo (Waterloo), University of Windsor (Windsor). From Quebec were Concordia University (Montreal), Laval University (Quebec), McGill University (Montreal), University of Montreal (Montreal), University of Quebec At Montreal (Montreal), University of Quebec in Outaouais (Gatineau).

Section 4
Emerging Research and Practice Issues

Chapter 21
Expanding the CoI:
Finding the Hidden Wholeness in Online Learning and Online Working

Sebastián Romualdo Díaz
West Virginia University, USA

ABSTRACT

This chapter explores how the foundational principles of the Community of Inquiry survey can be used to assess and evaluate parallel processes for Knowledge Workers, given that online teaching and learning is quite similar to "online working." The phenomenon analogous to teaching presence in online learning is a knowledge worker's ability to create and disseminate knowledge. Communities of Practice provide a measurable phenomenon analogous to social presence. Finally, data-driven decision-making's use for evaluation, coupled with innovation, serves as a phenomenon parallel to cognitive presence. Together, these three measures, developed in parallel with teaching, social and cognitive presence, provide an effective framework for evaluating online work, which is quite similar to online learning.

INTRODUCTION

The late writer and Trappist monk Thomas Merton sought solitude at Gethsemane, and in separating himself from the other monks, he discovered a remarkable paradox. Ironically, the reflection in solitude at his hermitage ultimately prepared him for the discovery of what he referred to as "a hidden wholeness." Outside the confines of his abbey and hermitage one day, during a daytrip to nearby Louisville, Kentucky, Merton made the connection:

...the conception of "separation from the world" that we have in the monastery too easily presents itself as a complete illusion...We are in the same world as everybody else, the world of the bomb, the world of race hatred, the world of technology, the world of mass media, big business, revolution, and all the rest (Merton, 1966, pp. 140-141).

Imagine if you would that Merton were instead an academician, and that the single word *monastery* in his passage above was changed to *university*. Have we not all in the Academy heard

DOI: 10.4018/978-1-4666-2110-7.ch021

the criticisms from outside the ivory tower about our inability to connect with issues of real-world policy, social justice, technology innovation, dissemination of ideas, and commerce? Have we not all at one time considered our uniqueness as academicians? How might our views as teachers, researchers, students, and programmatic leaders be changed if we were to seek our own hidden wholeness with the outside world?

This idea is not only Merton's. Other writers have alluded to the same universal truth. Norman Maclean, author of *A River Runs Through It* (himself an academic) found his own version of hidden wholeness in the beautiful trout streams of his native Montana. "Eventually, all things merge into one, and a river runs through it" (Maclean, 1976)." This principle of hidden wholeness is certainly not limited to theology and fly fishing. The educator Parker Palmer explored the implications for hidden wholeness on the field of education. In his book titled, *The Hidden Wholeness,* he explores the use of Circles of Trust to help educators find the hidden wholeness in their work (2004).

This seemingly mystical introduction to a chapter on the Community of Inquiry (CoI) may seem misplaced. Yet this chapter focuses on this very hidden wholeness. The major premise of this chapter is that the world of online teaching and learning is not that much different from what the knowledge worker experiences during a typical day at the office. The chapter responds, in part, to a challenge my colleagues and I posed in an earlier manuscript exploring the CoI. Continued investigation and application of the CoI framework, we argued, is clearly needed given the importance of evaluating factors that promote growth in online communities, regardless of whether they involve conventional online universities or online communities of practice that continue to define the typical workday in the Knowledge Society (Díaz, Swan, Ice, & Kupczynski, 2010). In other words, there exists a common experience, a hidden wholeness in the teaching and learning processes assessed by the CoI survey (Arbaugh, Cleveland-Innes,

Diaz, Garrison, Ice, Richardson, Shea & Swan, 2008) and the processes typically experienced by a contemporary knowledge worker.

We should no longer think of teaching and learning and work as disparate elements. Teaching/learning is work, and vice versa. As Friedman warns, the first, and most important ability a person can develop in a flat world is to "learn how to learn (Friedman, 2007, p. 309). The importance of the production and dissemination of knowledge continues to increase as our knowledge economies emerge. Clark Kerr posited that "knowledge has certainly never in history been so central to the conduct of an entire society…and the university is at the center of the knowledge process" (2001, p. 66).

A variety of factors seek to camouflage this hidden wholeness. First and foremost, the scrutiny that is being applied on online education, especially in the for-profit sector, seeks to frantically distinguish online learning from conventional face-to-face instruction, often for the sake of self-preservation and resistance to change. Research and evaluation focused on refining this distinction all too often misses the mark. This approach distracts educators from focusing on more foundational principles of curriculum and pedagogy that transcend modes of delivery. Regrettably systematic efforts of scrutiny such as the committee hearings initiated by Iowa Senator Tom Harkin have much more to do with emerging economic competition than they do addressing foundational pedagogical principles of accountability. Further compounding these efforts at divisiveness are academicians' tendencies to overemphasize their unique specializations. There is a fine balance between developing one's own focused expertise while maintaining relevance and connection to the outside world.

Spiritually speaking, we in the Academy are at times a disjointed enterprise as we attempt to negotiate our role in the new knowledge society. As we deal with unprecedented changes that are bound to change irrevocably the nature of our work, we often act (quite justifiably) as lost souls. In particular for those of us who work in conventional colleges and universities, innovations in online learning, computation, information architecture and informal learning threaten the existence of our institutions, and maybe just as importantly the lifestyle of the traditional university professor. One major premise of this chapter is that the academy's long term viability is better served by proactively embracing these changes as opposed to resisting them. One way to embrace these changes is to explore how Knowledge Management principles as applied to the CoI framework help illustrate the commonalities between online learning and teaching and online working.

This chapter begins with a very basic and cursory review of the CoI framework. The chapter then explores the basic tenets of knowledge management (KM) with particular emphasis on how KM is revolutionizing the manner in which we evaluate students, faculty and academic programs. The chapter explores how we can expand the CoI framework to the world of work, particularly in the case of the knowledge worker. This section of the chapter demonstrates how the subscales of teaching, social and cognitive presence provide a valuable framework for defining processes inherent in knowledge work. Parallels between online learning and knowledge work are thus explored within the context of knowledge management.

BACKGROUND: FOUNDATIONAL REVIEW OF THE COI AND KNOWLEDGE MANAGEMENT

CoI Framework

At the risk of oversimplification, work on the CoI framework stemmed from a perceived overreliance on evaluating solely the inputs and outputs of teaching and learning, while ignoring other rich processes sandwiched between the two. In developing the CoI framework survey, a team of investigators generated Likert scale items for teaching, social and cognitive presence, and then revised these items over approximately 14 iterations of review. The CoI survey was born, and as one of the co-authors of the instrument, I can assure you that few if any of us ever anticipated the survey would be administered to the extent it has.

The CoI survey is being used in educational institutions throughout the world. It is used primarily for two purposes. At a pragmatic level, the CoI survey is used to evaluate the efficacy of online learning. When the instrument is used as part of a broader information architecture, it allows one to evaluate students, teachers and academic programs. At an epistemological level, the instrument is used to explore the relationship of teaching, social and cognitive presence to other variables.

Because the instrument is used primarily in online teaching and learning, the Learning Management System (LMS) architectures inherent in such settings naturally allow for the CoI survey results to be codified electronically, and thus be merged with other data in the LMS or Student Information System (SIS). Had the CoI survey been developed primarily for conventional face-to-face instruction, there is a likelihood it would have often been administered in paper fashion to students, and therefore much of this disparate data would have been eventually lost in the locked filing cabinets of researchers and evaluators. Yet because the CoI framework has been applied primarily to online learning environments, its electronic administration, storage and manipulation has allowed investigators and educators to benefit from robust sample sizes and rich cross examination of variables. As an example, Boston and his colleagues explored the relationship of CoI measures and student retention. Their study's sample size of almost (n=29,000) indicated that one particular social presence item accounted for the majority of variance in a logistic regression of CoI items towards retention (Boston, Díaz, Gibson, Ice, Richardson & Swan, 2009).

In this way, the advent of online learning is fundamentally changing our expectations for sample sizes in educational research. Actually, it is not online learning, per se, responsible for this change. Rather, it is the information systems needed for online and blended learning that are making it possible to administer surveys like the CoI at unprecedented levels of sample size. Electronic mechanisms for facilitating teaching and learning invariably will fundamentally change how we conduct educational research. These information systems that draw from the principles of Knowledge Management are revolutionizing how we evaluate our students, our faculty, and our academic programs. For this reason, it is important to review briefly the implications of Knowledge Management on postsecondary education.

Knowledge Management

In her exploration of how Chaos Theory relates to organizations, Margaret Wheatley touched upon a characterization that is germane to the university. "One of an organization's most critical competencies," she states, "is to create conditions that both generate new knowledge and help it to be freely shared" (Wheatley, 2006, p. 110). This particular characterization reveals how our work in the Academy, which is primarily to produce and disseminate knowledge, is no longer a domain we solely own. The bad news is that for those of us in academia, our roles are being usurped by competitive forces. The good news is that whereas the ivory tower has historically been viewed as distinct from the world of real work, in the new knowledge society those of us in the university provide a model that help define the day to day experiences of the knowledge worker. This good news, however, assumes that we in the Academy embrace the technological and computational changes inherent in online learning. While we worry in the present about the impact of online learning on our viability, all of us should keep an equally watchful eye on how informal learning and the wealth of open educational resources will change our institutions even further. The very tech-

nologies that have revolutionized distance learning are revolutionizing how we manage knowledge, regardless of whether we are a professor at a conventional or for-profit online university, or the manager of a Wal-Mart or video rental store.

Knowledge Management (KM) is defined as the leveraging of collective wisdom to increase responsiveness and innovation (Frappaolo, 2006, p. 8). It is the deliberate and systematic coordination of an organization's people, technology, processes, and organizational structure for the purpose of adding value through reuse and innovation (Dalkir, 2011, p. 4). Although KM is considered to be synonymous with phenomenon like Intellectual Capital or Data-Driven Decision Making, it is actually a broader construct. Gupta and colleagues describe KM involving a variety of activities such as 1) generating new knowledge; 2) acquiring valuable knowledge from outside sources; 3) using this knowledge in decision-making; 4) embedding knowledge in processes, products, and/or services; 5) coding information into documents, databases and software; 6) facilitating knowledge growth; 7) transferring knowledge to other parts of the organization, and; 8) measuring the value of knowledge assets and/or the impact of KM (Gupta, Sharma, & Hsu, 2004, p. 3). The organization that knows how to convert information into knowledge, knows what it knows, and can act with greater intelligence and discernment are the organizations that will make it into the future (Wheatley, 2005, p. 145).

Disparate perspectives of knowledge, impact how one conceptualizes Knowledge Management. Jakubik (2007, p. 11) compares and contrasts four approaches to knowledge. The epistemological perspective views knowledge as a scientific construct, whereas the community perspective views it as a social construct. These disparate views may impact, for example, whether phenomena like teaching, social and cognitive presence are measured quantitatively via a self-report survey, or qualitatively using semantic analysis of student's postings within a Learning Management System.

The ontological perspective views how the reality of knowledge is constructed, while the commodity view examines knowledge as an asset. It is this latter perspective, more traditionally reserved for econometricians and others interested in Return on Investment (ROI), that we need to embrace more so as outside stakeholders increase the scrutiny upon the academy.

Drucker, by contrast, identifies three major types of knowledge: 1) continuing improvement of process, product, service; 2) continuous exploitation of existing knowledge to develop new and different products, processes, and services, and; 3) genuine innovation (1993, p. 185). The first type, which focuses on continuous improvement of existing processes, products and services, is in most cases already regular part of business intelligence within colleges and universities. The second type that focuses on exploiting existing knowledge to develop new products, processes and service is not as common. And innovation, the last of the three types of knowledge as categorized by Drucker, is something that many in the University lack the capacity to pursue.

A theoretical explanation of knowledge management can be well balanced by painting a picture of how it actually manifests in organizations. Many of us are already familiar with KM when we consider the manner in which Amazon.com or Netflix.com interacts with its customers. An equally illustrative example is the experience we have at a McDonald's restaurant.

When you purchase a Big Mac, fries and soft drink at McDonald's, the motions of the teenage employee behind the counter may seem banal. However, there is an intelligent structural capital design at work that contributes to a sophisticated system of KM. As the worker takes your order, data is electronically stored in a central database. The information included in this database includes the employee's identity, a date stamp, a time stamp, the items ordered, and the total price of your order. If you notice carefully, just before placing the last item on your tray, the worker hits a keypad,

usually placed at eye-level directly behind the counter, letting the database know the exact time at which your order was completed.

From this database, data mining experts can readily determine: 1) the average time it takes for an order to be filled; 2) the spending habits of customers given a particular time of day, day of the week, or month of the year, and 3) the frequency with which particular items tend to be sold together. Since this information system is standard throughout all McDonald's restaurants, it allows for comparisons in efficacy and efficiency among individual employees, teams or shifts, restaurants, and geographical regions. The system also allows for thorough sales analyses to determine which particular burger sells best in contexts such as geographic regions, time of day, or time of year. From an even more pragmatic perspective, the system can automatically alert managers and distributers when more French fries or paper cups are needed for a particular restaurant. Rather than having the manager manually order these supplies, the system can place the orders in automated fashion, saving the restaurant significant personnel costs while increasing accuracy of record keeping. Simple descriptive comparisons of supplies utilization among different restaurants may even be used to detect potential incidents of employee theft or fraud.

In addition to the database, the McDonald's corporation has invested heavily in its structural capital by incorporating a standardized training program that quickly gets new employees "on board," helping ensure their contribution to the organization's success. This interplay between the KM system and the professional development training program provides valuable insights for those of us in postsecondary education. This McDonald's example may seem far-fetched as it relates to online learning or work in the knowledge economy. After all, from a human resources perspective, postsecondary students and educators, along with workers in the knowledge economy are often considered the elite, while McDonald's workers have skill sets that can seemingly be more easily replaced. Imagine, however, that universities armed themselves with the level of structural capital typically found in a McDonald's restaurant…Well, this actually happened quite accidentally with the introduction of learning management systems traditionally reserved for online learning.

Learning management systems (LMS) were not originally developed for the primary purpose of evaluation. Instead these systems were developed to help facilitate the electronic transactions necessary for synchronous and asynchronous instruction in online and blended environments. In a rather unintended and accidental fashion these LMSs created repositories of rich quantitative and qualitative data related to students' and instructors' behaviors as they negotiated the teaching and learning process.

Compare and contrast the highly sophisticated KM system utilized by the McDonald's chain with the information system utilized by a mom-and-pop hamburger stand. LMSs unknowingly created for online education an information system synonymous with the more sophisticated KM systems of McDonald's. By contrast, those of us who teach conventional courses in conventional universities continue to utilize information systems synonymous with a failing mom-and-pop hamburger stand. While our online colleagues amass remarkably informative and well codified records of the teaching and learning process, many of us who teach courses conventionally collect assessment data that is about as sophisticated as maintaining financial bookkeeping records on the back of an envelope.

There exists a very real possibility that over time, online learning will be perceived as being more credible than conventional face-to-face instruction because the former provides better data with which to gauge efficacy and efficiency (Diaz, 2011, p. 80). As a faculty member at a land grant university, it is very difficult for me to obtain data that allows me to compare and con-trast my workload with that of my colleagues. It is of particular concern to me that I serve on too many dissertation committees. I have often been curious to ascertain what the relative dissertation committee loads are for my colleagues. The only way for me to obtain this information is to manu-ally review the individual, paper-based workload reports generated by individual faculty as part of our annual review process. This simple need for information to inform my own productivity in a comparative fashion becomes almost impossible because of our lack of a federated repository of electronic data related to our teaching, research and service activities. And this is but one of many information needs.

Compare that scenario to the information system I experienced when working with medi-cal librarians at another public university. When this particular public medical college was cre-ated, stakeholders chose to invest heavily in the electronic infrastructure of the library. As opposed to investing heavily in bricks and mortar, the library invested heavily in allowing patrons to have electronic access to the maximum number of resources possible. One of the librarians from this medical college shared with me data that had been automatically generated through their existing information system. A report showed the frequency and relative depth with which faculty utilized online library resources, and comparisons were drawn by departmental focus as well as by campus. Faculty development experts were thus able to assess the efficacy of their training programs not through self-report instruments, but instead by comparing and contrasting how workshop participants utilized library resources as compared to those who did not attend training. The library's information system automatically generated a central data warehouse easily acces-sible by researchers and evaluators who wanted to conduct evaluations of library programs. Aside from addressing evaluation needs, the technical infrastructure of the library facilitates easy access to materials for students, faculty members, and staff, thus helping to engender evidence-based practices.

The purpose of this manuscript is neither to denigrate traditional universities nor to proclaim the superiority of online education. It is important, however, to recognize the inherent advantage that online education has with respect to its capacity for sound assessment and evaluation of efficacy and efficiency. Learning management systems, albeit imperfect, provide educators with an intimate experience with KM systems. Those of us who have experienced teaching online understand the implications for transparency and accountability that result from the automated storage of data into the LMS repository. For that reason, we need to consider the utility of the CoI framework survey in the context of these emerging electronic repositories.

MAIN FOCUS OF THE CHAPTER

A Model for the Hidden Wholeness of Online Learning and Knowledge Work

The CoI framework focuses on the process of teaching and learning in online and blended educational environments. The framework assumes effective learning in online blended environments requires a community of learners that support meaningful inquiry and deeper levels of learning. Teaching presence refers primarily to three components or areas of responsibility for the instructor. These are design, facilitation and direct instruction (Arbaugh, et al., 2008). Social presence refers to the ability of participants in a CoI to project themselves socially and emotionally, as real people with authentic identities despite any limitations inherent in online or blended learning. Social presence, therefore, challenges the notion that students can feel connected only in face-to-face learning environments. Fortunately, the Facebook phenomenon has entirely eradicated that

particular argument. Cognitive presence refers to learners' ability to construct and confirm meaning through reflection and discourse in a community of inquiry.

The CoI framework survey presents respondents with 34 Likert-scale items that address teaching presence, social presence and cognitive presence. Based on the perceptions of respondents of their online or blended learning experience, the CoI survey allows investigators and educators to assess quantitatively the extent to which these phenomena were present. Despite its success as evidenced by its use in universities throughout the world, the CoI survey does have inherent limitations. As with any self-report instrument, the CoI's quantitative score depends heavily on the biases of the respondent. Another limitation and potential strength of the survey is that it detects these presences differently depending on the cultural context in which it is administered. In other words, students in societies that view the role of teachers much more traditionally will respond differently to the teaching presence items than students raised in a more progressive educational environment. Regardless, the CoI framework survey provides educators and researchers with a concise instrument that serves as a useful measure to inform teaching and learning efficacy.

As alluded to earlier in this document, the apparent utility this instrument caused several of its original authors to consider its applicability to inform efficacy of work processes that mirror those in the online and blended learning environments. Much of the work conducted by knowledge workers mirrors the asynchronous communication and sharing of information that occurs in online and blended learning environments. For example, as one of the individuals who originally created the CoI framework survey, I have yet to meet in person one of my co-authors. Our collective work in developing the CoI framework survey occurred in much the same fashion as a group assignment within an online class. The instrument's co-authors participated in a variety of discussions, both synchronously and asynchronously. Synchronous discussions often occurred over distance using conference call technology. We shared our work via online technologies, using email or online connect rooms similar to those used in learning management systems.

This peculiar similarity between online course participation and the work involved in developing an educational research survey tool caused us to consider the potential applicability of the CoI survey in work environments typical of knowledge economies. Consider the very writing of this book chapter and how it mirrors the online teaching and learning process. Much as an online instructor would solicit assignments from her students, the book's editors (neither of whom I've ever met face to face) solicited proposals from me and other academicians. We "posted our assignments" online, and the editors provided feedback using the same technology. My final work product, as well as its subsequent revision, will all be conducted in a fashion very similar to what we demand of our online students. And yet we continue to question the relevance of online learning to the "real-world" experiences of knowledge workers.

Obviously the CoI survey requires some translation before it can be used effectively to assess work environments in emerging knowledge economies. Creating that new survey is well beyond the scope of this chapter. What this chapter does explore, however, is how the principles embedded within the CoI framework can be used to inform the efficacy of work in the knowledge society, work which often simulates the very processes used in online learning.

Figure 1 helps illustrate how the subscales of teaching, social and cognitive presence may serve as the basis for a framework that is more generally applied to knowledge work.

Note that teaching, social and cognitive presences occupy a visual silo. The metaphorical use of a silo is intentional, since it reminds us that data used to measure these phenomena are warehoused within a KM system that allows for more thorough and rich analysis. Gray shaded arrows connect teaching, social and cognitive presence to their corollaries in the knowledge work process. These corollary phenomenon are: 1) knowledge production and dissemination; 2) communities of practice, and; 3) evaluation [D3M-data driven

Figure 1. Parallels between online learning and knowledge work

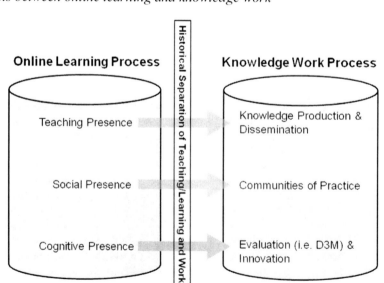

decision making] and innovation. Much as is the case for measures of teaching, social and cognitive presence, the three elements of the knowledge work process are also contained within a metaphorical silo.

What separates these two metaphorical silos is simply a historical tradition. Traditionally we have tended to view postsecondary teaching and learning as being quite distinct from "real-world" work. We are now discovering, however, that many of the processes used in online teaching and learning are transforming, if not defining, how we work in knowledge economies. By finding commonalities between online learning and knowledge work, we may be able to erode this distinction over time. Conceptually, this will allow us to explore more in-depth the similarities among online learning in postsecondary education and work in a knowledge economy.

SOLUTIONS AND RECOMMENDATIONS

Teaching Presence → Knowledge Production and Dissemination

The work-related corollary to teaching presence is knowledge production and dissemination. In the online classroom environment teaching presence focuses on the instructor's ability to design online instruction, her ability to facilitate online instruction and her skill in providing direct instruction to others. At the risk of sounding corny, knowledge workers all assume the roles of both teacher and learner throughout their daily work. A knowledge worker is expected to learn continuously by improving her human capital. That same knowledge worker is expected to contribute to the production of knowledge and also to disseminate it effectively to customers and other stakeholders. One of the main distinctions between measures for teaching presence and measures for knowledge production and dissemination in the workplace is that the

latter assumes that the subject serves both roles. In hindsight, the CoI survey should have emphasized the respondent's role as teacher in addition to focusing on her role as learner. Therefore, the knowledge work corollary to teaching presence examines the process by which a knowledge worker produces knowledge and successfully disseminates it so that it may become actionable.

In order to explore the potential utility of a measure for knowledge production and dissemination (parallel to teaching presence) in the workplace, it is useful to explore briefly how the existing teaching presence components of the CoI survey can be used as part of a larger KM approach to evaluate the efficacy of teaching and learning. In those instances where the CoI survey is administered to every student in the institution each time he or she completes an online or blended course, the data yield rich information for student and teacher as well as categorical designations of program, department, or college. For example aggregate measures of teaching presence items across multiple courses for an individual student may lend insights into that student's orientation towards faculty. These types of aggregate measures may reveal, for example, that a particular student tends to view his professors in a more positive or negative light as compared to the general student population. Aggregation can also occur at the instructor level, yielding insights into all students' perceptions about a particular faculty member. Simple descriptive statistical results of these teaching presence items (e.g. means and standard deviations) yield rich comparative data that can inform curriculum development, faculty development and intervention of students potentially at risk. At this simplistic level, therefore, aggregate results from the CoI survey can serve a variety of continuous quality improvement purposes within the university.

At a more complex level, we can expand the sophistication of data collection related to teaching presence. Narrative and semantic analyses of all interactions occurring within a learning management system may yield insights into the efficacy of the particular instructor's teaching presence. Student behaviors within the LMS can be correlated with their teaching presence ratings, possibly exposing associative relationships between the two. Regardless of the relative complexity or simplicity with which educators address teaching presence in online blended environments, comprehensive KM systems have heightened immensely the utility of this data. Simply having the ability to aggregate survey data across students or courses or faculty members increases the utility of the CoI survey. When survey data is linked to other variables in either an LMS or student information system, its utility for evaluation and planning increases exponentially.

In order to manifest a KM approach to the utilization of the CoI survey, institutions must design processes and systems to help students codify their interpretations of information and data. The same requirement applies for expansion of the CoI principles into assessing knowledge production and dissemination in the workplace. For students, universities will need to build data repositories into which students can store artifacts of their work. These artifacts, representing a range of multimedia formats, best represent the students' acquisition of knowledge, and more importantly their interpretation of that knowledge. For the knowledge worker, employers need to invest in information architectures that allow for the codification and dissemination of knowledge, both within the organization and to customers and stakeholders outside the organization.

The main implications for measurement and assessment is that we need to employ more direct measures of student and worker productivity, and rely less on indirect measures. For example, the CoI survey utilizes indirect measures of self perception to gauge teaching presence within a given course. In the future, while the foundational principle remains the same, measurement of teaching presence will be conducted using complex semantic analyses of narrative data stored within

the LMS. Artifacts of students' work will similarly be combed by complex computational engines that analyze narrative, visual and other metadata embedded within the students' assignments. For the knowledge worker, a similar process will be used to analyze the wealth of electronic data the worker produces and disseminates.

It is important to note that these highly automated approaches to review of narrative data will never fully replace the more complex intuition and analysis of a skilled leader. Regardless, these automated approaches will heighten our awareness for utilizing authentic assessment in both the classroom and the workplace. Furthermore, these approaches will focus primarily on evaluating aggregate trends among curricular programs or workplaces, and secondarily on evaluating students and workers individually.

Several implications for change arise from the utilization of KM systems to inform teacher presence in the classroom and knowledge production and dissemination in the workplace. From a curricular perspective, this approach will refocus teaching and learning on actionability. While continuing to allow students the esoteric pursuit of knowledge, institutions of higher education will need to develop and implement new evaluation systems that focus alternatively on a student's ability to take what she has learned and to consider how it can be applied to their future career as a knowledge worker. As Boyer (1990) noted, "we are faced today with the need to clarify campus missions and relate the work of the academy more directly to the realities of contemporary life" (p. 13).

A second implication arising from this use of KM systems is that increased knowledge sharing will threaten existing organizational hierarchies. Because knowledge is doubling at a remarkable rate, the structures (schools) and strategies historically used to deliver that knowledge in prescriptive and linear ways are now being challenged by knowledge-based institutions that recognize the need for continuous workplace learning (Marshall,

1997, p. 181). Drucker warned that when an organization focuses its data-processing capacity on producing information, it becomes clear that both the number of management levels and the number of managers can be sharply cut since whole layers of management neither make decisions nor lead (2006, p. 128). We should anticipate therefore that tensions will be created as knowledge workers seek to disseminate their knowledge for capitalization within historical hierarchies that are designed primarily to hoard information, data and knowledge. In other words, these knowledge workers will invariably threaten existing power structures in typical organizations. As one example, consider that a faculty member at a traditional University may seek to work more actively with colleagues outside the institution than collaborating with colleagues within. These new contexts for our academic work call to question long-established organizational structures. Couple this trend with economic challenges to higher education, and the process naturally calls to question why we support these antiquated hierarchies.

A third implication arising from the use of KM systems for addressing either teaching presence in the classroom or knowledge production and dissemination in the workplace is that the emphasis on this sharing and dissemination of data demands us to reevaluate the efficacy of our intellectual property policies, both at the institutional level and also at the national level. Moore & Craig, for example, argue that courts' interpretations of existing statutes for infringement of intellectual property rights are sometimes intended to be in support of the public policy for or against monopolies, and in furtherance of the needs of business (2008, p. 46). Although educators view their enterprise as distinct from business and/or monopolies, the tensions that exist between for profit online universities and conventional face to face institutions are often based on these very issues.

Two conflicting movements in education need to somehow be synergized. On the one hand, we need to incentivize the creativity of individuals who develop new ideas, systems, and technologies that enhance teaching and learning at the University and knowledge production and dissemination in the workplace. On the other hand, there is a movement afoot to create open educational resources (OER) that are available for free on the Internet. Lessig (2001), a proponent of creative commons, argues that "when future uses of a technology cannot be predicted – then leaving the technology uncontrolled is a better way of helping it find the right sort of innovation" (p. 39). By contrast, a university's technology transfer program naturally seeks ways to protect the institution's intellectual property. Rather than viewing these two movements as oppositional, we need to find creative ways to allow them to exist in harmony.

Social Presence → Communities of Practice

Social presence in an online learning environment manifests as a sense of belonging despite the lack of face-to-face interaction. Its corollary for knowledge workers is the manifestation of communities of practice (CoP). Communities of practice, also known as online knowledge communities or online social networks, are groups of people in an organization who extend their natural workspace by working in a common area online with the intent of improving their ability to deliver services or products for clients (Neff, 2002, p. 335). Since information knows no national boundaries, it will also form new "transnational" communities of people who, maybe without ever seeing each other in the flesh, are in communion because they are in communication (P. Drucker, 1989, p. 258). The term *community* suggests that these groups are not constrained by typical geographic, business unit, or functional boundaries, but rather by common tasks, contexts, and interests. The word practice implies knowledge and action -- how individuals actually perform their jobs and the day-to-day basis as opposed to more formal policies and procedures that reflect how work should be performed (Dalkir, 2011, p. 145).

With respect to the particular manifestation of communities of practice in the workplace, they are unique in that they occur regardless of whether or not the organization supports their development. Knowledge workers everywhere are struggling with the fact that, to do their work, they frequently need to cross the boundaries of the organization, and to get their work done, they must abandon the formal organizational structure and move into the informal organization (Pinchot, 1998, p. 129). One challenge that communities of practice pose is that these often invisible groups are virtually immune to management in a conventional sense – indeed, managing them can kill them (Stewart, 2001, p. 97).

Much of conventional university curriculum is hampered by our evaluation and assessment techniques, in which we grade a student's performance at the individual level as opposed to the group level. Therefore, to establish CoP in postsecondary education, and also to further increase social presence, we need to work harder to establish learning communities in which groups of individuals come together to solve problems. The problem-based learning (PBL) movement is one example of how curricular design enhances group level work that is more consistent with the realities that knowledge workers will face upon graduation from university. We need to replicate these efforts in online learning so that students are experiencing more often the type of group work they will encounter as knowledge workers.

We also need to consider, however, the possibility that our students will form CoPs that extend beyond the borders of our campus. If a particular student shares a common research interest with another student at a competing university, should

we not find ways to facilitate their collective interaction? Regardless of whether we in the university take this initiative, rest assured that contemporary students will utilize existing social network innovations to initiate these types of interactions on their own. This is a unique manifestation of transparency in postsecondary education. Whereas in the past students often relied on the university to make available to them the technologies needed for this type of collaboration, the ubiquity of educational and social networking technologies provides students the opportunity for initiating outreach beyond institutional membership to develop their own social capital.

Measuring the efficacy of CoP is not an easy task. Social capital is also not easy to measure. The measurement problem is made significantly more difficult when we consider the issue of cultural differences in the expression of social capital (Halpern, 2005, p. 36). Whereas the CoI survey measures in large part a respondent's satisfaction with the social network created through his online learning experience, we need a measure for the knowledge worker that incorporates both satisfaction with the existing social network as well as more objective measures of the efficacy of those networks or communities of practice. One possible strategy for measurement is to conduct semantic analyses of the work created within the respective commons. An alternative yet simpler approach is to develop a simple survey instrument that knowledge workers complete on a regular basis related to their workgroups. The challenge here, however, is that CoP do not always form at the behest of organizational leadership. They tend to form more organically and in a less planned manner. As both online learning and knowledge work shift towards more user-centric approaches, the need for KM systems increases. If students and knowledge workers responded only to the commands of superiors at their respective organizations/institutions, assessment would be relatively easy and would be planned according to the organizational schedule.

In reality, however, learning environments are becoming increasingly student-directed. Similarly in knowledge economies work is becoming increasingly worker-directed. This challenges us to explore alternative and more flexible means of assessment and evaluation that respond "just-in-time" as opposed to "right on schedule."

Regardless, the notion of social presence in online learning is clearly analogous to the sense of belonging felt by a knowledge worker when participating actively in CoP. These CoP do have serious implications for change. As alluded to earlier, one challenge inherent in the proliferation of CoP is that they threaten existing organizational structures into which so much has been invested. For example, within a conventional university a tenure-track professor is expected to participate in service activities that are often framed in the structure of committees, editorial review boards, and task forces. How should a university respond when a professor clearly feels more empowered and more at home in an informally created CoP as compared to the standard committees and task forces within his own institution? More importantly, if over time the research demonstrates that these CoP that transcend the bounds of institutional borders are more efficient and effective than the contrived committees created within the institution, do we dismantle these committees accordingly to more efficiently use scant resources?

The challenges are actually quite similar in both online education and the knowledge-based workplace. In online education instructors are learning that they must let go of the sense of control they may have experienced in traditional face-to-face lecture-based learning environments. Not only must they let go, they must also embrace the increased transparency that results from technologies and information systems that disseminate information and knowledge much more widely throughout the organization. For organizational leaders who supervise today's highly skilled knowledge worker, the challenges are quite similar.

Cognitive Presence → Evaluation and Innovation

In an online learning environment, cognitive presence manifests when a student engages in deep critical thought and reflection, and from these constructs develops his own meaning. Two corollary manifestations of cognitive presence are particularly germane to the knowledge worker. The first of these manifestations is that the knowledge worker engages in the highest level of cognitive reasoning as identified by the late educator Benjamin Bloom (1964), namely evaluation. In particular, what is of most interest to the knowledge worker is the evaluation of: 1) data; 2) information, and; 3) knowledge. In other words, manifestations of data-driven decision-making (D3M) serve as a valuable corollary to cognitive presence.

Innovation is yet another corollary to cognitive presence, and is germane to work in the knowledge economy. The world wide web that has revolutionized access to information for online students and knowledge workers is a driver of innovation. Along with the modern city, Johnson (2010) identifies the world wide web "as an engine of innovation because, for complicated historical reasons, it is an environment that is powerfully suited for the creation, diffusion, and adoption of good ideas" (p. 17). The KM systems that can better synergize online learning and knowledge work is also an engine for innovation. Knowledge management's primary role is the sharing of knowledge throughout the organization in a way that each individual or group understands the knowledge with sufficient depth and in sufficient context as to apply it effectively in decision making and innovation (Frappaolo, 2006, p. 19). Given the interrelationships among information access on the internet, knowledge management, and innovation, the frequency and depth with which knowledge workers engage in data driven decision-making and innovation serve as valuable measures for cognitive presence in the workplace. Yet, how does evidence of evaluation and innovation manifest in online learning and knowledge work?

In online learning, one possible manifestation of evidence of a student engaging in data driven decision-making is their information literacy. A student's ability to process data information and knowledge is highly indicative of their ability to do the same in a subsequent world of work. An even more complex manifestation of evidence of data driven decision-making involves the artifacts of work a student produces during his or her studies. These forms of evidence may require more complex subjective reviews by faculty members or highly automated yet sophisticated semantic analyses of students' narrative work. Despite the need for this complex analysis, we need to emphasize data-driven decision-making (as a manifestation of evaluation) and innovation in how we grade students' work. We need to do the same for knowledge workers.

Several challenges arise when emphasizing data driven decision-making and innovation for both students and knowledge workers. The first challenge is that innovation itself is often a threat to existing power structures in organizations. Thomas Friedman (2007) refers to this type of threat as the coefficient of flatness. The fewer natural resources one's company or country has, he argues, the more its members will dig inside themselves for innovation in order to survive (p. 157). We may find therefore, that organizations outside the university with scant resources and nonexistent endowments outperform us with respect to teaching and learning innovations.

The good news is we are leaders in innovation. Drucker (1986) claims that no better text for a *History of Entrepreneurship* could be found than the creation and development of the modern university, and especially the modern American university (p. 23). The bad news is that we cannot be complacent with our past successes. Drucker also reminds us, however, that the basic architectural plan on which our schools and universities are built go back at least three hundred years. He further argues that "new, in some cases radically new, thinking and new, in some cases radically new, approaches are required to education, and on all levels" (1986, pp. 264-265). It may be that the needs of today's knowledge worker cannot be adequately addressed by the university as we know it today, and new institutions will emerge to fill the vacuum between traditional higher education and demands of the knowledge-intensive workplace (LaRue, 2002).

FUTURE RESEARCH DIRECTIONS

This chapter provides only a cursory explanation of the CoI framework, the nature of the Knowledge Worker, and Knowledge Management. Future research can continue to explore the deeper complexity of each of these phenomena. With respect to the CoI, we need more in-depth research that explores its utility in a variety of contexts and cultural settings. Qualitative methodologies can be used to explore how end-users of the CoI survey perceive its utility. Furthermore, the academic community needs to learn more about how the use of the CoI survey has impacted curriculum development, faculty development, and student development. In particular, we need more research that informs the impact of widely used instruments like the CoI survey on a higher education institution's processes and structures.

The role of the knowledge worker continues to evolve, and we need continued research that informs postsecondary educators of the realities their students will face upon graduation. There is no simple solution for how best to prepare today's students for the ever-changing demands of the workplace. Yet, what we can realistically achieve is to commit more fully to investigating candidly which aspects of the higher education enterprise actually add value to students, and more importantly, which aspects of our enterprise do not add value. Given the external scrutiny falling like a hard rain on much of academia, it is natural that those inside the academy react defensively by metaphorically circling our wagons. Yet, if we do not take the initiative for streamlining our processes by removing waste, others outside the institution will do so in less thoughtful a fashion. Our research should inform these difficult decisions.

Finally, given that much of the work in Knowledge Management is from the for-profit business perspective, we need more work on how KM can be manifested within the academy. Technical research can explore how best to adopt hardware and software infrastructures for the adoption of KM. Yet the major challenge remains the human factor, and more research, both quantitative and qualitative, is needed in this area. Knowledge management principles continue to revolutionize how we evaluate faculty, students and academic programs, and in so doing increase organizational transparency within academia to unprecedented levels. Knowledge management also contributes to the availability of informal learning resources, which someday may threaten online learning much as online learning now threatens face-to-face.

CONCLUSION

Those of us who work outside the university are equally as guilty as those within for furthering a collective belief that postsecondary education has relatively little to do with the "real world." Online learning may help us to change that belief as we recognize that the use of technologies to facilitate interactions among teachers and learners mirrors quite similarly the daily experiences of the knowledge worker. And much as the Community of Inquiry framework survey helps us to assess the process inherent in online teaching and learning, it also provides a framework for assessing and evaluating parallel processes for the knowledge worker.

Much like Thomas Merton was drawn to solitude and reflection at his hermitage, many of us in the academy are drawn to the solitude and reflection of contemplative intellectual work. In fact, this is one of the greatest joys and privileges of academic life. Yet also like Merton, we may one day find ourselves in a situation where we look around and suddenly realize the connections and wholeness that exist between the world of online learning and the world of the professional knowledge worker. When we do this, we will have become better educators.

REFERENCES

Arbaugh, J. B., Cleveland-Innes, M., Diaz, S. R., Garrison, D. R., Ice, P., & Richardson, J. C. (2008). Developing a community of inquiry instrument: Testing a measure of the Community of Inquiry framework using a multi-institutional sample. *The Internet and Higher Education, 11*, 133–136. doi:10.1016/j.iheduc.2008.06.003

Bloom, B. S. (1964). *Stability and change in human characteristics.* New York, NY: John Wiley & Sons, Inc.

Boston, W., Diaz, S. R., Gibson, A. M., Ice, P., Richardson, J., & Swan, K. (2009). An exploration of the relationship between indicators of the community of inquiry framework and retention in online programs. *Journal of Asynchronous Learning Networks, 13*(3), 67–83.

Boyer, E. (1990). *Scholarship reconsidered: Priorities of the professoriate.* San Francisco, CA: Jossey-Bass.

Dalkir, K. (2011). *Knowledge management in theory and practice* (2nd ed.). Cambridge, MA: The MIT Press.

Diaz, S. R. (2011). Knowledge management as an approach to evaluating advanced graduate programs. In Perez, D. C., Fain, S., & Slater, J. (Eds.), *Higher education and human capital: Re/thinking the doctorate in America*. Rotterdam, The Netherlands: Sense Publishers. doi:10.1007/978-94-6091-418-8_6

Díaz, S. R., Swan, K., Ice, P., & Kupczynski, L. (2010). Student ratings of the importance of survey items, multiplicative factor analysis, and the validity of the community of inquiry survey. *The Internet and Higher Education, 13*, 22–30. doi:10.1016/j.iheduc.2009.11.004

Drucker, P. (1986). *Innovation and entrepreneurship: Practice and principles*. New York, NY: HarperBusiness.

Drucker, P. (1989). *The new realities*. New York, NY: Harper & Row.

Drucker, P. (2006). *The coming of the new organization. Classic Drucker*. Harvard Business School Publishing Corporation.

Drucker, P. F. (1993). *Post-Capitalist society*. New York, NY: Harper Business.

Frappaolo, C. (2006). *Knowledge management*. Chichester, England: Capstone Publishing Ltd.

Friedman, T. L. (2007). *The world is flat: A brief history of the 21st century* (3rd ed.). New York, NY: Picador.

Gupta, J., Sharma, S., & Hsu, J. (2004). An overview of knowledge management. In Gupta, J., & Sharma, S. (Eds.), *Creating knowledge based organizations* (p. 360). Hershey, PA, USA: Idea Group Publishing. doi:10.4018/978-1-59140-162-9.ch001

Halpern, D. (2005). *Social capital*. Malden, MA: Polity Press.

Jakubik, M. (2007). Exploring the knowledge landscape: four emerging views of knowledge. *Journal of Knowledge Management, 11*(4), 6–19. doi:10.1108/13673270710762675

Johnson, S. (2010). *Where good ideas come from: The natural history of innovation*. New York, NY: Riverhead Books.

Kerr, C. (2001). *The uses of the university* (5th ed.). Cambridge, MA: Harvard University Press.

LaRue, B. (2002). In Rudestam, K. E., & Schoenholtz-Read, J. (Eds.), *Synthesizing higher education and corporate learning strategies* (p. 460). Thousand Oaks, CA: Sage Publications.

Lessig, L. (2001). *The future of ideas*. New York, NY: Random House.

Maclean, N. (1976). *A river runs through it and other stories*. Chicago, IL: The University of Chicago Press.

Marshall, S. P. (1997). Creating sustainable learning communities for the twenty-first century. In Hesselbein, F., Goldsmith, M., & Beckhard, R. (Eds.), *The organization of the future*. San Francisco, CA: Jossey-Bass.

Merton, T. (1966). *Conjectures of a guilty bystander*. Garden City, NY: Doubleday.

Moore, L., & Craig, L. (2008). *Intellectual captial in enterprise success*. Hoboken, NJ: Wiley & Sons, Inc.

Neff, M. D. (2002). Online knowledge communities and their role in organizational learning. In Rudestam, K. E., & Schoenholtz-Read, J. (Eds.), *Handbook of online learning: Innovations in higher education and corporate training*. Thousand Oaks, CA: Sage Publications.

Palmer, P. (2004). *A hidden wholeness: The journey toward an undivided life*. San Francisco, CA: Jossey-Bass.

Pinchot, G. (1998). Building community in the workplace. In Hesselbein, F., Goldsmith, M., Beckhard, R., & Schubert, R. F. (Eds.), *The community of the future*. San Francisco, CA: Jossey-Bass.

Stewart, T. (2001). *The wealth of knowledge: Intellectual capital and the 21st century organization*. New York, NY: Currency Books.

Wheatley, M. (2005). *Finding our way: Leadership for an uncertain time*. San Francisco, CA: Berrett-Koehler Publishers, Inc.

Wheatley, M. (2006). *Leadership and the new science: Discovering order in a chaotic world* (3rd ed.). San Francisco, CA: Berrett-Koehler Publishers, Inc.

KEY TERMS AND DEFINITIONS

Cognitive Presence: The extent to which learners are able to construct and confirm meaning through sustained reflection and discourse.

Communities of Practice: Groups of people in an organization who extend their natural workspace by working in a common area online with the intent of improving their ability to deliver services or products for clients.

Community of Inquiry: A learning community where participants collaboratively engage in purposeful critical discourse and reflection to construct personal meaning and shared understanding through negotiation.

Hidden Wholeness: (In online learning and online working) is the integrity that exists between the world of online learning and the world of the professional knowledge worker.

Knowledge Management: The leveraging of collective wisdom to increase responsiveness and innovation. It is the deliberate and systematic coordination of an organization's people, technology, processes, and organizational structure for the purpose of adding value through reuse and innovation.

Social Presence: The ability of participants to identify with the community (e.g., course of study), communicate purposefully in a trusting environment, and develop inter-personal relationships by way of projecting their individual personalities.

Teaching Presence: The design, facilitation, and direction of cognitive and social processes for the purpose of realizing personally meaningful and educationally worthwhile learning outcomes.

Chapter 22
Through the Looking Glass:
Emerging Technologies and the Community of Inquiry Framework

Phil Ice
American Public University System, USA

Melissa Burgess
American Public University System, USA

ABSTRACT

This chapter explores how emerging technologies may challenge the CoI framework to evolve and account for new types of learner and instructor interactions. An exploration of processes inherent within the three presences is contextualized against the architecture of learning management systems, with attention given to those elements that are most likely to be impacted moving forward. As examples, innovations in digital publishing, multi-screen, multi-user virtual environments, on-demand education, adaptive learning environments and analytics are discussed, with a focus on how advancements in these areas may require rethinking and realignment of some aspects of the CoI framework.

INTRODUCTION

"Would you tell me, please, which way I ought to go from here?" asked Alice.
"That depends a good deal on where you want to get to," said the Cat.
- Lewis Carroll, Alice in Wonderland

In many ways Alice's exchange with the Cheshire Cat is reflective of the current state of online learning. Within the last few years technological advancements have been occurring at an unprecedented pace. Until now, education has largely immunized itself from these changes, preferring the comfort of rigid, outdated modes of delivery. However, the proliferation and adoption of these technologies have become so ubiquitous in other segments of society that the education sector has little choice but to modernize. While implementing such changes will cause major disruptions to institutional infrastructure, there will also be

DOI: 10.4018/978-1-4666-2110-7.ch022

significant change to the pedagogical structures which have evolved around infrastructures.

Prior to 1993, communication on the world wide web was largely relegated to bulletin board and file transfer services. In that year, Mosaic, the first graphic web browser was introduced, followed by Netscape and Microsoft IE by the end of 1995. While leveraging html to create a unified environment for viewing text and graphics, designing basic content (let alone entire courses) remained a challenge, especially in the education sector where few expert developers existed. In response, various learning management systems (LMS) began to appear in the mid 1990's. Though platform technology differs from LMS to LMS (architecture and component availability), the primary purpose of these products is to allow authors to rapidly create online course content, develop learning activities, post resources, establish areas for discussion, provide mechanisms for submission of work products, establish a centralized grading mechanism, and facilitate communication between instructors and students.

While ancillary materials may be referenced or ported into the LMS, these highly compartmentalized systems have been the primary vehicle for delivering courses and where related scholarly communities have emerged over the last 15 years. As a result, the vast majority of pedagogical strategies and best practices for online learning have been developed against the LMS framework.

Based upon a constructivist collaborative approach to learning, the Community of Inquiry framework (CoI) has been developed and, with a few exceptions, researched within the context of the LMS. This backdrop calls to question which portions of CoI research may be platform dependent and which portions may be generalized across all contemporary and emerging learning environments. In addition, critical questions need to be asked about how emerging technologies may alter the nature of virtual communities and how these changes should be conceptualized from a research paradigm.

This chapter begins with an overview of how the three CoI presences can be viewed in terms of process architectures related to the structural elements of the LMS. Here it is important to note that the processes described and analogies drawn are not meant to be all inclusive, rather the narrative is intended to depict a high level view of workflows associated with LMS based course construction and their relationship to the process model described by the CoI. Following is a discussion of how emerging trends in digital publishing, multi-screen and applications, virtual environments, on-demand environments, adaptive learning environments, and analytics may impact one or more of the presences.

CONTEXTUALIZING THE EMERGENCE OF THE COI FRAMEWORK AGAINST THE LMS DELIVERY PARADIGM

When deconstructed against the LMS architecture, associations between the three presences and building blocks become readily apparent. While there is certainly some amount of variation between the structure and naming of components across LMS's, it is not the intention of this section to map out how any one LMS provides the ability to develop and deliver courses that are optimally aligned with the CoI. Rather, the goal is to demonstrate that as a set of tools, LMS's have provided a means for easily facilitating Communities of Inquiry.

When viewed as a blank canvas for course creation, the LMS can be conceptualized as a collection of lightweight authoring tools and communication devices against which content and activities are developed. Depending upon the instructional design paradigm being utilized, courses are systematically constructed to move learners from a set of goals through a series of activities and culminating assessment activities. Notably, with the exception of a few emerging platforms, instructional designers must follow a very linear pathway in which there is little potential for deviation. However, the ease of which courses can be designed and developed has almost always outweighed limitations inherent in LMS. In academia this trade-off has been reinforced by the need to insure student privacy by utilizing systems that can reside entirely behind firewalls; another attribute of the LMS. It is against this backdrop that online learning has evolved and provided a test-bed for research related to teaching and learning – including the CoI.

Using the blank canvas metaphor, the LMS provides multiple tools such as announcements, calendars, and alerts that allow for clearly posting due dates, goals, objectives and directions for participation; all aspects of the Instructional Design and Organization component of Teaching Presence. Once these foundational instructional design goals are achieved, provisioning of learning activities is the next activity typically undertaken.

In this phase, some of the previous tool sets may be utilized in a cursory fashion; however, activities are usually developed with very basic html editors or through importing externally developed materials into content areas, lesson packets, or other similar functional areas. These typically include advanced organizers, activity instructions or problem based introductions. When viewed within the context of the CoI framework, these elements can be described as meeting the criteria for establishing a Triggering Event in the Cognitive Presence construct. Typically this will be immediately proceeded by engagement with course based content or instructions that guide the student to seek out and import external content. Regardless of the approach, this structure can be viewed as the Exploration phase of Cognitive Presence.

The next phase of course construction and related LMS utilization is less clear cut than the preceding as there are a variety of ways in which students may be asked to interact with each other and the instructor around the content. However, as some of the more dynamic means of interaction have only recently become available, this narrative will use the traditional discussion forum case; the format around which much of the foundational CoI transcript analysis was based. Though there may be stand-alone, introductory activities, such as biography and get-acquainted posts, discussion forums are typically associated with most course topics. It is here that learners engage in interactions around course problems, progress through the phases of Social Presence, and extend Exploration. Under certain circumstances, aspects of the Integration and Resolution phases of Cognitive Presence may also emerge in discussion forums. Indeed, seminal works in the development of the CoI were based upon Cognitive Presence manifesting in socially-driven academic discussions (Swan & Shih, 2005).

As learners progress through discussion forums, instructors engage in Facilitating Discourse by remediating misconceptions, providing suggestions, establishing pace, providing directionality and generally maintaining dialogue. At the conclusion of discussion threads, instructors provide both group and individualized feedback related to learner performance through the injection of expert advice. Doing so in a timely fashion helps learners clarify their thinking around topics and bring closure to learning units (Garrison & Arbaugh, 2007). Despite the fact that recent work indicates that elements of the CoI are likely tied to other activities such as group projects, external contact venues and cross-course collaboration, it is important to remain cognizant of the fact that discussion forums were the basis for the theory's development and elaboration (Archer, 2010).

As noted earlier, this crosswalk of LMS functionalities to processes within the CoI framework is intentionally cursory in nature. The purpose is not to describe all possible transactions with their corresponding theoretical elements, but to demonstrate how inexorable the linkages are between the dominant means of delivery, over the last decade and a half, and the CoI framework.

This should not be construed as implying that a given technology dictates pedagogy, but rather when a given technology, especially when it is as ubiquitous as the LMS, plays an extended, dominate role, it must shape the way in which theories are conceptualized and practices implemented.

Here it is important to note that in the context of media vs. pedagogy debate, this chapter takes the perspective, espoused by Kozma (1994), that different media possess different types of characteristics that make learning more or less accessible. With respect to the LMS, the ability to facilitate learning has been constrained by the extensibility and robustness of the systems components. These limitations thus definewhat Salamon (1997) terms the cognitively relevant capabilities of a given technology. In more modern works, Schneider (2011) argues that if to think of cognition as only a mental process we overlook the impact of interactions and tools that are used in the acquisition of knowledge. It is in this later vein that this chapter approaches the impact of emerging technologies; that as technologies advance the input changes, which in turn modifies the overall learning experience.

With this backdrop, the next sections of this chapter will discuss some emerging technologies that have the potential to drastically reshape the online learning landscape and significantly alter the corresponding pedagogical foundations. With respect to the CoI, the following will examine to what degree the framework will need to change as the landscape is transformed.

EXPLORING THE POTENTIAL IMPACT OF EMERGING TECHNOLOGIES ON THE COI

Digital Publishing

In the most general of terms, digital publishing can be classified as any means by which content can be rendered and consumed on digital devices.

However, when digital publishing is used in academic settings it is typically used to describe means by which content that would normally reside in a textbook is displayed in a format that is accessible online. Though digital versions of textbooks and ancillary materials have been available in CD ROM format since at least the early 1990s, they have been considered supplemental to publishers primary business channel and limited to select titles. Within the last few years, availability of publisher-produced digital titles have significantly increased as a function of market pressures from the open education resource community, demands by online institutions/programs to provide materials in a format compatible with other resources, and learners consumer orientation that has been driven by Kindle, Sony Reader and other devices. What still remains unclear are issues around formatting, accessibility, and the ability to integrate digital texts created using different workflows. Regardless, while on the surface, providing digital textbooks may not appear to be a catalyst for change that would alter the formation of online learning communities, a deeper analysis of what new asset classes may be included in digital texts, and how they will be consumed, is needed.

At present, publishing roadmaps all point toward the emergence of "textbooks" that include videos, simulations, and interactive components along with static text and visual elements. Notably, the ability to mark-up, add content, and share with others is key to product strategy. Interacting with content using touch gestures on portable tablet devices further distances the new generation of digital texts from the scrollable PDF paradigm (Johnson, Smith, Willis, Levine & Haywood, 2011).

From a pedagogical perspective, these factors portend significant change for online learning. While online courses have included components that can be downloaded and accessed offline since at least the mid 1990's, these resources seldom have included interactive components, let alone the ability to add content or create narratives around those components while disconnected from the online environment. Thus, if we are to suppose that digital publishing will emerge along the lines of current roadmaps, we have to ask what conceptual effect removing large chunks of a course from the traditional LMS-centric model will have on the development of community. Specifically, do students view the learning environment as analogous with community, or can alternate models of embedded communication and spontaneous social network-based discussion form the same sense of community as described in the CoI?

As advancements in digital publishing move forward, CoI research will need to develop means for assessing how learners and faculty interact in environments outside the discussion forum. Specifically, if digital publishing formats allow for students to comment directly around assets, will Affective Expression form in response to narrowly-focused topical interests that learners select? Will Group Cohesion emerge, dissipate, and reemerge? If so, this will precipitate a re-thinking of the community building strategies that are implicit in the LMS-centric environment. Likewise, if learners are able to add to and share content within core materials will they attain an expert status in the eyes of their peers? While certainly this occurs in contemporary discussion forums, through the attachment of or linking to content, the perception may be reinforced when additions become part of foundational course materials. However, this later scenario may be tempered by learners experience with wikis, wherein collaborative construction of knowledge is an expectation rather than an exception. Regardless, these are scenarios, related to digital publishing, that promise to empower students and may impact the role of community development.

From a Teaching Presence perspective, digital publishing may present unique challenges with respect to Facilitation of Discourse. Given that students will have the ability to create discussions around specific content objects, in addition to traditional forums, the instructor will have to be cognizant of when and where these spontaneous threads emerge. For instructors, this may significantly increase the time required to monitor and facilitate discussions. Conversely, there is also the potential for such threads to become points for resolution of extremely granular topics that are then refined in larger discussion forums. Either way, this ability to interact with and modify content at a micro level can be expected to cause disruption to established instructor roles.

Despite components of digital publishing products that have the potential to significantly alter (both positively and negatively) the development of community, the ability to use touch gestures may have the potential to facilitate change and provide support for the CoI. Even despite the control afforded by the mouse, touch pads, digital pens, etc., users have been limited in their interactions with the computer by a secondary layer – the input device. The ability to use touch gestures such as swiping, hand drawing, zooming, panning, and drilling provide for an enhanced sensory experience. In relationship to the CoI, the impact of touch gestures is likely to manifest most strongly in the Cognitive Presence domain. Specifically, the ability to add a kinesthetic layer, that facilitates direct input, may provide a sense of personalization and enhanced engagement, which in turn could strengthen the Triggering Event by catalyzing curiosity around problems posed. Subsequently, the ease of using touch gestures has the potential to accelerate the Exploration process and increase learner contact with a variety of assets.

Here it should be noted that the ability of the individual to possess, modify and spontaneously share content may be viewed as the creation of information and social nodes. In this respect, it may be argued that parallels can be drawn to Connectivist Theory; however, this is not the case as even though content and activities may manifest differently, learners remain bound by a common purpose that is provided in the Triggering Event phase of Cognitive Presence. This also does not presuppose that as communities become more distributed that Social Presence will be diluted, however, there may need to be significant tactical changes to the processes implied by the CoI.

Multi-Screen and Applications

Multi-screen is the term given to the ability to access content across a variety of devices including smart phones, tablets, laptops, desktops and web-enabled televisions. While it is often taken for granted that we can pay a bill on the iPhone, watch a just released movie on an Android tablet, or access on-demand services through TV top boxes, the same openness is not true for educational content. As with the rationale for relying on the LMS, education simply has not had developers who have been able to mass produce learning assets and environments that can be consumed easily across device types. In large part, this has been due to the fact that, unlike the laptop/desktop market, up until approximately 2009 there were numerous operating systems being used across smart phones and tablets.

With the rise of Android, the vast majority of devices operate on either the Google backed platform or the Apple produced iOS, with a small market share taken by RIM, Microsoft and other niche platforms. In practice this has streamlined coding onto two major platforms and with the use of certain software, developers can frequently write code one time that can be compiled for the other platform (with the most common sequence being to write for Android and recompile into Objective C for iOS). Beyond the technical benefits of this consolidation, developers are now able to build once, create iterations to match device appropriate form factors, and deploy across multiple devices (Green, 2011).

For education, the impact of this simplified marketplace will be the rapid escalation of the number of smart phone and tablet deployments in the coming years to replace or supplement traditional computer-based learning assets. It is anticipated that TV-based deployments, in education, will be further along the timeline. However, increased access does not automatically insure that the quality of learning will be dramatically improved. As with the preceding section on digital publishing, multi-screen holds both promise and peril for online learning and the CoI.

While creation of applications is becoming much easier, understanding the appropriate construction of those applications for educational deployment is another matter. As an example, while it is certainly possible to create an application that will render large amounts of text on a smart phone it may not be pedagogically sound – designers have to think about who would want to read more than about 100 words on a smart phone and if they did how aggravated would they be after the excessive scrolling that would be involved. However, providing audio or video would provide a format that could be easily consumed by a learner and be accessed virtually anywhere. Likewise, if learners are expected to comment using a mobile device it would be much easier to use tools such as voice boards as opposed to thumb-typing lengthy thought pieces or replies. Thus, when form factor appropriate content and tools are provided, multi-screen provides the opportunity to enhance the Exploration and Integration phases of Cognitive Presence, as well as strengthen Social Presence through frequent and diverse interaction. Conversely, if inadequate attention is giving to the development of learning assets and applications for multi-screen, then it is likely that these same areas could be significantly damaged.

As multi-screen applications begin to proliferate, researchers and practitioners will need to closely monitor learner and instructor interaction with these assets. Key research questions should revolve around if Cognitive Presence is being influenced in either a positive or negative fashion, as posited here, and if so, what correlations can be made. Additionally, it should be noted that, at least initially, it may be difficult to understand what areas of the CoI might be impacted by this technology. As such, researchers should consider substantive qualitative work that explores learners and instructors perceptions of multi-screen interaction. This would lead to classification within the existing CoI schema or potentially result in the realization that the technology has so altered the process that adjustment needs to be made to the current structure, as is the case with the Multi-User Virtual Environment Education Evaluation Tool (MUVEEET) and on-demand versions of the CoI presented next.

Multi-User Virtual Environments (MUVEs)

In recent years, a new breed of online learning platforms have paved the way for learning in educational, commercial, political, social, and organizational sectors. These platforms have similar components to the LMS, however, they differ greatly in architecture. Multi-User Virtual Environments (MUVEs) are 3D applications whereby users, represented as avatars, have the ability to engage in immersive, synchronous or asynchronous, and highly social experiences. Additionally, the ability to create and customize learning using in – world tools provides a more malleable and flexible environment — much less constrained than an LMS.

Although there are a variety of MUVEs available, some of the most notable include Second Life, OpenSimulator, Active Worlds, EduSim, There, and Quest Atlantis. Tools common to most MUVEs include voice chat, instant text messaging, email, file sharing, whiteboards, and public link sharing. It is important to note that the discourse among avatars — whether synchronous or asynchronous, may also be recorded for assessment and/or research purposes.

Two of the most appealing tools within MUVEs, however, provide the (1) ability to create

objects using a variety of programming/designing tools that are available within the environment and (2) customization of avatar appearance. The object development tools provide the means for users to develop important twenty-first century skills including creativity, problem-solving, collaboration, critical thinking, and effective communication (Partnership for 21st Century Skills, 2009) coupled with a heightened sense of purpose and collaborative community. Burgess and Ice (2011a)) posit that in addition to supporting 21st century skills, MUVEs also elicit optimal experiences including personal relevance, sense of loss of time, positive challenge, and sense of control. Avatar appearance customization tools allow users to present themselves with characteristics either similar to, or completely different from, their real-life physical characteristics. This capability may initially seem trivial, however, several researchers have examined the role appearance plays regarding representation, immersion and presence, and social behaviors (Blascovich, 2002; Lombard & Ditton, 1997). Overall, these two tools within the MUVE platform provide opportunities for personalized learning experiences, which are becoming increasingly important in educational applications. As mentioned earlier in the chapter, the CoI framework has been largely researched within learning management systems, therefore it becomes important to examine the existence and/or relevance the three CoI presences and associated indicators may have in MUVEs. Not surprisingly, research studies have recently emerged involving MUVEs and CoI. In their exploratory study, McKerlich and Anderson (2007) ascertained that the CoI was recognizable in MUVEs, and further established that Social Presence was enhanced, hence challenging the original definition of social presence, "the ability of participants…. to project their personal characteristics into the community, thereby presenting themselves to the other participants as 'real people'" (p. 91). The notion of "real" within MUVEs becomes somewhat blurred.

Additionally, the authors noted enhanced logistical, navigational, and in-world tool use considerations, and included these changes in their Multi-User Virtual Environment Education Evaluation Tool (MUVEEET) observation checklist. Building upon McKerlich and Anderson's study, Burgess, Slate, Rojas-LeBouef, and LaPrairie, (2010) used the MUVEEET instrument to document evidenced CoI components, however, observational data were analyzed differently. A category occurrence range was developed by the observers to rate each category as having a low, medium, or high occurrence within each corresponding presence. Burgess and Ice (2011a or b) developed a pedagogical framework based upon the fusion of the CoI and Bloom's revised taxonomy. The authors suggest that these two frameworks provide both asynchronous and synchronous online learning activities that elicit critical thinking skills.

It is worth noting that as new learning platforms emerge, it is not only important to evaluate the applicability of the CoI presences and components within the platform, it will also be necessary to re-evaluate the definitions of each presence against the platform, as well as adequately measuring learning for each presence according to emerging paradigms. For example, modern instructional practices call for educators to shift from a teacher-centric delivery to a more learner-centric delivery, therefore necessitating the alteration of teaching presence indicators to reflect a teacher's role as being more collaborative and less teacher-directed. Further, emerging learning platforms offer tools that allow for adaptive learning. Adaptive learning platforms provide the content to the learner, and through the use of Artificial Intelligence, learning paths are generated based upon an automated analysis of learning styles, actual knowledge, learning habits, and engagement-- all culled by real-time learning analytic data. This type of platform will require a self-directed learner, thus altering teaching presence components.

On-Demand Learning Platforms

While many current learning platforms involve varying degrees of instructor guidance and support as well as tools to support social presence, one platform for instructional delivery does not include either teaching or social presence as originally intended in the CoI framework. On-demand platforms may include webinars or eLearning courses that have been developed and/or are delivered using course authoring tools such as Adobe Captivate, Adobe Connect, Articulate, and Lectora. While some forms of on-demand may include synchronous instruction with a live instructor and synchronous communication tools, some forms of on-demand are non-facilitated, nor are there tools to communicate with other learners.

The on-demand learning platform is growing in popularity for the deliverance of non-facilitated, anytime, anywhere instruction. Seemingly incompatible to the CoI framework, due to the absence of two important CoI components, researchers would be remiss to reject the notion that the CoI framework cannot support non-facilitated instruction. In the absence of social and teaching presence in an on-demand platform, it is necessary to explore innovative design elements that potentially elicit virtual teaching presence, and virtual social presence. This new concept challenges researchers to look past obvious communication tools (discussion board, chat, social networks) and shift focus toward innovative design. Drawing from existing distance education standards and instructional design models (iNacol, ADDIE), coupled with the integration of CoI constructs, the authors of this chapter present a new set of standards and an evaluation instrument to measure CoI presence within an on-demand learning platform.

Virtual Teaching and Virtual Social Presence

Creating a virtual teaching presence and a virtual social presence within the on-demand platform requires a focus on innovative instructional design principles and the tools to leverage them. In addition to instructional design principles, instruction of this nature will require knowledge of the entire development process along with knowledge and skills in graphic design, narration, multimedia, as well as the course authoring tools and software needed to effectively present these elements. Learning in this environment will undoubtedly appeal to the self-regulated learner, therefore the design is crucial to positive learner outcomes.

Research addressing the notion of simulated, or virtual social and teaching interaction, however is scarce but growing. Studies by Kim and Baylor (2006a, 2006b) contend that pedagogical agents as learning companions (PALs), which are "animated digital characters functioning to simulate human-peer-like interaction" (Kim & Baylor, 2006, p. 223) serve as virtual instructors with four major roles: (1) an expert who provides information, (2) a mentor who advises, (3) a motivator who encourages, and (4) a companion who collaborates. Baylor and Kim (2005) further conducted a study which demonstrated that the interest and self-efficacy of a learner significantly increased when the learner was accompanied by a pedagogical agent that served as a virtual learning companion and that was also sensitive to the learner's affect. The overall area of Artificial Intelligence in on-demand environments will likely become a research focus for educators at all academic levels, as learning increasingly becomes more independent and adaptive. Therefore, expertise in the area of design and development of on-demand courses will also become increasingly important.

The on-demand course development process is guided by four main areas: (1) content, (2) instructional design and organization, (3) assessments, and (4) course management and evaluation. Although this process helps guide the designer of the on-demand course, to fully understand the potential for learning, the designer must design learning through the eyes of an instructor and a learner. When mapped against the CoI framework, this process makes clear the elements and activities that enhance social, teaching, and cognitive presence, as illustrated in Table 1.

The most notable deviations from the original CoI instrument include:

- A heavy reliance upon the design of the on-demand course to create a virtual teaching and social presence
- A shift from a "real" facilitator to a virtual facilitator
- Group cohesion is not possible
- Self-directed/individual learning
- Re-defining teaching and social presence

As with other sections in this chapter, the ODLEET instrument should be viewed as a means of exploring the applicability of the CoI framework as this medium continues to expand and mature. However, as it is based on considerable work that originated in another alternate environment, the MUVEEET, there are likely many suggestions that merit serious inquiry.

Adaptive Learning Environments (ALEs)

Caterpillar: Who... are... you?
Alice: Why, I hardly know, sir. I've changed so much since this morning, you see...
Caterpillar: No, I do not C, explain yourself.
Alice: I'm afraid I can't explain myself, you see, because I'm not myself, you know.
Caterpillar: I do not know.
Alice: I can't put it any more clearly, sir, because it isn't clear to me.
—Lewis Carroll, Alice in Wonderland

If you were to ask the average learner to define their own learning styles/preferences, cognitive levels, and in which ways they learn material best, chances are they may not clearly know. Yet, educators and researchers alike have earnestly

Table 1. On-demand learning environment education evaluation tool (ODLEEET)

ODLEEET
"Virtual" Teaching Presence **The design, virtual facilitation, and virtual direction of cognitive and social processes for the purpose of realizing personally meaningful and educationally worthwhile learning outcomes.**

Design and Organization	22) Are course topics presented? (syllabus, table of contents) 23) Are the objectives clearly stated and measurable? (narration with audio or video or text) 24) Are clear instructions presented on how to participate in course activities? (video tutorial, scavenger hunt activity, a key for the tools/interactions) 25) Are clear deadlines (if any) provided for completion? 26) Do content and embedded activities align with state or accreditation standards? 27) Do the assessments align with state or accreditation standards? 28) Is sufficient rigor, depth, and breadth integrated to teach the objectives? 29) Are digital literacy skills embedded? 30) Is there a table of contents to help guide the learner? 31) Are course requirements listed that are consistent with goals and objectives and represent the scope of the course? 32) Are clear and understandable scoring policies and practices provided? 33) Does the design of the course accommodate various learning styles/experiences? 34) Is the appropriate eLearning used to deliver the instruction (information, procedure, decision)?
Facilitation	35) Are there areas of agreement and disagreement on course topics embedded? ("tips" sections included where relevant) 36) Is the course presented in a logical, sequential, easy-to- navigate fashion to facilitate the understanding of course topics? 37) Is the training/course engaging for the learner (interactivity components such as knowledge checks, games, branching scenarios)? 38) Are there components that keep the learner on task (table of contents, navigation arrows, progress bar, motivational phrases through audio/video) 39) Are supplemental resources and materials provided to extend learning and/or encourage further exploration? (outside resources, "Did You Know?" activity) 40) Does the design of the course develop a virtual sense of community? (animations, audio/video, interactions with the narrator, feedback, posting answers/responses from students who previously took the course (Twitter back feed widget)
Direct Instruction	41) The design of the course helps the student focus on relevant issues that aid learning. (table of contents, providing current and relevant information) 42) There are several opportunities where immediate feedback is embedded to help the student understand strengths and weaknesses (audio or text, pop-up boxes, referring student back to the page/slide where the information was initially presented).
Emotional Presence **The outward expression of emotion by individuals, and among individuals, in a community of inquiry, as they relate to and interact with course content, peers and the instructor (Cleveland-Innes, 2007)**	
Triggering Event	22) Are aesthetic principles integrated to trigger or enhance emotion (i.e., visuals, graphics, text, colors)? 23) Are multimedia elements integrated to trigger or enhance emotion? (graphics, audio, video) 24) Are instructional strategies used to trigger students' emotion? (Perception, Motivation, Attention, Memory--telling stories, risky behavior, role play, creating cognitive dissonance, behavior modeling, appealing to the intellect, being subtle)
Interactive	25) Is interactivity integrated into the course intended to elicit emotion? 26) Are course activities integrated into the course intended to elicit action, application of knowledge, or a response based upon emotions?

continued on following page

Table 1. Continued

ODLEEET
"Virtual" Social Presence **"the ability of participants in a community of inquiry to project themselves socially and emotionally, as 'real' people (i.e. their full personality), through the medium of communication being used"**

Affective Expression	27) Are multimedia elements embedded to provide a virtual sense of belonging? (multimedia, animation, narration) 28) Are diverse perspectives on course topics presented? 29) Are there areas in the course that provide a virtual sense of social interaction? Multimedia, animation, narration, Twitter backfeed widget, also look into the webcam widget)
Open Communication	30) Are there opportunities throughout the course (where relevant) for students to provide thoughts and opinions? (i.e., dropdown menu of opinion choices with accompanying audio or text feedback or comments) 31) Are virtual characters, narrators included to support or initiate interactivity with the student?
Group Cohesion	32) Does feedback and/or comments encourage the student to express his/her opinions—even if they are in disagreement with the course information? (i.e. drop-down, multiple choice, short answer, essay maybe somehow use text analytics so qualitative responses could be accepted). 33) Does audio or text feedback allow the student to feel his/her point of view was acknowledged? (via audio or text feedback). 34) Are there embedded interactions that allow the student to feel a "virtual" sense of collaboration?

Cognitive Presence
Cognitive Presence Extent to which participants critically reflect, (re)construct meaning, and engage in discourse for the purpose of sharing meaning and confirming understanding. Note: When designing course goals, objectives, activities, and assessments, it is very helpful to use Bloom's Digital Taxonomy for this particular platform

Triggering Event	35) Are there problems posed to pique students' interest? (i.e. myth or fact? Did you know? Anticipation guide where students answer questions at the beginning of the course and find out at the end of the course if they responded incorrectly or correctly). 36) Are there activities embedded to pique students' interest? (games, branching scenarios, knowledge checks, webquests, hotspot) 37) Are there embedded motivators that encourage students to explore content-related questions? (scavenger hunt, webquest, incentives).
Exploration	38) Are there a variety of supplemental resources that allow the student to explore problems in the course? (links, documents, videos, audio clips – this is where we can utilize semantic mapping learning objects) 39) Are motivators/ prompts provided that lead a student to explore further information on a course topic that will aid in resolving questions? (providing clues, hints, fact or myth, did you know?) 40) Does the course represent an appreciation of diverse perspectives?
Integration	41) Combining new information helped me answer questions raised in course activities. 42) Do the course activities help the student construct explanations/solutions? 43) Are students encouraged to reflect on course content toward understanding fundamental concepts in the course?
Resolution	44) Are students provided opportunities where they can test or apply their knowledge? (knowledge checks, quizzes, tests) 45) Are students provided opportunities to develop solutions to course topics that can be applied in practice? 46) Are students provided opportunities to apply knowledge in this course to their job or non-class related activities. (i.e. assessment where the student chooses from a drop-down menu and they choose an activity where they can apply their knowledge. The activity chosen is linked to an assessment that reflects knowledge need to complete the activity)

tried to parlay cognitive processes (Witkin and Goodenough, 1981; Zimmerman, 1989) and learning styles, (Kolb, 1984; Gardner, Kornhaber, and Wake, 1997) based upon interactions between metacognitive knowledge, goals, metacognitive experience, and actions (Flavell, 1992, 1987, 1979; Masur, McIntyre, and Flavell, 1973). Glaser (1984, 1976, 1972) also contributed his perspectives regarding the management of cognitive learning processes (i.e., cognitive preferences, learning styles, skills, processes, and strategies). The first reference to the term "adaptive learning" however, was made by Cronbach (1957) when he urged those in the field to discover "for each individual the treatment to which he can most easily adapt"(p. 671). He further posited that by combining cognitive models with individual characteristics, educators would come closer to uncovering instructional best practices.

Interestingly, however, recent advances in e-learning have made quite clear the disparities between traditional pedagogy and pedagogy that is developed around the learner's individual needs. This type of personalized, or personalizable learning—especially in emerging e-learning platforms, is a current focal point in education (Collins and Halverson, 2009; Darling-Hammond, 2010)—a direct result of academic globalization, where past barriers such as time, space, an place, have been overcome by distance education. Moreover, discourse among proponents of e-learning argue that classrooms at all academic levels should adjust any existing traditional pedagogical practices to practices that have relevance to learners' lives, using technologies that are prevalent in present day society. Students are quickly becoming unengaged and confused with instruction that does not accompany context or real-world application (just as Alice finds herself confused in her conversation with the Caterpillar). Providing students with learning environments that are capable of molding instruction around their individual learning needs is an educational imperative.

Adaptive Learning Environments (ALEs) are considered environments that adjust, or adapt to the needs of the learner. Additionally, an ALE has the ability to monitor, interpret, and evaluate learner activity. From this point, the ALE system analyzes the learner activity data and presents activities based upon associated learning models. Situated within the associated learning models are rules, user misconception exceptions as well as content being questioned (Pedrazzoli, 2010). Such systems have the ability to adapt to learning styles, cognitive levels, and learning activity thus maximizing the opportunities for the student to learn. An intuitive ALE has the potential to provide detailed data on both individual and group learning, thus informing the development of future instruction. Using the Multidimensional Instructional Design Model, Pedralozzi (2010) and colleagues developed an extension for learning management systems, the OPUS One, which relies on real-time data and profiles, whereby the appropriate learning path is summoned and presented to the user by an Artificial Intelligence system. The generation of real-time data allows course designers to monitor learning activity that is based upon established learning paths, thus providing optimum levels of adaptive learning. Thus begs the question, could learning based upon instruction designed around the CoI Framework be measured in an adaptive learning system? A literature review on ALEs and social, teaching, and cognitive presence research suggests that it can.

ALEs and Social Presence

Placing learners in a collaborative learning environment assigned with group tasks does not necessarily ensure a meaningful learning experience (Soller, 2001). Therefore, it is the responsibility of the teacher/designer to create activities that foster collaborative learning. Soller (2001) demonstrated the ability to achieve meaningful collaboration in an ALE with his Intelligent Collaborative system.

Soller identified five behaviors conducive to rich collaborative learning:

1. Participation
2. Social grounding
3. Performance analysis
4. Group processing and application of active learning conversation skills
5. Promotive interaction.

He further paired these characteristics with Intelligent Assistants which included:

- A collaborative learning skill coach
- An instructional planner
- A student or group model
- A learning companion
- A personal learning assistant.

Similarly, Erkens (1997) used Intelligent Coaches in a variety of ways to support collaborative groups that included serving as a partner that may take on lower-order tasks while the student works on higher-order tasks and too act as a co-learner or partner during learning activities. OPUS One (Pedralozzi, 2010) / OLAT supports both standalone and as integrated tutored collaborative activities including the e-Tutor facility that offers additional resources and activities to student groups who may require extra instruction.

ALEs and Teaching Presence

One of the main components of adaptive learning environments is the presence of an assistive tutor. The assistive tutor serves in a variety of capacities including determining student capacity, target orientation, and expert based/rule driven subject matter. These functions may be carried out through learning paths, adaptive selection of learning materials, course re-structuring, etc., and are adapted according to real-time data generated by the learner's actions and/or input. For example, the OPUS One system (Pedralozzi, 2010) inte-

grates a Behavior Recorder Controller (BRC) that supervises and monitors the learner based upon requests for additional help or by the detection of learner difficulty. Additionally, based upon the subject matter sequence, grading value, and session position, individualized problem-solving content is offered to the learner.

ALEs and Cognitive Presence

ALEs most commonly integrate functionality that supports and adapts to cognitive learning styles. Mirroring similar functionalities to foster social and teaching presence, this particular component is structured to identify context-sensitive subject matter knowledge, misconceptions, adaptation rules, etc. according real-time adaptable learning paths and student input. Lo, Chan and Ye (2012) developed an adaptive web-based learning system that collected learners' browsing behaviors toward targeting cognitive learning styles. Holden and Westfall (2010, p. 5) however, warn against using *cognitive learning style* interchangeably with *learning styles* as they assert that "a learning style or modality describes how information enters the brain: visually, aurally, or tactically, whereas cognitive style refers to how the information is processed once the information gets to the brain." Dembro and Howard (2007) further this notion by adding that there is no evidence that application of a particular learning style to instruction increases student achievement. Other adaptive learning developers have focused on cognitive functioning processes based upon Cronbach and Snow's (1977) research, maintaining that adaptive instruction should include treatments that vary in structure, completeness, and ability. Their pivotal research could be considered foundational to the CoI Framework, further asserting that "an understanding of cognitive abilities considered alone would not be sufficient" to assess learning experiences, differences in learning styles, and aptitude treatment interactions.

To conclude, as new research studies are conducted in this intriguing--yet evolving field, adaptive learning environment developers would be well-informed to develop ALEs around cognitive, teaching, and social presence toward a "clearer" understanding of the interactions among these components toward learner experience. Otherwise, there will be learners--much like Alice, who "can't put it any more clearly, sir, because it isn't clear to me."

While some unique questions reside within this discussion on ALEs and the assessment of CoI presences, they serve as an extension to the previous section, On-Demand Platforms, and as a prelude to the topic on web optimization engines discussed in the following section, Learning Analytics.

Learning Analytics

At the time of this chapter's authoring, analytics has become a buzzword in higher education, especially in online education. Interestingly, when confronted with what exactly analytics are, no one is yet able to provide a concise definition. In the broadest sense, analytics can be defined as the application of quantitative techniques to solving problems. In the academic context these problems may take the form of business intelligence, learning outcomes assessment, predicting retention, gaining insight into qualitative data through semantic analysis, marketing, informing student success, and a host of other topics. Suffice it to say that analytics is a field that is still quite amorphous but has been recognized as the means for helping institutions make meaning of oceans of data that, until recent calls for accountability, have not even been fractionally utilized (Siemens & Long, 2011).

In attempting to shed some light on what role analytics may play in education, the 2011 Horizon Report (Johnson, et al., 2011) is informative in describing the benefit for students as identifying their learning needs and tailoring instruction

appropriately. Historically such analyses have been the role of institutional research offices, instructional designers, and faculty engaged in pedagogical research. However, despite best intentions, traditional research paradigms do not provide actionable intelligence that can be leveraged to implement near-term change, let alone provide real-time intelligence. Now, with the national drumbeat for transparency in education growing louder, institutions are scrambling to modify long tested business intelligence techniques to solve academic problems. Whether there is sufficient intellectual capital, monetary resources, and internal motivation to allow all institutions to achieve this type of integration is debatable. However, for those who are able to successfully implement change the following is intended to provide a glimpse into how analytics may impact their futures and, for purposes of this chapter, the application of the CoI framework. As noted, there are multiple classes of analytics that can be deployed across the institution, however, exploration in this chapter will be limited to a sampling of those techniques and tools that will likely have the greatest impact on, or directly related to, online learning environments.

Presently, there are several analytics products that capture some degree of data across institutional systems and conduct automated analysis to identify students who are at varying levels of risk for disenrollment, performing poorly on an assessment, falling behind in their coursework, and various other factors. Derived from traditional inferential techniques, the overwhelming majority of these applications lack high degrees of accuracy and do not use forward looking techniques such as neural network analysis or Bayesian modeling. However, even at their current level of implementation, analytics may be impacting the way in which communities emerge and evolve.

As an example, consider the case in which a 28 year-old, Asian female taking English 101 is not overly active in discussion forums. Tracking mechanisms collect this data and pair it with demographic information contained in the student information system. From there, an analysis engine performs various tests, ranging from comparison of descriptive statistics to some form of regression analysis. The output from these tests reveals that this student has a 70% chance of failing the course, if her discussion forum activity does not increase, when compared to all other 28 year-old Asian females who previously completed English 101. An automated email is generated informing the course instructor of these findings. In response, the instructor sends this student a note stating that he has noticed she has not been overly active in discussion forums and urges her to participate more. Though facilitating discourse and helping foster the development of Social Presence are key responsibilities of an instructor, decisions to intervene and provide guidance have been long made based upon intuition and application of personal experience. Automating the process, while likely more accurate than subjective interpretation of performance, may have unintended consequences. At the very least such actions will definitely alter the manner in which online learning is perceived from both the student and instructor perspectives.

While intended to be beneficial, it is possible that automated notifications and other such actions may cause learners to feel as if they are being unduly coerced to participate. Conversely, other learners may perceive these actions as being representative of instructor caring and become more involved. Regardless of whether one of these results is obtained, or countless other possible variations, the CoI would be impacted in some manner. When moving from a state in which community is formed as a result of natural interactions, to one in which data informs the decision-making process, macro level trends will certainly become visible over time. Given current trends around measuring activity, it is likely that the Facilitation of Discourse component of Teaching Presence, Social Presence and the Exploration phase of Cognitive Presence are the most likely to be impacted. However, this assumption is based on

familiarity with the CoI and certainly should not be considered as the only avenues for research.

Moving forward, it is likely that web analytics will be leveraged to enhance the types of analyses that are conducted in the learning space. As the name implies, web analytics are tools that capture online user interactions. This is typically accomplished by inserting snippets of Java code onto web pages. This code then captures information such as where did the user come from before they were on their current page, what page did they go to next, when did they abandon the site altogether, what type of device were they using to access they site, what is their physical location, what content did they access on the page, etc. Currently there are several products on the market, such as Google Analytics, Omniture and Core Metrics, that are classified as web analytics tools. As with any other software, there are variations, often quite dramatic, in the degree of functionality between products. While all provide numerical output and simple visualizations, others are dramatically more powerful and have capabilities such as content suggestion engines, user profiling tools and website optimization engines (Ice, 2011).

Notably, none of the web analytics tools currently available are optimized for use in learning environments. Though long used in online marketing and sales, academia has lagged in adoption of these tools, largely because of the large costs involved in refitting them to predict learning outcomes rather than points of sale. However, it should be noted that conceptually the two outcomes do not differ significantly from a statistical perspective, making it likely that there will be forays into modifying existing web analytics tools for online learning (Schuman & Ice, 2011). Figure 1 is a screenshot taken from a commercial implementation of Adobe Omniture. This pathing diagram visualizes the various navigational routes taken by customers on a commercial website and how they lead to points of purchase. Applying this same technique to utilization of educational resources would yield a virtual treasure trove

Figure 1. Adobe Omniture pathing diagram

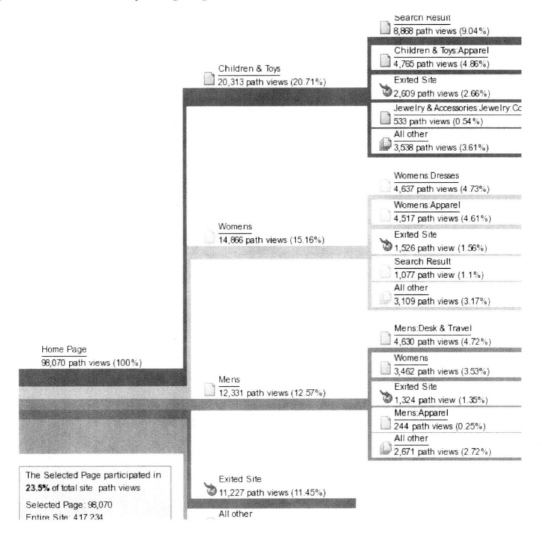

of data for instructional designers, instructors, and administrators. Learners would also benefit from similar outputs that would allow them to compare their progress to all other learners in a course. In addition, the data used to produce these visualizations can be utilized to produce robust predictive models.

In practice, this type of integration has the very real potential of creating the equivalent of suggestion engines such as those that power Amazon. com. These types of systems would develop detailed profiles of learners and their interactions to predict what types of content (both from a media and pedagogical perspective) would likely be most beneficial in helping learners achieve optimal learning outcomes. Significantly, rather than simply suggesting what content would be most beneficial, the most powerful web analytics systems have the ability to integrate with sophisticated digital asset management systems to provision individualized learning experiences on the fly. With respect to on-demand platforms, these optimization engines may be highly beneficial in enhancing virtual Teaching Presence, through allowing designers to build out sequences of pedagogically diverse learning activities that can be co-mingled to provide customized learning experience in the absence of an instructor. While somewhat disconcerting, the implication of this approach is that teaching presence may eventually be divided into human teaching presence and data driven teaching presence.

In traditional instructor-lead learning environments, optimization engines present an interesting scenario. Suppose that an institution has built out an array of learning objects, each aligned to various learning styles, levels of remediation or enrichment, type of device used for access (multi-screen), etc. When paired with web analytics engines it is very possible that each learner in a course could be provided with different learning pathways to achieve the same course goals or objectives. How would this impact the nature of group discussions? Would students truly benefit from multiple perspectives, as posited in the CoI framework, would the perspectives be too diverse, or would the underlying optimization engines be accurate enough that there would be a high degree of symmetry between student perspectives? Given any of these scenarios, how would Facilitation of Discourse be transformed? The above are but a few of the questions that must be confronted as analytics are used more and more frequently; not just to inform what is going on in learning environments, but to actually create those environments.

CONCLUSION

The technologies and scenarios presented in this chapter are by no means meant to be exhaustive or provide an in-depth review of the technologies that will impact online learning in the coming years. Rather, the technologies presented are ones that the authors believe will have the most significant impact and the scenarios are ones that will hopefully create a great deal of discomfort among readers who are attempting to reconcile current and emerging paradigms. Of course, as with any attempt to predict the future, there is every chance

that at best one of the scenarios presented will materialize. As such, our hope is that readers will use this chapter as a springboard to help them create their own discomforting scenarios and methods for exploring the impact of technologically driven change. As firm believers in the CoI framework, we would also like to note that even though the applicability of the three Presences and components are continuously challenged we do not believe that it will become irrelevant. Rather, we believe that the CoI framework was conceptualized around sound pedagogical principals, but in the context of a very rigid technical environment. As such, it is our hope that as academia confronts several transformational technologies, the CoI framework will be organically adapted to contextualize these affordances.

REFERENCES

Archer, W. (2010). Beyond online discussions: Extending the Community of Inquiry Framework to entire courses. *The Internet and Higher Education*, *13*(1-2), 69–70. doi:10.1016/j.iheduc.2009.10.005doi:10.1016/j.iheduc.2009.10.005

Baylor, A. L., & Kim, Y. (2005). Simulating instructional roles through pedagogical agents. *International Journal of Artificial Intelligence in Education*, *15*(1), 95–115.

Blascovich, J. (2002). A theoretical model of social influence for increasing the utility of collaborative virtual environment. *4th International Conference on Collaborative Virtual Environments, Bonn, Germany, 2002*, (pp. 25-30).

Burgess, M. L., & Ice, P. (2011a). Optimal experience in virtual environments among college level developmental readers. *Journal of Educational Computing Research*, *44*(4), 429–451. doi:10.2190/EC.44.4.ddoi:10.2190/EC.44.4.d

Burgess, M. L., & Ice, P. (2011b). Using the Community of Inquiry (CoI) model to support 21st century online teaching and learning in multi-user virtual environments. In R. Hinrichs & C. Wankel (Eds.), *Transforming virtual world learning: Cutting edge technologies in higher education*. Emerald Press.

Burgess, M. L., Slate, J. R., Rojas-LeBouef, A., & LaPrairie, K. (2010). Teaching and learning in Second Life: Using the Community of Inquiry (CoI) model to support online instruction with graduate students in instructional technology. *Special Issue of Internet & Higher Education*, *13*(1/2), 84–88. doi:10.1016/j.iheduc.2009.12.003doi:10.1016/j.iheduc.2009.12.003

Collins, A., & Halverson, R. (2009). *Rethinking education in the age of technology: The digital revolution and schooling in America*. New York, NY: Teachers College Press.

Cronbach, L., & Snow, R. (1977). *Aptitudes and instructional methods: A handbook for research on interactions*. New York, NY: Irvington Publishers.

Cronbach, L. (1957). The two disciplines of scientific psychology. *The American Psychologist*, *12*, 671–684. doi:10.1037/h0043943doi:10.1037/h0043943

Darling-Hammond, L. (2010). *The flat world and education*. New York, NY: Teachers College Press.

Dembo, M., & Howard, K. (2007). Advice about the use of learning styles: A major myth in education. *Journal of College Reading and Learning*, *37*(2), 101–109. Retrieved from http://www.eric.ed.gov/ERICWebPortal/search/detailmini.jsp?_nfpb=true&_&ERICExtSearch_SearchValue_0=EJ767768&ERICExtSearch_SearchType_0=no&accno=EJ767768

Flavell, J. (1992). Cognitive development: Past, present, and future. *Developmental Psychology*, *28*(6), 998–1005. doi:10.1037/0012-1649.28.6.998doi:10.1037/0012-1649.28.6.998

Flavell, J. H. (1979). Metacognition. *The American Psychologist*, *34*, 906–911. doi:10.1037/0003-066X.34.10.906doi:10.1037/0003-066X.34.10.906

Flavell, J. H. (1987). Speculations about the nature and development of metacognition. In F. Weinert & R. Kluwe (Eds.), *Metacognition, motivation, and understanding* (pp. 21–29). Hillsdale, NJ: Erlbaum Associates.

Gagné, R. (1967). *Learning and individual differences*. Columbus, OH: Merrill.

Gardner, H., Kornhaber, M., & Wake, W. (1997). *Intelligence: Multiple perspectives*. Philadelphia, PA: Harcourt Brace College Publishers.

Garrison, D. R., & Arbaugh, J. B. (2007). Researching the community of inquiry framework: Review, issues, and future directions. *The Internet and Higher Education*, *10*(3), 157–172. doi:10.1016/j.iheduc.2007.04.001doi:10.1016/j.iheduc.2007.04.001

Glaser, R. (1972). Individuals and learning: The new aptitudes. *Educational Researcher*, *1*(6), 5–13.

Glaser, R. (1976). Components of a psychology of instruction: Toward a science of design. *Review of Educational Research*, *46*(1), 1–24.

Glaser, R. (1984). Education and thinking: The role of knowledge. *The American Psychologist*, *39*, 93–104. doi:10.1037/0003-066X.39.2.93doi:10.1037/0003-066X.39.2.93

Green, T. (2011, October). *Multi-screen madness: Your life just got interesting*. Paper presented at the Adobe MAX Education Preconference, Los Angeles, CA.

Holden, J. T., & Westfall, P. (2010). *Learning styles and generational differences: Do they matter?* Federal Government Distance Learning Association.

Ice, P. (2011, November). *Applying analytics to instructional design.* Paper presented at the DevLearn Conference, Las Vegas, NV.

Johnson, L., Smith, R., Willis, H., Levine, A., & Haywood, K. (2011). *The 2011 horizon report.* Austin, TX: The New Media Consortium.

Kim, Y., & Baylor, A. L. (2006a). Pedagogical agents as learning companions: The role of agent competency and type of interaction. *Educational Technology Research and Development, 54*(3), 223–243. doi:10.1007/s11423-006-8805-zdoi:10.1007/s11423-006-8805-z

Kim, Y., & Baylor, A. L. (2006b). A social cognitive framework for designing pedagogical agents as learning companions. *Educational Technology Research and Development, 54*(6), 569–596. doi:10.1007/s11423-006-0637-3doi:10.1007/s11423-006-0637-3

Kolb, D. A. (1984). *Experiential learning: Experience as the source of learning and development.* New Jersey: Prentice-Hall.

Kozma, R. B. (1994). The influence of media on learning: The debate continues. *School Library Media Research, 22*(4). Retrieved from http://www.ala.org/aasl/aaslpubsandjournals/slmrb/editorschoiceb/infopower/selctkozmahtml

Lo, J., Chan, Y., & Yeh, S. (2012). Designing an adaptive web-based learning system based on students' cognitive styles identified online. *Computers & Education, 58*(1), 209–222. doi:10.1016/j.compedu.2011.08.018doi:10.1016/j.compedu.2011.08.018

Lombard, M., & Ditton, T. (1997). At the heart of it all: The concept of presence. *Journal of Computer-Mediated Communication, 3*(2).

Masur, E. F., McIntyre, C. W., & Flavell, J. H. (1973). Developmental changes in apportionment of study time among items in a multi-trial free recall task. *Journal of Experimental Child Psychology, 15*, 237–246. doi:10.1016/0022-0965(73)90145-8doi:10.1016/0022-0965(73)90145-8

McKerlich, R., & Anderson, T. (2007). Community of Inquiry and learning in immersive environments. *Journal of Asynchronous Learning Networks, 11*(4), 35–52.

Pedralozzi, A. (2010). *OPUS One: Intelligent adaptive learning environment using artificial intelligence support.* Paper presented at the American Institute of Physics (AIP), Lugano, Switzerland.

Salomon, G. (1997). *Interaction of media, cognition, and learning.* San Francisco, CA: Jossey Bass.

Schneider, D. (2011). *The media debate.* Retrieved from http://edutechwiki.unige.ch/en/The_media_debate

Schuman, J., & Ice, P. (2011, October). *The art of using online analytics tools from Adobe.* Paper presented at Educause Annual Conference, Philadelphia, PA.

Siemens, G., & Long, P. (2011). Penetrating the fog: Analytics in learning and education. *EDUCAUSE Review, 46*(5).

Soller, A. L. (2001). Supporting social interaction in an intelligent collaborative learning system. *International Journal of Artificial Intelligence in Education, 12*, 40–62.

Swan, K., & Shih, L. F. (2005). On the nature and development of social presence in online course discussions. *Journal of Asynchronous Learning Networks, 9*(3), 115–136.

Witkin, H. A., & Goodenough, D. R. (1981). *Cognitive styles: Essence and origins.* New York, NY: International Universities.

Zimmerman, B. J. (1989). A social cognitive view of self-regulated academic learning. *Journal of Educational Psychology, 81*, 329–339. doi:10.1037/0022-0663.81.3.329doi:10.1037/0022-0663.81.3.329

KEY TERMS AND DEFINITIONS

Adaptive Learning Environments (ALEs): Has the ability to monitor, interpret, and evaluate learner activity. Additionally, they adjust, or adapt to the needs of the learner based upon the data collected from the learning processes.

Analytics: A broad term that is currently used when referring to multiple classes of data driven decision making techniques used across institutions. This includes research, predictive modeling, business intelligence, web analytics and a host of other quantitative procedures that are intended to improve learning effectiveness and institutional effectiveness.

Digital Publishing: Delivery of content, including related interactive components, in digital formats that can be consumed on a variety of devices.

Multi-Screen: The ability to develop content that can be accessed across a variety of devices including smart phones, tablets, laptops, desktops and web-enabled televisions.

Multi-User Virtual Environment (MUVE): 3D applications whereby users, represented as avatars, have the ability to engage in immersive, synchronous or asynchronous, and highly social experiences.

Multi-User Virtual Environment Education Evaluation Tool (MUVEEET): Instrument developed by McKerlich and Anderson (2007) to measure the existence of social, cognitive, and teaching presence within a MUVE.

On-Demand: Online self-paced tutorials that integrate interactive and exploratory learning experiences that are accessible anywhere and at any time.

On-Demand Learning Environment Evaluation Tool (ODLEET): Instrument developed by Burgess and Ice (2011) to measure the existence of social, cognitive, and teaching presence within an on-demand learning environment.

Chapter 23

An Exploratory Study of Cross–Cultural Engagement in the Community of Inquiry:
Instructor Perspectives and Challenges

Viviane Vladimirschi
E-Connection, Brazil

ABSTRACT

This chapter examines instructor multicultural efficacy in global online learning communities. To explore this phenomenon in the CoI framework, a two-phase study was conducted with 10 instructors from two Alberta higher education institutions. Phase one comprised creating intercultural competency indicators to test how they developed and expanded existing teaching and social presence indicators. Qualitative data revealed that in the lack of any cross-cultural design, instructors utilize facilitation and open communication strategies to foster learning and prevent conflict. Phase two involved augmenting the 34-item CoI survey instrument. Additional roles that relate to instructor cross-cultural efficacy were incorporated into both teaching and social presence elements based on qualitative findings. Quantitative data revealed that the incorporated cultural indicators correlated highly with the teaching and social indicators, indicating their usefulness to measure multicultural efficacy in the CoI framework.

INTRODUCTION

The range of what we think and do is limited by what we fail to notice. And because we fail to notice that we fail to notice there is little we can do to change until we notice how failing to notice shapes our thoughts and deeds (R.D. Laing, 1972 as cited in Harrington & Hathaway, 1994, p. 1).

Asynchronous text-based computer-mediated communication (CMC) learning communities have afforded a growing number of cross-cultural learners the opportunity to study in internationally renowned universities or institutions without being bound by geographical or temporal constraints (McIssac, 2002). However, as learners cross educational borders, cross-cultural learners are

DOI: 10.4018/978-1-4666-2110-7.ch023

faced with myriad issues and challenges. Factors such as language and technological limitations are just some examples that barely scratch the surface of this complex subject. There are indeed other major cultural issues that may negatively impact cross-cultural online learners. Moreover, the limited theoretical underpinnings used in online education largely ignore culture as a significant factor (Wang & Reeves, 2007). Thus, instructors who fail to understand the differing needs and worldviews of these learners may in fact adversely affect successful educational outcomes in online communities of inquiry.

This study explores how instructors of asynchronous text-based online courses accommodate and make provisions for culturally diverse learners in online communities of inquiry. The main premise of this research was that, because instructors project their individual personalities in the online environment via their teaching and social presence, both of which are largely rooted in their dominant culture, their values, beliefs, and attitudes will significantly affect learners' social and cognitive presence. The term culture is defined in this study as "the set of attitudes, values, beliefs, and behaviors shared by a group of people, but different for each individual" (Matsumoto, 1996, p. 16). Further, cross-cultural students may find it more difficult to project themselves socially in asynchronous online learning environments due to inherent cultural differences and backgrounds. "Cross-cultural" refers to interaction among individuals from different cultures (http://tinyurl.com/44vlwv3). In the context of this study "cross-cultural" specifically refers to individuals who may or may not be currently living in Canada but were born in another country and whose native language is notably not English or individuals who identify with a culturally distinct group (e.g., Aboriginals, French Canadians, or a new immigrant group now residing in Canada).

Based on data collected from two survey instruments, the Adapted Multicultural Efficacy Questionnaire (AMEQ) and the CoI questionnaire,

this chapter proposes a revised 37-item CoI survey instrument for measuring instructor multicultural efficacy in an online community of inquiry.

REVIEW OF RELATED LITERATURE

There is great consensus among scholars that culture plays a major role in online learning (Bates & Gpe, 1997; Morse, 2003; Hewling, 2005; Moore, 2006; Edmundson, 2007, 2009). However, literature on this topic is still in its infancy and there are deficiencies in research-based studies especially in regards to globalization of education and cross-cultural issues (Gunawardena, Wilson, & Nolla, 2003; Edmundson, 2007; Zawacki-Richter, Bäcker & Vogt, 2009).

Studies have revealed that some of the factors that hinder successful online learning are as follows:

- Inability to understand specific cultural references
- Language limitations
- Inability to question authority (instructor or peers)
- Differing emotional needs
- Time zone limitations
- Technological limitations (Zhao & McDougall, 2008; Uzner, 2009; Zhang & Kenny, 2010).

Considering the exponential growth and needs of online learning programs and degree programs offered internationally, it is pivotal to increase intercultural awareness and efficacy of teachers in addressing the needs of a global population in order to achieve successful educational outcomes (Lim, 2004).

In a globalized online environment, although teaching should not be based on one dominant set of values or pedagogical assumptions, instructors quite often bring their own beliefs and stereotypes into the learning environment (Banks, Cookson,

Gay, Hawley, Irvine, Nieto, Schofield, & Stephan, 2001). Existing "essentialist" or nation-based models of cultural competence may fail to take into account the complexities of intercultural exchange in text-based asynchronous learning environments that foster critical reflection and higher-order learning (Hewling, 2005). Notwithstanding, asynchronous text-based computer-mediated communication (CMC) grounded on constructivist teaching and learning principles have become a major education delivery medium inasmuch as these environments are able to lift geographic and temporal limitations for global learners. For an international learner whose cultural experiences differ from the dominant educational cultures, a constructivist-based pedagogy couched in a highly interactive communication world can be a very lonely place (Shattuck, 2005).

The CoI framework is geared toward providing a theoretical framework that addresses how learning and teaching can be achieved in dynamic yet intricate online learning environments through the use of effective communities of practical inquiry. The model contemplates the complexities of written communication in achieving and fostering higher-order thinking skills in online and blended higher education. Although the CoI framework is becoming increasingly influential for explaining and prescribing effective conduct of collaborative constructivist online learning and teaching (Arbaugh, Cleveland-Innes, Diaz, Garrison, Ice, Richardson, Shea, & Swan, 2008; Garrison, 2011), it fails to take into consideration cultural issues and multicultural online engagement (Morgan, 2011).

The core elements that constitute the CoI framework are as follows: teaching presence, social presence, and cognitive presence. Cognitive presence is perceived as vital to achieving effective educational outcomes and it "reflects the inquiry and learning process" (Garrison, Cleveland-Innes, & Fung, 2010, p. 33). The function of teaching presence is to design, facilitate, and direct the cognitive and social processes of learners for the

purpose of realizing educational goals (Garrison, Anderson & Archer, 2000). The main challenge of teaching presence is to bring together all elements of a community of inquiry in a balanced and functional relationship congruent with the intended outcomes, needs, and capabilities of the learners (Garrison, 2011). Social presence is the degree to which a person is able to identify with the group or course study, communicate effectively in a trusting environment, and develop personal and affective relationships by projecting his/her individual personality in CMC (Garrison, 2009b as cited in Garrison, 2011). Learning is a social process (Tu, 2000) and discourse plays a fundamental role in the social process of learning (Harasim, 2002). While there is a positive correlation between social presence and learner's satisfaction with online learning (Arbaugh & Benbunan-Fich, 2006), the demand for academic discourse in contrast with the need and desire of the cross-cultural learner to connect with others on a personal level is a challenge for both instructor and student to overcome.

Absent or inappropriate teaching presence may not only negatively impact student discourse (Finegold & Cooke, 2006) but also learner's ability to project themselves socially in the online environment (Gilbert & Dabbagh, 2005; Shea, Li & Picket, 2006). Instructors play a key role not only in establishing an effective online community of practical inquiry but also in helping learners project their identities in this environment in order to achieve deep and meaningful learning. For example, learners who are used to rote memorization may feel uncomfortable with inquiry-based learning (Farmer, 2010). Provided the substantial influence instructors have on learners, prioritizing culture in education is ultimately an ethical concern that all distance education theoretical frameworks should contemplate (Parrish & Linder-VanBerschot, 2010). Thus, it is apropos to investigate how instructors in the context of the CoI framework are dealing with cross-cultural learners.

STUDY

This study was guided by two theoretical frameworks: the CoI framework and the Multicultural Efficacy Scale (MES) framework (See Appendix A). As the MES was originally developed for traditional face-to-face classroom environments and was applied to undergraduate and graduate teacher education students from several geographic regions across the United States, it underwent adaptations and was transformed into an open-ended survey questionnaire, the Adapted Multicultural Efficacy Scale (AMEQ). This enabled verification of the scale's applicability and reliability in a different context. Before being administered to the respondents, the AMEQ was pre-tested for face validation and clarity by four volunteers from two Alberta post-secondary institutions.

Methodology

The main research question leading this research is as follows: How do instructors accommodate and make provisions for cross-cultural learners in an online community of learning? To better understand this phenomenon and build on the existing CoI framework, this study applied a sequential exploratory strategy in which the level of mixing was partially mixed, time orientation was sequential, and greater emphasis was placed on the qualitative phase of the study than on the quantitative one. The sequential approach enables the researcher to obtain themes and specific statements from participants in an initial qualitative data collection, and then use these statements as specific items and the themes for scales to add on to an existing survey instrument (Creswell & Plano Clark, 2007). For this purpose, instructors from two Alberta higher education institutions who were currently teaching predominantly asynchronous text-based online undergraduate or graduate courses in which there were individuals who may or may not be currently living in Canada but were born in another country and whose native language is notably not English or individuals who identify with a culturally distinct group (e.g., Aboriginals, French Canadians or a new immigrant group now residing in Canada) constituted the context of this study. Ten online instructors from two Alberta post-secondary institutions volunteered to participate in the study. The demographic data shows that seven of the instructors were female and three were male. Four instructors were in the 35-44 years age bracket; one in the 45-54 years age bracket; four in the 55-64 age bracket; and one in the 65-74 age bracket. Seven of the 10 instructors were Canadian. One instructor was Indian, one Greek, and one Dutch. Instructors who responded they were Canadian also provided additional information on their cultural background. This included stating their race, religious identification, and mother tongue. Five respondents self-identified as being Caucasian, one respondent reported being Protestant and coming from Ukrainian ancestry, and one respondent reported being an English speaker. The Greek respondent reported being an Orthodox Christian. It is also important to mention that the sequential design used identical samples for both qualitative and quantitative components of this study.

Data Collection and Analysis for Phase 1

Participants were invited to respond to two online surveys over the course of the Spring/Summer 2011 Semester. Data for the qualitative phase (phase 1) of this study was collected using the Adapted Multicultural Efficacy Questionnaire (AMEQ). The AMEQ, Online Survey 1, was designed to assess instructors' perceived multicultural efficacy in teaching cross-cultural students online. This survey comprised fifteen open-ended survey questions. The AMEQ was administered to all 10 participants during the months of June and July, 2011.

Table 1. Cultural indicators and descriptors

Indicator abbreviation	Definition
ACC	**accommodation** - instructor adapts or modifies instructional material to address cross-cultural students' needs (also includes ways in which instructor adapts or modifies instructional material for cross-cultural learners)
CON	**contextualization** - instructor takes into account specific cultural factors when adapting curricula and activities
CSS	**creation of safe spaces** - instructor develops and incorporates activities designed to promote the success of cross-cultural learners
ENC	**encouragement** - instructor encourages cross-cultural collaborative online engagement
ANT	**anticipation** - instructor can anticipate online cross-cultural learner difficulties
PREV	**prevention** - instructor can take preventative measures to lessen or relieve learner difficulties
ADAP	**adaptation** - instructor can adapt to concerns and expectations of culturally diverse learners
ID	**identification** - instructor can identify solutions to possible online cultural clashes
KOD	**knowledge of diversity** - instructor can identify ways in which culturally diverse learners contribute to the online learning community and environment
SOD	**supportive of diversity** - instructor encourages online learners to assimilate and accept the perspective of ethnic and cultural groups different from their own

For this study the researcher opted to make use of a "grounded theory" approach to the analysis and interpretation of data as advocated by Strauss and Corbin (1998). Thus, in line with this approach, coding category names and cultural indicators and descriptors were devised based on two conceptual frameworks (CoI and AMEQ instrument), research questions, literature review, and other key variables brought to the study (Basit, 2003).

Three stages of coding were carried out. First, "open coding" was utilized to identify, name, categorize, and describe cultural descriptors and indicators present in the AMEQ instrument. From this instrument, 10 coding categories were extracted based on the questions contained in the AMEQ instrument. Codes for cultural indicators were devised to be relatively straightforward and explicit in meaning. These coding categories were then assigned abbreviations. Garrison, Cleveland-Innes, Koole and Kappelman (2006) hold that categories must be meaningful and indicators must be relatively discernible (i.e., explicit), if coding is to have reliability. Cultural indicator categories were loaded into NVivo, version 9.0, to determine how they related to the CoI elements of teaching presence and social presence. Table 1 provides

a breakdown of the cultural descriptors, corresponding abbreviations and definitions. The unit of analysis was of each of the open-ended survey responses in the form of utterances, sentences, or paragraphs submitted by the respondents. As Jackson and Trochim (2002) postulate:

The list-like format of open-ended survey question text lends itself to relatively easy creation of units of analysis. A unit of analysis consists of a sentence or phrase containing only one concept—units can often be lifted intact from the response because respondents tend to express one idea for each concern or opinion they list (p. 313).

Only one cultural indicator code was assigned at the response level. Some responses were too vague to be coded at all, while other respondents indicated that they did not accommodate or otherwise alter their teaching activities to account for cultural differences. In each of these instances, their responses were not coded according to cultural indicators. Survey responses were first coded for cultural indicators and subsequently for CoI indicators.

It is important to highlight that the focus of this study was to consider the way instructors addressed cultural differences in the overlap between teaching and social presence. From the perspective of the author of this chapter, issues of cross-cultural relations are related more to social and teaching presence and less to cognitive presence. Therefore, the construct of cognitive presence was not included or tested because it was not considered a first point of consideration in instructional differences. Categories for teaching presence and social presence were also loaded into NVivo. Social presence was analyzed in the responses to the open-ended questionnaire by coding for affective expression, open communication, and group cohesion (Garrison, 2011). Social presence was divided into three sub-elements: affective expression (SP-AE), group cohesion (SP-GC), and open communication (SP-OC). Teaching presence was coded for design and organization, facilitating discourse, and direct instruction (Garrison, 2011). Teaching presence was also divided into three sub-elements: design (TP-D), facilitation (TP-F), and direct instruction (TP-DI). Concepts and CoI model indicators associated with teaching presence and social presence were used as reference. The author of this chapter looked for evidence within and underneath the discussions about cultural differences to evaluate if social presence and teaching presence would emerge from the data. In other words, the author of this chapter evaluated the extent to which instructors referred to concepts of social presence and teaching presence in their discussion of cultural differences. CoI indicators were also coded at the response level; however, responses were double coded. For example, some responses were coded as being both teaching presence – design and teaching presence – facilitation. Hence, frequency results might have been different if the CoI indicators had been single coded. However, instructor responses appeared to fit in with more than one category. Next, an "axial coding" procedure was under-

taken to make explicit connections between the CoI and cultural indicators. The objective of this stage was to explain and understand relationships among categories in order to better understand the phenomena to which they relate, thus hypothesizing causal and generic relationships based on the cross-referencing of the CoI indicators with the cultural indicators. Finally, "selective coding" was utilized to detect the emergence of patterns to generate and validate theory with data.

To better illustrate the coding process, direct quotes from instructor responses to the AMEQ as they relate to the cross-referencing of the cultural indicators with each presence and its sub-element have been provided. The results section of this chapter summarizes these qualitative data findings.

Some examples of instructor responses that indicated the cultural indicator accommodation (ACC) was present in teaching presence – design are as follows: "Only in so much as the assignments can be customized to something that is relevant to them in their work but this option is open to all students in the course," "The instructional activities encourage students to share their own experiences including business experiences from other countries. The activies [sic] and curricula were not spectifically [sic] designed to cater to needs of students from other cultures" and "I don't specifically create instructional activities designed for non-Canadian cultures or even teach in French. However, many of my assignments and discussions are designed to allow for considerable individual input (i.e., applied such that theory or research, etc., is applied by the individual student to a situation or context of their own choosing)."

Examples of how instructor responses were coded for teaching presence – facilitation when cross-referenced with the cultural indicator encouragement (ENC) are illustrated in the following statements: "…yes - it is important for cross-cultural learners to interact with all students. In an online forum students learn much from each other regardless of cultural background -

they learn because they all have different [sic] backgrounds and experiences to draw from. Cross-cultural learners have the opportunity to learn "Canadian" things but the Canadians have the opportunity to learn from the students of other cultures" and "Yes, one of the strengths of taking online courses which have students from different cultures is students can share their cultural experiences. So I encourage students from different cultures to work collaboratively so that they can learn from each other." A clear example of the cultural indicator adaptation (ADAP) and teaching presence – facilitation is "Our department has had many discussions about the appropriate choice of technology for allowing access to our courses by International students and I will take bandwidth issues into account for students living in less developed parts of the world or, in fact, even Canadian students living in remote and rural parts of Canada (e.g., First Nations students living on reserves). Asynchronous delivery methods like Moodle work well in most situations, but we do sometimes have to be careful about the inclusion of items like large graphics and streaming video and audio conferencing can be problematic for such students." In conclusion, the following instructor responses illustrate coding of teaching presence – facilitation when cross-referenced with the cultural indicator accommodation (ACC): "I make every effort to accommodate my students who may be located in developing countries, new to Canada or English is their second language, to help them grasp/engage in the context of the course learning" and "I do not adjust the curricula, but I offer phone conversations, Skype conversations and electronic connections to provide whatever support the student may require to find success within each course that I teach."

Examples of how the indicator for social presence – open communication was coded when cross-referenced with the cultural indicator knowledge of diversity (KOD) may be detected in instructor responses that express appreciation for contributions from cross-cultural learners: "…but I do think that culturally diverse groups tend to enrich the discussions in courses because students bring in examples from their own cultures and life experiences that can be potentially quite different than those of other students"; "Their different perspectives enhance our learning and open other students' minds to difference"; "It is quite common to have students from different environments and students who are working overseas in our courses. In general, they are ex-pat Canadians or very well acculturized [sic] citizens of the world. These people do often bring some excellent examples of the difficult economic, social and cultural issues in their environments. For example, a recent student described the problems she is having in serving Muslim [sic] women and girls who are trying to achieve an academic credential in Kabul" and "Yes, getting back to the example of color, it is fascinating when students from different colors share their interpretations and feelings about red, for example. The sharing of such seemingly minor details helps the other students hone their sensitivity to such design decisions. Cultural diversity is extremely important."

To achieve coder inter-rater reliability, data from the AMEQ was coded by the author of this chapter and a research assistant. The researchers analyzed the survey data by applying a negotiated coding approach (Garrison et al., 2006). Prior to loading data on the analytic tool NVivo, the researchers discussed the overall structure of the codes, devising a set of rules about "how" to code, measure, classify, and record the data. Both the author of this chapter and the research assistant made two passes through the data. During the first pass, each researcher created a series of free nodes representing the 10 cultural indicators. The researchers then coded the data using the cultural indicators as reference. The research assistant then compared her coding with the author of this chapter and negotiated an agreement on cultural indicators. A second pass through the data was

Table 2. CoI instrument and incorporated indicators

Core Codes	Cultural Indicator
Teaching Presence – Design & Organization	The instructor allows for adjustments to the design and organization when necessary to accommodate cultural diversity.
Teaching Presence – Facilitation	The instructor supports interaction among culturally diverse learners.
Social Presence – Open Communication	Open communication in this community allows for culturally diverse presentation.

made, coding for the CoI presences, using the indicators for teaching presence (design, direct instruction, and facilitation) and social presence (open communication, group cohesion, and affective expression). Once again, coding was compared with that performed by the author of this chapter and negotiations occurred to arrive at an overall agreement regarding teaching and social presence indicators.

Building onto the CoI Instrument

The AMEQ was intended to explore instructors' perceived multicultural efficacy in an online community of learning. The intent of the analysis was to explore what categories or themes would emerge from the sample as a whole at the time of measurement taking into consideration instructor perspectives and challenges in this environment. From a grounded theory perspective, the author of this chapter was interested in discovering if indicators for teaching and social presence would emerge from instructor responses to the questionnaire. While the questions were not designed specifically to ask about instructor teaching and social presence, the author of this chapter coded for evidence of the emergence of social presence and teaching presence indicators in instructors' discussion of teaching and attention to cultural differences. Data analysis of the AMEQ showed that within and underneath instructors' discussions on teaching and attention to cultural differences, the elements of teaching presence and social presence were present. The author of this

chapter initially searched for CoI evidence in the AMEQ questionnaire, but did not specifically ask for this evidence.

Matrix coding queries that combined the CoI presences with the cultural descriptors and indicators were run to cross-reference data. The objective of this was to determine frequencies and patterns in relation to the impact of the 10 cultural indicators and descriptors on the CoI teaching presence and social presence elements. Cultural indicators that correlated highly with design, facilitation, and open communication generated a final coding scheme or a code family. In light of the matrix query results, additional roles were added to the elements of teaching and social presence. Table 2 illustrates the incorporated cultural indicators into the CoI survey instrument. Three new indicators, two for teaching presence and one for social presence, which consider the role of instructors in an intercultural context, were incorporated into the original 34-item CoI survey instrument. Thus, the revised version of the CoI instrument administered to the sample population contained 37 items.

Data Collection and Analysis for Phase 2

Data for the quantitative phase of this study (phase 2) was collected using the revised version of the CoI survey instrument (See Appendix B). The revised CoI instrument was administered to the same sample population during the months of August and September, 2011. However, only

9 participants ($N = 9$) out of 10 of the sample population responded to the questionnaire.

Ordinal responses were scored using a Likert-like scale that ranged from 1 to 5 (1 = strongly disagree, 2 = disagree, 3 = neutral, 4 = agree, 5 = strongly agree). To obtain frequency distributions, CoI survey questions were grouped in the following manner: (i) teaching presence indicators comprised 13 questions in the CoI survey instrument; (ii) social presence indicators comprised 9 questions in the CoI survey instrument; and (iii) cultural indicators comprised 3 questions that were incorporated into the CoI survey instrument after the qualitative analysis (questions 35, 36, and 37). Frequency distributions expressed as percentages were calculated according to the total number of respondents.

To calculate whether there was any degree of association among the variables, teaching presence, social presence, and cultural indicators, Spearman's rank correlation non-parametric measure was utilized. The null hypothesis was that there would be no association between the variables in the underlying population. It is also important to note that the Spearman's rank correlation test does not make any assumptions about the distribution.

RESULTS

For the sake of clarity, the reporting of results has been divided into two sections: *Qualitative Data Findings: Matrix Results*, and *Quantitative Data Findings: CoI Results*.

Qualitative Data Findings: Matrix Results

Analysis of survey responses yielded a variety of cultural indicators closely associated with the CoI elements. Figure 1 shows the frequency counts obtained for each cultural indicator when cross-referenced with the core elements of teaching presence and social presence and their respective sub-elements. Matrix cell shadings in a darker blue indicate obtained higher frequencies. Note that there is no information on how affective expression and group cohesion would play out when cross-referenced with the cultural indicators, because of how data was collected. These two components were not the focus of this study as the instructors reported mainly what they do and how they handle cross-cultural learners in the online environment. This is a limitation of the study. Further, there is little data to report on direct instruction. Low frequencies are shown scattered throughout 7 of the 10 cultural indicators. This is perhaps due to the way data was collected

Figure 1. Matrix coding query results

	A:SP-OC	B:SP-GC	C:SP-AE	D:TP-D	E:TP-DI	F:TP-F
1 : ACC	0	0	0	8	0	6
2 : ADAP	3	0	0	6	2	6
3 : ANT	0	0	0	0	2	4
4 : CON	1	0	0	7	3	3
5 : CSS	4	0	0	3	3	5
6 : ENC	4	0	1	0	0	7
7 : ID	4	0	0	2	1	6
8 : KOD	8	0	0	1	1	1
9 : PREV	1	0	0	3	4	6
10 : SOD	5	0	0	1	0	6
Total Frequency	30	0	1	31	16	53

focusing mainly on design and facilitation issues. Thus, these elements are worthy of more studies.

Cultural Indicators and Teaching Presence

Design

Garrison (2011) indicates that "design refers to structural decisions made before the process begins, while organization refers to similar decisions that are made to adjust to changes during the educational transaction (i.e., *in situ* design)" (p. 57). The cultural indicators accommodation (ACC) and contextualization (CON) appear to significantly impact teaching presence – design with a total reported frequency of respectively 8 and 7 for both datasets. The cultural indicator ACC refers to if and in what ways instructors adapt curricula and activities to cater to the needs of students from other cultures. CON means the instructor takes into account specific cultural factors such as language barriers, gender issues, salutation issues, religious issues, technological issues, etc. when adapting curricula and activities. It is important to highlight that instructors were not asked on the AMEQ instrument to indicate whether they designed the courses they taught. Notwithstanding, based on instructors' responses it appears that instructors have the liberty of modifying or adapting instructional material and activities whenever necessary.

In regards to the cultural indicator ACC, findings revealed that three instructors adapted curricula and instructional activities to cater to the needs of culturally diverse students, one instructor would modify assignments to align with the student's context and four instructors stated that although they did not design instructional activities for non-Canadian cultures, learners were free to apply the instructional material to their own personal context or culture. Instructors were also asked in what ways they adapted curricula and activities to cater to the needs of cross-cultural students. Answers ranged from changing the language in which they posted their responses so that it would be more cross-cultural and choosing more culturally "neutral" assignments to incorporating international cultural examples throughout the courses they teach. Learners are also encouraged to bring examples from their own cultural realities in the online discussions.

In relation to the cultural indicator CON when cross-referenced with teaching presence – design, data showed that three instructors are sensitive to and take into account religious and demographic issues when adapting curricula and activities; two instructors take into account the gender of the student and five instructors take into account language limitations and barriers.

Although adaptation (ADAP) correlated more highly with teaching presence – facilitation, it appears to also impact the teaching presence – design construct with a reported frequency of 6. ADAP refers to the ability of the instructors to adapt to the concerns and expectations of culturally diverse learners. In regards to technology limitations, data for ADAP showed that three instructors regularly consult with the class to establish synchronous sessions, are more flexible in relation to assignment deadlines, and/or provide alternative communication modes to cater to cross-cultural students' needs.

Facilitation

Instructor facilitation of reflection and discourse to build understanding is just as central to the online learning experience as it is to the face-to-face learning environment. It is within this sub-element of teaching presence that interest, engagement, and learning converge (Garrison, 2011). The highest frequency count for both datasets was observed in the sub-element teaching presence – facilitation (53). This fact was not surprising since the majority of the respondents stated they did not design specific instructional activities for cross-cultural learners. Thus, effective facilitation strategies can compensate for the lack of a proper design when dealing with cross-cultural learners. Findings demonstrated that the cultural indicators that appeared to correlate highly with facilitation were as follows: adaptation (ADAP) with a frequency of 9, encouragement (ENC) with a frequency of 7, and the cultural indicators accommodation (ACC), identification (ID), prevention (PREV), and support of diversity (SOD) with an equal total reported frequency of 6.

ADAP, as mentioned in the previous section, refers to the ability of the instructors to adapt to the concerns and expectations of culturally diverse learners. Instructor responses for ADAP in regards to teaching presence – facilitation include the following: deciding on the appropriate choice of technology for international students, being flexible in relation to what the learner needs to achieve from a particular assignment, being flexible in due dates, acquiring knowledge on culturally diverse student populations, promoting collaborative work between students from different cultures, and making adaptations or modifications in assignments based on the personal requirements and needs of the learners.

The cultural indicator encouragement (ENC) relates to whether instructors encourage cross-cultural collaborative engagement. Data for ENC revealed that eight instructors agreed that promoting cross-cultural collaborative engagement was important in the online environment.

ID means the instructor is able to identify solutions to possible online cultural clashes. Findings for ID indicated that only four instructors were able to identify solutions to possible online cultural clashes in addition to presenting solutions to remedy these cultural clashes.

PREV signifies the instructor is able to take preventative measures to lessen or relieve learner difficulties. The cultural indicator PREV, as reported by instructors, includes developing assignments and exams to be understood by all, checking the "user profile" in Moodle and the "welcome forum" to detect potential cultural or language difficulties,

offering extra support to students with language proficiency problems, encouraging students with language limitations to proofread their work, and checking language issues to make amendments as appropriate. Interestingly, instructors seem to be able to anticipate (ANT) more readily language proficiency problems but not specific cultural differences and problems.

Finally, SOD occurs when instructors encourage online learners to assimilate and accept the perspective of ethnic and cultural groups different from their own. Data for SOD reinforces the notion that instructors not only support diversity but also foster cross-cultural collaboration.

Cultural Indicators and Social Presence

Open Communication

Open communication is vital to establishing learner trust and acceptance of questioning in an online community of inquiry. Moreover, being able to communicate effectively across cultures is paramount in achieving intercultural competence (Liaw, 2006). Eight of the 10 cultural indicators appear to impact the sub-element social presence – open communication with a total reported frequency of 30 for both datasets. The cultural indicator knowledge of diversity (KOD) ranked in first place for the sub-element open communication (8 frequencies). KOD indicates the instructor is able to identify ways in which culturally diverse learners contribute to the online learning community and environment.

In practice what this means is that 50% of the instructors not only value the different perspectives and experiences of culturally diverse learners because it enhances their learning experience but also agree that these different perspectives contribute to the overall quality of the online discussions. These findings are important because as Garrison (2011) maintains, "a sense of isolation or of not being connected will not encourage or support critical inquiry" (p. 92). Hence, the more cross-cultural

Table 3. Percentage of agreement/disagreement per indicator

	Strongly disagree (1)	Disagree (2)	Neutral (3)	Agree (4)	Strongly agree (5)	No answer	Not displayed
Frequency distribution of Likert-type scale for questions of the Teaching Presence Indicators **Data expressed as count (percentage)**							
Q02	0 (0)	0 (0)	3 (33)	0 (0)	6 (67)	0 (0)	0 (0)
Q05	0 (0)	0 (0)	0 (0)	0 (0)	9 (100)	0 (0)	0 (0)
Q07	0 (0)	0 (0)	0 (0)	6 (67)	3 (33)	0 (0)	0 (0)
Q08	0 (0)	0 (0)	0 (0)	6 (67)	3 (33)	0 (0)	0 (0)
Q09	0 (0)	0 (0)	0 (0)	6 (67)	3 (33)	0 (0)	0 (0)
Q10	0 (0)	0 (0)	0 (0)	3 (33)	3 (33)	0 (0)	3 (33)
Q14	0 (0)	0 (0)	0 (0)	6 (67)	3 (33)	0 (0)	0 (0)
Q15	0 (0)	0 (0)	0 (0)	6 (67)	3 (33)	0 (0)	0 (0)
Q20	0 (0)	0 (0)	0 (0)	3 (33)	6 (67)	0 (0)	0 (0)
Q22	0 (0)	0 (0)	3 (33)	3 (33)	3 (33)	0 (0)	0 (0)
Q24	0 (0)	0 (0)	0 (0)	3 (33)	6 (67)	0 (0)	0 (0)
Q29	0 (0)	0 (0)	3 (33)	0 (0)	6 (67)	0 (0)	0 (0)
Q33	0 (0)	0 (0)	0 (0)	6 (67)	3 (33)	0 (0)	0 (0)
Frequency distribution of Likert-type scale for questions of the Social Presence Indicators **Data expressed as count (percentage)**							
	Strongly disagree (1)	Disagree (2)	Neutral (3)	Agree (4)	Strongly agree (5)	No answer	Not displayed
Q06	0 (0)	3 (33)	0 (0)	6 (67)	0 (0)	0 (0)	0 (0)
Q11	0 (0)	0 (0)	3 (33)	6 (67)	0 (0)	0 (0)	0 (0)
Q19	0 (0)	0 (0)	0 (0)	6 (67)	0 (0)	0 (0)	3 (33)
Q23	0 (0)	0 (0)	0 (0)	6 (67)	3 (33)	0 (0)	0 (0)
Q25	0 (0)	0 (0)	3 (33)	0 (0)	3 (33)	0 (0)	3 (33)
Q26	0 (0)	0 (0)	0 (0)	6 (67)	3 (33)	0 (0)	0 (0)
Q27	0 (0)	0 (0)	3 (33)	6 (67)	0 (0)	0 (0)	0 (0)
Q31	0 (0)	0 (0)	0 (0)	6 (67)	3 (33)	0 (0)	0 (0)
Q34	0 (0)	0 (0)	0 (0)	6 (67)	3 (33)	0 (0)	0 (0)
Frequency distribution of Likert-type scale for questions of the Incorporated Cultural Indicators **Data expressed as count (percentage)**							
	Strongly disagree (1)	Disagree (2)	Neutral (3)	Agree (4)	Strongly agree (5)	No answer	Not displayed
Q35	0 (0)	3 (33)	0 (0)	6 (67)	0 (0)	0 (0)	0 (0)
Q36	0 (0)	3 (33)	0 (0)	3 (33)	3 (33)	0 (0)	0 (0)
Q37	0 (0)	0 (0)	0 (0)	6 (67)	3 (33)	0 (0)	0 (0)

learners are encouraged to project their individual personalities in an environment that respectfully acknowledges their cultural differences, the less isolated they will feel.

Quantitative Data Findings: CoI Results

Data analysis of the frequency distributions of the teaching presence questions in the CoI survey instrument showed that 52% of the respondents agreed and 43% of the respondents strongly agreed with the 13 teaching presence indicators. Frequency distributions for social presence questions revealed that 68% of the respondents agreed, 14% strongly agreed, 14% were neutral, and 4% disagreed with the 9 indicators for social presence. Lastly, results of the frequency distributions for the three incorporated cultural indicator questions to the CoI survey instrument showed that 45% of the respondents agreed, 40% strongly agreed, 7% were neutral, and 7% disagreed. Table 3 shows the percentage of agreement or disagreement to the indicators for teaching presence, social presence, and incorporated cultural indicators. To aid understanding of data, corresponding question numbers for each indicator have been provided.

Spearman's rank correlation test was conducted to determine the degree of correlation among the ordinal variables: teaching presence, social presence, and cultural indicators. Table 4 presents the data results for Spearman's rank correlation test ($N = 9$).

Results for Spearman's rank correlation test showed that there was a high degree of correlation between the cultural indicators and the teaching presence indicators ($0,86\ r_s$). When r_s is high (close to 1) it means that the two variables are strongly correlated. The degree of correlation between the cultural indicators and indicators for social presence was good but a bit more moderate ($0,73\ r_s$). Findings demonstrate that the variables have a strong relationship, indicating that the cultural indicator is first an artifact of teaching presence, and also a concept that relates to social presence.

DISCUSSION

This study aimed to elucidate how instructors accommodate and make provisions for cross-cultural learners in an online community of learning. The findings of this study provided three insights: (i) there is evidence that 10 cultural indicators appear to impact and span across all three teaching presence categories, some to a higher degree than others; (ii) effective facilitation and open communication strategies aimed at building trust and improving cross-cultural relationships in a learning community are crucial factors in establishing a successful online community of learning; and (iii) high and good degrees of correlation between the cultural indicators and the indicators for teaching presence and social presence suggest the incorporated cultural indicators are in fact playing an additional role to these two presences as a result of an intercultural context for this sample group. The first insight is not surprising as several studies have emphasized the fact that teaching presence plays a central role in the development of a community of inquiry (Akyol & Garrison, 2008; Garrison et al. 2010). In regards to the second insight, Gunawardena and Lapointe (2007) have put forward that the greater the bond between participants (the greater the sense of social presence), the greater the ability to resolve conflict and adopt face-saving strategies. Consequently, these strategies and skills are pivotal especially in the lack of a design that caters to the needs of cross-cultural students.

The core components of intercultural competence espoused by Bennett, Nigle and Stage (1990) comprise knowledge of the culture and values of culturally diverse learners and skills to plan and provide for effective multicultural practices, espe-

Table 4. Data results for Spearman's rank correlation test

	Teaching Presence	Social Presence	Cultural Indicators
Teaching Presence	1,00	0,91	0,86
Social Presence	0,91	1,00	0,73
Cultural Indicators	0,86	0,73	1,00

cially in the absence of a culturally sensitive design and attitudes that minimize one's own prejudices and misconceptions in regards to cross-cultural students. Results from the qualitative dataset revealed that instructors appear to be quite cognizant of cultural diversity and have strong multicultural efficacy in terms of their knowledge of diversity and the strategies that they use to promote learning and prevent conflict. When design is lacking, instructors seem willing to alter it through use of facilitation activities that take into account cultural diversity in group work, encouraging learners to apply the course contents to their own personal contexts, and by encouraging multiple perspectives in online discussions. Open communication seems to be a strategy for promoting learning and preventing conflict as well. This strategy is of chief importance since the perception of an increased cultural gap among communicators may lead to a feeling of anxiety which may, in turn, result in increased miscommunication (Chase, Macfadyen, Reeder & Roche, 2002).

Results from the quantitative dataset indicated that most instructors are not only aware of the importance of design and organization in the CoI context, but also willing to make necessary adjustments to accommodate culturally diverse learners. Data also corroborates the notion that supporting interaction between culturally diverse learners via facilitation is a practice adopted by most respondents. Further, 56% of the respondents agreed that open communication enables learners to present themselves as culturally diverse. This is in line with Garrison's (2011) argument that "the design must be inherently flexible and adaptable to unpredictable and individual learning needs as they arise" (p. 87). In regards to the lower degree of correlation between the cultural indicators and the indicators for social presence, perhaps more roles that take into consideration an intercultural context might need to be added to this element so as to obtain a higher degree of correlation. More

studies will help clarify this issue. Finally, further studies conducted with larger samples and within different contexts will help validate this data.

FUTURE RESEARCH DIRECTIONS

This study presents a revised 37-item CoI instrument for dealing with cross-cultural students in an online community of practical inquiry. However, this research was exploratory in nature and future research should seek to expand and confirm these findings. The limitations of the study could be regarded as fruitful avenues for future research on multicultural engagement in distance education institutions that utilize the CoI model. First, a larger and more diverse sample should be used to test and validate the revised 37-item CoI survey instrument. More online or blended-learning higher education institutions in Canada and in other countries should be investigated to further clarify how instructors are accommodating and making provisions for cross-cultural learners using the CoI framework. Second, more studies are needed to examine more closely how the cultural indicators correlate and play out with the sub-elements of direct instruction, affective expression, and group cohesion. It would be worthwhile to develop an open-ended survey questionnaire that focused more on instructor actions in regard to these sub-elements and cross-reference them with the cultural indicators in order to elucidate their importance and impact when dealing with an intercultural context. Depending on findings, additional roles and indicators could be incorporated to these sub-elements in the CoI survey instrument. Third, further studies could investigate how cognitive presence and its four distinct phases may vary across culture, although the practical inquiry process is not amenable to cultural differences. While cognitive presence was not included in this study because it was not considered the first point of consideration in instructional differences, the way it emerges as cognitive presence in the practical inquiry process may be unique and is worthy of additional studies. It would also be very interesting to explore to what extent the lack of a cross-cultural design impacts learner's critical discourse and meaningful, deep learning. Last but not least, it would be indispensable to obtain cross-cultural students perspectives and challenges as they relate to multicultural engagement in an online community of inquiry.

CONCLUSION

An online community of inquiry environment is a space where students from different countries and cultural backgrounds are afforded an opportunity to bond and learn regardless of place and time. The concept of community as applied to education implies that who we are as social beings drives learning and that the social aspects of learning are the most important factors in establishing a sense of belonging (Pallof & Pratt, 2007). Asynchronous online text-based discussions have the potential to promote deep knowledge and higher-level thinking skills for learners. In addition, asynchronous text-based discussions offer students additional time for research and considered response in addition to encouraging reflection (Redmond, 2010). However, the achievement of such goals cannot be realized to its fullest potential without careful pedagogical planning and support that takes into account cultural diversity. When teaching courses in these communities of inquiry, educators need to rethink their mindset in relation to culturally diverse learners and adopt instructional practices that cater to the needs of such populations (Farmer, 2010).

This study has revealed that instructor intercultural competence in the form of efficacious fa-cilitation and open communications strategies can compensate for the lack of an instructional design that is culturally oriented and inclusive. Moreover, this study has produced a revised 37-item CoI survey instrument informed by professionals in the field. Therefore, it makes a contribution to the literature by illustrating how instructors are accommodating and making provisions for cross-cultural learners in the CoI framework and by proposing a revised CoI survey instrument that takes into account an online intercultural teaching and learning environment. Teaching and social presence in this context needs to be flexible to adapt to multiple needs and limitations of cross-cultural students.

The objective of the proposed revised CoI survey instrument is to raise awareness of and appreciation for cultural diversity in addition to providing indicators aimed at measuring instructor multicultural efficacy. The goal is to persuade higher education institutions and educators to acknowledge the necessity for such cultural considerations when using the CoI framework. Those institutions that offer global e-learning must consider the varying cultural backgrounds of their learners to offer customized value-added higher education. As an increasing number of online higher education institutions tap into new global education markets, research into the potential of existing distance education frameworks, such as the CoI framework, to address effectively cross-cultural aspects, is not only necessary but also imperative to the survival and propagation of such teaching and learning transactional theories. In sum, expansion of the CoI model will ensure its effectiveness and success in global education markets.

REFERENCES

Akyol, Z., & Garrison, D. R. (2008). The development of a community of inquiry over time in an online course: Understanding the progression and integration of social, cognitive and teaching presence. *Journal of Asynchronous Learning Networks, 12* (3-4), 3-22. Retrieved March 28, 2011, from http://eric.ed.gov/PDFS/EJ837483.pdf

Arbaugh, J. B., & Benbunan-Fich, R. (2006). Separating the effects of knowledge construction and group collaboration in learning outcomes of web-based courses. *Information & Management, 43*(6), 778–793. doi:10.1016/j.im.2005.09.001

Arbaugh, J. B., Cleveland-Innes, M., Diaz, S., Garrison, D. R., Ice, P., & Richardson, J. C. (2008). Developing a community of inquiry instrument: testing a measure of the Community of Inquiry framework using a multi-institutional sample. *The Internet and Higher Education, 1,* 133–136. Elsevier Inc. doi:10.1016/j.iheduc.2008.06.003

Banks, J. A., Cookson, P., Gay, G., Hawley, W. D., Irvine, J. J., & Nieto, S. … Stephan, W. G. (2001). *Diversity within unity: Essential principles for teaching and learning in a multicultural society.* Center for Multicultural Education, University of Washington. Retrieved July 6, 2010 from http://education.washington.edu/cme/DiversityUnity.pdf

Basit, T. N. (2003). Manual or electronic? The role of coding in qualitative data analysis. *Educational Research, 45*(2), 143–154. doi:10.1080/0013188032000133548

Bates, A. W., & Gpe, J. (1997). Crossing boundaries: making global distance education a reality. *Journal of Distance Education, 12*(1/2), 49–66.

Bennett, C., Niggle, T., & Stage, F. (1990). Preservice multicultural teacher education: Predictors of student readiness. *Teaching and Teacher Education, 6*(3), 243–254. doi:10.1016/0742-051X(90)90016-X

Chase, M., Macfadyen, L., Reeder, K., & Roche, J. (2002). Intercultural challenges in networked learning: hard technologies meet soft skills. *First Monday, 7*(8), 1-22. doi: 10.1.1.131.9140

Creswell, J. W., & Plano Clark, V. L. (2007). *Designing and conducting mixed methods research.* New Delhi, India: Sage Publications, Inc.

Edmundson, A. (Ed.). (2007). *Globalized e-learning cultural challenges.* Hershey, PA: Information Science Publishing.

Edmundson, A. (2009). *Culturally accessible e-learning: An overdue global business imperative.* The American Society for Training and Development. Retrieved May 24, 2010, from http://www.astd.org/LC/2009/0509_edmundson.htm

Farmer, L. S. J. (2010). Culturally-sensitive e-learning practices for teacher education. In C. D. Maddux, D. Gibson, & B. Dodge (Eds.), *Research Highlights in Technology and Teacher Education 2010* (pp. 203-210). Society for Information Technology & Teacher Education (SITE).

Finegold, A. R. D., & Cooke, L. (2006). Exploring the attitudes, experiences and dynamics of interaction in online groups. *Internet and Higher Education, 9*(3), 201–215. Retrieved March 28, 2011, from http://hdl.handle.net/2134/3279

Garrison, D. R. Cleveland- Innes, M., Koole, M., & Kappleman, J. (2006). Revisiting methodological issues in transcript analysis: negotiated coding and reliability. *Internet and Higher Education, 9*(2006), 1 -8. Retrieved August 9, 2011, from http://auspace.athabascau.ca:8080/dspace/bitstream/2149/611/1/sdarticle.pdf

Garrison, D. R. (2011). *E-learning in the 21st century: A framework for research and practice* (2nd ed.). London, UK: Routledge, Taylor & Francis Group.

Garrison, D. R., Anderson, T., & Archer, W. (2000). Critical inquiry in a text-based environment: Computer conferencing in higher education. *The Internet and Higher Education, 2*(2-3), 87-105. Retrieved May 24, 2010, from http://hdl.handle.net/2149/739

Garrison, D. R., Cleveland-Innes, M., & Fung, T. S. (2010). Exploring causal relationships among teaching, cognitive and social presence: Students perceptions of the community of inquiry framework. *The Internet and Higher Education, 13,* 31–36. doi:10.1016/j.iheduc.2009.10.002

Gilbert, P. K., & Dabbagh, N. (2005). How to structure online discussions for a meaningful discourse: A case study. *British Journal of Educational Technology, 36*(1), 5-18. Retrieved March 28, 2011, from http://ritv.les.inf.puc-rio.br/groupware/temp/denise/071212/structured.foruns_j.1467-8535.2005.00434.pdf

Gunawardena, C., & Lapointe, D. (2007). Cultural dynamics of online learning. In Moore, M. G. (Ed.), *Handbook of distance education* (2nd ed., pp. 593–607). Mahwah, NJ: Lawrence Erlbaum Associates.

Gunawardena, C., Wilson, P. L., & Nolla, A. C. (2003). Culture and online education. In Moore, M. G., & Anderson, W. G. (Eds.), *Handbook of distance education* (pp. 753–775). Mahwah, NJ: Lawrence Erlbaum Associations.

Guyton, E. M., & Wesche, M. V. (2005). The multicultural efficacy scale: Development, item selection, and reliability. *Multicultural Perspectives, 7*(4), 21–29. doi:10.1207/s15327892mcp0704_4

Harasim, L. (2002). What makes online learning communities successful? The role of collaborative learning in social and intellectual development. In Vrasidas, C., & Glass, G. V. (Eds.), *Distance Education and Distributed Learning* (pp. 181–200). Greenwich, CT: Information Age Publishing.

Harrington, H. L., & Hathaway, R. S. (1994). Computer conferencing, critical reflection, and teacher development. *Teaching & Teacher Education, 10*(5), 543- 554. Retrieved July 19, 2010, from http://deepblue.lib.umich.edu/bitstream/2027.42/31371/1/0000284.pdf

Hewling, A. (2005). Culture in the online class: Using message analysis to look beyond nationality-based frames of reference. *Journal of Computer-Mediated Communication, 11*(1), 16. doi:10.1111/j.1083-6101.2006.tb00316.x

Jackson, K. M., & Trochim, W. M. K. (2002). Concept mapping as an alternative approach for the analysis of open-ended survey responses. *Organizational Research Methods, 5*(4), 307–336. doi:10.1177/109442802237114

Liaw, M.-L. (2006). E-learning and the development of intercultural competence. *Language Learning & Technology, 10*(3), 49-64. doi: 10.1.1.110.1555.

Lim, D. H. (2004). Cross cultural differences in online learning motivation. *Educational Media International, 41*(2), 163–175. doi:10.1080/09523980410001685784

Matsumoto, D. (1996). *Culture and psychology.* Pacific Grove, CA: Brooks/Cole Publishing Company.

McIssac, M. (2002). Online learning from an international perspective. *Education Media International.* Online © 2002 International Council for Education Media. doi: 10.1080/09523980210131196

Moore, M. (2006). Editorial: Questions of culture. *American Journal of Distance Education, 20*(1), 1–5. doi:10.1207/s15389286ajde2001_1

Morgan, T. (2011). Online classroom or community-in-the-making? Instructor conceptualizations and teaching presence in international online contexts. *The Journal of Distance Education, 25*(1), 1-15. Retrieved March 24, 2011, from http://www.jofde.ca/index.php/jde/article/view/721/1190

Morse, K. (2003). Does one size fit all? Exploring asynchronous learning in a multicultural environment. *The Journal of Asynchronous Learning Networks, 7*(1). Retrieved May 24, 2010, from citeseerx.ist.psu.edu/viewdoc/download *doi:10.1.1.138.6050.*

Pallof, R. M., & Pratt, K. (2007). *Building online learning communities* (2nd ed.). San Francisco, CA: Jossey-Bass.

Parrish, P., & Linder-VanBerschot, J. A. (2010). Cultural dimensions of learning: Addressing the challenges of multicultural instruction. *International Review of Research in Open and Distance Learning, 11*(2). Retrieved May 28, 2010 from http://www.irrodl.org/index.php/irrodl

Redmond, P. (2010). Investigating the use of online discussions in an undergraduate face-to-face course (pp. 27 – 33). In C. D. Maddux, D. Gibson, & B. Dodge (Eds.), *Research Highlights in Technology and Teacher Education 2010* (pp. 27-33). Society for Information Technology & Teacher Education (SITE).

Shattuck, K. (2005). *Cultures meeting cultures in online distance education: Perceptions of international adult learners of the impact of culture when taking online distance education courses designed and delivered by an American university.* Unpublished doctoral dissertation, The Pennsylvania State University, University Park.

Shea, P., Li, C. S., & Picket, A. (2006). A study of teaching presence and student sense of learning community in fully online and web-enhanced college courses. Retrieved March 28, 2011, from http://gpc.edu/~onlineis/teaching_presence.pdf. *The Internet and Higher Education, 9*, 175–190. Retrieved March 28, 2011 doi:10.1016/j.iheduc.2006.06.005

Strauss, A., & Corbin, J. (1998). *Basics of qualitative research: Techniques and procedures for developing grounded theory*. Thousand Oaks, CA: Sage Publications.

Tu, C.-H. (2000). On-line learning migration: From social learning theory to social presence theory in a CMC environment. *Journal of Network and Computer Applications, 2*, 27–37. doi:10.1006/jnca.1999.0099

Uzner, S. (2009). Questions of culture in distance learning: A research review. *International Review of Research in Open and Distance Learning, 10*(3).

Wang, C. M., & Reeves, T. C. (2007). The meaning of culture in online education: Implications for teaching, learning, and design. In Edmundson, A. (Ed.), *Globalized e-learning cultural challenges* (pp. 1–17). Hershey, PA: Information Science.

Zawacki-Richter, O., Bäcker, E. M., & Vogt, S. (2009). Review of distance education research (2000 to 2008). Analysis of research areas, methods, and authorship patterns. *International Review of Research in Open and Distance Learning, 10*(6), 1-30. Retrieved June 14, 2010, from http://www.irrodl.org/index.php/irrodl/article/view/741/1461

Zhang, Z., & Kenny, R. F. (2010). Learning in an online distance education course: Experiences of three international students. *International Review of Research in Open and Distance Learning, 11*(1).

Zhao, N., & McDougall, D. (2008). Cultural influences on Chinese students' asynchronous online learning in a Canadian university. *Journal of Distance Education, 22*(2).

KEY TERMS AND DEFINITIONS

Adapted Multicultural Efficacy Questionnaire (AMEQ): A tool comprising 15 open-ended survey questions geared toward assessing instructor perceived multicultural efficacy in teaching cross-cultural online students. Adapted from the MES framework.

Asynchronous: Asynchronous online learning, the opposite of synchronous, means that communication occurs at different times. Time delay allows participants to respond at a different time from when the message is sent. Interactions in this mode of delivery are mainly text-based (Moore & Kearsley, 2005).

Computer Mediated Communication CMC: Threaded forum group discussions that address specific questions, tasks, problems, or other mediating artifacts posed by the instructor or other students that require reflection. CMC in this context has the ability to support a truly collaborative learning experience at a distance, independent of time or space.

Cognitive Presence: The extent to which learners are able to construct and confirm meaning through course activities, sustained reflection, and discourse (Garrison, Anderson, & Archer, 2000).

Community of Inquiry Framework: A theoretical distance education model that consists of three overlapping presences (social, cognitive, and teaching). The model "is grounded in a collaborative constructivist view of higher education and assumes that effective online learning requires the development of a community" (Rovai, 2002; Shea, 2006 as cited in Swan, 2010, p. 122). The main objective of the model is to foster deep meaningful learning in an online community of learners.

Constructivism: A philosophy of teaching and learning based on the principle that individuals construct meaning and understanding as they experience and engage the world. "Learning is viewed as a process of creating and adjusting mental models to accommodate new experiences" (Swan, 2010, p. 127).

Cross Cultural: Interaction among individuals from different cultures. The term cross-cultural is generally used to describe comparative studies of cultures. Intercultural has the same meaning and is used interchangeably. (http://www.dot-connect.com/Dictionary_of_Cross-Cultural_terminology_Inter_cultural_terminology.html).

Culture: For the purpose of this study culture is defined as "the set of attitudes, values, beliefs, and behaviors shared by a group of people, but different for each individual, communicated from one generation to the next" (Matsumoto, 1996, p. 16).

E-Learning: Broadly defined as the use of computer technology, primarily over an intranet or through the Internet, to deliver information and instruction to individuals. (Welsh, Wanberg, Brown & Simmering, 2003).

MES Framework: A tool developed to measure teacher multicultural efficacy in multicultural environments "along with the multicultural teacher education dimensions of intercultural experiences, minority group knowledge, attitudes about diversity, and knowledge of teaching skills in multicultural settings" (Guyton & Wesche, 2005, p. 23). Guyton & Wesche (2005) conducted a pilot study with a total of 665 undergraduate and graduate teacher education students from several geographic regions across the United States. The MES was finalized as a 35-instrument scale, with subscales for experience, attitude, efficacy, and instructors' views on multicultural teaching (Guyton & Wesche, 2005). Both the confirmatory factor analysis and reliability analysis have attested to the usefulness of the MES as an instrument to research multicultural teacher education.

Multiculturalism: A belief or policy that endorses the principle of cultural diversity of different cultural and ethnic groups so that they retain distinctive cultural identities. The term multiculturalism is also used to refer to strategies and measures intended to promote diversity (http://www.dot-connect.com/Dictionary_of_Cross-

Cultural_terminology_Inter_cultural_terminology.html).

Social Presence: The ability of participants in a community of inquiry "to identify with a group, communicate purposefully in a trusting environment, and develop personal and affective relationships progressively by way of projecting their individual personalities" (Garrison, 2009b as cited in Garrison, 2011, p.23).

Teaching Presence: "The design, facilitation, and direction of cognitive and social processes for the purpose of realizing personally meaningful and educationally worthwhile learning outcomes" (Anderson, Rourke, Garrison & Archer, 2001 as cited in Garrison, 2011, p. 24).

Text-Based Communication: The use of written communication for teaching and learning purposes in e-learning. Text-based communication is the primary mode of communication in asynchronous computer-mediated conferencing. Text-based communication facilitates critical discourse and reflection and supports collaborative, constructivist approaches to learning (Garrison & Anderson, 2003).

APPENDIX A

Online Survey 1- Adapted Multicultural Efficacy Questionnaire (AMEQ)

Demographic Information

TO THE RESPONDER: The demographic information requested is necessary for the research process. Completion of these items is mandatory for the research process since data obtained in Online Survey 1 will be compared to that of the Online Survey 2. However, participants may opt out from answering any questions. Please rest assured that this information and all your responses on this questionnaire will be kept **strictly confidential**. Data will be reported in such a way that identification of individuals will be impossible.

Token ID #: _____

Gender (Check one): _____Male _____Female

Age (Check one group):

_____under 25

_____25 to 34

_____35 to 44

_____45 to 54

_____55 to 64

_____65 to 74

_____ over 75

Are there students participating in your course(s) who are culturally distinct from the mainstream Canadian culture? (Check one): _____Yes_____No

What is your cultural background? Cultural background in this context refers to what group you identify most in terms of activities, beliefs, and customs.

Questionnaire

Please provide complete answers to the questions that follow.

Definition of terms:

a. The term "culture" is defined here as "the set of attitudes, values, beliefs, and behaviors shared by a group of people, but different for each individual" (Matsumoto, 1996, p.16).

b. *Cross-cultural online engagement is defined in this study* as interaction between individuals from different cultures in an asynchronous text-based Computer Mediated Communication (CMC) online environment. *For this particular study, individuals from different cultures fall into two categories: 1) foreign or international students enrolled who may or may not be currently living in Canada but were born in another country and whose native language is notably not English and 2) students enrolled whose native language is not English and they identify with a culturally distinct group (e.g., Aboriginals, French Canadians, or a new immigrant group now residing in Canada).*

1. In the online courses you teach, do you usually adapt curricula and instructional activities to cater to the needs of students from other cultures?
2. In what ways do you adapt curricula and activities to cater to the needs of students from other cultures?
3. What specific cultural factors or issues do you take into account? If not, why not?
4. In your online lesson plans, do you develop or incorporate activities that are designed to promote the success of cross-cultural or international learners studying online? In what ways?
5. Do you find it important to encourage cross-cultural learners to work collaboratively with mainstream Canadian culture learners? Please explain why or why not.
6. Are you able to anticipate certain learning difficulties an online cross-cultural learner might have to face during the course?
7. If so, what actions or preventative measures do you take before the semester begins and during the semester to lessen or relieve these difficulties? If not, why not?
8. Studies have revealed that the inability to understand specific cultural references, language barriers, and/or limitations, the inability to question authority (instructors or peers), differing emotional needs, time zone limitations, and technological limitations are just some of the factors that hinder successful online learning (Zhao & McDougall, 2008; Uzner, 2009; Zhang & Kenny, 2010). Taking these facts into consideration, are you able to adapt to the expectations and concerns of culturally diverse learners in the online learning environment?
9. Cultural clashes in the online environment may arise from learners having attitudes, values, and beliefs that differ from the mainstream Canadian population and/or from learners having to deal with instructional material or curricula that do not speak to them. Are you usually able to identify solutions to problems that arise from possible cultural clashes in this teaching setting? If so, please explain the measures taken to remedy or alleviate existing cultural clashes.
10. Does the lack of face-to-face interaction tend to increase or decrease potential online cultural clashes in the online learning environment? In what ways?
11. Are you able to identify ways in which culturally diverse groups contribute in a different way than other, non-diverse students to the online learning community and environment?
12. Do you encourage your online students to assimilate and accept the perspective of ethnic and cultural groups different from their own? If so, in what ways?
13. Can you identify any institutional policies and practices that may harm or adversely impact the educational outcomes of online learners? Conversely, can you identify any policies that are culturally uplifting? If so, please state which ones.
14. The Community of inquiry framework is a theoretical distance education model that consists of three overlapping presences: social, cognitive, and teaching. The model "is grounded in a collaborative constructivist view of higher education and assumes that effective online learning requires the development of a community" (Rovai, 2002; Shea, 2006 as cited in Swan, 2010, p. 122). The main objective of the model is to foster deep meaningful learning in an online community of learners. Researchers believe that all three presences are equally important in promoting higher-order learning based on reflective and collaborative discourse. How do you think cultural presence would fit in this grouping?
15. Please use the space below to add any other additional comments or statements regarding cross-cultural engagement in the asynchronous text-based CMC online educational context.

"When you press the SUBMIT button, your data will be included in the study. If you decide to withdraw after submitting simply contact Viviane Vladimirschi (vladimirschi@uol.com.br), and provide your participation identifier. Your data will then be destroyed and will not be included within the study."

Note: Adapted from Guyton, E.M. & Wesche, M.V. (2005). The multicultural efficacy scale: development, item selection, and reliability. *Multicultural Perspectives*, 7 (4), 21-29. Lawrence Erlbaum Associates, Inc.

APPENDIX B

Online Survey 2- Revised Community of Inquiry Survey Instrument

1. Students in this course can describe ways to test and apply the knowledge created in this course.
2. My actions reinforced the development of a sense of community among course participants.
3. Students in this course are motivated to explore content-related questions.
4. Course activities piqued students' curiosity.
5. I clearly communicated important due dates/time frames for learning activities.
6. Students in this course are able to form distinct impressions of some other course participants.
7. I clearly communicated important course goals.
8. I provided feedback in a timely fashion.
9. I provided feedback that helped students understand strengths and weaknesses relative to the course goals and objectives.
10. I helped to identify areas of agreement and disagreement on course topics that helped students to learn.
11. Students felt comfortable disagreeing with other course participants while still maintaining a sense of trust.
12. Reflection on course content and discussions helped students understand fundamental concepts in this class.
13. Online discussions were valuable in helping students appreciate different perspectives.
14. I encouraged course participants to explore new concepts in this course.
15. I clearly communicated important course topics.
16. Combining new information helped students answer questions raised in course activities.
17. Brainstorming and finding relevant information helped students resolve content related questions.
18. Learning activities helped students construct explanations/solutions.
19. Students felt his/her point of view was acknowledged by other course participants.
20. I keep the course participants on task in a way that helps students to learn.
21. Students utilized a variety of information sources to explore problems posed in this course.
22. I keep course participants engaged and participating in productive dialogue.
23. Students felt comfortable interacting with other course participants.
24. I provided clear instructions on how to participate in course learning activities.
25. Getting to know other course participants gave students a sense of belonging in the course.
26. Students felt comfortable conversing through the online medium.

27. Online or web-based communication is an excellent medium for social interaction.
28. Problems posed increased student interest in course issues.
29. I helped to focus discussion on relevant issues in a way that helped students to learn.
30. Students can apply the knowledge created in this course to his/her work or other non-class related activities.
31. Students felt comfortable participating in the course discussions.
32. Students developed solutions to course problems that can be applied in practice.
33. I was helpful in guiding the class toward understanding course topics in a way that helped students clarify their thinking.
34. Online discussions helped students to develop a sense of collaboration.
35. I allowed for adjustments to the design and organization when necessary to accommodate cultural diversity.
36. I supported interaction among culturally diverse learners.
37. Open communication in this community allows for culturally diverse presentation.

Five point Likert-type scale
1 = strongly disagree, 2 = disagree, 3 = neutral, 4 = agree, 5 = strongly agree

Note: From Arbaugh, J. B., Cleveland-Innes, M., Diaz, S., Garrison, D. R., Ice, P, Richardson, J. C., Shea, P., & Swan, K. (2008). Developing a community of inquiry instrument: testing a measure of the Community of Inquiry framework using a multi-institutional sample. *The Internet and Higher Education. 11*(2008), 133-136. © 2008 Elsevier Inc. Adapted with permission.

Chapter 24
Developing Communities of Inquiry in Online Courses:
A Design–Based Approach

Daniel Matthews
University of Illinois Springfield, USA

Leonard Bogle
University of Illinois Springfield, USA

Emily Boles
University of Illinois Springfield, USA

Scott Day
University of Illinois Springfield, USA

Karen Swan
University of Illinois Springfield, USA

ABSTRACT

This chapter reports on ongoing design-based research being conducted in the fully online Master of Arts in Teacher Leadership (MTL) program at the University of Illinois Springfield. After an initial Quality Matters (QM) review and redesign, semester-to-semester implementation issues identified by the Community of Inquiry (CoI) survey form the basis for ongoing course improvements. Preliminary results from a four-semester iterative redesign of one course demonstrated the efficacy of using this design-based process for significantly improving learning outcomes. Currently, departmental faculty are collaborating on the redesign of all core courses in the MTL program using a similar process guided by an initial QM redesign followed by iterative and incremental changes driven by CoI survey results.

DOI: 10.4018/978-1-4666-2110-7.ch024

INTRODUCTION

This chapter reports on the authors' experiences with a program-wide, multi-semester online course improvement project that is driven primarily by the Community of Inquiry framework. While originally conceived as a one-semester, quasi-experimental test of the revision of a single course in the fall of 2009, the project evolved into a design experiment which will continue at least through 2012 and involves all core courses in a graduate program in teacher leadership.

In this chapter, we will describe our original research and how our results caused us to change our approach from a single course redesign effort to an ongoing redesign based on student perceptions of learning processes as reflected on the Community of Inquiry (CoI) survey. We will further describe how we are expanding our efforts to include the core courses in our fully online MTL program, and provide recommendations for others who would similarly pursue program-wide improvements in student learning outcomes.

BACKGROUND

This chapter reflects on our experiences in using an iterative, collaborative, theory-based and data-driven approach to improving online courses based on student perceptions of social, teaching and cognitive presence. Across several semesters of recursive modifications to online graduate courses in the MTL program, we came to situate our improvement efforts within a design experiment perspective. Specifically, we applied a design-based approach to fully online courses and used the Community of Inquiry (CoI) framework as a theoretical compass to guide iterative course modifications.

We are not the first to use the Community of Inquiry framework as a conceptual guide for program-wide change (see, for example, Bogle, Cook, Day, & Swan, 2009, and Vaughan & Gar-

rison, 2006). Our project builds on that earlier program-level work, with some important implementation and methodological differences. The redesign project described in this chapter is within a fully online program; the work described by Bogle, Cook, Day and Swan and by Vaughan and Garrison was done within blended programs. In addition, the redesign project we describe in this chapter was a faculty-initiated grassroots effort by program faculty, with no university-wide initiative providing a catalyst for this ongoing course improvement work. Perhaps most importantly, our work is guided not just conceptually by the Community of Inquiry framework; it is directly and repeatedly informed by course-level CoI survey data. We thus use theoretically-derived empirical evidence from our online courses to guide their redesign.

When we began the project, we had planned no further than to do what we assumed would be a one-time, quasi-experimental pre-post study in the fall semester of 2009 to explore the effects of a single course redesign. The initial revisions made were based on a Quality Matters (Quality Matters, 2005) review of an Educational Research Methods course. We sought to measure the effects of the revisions, not just on learning outcomes, but also on learning processes as measured by the Community of Inquiry (CoI) survey (Swan, Richardson, Ice, Garrison, Cleveland-Innes, & Arbaugh, 2008). We imagined that an improved course design would result immediately in improved learning processes and that improved learning processes would, in turn, support improved student outcomes.

Quality Matters Rubric

Quality Matters is a faculty-oriented, peer review process designed to assure quality in online courses and structured around a rubric (Appendix A) based on instructional design principles (Quality Matters, 2005; Shattuck, 2007). The rubric consists of 41 standards which are assigned point values of 1, 2, or 3, and are organized into eight categories --

course overview, learner objectives, assessment and measurement, instructional materials, learner interaction and engagement, course technology, learner support, and accessibility. Three reviewers assess whether or not a course meets or does not meet each of the standards. All three point standards, of which there are 21, as well as a minimum score must be met. Nine of the 21 essential (3 point) standards involve learning objectives.

Community of Inquiry Survey

The Community of Inquiry (CoI) survey (Appendix B), which is based on Garrison, Anderson, and Archer's (2000) Community of Inquiry framework, is designed to measure student perceptions of learning processes in online courses. The survey consists of 34 statements related to the three presences – teaching, social, and cognitive – that the CoI model identifies as collectively supporting learning online. Survey respondents are asked to rate their agreement on a 5-point Likert scale (1=strongly disagree; 5=strongly agree) with each statement. The survey has been validated through a factor analysis (Arbaugh, et al., 2008) in which all items loaded cleanly onto the factors representing the expected presences.

Initial Research

In the fall of 2009, three QM reviewers, including a QM expert, an instructional designer, and a faculty member in the educational leadership program, reviewed a version of the core Educational Research Methods course in the MTL program. The course failed to meet several of the essential (3 point) standards, all of which had to do with learning objectives and their assessments. These deficits were addressed in the spring 2010 version of the course, which was reviewed again and met all but one 1 point standard. The changes made centered on the development of complete objectives for every unit in the course, the linking of

objectives to assessments, and clear provision of this information to learners.

We began our course redesign project with the unspoken assumption that it would be a two-semester project consisting of three steps: an initial collection of baseline data, a between-semesters course redesign, and a second-semester data collection and analysis. Data collected each semester consisted of student responses to the CoI survey, which was given the week after midterms, and outcomes measures consisting of student scores on the final exam and a major paper, representing two of the major course goals respectively, as well as overall course grades, all standardized to percent correct.

How the Data Forced the Authors to Rethink

At the start of this project, our assumptions were that the QM redesign would result in improved learning processes (as measured by the CoI survey) and that improved learning processes would result in improved learning outcomes. Our results, however, confounded these original assumptions: we found increases, although not significant ones, in all three learning outcomes measures, but decreases in CoI scores (i.e., the learning processes), mostly related to the perceived teaching presence subscale (Swan, Matthews, Bogle, Boles, & Day, 2011).

Our faculty research team had some lively discussions in our efforts to make sense of the findings. First, we realized something we should have known from the start; namely, that the QM and CoI models view learning from very different epistemological perspectives. QM is an objectivist, instructional design-based model and the CoI framework is a social constructivist, process model. There was no reason to believe the former would affect the latter, and in fact, it did not.

Our second, and perhaps more important, insight was that the redesign work could and should not be confined to a single cycle, between-semesters effort. We realized that, during the initial semester of systematically implementing changes into the course, the QM emphasis on instructional design and learning objectives may have distracted the course instructor from learning process issues, leading to the lower teaching presence ratings. We further realized we should use the CoI survey data to guide course improvements on a semester-to-semester basis.

Iterative Course Improvements Based on CoI Survey Scores

Once we had CoI data on the QM-revised course, we began the process of making course improvements directly based on CoI survey data. In revising the online Educational Research Methods course for the summer of 2010, for example, spring 2010 CoI survey items whose average scores were less than 3.75, or slightly less than "agree" (4), were selected by the instructor as indicating problem areas. These seemed to be mainly focused on online discussion and collaborative group work (See Figure 1). Revisions for the Summer 2010 version of the course thus centered on changing the grading of the discus-

sion from counting for extra credit to counting for 16% of the course grade (to show students it was valued), and asking student groups to agree on participation expectations before they began group work (to avoid time on task issues).

CoI scores improved considerably after the spring revisions outlined above; so much so that no items had average scores under 3.75. Some items still had scores under 4, however, including numbers 11 and 16 (identified in the spring results and not much improved by summer) and two new cognitive presence items. These items still seemed focused on discussion, but not on collaborative work, and moreover seemed focused on the content of discussion (See Figure 2). Thus, for the fall 2010 version of Educational Research Methods, discussion questions were changed to call upon students' experience (when previously they involved specific data related problems).

In the fall 2010 semester, CoI scores on individual survey items again increased, with no items scores falling below a 4. Figure 3 shows the progression of CoI survey results for the three composite scales, teaching presence, social presence, and cognitive presence, across semesters from fall 2009 through fall 2010. Please note the initial decline (SP2010) after the QM redesign and the

Figure 1. Items on CoI survey with average scores of less than 3.75 in spring 2010 (boldface added)

- **TP 7 (3.5)** The instructor helped to **keep course participants engaged and participating** in productive dialogue.
- **TP 9 (3.3)** The instructor helped **keep the course participants** on task in a way that helped me learn.
- **TP 11 (3.7)** The instructor helped to **focus discussion on relevant issues** in a way that helped me to learn.
- **SP 14 (3.7) Getting to know other course participants** gave me a sense of belonging in the course.
- **SP 16 (3.7) Online or web-based communication** is an excellent medium for interaction.
- **CP 27 (3.5) Brainstorming** and finding relevant information helped me resolve content related questions.

Figure 2. Items on CoI survey with average scores of less than 4.0 in summer 2010 (boldface added)

- **TP 11 (3.83)** The instructor helped to **focus discussion on relevant issues** in a way that helped me to learn.
- **SP 16 (3.83)** Online or web-based communication is an **excellent medium for social interaction.**
- **CP 24 (3.83)** Course activities **piqued my curiosity.**
- **CP 28 (3.83)** Online discussions were valuable in **helping me appreciate different perspectives.**

subsequent incremental improvements resulting from small changes to the course made to address areas identified by CoI survey items.

Effects on Learning Outcomes

Even more important than the finding of an upward trend in CoI presences was the finding that iterative improvements in CoI survey results corresponded with additional improvements in learning outcomes (Figure 4). There was a slight slump in outcomes scores in the summer 2010 semester in which CoI changes were first intro-

duced, but this most likely resulted from the same demanding course content being covered in eight rather than sixteen weeks. However, outcomes improved considerably in the fall of 2010 and the data show that the combination of both the QM and CoI revisions across four semesters brought average scores on the research proposal from a 91 to a 97 and on the final exam from an 82 to a 90, while overall course grades went from a 90 to a 99.

Moreover, analysis of variance shows these differences are significant for the final exam scores at the p=.05 level and for overall course grades at the p=.001 level. That is, increases in learning

Figure 3. Comparison of CoI survey scores over four semesters (from: Swan, Matthews, Bogle, Boles, & Day, 2011)

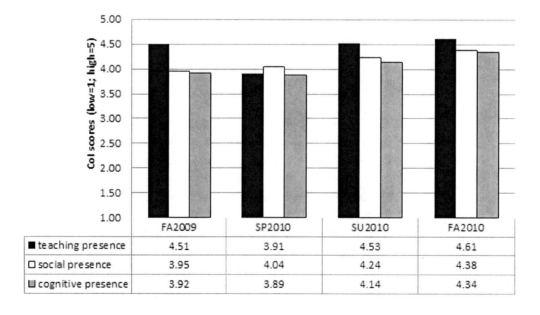

	FA2009	SP2010	SU2010	FA2010
■ teaching presence	4.51	3.91	4.53	4.61
□ social presence	3.95	4.04	4.24	4.38
▨ cognitive presence	3.92	3.89	4.14	4.34

Figure 4. Comparison of learning outcomes across four semesters (from: Swan, Matthews, Bogle, Boles, & Day, 2011)

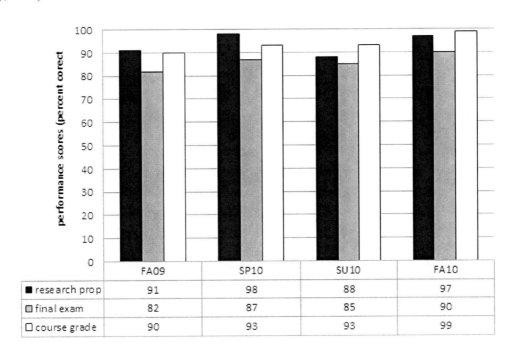

	FA09	SP10	SU10	FA10
■ research prop	91	98	88	97
▨ final exam	82	87	85	90
▢ course grade	90	93	93	99

outcomes that were not significant after the initial semester of the QM revisions alone were significant after several semesters of the combined initial QM/iterative CoI revision process. Using Cohen's (1992) analysis of eta squared results, effect sizes of the cumulative QM/CoI revisions were small for the research proposal (.11) and the final exam (.16), but moderate in terms of the overall course grades (.29). It should also be noted that these results were meaningful despite what appears to be a ceiling effect affecting potential gains.

DESIGN-BASED RESEARCH

We believe that adopting the iterative processes and pragmatic goals of design research guided by CoI theory was essential to the eventual success of our improvement efforts. The design-based approach to the iterative "tweaking" of the Educational Research Methods course was extremely successful, and, over four semesters, led to significant increases in both student perceptions of learning and student scores on multiple outcome measures. It also should be noted that our original belief in the efficacy of the Community of Inquiry model was confirmed by these results. Our initial success, in turn, led us to embrace a multi-semester, multi-course effort to improve core courses in our fully online Masters of Arts in Teacher Leadership (MTL) program.

Our success with the CoI-guided redesign of the Educational Research Methods course encouraged us to apply a similar heuristic to other courses in our fully online Master of Arts in Teacher Leadership (MTL) program. As a group, we decided to extend to all the core, required courses in the program the same ongoing course improvement process: initial QM revisions followed by iterative, CoI-guided, incremental improvements across semesters. Just as importantly, we stopped thinking about our work as traditional pre-post, quasi-experimental research; instead, we began viewing it as design-based. Design-based approaches blend empirical research with the theory-based design of learning environments. They center on the systematic investigation of innovations designed to improve educational practice through an iterative process of design, development, implementation and analysis in real-world settings (Wang & Hannafin, 2005) to help us understand "how, when, and why educational innovations work in practice" (Design-based Research Collective, 2003, p. 5). Gorard, Roberts, and Taylor's (2004) description of design research nicely summarizes our implementation of this methodological approach. They note that, "Within a design science approach…, currently accepted theory is used to develop an educational artifact or intervention that is tested, modified, retested and redesigned… until a version is developed that both achieves the education aims… and allows reflection on the educational processes involved in attaining those aims" (Gorard, Roberts, & Taylor, 2004, p. 579).

Community of Inquiry Guided, Design-Based Program Improvement

The program-level work we are doing has led us to identify benefits and challenges that make developing and improving CoI-guided courses distinct from similar work with more traditional, lecture-oriented approaches. As noted earlier, we began our course improvement project thinking that our initial course revisions would lead to immediate improvements in both learning processes and learning outcomes for the initial course studied. We implicitly assumed that were we to expand our work to other courses in the program, it would entail no more than a series of single-semester projects with the improvement efforts for each course completed in one semester. Our results, however, suggested that the relationships among course redesign, enhanced learning processes, and improved learning outcomes are not necessarily linear, making a multi-semester approach necessary. Indeed, it was only after four semesters of

data-based design and implementation changes that we saw significantly better outcomes in the first course we explored. We also believe that the ever-changing social contexts within each online course call for ongoing, multi-semester data collection and analyses. This ongoing data collection is particularly important given the interactive, social constructivist processes that are central to the CoI framework (Swan, Garrison, & Richardson, 2009).

The interactive, social constructivist aspects of the CoI framework, in particular, the grounding of cognitive presence in a somewhat adapted version of Dewey's (1938) practical inquiry model (Garrison, Anderson, & Archer, 2001) and the critical importance of social presence to the CoI model (Swan & Shih, 2005), make design research methodology particularly relevant to CoI-guided course improvement research. Design research typically includes iterative designs and the approach assumes that "designed contexts are conceptualized as interacting systems rather than as either a collection of activities or a list of separate factors that influence learning" (Cobb, Confrey, diSessa, Lehrer, & Schauble, 2003, p. 9). Design research addresses "the need to derive research findings from formative evaluation" (Collins, Joseph, & Bielaczyc, 2004, p. 16), which is a particularly relevant issue for us because of the multi-year nature of our course improvement work.

Collaborative, Design-Based Continuous Improvement

The MTL program has a long history of collaboration. It was developed in 2000 through a collaborative, multi-program effort aimed at creating a fully online program to cultivate teacher leaders. Throughout the online program's existence, the faculty and department leadership have worked to create a safe, non-threatening teaching environment in which colleagues would be willing to share their course designs and teaching experiences with others and be open to making ongoing change to online courses.

Our current redesign project began with faculty agreeing to open their courses for peer review using the QM rubric, which faculty understood was demanding and would likely point out the need for improvements. The faculty also voluntarily agreed to allow the CoI survey to be administered to students in their courses and to share learning outcomes. It is our belief that a culture of collaboration and trust is essential for sustaining an ongoing program of this duration and critical nature.

The collaborative, design-based, continuous improvement model we adopted is grounded in the collection and analysis of three sets of data. The first set is focused on design and involves a Quality Matters review. The second set is focused on implementation and learning processes and is based on student perceptions of teaching, social, and cognitive presence in their courses, gleaned from their responses on the CoI survey, which is given every semester just after midterms. The final set of data is focused on learning outcomes and is taken from scores on course assessments linked to major course goals standardized to percent correct scores to make them more consistent across courses. Before we initiated any redesign effort in a course, baseline data in all three areas was collected for it.

The first step in the redesign of our core courses was a Quality Matters review. Two MTL faculty members and an instructional designer from our Center for Online Learning, Research, and Service (COLRS) reviewed each course separately and then came together to decide on final QM scoring. The QM review team provided detailed data to each instructor on which QM standards their courses met and which they did not, identifying specific areas that needed improvement. The faculty modified their courses based on the specific areas noted in the QM review between semesters, and then met as a group to share how they had revised each component of the course to

meet the QM criteria. The group reached consensus that each of the deficiencies were addressed and all core courses met QM standards. The sharing also resulted in faculty being exposed to many good ideas for the design of their own courses.

The reviews of the QM data led to several specific changes in the courses. Most faculty added explicit learning objectives (a major component of the QM rubric) to their courses. The need to explicitly state objectives resulted in faculty discussions of key course goals and objectives the program expected for each of those core courses. The QM reviews brought about other changes including an increase in the variety of technology tools used in the courses. For example, as a result of the QM review, one professor added lectures via podcasting and YouTube.

The research team is currently in the midst of a voluntary, collaborative data generation and analysis stage that extends to all of the program's core courses. Most of the remaining core courses in our program are currently being taught for the first time since they underwent QM reviews and revisions. At this time, CoI survey data and major outcomes are being collected for each of these core courses. The data analyses are a cooperative project. The research team will provide program-level data to the group to track the improvement project's overall progress. The research team also assures the initial detailed QM review and the ongoing CoI survey data are provided to the individual professors to guide specific course improvements. Individual professors, in turn, provide learning outcome data for each semester to the team. The program-level and course-level information collected by the team includes the following: (1) whether courses met the QM review (pre- and post-revision), (2) the CoI survey results for each semester, and (3) the learning outcomes for each semester which thus far include exams, major projects, and overall grades standardized to percent correct scores.

The actual revisions and redesign of the courses are designed to be iterative and collaborative. Each semester, the instructors will review the prior semester's CoI survey and outcomes data. They will look for stronger CoI scores and improved outcomes, but also identify the lowest CoI items and problem areas in the outcomes data in order to focus the next round of course improvements. It is anticipated that the review of the data will lead to discussion on strategies or techniques to address the lowest scoring areas. For example, as previously noted, relatively low scores on several CoI social presence items led one instructor to give points for contributing to interactive, online discussions in order to encourage that activity. That professor then saw an improvement in those areas over the next semester and recommended similar changes to peers in the program. We believe that the same process will work with all our core courses over time.

We should reiterate that the collaborative approach that facilitated this work emerged from a faculty that has a history of working cooperatively and with a shared sense of trust and respect for their departmental colleagues. It is a department where professors value the collaborative approach and are willing to share ideas in order to advance the program and improve their courses. The faculty has a history of sharing instructional strategies, along with new technologies. From the beginning of this course improvement project, faculty members were willing to open their courses for peer review.

Design-Based, QM/CoI-Driven Course Redesign Model

Our designed-based course redesign is focused on the goals of improving course processes and learning outcomes and has three main mechanisms for guiding and effecting change: theory, data, and collaboration. The CoI framework provided a means to operationalize improvements in course implementation and learning processes grounded social constructivist theory. The QM framework offered an instantiation of a more objectivist

theoretical perspective and an instructional design focus. Our ongoing course improvement work is situated within those theoretical perspectives, and tested by collaborative review of semester to semester changes in learning outcomes which together inform specific, course-level revisions that are inherently tied to both the theoretical frameworks and the practical outcomes. The data generation, analysis, and resulting course modifications are done collaboratively. Because the specific course-level revisions are done by the course instructors themselves, this assures faculty acceptance of change; the collaborative nature of the process assures that faculty's creative course-level modifications in response to data-identified needs are shared and can be adopted by their colleagues. The process consists of a multi-semester, iterative cycle that begins with the use of the CoI and QM frameworks and culminates in continuous data-driven and collaborative improvement focused on learning outcomes. Figure 5 summarizes the key elements of our course redesign model.

RECOMMENDATIONS FOR DEVELOPING COMMUNITIES OF INQUIRY USING A DESIGN-BASED APPROACH

From our department's experiences using the Community of Inquiry and Quality Matters frameworks to guide our course redesign and improvement work, we developed a set of recommendations for others who would use a design-based approach to improve courses, either individually or within a program. These recommendations are discussed below.

Figure 5. Collaborative design-based course redesign model

Focus on the Theoretical Models and their Key Components to Provide Direction for the Course Improvement Efforts

We recommend using the Community of Inquiry (CoI) and Quality Matters (QM) frameworks because they have proved invaluable in guiding our redesign work. To begin with, the CoI and QM frameworks are designed specifically for online learning. Moreover, while they view online learning from seemingly orthogonal perspectives, in practice these have given us a richer understanding of the landscape of teaching and learning (Wittgenstein, 1953). As theory-driven models, the CoI and QM frameworks make possible meaningful empirical analyses of how well our course redesigns are implemented. In addition, the use of these frameworks provides us with widely-accepted and validated instruments – the

CoI survey and the QM rubric. The CoI survey and the QM rubric, in turn, are allowing us to go beyond the constraints of typical "outcomes-only" analyses that lack empirical measures of how well the intended models were actually implemented. In addition, the CoI and QM frameworks serve as a compass to guide our ongoing redesign and instructional efforts across multiple semesters.

The theory-based educational models we used identify key components of quality online education: teaching, social, and cognitive presences for the CoI model; explicit learning objectives aligned with assessments for the QM framework. As noted below, those key components of the CoI and QM frameworks became the primary focus of our work to improve our courses' design, processes, and outcomes.

Generate and Analyze Data on Course Design, Course Processes, and Learning Outcomes

While we agree that when evaluating educational offerings, it is necessary to analyze outcomes data, we view outcomes data alone as insufficient to guide change. From our perspective, generating and analyzing data on course design and course processes is essential and is what distinguishes our effort from routine, "Did the program work?" outcomes-only evaluations. Clearly inputs, such as course design, and processes, such as the learning processes specified in the CoI framework, affect course outcomes and therefore must be the focus of redesign efforts. Before data on course design and processes can be generated, course developers and instructors should come to a consensus regarding what constitutes good course design, what are worthwhile course processes, and how each of these can be measured. While it might be possible for a program's stakeholders to generate these influential components intuitively from their own experiences, we recommend the use of CoI and QM frameworks because they are two widely accepted, contemporary theory-based models specifically developed for online learning. They have served us well by guiding our redesign work, data generation, and data interpretation. The use of the CoI and QM frameworks allowed our local course improvement efforts to use published, validated data collection instruments, which provide better reliability and external credibility than would locally designed instruments, and to empirically analyze design and processes changes over time. A second advantage to using an established theory, framework, or model to guide data generation and analysis is that one's local effort might then contribute to the literature in that field, as our work is doing.

Of course, those analyses of data on initial course designs and within-semester course processes, as important as they are, are insufficient without similar attention to the analysis of learning outcomes. In the past decade, there have been increasing demands that educational institutions include empirical assessments of learning, and findings of measurable effects on outcomes are considered by most to be an essential component of any evaluation of a course redesign project. We have identified ways to analyze course-specific learning outcomes from end-of-semester data. The course instructors choose two or three assessments or summary scores linked to stated course goals, such as a paper, a final exam, or composite scores addressing a major goal, as the operational measures of their learning outcomes. The outcomes data are summarized at the class level as average percent correct to make comparisons across semesters and courses possible.

We initially found it to be a considerable practical challenge to organize the outcomes data in ways that allowed it to be summarized and compared across semesters, among differing courses in different stages of the redesign process, and in a ways that could provide useful feedback to individual course designers/instructors to use in their ongoing course modifications. Unlike the initial design data and the course processes data, which were generated in consistent formats using the QM and CoI tools respectively, there are not (and cannot be) shared assessments for the different courses we are revising. In addition, we had to accomplish all of our data analysis goals without a budget or extra staffing dedicated to the project. We were able to accomplish most of our outcomes data analysis goals by developing data file templates for Excel that had columns for the following variables: Course, Instructor, Study Semester (where "1" was baseline, "2" was first post-revision semester, and additional numbers indicated additional semesters of involvement and iterative, data-informed tweaking), followed by columns for each of the 34 items on the CoI survey as well composite items for teaching presence, social presence, and cognitive presence, and course-specific learning outcomes measures. We run descriptive statistics while within Excel and then import the data into SPSS to run inferential statistics.

In short, we analyze the processes and outcomes data at the most detailed levels possible in order to report it to the individual course instructors so they can make specific, data-informed modifications to their courses. We also analyze the data on an ongoing basis for overall trends in terms of improvements in course processes and outcomes. The detailed, course-level data analyses are the backbone of our course-level formative evaluations; the ongoing analyses of overall trends at the program level will inform our program-level evaluations of our course improvement efforts.

We believe an ongoing, multi-semester approach, such as that involved in design research, is particularly important when working within a social constructivist, process-oriented framework such as the Community of Inquiry model. More specifically, each semester a course is offered, the social milieu within the class – the mix of students, the rapport and backgrounds of the instructors and participants – can differ substantially. It is quite likely that such semester-to-semester social variation could dramatically affect the development of teaching, social, and cognitive presences. In addition, with online education, technical innovations could reasonably affect learning processes within online courses. As a result, no single semester's results regarding learning processes can be considered definitive and final, and ongoing assessments of such factors are essential.

Create a Collaborative Community of Educators to Share Responsibility for Ongoing Course Improvement and Redesign

We noted above the history of trust and collaboration among faculty that we believe has been central to our success in implementing this ongoing course redesign work. Our first semester of course redesign work for this project began with a small grant that initiated the revision of a single Educational

Research Methods course. The work on that initial course was open to collaboration from the beginning because the research team included not just the research course faculty but also other professors who taught core courses in our online program. Our program-wide course improvement project grew out of our initial course's redesign successes and is supported not by internal or external funding but by the intrinsic interest of the department's faculty in continuing that work and expanding it to all of the core courses in the program. The benefits to our faculty include an opportunity to make data- and theory-informed improvements to their courses. As faculty in a college of education, we are fortunate that we are able to involve our students, who are educators in K12 settings, in the course improvement process via the CoI surveys. In the process, we have the opportunity to model for our students how we use theory and data in our own teaching. In addition, we are in an institution that values teacher-scholars, and aligning our course improvement research within the CoI and QM theoretical frameworks has resulted in opportunities for faculty on the redesign team to share more broadly with our university colleagues and to present at several academic conferences, and has generated opportunities for publication.

CONCLUSION

Our experiences demonstrate the value of an iterative approach to improving online courses using the Quality Matters (QM) and the Community of Inquiry (CoI) frameworks as assessment and redesign guides. While the QM and CoI models view learning from different epistemological perspectives, they complement each other and together their use resulted in significant increases in student learning outcomes over a four semester period of time. The Quality Matters design analysis provides a faculty-oriented, peer review process designed to assure quality in online course structure and combined with the CoI model provides instructors with two separate but important views designed to enhance student learning. The Community of Inquiry survey provides a structure to determine student perceptions of teaching, social and cognitive presence within a course, and adjust the presentations accordingly. Our experiences suggest three recommendations for those programs and departments wishing to systematically enhance student achievement through improved course design and analysis of student opinions regarding the teaching, cognitive and social processes of the course. These recommendations are:

1. Focus on one or two recognized educational theories, frameworks, or models to provide direction for the course improvement efforts. For online education, we specifically recommend the use of the QM framework to guide initial course redesign and the CoI framework to inform change directed toward improving learning processes.
2. Generate and analyze data on course design (QM rubric), learning processes (CoI survey), and on learning outcomes. Analyze the outcomes in relationship to inputs and processes.
3. Create a collaborative community of educators to share responsibility for ongoing course improvement and redesign.

We recommend that educators taking on the important task of CoI-guided course improvement recognize that the adjustments to their course designs and the analysis of student achievement must be ongoing and collaborative. An iterative, theory- and data-driven course improvement project such as described in this chapter can work only if instructors make their courses available for analyses, adjust their course designs based on such analyses, and collaborate with their colleagues in making substantive changes to their courses. In this situation, a bottom-up, rather than top-down approach worked best (Bolman & Deal, 2008). This requires a trusting environ-

ment where improvement is an important goal and where collaboration is valued and rewarded, as is the case among the faculty involved in the work described here.

In sum, we found that using a design-based, collaborative approach to building communities of inquiry in online courses was quite productive and worthwhile. The CoI framework provided us with a clear, theory-based model that kept us focused throughout on improving the teaching, social, and cognitive presences that are central to developing communities of inquiry. The initial QM reviews strengthened the alignment of learning objectives to assessments within our courses and assured the courses met QM's widely accepted standards for quality. The empirical data from the CoI student surveys allowed faculty to identify specific, actionable areas for ongoing improvements to learning processes. The design-based research perspective provided us methodological flexibility while keeping us focused on both theoretical and pragmatic course improvement goals.

In addition, this CoI-guided, design-based course improvement work provided an opportunity for a faculty-initiated, collaborative project that has improved our online programs and, we believe, has provided some insights that can be useful to other online educators. While we note that this work is in process, and final results for the entire project are not yet in, the data to date provide empirical support for adopting a CoI-guided, design-based approach to improving online courses.

REFERENCES

Arbaugh, J. B., Cleveland-Innes, M., Diaz, S. R., Garrison, D. R., Ice, P., Richardson, J. C., & Swan, K. (2008). Developing a community of inquiry instrument: Testing a measure of the Community of Inquiry framework using a multi-institutional sample. *The Internet and Higher Education, 11*(3–4), 133–136. doi:10.1016/j.iheduc.2008.06.003

Bogle, L., Cook, V., Day, S., & Swan, K. (2009). Blended program development: Applying the quality matters and community inquiry frameworks to ensure high quality design and implementation. *Journal of the Research Center for Educational Technology (RCET)*, *5*(2), 51–66.

Bolman, L. G., & Deal, T. E. (2008). *Reframing organizations: Artistry, choice, and leadership*. San Francisco, CA: Jossey-Bass.

Cobb, P., Confrey, J., di Sessa, A., Lehrer, R., & Schauble, L. (2003). Design experiments in educational research. *Educational Researcher*, *32*(1), 9–13. doi:10.3102/0013189X032001009

Cohen, J. (1992). Statistics: A power primer. *Psychological Bulletin*, *112*(1), 155–159. doi:10.1037/0033-2909.112.1.155

Collins, A., Joseph, D., & Bielaczyc, K. (2004). Design research: Theoretical and methodological issues. *Journal of the Learning Sciences*, *13*(1), 15–42. doi:10.1207/s15327809jls1301_2

Design-Based Research Collective. (2003). Design-based research: An emerging paradigm for educational inquiry. *Educational Researcher*, *32*(1), 5–8. doi:10.3102/0013189X032001005

Dewey, J. (1938). *Experience and education*. New York, NY: Collier.

Garrison, D. R., Anderson, T., & Archer, W. (2000). Critical inquiry in a text-based environment: Computer conferencing in higher education. *The Internet and Higher Education, 2*, 87–105. doi:10.1016/S1096-7516(00)00016-6

Garrison, D. R., Anderson, T., & Archer, W. (2001). Critical thinking, cognitive presence and computer conferencing in distance education. *American Journal of Distance Education*, *15*(1), 7–23. doi:10.1080/08923640109527071

Gorard, S., Roberts, K., & Taylor, C. (2004). What kind of creature is design experiment? *British Educational Research Journal*, *30*(4), 577–590. doi:10.1080/0141192042000237248

Quality Matters. (2005). *Research literature and standards sets support for Quality Matters review standards*. Retrieved July 14, 2010, from http://www.qualitymatters.org/Documents/Matrix%20of%20Research%20Standards%20FY0506.pdf

Shattuck, K. (2007). Quality matters: Collaborative program planning at a state level. *Online Journal of Distance Learning Administration*, *10*(3), 1–10.

Swan, K., Garrison, D. R., & Richardson, J. C. (2009). A constructivist approach to online learning: The Community of Inquiry framework. In Payne, C. R. (Ed.), *Information technology and constructivism in higher education: Progressive learning frameworks* (pp. 43–57). Hershey, PA: IGI Global. doi:10.4018/978-1-60566-654-9.ch004

Swan, K., Matthews, D., Bogle, L., Boles, E., & Day, S. (2011). Linking online course design and implementation to learning outcomes: A design experiment. *The Internet and Higher Education*. doi:doi:10.1016/j.iheduc.2011.07.002

Swan, K., & Shih, L.-F. (2005). On the nature and development of social presence in online course discussions. *Journal of Asynchronous Learning Networks*, *9*(3), 115–136.

Swan, K. P., Richardson, J. C., Ice, P., Garrison, D. R., Cleveland-Innes, M., & Arbaugh, J. B. (2008). Validating a measurement tool of presence in online communities of inquiry. *E-mentor*, *2*(24). Retrieved from http://www.e-mentor.edu.pl/artykul_v2.php?numer=24&id=543

Vaughan, N. D., & Garrison, D. R. (2006). A blended faculty community of inquiry: Linking Leadership, course redesign and evaluation. *Canadian Journal of University Continuing Education, 32*(2), 67–92.

Wang, F., & Hannafin, M. J. (2005). Design-based research and technology enhanced learning environments. *Educational Technology Research and Development, 53*(4), 5–23. doi:10.1007/BF02504682

Wittgenstein, L. (1953). *Philosophical investigations*. Oxford, UK: Blackwell Publishing.

KEY TERMS AND DEFINITIONS

Cognitive Presence: The extent to which learners are able to construct and confirm meaning through sustained reflection and discourse in a critical community of inquiry.

Community of Inquiry (CoI) Framework: A social-constructivist, process model of learning in online and blended educational environments which assumes that effective learning in higher education requires the development of a community of learners that supports meaningful inquiry.

Community of Inquiry Survey: A 34 question Likert Scale survey designed to determine the level of the three presences identified in the CoI framework as supporting online learning, teaching (13), social (9) and cognitive (12), as measured by student responses. The intersection of these presences is where student learning in an online environment occurs and the higher the score the greater the opportunity for students to acquire the core material for the class.

Design-Based Research: An iterative approach to improvement that blends multi-stage empirical research with the theory-based design of learning environments.

Quality Matters (QM): A peer-review rating system designed to determine the quality of an online or blended class by rating the design of the class as it appears online.

Social Presence: The ability of participants in a virtual community of inquiry to project themselves socially and emotionally–as 'real' people.

Teaching Presence: The design, facilitation and direction of cognitive and social processes for the purpose of realizing personally meaningful and educationally worthwhile learning outcomes.

APPENDIX A

Table 1. Quality Matters Rubric

	Standards	Pts.
Course Overview and Introduction	1.1 Instructions make clear how to get started and where to find various course components.	3
	1.2 Students are introduced to the purpose and structure of the course.	3
	1.3 Etiquette expectations (sometimes called "netiquette") for online discussions, email, and other forms of communication are stated clearly.	2
	1.4 Course and/or institutional policies with which the student is expected to comply are clearly stated, or a link to current policies is provided.	2
	1.5 Prerequisite knowledge in the discipline and/or any required competencies are clearly stated.	1
	1.6 Minimum technical skills expected of the student are clearly stated.	1
	1.7 The self-introduction by the instructor is appropriate and available online.	1
	1.8 Students are asked to introduce themselves to the class.	1
Learning Objectives (Competencies)	2.1 The course learning objectives describe outcomes that are measurable.	3
	2.2 The module/unit learning objectives describe outcomes that are measurable and consistent with the course-level objectives.	3
	2.3 All learning objectives are stated clearly and written from the students' perspective.	3
	2.4 Instructions to students on how to meet the learning objectives are adequate and stated clearly.	3
	2.5 The learning objectives are appropriately designed for the level of the course.	3
Assessment and Measurement	3.1 The types of assessments selected measure the stated learning objectives and are consistent with course activities and resources.	3
	3.2 The course grading policy is stated clearly.	3
	3.3 Specific and descriptive criteria are provided for the evaluation of students' work and participation and are tied to the course grading policy.	3
	3.4 The assessment instruments selected are sequenced, varied, and appropriate to the student work being assessed.	2
	3.5 Students have multiple opportunities to measure their own learning progress.	2
Instructional Materials	4.1 The instructional materials contribute to the achievement of the stated course and module/unit learning objectives.	3
	4.2 The purpose of instructional materials and how the materials are to be used for learning activities are clearly explained.	3
	4.3 All resources and materials used in the course are appropriately cited.	2
	4.4 The instructional materials are current.	2
	4.5 The instructional materials present a variety of perspectives on the course content.	1
	4.6 The distinction between required and optional materials is clearly explained.	1
Learner Interaction and Engagement	5.1 The learning activities promote the achievement of the stated learning objectives.	3
	5.2 Learning activities provide opportunities for interaction that support active learning.	3
	5.3 The instructor's plan for classroom response time and feedback on assignments is clearly stated.	3
	5.4 The requirements for student interaction are clearly articulated.	2

continued on following page

Table 1. Continued

	Standards	Pts.
Course Technology	6.1 The tools and media support the course learning objectives.	3
	6.2 Course tools and media support student engagement and guide the student to become an active learner.	3
	6.3 Navigation throughout the online components of the course is logical, consistent, and efficient.	3
	6.4 Students can readily access the technologies required in the course.	2
	6.5 The course technologies are current.	1
Learner Support	7.1 The course instructions articulate or link to a clear description of the technical support offered and how to access it.	3
	7.2 Course instructions articulate or link to the institution's accessibility policies and services.	3
	7.3 Course instructions articulate or link to an explanation of how the institution's academic support services and resources can help students succeed in the course and how students can access the services.	2
	7.4 Course instructions articulate or link to an explanation of how the institution's student support services can help students succeed and how students can access the services.	1
Accessibility	8.1 The course employs accessible technologies and provides guidance on how to obtain accommodation.	3
	8.2 The course contains equivalent alternatives to auditory and visual content.	2
	8.3 The course design facilitates readability and minimizes distractions.	2
	8.4 The course design accommodates the use of assistive technologies.	2

APPENDIX B

Table 2. Community of Inquiry Survey

	Survey	
	The following statements relate to your perceptions of "**Teaching Presence**" – the design of this course and your instructor's facilitation of discussion and direct instruction within it. Please indicate your agreement or disagreement with each statement.	
#	Statement	Agreement 1 = strongly disagree; 5 = strongly agree
1	The instructor clearly communicated important course topics.	1 2 3 4 5
2	The instructor clearly communicated important course goals.	1 2 3 4 5
3	The instructor provided clear instructions on how to participate in course learning activities	1 2 3 4 5
4	The instructor clearly communicated important due dates/time frames for learning activities.	1 2 3 4 5
5	The instructor was helpful in identifying areas of agreement and disagreement on course topics that helped me to learn.	1 2 3 4 5
6	The instructor was helpful in guiding the class towards understanding course topics in a way that helped me clarify my thinking.	1 2 3 4 5
7	The instructor helped to keep course participants engaged and participating in productive dialogue.	1 2 3 4 5
8	The instructor helped keep the course participants on task in a way that helped me to learn.	1 2 3 4 5
9	The instructor encouraged course participants to explore new concepts in this course.	1 2 3 4 5
10	Instructor actions reinforced the development of a sense of community among course participants	1 2 3 4 5
11	The instructor helped to focus discussion on relevant issues in a way that helped me to learn.	1 2 3 4 5
12	The instructor provided feedback that helped me understand my strengths and weaknesses relative to the course's goals and objectives.	1 2 3 4 5
13	The instructor provided feedback in a timely fashion.	1 2 3 4 5
	The following statements refer to your perceptions of "**Social Presence**" -- the degree to which you feel socially and emotionally connected with others in this course. Please indicate your agreement or disagreement with each statement.	
#	Statement	Agreement 1 = strongly disagree; 5 = strongly agree
14	Getting to know other course participants gave me a sense of belonging in the course.	1 2 3 4 5
15	I was able to form distinct impressions of some course participants.	1 2 3 4 5
16	Online or web-based communication is an excellent medium for social interaction.	1 2 3 4 5
17	I felt comfortable conversing through the online medium.	1 2 3 4 5
18	I felt comfortable participating in the course discussions.	1 2 3 4 5

continued on following page

Table 1. Continued

	Survey	
19	I felt comfortable interacting with other course participants.	1 2 3 4 5
20	I felt comfortable disagreeing with other course participants while still maintaining a sense of trust.	1 2 3 4 5
21	I felt that my point of view was acknowledged by other course participants.	1 2 3 4 5
22	Online discussions help me to develop a sense of collaboration.	1 2 3 4 5

The following statements relate to your perceptions of "**Cognitive Presence**" -- the extent to which you were able to develop a good understanding of course topics. Please indicate your agreement or disagreement with each statement.

#	Statement	Agreement 1 = strongly disagree; 5 = strongly agree
23	Problems posed increased my interest in course issues.	1 2 3 4 5
24	Course activities piqued my curiosity.	1 2 3 4 5
25	I felt motivated to explore content related questions.	1 2 3 4 5
26	I utilized a variety of information sources to explore problems posed in this course.	1 2 3 4 5
27	Brainstorming and finding relevant information helped me resolve content related questions.	1 2 3 4 5
28	Online discussions were valuable in helping me appreciate different perspectives.	1 2 3 4 5
29	Combining new information helped me answer questions raised in course activities.	1 2 3 4 5
30	Learning activities helped me construct explanations/solutions.	1 2 3 4 5
31	Reflection on course content and discussions helped me understand fundamental concepts in this class.	1 2 3 4 5
32	I can describe ways to test and apply the knowledge created in this course.	1 2 3 4 5
33	I have developed solutions to course problems that can be applied in practice.	1 2 3 4 5
34	I can apply the knowledge created in this course to my work or other non-class related activities.	1 2 3 4 5

Chapter 25
Design–Based Approach for the Implementation of an International Cyberlearning Community of Inquiry for Medical Education

Yianna Vovides
George Washington University, USA

Kristine Korhumel
George Washington University, USA

ABSTRACT

This chapter describes the conceptualization and implementation of a cyberlearning environment as a community of inquiry (CoI). This environment includes 13 medical schools from Sub-Saharan Africa and their 50-plus partners from around the world. The theoretical foundations of Communities of Inquiry provided the framework that drove the design of the web-based platform used in this project. Through an emphasis on learning from conversations, the resulting cyberlearning environment was designed to foster engagement among faculty, staff, and students of the 13 medical schools and their partners. Recognizing that generating a virtual community of inquiry framed around the cognitive, social, and teaching presence is no easy task, the approach taken for the design was based on conceptualizing the development of such a community along a continuum that addressed the depth of interaction for each presence. This type of design assumes a phased-in implementation. The chapter describes this conceptualization by addressing the core communication strategy used, which underlies the interactions to support learning from conversations. In addition, the chapter addresses key environmental constraints and how these constraints guided operational decisions during implementation. In addition, the chapter discusses challenges and solutions, as well as lessons learned.

DOI: 10.4018/978-1-4666-2110-7.ch025

INTRODUCTION

This chapter describes the conceptualization and implementation of a cyberlearning environment as a community of inquiry (CoI) that includes 13 medical schools from Sub-Saharan Africa and their 50-plus partners from around the world. Cyberlearning is defined as the use of "networked computing and communications technologies to support learning" (NSF Report, 2008, p. 5). The theoretical foundations of Communities of Inquiry (Garrison, Anderson, & Archer, 2000) provided the framework that drove the design of the web-based platform used in this project. Through an emphasis on learning from conversations, this cyberlearning environment was designed to foster engagement among faculty, staff, and students of the 13 medical schools and their partners. Formal, non-formal, and informal learning opportunities are merged in the design of this environment. Definitions of formal, non-formal, and informal learning have been adopted from Colardyn and Bjornavold (2004, p. 71). Formal learning is intentional—recognized through earning a diploma, certificate, etc.—and occurs within an organized and structured context (formal education, formal training certification). Non-formal learning is also intentional but tends to be embedded in planned or structured activities that in and of themselves are not designated as learning activities. For example, in the design of the environment live webinars were aligned with key content themes (e-learning in medical education, medical education research methods, research support, and community-based education). These live webinars were archived and made available as resources. Learners could explore the archived webinars on their own and still move through a series of webinars following the structure provided based on the key content themes. In other words, a learner could explore webinars categorized as e-learning on topics such as digital libraries, open educational resources, etc. Finally, informal learning or experiential learning is learning that results from daily experiences

and tends to be incidental instead of intentional. A "who's online" extension was enabled as part of the cyberlearning environment to allow for opportunities among learners of impromptu conversations.

The merging of formal, non-formal, and informal learning within the design of the cyberlearning environment extends the utilization of the CoI framework as a process model beyond its traditional focus for use within formal educational environments. It is within this context that the chapter examines how the CoI framework could be used to serve as the process model for the design of a fused formal to informal cyberlearning environment. A design-based research approach is used as the lens of the exploration into whether the initial design of the cyberlearning environment would generate and support the cognitive, social, and teaching presence core to the CoI theoretical framework. In addition, to further identify participant needs, given the initial design, system data is collected and interviews are conducted with participants. Results inform re-design and expanded opportunities for learning.

BACKGROUND

The core team responsible for the design and development of the cyberlearning environment consisted of medical educators, senior programmer analysts, and instructional designers. This core team was based at a private university in the United States that coordinated efforts among the 13 schools in Sub-Saharan Africa.

It became apparent early on, due to the multi-dimensional elements that underscored this project (listed below), that the design of this cyberlearning environment needed to have flexibility to allow for both formal and informal opportunities for engagement among the 13 primary institutions and their partners. The elements that had to be accommodated were considered integral to the design of the cyberlearning environment and included:

- A diverse audience with varied priorities, needs, and uses of technology
- Infrastructure at each institution that supports limited web-based interaction
- Scheduling difficulties for synchronous communication due to the time differences at the various locations
- Lack of audience buy-in

Lack of buy-in among the 13 schools and their partners was at the core of the design challenge. The schools saw the value in designing a website rich in resources, but they did not necessarily see the value in having an active role and being part of a learning community. It seemed that the design of this cyberlearning environment needed to account for richness in content to establish relevance. To engage participants as learners and not simply as consumers of information, the design needed to allow for multiple types of interaction as well as account for participants' varied prior knowledge and motivation. Therefore, the design model for this cyberlearning environment combined the ARCS (Attention, Relevance, Confidence, Satisfaction) motivation model (Suzuki & Keller, 1996, Keller, 2010) with the following types of interaction: learner-learner, learner-content, learner-system, and learner-expert. Going into this level of depth at the conceptualization stage of the design of the cyberlearning environment allowed the project team to establish a plan for the development of a learning community spread over the 5-year lifespan of the project.

In summary, the trajectory of the purpose of the cyberlearning environment over the project's lifespan is as follows:

- Through structured formal and informal learning opportunities made available via the cyberlearning environment, to bring together participants (faculty and students from the 13 schools and their partners) to engage in information and knowledge sharing. The key learning outcome expected as

part of this initial step is for participants to recognize the usefulness of this environment as a resource for their work in medical education.

- Through expanded structured formal and informal learning opportunities made available via the cyberlearning environment, to engage participants in reflection on what it is they are learning and how it has or has not influenced their practice. The key learning outcome expected as part of this step is for participants to initiate knowledge exchanges.
- Through the work of technical working groups to engage participants in fully online formal education opportunities. The key learning outcome expected as part of this step is for participants to display a commitment to their own professional development through their participation in these formal education opportunities.

The rest of this Background section explores which learning community framework was best suited to support the progression of engagement and outcomes outlined above. An operational definition of a learning community is described along with a brief review of the communities of practice and the communities of inquiry frameworks for the purpose of supporting the design of the cyberlearning environment to develop the learning community.

Swan and Shea (2005) provide an overview of social learning theories as they relate to the development of virtual learning communities. They explain that "three common themes can be identified: cognition is situated in particular social contexts, knowing is distributed across groups, and learning takes place in communities" (p.3). With this in mind, learning can be thought of in terms of an individual going through a process of "making the strange familiar" and "the familiar strange" (Baker, Jensen, & Kolb, 2002) and thus enabling a back and forth internal to the individual through participation via conversations as part of a learning community. This can result in knowledge creation transcending the individual and can lead to deep learning (Baker, Jensen, & Kolb, 2002).

Kilpatrick, Barrett, and Jones (2003) compiled a composite definition of learning communities based on their review of common themes in the literature that link definitions and uses, which include: "common or shared purpose, interests or geography; collaboration, partnership and learning; respecting diversity, and enhanced potential and outcomes" (p.4). Based on this composite definition, the following operational definition of learning community was identified for the purposes of this project: a group of people connected by common interest generating learning resources in order to develop a participative environment, while respecting a variety of perspectives, through the provision of learning opportunities. The outcome of this type of activity is to enhance the potential of its members to create new knowledge within the context of medical education. Given this operational definition of the type of learning community to be developed over the life of the project as well as the expected outcome, a comparison of the Community of Practice and the Community of Inquiry frameworks was done to identify the best fit in driving the design of the cyberlearning environment.

Communities of Practice (CoP), as defined by Wenger, McDermott, and Snyder (2002), are "groups of people who share a concern, a set of problems, or a passion about a topic, and who deepen their knowledge and expertise in this area by interacting on an ongoing basis" (p. 4) while a Community of Inquiry (CoI) is defined as an "educational group of individuals who collaboratively engage in purposeful critical discourse and reflection to construct personal meaning and confirm mutual understanding" (Community of Inquiry, 2011).

Within the context of education, Wenger (2006) emphasizes that communities of practice can affect educational practices internally, exter-

nally, and over the lifetime of students. CoP can affect educational practices internally through the grounding of school learning in practice based on a domain of interest; externally, CoP can connect the academic experience to actual practice; and over the lifetime of students, CoP can extend and deepen the learning for a particular domain. It is important to note that CoP assumes a shared domain of interest and engagement in joint activities, and that its members are practitioners. Being part of a CoP "implies a commitment to the domain, and therefore shared competence that distinguishes members from other people" (Wenger, 2006). Such commitment to the domain engages its members to learn from each other and develop shared resources, thus forming a community of shared practice within mostly non-formal and informal learning settings (Wenger, 2006).

The Community of Inquiry framework proposed by Garrison, Anderson, and Archer (2000) is based on a conceptual framework that includes three types of "presences" that when coming together generate a worthwhile educational experience. These core elements include cognitive, social, and teaching presences. Cognitive presence can be thought of as participants' ability to create meaning through communication sustained over time (Garrison, Anderson, & Archer, 2001; Akyol & Garrison, 2008). Social presence stems from participants' sense of belonging and identifying with a community as well as being able to have purposeful communication and to develop interpersonal relationships; elements of trust and participants' individual personalities come into play within the social presence (Garrison, 2009). Finally, teaching presence provides design, facilitation, and direction to support the cognitive and social processes to reach the expected learning outcomes (Anderson, Rourke, Garrison, & Archer, 2001).

Within the context of online learning environments, there is often confusion as to what constitutes a community of practice and/or a community of inquiry (Swann, 2009). Online learning environments have traditionally been designed to address formal, non-formal, or informal learning, but rarely all three. The CoP framework, stemming from the anthropological perspective (Barab & Duffy, 2000), supports informal and non-formal learning (Gray, 2004). The CoI framework has been used as a design model for fully online and blended communities of inquiry (Akyol, Garrison, & Ozden, 2009) primarily for formal learning. The CoI framework accounts for a teaching presence as one of the core elements, in addition to the social and cognitive presences, which makes it the more appropriate model for formal learning. In fact, teaching presence is what does not tend to be present within the communities of practice framework. Communities of practice members are practitioners who seek to learn from and with other practitioners (Wenger, 2006), and within such a framework, there is no real need for teaching presence as defined by CoI. Communities of practice have the luxury to develop over time and, although difficult, are able to be theoretically sustained over time, due to the underlying intrinsic motivation of its members. This is a strength that is often not found in formal learning environments utilizing the CoI as its design model. Even though the CoI framework emphasizes the creation of effective learning communities that support deep learning (Akyol, Garrison, & Ozden, 2009), participants within communities of inquiry do not necessarily start out being intrinsically motivated to participate. Designing cyberlearning environments that establish and sustain a cognitive presence that supports deep learning requires a dynamic balancing act in relation to the social and teaching presences (Akyol, Vaughan, & Garrison, 2011).

Understanding the participants of a learning community is invariably at the core of effectively designing such an environment. Within the context of the 5-year project being described in this chapter, the participants had not initiated or even seen the need for a learning community. Why then design one? Much as in formal learning, classes and courses are not always designed and taken because the students see the need; rather, classes and courses are often simply required. In the same manner, the challenge for this project was to design a "required" cyberlearning community. Keeping in mind the operational definition of a learning community described earlier in this section, the CoI framework was deemed more appropriate than CoP to serve as the driver for the design decisions that guided the development of the cyberlearning environment.

The rest of the chapter explains in detail the design and implementation decisions associated with the teaching, social, and cognitive presences of CoI. The merging of formal, non-formal, and formal learning over time is accounted for in the design. In addition, motivational aspects are also accounted for both in the overall design of the cyberlearning environment as well as in the design of individual learning activities.

DESIGN DECISIONS: FROM CONCEPTUALIZATION TO IMPLEMENTATION

The 13 medical schools in Sub-Saharan Africa are located in 12 different countries and form the core community of learning. Their partners are U.S., European, and African institutions of higher education. At the initial stages of the project, a survey was drafted and sent to the 13 medical schools to better understand the information and communications technology (ICT) available at each school as well as technology acceptance. The survey questions focused on infrastructure and level of comfort with utilizing web-based tools. Although the infrastructure among the medical schools varied, some with many more computers in their computer labs than others, all schools indicated that they had internet access and were comfortable with email communication and web browsing but not particularly comfortable with audio or video web conferencing given the bandwidth limitations of their infrastructure. All

13 schools were also involved in e-learning efforts and were interested in learning more on this front. Therefore, it seemed that the community of inquiry could address, at least initially in years 1 and 2, issues surrounding e-learning for medical education.

To determine what constraints should be accounted for in the design, the ICT survey that was sent to the 13 schools provided the communications team with enough information to support the research being conducted on the selection of the web-based platform. A decision support tool was prepared to provide decision-makers with a breakdown of the options listing each platform's pros and cons focusing on flexibility of the system, support, and sustainability. Start-up costs and recurring costs were also key considerations. Weighing these options helped identify whether a custom-built solution was needed vs. a turn-key solution and whether a hosted or self-hosted model would be followed. This process resulted in the selection of an open source, hosted solution to serve as the platform for the cyberlearning environment.

Even though the design of the cyberlearning environment needed to account for immediate perceived usefulness, the project's lifespan of 5 years allowed enough flexibility to support a transformation from mere participant to learner. This transformation was accounted for in the environment's design decisions in order to enable participants to recognize the longer-term gains that could be realized through their own intellectual contributions. Recognizing that conversations generated by a group of participants at one point in time remain within such a cyberlearning environment to foster engagement for other groups at a different point in time has the potential to advance knowledge creation (Baker, Jensen, & Kolb, 2002). This was the key learning outcome for years 1 and 2 of the project. Designing conversations within a cyberlearning environment is complex (Luppicini, 2008), but it can enable informal, non-formal, and formal learning to occur.

For years 3 and 4, more structured engagement is planned to benefit the larger community of medical educators, including formal learning opportunities about community-based education, tracking, and e-learning. At 5 years, this community of inquiry is expected to support and contribute to transformative learning in medical education among the participants. Transformative learning is defined as "learning that transforms problematic frames of reference to make them more inclusive, discriminating, reflective, open, and emotionally able to change" (Mezirow, 2009, p. 22).

With this longer term goal of the project in mind, it became apparent that identifying ways to determine the impact that the cyberlearning environment had on decisions made by those participating was critical. In other words, what did the participants learn, given the formal, non-formal, and informal learning opportunities within this environment, and did what they learned inform their decisions and actions? A plan was created to monitor the use and interaction of the web-based platform used for the environment and described in more detail in the Design-based Approach section of the chapter. Figure 1 shows the progression of the macro-level design of the cyberlearning environment. The project is currently at year 2.

Design-Based Approach

As shown in Figure 1, the design of the cyberlearning environment was mapped to the three essential elements of communities of inquiry (CoI) - cognitive, social, and teaching presences (Garrison, Anderson, & Archer, 2000). Akyol and Garrison (2008) found that the three elements of CoI develop over time in different ways within an online learning environment and such progression could vary based on the context of the learning environment itself, such as informal learning. Their study, although limited in terms of generalization due to the small number of participants, found evidence that both social and teaching presence change over time; however, cognitive presence

Figure 1. Macro-level design progression over time

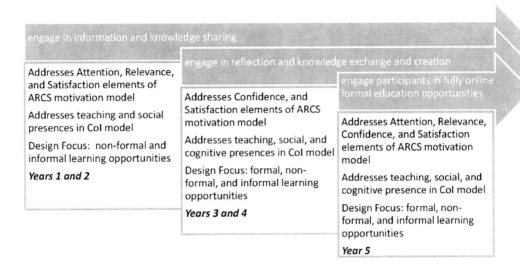

did not. In addition, they recommend that the "elements of a community of inquiry should be designed, facilitated and directed based on the purpose, participants and technological context of the learning experience" (Akyol & Garrison, 2008, p.18).

Taking into account the characteristics of the primary audience (13 medical schools) described earlier in this chapter, as well as the environmental constraints relating to internet access, the design of this cyberlearning environment focused on integrating the social and teaching presences initially (years 1-2) to be sustained through the end of the project in year 5. Cognitive presence is integrated in the design of the cyberlearning environment in year 3 and sustained through the end of the project (Figure 1). Given the dynamic nature of the social and teaching presences over time, a comprehensive communication strategy (Figure 2) was also designed to support the dynamic level of interaction expected in the participation within this environment. This was done by aligning the CoI categories for each of the elements (cognitive, social, and teaching presence) to the communication strategy, as shown in Figure 3, emphasizing two-way and multi-way interac-

tions. For years 1 and 2 of the project the focus was on knowledge exchange and sharing so that participants recognized the usefulness of the cyberlearning environment as a resource for their work in medical education.

Note that at the macro-level design shown in Figure 1, motivation is taken into account based on Keller's ARCS model, which was validated internationally as a systematic design model that accounts for motivational elements in e-learning environments (Keller & Suzuki, 2004). Keller (2006) defines motivational design as the "process of arranging resources and procedures to bring about changes in motivation" (p. 3). The ARCS model is an interaction-centered model stemming from social learning theory that addresses the relationships between effort, performance and satisfaction (Keller, 2006). It includes four categories of motivational variables: attention, relevance, confidence, and satisfaction, with each one of these categories including sub-categories: attention includes perceptual arousal, inquiry arousal, and variability; relevance includes goal orientation, motive matching, and familiarity; confidence includes learning requirements, success opportunities, and personal control; satisfac-

Figure 2. Communication strategy and process

Week 1	Week 2	Week 3	Week 4
Newsletter Distributed	Guest Speaker PPT received	Instructions to participants sent	Follow-up eDiscussion moderation continued
Notification to webinar guest speaker sent regarding presentation and a practice run	Practice Run completed	Webinar completed	Follow-up eDiscussion summarized
	Announcements via social media and other venues repeated	Follow-up eMail communication summarizing key points	
Webinar registration set up and tracked	Webinar registration tracked	Follow-up eDiscussion released	Resource package prepared and shared on web-based platform - recorded webinar session and discussion summary
Announcements via social media and other venues done		Follow-up eDiscussion moderated	

Figure 3. Linkage of cognitive, social, and teaching presences to cyberlearning environment design

Cognitive Presence	Triggering Event	Newsletter feature based on areas of interest determined from survey results
	Exploration	Newsletter hyper-links to community; webinar registration; feature articles; recommended links available on the Home page of community
	Integration	Integrated communication month-long strategy: newsletter editorial on a particular topic, followed by webinar on same topic, followed by eDiscussions on same topic
	Resolution	Follow-up with participants on implemented ideas in their own projects and internal group conversations
Social Presence	Emotional Expression	Social network options (friending with who's online function, messaging, email, posting on "walls")
	Open Communication	eDiscussion options (asynchronous discussion forum, moderated and unmoderated discussions)
	Group Cohesion	Social networking options (creating groups and events, group-specific asynchronous discussions)
Teaching Presence	Instructional Management	Site registration, moderated eDiscussions (asynchronous) participation, Guest lectures and expert panels (synchronous) attendance
	Building Understanding	Engagement with expert panels and guest lecturers via webinars and eDiscussion, topic-based interest groups, journal club (monthly)
	Direct Instruction	Newsletter - editorial and feature article, Webinar lecture series, quick guides, resources and literature

tion includes intrinsic reinforcements, extrinsic rewards, and equity (Keller, 2006). The sub-category variables were taken into account while determining the communication strategy and are shown in Figure 4.

With CoI forming the framework of the design model that also takes into account motivational design to address the interaction supported in the cyberlearning environment, the overlay of the informal, non-formal, and formal learning opportunities via conversations is described next. This overlay transitions the design macro to micro levels allowing the focus to shift from the overall environment to the design of the actual learning activities. Figure 5 was adapted from Clark (2010) to demonstrate a matrix of formal to informal learning ranging from intentional to incidental learning. In designing opportunities for learning within the cyberlearning environment for this project, the continuum between formal and informal learning as well as intentional and incidental was one of the considerations for designing learning activities.

According to Luppicini (2008), conversations involve "an exchange of ideas and mental processes between speakers and listeners" (p.2). According to conversation theory, conversations produce "mind-generating processes of which we are aware or can become aware" (Boyd, 2004, p.185). Given the primary learning outcome for years 1 and 2 of the project, the cyberlearning environment utilizes conversations to support interaction within the learning activities. With several obstacles to overcome in terms of limited

Figure 4. Linkage of cognitive, social, and teaching presence to motivation categories tied to cyberlearning environment design

Cognitive Presence	Triggering Event	Attention: perceptual arousal, inquiry arousal, variability; Relevance: goal orientation, familiarity	Newsletter feature based on survey results of areas of interest
	Exploration	Relevance: motive matching, and familiarity; Confidence: learning requirements	Links to community from newsletter, webinar registration, feature article, etc. Recommended links available on the Home page of community
	Integration	Relevance: goal orientation, motive matching, familiarity; Confidence: learning requirements; Satisfaction: intrinsic reinforcements, extrinsic reward	Integrated communication strategy: newsletter editorial on a particular topic, followed by webinar on same topic, followed by eDiscussions
	Resolution	Confidence: learning requirements, success opportunities, personal control	Follow-up with participants on whether implemented ideas in their own projects ideas and internal group conversations
Social Presence	Emotional Expression	Attention: variability; Relevance: goal orientation, motive matching, familiarity; Confidence: personal control; Satisfaction: intrinsic reinforcements, equity	Social network options (friending with who's online function, messaging, email, posting on "walls")
	Open Communication	Attention: inquiry arousal, variability; Relevance: motive matching, familiarity; Confidence: success opportunities, personal control; Satisfaction: intrinsic reinforcements, extrinsic rewards	eDiscussion options (asynchronous discussion forum, moderated and unmoderated discussions)
	Group Cohesion	Attention: inquiry arousal, variability; Confidence: personal control; Satisfaction: intrinsic reinforcements	Social networking options (creating groups and events, group-specific asynchronous discussions)
Teaching Presence	Instructional Management	Confidence: learning requirements, personal control; Satisfaction: equity	Site registration, moderated eDiscussions (asynchronous) participation, Guest lectures and expert panels (synchronous) attendance
	Building Understanding	Attention: perceptual arousal, inquiry arousal; Relevance: goal orientation, familiarity; Confidence: learning requirements, success opportunities, personal control	Engagement with expert panels and guest lecturers via webinars and eDiscussion, topic-based interest groups, journal club (monthly)
	Direct Instruction	Attention: inquiry arousal, variability; Confidence: learning requirements, personal control; Satisfaction: intrinsic reinforcements, extrinsic rewards, equity	Newsletter - editorial and feature article, Webinar lecture series, quick guides, resources and literature

Figure 5. Linkage of cognitive, social, and teaching presence to motivation categories tied to cyberlearning environment

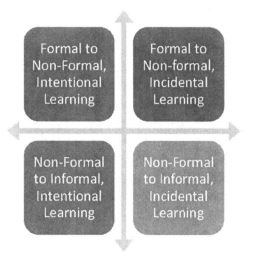

buy-in and use of web-based tools, the communication strategy and the design of conversations for learning were designed to address topics that would be of particular value to the participants. These included the following: digital libraries, open educational resources in Africa, social accountability, retention, and e-learning in medical education. The authenticated cyberlearning environment was launched in June 2011 and currently has 627 registered participants. However, only 201 of these participants have actually logged in to the site. As of October 2011, a total of 109 of those participants are users from the 13 medical schools in Sub-Saharan Africa, a steadily increasing number.

In terms of interest and attendance for the webinars offered synchronously via the cyberlearning environment, there has been a slow but steady increase ranging from four to 18 participants with the highest being the two most recent ones on retention and e-learning. This can be attributed partly to communication and outreach efforts as well as to potentially an increasing perceived usefulness of the cyberlearning environment. These webinars are archived and become a resource for

the asynchronous eDiscussion that follows the synchronous direct instruction to support building of understanding around the topic. These eDiscussions are moderated. The facilitation of these eDiscussions is designed with a focus on conversational learning. For years 1 and 2 of the project, the focus is on non-formal and informal learning opportunities across the intentional to incidental axis as shown in Figure 5. For example, the eDiscussions following the webinar are designed to support non-formal, intentional learning while participation in the ICTs in medical education group is designed to support informal, incidental learning. Formal learning opportunities become a focus for years 3 and 4 of the project. With this in mind, learning resources such as the archived webinars are added to the digital library of resources that is part of the site.

Building out the library of resources for the community has been a priority as part of the efforts to support a robust teaching presence for direct instruction. One of the major findings during the needs analysis stage of the process for designing the cyberlearning environment through the ICT survey and follow-up telephone interviews was the request for learning resources. This finding impacted the choices of the webinar topics, which focused on options around digital libraries, open educational resources, and e-learning. In addition, a major effort was launched to identify, categorize, and tag relevant resources to include as part of the library section of the cyberlearning environment. Over 300 resources are available and searchable by resource type (literature, tool, school, journal, funding opportunities) and by category and sub-category. The top-level categories are the following 15: Capacity Building for Research, Community Engagement, Costing and Financing, Curriculum Development, Directories, Faculty Development, Increasing Diversity, Increasing Health Workforce, Information and Communications Technology, Medical Disciplines, Monitoring and Evaluation, Retention Strategies, Teaching Methods, Policies and Regulations, Women and

Medicine. An interactive map is available for searching the library resources by country in addition to an overall keyword search option. The keywords used are available as a separate document to inform participants of the search terms and support them in locating relevant resources.

An instructional management plan was created to monitor the use and interaction of the web-based platform based on system analytics in order to be able to follow-up with personal e-mail communication to encourage participation and further conversation. This has become easier to accomplish as more activity is recorded on the system itself. Indicators include accessing the electronic monthly newsletter, forwarding it to others, participating in a monthly synchronous webinar, asking questions, participating in asynchronous eDiscussions, and becoming active within the community's social network through participating in interest groups. Evaluating the information collected can provide guidance for improvement and can provide evidence of CoI presences. The focus of such monitoring and evaluation is to be able to align goals with the activities and interaction within a community in a fairly dynamic manner. Reliance on system analytics is part of the effort for managing the cyberlearning environment to support conversational learning. This is coupled with monthly telephone conversations with each school's ICT contact to encourage familiarity with the environment itself and to serve as conduits for further engagement with the system. In addition, the ICT contacts function as usability agents testing the platform for technical enhancements and for getting feedback from the larger audience within each one of their schools for content-related enhancements.

Establishing personal connections at a distance is difficult enough, let alone trying to involve participants who have not yet accepted the technology fully as part of their daily routine. The Technology Acceptance Model (TAM) (Davis, Bagozzi, & Warshaw, 1989), a model widely used in e-commerce stemming from information systems theory,

identified perceived ease of use and perceived usefulness as constructs that impact individuals' attitude toward using a particular technology and their intention to use. It became apparent early on in the project, during audience analysis, that to support the development of a community of inquiry, the cyberlearning environment needed to be linked to the overall communication strategy outside of this environment in order to establish personal connections and perceived usefulness. Therefore, for years 1 and 2 the design focused on establishing social presence (see Figure 3) through informal learning opportunities mapped along the intentional to incidental axis shown in Figure 5.

Efforts focused on gaining information regarding the environment's ease of use as this was needed to be able to make adjustments to the platform to better meet the needs of the audience. Open communication (social presence) outside the environment was conducted via the monthly ICT contact telephone calls. The calls were organized around structured conversations that are part of the overall communication strategy. For example, the first such conversation was introducing each contact to the site and in particular to the location of their own school's page where participants could add their own news, activities, relevant resources, etc. Before this conversation, none of the 13 schools had added any of their own materials to their school's page even after email instructions and reminders. After this first conversation, 7 out of the 13 schools have added relevant content within the context of medical education to their school page. The second conversation focused on usability questions. Out of the conversations with all contacts, recommendations for re-design of the environment have emerged that are in the process of being implemented for testing.

Group cohesion is starting to emerge out of these conversations as well. An ICT in medical education group was created as part of the environment that currently has 20 members but 10 joined after the webinars and telephone conversations started to happen. Emotional expression (social presence) is being cultivated by offering opportunities for engagement, but this is not something that is prioritized in the design for a number of reasons. This is an authenticated site, and even though it utilizes its own social network tool, it is not open to the public, which is inherently limiting. This is one of the areas that is being proposed for re-consideration in terms of strategy as well as re-design in terms of the cyberlearning environment.

SOLUTIONS AND RECOMMENDATIONS

The design-based approach described so far in this chapter assumes development over time. The chapter focused on years 1 and 2 of the project to establish a cyberlearning community of inquiry environment. Recognizing that doing so in the context of medical education with faculty and students spread in multiple countries required an approach to design that is itself design-based. This allowed assumptions to be made and proven wrong so that a better design to support such a community of inquiry could emerge. This approach to design emphasizes long-term impacts and sustainability and is inherently itself a developmental process.

As part of this developmental process, it is important to take into account the following design recommendations:

- Determine initially the learners' motivational drivers as well as the level of technology acceptance of the core platform to be used.
- Depending on the complexity of the audience and context, utilize communication strategies that are both traditional and electronic.
- Design at both the macro- and micro-levels to account for learning opportunities across the spectrum of formal, non-formal, and informal as well as incidental and intentional.
- Establish a long-term design plan for monitoring and evaluation of both the system itself and of the learning to occur. In such a plan, account for the learning that occurs as part of the developmental process.

FUTURE RESEARCH DIRECTIONS

Designing a cyberlearning community of inquiry within the context of medical education for a diverse audience across many countries is a challenge welcome by most designers. It allows for innovation in design. Using the Community of Inquiry as the design framework allowed the design of the cyberlearning environment to be built across multiple dimensions at both macro- and micro-levels. The CoI framework was linked to motivational design to drive decisions on tools and strategy (Figure 5). An overlay of formal, non-formal, and informal learning across the incidental to intentional learning continuum was added to account for designing interaction through conversations. All this and following a design-based approach made this system quite complex. Why?

CoI has traditionally been implemented as a design model for formal learning. This project utilizes it as its core framework to design and form a community of inquiry that has yet to be developed. In other words, CoI is being implemented as a developmental framework to drive the design of a cyberlearning environment. It has been taken apart and implemented for design purposes across multiple years following a design-based approach. This type of design extends the CoI framework by adding these several dimensions and exploring their operationalization. This is an area that requires further research specifically to investigate instructional design using the CoI framework across time and with multiple dimensions.

CONCLUSION

The chapter addressed a design-based approach for implementing a cyberlearning environment to function as a community of inquiry within the context of medical education. The design of such an environment accounted for several different dimensions. At the macro-level it took into consideration the presences – teaching, social, and cognitive – of the CoI framework. It examined the design of the cyberlearning environment by considering ways to incorporate each one of the CoI presences in ways that would promote conversational learning across the continuum of formal to informal learning. It also addressed the need of a comprehensive communication strategy as part of the design of the community.

This is a multi-year project, and the focus of this chapter has been on the design decisions and implementation for years 1 and 2. Lessons learned have been identified throughout the design-based approach discussion and recommendations are provided. However, the work as well as lessons learned as the design-based approach for implementing such a cyberlearning community of inquiry continues. For years 3 and 4, the design focuses on expanded formal, non-formal, and informal learning opportunities made available via the cyberlearning environment, to engage participants in reflection on what it is they are learning and how it has or has not influenced their practice. The key learning outcome expected as part of this step is for participants to initiate knowledge exchanges. Through the work of an e-learning technical working group it is planned to engage participants in fully online formal educa-tion opportunities in medical education. The key learning outcome expected as part of this year 5 step is for participants to display a commitment to their own professional development through their participation in these formal education op-portunities.

Further research to explore the multi-di-mensionality of the instructional design model implemented for this cyberlearning environment is needed. As the project progresses such research is being planned to test and adjust the design decisions for the creation of this community of inquiry in medical education.

REFERENCES

Akyol, Z., & Garrison, D. R. (2008). The devel-opment of a community of inquiry over time in an online course: Understanding the progression and integration of social, cognitive and teaching presence. *Journal of Asynchronous Learning Networks, 12*(3-4), 3–22.

Akyol, Z., Garrison, D. R., & Ozden, M. (2009). Online and blended communities of inquiry: Exploring the developmental and perceptional differences. *International Review of Research in Open and Distance Learning, 10*(6), 65–83. Retrieved from http://www.irrodl.org/index.php/irrodl/article/view/765/1436

Akyol, Z., Vaughan, N., & Garrison, D. R. (2011). The impact of course duration on the development of a community of inquiry. *Inter-active Learning Environments, 19*(3), 231–246. doi:10.1080/10494820902809147

Anderson, T., Rourke, L., Garrison, D. R., & Archer, W. (2001). Assessing teaching presence in computer conferencing context. *Journal of Asynchronous Learning Networks, 5*(2), 1–17.

Baker, A. C., Jensen, P. J., & Kolb, D. A. (2002). *Conversational learning: An experiential approach to knowledge creation.* Westport, CT: Quorum Books.

Barab, S. A., & Duffy, T. M. (2000). From practice fields to communities of practice. In Jonassen, D. H., & Land, S. M. (Eds.), *Theoretical foundations of learning environments* (pp. 25–55). Mahwah, NJ: Lawrence Erlbaum Associates.

Boyd, G. (2004). Conversation theory. In Jonassen, D. H., & Jonassen, D. H. (Eds.), *Handbook of research on educational communications and technology* (2nd ed., pp. 179–197). Mahwah, NJ: Lawrence Erlbaum Associates Publishers.

Clark, D. R. (2010). Formal and informal learning. Retrieved November 15, 2011, from http://nwlink.com/~donclark/leader/leader.html

Colardyn, D., & Bjornawold, J. (2004). Validation of formal, non-formal and informal learning: policy and practices in EU member states. *European Journal of Education, 39*(1), 70–89. doi:10.1111/j.0141-8211.2004.00167.x

Community of Inquiry. (2011). COI model. Retrieved from http://communitiesofinquiry.com/model

Davis, F. D., Bagozzi, R. P., & Warshaw, P. R. (1989). User acceptance of computer technology: A comparison of two theoretical models. *Management Science, 35,* 982–1003. doi:10.1287/mnsc.35.8.982

Garrison, D. R. (2009). Communities of inquiry in online learning: Social, teaching and cognitive presence. In Howard, C. (Eds.), *Encyclopedia of distance and online learning* (2nd ed., pp. 352–355). Hershey, PA: IGI Global. doi:10.4018/978-1-60566-198-8.ch052

Garrison, D. R., Anderson, T., & Archer, W. (2000). Critical inquiry in a text-based environment: Computer conferencing in higher education. *The Internet and Higher Education, 2*(2-3), 87–105. doi:10.1016/S1096-7516(00)00016-6

Garrison, D. R., Anderson, T., & Archer, W. (2001). Critical thinking, cognitive presence, and computer conferencing in distance education. *American Journal of Distance Education, 15*(1). doi:10.1080/08923640109527071

Gray, B. (2004). Informal learning in an online community of practice. *Journal of Distance Education, 19*(1), 20–35.

Keller, J. M. (2006). What is motivational design? Retrieved from http://arcsmodel.com/pdf/Motivational%20Design%20Rev%20060620.pdf

Keller, J. M. (2010). *Motivational design for learning and performance: The ARCS model approach.* New York, NY: Springer. doi:10.1007/978-1-4419-1250-3

Keller, J. M., & Suzuki, K. (2004). Learner motivation and E-learning design: A multinationally validated process. *Journal of Educational Media, 29*(3), 229–239. doi:10.1080/1358165042000283084

Kilpartrick, S., Barrett, M., & Jones, T. (2003). Defining learning communities. Research and learning in Regional Australia, University of Tasmania, D1/2003. Retrieved from http://www.crlra.utas.edu.au/

Luppicini, R. (2008). Introducing conversation design. In Luppicini, R. (Ed.), *Handbook of conversation design for instructional applications* (pp. 1–18). Hershey, PA: IGI Global. doi:10.4018/978-1-59904-597-9.ch001

Mezirow, J. (2009). Transformative learning theory. In Mezirow, J., & Taylor, E. W. (Eds.), *Transformative learning in practice: Insights from community, workplace, and higher education* (pp. 18–32). San Francisco, CA: Jossey-Bass.

National Science Foundation. (2008). Fostering learning in the networked world: The cyberlearning opportunity and challenge. Retrieved from http://cyberlearningstem.org/assets/nsf08204.pdf

Rourke, L., & Kanuka, H. (2009). Learning in communities of inquiry: A review of the literature. *Journal of Distance Education, 23*(1), 19–48.

Suzuki, K., & Keller, J. M. (1996). Applications of the ARCS model in computer-based instruction in Japan. Annual Meeting of the Japanese Educational Technology Association, Kanazawa, Japan.

Swan, K., & Shea, P. (2005). The development of virtual learning communities. In Hiltz, S. R., & Goldman, R. (Eds.), *Asynchronous learning networks: The research frontier* (pp. 239–260). New York, NY: Hampton Press.

Swann, J. (2009). A dialogic approach to online facilitation. In Same Places, Different Spaces, Proceedings ASCILITE Auckland 2009. Retrieved from http://www.ascilite.org.au/conferences/auckland09/procs/swann.pdf

Wenger, E. (2002). Cultivating communities of practice: a quick start-up guide. Retrieved from http://www.ewenger.com/theory/start-up_guide_PDF.pdf

Wenger, E. (2006). Communities of practice: A brief introduction. Retrieved from http://www.ewenger.com/theory/

Wenger, E., McDermott, R., & Snyder, W. (2002). *Cultivating communities of practice: A guide to managing knowledge.* Boston, MA: Harvard Business School Press.

ADDITIONAL READING

Akyol, Z., & Garrison, D. (2011a). Assessing metacognition in an online community of inquiry. *The Internet and Higher Education, 14*(3), 183–190. doi:10.1016/j.iheduc.2011.01.005

Akyol, Z., & Garrison, D. (2011b). Understanding cognitive presence in an online and blended community of inquiry: Assessing outcomes and processes for deep approaches to learning. *British Journal of Educational Technology, 42*(2), 233–250. doi:10.1111/j.1467-8535.2009.01029.x

Allard, C. C., Goldblatt, P. F., Kemball, J. I., Kendrick, S. A., Millen, K., & Smith, D. M. (2007). Becoming a reflective community of practice. *Reflective Practice, 8*(3), 299–314. doi:10.1080/14623940701424801

Arbaugh, J. B., Bangert, A., & Cleveland-Innes, M. (2010). Subject matter effects and the Community of Inquiry (CoI) framework: An exploratory study. *The Internet and Higher Education, 13*(1/2), 37–44. doi:10.1016/j.iheduc.2009.10.006

Arbaugh, J. B., Cleveland-Innes, M., Diaz, S. R., Garrison, D., Ice, P., Richardson, J. C., & Swan, K. P. (2008). Developing a community of inquiry instrument: Testing a measure of the Community of Inquiry framework using a multi-institutional sample. *The Internet and Higher Education, 11*(3/4), 133–136. doi:10.1016/j.iheduc.2008.06.003

Bangert, A. W. (2009). Building a validity argument for the community of inquiry survey instrument. *The Internet and Higher Education, 12*(2), 104–111. doi:10.1016/j.iheduc.2009.06.001

Fusco, J., Haavind, S., Remold, J., & Schank, P. (2011). Exploring differences in online professional development seminars with the community of inquiry framework. *Educational Media International*, *48*(3), 139–149. doi:10.1080/095 23987.2011.607318

Garrison, D., & Arbaugh, J. B. (2007). Researching the community of inquiry framework: Review, issues, and future directions. *The Internet and Higher Education*, *10*(3), 157–172. doi:10.1016/j. iheduc.2007.04.001

Golding, C. (2011). Educating for critical thinking: thought-encouraging questions in a community of inquiry. *Higher Education Research & Development*, *30*(3), 357–370. doi:10.1080/07294360.20 10.499144

Jones, A. (2011). Teaching history at university through communities of inquiry. *Australian Historical Studies*, *42*(2), 168–193. doi:10.1080/103 1461X.2010.531747

Ke, F. (2010). Examining online teaching, cognitive, and social presence for adult students. *Computers & Education*, *55*(2), 808–820. doi:10.1016/j.compedu.2010.03.013

Lowenthal, P. R., & Dunlap, J. C. (2010). From pixel on a screen to real person in your students' lives: Establishing social presence using digital storytelling. *The Internet and Higher Education*, *13*(1/2), 70–72. doi:10.1016/j.iheduc.2009.10.004

Parsons, L. T. (2009). Readers researching their reading: Creating a community of inquiry. *Language Arts*, *86*(4), 257–267.

Powell, S., Tindal, I., & Millwood, R. (2008). Personalized learning and the Ultraversity experience. *Interactive Learning Environments*, *16*(1), 63–81. doi:10.1080/10494820701772710

Richmond, G., & Manokore, V. (2011). Identifying elements critical for functional and sustainable professional learning communities. *Science Education*, *95*(3), 543–570. doi:10.1002/sce.20430

Rubin, B., Fernandes, R., Avgerinou, M. D., & Moore, J. (2010). The effect of learning management systems on student and faculty outcomes. *The Internet and Higher Education*, *13*(1/2), 82–83. doi:10.1016/j.iheduc.2009.10.008

Saw, K. G., Majid, O., Abdul Ghani, N. N., Atan, H. H., Idrus, R. M., Rahman, Z. A., & Tan, K. E. (2008). The videoconferencing learning environment: Technology, interaction and learning intersect. *British Journal of Educational Technology*, *39*(3), 475–485. doi:10.1111/j.1467-8535.2007.00736.x

Shea, P., & Bidjerano, T. (2009). Community of inquiry as a theoretical framework to foster "epistemic engagement" and "cognitive presence" in online education. *Computers & Education*, *52*(3), 543–553. doi:10.1016/j.compedu.2008.10.007

Shea, P., Gozza-Cohen, M., Uzuner, S., Mehta, R., Valtcheva, A., Hayes, S., & Vickers, J. (2011). The Community of Inquiry framework meets the SOLO taxonomy: a process-product model of online learning. *Educational Media International*, *48*(2), 101–113. doi:10.1080/09523987.2 011.576514

Shea, P., Hayes, S., Vickers, J., Gozza-Cohen, M., Uzuner, S., & Mehta, R. (2010). A re-examination of the community of inquiry framework: Social network and content analysis. *The Internet and Higher Education*, *13*(1/2), 10–21. doi:10.1016/j. iheduc.2009.11.002

Stein, D. S., Wanstreet, C. E., Glazer, H. R., Engle, C. L., Harris, R. A., & Johnston, S. M. (2007). Creating shared understanding through chats in a community of inquiry. *The Internet and Higher Education, 10*(2), 103–115. doi:10.1016/j.iheduc.2007.02.002

Using Data to Improve Online Courses. (2011). *Distance Education Report, 15*(10), 5–7.

Wanstreet, C. E., & Stein, D. S. (2011). Presence over time in synchronous communities of inquiry. *American Journal of Distance Education, 25*(3), 162–177. doi:10.1080/08923647.2011.590062

Waterston, R. (2011). Interaction in online inter-professional education case discussions. *Journal of Interprofessional Care, 25*(4), 272–279. doi:10.3109/13561820.2011.566647

Compilation of References

Abrams, Z. (2001). Computer-mediated communication and group journals: Expanding the repertoire of participant roles. *System*, *29*, 489–503.

Abrams, Z. I. (2003). The effect of synchronous and asynchronous CMC on oral performance in German. *Modern Language Journal*, *87*(2), 157–167. doi:10.1111/1540-4781.00184

Ahern, T. C., Thomas, J. A., Tallent-Runnels, M. K., Lan, W. Y., Cooper, S., Lu, X., & Cyrus, J. (2006). The effect of social grounding on collaboration in a computer-mediated small group discussion. *The Internet and Higher Education*, *9*, 37–46. doi:10.1016/j.iheduc.2005.09.008

Akyol, Z. (2009). *Examining teaching presence, social presence, cognitive presence, satisfaction and learning in online and blended course contexts*. Doctoral dissertation, Middle East Technical University, 2009.

Akyol, Z., & Garrison, D. R. (2008). The development of a community of inquiry over time in an online course: Understanding the progression and integration of social, cognitive and teaching presence. *Journal of Asynchronous Learning Networks*, *12* (3-4), 3-22. Retrieved March 28, 2011, from http://eric.ed.gov/PDFS/EJ837483.pdf

Akyol, Z., Arbaugh, J. B., Cleveland-Innes, M., Garrison, D. R., Ice, P., Richardson, J. C., Swan, K. (2003). A response to the review of the community of inquiry framework. *Journal of Distance Education / Revue de l'Éducation à Distance*, *23*(2) 123-136.

Akyol, Z., & Garrison, D. R. (2008). The development of a community of inquiry over time in an online course: Understanding the progression and integration of social, cognitive and teaching presence. *Journal of Asynchronous Learning Networks*, *12*(2-3), 3–23.

Akyol, Z., & Garrison, D. R. (2011). Assessing metacognition in an online community of inquiry. *The Internet and Higher Education*, *14*(3), 183–190.

Akyol, Z., & Garrison, D. R. (2011). Understanding cognitive presence in an online and blended community of inquiry: Assessing outcomes and processes for deep approaches to learning. *British Journal of Educational Technology*, *42*(2), 233–250.

Akyol, Z., & Garrison, D. R. (2011). Understanding cognitive presence in an online and blended community of inquiry: Assessing outcomes and processes for deep approaches to learning. *British Journal of Educational Technology*, *42*(2), 233–250.

Akyol, Z., Garrison, D. R., & Ozden, M. Y. (2009). Online and blended communities of inquiry: Exploring the developmental and perceptual differences. *International Review of Research in Open and Distance Learning*, *10*(6), 65–83.

Akyol, Z., & Garrison, R. (2008). The development of a Community of Inquiry over time in an online course: Understanding the progression and integration of social, cognitive and teaching presence. *Journal of Asynchronous Learning Networks*, *12*(3-4), 3–22.

Akyol, Z., Vaughan, N., & Garrison, D. R. (2011). The impact of course duration on the development of a community of inquiry. *Interactive Learning Environments*, *19*(3), 231–246. doi:10.1080/10494820902809147

Alberta Assessment Consortium. (2002). *About classroom assessment*. Retrieved from http://www.aac.ab.ca/final2002.doc

Allen, E. I., & Seaman, J. (November, 2011). *Going the distance: Online education in the United States, 2011.* Babson Park, MA: Babson Survey Research Group and Quahog Research Group, LLC. Retrieved August 8, 2012, from http://www.onlinelearningsurvey.com/reports/goingthedistance.pdf

Allen, I. E., & Seaman, J. (2010). *Learning on demand: Online education in the United States, 2009.* (Research Report No. 7). Retrieved from http://www.sloanc.org/publications/survey/pdf/learningondemand.pdf

Allen, I. E., & Seaman, J. (2004). *Entering the mainstream: The quality and extent of online education in the United States, 2003 and 2004.* Needham, MA: Sloan-C.

Allen, I., & Seaman, J. (2007). *Online Nation: Five years of growth in online learning.* Needham, MA: Sloan Consortium.

Alverno College. (2001). *Assessment essentials: Definition of terms.* Retrieved from http://depts.alverno.edu/saal/terms.html

Amemado, D. (2010a). University models with high-growth probability, under ICT integration, during the next decade in North America. In J. Sanchez & K. Zhang (Eds.), *Proceedings of World Conference on E-Learning in Corporate, Government, Healthcare, and Higher Education 2010* (pp. 1309-1313). Chesapeake, VA: AACE.

Amemado, D. (2010b). *Changements et évolution des universités conventionnelles sous l'influence des technologies de l'information et de la communication (TIC): Le cas du contexte universitaire nord-américain.* Unpublished doctoral dissertation, University of Montreal, Canada.

American Association of Higher Education and Accreditation. (1996). *Nine principles of good practice for assessing student learning.* Retrieved from http://www.niu.edu/assessment/Manual/media/9Principles.pdf

Anderson, T. (2003). Getting the mix right again: An updated and theoretical rationale for interaction. *International Review of Research in Open and Distance Learning, 4*(2).

Anderson, T., & Garrison, D. R. (1998). Learning in a networked world: New roles and responsibilities. In Gibson, C. (Ed.), *Distance learners in higher education* (pp. 97–112). Madison, WI: Atwood Publishing.

Anderson, T., Rourke, L., Garrison, D. R., & Archer, W. (2001). Assessing teaching presence in a computer conference environment. *Journal of Asynchronous Learning Networks, 5*(2).

Anderson, T., Rourke, L., Garrison, D. R., & Archer, W. (2001). Assessing teaching presence in computer conferencing context. *Journal of Asynchronous Learning Networks, 5*(2), 1–17.

Andrews, J. (1980). The verbal structure of teacher questions: Its impact on class discussion. *POD Quarterly: Journal of Professional and Organizational Development Network in Higher Education, 2*(3&4), 129–163.

Andriessen, J. (2006). Collaboration in computer conferencing. In O'Donnell, A. M., Hmelo-Silver, C., & Erkens, G. (Eds.), *Collaborative learning, reasoning and technology* (pp. 197–232). Mahwah, NJ: Erlbaum.

Angelino, L. M., Williams, F. K., & Natvig, D. (2007). Strategies to engage online students and reduce attrition rates. *The Journal of Educators Online, 4*(2), 1–14.

Angelo, T. A., & Cross, K. P. (1993). *A handbook of classroom assessment techniques for college teachers.* San Francisco, CA: Jossey-Bass.

Anglin, G. J., & Morrison, G. R. (2002). Evaluation and research in distance education: Implications for research. In Vrasidas, C., & Glass, G. V. (Eds.), *Distance education and distributed learning* (pp. 157–180). Greenwich, CT: Information Age Publishing.

Antaki, C., & Lewis, A. (1986). Mental mirrors. In Antaki, C., & Lewis, A. (Eds.), *Mental mirrors: Metacognition in social knowledge and communication.* London, UK: Sage Publications.

Antón, M., DiCamilla, F., & Lantolf, J. (2003). Sociocultural theory and the acquisition of Spanish as a second language. In Lafford, B., & Salaberry, R. (Eds.), *Spanish second language acquisition. State of the science* (pp. 262–284). Washington, DC: Georgetown University Press.

Arbaugh, J. B., Cleveland-Innes, M., Diaz, D. P., Garrison, D. R., Ice, P., Richardson, J., Swan, K. (2007a). *Community of Inquiry survey instrument.*

Arbaugh, J. B., Cleveland-Innes, M., Diaz, S., Garrison, D. R., Ice, P., Richardson, J., et al. (November 2007). *Community of inquiry framework: Validation & instrument development.* 13th Annual Sloan-C Conference Presentation. Orlando, Florida.

Arbaugh, J. B. (2005). Is there an optimal design for online MBA courses? *Academy of Management Learning & Education, 4,* 135–149.

Arbaugh, J. B. (2007). An empirical verification of the community of inquiry framework. *Journal of Asynchronous Learning Networks, 11*(1), 73–84.

Arbaugh, J. B. (2008). Does the community of inquiry framework predict outcomes in online MBA courses? *International Review of Research in Open and Distance Learning, 9*(2), 1–21.

Arbaugh, J. B., Bangert, A., & Cleveland-Innes, M. (2010). Subject matter effects and the Community of Inquiry (CoI) framework: An exploratory study. *The Internet and Higher Education, 13,* 37–44. doi:10.1016/j.iheduc.2009.10.006

Arbaugh, J. B., & Benbunan-Fich, R. (2006). An investigation of epistemological and social dimensions of teaching in online learning environments. *Academy of Management Learning & Education, 5*(4), 435–447.

Arbaugh, J. B., & Benbunan-Fich, R. (2006). Separating the effects of knowledge construction and group collaboration in learning outcomes of web-based courses. *Information & Management, 43*(6), 778–793. doi:10.1016/j.im.2005.09.001

Arbaugh, J. B., Cleveland-Innes, M., Diaz, S. R., Garrison, D. R., Ice, P., Richardson, J. C., & Swan, K. P. (2008). Developing a community of inquiry instrument: Testing a measure of the Community of Inquiry framework using a multi-institutional sample. *The Internet and Higher Education, 11*(3-4), 133–136. doi:10.1016/j.iheduc.2008.06.003

Arbaugh, J. B., & Hwang, A. (2006). Does "teaching presence" exist in online MBA courses? *The Internet and Higher Education, 9*(1), 9–21.

Archer, W. (2010). Beyond online discussions: Extending the Community of Inquiry Framework to entire courses. *The Internet and Higher Education, 13*(1-2), 69–70. doi:10.1016/j.iheduc.2009.10.005doi:10.1016/j.iheduc.2009.10.005

Archibald, D. (2011). *Fostering cognitive presence in higher education through the authentic design, delivery, and evaluation of an online learning resource: A mixed methods study.* Unpublished doctoral dissertation, University of Ottawa, Ottawa

Archibald, D. (2010). Fostering the development of cognitive presence: Initial findings using the community of inquiry survey instrument. *The Internet and Higher Education, 13*(1-2), 73–74.

Arend, B. (2009). Encouraging critical thinking through online threaded discussions. *The Journal of Educators Online, 6*(1), 1–23.

Arnold, N., & Ducate, L. (2006). Future foreign language teachers' social and cognitive collaboration in an online environment. *Language Learning & Technology, 10*(1), 42–66.

Arnold, N., Ducate, L., Lomicka, L., & Lord, G. (2005). Using computer-mediated communication to establish social and supportive environments in teacher education. *CALICO Journal, 22,* 537–566.

Arnold, N., Ducate, L., Lomicka, L., & Lord, G. (2009). Assessing online collaboration among language teachers: A cross-institutional case study. *Journal of Interactive Online Learning, 8*(2), 121–139.

Artino, A. R. Jr. (2009). Think, feel, act: Motivational and emotional influences on military students' online academic success. *Journal of Computing in Higher Education, 21,* 146–166. doi:10.1007/s12528-009-9020-9

Artino, A. R. Jr. (2010). Online or face-to-face learning? exploring the personal factors that predict students' choice of instructional format. *The Internet and Higher Education, 13*(4), 272–276. doi:10.1016/j.iheduc.2010.07.005

Ashlie-Fridie, B. (2008). Take the fear out: Motivating faculty to design online courses. In K. McFerrin, et al. (Eds.), *Proceedings of Society for Information Technology & Teacher Education International Conference 2008,* (pp. 1325-1330). Chesapeake, VA: AACE.

Astin, A. (1984). Student involvement: A developmental theory for higher education. *Journal of College Student Personnel, 25*(3), 297–308.

Atkinson, M. P. (2001). The scholarship of teaching and learning: Reconceptualizing scholarship and transforming the academy. *Social Forces*, *79*(4), 1217–1229. doi:10.1353/sof.2001.0029

Averweg, U. R. (2010). Enabling role of an intranet to augment e-coaching. *Industrial and Commercial Training*, *42*(1), 47–52.

Bai, H. (2009). Facilitating students' critical thinking in online discussion: An instructor's experience. *Journal of Interactive Online Learning*, *8*(2), 156–164.

Baker, J. (September 2006). *Baker's guide to Christian distance education*. Retrieved September 17, 2006, from http://www.bakersguide.com/Distance_Education_Timeline/

Baker, A. C., Jensen, P. J., & Kolb, D. A. (2002). *Conversational learning: An experiential approach to knowledge creation*. Westport, CT: Quorum Books.

Baker, J., Redfield, K., & Tonkin, S. (2006). Collaborative coaching and networking for online instructors. *Online Journal of Distance Learning Administration*, *9*(4). Retrieved from www.westga.edu/~distance/ojdla/winter94/baker94.htm

Bangert, A. W. (2010). Building a validity argument for the community of inquiry survey instrument. *The Internet and Higher Education*, *12*, 104–111.

Banks, J. A., Cookson, P., Gay, G., Hawley, W. D., Irvine, J. J., & Nieto, S. … Stephan, W. G. (2001). *Diversity within unity: Essential principles for teaching and learning in a multicultural society*. Center for Multicultural Education, University of Washington. Retrieved July 6, 2010 from http://education.washington.edu/cme/DiversityUnity.pdf

Barab, S. A. (2003). An introduction to the special issue: Designing for virtual communities in the service of learning. *The Information Society*, *19*(3), 197–201.

Barab, S. A., & Duffy, T. M. (2000). From practice fields to communities of practice. In Jonassen, D. H., & Land, S. M. (Eds.), *Theoretical foundations of learning environments* (pp. 25–55). Mahwah, NJ: Lawrence Erlbaum Associates.

Barab, S. A., Kling, R., & Gray, J. H. (2004). Introduction. In Barab, S. A., Kling, R., & Gray, J. H. (Eds.), *Designing for virtual communities in the service of l earning* (pp. 3–15). New York, NY: Cambridge University Press. doi:10.1017/CBO9780511805080.005

Barber, T. C. (2011). The online crit: The community of inquiry meets design education. *Journal of Distance Education*, *25*(1). Retrieved from http://www.jofde.ca/index.php/jde/article/view/723/1189

Barkley, E., Cross, K. P., & Mayor, C. H. (2005). *Collaborative learning techniques: A handbook for college faculty*. San Francisco, CA: Jossey-Bass.

Barnes, S. B. (2008). Understanding social media from the media ecological perspective. In Konijn, E. A., Utz, S., Tanis, M., & Barnes, S. B. (Eds.), *Mediated interpersonal communication* (pp. 14–33). New York, NY: Routledge.

Barr, R. B., & Tagg, J. (1995). A new paradigm for undergraduate education. *Change*, *27*(6), 13–25. Retrieved from http://critical.tamucc.edu/~blalock/readings/tch2learn.htm

Basit, T. N. (2003). Manual or electronic? The role of coding in qualitative data analysis. *Educational Research*, *45*(2), 143–154. doi:10.1080/0013188032000133548

Bates, A. W., & Gpe, J. (1997). Crossing boundaries: making global distance education a reality. *Journal of Distance Education*, *12*(1/2), 49–66.

Bateson, G. (1972). *Steps to an ecology of mind*. New York, NY: Ballantine Books.

Baudrillard, J. (1998). Simulacra and simulations. In Poster, M. (Ed.), *Jean Baudrillard: Selected writings* (pp. 166–184). Palo Alto, CA: Stanford University Press.

Bauer, B., de Benedette, L., Furstenberg, G., Levet, S., & Waryn, S. (2006). The Cultura Project. In Belz, J. A., & Thorne, S. L. (Eds.), *Internet-mediated intercultural FL education* (pp. 31–62). Boston, MA: Heinle & Heinle.

Baylor, A. L., & Kim, Y. (2005). Simulating instructional roles through pedagogical agents. *International Journal of Artificial Intelligence in Education*, *15*(1), 95–115.

Bean, J. P., & Metzner, B. S. (1985). A conceptual model of nontraditional undergraduate student attrition. *Review of Educational Research*, *55*(4), 485–540.

Becerra Labra, C., Gras-Martí, A., Hernández Hernández, C., Montoya Vargas, J., Osorio Gómez, L. A., & Sancho Vinuesa, T. (2012). (accepted). Renovación de la Enseñanza Universitaria Basada en Evidencias (REUBE): Una metodología de acción flexible. *Perfiles Educativos*.

Bedford, L. A. (2009). The professional adjunct: An emerging trend in online instruction. *Online Journal of Distance Learning Administration, 12*(3).

Beers, P., Boshuizen, H., Kirschner, P. A., & Gijselaers, W. H. (2005). Computer support for knowledge construction in collaborative learning environment. *Computers in Human Behavior, 21*, 623–643.

Beers, P., Boshuizen, H., Kirschner, P. A., & Gijselaers, W. H. (2007). The analysis of negotiation of common ground in CSCL. *Learning and Instruction, 17*(4), 427–435.

Benbunan-Fich, R., & Hiltz, S. R. (1999). Impacts of asynchronous learning networks on individual and group problem solving: A field experiment. *Group Decision and Negotiation, 8*(5), 409–426.

Benbunan-Fich, R., Hiltz, S. R., & Harasim, L. (2005). The online interaction learning model: An integrated theoretical framework for learning networks. In Hiltz, S. R., & Goldman, R. (Eds.), *Learning together online - Research on asynchronous learning networks* (pp. 19–37). Mahwah, NJ: Lawrence Erlbaum Associates.

Benbunan-Fich, R., Hiltz, S. R., & Turoff, M. (2002). A comparative content analysis of face-to-face vs. asynchronous group decision making. *Decision Support Systems, 34*, 457–469.

Bender, T. (2003). *Discussion-based online teaching to enhance student learning: Theory, practice, assessment*. Sterling, VA: Stylus.

Benjamin, J. (2003). Interactive online educational experiences: E-volution of graded projects. In Reisman, S., Flores, J. G., & Edge, D. (Eds.), *Electronic learning communities: Current issues and best practices* (pp. 1–26). Greenwich, CT: Information Age Publishing.

Benner, P. (1984). *From novice to expert: Excellence and power in clinical nursing practice*. Menlo Park, CA: Addison-Wesley. doi:10.1097/00000446-198412000-00025

Bennett, C., Niggle, T., & Stage, F. (1990). Preservice multicultural teacher education: Predictors of student readiness. *Teaching and Teacher Education, 6*(3), 243–254. doi:10.1016/0742-051X(90)90016-X

Berge, Z. L., & Huang, Y. (2004). A model of sustainable student retention: A holistic perspective on the student dropout problem with special attention to e-learning. *DEOSNEWS, 13*(5). Retrieved from http://www.ed.psu.edu/acsde/deos/deosnews/deosnews13_5.pdf

Berge, Z. L. (1995). Facilitating computer conferencing: Recommendations from the field. *Journal of Educational Technology & Society, 35*(1), 22–30.

Bergquist, W. H., & Phillips, S. R. (1981). *A handbook for faculty development* (*Vol. 3*). Washington, DC: The Council of Independent Colleges.

Betts, K. S. (1998). Why do faculty participate in distance education? *The Technology Source*, October 1998.

Bielaczyc, K., & Collins, A. (1999). Learning communities: A reconceptualization of educational practice. In Reigeluth, C. M. (Ed.), *Instructional design theories and models* (*Vol. II*, pp. 30, 269–292). Mahwah, NJ: Lawrence Erlbaum Associates.

Bielaczyc, K., & Collins, A. (2006). Fostering knowledge-creating communities. In O'Donnell, A. M., Hmelo-Silver, C., & Erkens, G. (Eds.), *Collaborative learning, reasoning and technology* (pp. 37–60). Mahwah, NJ: Erlbaum.

Biggs, J. (1998). Assumptions underlying new approaches to assessment. In Stimson, P., & Morris, P. (Eds.), *Curriculum and assessment in Hong Kong: Two components, one system* (pp. 351–384). Hong Kong: Open University of Hong Kong Press.

Biggs, J. B., & Collis, K. F. (1982). *Evaluating the quality of learning: The SOLO taxonomy*. New York, NY: Academic Press.

Biggs, J., & Tang, C. (2007). *Teaching for quality learning at university* (3rd ed.). Maidenhead, UK: Open University Press.

Blanchette, J. (2010). Questions in the online learning environment. *Journal of Distance Education, 16*(2), 37–57.

Blascovich, J. (2002). A theoretical model of social influence for increasing the utility of collaborative virtual environment. *4th International Conference on Collaborative Virtual Environments, Bonn, Germany, 2002,* (pp. 25-30).

Blau, J. R., & Goodman, N. (Eds.). (1995). *Social role s & social institutions.* New Brunswick, NJ: Transaction Publishers.

Blignaut, S., & Trollip, S. (2003). A taxonomy for faculty participation in asynchronous online discussions. In D. Lassner & C. McNaught (Eds.), *Proceedings of World Conference on Educational Multimedia, Hypermedia and Telecommunications 2003,* (pp. 2043-2050).

Blin, F., & Munro, M. (2008). Why hasn't technology disrupted academics' teaching practices? Understanding resistance to change through the lens of activity theory. *Computers & Education, 50,* 475–490.

Bliss, C. A., & Lawrence, B. (2009). From posts to patterns: A metric to characterize discussion board activity in online courses. *Journal of Asynchronous Learning Networks, 13*(2), 15–32.

Bliss, C. A., & Lawrence, B. (2009). From posts to patterns: A metric to characterize discussion board activity in online courses. *Journal of Asynchronous Learning Networks, 13*(2), 15–32.

Bloom, B. (1956). *Taxonomy of educational objectives.* New York, NY: David McKay.

Bloom, B. S. (1964). *Stability and change in human characteristics.* New York, NY: John Wiley & Sons, Inc.

Bloom, B. S., Engelhart, M. D., Furst, E. J., Hill, W. H., & Krathwohl, D. R. (1956). *Taxonomy of educational objectives – The classification of educational goals, handbook 1, cognitive domain.* London, UK: Longman Group.

Bluckert, P. (2005). The foundations of a psychological approach to executive coaching. *Industrial and Commercial Training, 37*(4), 171–178.

Bogle, L., Cook, V., Day, S., & Swan, K. (2009). Blended program development: Applying the quality matters and community inquiry frameworks to ensure high quality design and implementation. *Journal of the Research Center for Educational Technology (RCET), 5*(2), 51–66.

Bohm, D. (1990). *On dialogue.* Ojai, CA: David Bohm Seminars.

Bohm, D. (1997). *Thought as a system.* New York, NY: Routledge.

Bolliger, D. U., & Wasilik, O. (2009). An analysis of the history of online graduate-level courses taught by an expert instructor. *MERLOT Journal of Online Learning and Teaching, 5*(1).

Bolman, L. G., & Deal, T. E. (2008). *Reframing organizations: Artistry, choice, and leadership.* San Francisco, CA: Jossey-Bass.

Bolton, M. (1999). The role of coaching in student teams: A just-in-time approach to learning. *Journal of Management Education, 23*(3), 233–250.

Bonk, C. J., & Graham, C. R. (2006). *The handbook of blended learning: Global perspectives, local designs* (1st ed.). San Francisco, CA: Pfeiffer.

Bonk, C. J., Wisher, R. A., & Lee, J.-Y. (2004). Moderating learner-centered e-learning: Problems and solutions, benefits and implications. In Roberts, T. S. (Ed.), *Online collaborative learning: Theory and practice* (pp. 54–85). Hershey, PA: Information Science Publishing.

Borkowski, J. G., Chan, L. K. S., & Muthukrishna, N. (2000). A process–oriented model of metacognition: Links between motivation and executive functioning. In Schraw, G., & Impara, J. C. (Eds.), *Issues in the measurement of metacognition* (pp. 1–42). Lincoln, NE: University of Nebraska-Lincoln.

Boston, W. (2010). *Online student retention.* Retrieved from http://wallyboston.com/2010/10/21/online-student-retention

Boston, W., & Ice, P. (2011). Assessing retention in online learning: An administrative perspective. *Online Journal of Distance Learning Administration, 14*(2).

Boston, W., Ice, P., Díaz, S. R., Richardson, J., Gibson, A. M., & Swan, K. (2009). An exploration of the relationship between indicators of the community of inquiry framework and retention in online programs. *Journal of Asynchronous Learning Networks, 13*(3), 67–76.

Boston, W., Ice, P., & Gibson, A. M. (2011). Comprehensive assessment of student retention in online learning environments. *Online Journal of Distance Learning Administration, 14*(1).

Boud, D. J. (2000). Sustainable assessment: rethinking assessment for the learning society. *Studies in Continuing Education, 22*(2), 151–167. Retrieved from http://www.education.uts.edu.au/ostaff/staff/publications/db_28_sce_00.pdfdoi:10.1080/713695728

Boud, D. J. (2007). *Rethinking assessment for higher education: Learning for the longer term*. London, UK: Routledge.

Bourne, K., & Seaman, J. (2005). *Sloan-C special survey report: A look at blended learning*. Needham, MA: The Sloan Consortium.

Boyce, L. A., & Hernez-Broome, G. (2010). E-coaching: Consideration of leadership coaching in a virtual environment. In Clutterbuck, D., & Hussain, Z. (Eds.), *Virtual coach, virtual mentor* (pp. 139–174). Charlotte, NC: Information Age Publishing.

Boyd, G. (2004). Conversation theory. In Jonassen, D. H., & Jonassen, D. H. (Eds.), *Handbook of research on educational communications and technology* (2nd ed., pp. 179–197). Mahwah, NJ: Lawrence Erlbaum Associates Publishers.

Boyer, E. (1990). *Scholarship reconsidered: Priorities of the professoriate*. San Francisco, CA: Jossey-Bass.

Bradley, M. E., Thom, L. R., Hayes, J., & Hay, C. (2008). Ask and you will receive: How question type influences quantity and quality of online discussions. *British Journal of Educational Technology, 39*, 888–900.

Branon, R. F., & Essex, C. (2001). Synchronous and asynchronous communication tools in distance education: A survey of instructors. *TechTrends, 45*, 36–42.

Brewer, S., & Klein, J. D. (2006). Type of positive interdependence and affiliation motive in an asynchronous, collaborative learning environment. *Educational Technology Research and Development, 54*(4), 331–354.

Brewer, S., Klein, J. D., & Mann, K. E. (2003). Using small group strategies with adult re-entry students. *College Student Journal, 37*(2), 286–297.

Bridges, D. (1990). The character of discussion: A focus on students. In Wilen, W. (Ed.), *Teaching and learning through discussion: The theory, research and practice of the discussion method* (pp. 97–112). Springfield, IL: Charles Thomas Publishers.

Brockbank, A. (2008). Is the coaching fit for purpose? A typology of coaching and learning approaches. *Coaching: An International Journal of Theory. Research and Practice, 1*(2), 132–144.

Brockhaus, A., Leppa, C., Bliquez, R., Goldstein, D., & Porter, I. (2011). *Technology Advisory Committee Hybrid Learning Subcommittee draft report, June 2011*. Retrieved November 20, 2011, from http://www.uwb.edu/getattachment/it/tac/tacdocs/TAC-hybrid-learning-report-2011.pdf

Brookfield, S. D. (2006a). *Developing critical thinkers*. Retrieved October 05, 2011, from http://www.stephenbrookfield.com/Dr._Stephen_D._Brookfield/Workshop_Materials_files/Critical_Thinking_materials.pdf

Brookfield, S. D. (2006b). *Discussion as a way of teaching*. Retrieved September 21, 2011, from http://www.stephenbrookfield.com/Dr._Stephen_D._Brookfield/Workshop_Materials.html

Brookfield, S. D. (1995). *Becoming a critically reflective teacher*. San Francisco, CA: Jossey-Bass.

Brookfield, S. D., & Preskill, S. (2005). *Discussion as a way of teaching: Tools and techniques for democratic classrooms* (2nd ed.). San Francisco, CA: Jossey-Bass.

Brown, S. (2004). Assessment for learning. *Learning and Teaching in Higher Education, 1*(1), 81-89. Retrieved from http://www2.glos.ac.uk/offload/tli/lets/lathe/issue1/articles/brown.pdf

Brown, A. (1987). Metacognition, executive control, self control, and other mysterious mechanisms. In Weinert, F., & Kluwe, R. (Eds.), *Metacognition, motivation, and understanding* (pp. 65–116). Hillsdale, NJ: Erlbaum.

Brown, J. S., & Adler, R. P. (2008). Minds on fire: Open education, the long tail, and learning 2.0. *EDUCAUSE Review, 43*(1), 17–32.

Brown, J. S., & Duguid, P. (2000). *The social life of information*. Boston, MA: Harvard Business School Press.

Brown, R. E. (2001). The process of community-building in distance learning classes. *The Internet and Higher Education, 5*(2), 18–35.

Bruffee, K. A. (1999). *Collaborative learning: Higher education, interdependence, and the authority of knowledge* (2nd ed.). Baltimore, MD: Johns Hopkins University Press.

Bruner, J. (1996). *The culture of education.* Cambridge, MA: Harvard University Press.

Buchler, J. (1990). *Metaphysics of natural complexes* (2nd ed.). Albany, NY: State University of New York Press.

Buck Institute for Education. (2011). *What is PBL?* (project based learning) Retrieved October 9, 2011, from http://www.bie.org/about/what_is_pbl

Burbles, N., & Callister, T. (2000). Universities in transition: The promise and challenge of new technologies. *Teachers College Record, 102*(2), 271–293.

Burbules, N. (1993). *Dialogue in teaching: Theory and practice.* New York, NY: Teachers College Press.

Burgess, M. L., & Ice, P. (2011a). Optimal experience in virtual environments among college level developmental readers. *Journal of Educational Computing Research, 44*(4), 429–451. doi:10.2190/EC.44.4.ddoi:10.2190/EC.44.4.d

Burgess, M. L., & Ice, P. (2011b). Using the Community of Inquiry (CoI) model to support 21st century online teaching and learning in multi-user virtual environments. In R. Hinrichs & C. Wankel (Eds.), *Transforming virtual world learning: Cutting edge technologies in higher education.* Emerald Press.

Burgess, M. L., Slate, J. R., Rojas-LeBouef, A., & LaPrairie, K. (2010). Teaching and learning in Second Life: Using the Community of Inquiry (CoI) model to support online instruction with graduate students in instructional technology. *Special Issue of Internet & Higher Education, 13*(1/2), 84–88. doi:10.1016/j.iheduc.2009.12.003doi:10.1016/j.iheduc.2009.12.003

Cacciamani, S., Cesareni, D., Martini, F., Ferrini, T., & Fujita, N. (2011). Influence of participation, facilitator styles, and metacognitive reflection on knowledge building in online university courses. *Computers & Education, 58*, 874–884.

Carnevale, D. (2000). New master plan in Washington State calls for more online instruction. *The Chronicle of Higher Education, 46*(22).

Cannon, D., & Weinstein, M. (1993). Reasoning skills: An overview. In Lipman, M. (Ed.), *Thinking children and education* (pp. 598–604). Dubuque, IA: Kendall Hunt.

Carr-Chellman, A. A. (2010). *Instructional design for teachers ID4T: Improving classroom practice.* New York, NY: Routledge.

Carr-Chellman, A., & Duchastel, P. (2000). The ideal online course. *British Journal of Educational Technology, 31*(3), 229–241.

Cavalier, J. C., Klein, J. D., & Cavalier, F. J. (1995). Effects of cooperative learning on performance, attitude, and group behaviors in a technical team environment. *Educational Technology Research and Development, 43*(3), 61–71.

Cavanaugh, J. (2005). Teaching online – A time comparison. *Online Journal of Distance Learning Administration, 8*(1).

Celentin, P. (2007). Online education: Analysis of interaction and knowledge building patterns among foreign language teachers. *Journal of Distance Education, 21*(3), 39–58.

Champion, D. P., Kiel, D. H., & McLendon, J. A. (1990). Choosing a consulting role. *Training and Development Journal, 44*(2), 66–69.

Chang, C., Paulus, T. M., Pawan, F., & Yalcin, S. (2003). Online learning: Patterns of engagement and interaction among in-service teachers. *Language Learning & Technology, 7*(3), 119–140.

Chang, S. (2004). The roles of mentors in electronic learning environments. *AACE Journal, 12*(3), 331–342.

Chapelle, C. A. (2001). *Computer applications in second language acquisition – Foundations for teaching, testing and research.* Cambridge, UK: Cambridge University Press.

Chase, M., Macfadyen, L., Reeder, K., & Roche, J. (2002). Intercultural challenges in networked learning: hard technologies meet soft skills. *First Monday, 7*(8), 1-22. doi: 10.1.1.131.9140

Chen, L. S., Cheng, Y. M., Weng, S. F., Lin, C. H., & Tan, Y. K. (2005). A computer-based clinical teaching-case system with emulation of time sequence for medical education. *IEICE Transactions on Information and Systems, E88*(5), 816–821.

Chen, N.-S., & Ko, H.-C., Kinshuk, & Lin, T. (2005). A model for synchronous learning using the Internet. *Innovations in Education and Teaching International, 42*(2), 181–194.

Chen, Y.-J., & Willits, F. K. (1999). Dimensions of educational transactions in a videoconferencing learning environment. *American Journal of Distance Education, 13*(1), 45–59.

Chickering, A. W., & Gamson, Z. F. (1987). Seven principles for good practice in undergraduate education. *American Association of Higher Education Bulletin*, 3-7.

Chidambaram, L. (1996). Relational development in computer-supported groups. *Management Information Systems Quarterly, 20*(2), 143–163.

Chin, C., & Langsford, A. (2004). Questioning students in the ways that encourage thinking. *Teaching Science, 5*(50), 16–22.

Chun, D. (1994). Using computer-assisted class discussion to facilitate the acquisition of interactive competence. In Swaffar, J., Romano, S., Arens, K., & Markley, P. (Eds.), *Language learning online: Theory and practice in the ESL and L2 computer classroom* (pp. 57–80). Austin, TX: Labyrinth Publications.

Cilliers, P. (1998). *Complexity and postmodernism*. London, UK: Routledge.

Clark, D. R. (2010). Formal and informal learning. Retrieved November 15, 2011, from http://nwlink.com/~donclark/leader/leader.html

Clark, H. H. (1994). Managing problems in speaking. *Speech Communication, 15*, 243–250. doi:10.1016/0167-6393(94)90075-2

Clark, R. C., & Mayer, R. E. (2008). *E-learning and the science of instruction: Proven guidelines for consumers and designers of multimedia learning* (2nd ed.). San Francisco, CA: Pfeiffer.

Cleveland-Innes, M., Sangra-Morer, A., & Garrison, R. (2008). *The art of teaching in an online community of inquiry: The online teacher as bricoleur.* Paper published in the 5th European Distance Education Network Research Workshop, Paris, France.

Cleveland-Innes, M., & Garrison, D. R. (2009). The role of learner in an online community of inquiry: Instructor support for first time online learners. In Karacapilidis, N. (Ed.), *Solutions and innovations in web-based technologies for augmented learning: Improved platforms, tools and applications* (pp. 167–184). Hershey, PA: IGI Global. doi:10.4018/978-1-60566-238-1.ch001

Cleveland-Innes, M., & Garrison, D. R. (2010). The role of learner in an online community of inquiry: Instructor support for first-time online learners. In Karacapilidis, N. (Ed.), *Web-based learning solutions for communities of practice: Developing virtual environments for social and pedagogical advancements* (pp. 167–184). Hershey, PA: IGI Global.

Cleveland-Innes, M., & Garrison, D. R. (2012). Higher education and post-industrial society: New ideas about teaching, learning, and technology. In Moller, L., & Huett, J. (Eds.), *The next generation of distance education: Unconstrained learning* (pp. 221–248). New York, NY: Springer. doi:10.1007/978-1-4614-1785-9_15

Cleveland-Innes, M., Garrison, D. R., & Kinsel, E. (2007). Role adjustment for learners in an online community of inquiry: Identifying the challenges of incoming online learners. *International Journal of Web-Based Learning and Teaching Technologies, 2*(1), 1–16. doi:10.4018/jwltt.2007010101

Cobb, P., Confrey, J., di Sessa, A., Lehrer, R., & Schauble, L. (2003). Design experiments in educational research. *Educational Researcher, 32*(1), 9–13. doi:10.3102/0013189X032001009

Cogburn, D. L., & Levinson, N. (2003). U.S.-Africa virtual collaboration in globalization studies: Success factors for complex, cross-national learning teams. *International Studies Perspectives, 4*, 34–51.

Cohen, E. B., & Nycz, M. (2006). Learning objects: An informing science perspective. *Interdisciplinary Journal of Knowledge and Learning Objects, 2*, 23–34.

Cohen, E. G. (1994). Restructuring the classroom: Conditions for productive small groups. *Review of Educational Research, 64*(1), 1–35.

Cohen, J. (1992). Statistics: A power primer. *Psychological Bulletin, 112*(1), 155–159. doi:10.1037/0033-2909.112.1.155

Cohen, J., Cohen, P., West, S., & Aiken, L. (2003). *Applied multiple regression/correlation analysis for the behavioral sciences* (3rd ed.). Hillsdale, NJ: Lawrence Erlbaum Associates.

Colachico, D. (2007). Developing a sense of community in an online environment. *International Journal of Learning, 14*(1), 161–165.

Colardyn, D., & Bjornawold, J. (2004). Validation of formal, non-formal and informal learning: policy and practices in EU member states. *European Journal of Education, 39*(1), 70–89. doi:10.1111/j.0141-8211.2004.00167.x

Collins, A., & Halverson, R. (2009). *Rethinking education in the age of technology: The digital revolution and schooling in America.* New York, NY: Teachers College Press.

Collins, A., Joseph, D., & Bielaczyc, K. (2004). Design research: Theoretical and methodological issues. *Journal of the Learning Sciences, 13*(1), 15–42. doi:10.1207/s15327809jls1301_2

Collison, G., Elbaum, B., Haavind, S., & Tinker, R. (2000). *Facilitating online learning: Effective strategies for moderators.* Madison, WI: Atwood Publishing.

Colorado, J. T., & Eberle, J. (2010). Student demographics and success in online learning environments. *The Emporia State Research Studies, 46*(1), 4–10.

Community of Inquiry. (2011). COI model. Retrieved from http://communitiesofinquiry.com/model

Conrad, D. (2005). Building and maintaining community in cohort-based online learning. *Journal of Distance Education, 20*(1), 1–21.

Contreras-Castillo, J., Favela, J., Perez-Fragoso, C., & Santamaria-del-Angel, E. (2004). Informal interactions and their implications for online courses. *Computers & Education, 42,* 149–168.

Cooper, J., & Mueck, R. (1990). Student involvement in learning: Cooperative learning and college instruction. *Journal on Excellence in College Teaching, 1,* 68–76.

Costa, A. (1990). Teacher behaviors that promote discussion. In Wilen, W. (Ed.), *Teaching and learning through discussion: The theory, research and practice of the discussion method* (pp. 45–77). Springfield, IL: Charles Thomas Publishers.

Cotton, K. (1988). *Classroom questioning.* School improvement research series close up #5. North West Regional Educational Laboratory. Retrieved October 5, 2011, from the from http://educationnorthwest.org/webfm_send/569

Creswell, J. W. (1997). *Qualitative inquiry and research design: Choosing among five traditions.* Thousand Oaks, CA: Sage.

Creswell, J. W., & Clark, V. L. P. (2011). *Designing and conducting mixed methods research* (2nd ed.). Thousand Oaks, CA: Sage.

Creswell, J. W., & Plano Clark, V. L. (2007). *Designing and conducting mixed methods research.* New Delhi, India: Sage Publications, Inc.

Cronbach, L. (1957). The two disciplines of scientific psychology. *The American Psychologist, 12,* 671–684. doi:10.1037/h0043943doi:10.1037/h0043943

Cronbach, L., & Snow, R. (1977). *Aptitudes and instructional methods: A handbook for research on interactions.* New York, NY: Irvington Publishers.

Crouch, C. H., & Mazur, E. (2001). Peer instruction: Ten years of experience and results. *American Journal of Physics, 69*(9), 970–977. doi:10.1119/1.1374249

Curtis, R. (2004). Analyzing students' conversations in chat room discussion groups. *College Teaching, 52*(4), 143–148.

Cuseo, J. (1992). Collaborative and cooperative learning in higher education: A proposed taxonomy. *Cooperative Learning and College Teaching, 2*(2), 2–4.

D'Angelo, E. (1971). *The teaching of critical thinking.* Amsterdam, The Netherlands: B. R. Gruner N. V.

Dabbagh, N. (2005). Pedagogical models for e-learning: A theory-based design framework. *International Journal of Technology in Teaching and Learning, 1*(1), 25–44.

Dalkir, K. (2011). *Knowledge management in theory and practice* (2nd ed.). Cambridge, MA: The MIT Press.

Dallimore, E., Hertenstein, J., & Platt, M. (2006). Nonvoluntary class participation in graduate discussion courses: Effects of grading and cold calling. *Journal of Management Education, 30*(2), 354–377.

Dana, H., Havens, B., Hochanadel, C., & Phillips, J. (2010). An innovative approach to faculty coaching. *Contemporary Issues in Education Research, 3*(11), 29–34.

Darabi, A., Arrastia, M. C., Nelson, D. W., Cornille, T., & Liang, X. (2011). Cognitive presence in asynchronous online learning: A comparison of four discussion strategies. *Journal of Computer Assisted Learning, 27*(3), 216–227. doi:doi:10.1111/j.1365-2729.2010.00392.x

Darling-Hammond, L. (2010). *The flat world and education.* New York, NY: Teachers College Press.

Davidson-Shivers, G. V. (2009). Frequency and types of instructor-interactions in online instruction. *Journal of Interactive Online Learning, 8*(1). Retrieved September 28, 2010, from www.ncolr.org/jiol/issues/PDF/8.1.2.pdf

Davidson-Shivers, G. V., Muilenburg, L. Y., & Tanner, E. J. (2001). How do students participate in synchronous and asynchronous online discussions? *Journal of Educational Computing Research, 25*(4), 351–366.

Davis, F. D., Bagozzi, R. P., & Warshaw, P. R. (1989). User acceptance of computer technology: A comparison of two theoretical models. *Management Science, 35*, 982–1003. doi:10.1287/mnsc.35.8.982

Davis, G. A., & Thomas, M. A. (1989). *Effective schools and effective teachers.* Needham Heights, MA: Allyn & Bacon.

Davis, J. R., & Davis, A. B. (1998). *Effective training strategies.* San Francisco, CA: Berrett-Koehler.

Dawson, S. (2006). Online forum discussion interactions as an indicator of student community. *Australasian Journal of Educational Technology, 22*(4), 495–510. Retrieved from http://www.ascilite.org.au/ajet/ajet22/ajet22.html

Dawson, S. (2006). A study of the relationship between student communication interaction and sense of community. *The Internet and Higher Education, 9*(3), 153–162. doi:10.1016/j.iheduc.2006.06.007

De Laat, M., Lally, V., Lipponen, L., & Simons, R.-J. (2007). Online teaching in networked learning communities: A multi-method approach to studying the role of the teacher. *Instructional Science, 35*(3), 257–286.

De Marzio, D. M. (1997). *Robert Corrington and the Philosophy for Children program: Communities of interpretation and communities of inquiry.* Unpublished masters thesis, Montclair State University, Montclair NJ.

De Wever, B., Schellens, T., Valcke, M., & Van Keer, H. (2006). Content analysis schemes to analyze transcripts of online asynchronous discussion groups: A review. *Computers & Education, 46*(1), 6–28.

Debord, G. (1983). *Society of the spectacle.* Detroit, MI: Black and Red.

DeCorte, E. (1996). New perspectives on learning and teaching in higher education. In Burgen, A. (Ed.), *Goals and purposes of higher education in the 21st century.* London, UK: Jessica Kingsley.

Deleuze, G., & Guattari, F. (1980). *A thousand plateaus: Capitalism and schizophrenia* (Massumi, B., Trans.). Minneapolis, MN: University of Minnesota Press.

Delfino, M., & Manca, S. (2007). The expression of social presence through the use of figurative language in a web-based learning environment. *Computers in Human Behavior, 23*, 2190–2211. doi:10.1016/j.chb.2006.03.001

Dembo, M., & Howard, K. (2007). Advice about the use of learning styles: A major myth in education. *Journal of College Reading and Learning, 37*(2), 101–109. Retrieved from http://www.eric.ed.gov/ERICWebPortal/search/detailmini.jsp?_nfpb=true&_&ERICExtSearch_SearchValue_0=EJ767768&ERICExtSearch_SearchType_0=no&accno=EJ767768

Design-Based Research Collective. (2003). Design-based research: An emerging paradigm for educational inquiry. *Educational Researcher, 32*(1), 5–8. doi:10.3102/0013189X032001005

DeWeaver, B., Schellens, T., Valcke, M., & Van Keer, H. (2006). Content analysis schemes to analyze transcripts of online asynchronous discussion groups: A review. *Computers & Education, 46*(1), 6–28.

Dewey, J. (1910). *How we think.* Boston, MA: D. C. Heath & Co.doi:10.1037/10903-000

Dewey, J. (1916). *Democracy and education.* New York, NY: Free Press.

Dewey, J. (1933). *How we think* (rev. ed.). Boston, MA: D.C. Heath.

Dewey, J. (1933). *How we think: A restatement of the relation of reflective thinking to the educative process.* Boston, MA: D. C. Heath.

Dewey, J. (1938). *Experience and education.* New York, NY: Collier Macmillan.

Dewey, J. (1938). *Logic: The theory of inquiry.* New York, NY: Holt, Rinehart and Winston.

Dewey, J. (1990). *The school and society & The child and the curriculum.* Chicago, IL: University of Chicago Press. (Original work published 1902)

Dewiyanti, S., Brand-Gruwel, S., Jochems, W., & Broers, N. J. (2007). Students' experience with collaborative learning in asynchronous Computer-Supported Collaborative Learning environments. *Computers in Human Behavior, 23*(1), 496–514.

Diaz, D. P., & Cartnal, R. B. (1999). Students' learning styles in two classes: Online distance learning and equivalent on-campus. *College Teaching, 47*(4), 130–135.

Diaz, S. R. (2011). Knowledge management as an approach to evaluating advanced graduate programs. In Perez, D. C., Fain, S., & Slater, J. (Eds.), *Higher education and human capital: Re/thinking the doctorate in America.* Rotterdam, The Netherlands: Sense Publishers. doi:10.1007/978-94-6091-418-8_6

Diaz, S. R., Swan, K., Ice, P., & Kupczynski, L. (2010). Student ratings of the importance of survey items, multiplicative factor analysis, and the validity of commuity of inquiry survey. *The Internet and Higher Education, 13*, 22–30.

Dickey, M. D. (2004). The impact of web-logs (blogs) on student perceptions of isolation and alienation in a web-based distance-learning environment. *Open Learning, 19*(3), 279–291.

Dick, W., Carey, L., & Carey, J. O. (2009). *The systematic design of instruction* (7th ed.). Upper Saddle River, NJ: Pearson.

Digiano, C., Goldman, S., & Chorost, M. (2008). *Educating learning technology designers.* New York, NY: Routledge.

Dillenbourg, P., Baker, M., Blaye, A., & O'Malley, C. (1996). The evolution of research on collaborative learning. In Spada, E., & Reiman, P. (Eds.), *Learning in humans and machine: Towards an interdisciplinary learning science* (pp. 189–211). Oxford, UK: Elsevier.

Dillon, J. T. (1994). The effect of questions in education and other enterprises. *Journal of Curriculum Studies, 14*, 127–152.

Doherty, W. (2006). An analysis of multiple factors affecting retention in web-based community college courses. *The Internet and Higher Education, 9*, 245–255. doi:10.1016/j.iheduc.2006.08.004

Donald, J. (2002). *Learning to think: Disciplinary perspectives.* San Francisco, CA: Jossey-Bass Publishers.

Doymus, K. (2008). Teaching chemical equilibrium with the jigsaw technique. *Research in Science Education, 38*(2), 249–260.

Dreyfus, H. L., & Dreyfus, S. E. (1986). *Mind over Machine: the power of human intuition and expertise in the age of the computer.* Oxford, UK: Basil Blackwell.

Dringus, L. P. (2000). Towards active online learning: A dramatic shift in perspective for learners. *The Internet and Higher Education, 2*(4), 189–195. doi:10.1016/S1096-7516(00)00023-3

Dringus, L. P., & Scigliano, J. A. (2000). From early to current developments in online learning at Nova Southeastern University: Reflections on historical milestones. *The Internet and Higher Education, 3*(1-2), 23–40. doi:10.1016/S1096-7516(00)00031-2

Drucker, P. (1986). *Innovation and entrepreneurship: Practice and principles.* New York, NY: HarperBusiness.

Drucker, P. (1989). *The new realities*. New York, NY: Harper & Row.

Drucker, P. (2006). *The coming of the new organization. Classic Drucker*. Harvard Business School Publishing Corporation.

Drucker, P. F. (1993). *Post-Capitalist society*. New York, NY: Harper Business.

Ducate, N., & Lomicka, L. (2005). Exploring the Blogosphere: Use of web logs in the foreign language classroom. *FL Annals*, *38*(3), 410–421.

Duell, O. K. (1994). Extended wait time and university student achievement. *American Educational Research Journal*, *31*, 397–414.

Duffy, G. G., Miller, S. D., Parson, S. A., & Meloth, M. (2009). Teachers as metacognitive professionals. In Hacker, D. J., Dunlosky, J., & Graesser, A. C. (Eds.), *Handbook of metacognition in education* (pp. 240–256). Mahwah, NJ: Lawrence Erlbaum.

Duffy, T. M., & Kirkley, J. R. (Eds.). (2004). *Learner-centered theory and practice in distance education: Cases from Higher Education*. Mahwah, NJ: Lawrence Erlbaum.

Duncan, H. E., & Stock, M. J. (2010). Mentoring and coaching rural school leaders: What do they need? *Mentoring & Tutoring: Partnership in Learning*, *18*(3), 293–311.

Duphorne, P., & Gunawardena, C. N. (2005). The effect of three computer conferencing designs on critical thinking skills of nursing students. *American Journal of Distance Education*, *19*(1), 37–50.

Durrington, V. A., Berryhill, A., & Swafford, J. (2006). Strategies for enhancing student interactivity in an online environment. *College Teaching*, *54*(1), 190–193.

Dweck, C. (1999). *Self-theories: Their role in motivation, personality and development*. Philadelphia, PA: Psychology Press.

Dziuban, C., Moskal, P., Brophy, J., Shea, P., & Lorenzo, G. (2008). *An underling structure for student satisfaction with asynchronous learning networks*. Paper presented at the 14th Annual Sloan-C International COnference on Online Learning, Orlando, FL.

Edmundson, A. (2009). *Culturally accessible e-learning: An overdue global business imperative*. The American Society for Training and Development. Retrieved May 24, 2010, from http://www.astd.org/LC/2009/0509_edmundson.htm

Edmundson, A. (Ed.). (2007). *Globalized e-learning cultural challenges*. Hershey, PA: Information Science Publishing.

Eley, M. G. (1992). Differential adoption of study approaches within individual students. *Higher Education*, *23*(3), 231–254.

Elliot, J. (1990). Teachers as researchers: Implications for supervision and for teacher education. *Teaching and Teacher Education*, *6*(1), 1–26. doi:10.1016/0742-051X(90)90004-O

Ellis, A. (December, 2001). Student-centered collaborative learning via face-to-face and asynchronous online communication: What's the difference? *ASCILITE Conference Proceedings*. Retrieved April 16, 2008, from http://www.ascilite.org.au/conferences/melbourne01/pdf/papers/ellisa.pdf

Ellis, J., & Romano, D. (2008). Synchronous and asynchronous online delivery: How much interaction in e-learning is enough in higher education? In G. Richards (Ed.), *Proceedings of World Conference on E-Learning in Corporate, Government, Healthcare, and Higher Education 2008* (pp. 2615-2620). Chesapeake, VA: AACE.

Emerson, J. D., & Mosteller, F. (2004). Cooperative learning in schools and colleges: II. A review of reviews. In Orey, M., Fitzgerald, M. A., & Branch, R. M. (Eds.), *Educational media and technology yearbook* (*Vol. 29*, pp. 148–170). Westport, CT: Libraries Unlimited.

Entwistle, N. J. (2000). Approaches to studying and levels of understanding: The influences of teaching and assessment. In Smart, J. C. (Ed.), *Higher education: Handbook of theory and research* (*Vol. XV*, pp. 156–218). New York, NY: Agathon Press.

Ertmer, P. A., & Stepich, D. A. (2004, July). Examining the relationship between higher-order learning and students' perceived sense of community in an online learning environment. *Proceedings of the 10th Australian World Wide Web conference*, Gold Coast, Australia.

Ertmer, P. A., Sadaf, A., & Ertmer, D. (2011a). Student-content interactions in online courses: The role of question prompts in facilitating higher-level engagement with course content. *Journal of Computing in Higher Education.* doi:doi:10.1007/s12528-011-9047-6

Ertmer, P. A., Sadaf, A., & Ertmer, D. (2011b). Designing effective question prompts to facilitate critical thinking in online discussions. *Design Principles and Practices: An International Journal, 5*(4), 1–28.

Facione, P. (1990). *Executive summary – Critical thinking: A statement of expert consensus for purposes of educational assessment and instruction.* Millbrae, CA: The California Academic Press.

Fairweather, J. S. (2002). The mythologies of faculty productivity: Implications for institutional policy and decision making. *The Journal of Higher Education, 73*(1). Retrieved September 23, 2010 from http://202.198.141.77/upload/soft/0000/73.1fairweather02%5B1%5D.pdf

Farmer, L. S. J. (2010). Culturally-sensitive e-learning practices for teacher education. In C. D. Maddux, D. Gibson, & B. Dodge (Eds.), *Research Highlights in Technology and Teacher Education 2010* (pp. 203-210). Society for Information Technology & Teacher Education (SITE).

Fasco, D. Jr., (Ed.). (2003). *Critical thinking and reasoning: Current research, theory, and practice.* Cresskill, NJ: Hampton Press.

Felton, M. K. (2005). Approaches to argument in critical thinking instruction. *Thinking Classroom, 6*(4), 6-6-13.

Finegold, A. R. D., & Cooke, L. (2006). Exploring the attitudes, experiences and dynamics of interaction in online groups. *Internet and Higher Education, 9*(3), 201–215. Retrieved March 28, 2011, from http://hdl.handle.net/2134/3279

Fjermestad, J., & Hiltz, S. R. (1998). An assessment of group support systems experimental research: Methodoogy and results. *Journal of Management Information Systems, 15*(3), 7–149.

Flanagin, A. J., Park, H. S., & Seibold, D., R. (2004). Group performance and collaborative technology: A longitudinal and multilevel analysis of information quality, contribution equity, and members' satisfaction in computer-mediated groups. *Communication Monographs, 71*(3), 352–372.

Flavell, J. (1992). Cognitive development: Past, present, and future. *Developmental Psychology, 28*(6), 998–1005. doi:10.1037/0012-1649.28.6.998doi:10.1037/0012-1649.28.6.998

Flavell, J. H. (1979). Metacognition. *The American Psychologist, 34*, 906–911. doi:10.1037/0003-066X.34.10.906doi:10.1037/0003-066X.34.10.906

Flavell, J. H. (1987). Speculations about the nature and development of metacognition. In F. Weinert & R. Kluwe (Eds.), *Metacognition, motivation, and understanding* (pp. 21–29). Hillsdale, NJ: Erlbaum Associates.

Flavell, J. H. (1979). Metacognition and cognitive monitoring: A new area of cognitive developmental inquiry. *The American Psychologist, 34*(10), 906–911.

Flavell, J. H. (2004). Theory-of-mind development: Retrospect and prospect. *Merrill-Palmer Quarterly, 50*(3), 274–290.

Fortune, M. F., Shifflett, B., & Sibley, R. E. (2006). A Comparison of online (high tech) and traditional (high touch) learning in business communication courses in Silicon Valley. *Journal of Education for Business, 81*(4), 210–214.

Foucault, M. (2005). *The hermeneutics of the subject: Lectures at the College de France, 1981-82.* New York, NY: Palgrave Macmillan.

Foundation Coalition. (2002). *Peer assessment and peer evaluation.* Retrieved from http://www.foundationcoalition.org/publications/brochures/2002peer_assessment.pdf

Francescato, D., Porcelli, R., Mebane, M., Cuddetta, M., Klobas, J., & Renzi, P. (2006). Evaluation of the efficacy of collaborative learning in face-to-face and computer-supported university contexts. *Computers in Human Behavior, 22*, 163–176.

Frappaolo, C. (2006). *Knowledge management.* Chichester, England: Capstone Publishing Ltd.

Freire, P. (1965). *Pedagogy of the oppressed.* New York, NY: Seabury.

Friedman, T. L. (2007). *The world is flat: A brief history of the 21st century* (3rd ed.). New York, NY: Picador.

Friedman, V. (2001). Creating communities of inquiry in communities of practice. In Reason, P., & Bradbury, H. (Eds.), *Handbook of action research. Participative inquiry and practice*. London, UK: Sage.

Furstenberg, G. (1987). Teaching with technology: What is at stake? *ADFL Bulletin, 28*(3), 21–25.

Gagné, R. (1967). *Learning and individual differences*. Columbus, OH: Merrill.

Gallagher, J. J., & Aschner, M. J. (1963). A preliminary report on analyses of classroom interaction. *Merrill-Palmer Quarterly, 9*, 183–194.

Galusha, J.M. (1997). Barriers to learning in distance education. *Interpersonal Computing and Technology: An Electronic Journal for the 21st Century, 5*(3/4), 6-14.

Galvis Panqueva, Á. H., & Leal Fonseca, D. E. (2006). Aprendiendo en comunidad: más allá de aprender y trabajar en compañía. *Eduweb. Revista de Tecnología de Información y Comunicación en Educación, 1*, 9–32.

Gardner, H., Kornhaber, M., & Wake, W. (1997). *Intelligence: Multiple perspectives*. Philadelphia, PA: Harcourt Brace College Publishers.

Garrison, D. R. (2004). Transformative leadership and e-learning. In K. Matheos & T. Carey (Eds.), *Advances and challenges in eLearning at Canadian research universities* (pp. 46–54). CHERD Occasional Papers in Higher Education, 12, University of Manitoba.

Garrison, D. R. Cleveland- Innes, M., Koole, M., & Kappleman, J. (2006). Revisiting methodological issues in transcript analysis: negotiated coding and reliability. *Internet and Higher Education, 9*(2006), 1 -8. Retrieved August 9, 2011, from http://auspace.athabascau.ca:8080/dspace/bitstream/2149/611/1/sdarticle.pdf

Garrison, D. R., & Arbaugh, J. B. (2007). Researching the community of inquiry framework: Review, issues, and future directions. *The Internet and Higher Education, 10*(3), 157–172. doi:10.1016/j.iheduc.2007.04.001doi:10.1016/j.iheduc.2007.04.001

Garrison, D. R., Anderson, T., & Archer, W. (2000). Critical inquiry in a text-based environment: Computer conferencing in higher education. *The Internet and Higher Education, 2*(2-3), 87-105. Retrieved May 24, 2010, from http://hdl.handle.net/2149/739

Garrison, D. R., Anderson, T., & Archer, W. (2004). *Critical thinking, cognitive presence and computer conferencing in distance education*. Retrieved February 20, 2011, from http://communityofinquiry.com/files/CogPres_Final.pdf

Garrison, D. R., Arbaugh, J. B., Cleveland-Innes, M., Diaz, S., Ice, P., Richardson, J., et al. (2008). *Community of inquiry framework: Instrument development, validation and application*. Paper presented at the First International Conference of the new Canadian Network for Innovation in Education (CNIE), Banff, Alberta, CA. http://communitiesofinquiry.com/sites/communityofinquiry.com/files/CNIE_CoI_2008_Survey.pdf

Garrison, D. R., Cleveland-Innes, M., & Fung, T. (2004). Student role adjustment in online communities of inquiry: Model and instrument validation. *Journal of Asynchronous Learning Networks, 8*(2), 61-74. Retrieved January 8, 2009, from http://www.sloan-c.org/publications/jaln/v8n2/pdf/v8n2_garrison.pdf

Garrison, D. (2007). Online community of inquiry review: Social, cognitive, and teaching presence issues. *Journal of Asynchronous Learning Networks, 11*(1), 61–72.

Garrison, D. (2011). *E-learning in the 21st century: A framework for research and practice* (2nd ed.). London, UK: Routledge/Taylor and Francis.

Garrison, D. R. (1985). Three generations of technological innovations in distance education. *Distance Education, 6*(2), 235–241.

Garrison, D. R. (1991). Critical thinking and adult education: A conceptual model for developing critical thinking in adult learners. *International Journal of Lifelong Education, 10*(4), 287–303.

Garrison, D. R. (1993). Multifunction microcomputer enhanced audio teleconferencing: Moving into the third generation of distance education. In Harry, K., Keegan, D., & Magnus, J. (Eds.), *Distance education: New perspectives* (pp. 200–208). London, UK: Routledge.

Garrison, D. R. (1997). Computer conferencing: The post-industrial age of distance education. *Open Learning, 12*(2), 3–11.

Garrison, D. R. (2003). Cognitive presence for effective asynchronous online learning: The role of reflective inquiry, self-direction and metacognition. In Bourne, J., & Moore, J. C. (Eds.), *Elements of quality online education: Practice and direction*. Needham, MA: The Sloan Consortium.

Garrison, D. R. (2006). Online collaboration principles. *Journal of Asynchronous Learning Networks, 10*(1), 25–33.

Garrison, D. R. (2007). Online community of inquiry review: Social, cognitive and teaching presence issues. *Journal of Asynchronous Learning Networks, 11*(1), 61–72.

Garrison, D. R. (2009). Communities of inquiry in online learning. In Rogers, P. L. (Ed.), *Encyclopedia of distance learning* (2nd ed., pp. 352–355). Hershey, PA: IGI Global.

Garrison, D. R. (2009). Communities of inquiry in online learning: Social, teaching and cognitive presence. In Howard, C. (Eds.), *Encyclopedia of distance and online learning* (2nd ed., pp. 352–355). Hershey, PA: IGI Global. doi:10.4018/978-1-60566-198-8.ch052

Garrison, D. R. (2011). *E-learning in the 21ˢᵗ century: A framework for research and practice* (2nd ed.). London, UK: Routledge, Taylor & Francis Group.

Garrison, D. R. (2012). Theoretical foundations and epistemological insights. In Akyol, Z., & Garrison, D. R. (Eds.), *Educational communities of inquiry: Theoretical framework, research and practice* (p. xx). Hershey, PA: IGI Global.

Garrison, D. R., Cleveland- Innes, M., Koole M., & Kappelman, J. (2006). Revisiting methodological issues in transcript analysis: Negotiated coding and reliability. *The Internet and Higher Education, 9*, 1–8.

Garrison, D. R., Anderson, R. T., & Archer, W. (2000). Critical inquiry in a text-based environment: Computer conferencing in higher education. *The Internet and Higher Education, 2*(2-3), 87–105.

Garrison, D. R., & Anderson, T. (2003). *E-learning in the 21st century: A framework for research and practice*. London, UK: Routledge Falmer.

Garrison, D. R., Anderson, T., & Archer, W. (2000). Critical inquiry in a text based-environment: Computer conferencing in higher education. *The Internet and Higher Education, 2*(2-3), 87–105.

Garrison, D. R., Anderson, T., & Archer, W. (2001). Critical thinking, cognitive presence and computer conferencing in distance education. *American Journal of Distance Education, 15*(1), 7–23.

Garrison, D. R., Anderson, T., & Archer, W. (2001). Critical thinking, cognitive presence, and computer conferencing in distance education. *American Journal of Distance Education, 15*(1), 7–23.

Garrison, D. R., Anderson, T., & Archer, W. (2010). The first decade of the community of inquiry framework: A retrospective. *The Internet and Higher Education, 13*, 5–9. doi:10.1016/j.iheduc.2009.10.003

Garrison, D. R., & Arbaugh, J. B. (2007). Researching the community of inquiry framework: Review, issues, and future directions. *The Internet and Higher Education, 10*(3), 157–172.

Garrison, D. R., & Archer, W. (2000). *A transactional perspective on teaching and learning. A framework for adult and higher education*. Oxford, UK: Pergamon.

Garrison, D. R., & Archer, W. (2007). A community of inquiry framework for online learning. In Moore, M., & Anderson, W. G. (Eds.), *Handbook of distance education* (2nd ed., pp. 77–88). New York, NY: Lawrence Erlbaum.

Garrison, D. R., & Cleveland-Innes, M. (2003). Critical factors in student satisfaction and success: Facilitating student role adjustment in online communities of inquiry. In Bourne, J., & Moore, J. (Eds.), *Elements of quality online education: Into the mainstream* (pp. 29–38). Needham, MA: Sloan-C.

Garrison, D. R., & Cleveland-Innes, M. (2005). Facilitating cognitive presence in online learning: Interaction is not enough. *American Journal of Distance Education, 19*(3), 133–148.

Garrison, D. R., & Cleveland-Innes, M. (2010). Conclusion. In Cleveland-Innes, M. F., & Garrison, D. R. (Eds.), *An introduction to distance education: Understanding teaching and learning in a new era* (pp. 137–164). New York, NY: Routledge.

Garrison, D. R., Cleveland-Innes, M., & Fung, T. (2009). Exploring causal relationships among cognitive, social and teaching presence: Student perceptions of the community of inquiry framework. *The Internet and Higher Education.* doi:doi:10.1016/j.iheduc.2009.10.002

Garrison, D. R., Cleveland-Innes, M., & Fung, T. S. (2010). Exploring causal relationships among teaching, cognitive and social presence: Student perceptions of the community of inquiry framework. *The Internet and Higher Education, 13*(1-2), 31–36.

Garrison, D. R., Cleveland-Innes, M., Koole, M., & Kappelman, J. (2006). Revisting methodological issues in the analysis of transcripts: Negotiated coding and reliability. *The Internet and Higher Education, 9*(1), 1–8. doi:10.1016/j.iheduc.2005.11.001

Garrison, D. R., & Kanuka, H. (2004). Blended learning: Uncovering its transformative potential in higher education. *The Internet and Higher Education, 7*(2), 95–105.

Garrison, D. R., & Vaughan, N. (2008). *Blended learning in higher education: Framework, principles and guidelines.* San Francisco, CA: Jossey-Bass.

Garrison, D., Anderson, T., & Archer, W. (2000). Critical inquiry in a text-based environment: Computer conferencing in higher education. *The Internet and Higher Education, 2*(2), 87–105.

Garrison, D., Anderson, T., & Archer, W. (2001). Critical thinking, cognitive presence, and computer conferencing in distance education. *American Journal of Distance Education, 15*(1).

Garrison, D., & Arbaugh, J. B. (2007). Researching the community of inquiry framework: Review, issues, and future directions. *The Internet and Higher Education, 10*(3), 157–172.

Garrison, R. (2000). Theoretical challenges for distance education in the 21st century: A shift from structural to transactional issues. *International Review of Research in Open and Distance Learning, 1*(1), 1–17.

Gibbs, G. (1993). The CNAA improving student learning project. *Research and Development in Higher Education, 14*, 8–19.

Gibbs, G. (2006). How assessment frames student learning. In Bryan, C., & Clegg, K. (Eds.), *Innovative assessment in higher education* (pp. 23–36). London, UK: Routledge.

Gibbs, G., & Simpson, C. (2004). Conditions under which assessment supports students' learning? *Learning and Teaching in Higher Education, 1*, 3–31.

Gibson, J. (1999). Discussion approach to instruction. In C. M. Reigeluth (Ed.), *Instructional-design theories and models, Vol. III: Building a common knowledge base* (pp. 99-116). New York, NY: Taylor and Francis.

Giesbers, B., Rienties, B., Gijselaers, W. H., Segers, M., & Tempelaar, D. T. (2009). Social presence, web-videoconferencing and learning in virtual teams. *Industry and Higher Education, 23*(4), 301–310.

Gilbert, P. K., & Dabbagh, N. (2005). How to structure online discussions for a meaningful discourse: A case study. *British Journal of Educational Technology, 36*(1), 5-18. Retrieved March 28, 2011, from http://ritv.les.inf.puc-rio.br/groupware/temp/denise/071212/structured.foruns_j.1467-8535.2005.00434.pdf

Gillani, B. B. (2000). Using the web to create student-centered curriculum. In Cole, R. A. (Ed.), *Issues in web-based pedagogy: A critical primer* (pp. 161–181). Westport, CT: Greenwood press.

Gill, J., Kostiw, N., & Stone, S. (2010). Coaching teachers in effective instruction: A Victorian perspective. *Literacy Learning: The Middle Years, 18*(2), 49–53.

Gilmore, T., Krantz, J., & Ramirez, R. (1986). Action based modes of inquiry and the host-researcher relationship. *Consultation, 5*(3), 161.

Gitai, A. (2005). *Free zone. Agav Films (France), Agat Films & Cie (France), Golem (Spain), Artémis Productions, Agav Hafakot (Israel), Hammon Hafakot (Israel), Arte France Cinéma.* Belgium: Cinéart.

Glaser, R. (1972). Individuals and learning: The new aptitudes. *Educational Researcher, 1*(6), 5–13.

Glaser, R. (1976). Components of a psychology of instruction: Toward a science of design. *Review of Educational Research, 46*(1), 1–24.

Glaser, R. (1984). Education and thinking: The role of knowledge. *The American Psychologist*, *39*, 93–104. doi:10.1037/0003-066X.39.2.93doi:10.1037/0003-066X.39.2.93

Goldstein, D. S. (2010). Once more, with feeling: Whole people and partial lessons. *National Teaching and Learning Forum*, *20*(1), 5–7.

Goldstein, D. S., Leppa, C., Brockhaus, A., Bliquez, R., & Porter, I. (2012). Fostering social presence in a blended learning faculty development institute. In Akyol, Z., & Garrison, D. (Eds.), *Educational communities of inquiry: Theoretical framework, research and practice*. Hershey, PA: IGI Global.

Goldstein, D., Tippens, B., Behler, C., Brockhaus, A., Collins, P., Erdley, B., & Van Galen, J. (2009). *Technology and Teaching Innovation Task Force final report: May 28, 2009*. University of Washington Bothell.

Goodyear, P. (2001). *Effective networked learning in higher education: notes and guidelines*. Networked Learning in Higher Education Project (JCALT), Centre for Studies in Advanced Learning Technology, University of Lancaster. Retrieved February 24, 2010, from http://www.csalt.lancs.ac.uk/jisc/guidelines_final.doc

Gorard, S., Roberts, K., & Taylor, C. (2004). What kind of creature is design experiment? *British Educational Research Journal*, *30*(4), 577–590. doi:10.1080/01411 92042000237248

Gorsky, P., & Blau, I. (2009). Online teaching effectiveness: A tale of two instructors. *International Review of Research in Open and Distance Learning*, *10*(3), 1–27.

Gorsky, P., Caspi, A., & Trumper, R. (2006). Campus-based university students' use of dialogue. *Studies in Higher Education*, *31*(1), 71–87. Retrieved from http://old.oranim.ac.il/Docs/CSHE_A_139217.pdf-doi:10.1080/03075070500392342

Gourgey, A. F. (2001). Metacognition in basic skills instruction. In Hartman, H. J. (Ed.), *Metacognition in learning and instruction* (pp. 17–32). Netherlands: Kluwer Academic Publishers.

Grabe, M., & Christopherson, K. (2005). Evaluating the advantages and disadvantages of providing lecture notes: The role of Internet technology as a delivery system and research tool. *The Internet and Higher Education*, *8*(4), 291–298. doi:10.1016/j.iheduc.2005.09.002

Graham, C. R., & Misanchuk, M. (2004). Computer-mediated learning groups: Benefits and challenges to using groupwork in online learning environments. In Roberts, T. S. (Ed.), *Online collaborative learning: Theory and practice* (pp. 181–202). Hershey, PA: Information Science Publishing.

Gray, B. (2004). Informal learning in an online community of practice. *Journal of Distance Education*, *19*(1), 20–35.

Green, T. (2011, October). *Multi-screen madness: Your life just got interesting*. Paper presented at the Adobe MAX Education Preconference, Los Angeles, CA.

Green, S. G., & Taber, T. D. (1980). The effects of three social decision schemes on decision group processes. *Organizational Behavior and Human Performance*, *25*, 97–106.

Grosset, J. M. (1991). Patterns of integration, commitment, and student characteristics and retention among younger and older students. *Research in Higher Education*, *32*(2), 159–178. doi:10.1007/BF00974435

Gudea, S. R. (2008). *Expectations and demands in online teaching: Practical experiences*. Hershey, PA: IGI Global. doi:10.4018/978-1-59904-747-8

Guglielmino, L. M., & Guglielmino, P. J. (1991). *The learner preference assessment*. Organization Design and Development.

Gunawardena, C. N. (1995). Social presence theory and implications for interaction and collaborative learning in computer conferences. *International Journal of Educational Telecommunications*, *1*(2/3), 147–166.

Gunawardena, C. N., & McIsaac, M. S. (2004). Distance education. In Jonassen, D. H. (Ed.), *Handbook of research on educational communications and technology* (2nd ed., pp. 355–395). Mahwah, NJ: Lawrence Erlbaum Associates Publishers.

Gunawardena, C. N., Nolla, A. C., Wilson, P. L., Lopez-Islas, J. R., Ramirez-Angel, N., & Megchun-Alpizar, R. M. (2001). A cross-cultural study of group process and development in online conferences. *Distance Education*, *22*(1), 85–121.

Gunawardena, C. N., Ortegano-Layne, L., Carabajal, K., Frechette, C., Lindemann, K., & Jennings, B. (2006). New model, new strategies: Instructional design for building online wisdom communities. *Distance Education*, *27*(2), 217–232.

Gunawardena, C. N., & Zittle, F. J. (1997). Social presence as a predictor of satisfaction within a computer-mediated conferencing environment. *American Journal of Distance Education*, *11*(3), 8–26.

Gunawardena, C., & Lapointe, D. (2007). Cultural dynamics of online learning. In Moore, M. G. (Ed.), *Handbook of distance education* (2nd ed., pp. 593–607). Mahwah, NJ: Lawrence Erlbaum Associates.

Gunawardena, C., Wilson, P. L., & Nolla, A. C. (2003). Culture and online education. In Moore, M. G., & Anderson, W. G. (Eds.), *Handbook of distance education* (pp. 753–775). Mahwah, NJ: Lawrence Erlbaum Associations.

Gupta, J., Sharma, S., & Hsu, J. (2004). An overview of knowledge management. In Gupta, J., & Sharma, S. (Eds.), *Creating knowledge based organizations* (p. 360). Hershey, PA, USA: Idea Group Publishing. doi:10.4018/978-1-59140-162-9.ch001

Guri-Rosenblit, S. (2001). Virtual universities: Current models and future trends. *Higher Education in Europe*, *26*(4), 487–499. doi:10.1080/03797720220141807

Gustafson, K. L. (2002). What is instructional design. In Reiser, R. A., & Dempsey, J. V. (Eds.), *Trends and issues in instructional design and technology* (pp. 16–25). Upper Saddle River, NJ: Merrill Education/Prentice.

Guyton, E. M., & Wesche, M. V. (2005). The multicultural efficacy scale: Development, item selection, and reliability. *Multicultural Perspectives*, *7*(4), 21–29. doi:10.1207/s15327892mcp0704_4

Haavind, S. (2006). *Key factors of online course design and instructor facilitation that enhance collaborative dialogue among learners*. Paper presented at the annual meeting of the American Educational Research Association, San Francisco, CA.

Habermas, J. (1984). *The theory of communicative action*. Boston, MA: Beacon Press.

Hacker, D. J. (1998). Definitions and empirical foundations. In Hacker, D. J., Dunlosky, J., & Graesser, A. C. (Eds.), *Metacognition in educational theory and practice* (pp. 1–23). Mahwah, NJ: Erlbaum.

Hacker, D. J., Keener, M. C., & Kircher, J. C. (2009). Writing is applied metacognition. In Hacker, D. J., Dunlosky, J., & Graesser, A. C. (Eds.), *Handbook of metacognition in education*. New York, NY: Routledge, Taylor & Francis Group.

Hall, D. (1997). Computer mediated communication in post-compulsory teacher education. *Open Learning*, *12*(3), 54–57.

Hall, R. H., Rocklin, T. R., Dansereau, D. F., Skaggs, L. P., O'Donnell, A. M., Lambiotte, J. G., & Young, M. D. (1988). The role of individual differences in the cooperative learning of technical material. *Journal of Educational Psychology*, *80*(2), 172–178.

Halpern, D. (2005). *Social capital*. Malden, MA: Polity Press.

Hammond, M. (2000). Communication within on-line forums: the opportunities, the constraints and the value of a communicative approach. *Computers & Education*, *35*(4), 251–262.

Hanley, S. (2010). A sports metaphor in career coaching. *Career Planning and Adult Development Journal*, *26*(1), 96–100.

Hara, N., Bonk, C. J., & Angeli, C. (1998). Content analysis of online discussion in an applied educational psychology course. *Instructional Science*, *28*(2), 115–152.

Harasim, L. (March, 2006). *Online collaborative learning: The next generation for elearning*. Public Presentation Sao Paulo, Brazil. Retrieved May 16, 2009, from http://www.slideshare.net/aquifolium/linda-harasim-on-online-collaborative-learning

Harasim, L. (2001). Shift happens: Online education as a new paradigm in learning. *The Internet and Higher Education, 3*(1), 41–61.

Harasim, L. (2002). What makes online learning communities successful? The role of collaborative learning in social and intellectual development. In Vrasidas, C., & Glass, G. V. (Eds.), *Distance Education and Distributed Learning* (pp. 181–200). Greenwich, CT: Information Age Publishing.

Hardt, M., & Negri, A. (2004). *Multitude: War and democracy in the age of empire*. New York, NY: Penguin Books.

Harker, M., & Koutsantoni, D. (2005). Can it be as effective? Distance versus blended learning in a web-based EAP programme. *ReCALL, 17*(1), 197–216.

Harre, R. (2001). The discursive turn in social psychology. In Schiffrin, D., Tannen, D., & Hamilton, H. E. (Eds.), *The handbook of discourse analysis*. Malden, MA: Blackwell Publishing.

Harrington, H. L., & Hathaway, R. S. (1994). Computer conferencing, critical reflection, and teacher development. *Teaching & Teacher Education, 10*(5), 543- 554. Retrieved July 19, 2010, from http://deepblue.lib.umich.edu/bitstream/2027.42/31371/1/0000284.pdf

Hartman, H. J. (2001). Teaching metacognitively. In Hartman, H. J. (Ed.), *Metacognition in learning and instruction: Theory, research and practice* (pp. 149–172). Boston, MA: Kluwer Academic.

Hartman, J., Dziuban, C., & Brophy Ellison, J. (2007). Faculty 2.0. *EDUCAUSE Review, 42*(5), 62–77.

Hedberg, J., & Corrent-Agostinho, S. (1999). Creating a postgraduate virtual community: Assessment drives learning. In B. Collis & R. Oliver (Eds.), *Proceedings of World Conference on Educational Multimedia, Hypermedia and Telecommunications.* (pp. 1093-1098). AACE: Chesapeake, VA. Retrieved from http://www.editlib.org/p/7040

Heinich, R., Molenda, M., Russell, J. D., & Smaldino, S. E. (2002). *Instructional media and technologies for learning* (7th ed.). Upper Saddle River, NJ: Pearson.

Henri, F. (2001). Des cours sur le web à l'université. In T. Karsenti & L. Larose (Eds.), *Les TIC...au cœur des pédagogies universitaires* (117-143). Québec, Canada: Presses de l'Université du Québec.

Henri, F. (1992). Computer conferencing and content analysis. In O'Malley, C. (Ed.), *Computer supported collaborative learning*. Heidelberg, Germany: Springer-Verlag.

Henri, F., & Rigault, C. R. (1996). Collaborative distance learning and computer conferencing. In Liao, T. (Ed.), *Advanced educational technology: Research issues and future potential* (pp. 45–76). Berlin, Germany: Springer Verlag.

Herron, T. L. (1998). Teaching with the Internet. *The Internet and Higher Education, 1*(3), 217–222. doi:10.1016/S1096-7516(99)80168-7

Hewling, A. (2005). Culture in the online class: Using message analysis to look beyond nationality-based frames of reference. *Journal of Computer-Mediated Communication, 11*(1), 16. doi:10.1111/j.1083-6101.2006.tb00316.x

Higgins, R., Hartley, P., & Skelton, A. (2001). Getting the message across: The problem of communicating assessment feedback. *Teaching in Higher Education, 6*(2), 269–274. doi:10.1080/13562510120045230

Hillard, A. (2006). *Evaluation of different methods of online collaboration/group work forming the coursework assessment in a blended learning module.* Paper presented at the 5th European Conference on e-Learning, University of Winchester, UK.

Hillman, D. C., Willis, D. J., & Gunawardena, C. N. (1994). Learner-interface interaction in distance education: An extension of contemporary models and strategies for practitioners. *American Journal of Distance Education, 8*(2), 30–42.

Hill, W. F. (1991). *Learning thru discussion* (2nd ed.). Newbury Park, CA: Sage.

Hiltz, S. R., & Goldman, R. (2005). What are asynchronous learning networks? In Hiltz, S. R., & Goldman, R. (Eds.), *Learning together online: Research on asynchronous learning networks* (pp. 3–18). Mahwah, NJ: Lawrence Erlbaum Associates.

Hmelo-Silver, C., Duncan, R. G., & Chinn, C. A. (2007). Scaffolding and achievement in problem-based and inquiry learning: A response to Kirschner, Sweller, and Clark (2006). *Educational Psychologist, 42*(2), 99–107.

Holcomb, L. B., King, F. B., & Brown, S. W. (2004). Student traits and attributes contributing to success in online courses: Evaluation of university online courses. *The Journal of Interactive Online Learning, 2*(3), 1–17.

Holden, J. T., & Westfall, P. (2010). *Learning styles and generational differences: Do they matter?* Federal Government Distance Learning Association.

Holder, B. (2007). An investigation of hope, academics, environment, and motivation as predictors of persistence in higher education online programs. *The Internet and Higher Education, 10*, 245–260. doi:10.1016/j.iheduc.2007.08.002

Hooper, S. (1992). Cooperative learning and computer-based instruction. *Educational Technology Research and Development, 40*(3), 21–38.

Hrastinski, S. (2006). Introducing an informal synchronous medium in a distance learning course: How is participation affected? *The Internet and Higher Education, 9*(2), 117–131.

Huang, H. (2002). Toward constructivism for adult learners in online learning environments. *British Journal of Educational Technology, 33*(1), 27–37.

Hughes, J. (2004). Supporting the online learner. In Anderson, T., & Elloumi, F. (Eds.), *Theory and practice of online learning*. Canada: Athabasca University.

Hughes, M., Ventura, S., & Dando, M. (2007). Assessing social presence in online discussion groups: A replication study. *Innovations in Education and Teaching International, 44*(1), 17–29.

Ice, P. (2008). How do we assess the effectiveness of new technologies and learning environments? *Sloan-C View, 7*(2). Retrieved from http://www.sloanconsortium.org/publications/view/v7n2/viewv7n2.htm#Assess

Ice, P. (2011, November). *Applying analytics to instructional design.* Paper presented at the DevLearn Conference, Las Vegas, NV.

Ice, P., Arbaugh, B., Diaz, S., Garrison, D. R., & Richardson, J. Shea, P., & Swan, K. (2007, November). *Community of inquiry framework: validation and instrument development.* Paper Presented at the 13th Annual Sloan-C International Conference on Online Learning, Orlando, Florida. Received April 10, 2009, from http://communitiesofinquiry.com/files/Sloan%20CoI%20Orlando%2007.pdf

Ice, P., Curtis, R., Phillips, P., & Wells, J. (2007). Using asynchronous audio feedback to enhance teaching presence and students' sense of community. *Journal of Asynchronous Learning Networks, 11*(2), 3-25. Retrieved January 31, 2011, from http://sloanconsortium.org/jaln/v11n2/using-asynchronous-audio-feedback-enhance-teaching-presence-and-students%E2%80%99-sense-community

Ice, P., Kupczynski, L., & Mitchell, R. (2008). *Instructional design strategies and the Community of Inquiry framework.* Paper presented at the 14th Annual Sloan-C Conference on Online Learning, Orlando, FL.

Ice, P., Gibson, A., Boston, W., & Becher, D. (2011). An exploration of differences between community of inquiry indicators in low and high disenrollment online courses. *Journal of Asynchronous Learning Networks, 15*(2), 44–69.

Ice, P., Kupczynski, L., Wiesenmeyer, R., & Phillips, P. (2008). Student perceptions of the effectiveness of group and individualized feedback in online courses. *First Monday, 13*(11).

Iskala, T., Vauras, M., Lehtinen, E., & Salonen, P. (2011). Socially shared metacognition of dyads of pupils in collaborative mathematical problem-solving processes. *Learning and Instruction, 21*, 379–393.

Ivanic, R., Clark, R., & Rimmershaw, R. (2000). What am I supposed to make of this? The messages conveyed to students by tutors' written comments. In Lea, M. R., & Stierer, B. (Eds.), *Student writing in higher education: New contexts*. Buckingham, UK: Open University Press.

Jackson, K. M., & Trochim, W. M. K. (2002). Concept mapping as an alternative approach for the analysis of open-ended survey responses. *Organizational Research Methods, 5*(4), 307–336. doi:10.1177/109442802237114

Jakubik, M. (2007). Exploring the knowledge landscape: four emerging views of knowledge. *Journal of Knowledge Management, 11*(4), 6–19. doi:10.1108/13673270710762675

Jang, H., Reeve, J., & Deci, E. L. (2010). Engaging students in learning activities: It is not autonomy support or structure but autonomy support and structure. *Journal of Educational Psychology, 102*(3), 588–600.

Jaques, D. (2000). *Learning in groups.* London, UK: Kogan Page Ltd.

Järvelä, S., Hurme, T., & Järvenoja, H. (2011). Self-regulation and motivation in computer-supported collaborative learning environments. In Ludvigson, S., Lund, A., Rasmussen, I., & Säljö, R. (Eds.), *Learning across sites: New tools, infrastructure and practices.* New York, NY: Routledge.

Järvelä, S., Järvenoja, H., & Veermans, M. (2008). Understanding the dynamics of motivation in socially shared learning. *International Journal of Educational Research, 47*(2), 122–135.

Järvelä, S., Volet, S., & Järvenoja, H. (2010). Research on motivation in collaborative learning: Moving beyond the cognitive-situative divide and combining individual and social processes. *Educational Psychologist, 45*(1), 15–27.

Jenkins, R. (2011, May 22). Why are so many students still failing online? *The Chronicle of Higher Education.*

Jezegou, A. (2010). Community of inquiry in e-learning: Concerning the Garrison and Anderson model. *Journal of Distance Education, 24*(3).

Johansson, P., & Gardenfors, P. (2005). *Cognition, education, and communication technology.* Mahwah, NJ: Lawrence Erlbaum Associates.

John, P., & Sutherland, R. (2005). Affordance, opportunity and the pedagogical implications of ICT. *Educational Review, 57*(4), 405–415. doi:10.1080/00131910500278256

Johnson, L., Smith, R., Willis, H., Levine, A., & Haywood, K. (2011). *The 2011 horizon report.* Austin, TX: The New Media Consortium.

Johnson, R. T., & Johnson, D. W. (1994). An overview of cooperative learning. In J. Thousand, A. VIlla & A. Nevin (Eds.), *Creativity and collaborative learning.* Baltimore, MD: Brookes Press.

Johnson, D. W., & Johnson, R. T. (1991). *Learning together and alone: Cooperative, competitive and individualistic learning* (3rd ed.). Needham Heights, MA: Allyn and Bacon.

Johnson, D. W., & Johnson, R. T. (1996). Cooperation and the use of technology. In Jonassen, D. H. (Ed.), *Handbook of research for educational communications and technology.* New York, NY: Simon & Schuster Macmillan.

Johnson, S. (2010). *Where good ideas come from: The natural history of innovation.* New York, NY: Riverhead Books.

Jonassen, D. H. (1997). Instructional design model for well-structured and ill-structured problem-solving learning outcomes. *Educational Technology Research and Development, 45*(1), 65–95.

Jonassen, D. H. (2000). Transforming learning with technology: Beyond modernism and post-modernism or whoever controls the technology creates the reality. *Educational Technology, 40*(2), 21–25.

Jonassen, D. H. (2006). Typology of case-based learning: The content, form, and function of cases. *Educational Technology, 46*(4), 11–15.

Jonassen, D. H., Peck, K. L., & Wilson, B. G. (1999). *Learning with technology: A constructivist perspective.* Columbus, OH: Prentice Hall.

Joo, Y. J., Lim, K. Y., & Kim, E. K. (2011). Online university students' satisfaction and persistence: Examining perceived level of presence, usefulness and ease of use as predictors in a structural model. *Computers & Education, 57,* 1654–1664. doi:doi:10.1016/j.compedu.2011.02.008

Joubert, J. (1842). *Pensees.* Retrieved from http://www.doyletics.com/art/notebook.htm

Jung, I. S. (2001). Building a theoretical framework of Web-based instruction in the context of distance education. *British Journal of Educational Technology, 32*(5), 525–534.

Kahneman, K. (2011). *Thinking, fast and slow*. New York, NY: Farrar, Straus and Giroux.

Kamin, C. O'Sullivan, P., Deterding, R., Younger, M., & Wade, T. (2006). A case study of teaching presence in virtual problem-based learning groups. *Medical Teacher, 28*(5), 425–428.

Kanuka, H. (2005). An exploration into facilitating higher levels of learning in a text-based internet learning environment using diverse instructional strategies. *Journal of Computer-Mediated Communication, 10*(3).

Kanuka, H., & Anderson, T. (1998). Online social interchange, discord, and knowledge construction. *Journal of Distance Education, 13*(1), 57–74.

Kanuka, H., & Garrison, D. R. (2004). Cognitive presence in online learning. *Journal of Computing in Higher Education, 15*(2), 21–39.

Kanuka, H., Rourke, L., & Laflamme, E. (2007). The influence of instructional methods on the quality of online discussion. *British Journal of Educational Technology, 38*(2), 260–271.

Kanwar, M., & Swenson, D. (2000). *Canadian sociology*. Iowa: Kendall/Hunt Publishing Company.

Kearsley, G. (1995, May). *The nature and value of interaction in distance learning*. Paper presented at the Third Distance Education Research Symposium, College Park, PA: American Center for the Study of distance Education.

Keegan, D. (1995). *Distance education technology for the new millennium: Compressed video teaching*. ZIFF Papiere. Hagen, Germany: Institute for Research into Distance Education. (Eric Document Reproduction Service No. ED 389 931).

Ke, F. (2010). Examining online teaching, cognitive, and social presence for adult students. *Computers & Education, 55*, 808–820. doi:10.1016/j.compedu.2010.03.013

Kehrwald, B. (2008). Understanding social presence in text-based online learning environments. *Distance Education, 29*(1), 89–106.

Keller, J. M. (2006). What is motivational design? Retrieved from http://arcsmodel.com/pdf/Motivational%20Design%20Rev%20060620.pdf

Keller, J. M. (2010). *Motivational design for learning and performance: The ARCS model approach*. New York, NY: Springer. doi:10.1007/978-1-4419-1250-3

Keller, J. M., & Suzuki, K. (2004). Learner motivation and E-learning design: A multinationally validated process. *Journal of Educational Media, 29*(3), 229–239. doi:10.1080/1358165042000283084

Kelm, O. (1992). The use of synchronous computer networks in second language instruction: A preliminary report. *Foreign Language Annals, 25*(5), 441–454. doi:10.1111/j.1944-9720.1992.tb01127.x

Kendall, D., Murray, J., & Linden, R. (2010). *Sociology in our times* (2nd ed.). Ontario, Canada: Canadian Cataloguing in Publication.

Kennedy, N., & Kennedy, D. (2010b). Between chaos and entropy: Community of inquiry from a systems perspective. *Complicity: An International Journal of Complexity and Education, 7*(2). http://ejournals.library.ualberta.ca/index.php/complicity/index

Kennedy, D. (1990). Hans-Georg Gadamer's dialectic of dialogue and the epistemology of the community of inquiry. *Analytic Teaching, 11*(1), 43–51.

Kennedy, D. (1993). *Community of inquiry and educational structure. Thinking children and education* (pp. 352–357). Dubuque, IA: Kendall Hunt.

Kennedy, D. (1999). Philosophy for children and the reconstruction of philosophy. *Metaphilosophy, 30*(4), 338–359.

Kennedy, D. (2004a). The role of a facilitator in a community of philosophical inquiry. *Metaphilosophy, 35*(4), 744–765.

Kennedy, D. (2004b). Communal philosophical dialogue and the intersubject. *International Journal for Philosophical Practice, 18*(2), 203–208.

Kennedy, D. (2006). What some second graders say about conflict. In *Changing conceptions of the child from the Renaissance to post-modernity: A philosophy of childhood* (pp. 171–255). Lewiston, NY: The Edwin Mellen Press.

Kennedy, D. (2010a). *Philosophical dialogue with children: Essays on theory and practice*. Lewiston, NY: The Mellen Press.

Kennedy, D. (in press). Rhizomatic curriculum development in community of philosophical inquiry. In Santi, M., & Oliverio, S. (Eds.), *Educating for complex thinking through philosophical inquiry. Models, advances, and proposals for the new millennium*. Napoli, Italy: Liguori.

Kennedy, N. S., & Kennedy, D. (2010). Between chaos and entropy: Community of inquiry from a systems perspective. *Complicity: An International Journal of Complexity and Education, 2*, 1–15.

Kennedy, N., & Kennedy, D. (2012). Community of philosophical inquiry as a discursive structure, and its role in school curriculum design. In Vansieleghem, N., & Kennedy, D. (Eds.), *Philosophy for children in transition: Problems and prospects* (pp. 97–116). London, UK: Blackwell.

Kerr, C. (2001). *The uses of the university* (5th ed.). Cambridge, MA: Harvard University Press.

Keyton, J. (1999). Analyzing interaction patterns in dysfunctional teams. *Small Group Research, 30*(4), 491–518.

Kilpartrick, S., Barrett, M., & Jones, T. (2003). Defining learning communities. Research and learning in Regional Australia, University of Tasmania, D1/2003. Retrieved from http://www.crlra.utas.edu.au/

Kim, Y., & Baylor, A. L. (2006a). Pedagogical agents as learning companions: The role of agent competency and type of interaction. *Educational Technology Research and Development, 54*(3), 223–243. doi:10.1007/s11423-006-8805-zdoi:10.1007/s11423-006-8805-z

Kim, Y., & Baylor, A. L. (2006b). A social cognitive framework for designing pedagogical agents as learning companions. *Educational Technology Research and Development, 54*(6), 569–596. doi:10.1007/s11423-006-0637-3doi:10.1007/s11423-006-0637-3

Kim, K. J., & Bonk, C. J. (2006). The future of online teaching and learning in higher education: The survey says. *EDUCAUSE Quarterly, 29*(4), 22–30.

Kim, K.-J., Liu, S., & Bonk, C. J. (2005). Online MBA students' perceptions of online learning: Benefits, challenges, and suggestions. *The Internet and Higher Education, 8*(4), 335–344.

King, A. (2007). Scripting collaborative learning processes: A cognitive perspective. In Fischer, F., Koller, I., Mandl, H., & Haake, J. M. (Eds.), *Scripting computer-supported collaborative learning – Cognitive, computational and educational perspectives*. New York, NY: Shpringer. doi:10.1007/978-0-387-36949-5_2

King, P. M., & Kitchener, K. S. (1994). *Developing reflective judgment: Understanding and promoting intellectual growth and critical thinking in adolescents and adults*. San Francisco, CA: Jossey-Bass.

Kirschner, P. A. (2001). Using integrated electronic environments for collaborative teaching/learning. *Research Dialogue in Learning and Instruction, 2*(Supplement 1), 1–9.

Kirschner, P. A., Beers, P., Boshuizen, H., & Gijselaers, W. H. (2008). Coercing shared knowledge in collaborative learning environments. *Computers in Human Behavior, 24*(2), 403–420.

Kirschner, P. A., Sweller, J., & Clark, R. E. (2006). Why minimal guidance during instruction does not work: An analysis of the failure of constructivist, discovery, problem-based, experiential, and inquiry-based teaching. *Educational Psychologist, 41*(2), 75–86.

Kitchen, D., & McDougall, D. (1998). Collaborative learning on the internet. *Journal of Educational Technology Systems, 27*(3), 245–258.

Klein, J. D., & Doran, M. S. (1999). Implementing individual and small group learning structures with a computer simulation. *Educational Technology Research and Development, 47*(1), 97–110.

Knuttila, M. (2002). *Introducing sociology: A critical perspective*. Don Mills, Canada: Oxford University Press.

Kolb, D. A. (1984). *Experiential learning: Experience as the source of learning and development*. New Jersey: Prentice-Hall.

Kol, S., & Schcolnik, M. (2008). Asynchronous forums in EAP: Assessment issues. *Language Learning & Technology, 12*(2), 49–70. Retrieved from http://llt.msu.edu/vol12num2/kolschcolnik.pdf

Kostin, M., & Haeger, M. (2006). Coaching schools to sustain improvement. *Education Digest, 71*(9), 29–33.

Kozma, R. B. (1994). The influence of media on learning: The debate continues. *School Library Media Research, 22*(4). Retrieved from http://www.ala.org/aasl/aaslpubsandjournals/slmrb/editorschoiceb/infopower/selctkozmahtml

Krashen, S. (1985). *The input hypothesis: Issues and implications*. London, UK: Longman.

Krathwohl, D. R. (2002). A revision of Bloom's taxonomy: An overview. *Theory into Practice, 41*(4), 212–218.

Kubala, T. (1998). Addressing student needs: teaching on the internet. *T.H.E. Journal, 25*(8), 71–74.

Kupczynski, L., Davis, R., Ice, P., & Callejo, D. (2008). Assessing the impact of instructional design and organization on student achievement in online courses. *International Journal of Instructional Technology and Distance Learning, 5*(1). Retrieved from http://itdl.org/Journal/Jan_08/article01.htm

Kupczynski, L., Ice, P., Wiesenmayer, R., & McCluskey, F. (2010). Student perceptions of the relationship between indicators of teaching presence and success in online courses. *Journal of Interactive Online Learning, 9*(1).

Lam, R. (2010). A peer review training workshop: Coaching students to give and evaluate peer feedback. *TSEL Canada Journal/Revue TESL du Canada, 27*(2), 114–127.

Lamy, M.-N., & Hampel, R. (2007). *Online communication in language learning and teaching*. Hampshire, UK: Pagrave Macmillan. doi:10.1057/9780230592681

Langan, M. A., & Wheater, C. P. (2003). Can students assess students effectively? Some insights into peer-assessment. *Learning and Teaching in Action, 2*(1). Retrieved from http://www.celt.mmu.ac.uk/ltia/issue4/langanwheater.pdf

Langford, G. (1986). The philosophical basis of cognition and metacognition. In Antaki, C., & Lewis, A. (Eds.), *Mental mirrors: Metacognition in social knowledge and communication*. London, UK: Sage Publications.

LaPointe, D. K., & Gunawardena, C. N. (2004). Developing, testing, and refining a model to understand the relationship between peer interaction and learning outcomes in computer-mediated conferencing. *Distance Education, 25*(1), 83–106.

Larkin, S. (2009). Socially mediated metacognition and learning to write. *Thinking Skills and Creativity, 4*(3), 149–159.

Larramendy-Joerns, J., & Leinhardt, G. (2006). Going the distance with online education. *Review of Educational Research, 76*(4), 567–605.

LaRue, B. (2002). In Rudestam, K. E., & Schoenholtz-Read, J. (Eds.), *Synthesizing higher education and corporate learning strategies* (p. 460). Thousand Oaks, CA: Sage Publications.

Laszlo, E. (1975). Basic constructs of systems philosophy. In Ruben, B., & Kim, J. (Eds.), *General systems theory and human communication* (pp. 66–77). Rochelle Park, NJ: Hayden Book Company.

Latour, B. (2005). *Reassembling the social*. New York, NY: Oxford University Press.

Laurillard, D. (2002). *Rethinking university teaching. A conversational framework for the effective use of learning technologies*. London, UK: Routledge. doi:10.4324/9780203304846

Lea, S. J., Stephenson, D., & Troy, J. (2003). Higher education students' attitudes to student centred learning: Beyond 'educational bulimia'. *Studies in Higher Education, 28*(3), 321–334. doi:10.1080/03075070309293

Lee, C. D., & Smagorinsky, P. (2000). Introduction: Constructing meaning through collaborative inquiry. In Lee, C. D., & Smagorinsky, P. (Eds.), *Vygotskian perspectives on literacy research: Constructing meaning through collaborative inquiry* (pp. 1–15). New York, NY: Cambridge University Press.

Leech, N. L., & Onwuegbuzie, A. J. (2007). An array of qualitative data analysis tools: A call for data analysis triangulation. *School Psychology Quarterly, 22*(4), 557.

Leeds, E., Campbell, S., Ali, R., Brawley, D., & Crisp, J. (in press). The impact of student retention strategies: An empirical study. *International Journal of Management in Education*.

Leedy, P. D., & Ormrod, J. E. (2005). *Pratical research: Planning and design* (8th ed.). Upper Saddle River, NJ: Pearson Prentice Hall.

Lee, L. (2002). Synchronous online exchanges: A study of modification devices on non-native discourse. *System, 30*, 275–288. doi:10.1016/S0346-251X(02)00015-5

Lefoe, G., & Hedberg, J. (2006). Blending on and off campus: A tale of two cities. In Bonk, C., & Graham, C. (Eds.), *Handbook of blended learning environments: Global perspectives, local designs*. San Francisco, CA: Pfeiffer.

Leh, A. S. (2002). Action research on hybrid courses and their online communities. *Educational Media International, 39*(1), 31–38.

Leiss, P. D. (2010). *Does synchronous communication technology influence classroom community? A study on the use of a live Web conferencing system within an online classroom*. Unpublished doctoral dissertation. Capella University, Minneapolis.

Leppa, C., Brockhaus, A., & Planchon-Wolf, J. (2005). Developing online teaching and learning resources that engage faculty. In G. Richards (Ed.), *Proceedings of World Conference on E-Learning in Corporate, Government, Healthcare, and Higher Education*, (pp. 866-871). Chesapeake, VA: AACE.

Lessig, L. (2001). *The future of ideas*. New York, NY: Random House.

Liaw, M.-L. (2006). E-learning and the development of intercultural competence. *Language Learning & Technology, 10*(3), 49-64. doi: 10.1.1.110.1555.

Lieblein, E. (2000). Critical factors for successful delivery of online programs. *The Internet and Higher Education, 3*(3), 161–174. doi:10.1016/S1096-7516(01)00036-7

Limbach, B., & Waugh, W. (Fall, 2005). Questioning the lecture format. *The NEA Higher Education Journal: Thought and Action, 20*(1) 47-56. Retrieved on January 18, 2011, from http://www.nea.org/assets/img/PubThoughtAndAction/TAA_05_05.pdf

Lim, D. H. (2004). Cross cultural differences in online learning motivation. *Educational Media International, 41*(2), 163–175. doi:10.1080/09523980410001685784

Lim, D. H., Morris, M. L., & Kupritz, V. (2007). Online vs. blended learning: Differences in instructional outcomes and learner satisfaction. *Journal of Asynchronous Learning Networks, 11*(2), 27–42.

Lin, Q. (2008). Student satisfaction in four mixed courses in an elementary teacher education program. *The Internet and Higher Education, 11*, 53–59.

Lin, X., Hmelo, C., Kinzer, K., & Secules, T. J. (1999). Designing technology to support reflection. *Educational Technology Research and Development, 47*(3), 43–62. doi:10.1007/BF02299633

Lipman, M. (1991). *Thinking in education*. New York, NY: Cambridge University Press.

Lipman, M. (1992). Critical thinking: What can it be? In Oxman, W., Michelli, N. M., & Coia, L. (Eds.), *Critical thinking and learning* (pp. 79–97). Montclair, NJ: Montclair State University.

Lipman, M. (2003). *Thinking in education* (2nd ed.). Cambridge, UK: Cambridge University Press.

Lipman, M. (Ed.). (1993). *Thinking children and education*. Dubuque, IA: Kendall Hunt.

Lipman, M., Sharp, A. M., & Oscanyan, F. S. (1980). *Philosophy in the classroom* (2nd ed.). Philadelphia, PA: Temple University Press.

Lipponen, L. (2002). *Exploring foundations for computer-supported collaborative learning*. Paper presented at the 4th Computer Support for Collaborative Learning: Foundations for a CSCL Community, (CSCL-2002), Boulder, Colorado.

Liu, S., Gomez, J., & Yen, C. (2009). Community college online course retention and final grade: Predictability of social presence. *Journal of Interactive Online Learning, 8*(2), 165–182.

Liu, X., Magjuka, R., Bonk, C., & Lee, S. (2007). Does sense of community matter? *Quarterly Review of Distance Education, 8*(1), 9–24.

Lo, J., Chan, Y., & Yeh, S. (2012). Designing an adaptive web-based learning system based on students' cognitive styles identified online. *Computers & Education, 58*(1), 209–222. doi:10.1016/j.compedu.2011.08.018doi:10.1016/j.compedu.2011.08.018

Lombard, M., & Ditton, T. (1997). At the heart of it all: The concept of presence. *Journal of Computer-Mediated Communication, 3*(2).

Lombard, M., Snyder-Duch, J., & Campanella Bracken, C. (2002). Content analysis in mass communication: Assessment and reporting of intercoder reliability. *Human Communication Research, 28*(4), 587–604.

Lomicka, L., & Lord, G. (2007). Social presence in virtual communities of foreign language (FL) teachers. *System, 35*, 208–228.

Long, M. (1989). Task, group, and task-group interactions. *University of Hawaii's Working Papers in ESL, 8*(2), 1-26.

Long, M. (1981). Input, interaction, and second language acquisition. *Annals of the New York Academy of Sciences, 379*, 259–279. doi:10.1111/j.1749-6632.1981.tb42014.x

Longnecker, C. O. (2010). Coaching for better results: Key practices of high performance leaders. *Industrial and Commercial Training, 42*(1), 32–40.

Lou, Y., Abrami, P. C., & d'Apollonia, S. (2001). Small group and individual learning with technology: A meta-analysis. *Review of Educational Research, 71*(3), 449–521.

Lowenthal, P. R. (2009). Social presence. In Rogers, P., Berg, G., Boettcher, J., Howard, C., Justice, L., & Schenk, K. (Eds.), *Encyclopedia of distance and online learning* (2nd ed., Vol. 1, pp. 1900–1906). Hershey, PA: IGI Global.

Lowenthal, P., & Dunlap, J. (2010). From pixel on a screen to real person in you students' lives: Establishing social presence using digital storytelling. *The Internet and Higher Education, 13*(1-2), 70–72.

Ludwig-Hardman, S., & Dunlap, J. C. (2003). Learner support services for online students: Scaffolding for success. *International Review of Research in Open and Distance Learning, 4*(1).

Lueddeke, G. R. (1999). Toward a constructivist framework for guiding change and innovation in higher education. *The Journal of Higher Education, 70*(3), 235–260. doi:10.2307/2649196

Luhmann, N. (1995). *Social systems*. Palo Alto, CA: Stanford University Press.

Luke, C. (1989). *Pedagogy, printing, and Protestantism: The discourse on childhood*. Albany, NY: SUNY Press.

Luppicini, R. (2008). Introducing conversation design. In Luppicini, R. (Ed.), *Handbook of conversation design for instructional applications* (pp. 1–18). Hershey, PA: IGI Global. doi:10.4018/978-1-59904-597-9.ch001

Lushyn, P., & Kennedy, D. (2002). Power, manipulation, and control in a community of inquiry. *Analytic Teaching, 23*(2), 103–110.

Lynch, C. L., & Wolcott, S. K. (2001). *Helping your students develop critical thinking skills. (IDEA Paper No. 37)*. Manhattan, KS: The IDEA Center.

Lyons, N. (2010). Reflective inquiry: Foundational issues – A deepening of conscious life. In Lyons, N. (Ed.), *Handbook of reflection and reflective inquiry*. US: Springer.

MacDonald, C. J., Stodel, E. J., & Farres, L. G. (2005). The future of university and organisational learning. In Howard, C. (Eds.), *Encyclopedia of distance learning* (*Vol. II*, pp. 960–968). Hershey, PA: Idea Group.

MacDonald, C. J., Stodel, E. J., Thompson, T.-L., & Casimiro, L. (2009). W(e)Learn: A framework for inter-professional education. *International Journal of Electronic Healthcare, 5*(1), 33–47.

Macdonald, J. (2003). Assessing online collaborative learning: Process and product. *Computers & Education, 40*(4), 377–391.

Mackinnon, G. R. (2004). Computer-mediated communication and science teacher training: Two constructivist examples. *Journal of Technology and Teacher Education, 12*(1), 101–114.

MacKnight, C. B. (2000). Teaching critical thinking through online discussions. *EDUCAUSE Quarterly, 23*, 38–41.

Maclean, N. (1976). *A river runs through it and other stories*. Chicago, IL: The University of Chicago Press.

Maki, R. H., & McGuire, M. J. (2004). Metacognition for text: findings and implications for education. In Perfect, T. J., & Schwartz, B. L. (Eds.), *Applied metacognition* (pp. 39–67). Cambridge, UK: Cambridge University Press.

Mandernach, B. J., Gonzales, R. M., & Garrett, A. L. (2006). An examination of online instructor presence via threaded discussion participation. *Journal of Online Learning and Teaching, 2*(4), 248–260.

Marshall, S. P. (1997). Creating sustainable learning communities for the tweny-first century. In Hesselbein, F., Goldsmith, M., & Beckhard, R. (Eds.), *The organization of the future*. San Francisco, CA: Jossey-Bass.

Marton, F., & Saljo, R. (1984). Approaches to learning. In Marton, F., Hounsell, D., & Entwistle, N. (Eds.), *The experience of learning*. Edinburgh, UK: Scottish Academic Press.

Mason, R. (1991). Moderating educational computer conferencing. *Deosnews, 1*(19).

Masur, E. F., McIntyre, C. W., & Flavell, J. H. (1973). Developmental changes in apportionment of study time among items in a multi-trial free recall task. *Journal of Experimental Child Psychology, 15*, 237–246. doi:10.1016/0022-0965(73)90145-8doi:10.1016/0022-0965(73)90145-8

Matsumoto, D. (1996). *Culture and psychology*. Pacific Grove, CA: Brooks/Cole Publishing Company.

Maurino, P. S. (2007). Looking for critical thinking in online threaded discussions. *Journal of Educational Technology Systems, 35*(3), 241–260.

Maushak, N. J., & Ou, C. (2007). Using synchronous communication to facilitate graduate students' online collaboration. *The Quarterly Review of Distance Education, 8*(2), 161–169.

Maxwell, J. A. (2005). *Qualitative research design. An interactive approach* (2nd ed.). New York, NY: Sage Publications.

McBrien, J. L., Jones, P., & Cheng, R. (2009). Virtual spaces: Employing a synchronous online classroom to facilitate student engagement in online learning. *International Review of Research in Open and Distance Learning, 10*(3).

McCall, C. (1993). Young children generate philosophical ideas. In Lipman, M. (Ed.), *Thinking children and education* (pp. 569–592). Dubuque, IA: Kendall Hunt.

McCombs, B. L., & Miller, L. (2007). *Learner-centered classroom practices and assessments: Maximizing student motivation, learning, and achievement*. Thousand Oaks, CA: Corwin Press.

McDonald, J. H. (2009). *Handbook of biological statistics* (2nd ed.). Baltimore, MD: Sparky House Publishing. Retrieved from http://udel.edu/~mcdonald/statintro.html

McIsaac, M. S., & Gunawardena, C. N. (1996). Distance education. In Jonassen, D. H. (Ed.), *Handbook of research for educational communication and technology* (pp. 403–437). New York, NY: Simon & Schuster Macmillan.

McIssac, M. (2002). Online learning from an international perspective. *Education Media International*. Online © 2002 International Council for Education Media. doi:10.1080 /09523980210131196

McKeachie, W. J., Pintrich, P. R., Lin, Y. G., & Smith, D. A. F. (1986). *Teaching and learning in the college classroom: A review of the research literature*. Ann Arbor, MI: University of Michigan.

McKenzie, W., & Murphy, D. (2000). "I hope this goes somewhere": Evaluation of an online discussion group. *Australian Journal of Educational Technology, 16*(3), 239–257. Retrieved from http://www.ascilite.org.au/ajet/ajet16/mckenzie.html

McKerlich, R., & Anderson, T. (2007). Community of Inquiry and learning in immersive environments. *Journal of Asynchronous Learning Networks, 11*(4), 35–52.

McKlin, T., Harmon, S. W., Evans, W., & Jones, M. G. (2001). Cognitive presence in web based learning: A content analysis of students' online discussions. *American Journal of Distance Education, 15*(1), 7–23.

McLellan, H. (2006). Digital storytelling: Bridging old and new. *Educational Technology, 46*(2), 26–31.

McLoughlin, D., & Mynard, J. (2009). An analysis of higher order thinking in online discussions. *Innovations in Education and Teaching International, 46*(2), 147–160.

McLuhan, M. (1995). *Understanding media: The extensions of man*. Cambridge, MA: The MIT Press.

McMillan, J. H., & Schumacher, S. (2001). *Research in education: A conceptual introduction* (5th ed.). New York, NY: Longman.

McPeck, J. (1981). *Critical thinking and education*. Oxford, UK: Martin Robertson.

Mead, G. H. (1934). *Mind, self and society*. Chicago, IL: University of Chicago Press.

Means, B., Toyama, Y., Murphy, R., Bakia, M., & Jones, K. (2009). *Evaluation of evidence-based practices in online learning: A meta-analysis and review of online learning studies.* U.S. Department of Education. Retrieved July 29, 2010 from http://www2.ed.gov/rschstat/eval/tech/evidence-based-practices/finalreport.pdf

Means, B., Toyama, Y., Murphy, R., Bakia, M., & Jones, K. (2010). *Evaluation of evidence-based practices in online learning*. Washington, DC: U.S. Department of Education. Retrieved November 10, 2011, from http://www2.ed.gov/rschstat/eval/tech/evidence-based-practices/finalreport.pdf.

Mejias, R. J. (2007). The interaction of process losses, process gains, and meeting satisfaction within technology-supported environments. *Small Group Research*, *38*(1), 156–194.

Mergel, B. (May, 1998). *Instructional design and learning theories*. Retrieved March 13, 2007, from http://www.usask.ca/education/coursework/802papers/mergel/brenda.htm

Merton, T. (1966). *Conjectures of a guilty bystander*. Garden City, NY: Doubleday.

Meskill, C., & Anthony, N. (2007). Form-focused CMC: What language learners say. *CALICO Journal*, *25*(1), 69–90. Retrieved from https://www.calico.org/html/article_677.pdf

Metzner, B. S., & Bean, J. P. (1987). The estimation of a conceptual model of nontraditional undergraduate student attrition. *Research in Higher Education*, *27*(1), 15–38. doi:10.1007/BF00992303

Meyer, K. (2003). Face-to-face versus threaded discussions: The role of time and higher-order thinking. *Journal of Asynchronous Learning Networks*, *7*(3), 55–65.

Meyer, K. (2004). Evaluating online discussions: Four different frames of analysis. *Journal of Asynchronous Learning Networks*, *8*(2), 101–114.

Meyer, K. A. (2004). Evaluating online discussions: Four different frames of analysis. *Journal of Asynchronous Learning Networks*, *8*(2), 101–114.

Meyer, K. A., Bruwelheide, J., & Poulin, R. (2006). Why they stayed: Near-perfect retention in an online certification program in library media. *Journal of Asynchronous Learning Networks*, *10*(4), 99–115.

Mezirow, J. (2009). Transformative learning theory. In Mezirow, J., & Taylor, E. W. (Eds.), *Transformative learning in practice: Insights from community, workplace, and higher education* (pp. 18–32). San Francisco, CA: Jossey-Bass.

Miell, D. K., & Miell, D. E. (1986). Recursiveness in interpersonal cognition. In Antaki, C., & Lewis, A. (Eds.), *Mental mirrors: Metacognition in social knowledge and communication*. London, UK: Sage Publications.

Millis, B. J., & Cottell, P. G. (1998). *Cooperative learning for higher education faculty*. Phoenix, AZ: Oryx Press.

Molenda, M. (2003). In search of the elusive ADDIE model. *Performance Improvement*, *42*(5), 34–36. doi:doi:10.1002/pfi.4930420508

Molinari, D. L. (2004). The role of social comments in problem-solving groups in an online class. *American Journal of Distance Education*, *18*(2), 89–101.

Moon, J. (2008). *Critical thinking: An exploration of theory and practice*. New York, NY: Routledge.

Moore, A., Moore, J., & Fowler, S. (2005). Faculty development for the net generation. In D. Oblinger & J. Oblinger (Eds.), *Educating the Net generation,* (pp. 11.1-11.15). Retrieved November 20, 2011, from http://www.educause.edu/educatingthenetgen

Moore, A. H., Fowler, S. B., & Watson, C. E. (2007). Active learning and technology: Designing Change for faculty, students, and institutions. *EDUCAUSE Review*, *42*(5), 43–60.

Moore, J. C. (2002). *Elements of quality: The Sloan-C framework*. Needham, MA: Sloan Consortium.

Moore, J. C. (2005). Is higher education ready for transformative learning? A question explored in the study of sustainability. *Journal of Transformative Education*, *3*, 76–91.

Moore, J., & Marra, R. (2005). A comparative analysis of online discussion participation protocols. *Journal of Research on Technology in Education*, *38*(2), 191–212.

Moore, L., & Craig, L. (2008). *Intellectual captial in enterprise success*. Hoboken, NJ: Wiley & Sons, Inc.

Moore, M. (1989). Three types of interaction. *American Journal of Distance Education, 3*(2), 1–16.

Moore, M. (2006). Editorial: Questions of culture. *American Journal of Distance Education, 20*(1), 1–5. doi:10.1207/s15389286ajde2001_1

Moore, M., & Kearsley, G. (1995). *Distance education: A systems view*. California: Wadsworth.

Morgan, C., & Metni, E. (2006). *United beyond our diversity, a global panorama - Tiles of unity*. Presented at The role of Information Communications Technology (ICT) in Bridge Building and Social Inclusion. University of Ulster, Northern Ireland. Retrieved December 2, 2010 from http://www.socsci.ulster.ac.uk./education/ict_conf/abstract/morgan.html

Morgan, T. (2011). Online classroom or community-in-the-making? Instructor conceptualizations and teaching presence in international online contexts. *The Journal of Distance Education, 25*(1), 1-15. Retrieved March 24, 2011, from http://www.jofde.ca/index.php/jde/article/view/721/1190

Morris, F. (2005). Child-to-child interaction and corrective feedback in a computer mediated L2 class. *Language Learning & Technology, 9*(1), 29–45.

Morris, L. V., Finnegan, C., & Wu, S. (2005). Tracking student behavior, persistence and achievement in online courses. *The Internet and Higher Education, 8*, 221–231. doi:10.1016/j.iheduc.2005.06.009

Morrison, G. R., Ross, S. M., & Kemp, J. E. (2010). *Designing effective instruction* (6th ed.). Hoboken, NJ: John Wiley & Sons, Inc.

Morse, K. (2003). Does one size fit all? Exploring asynchronous learning in a multicultural environment. *The Journal of Asynchronous Learning Networks, 7*(1). Retrieved May 24, 2010, from citeseerx.ist.psu.edu/viewdoc/download*doi:10.1.1.138.6050.*

Mudrack, P. E., & Farrell, G. M. (1995). An examination of functional role behavior and its consequences for individuals in group settings. *Small Group Research, 26*(4), 542–571.

Murphy, E. (2004). An instrument to support thinking critically about critical thinking in online asynchronous discussions. *Australasian Journal of Educational Technology, 20*(3), 295–315.

Murphy, E. (2004). Identifying and measuring ill-structured problem formulation and resolution in online asynchronous discussions. *Canadian Journal of Learning and Technology, 30*(1), 5–20.

Murphy, E. (2004). Recognising and promoting collaboration in an online asynchronous discussion. *British Journal of Educational Technology, 35*(4), 421–431.

Murphy, K. L., Mahoney, S. E., Chen, C.-Y., Mendoza-Diaz, N. V., & Yang, X. (2005). A constructivist model of mentoring, coaching, and facilitating online discussions. *Distance Education, 26*(3), 341–366.

Muse, H. E. Jr. (2003). The web-based community college student: An examination of factors that lead to success and risk. *The Internet and Higher Education, 6*, 241–261. doi:10.1016/S1096-7516(03)00044-7

Nadolski, R. J., Kirschner, P. A., & Van Merriënboer, J. J. G. (2005). Optimizing the number of steps in learning tasks for complex skills. *The British Journal of Educational Psychology, 75*(2), 223–237.

National Science Foundation. (2008). Fostering learning in the networked world: The cyberlearning opportunity and challenge. Retrieved from http://cyberlearningstem.org/assets/nsf08204.pdf

Neal, E. (1996). Leading the seminar: Graduate and undergraduate. *Essays on Teaching Excellence*, a Professional & Organizational Development Network in Higher Education publication. Retrieved September 8, 2009, from http://www.podnetwork.org/publications/essayseries.htm#1995-96

Necka, E., & Orzechowski, J. (2005). Higher order cognition and intelligence. In Sternberg, R. J., & Pretz, J. E. (Eds.), *Cognition and intelligence: Identifying mechanisms of the mind*. Cambridge University Press.

Neff, M. D. (2002). Online knowledge communities and their role in organizational learning. In Rudestam, K. E., & Schoenholtz-Read, J. (Eds.), *Handbook of online learning: Innovations in higher education and corporate training*. Thousand Oaks, CA: Sage Publications.

Nelson, L. M. (1999). Collaborative problem solving. In Reigeluth, C. M. (Ed.), *Instructional-design theories and models, II*. Mahwah, NJ: Lawrence Erlbaum Associates.

Newman, D. R., Johnson, C., Cochrane, C., & Webb, B. (1996). An experiment in group learning technology: Evaluating critical thinking in face-to-face and computer-supported seminars. *Interpersonal Computing and Technology: An Electronic Journal for the 21st Century, 4*(1), 57–74. Retrieved from http://www.helsinki.fi/science/optek/1996/ n1/newman.txt

Newman, D. R., Webb, B., & Cochrane, C. (1995). A content analysis method to measure critical thinking in face-to-face and computer supported group learning. *Interpersonal Computing and Technology: An Electronic Journal for the 21st Century, 3*(2), 56–77. Retrieved from http://www.helsinki.fi/science/optek/1995/n2/newman.txt

Nicol, D. J., & Macfarlane-Dick, D. (2006). Formative assessment and self-regulated learning: A model and seven principles of good feedback practice. *Studies in Higher Education, 31*(2), 199–218. doi:10.1080/03075070600572090

Nippard, E., & Murphy, E. (2007). Social presence in the web-based synchronous secondary classroom. *Canadian Journal of Learning and Technology, 33*(1). Retrieved from http://www.cjlt.ca/content/vol33.1/nippard.html

Ni, S., & Aust, R. (2008). Examining teacher verbal immediacy and sense of classroom community in online classes. *International Journal on E-Learning, 7*(3), 477–498.

Nora, A. (1987). Determinants of retention among Chicano college students. *Research in Higher Education, 26*(1), 31–59. doi:10.1007/BF00991932

O'Donnell, A. M. (2006). The role of peers and group learning. In Alexander, P., & Winne, P. (Eds.), *Handbook of educational psychology* (2nd ed., pp. 781–802). Mahwah, NJ: Lawrence Erlbaum.

O'Dowd, R. (2006). The use of videoconferencing and e-mail as mediators of intercultural student ethnography. In Belz, J., & Thorne, S. (Eds.), *Internet-mediated intercultural FL education* (pp. 86–120). Boston, MA: Thomson Heinle.

O'Sullivan, P. B. (2000). Communication technologies in an education environment: Lessons from a historical perspective. In Cole, R. A. (Ed.), *Issues in Web-based pedagogy: A critical primer* (pp. 49–64). Westport, CT: Greenwood Press.

Oberst, U., Gallifa, J., Farriols, N., & Villaregut, A. (2009). Training emotional and social competences in higher education: The seminar methodology. *Higher Education in Europe, 34*, 3–4.

Ocker, R. J., & Yaverbaum, G. J. (1999). Asynchronous computer-mediated communication versus face-to-face collaboration: Results on student learning, quality and satisfaction. *Group Decision and Negotiation, 8*, 427–440.

Ocker, R. J., & Yaverbaum, G. J. (2001). Collaborative learning environments: Exploring student attitudes and satisfaction in face-to-face and asynchronous computer conferencing settings. *Journal of Interactive Learning Research, 12*(4), 427–448.

Olaniran, B. A. (1996). A model of group satisfaction in computer-mediated communication and face-to-face meetings. *Behaviour & Information Technology, 15*(1), 24–36.

Oliver, R., & Omari, A. (2001). Student responses to collaborating and learning in a web-based environment. *Journal of Computer Assisted Learning, 17*(1), 34–47.

Ong, W. (1982). *Orality and literacy: The technologizing of the word*. New York, NY: Methuen.

O'Reilly, T. (2005). What is web 2.0? *O'Reilly Network*. Retrieved from http://oreilly.com/web2/archive/what-is-web-20.html

Osborn, D. S. (2009). Wikis, podcasts and more… program policy considerations with online teaching. In Walz, G. R., Bleuer, J. C., & Yep, R. K. (Eds.), *Compelling counselling interventions: VISTAS 2009* (pp. 329–336). Alexandria, VA: American Counselling Association.

Overbaugh, R., Nickel, C., & Brown, H. M. (2006). *Student characteristics in a university-level foundations course: An examination of orientation toward learning and the role of academic community*. Paper presented at the Eastern Educational Research Association Annual Conference, Hilton Head, SC.

Overbaugh, R., & Nickel, C. (2008). *A comparison of student satisfaction and value of academic community between blended and online sections of a university-level educational foundations course.* Norfolk, VA: Old Dominion University.

Pachnowski, L. M., & Jurczyk, J. P. (2003). Perceptions of faculty on the effect of distance learning technology on faculty preparation time. *Online Journal of Distance Learning Administration, 6*(3).

Palloff, R. M., & Pratt, K. (1999). *Building learning communities in cyberspace: Effective strategies for the online classroom.* San Francisco, CL: Jossey-Bass Publishers.

Palloff, R. M., & Pratt, K. (2005). *Collaborating online: learning together in community.* San Francisco: Jossey-Bass.

Palloff, R., & Pratt, K. (2001). *Lessons from the cyberspace classroom: The realities of online teaching.* San Francisco, CA: Jossey-Bass.

Pallof, R. M., & Pratt, K. (2007). *Building online learning communities* (2nd ed.). San Francisco, CA: Jossey-Bass.

Palmer, P. (1998). *The courage to teach: Exploring the inner landscape of a teacher's life.* San Francisco, CA: Jossey-Bass.

Palmer, P. (2004). *A hidden wholeness: The journey toward an undivided life.* San Francisco, CA: Jossey-Bass.

Park, Y. J., & Bonk, C. (2007). Synchronous learning experiences: distance and residential learners' perspectives in a blended graduate course. *Journal of Interactive Online Learning, 6*(3), 245-264. Retrieved June 22, 2008 from http://www.ncolr.org/jiol/issues/PDF/6.3.6.pdf

Park, C. L. (2009). Replicating the use of a cognitive presence measurement tool. *Journal of Interactive Online Learning, 8,* 140–155.

Parrish, P., & Linder-VanBerschot, J. A. (2010). Cultural dimensions of learning: Addressing the challenges of multicultural instruction. *International Review of Research in Open and Distance Learning, 11*(2). Retrieved May 28, 2010 from http://www.irrodl.org/index.php/irrodl

Pascarella, E. T., & Terenzini, P. (1980). Predicting persistence and voluntary dropout decisions from a theoretical model. *The Journal of Higher Education, 51*(1), 60–75. doi:10.2307/1981125

Pask, G. (1976). *Conversation theory: Applications in education and epistemology.* Amsterdam, The Netherlands: Elsevier.

Patton, B. A. (2008). Synchronous meetings: A way to put personality in an online class. *Turkish Online Journal of Distance Education, 9*(4). Retrieved January 15, 2009, from http://tojde.anadolu.edu.tr/

Patton, M. Q. (1990). *Qualitative evaluation and research methods* (2nd ed.). Newbury Park, CA: Sage Publications.

Paul, R. (1985). The critical thinking movement. *National Forum, 65*(1), 2–3.

Paul, R., & Elder, L. (2001). *Critical thinking: Tools for talking charge of your learning and your life.* Upper Saddle River, NJ: Prentice Hall.

Paulsen, M. F. (1995). Moderating educational computer conferences. *Computer Mediated Communication and the Online Classroom, 3,* 81–89.

Paulus, T. M. (2005). Collaborative and cooperative approaches to online group work: The impact of task type. *Distance Education, 26*(1), 111–125.

Pawan, F., Paulus, T. M., Yalcin, S., & Chang, C. F. (2003). Online learning: Patterns of engagement and interaction among in-service teachers. *Language Learning & Technology, 7*(3), 119–140.

Pedralozzi, A. (2010). *OPUS One: Intelligent adaptive learning environment using artificial intelligence support.* Paper presented at the American Institute of Physics (AIP), Lugano, Switzerland.

Peirce, C. S. (1958). *Values in a universe of chance* (Weiner, P., Ed.). Garden City, NY: Doubleday Anchor Books.

Peirce, C. S. (1966). The fixation of belief. In Weiner, P. (Ed.), *Selected writings* (pp. 27–40). New York, NY: Dover Publications.

Peirce, C. S. (2011). *The philosophical writings of Peirce (J. Buchler* (New York, N. Y., Ed.). Dover.

Pena-Shaff, J. B., & Nicholls, C. (2004). Analyzing student interactions and meaning construction in computer bulletin board discussions. *Computers & Education, 42*(3), 243–265.

Perkins, D. (1986). On creativity and thinking skills: A conversation with David Perkins. *Educational Leadership, 43*(8), 12–18.

Perry, B., & Edwards, M. (2005). Exemplary online educators: Creating a community of inquiry. *Turkish Online Journal of Distance Education, 6*(2).

Perry, R. P., & Smart, J. C. (2007). *Scholarship of teaching and learning in higher education.* New York, NY: Springer. doi:10.1007/1-4020-5742-3

Peters, O. (1993). Distance education in a postindustrial society. In Keegan, D. (Ed.), *Theoretical principles of distance education* (pp. 39–58). London, UK: Routledge.

Petrie, H. G. (1981). *The dilemma of enquiry and learning.* Chicago, IL: University of Chicago Press.

Phillips, H. J., & Powers, R. B. (1979). The college seminar: Participation under instructor-led and student-led discussion groups. *Teaching of Psychology, 6*(2).

Piaget, J. (1977). *The development of thought: Equilibration of cognitive structures.* New York, NY: Viking.

Picciano, A. G. (2002). Beyond student perceptions: Issues of interaction, presence, and performance in an online course. *Journal of Asynchronous Learning Networks, 6*(1), 21–40.

Piccoli, G., Ahmad, R., & Ives, B. (2001). Web-based virtual learning environments: A research framework and a preliminary assessment of effectiveness in basic IT training. *Management Information Systems Quarterly, 25*(4), 401–426.

Pinchot, G. (1998). Building community in the workplace. In Hesselbein, F., Goldsmith, M., Beckhard, R., & Schubert, R. F. (Eds.), *The community of the future.* San Francisco, CA: Jossey-Bass.

Pintrich, P. R., Wolters, C. A., & Baxter, G. P. (2000). Assessing metacognition and self-regulated learning. In Schraw, G., & Impara, J. C. (Eds.), *Issues in the measurement of metacognition.* Lincoln, NE: University of Nebraska-Lincoln.

Plato,. (1961). Phaedrus. In Hamilton, E., & Cairns, H. (Eds.), *The collected dialogues of Plato* (pp. 475–525). Princeton, NJ: Princeton University Press.

Power, M. (2008). The emergence of blended online learning. *Journal of Online Teaching & Learning, 4*(4).

Power, M., & Gould-Morven, A. (2011). Head of gold, feet of clay: The online learning paradox. *International Review of Research in Open and Distance Learning, 12*(2).

Power, M., & Vaughan, N. (2010). Redesigning online learning for graduate seminar delivery. *Journal of Distance Education, 24*(2).

Power, M., Vaughan, N., & Saint-Jacques, A. (2010). *Revisiting the graduate seminar through blended online learning design. American Educational Research Association* (pp. 30–May-4). Denver: Co. April.

Powers, S. M., & Mitchell, J. (1997). *Student perceptions and performance in a virtual classroom environment.* Paper presented at the Annual Meeting of the American Educational Research Association, Chicago, IL.

Priluck, R. (2004). Web-assisted courses for business education: An examination of two sections of principles of marketing. *Journal of Marketing Education, 26*(2), 161–173.

Privateer, P. M. (1999). Academic technology and the future of higher education. *The Journal of Higher Education, 70*(1), 60–79. doi:10.2307/2649118

Quality Matters. (2005). *Research literature and standards sets support for Quality Matters review standards.* Retrieved July 14, 2010, from http://www.qualitymatters.org/Documents/Matrix%20of%20Research%20Standards%20FY0506.pdf

Quintana, C., Reiser, B. J., Davis, E. A., Krajcik, J., Fretz, E., & Duncan, R. G. (2004). A scaffolding design framework for software to support science inquiry. *Journal of the Learning Sciences, 13*(3), 337–386.

Ramprasad, A. (1983). On the definition of feedback. *Behavioral Science, 28*, 4–13.

Ramsden, P. (2003). *Learning to teach in higher education* (2nd ed.). London, UK: Routledge.

Redmond, P. (2010). Investigating the use of online discussions in an undergraduate face-to-face course (pp. 27–33). In C. D. Maddux, D. Gibson, & B. Dodge (Eds.), *Research Highlights in Technology and Teacher Education 2010* (pp. 27-33). Society for Information Technology & Teacher Education (SITE).

Reigeluth, C. M., & Carr-Chellman, A. A. (2010). Understanding instructional theory. In Reigeluth, C. M., & Carr-Chellman, A. A. (Eds.), *Instructional design theory and models* (*Vol. III*). New York, NY: Routledge.

Rendon, L. (1994). Validating culturally diverse students: Toward a new model of learning and student development. *Innovative Higher Education*, *9*(1), 33–52. doi:10.1007/BF01191156

Reneland-Forsman, L., & Ahlbäck, T. (2007). Collaboration as quality interaction in web-based learning. *Journal Advanced Technology for Learning*, *4*, 30–35.

Rennie, F., & Morrison, T. (2007). *E-learning and social networking handbook: Resources for higher education.* New York, NY: Routledge.

Rhoades, G., & Maitland, C. (2004). Bargaining workload and workforce on the high tech campus. *The NEA 2004 Almanac of Higher Education* (pp. 75-81). Retrieved from http://www.nea.org/assets/img/PubAlmanac/ALM_04_06.pdf

Rhoades, G. (2006). The higher education we choose: A question of balance. *The Review of Higher Education*, *29*(3), 381–404. Project MUSE database. doi:10.1353/rhe.2006.0015

Rhode, J. F. (2008). *Interaction equivalency in self-paced online learning environments: An exploration of learner preferences.* ProQuest.

Richardson, J., & Swan, K. (2000). How to make the most of online interaction. In J. Bourdeau & R. Heller (Eds.), *Proceedings of World Conference on Educational Multimedia, Hypermedia and Telecommunications* (pp. 1488-1489). Chesapeake, VA: AACE.

Richardson, J. C., & Ice, P. (2010). Investigating students' level of critical thinking across instructional strategies in online discussions. *The Internet and Higher Education*, *13*(1/2), 52–59.

Richardson, J. C., Sadaf, A., & Ertmer, P. G. (2012). Relationship between types of question prompts and critical thinking in online discussions. In Akyol, Z., & Garrison, D. (Eds.), *Educational communities of inquiry: Theoretical framework, research and practice.* Hershey, PA: IGI Global.

Richardson, J. C., & Swan, K. (2003). Examining social presence in online courses in relation to students' perceived learning and satisfaction. *Journal of Asynchronous Learning Networks*, *7*(1), 68–88.

Rienties, B. (2010). *Understanding social interaction in computer-supported collaborative learning: The role of motivation on social interaction.* Unpublished manuscript, Maastricht.

Rienties, B., Giesbers, B., Tempelaar, D. T., Lygo-Baker, S., Segers, M., & Gijselaers, W. H. (2012). The role of scaffolding and motivation in CSCL. *Computers & Education*, *59*(3), 893–906. doi:10.1016/j.compedu.2012.04.010

Rienties, B., Kaper, W., Struyven, K., Tempelaar, D. T., Van Gastel, L., & Vrancken, S. (2011). (in press). A review of the role of information communication technology and course design in transitional education practices. *Interactive Learning Environments*. doi:doi:10.1080/10494820.10492010.10542757

Rienties, B., Tempelaar, D. T., Van den Bossche, P., Gijselaers, W. H., & Segers, M. (2009). The role of academic motivation in computer-supported collaborative learning. *Computers in Human Behavior*, *25*(6), 1195–1206.

Rienties, B., Tempelaar, D. T., Waterval, D., Rehm, M., & Gijselaers, W. H. (2006). Remedial online teaching on a summer course. *Industry and Higher Education*, *20*(5), 327–336.

Riva, G. (2009). Is presence a technology issue? Some insights from cognitive sciences. *Virtual Reality (Waltham Cross)*, *13*, 159–169. doi:doi:10.1007/s10055-009-0121-6

Rivera, J. C., McAlister, M. K., & Rice, M. L. (2002). A comparison of student outcomes & satisfaction between traditional & web based course offerings. *Online Journal of Distance Learning Administration*, *5*(3). Retrieved from http://www.westga.edu/~distance/ojdla/fall53/rivera53.html

Roberts, T. S. (2004). Self, peer and group assessment in e-Learning: An introduction. In Roberts, T. S. (Ed.), *Self, peer, and group assessment in e-learning* (pp. 1–16). Hershey, PA: Information Science Publishing.

Rockinson-Szapkiw, A. G. (2009). *The impact of asynchronous and synchronous instruction and discussion on cognitive presence, social presence, teaching presence and learning*. Unpublished doctoral dissertation, Regent University, Virginia.

Rodriguez, J., Plax, T. G., & Kearney, P. (1996). Clarifying the relationship between teacher nonverbal immediacy and student cognitive learning: Affective learning as the central causal mediator. *Communication Education, 45,* 293–305. doi:10.1080/03634529609379059

Rogers, P., Berg, G. A., Boettcher, J., Howard, C., Justice, L., & Schenk, K. D. (2009). (Eds.), *Encyclopedia of distance learning* (2nd ed.). Hershey, PA: Information Science Reference.

Rogers, E. M. (1995). *Diffusion of innovations* (4th ed.). New York, NY: Free Press.

Rogers, P., & Lea, M. (2005). Social presence in distributed group environments: The role of social identity. *Behaviour & Information Technology, 24*(2), 151–158.

Romiszowski, A. (1999). The development of physical skills: Instruction in the psychomotor domain. In Reigeluth, C. M. (Ed.), *Instructional design theories and models* (*Vol. II*). Mahwah, NJ: Erlbaum.

Roschelle, J., & Teasley, S. (1995). The construction of shared knowledge in collaborative problem solving. In O'Malley, C. (Ed.), *Computer supported collaborative learning* (pp. 69–97). Berlin, Germany: Springer-Verlag.

Rose, M. A. (2002). *Cognitive dialogue, interaction patterns, and perceptions of graduate students in an online conferencing environment under collaborative and cooperative structures.* Doctor of Education Dissertation, Indiana University.

Rose, M. A. (2004). Comparing productive online dialogue in two group styles: Cooperative and collaborative. *American Journal of Distance Education, 18*(2), 73–88.

Rourke, L., & Anderson, T. (2002). Using peer teams to lead online discussions. *Journal of Interactive Media in Education, 1,* 1–21.

Rourke, L., & Anderson, T. (2004). Validity in quantitative content analysis. *Educational Technology Research and Development, 52*(1), 5–18.

Rourke, L., Anderson, T., Garrison, D. R., & Archer, W. (1999). Assessing social presence in asynchronous text-based computer conferencing. *Journal of Distance Education, 14*(2), 50–71.

Rourke, L., Anderson, T., Garrison, D. R., & Archer, W. (2001). Methodological issues in the content analysis of computer conference transcripts. *International Journal of Artificial Intelligence in Education, 12*(1), 8–22.

Rourke, L., Anderson, T., Garrison, R. D., & Archer, W. (2001). Assessing social presence in asynchronous text-based computer conferencing. *Journal of Distance Education, 14*(2). Retrieved from http://cade.athabascau.ca/vol14.2/rourke_et_al.html

Rourke, L., & Kanuka, H. (2009). Learning in communities of inquiry: A review of the literature. *Journal of Distance Education, 23*(1), 19–48.

Rovai, A. P. (2001). Building classroom community at a distance: A case study. *Educational Technology Research and Development, 49*(4), 33–48.

Rovai, A. P. (2002). A preliminary look at structural differences in sense of classroom community between higher education traditional and ALN courses. *Journal of Asynchronous Learning Networks, 6*(1), 41–56.

Rovai, A. P. (2002). Building sense of community at a distance. *International Review of Research in Open and Distance Learning, 3*(1).

Rovai, A. P. (2002). Development of an instrument to measure classroom community. *The Internet and Higher Education, 5*(3), 197–211.

Rovai, A. P. (2002). Sense of community, perceived cognitive learning, and persistence in asynchronous learning networks. *The Internet and Higher Education, 5*(4), 319–332.

Rovai, A. P. (2003). In search of higher persistence rates in distance education online programs. *The Internet and Higher Education, 6,* 1–16. doi:10.1016/S1096-7516(02)00158-6

Rovai, A. P. (2004). A constructivist approach to online college learning. *The Internet and Higher Education, 7*(2), 79–93. doi:10.1016/j.iheduc.2003.10.002

Rovai, A. P., & Jordan, H. M. (2004). Blended learning and sense of community: A comparative analysis with traditional and fully online graduate courses. *International Review of Research in Open and Distance Learning, 5*(2).

Rovai, A. P., & Lucking, R. (2003). Sense of community in a higher education television-based distance education program. *Educational Technology Research and Development, 51*(2), 5–16.

Rovai, A. P., & Ponton, M. K. (2005). An examination of sense of classroom community and learning among African American and Caucasian graduate students. *Journal of Asynchronous Learning Networks, 9*(3), 75–90.

Rovai, A. P., Ponton, M. K., & Baker, J. D. (2008). *Distance learning in higher education: A programmatic approach to planning, design, instruction, evaluation, and accreditation.* New York, NY: Teachers College Press.

Rusman, E., Van Bruggen, J., Cörvers, R., Sloep, P., & Koper, R. (2009). From pattern to practice: Evaluation of a design pattern fostering trust in virtual teams. *Computers in Human Behavior, 25*(5), 1010–1019.

Russell, T. L. (1999). *No significant difference phenomenon.* Raleigh, NC: North Carolina State University.

Russell, T. L. (2001). *The no significant difference phenomenon: A comparative research annotated bibliography on technology for distance education.* Montgomery: AL The International Distance Education Certification Center.

Russo, T. C., & Benson, S. (2005). Learning with invisible others: Perceptions of online presence and their relationship to cognitive and affective learning. *Journal of Educational Technology & Society, 8*(1), 54–62.

Rust, C. (2002). The impact of assessment on student learning: How can the research literature practically help to inform the development of departmental assessment strategies and learner-centred assessment practices? *Active Learning in Higher Education, 3*(2), 145–158. doi:10.1177/1469787402003002004

Sadler, D. R. (1998). Formative assessment: revisiting the territory. *Assessment in Education, 5*(1), 77–84. doi:10.1080/0969595980050104

Sailors, M., & Shanklin, N. L. (2010). Growing evidence to support coaching in literacy and mathematics. *The Elementary School Journal, 111*(1), 1–6.

Saint-Jacques, A. (2012). Effective teaching practices to foster vibrant communities of inquiry in synchronous online learning. In Akyol, Z., & Garrison, D. R. (Eds.), *Educational communities of inquiry: Theoretical framework, research and practice* (p. xx). Hershey, PA: IGI Global.

Salomon, G. (1997). *Interaction of media, cognition, and learning.* San Francisco, CA: Jossey Bass.

Sammons, M., & Ruth, S. (2007). The invisible professor and the future of virtual faculty. *International Journal of Teaching and Technology, 4*(1).

Schacht, S., & Aspelmeier, J. (2005). *Social and behavioral statistics: A user-friendly approach* (2nd ed.). Boulder, CO: Westview Press.

Schellens, T., & Valcke, M. (2005). Collaborative learning in asynchronous discussion groups: What about the impact on cognitive processing? *Computers in Human Behavior, 21*(6), 957–975.

Schellens, T., & Valcke, M. (2006). Fostering knowledge construction in university students through asynchronous discussion groups. *Computers & Education, 46*(4), 349–370.

Schellens, T., Van Keer, H., & Valcke, M. (2005). The impact of role assignment on knowledge construction in asynchronous discussion groups: A multilevel analysis. *Small Group Research, 36*, 704–745.

Schiffrin, D., Tannen, D., & Hamilton, H. E. (Eds.). (2001). *The handbook of discourse analysis.* Malden, MA: Blackwell Publishing.

Schlosser, L. A., & Simonson, M. (2002). *Distance education: Definition and glossary of terms.* Bloomington, IN: Association for Educational Communications and Technology.

Schmidt, H. G., Loyens, S. M. M., Van Gog, T., & Paas, F. (2007). Problem-based learning is compatible with human cognitive architecture: Commentary on Kirschner, Sweller, and Clark (2006). *Educational Psychologist, 42*(2), 91–97.

Schmidt, H. G., Van Der Molen, H. T., Te Winkel, W. W. R., & Wijnen, W. H. F. W. (2009). Constructivist, problem-based learning does work: a meta-analysis of curricular comparisons involving a single medical school. *Educational Psychologist, 44*(4), 227–249.

Schneider, D. (2011). *The media debate.* Retrieved from http://edutechwiki.unige.ch/en/The_media_debate

Schraw, G. (2001). Promoting general metacognitive awareness. In Hartman, H. J. (Ed.), *Metacognition in learning and instruction: Theory, research and practice* (pp. 3–16). Boston, MA: Kluwer.

Schrire, S. (2004). Interaction and cognition in asynchronous computer conferencing. *Instructional Science, 32*, 475–502.

Schrire, S. (2006). Knowledge building in asynchronous discussion groups: Going beyond quantitative analysis. *Computers & Education, 46*(1), 49–70.

Schullo, S. J. (2005). *An analysis of pedagogical strategies: Using synchronous Web-based course systems in the online classroom.* Unpublished doctoral dissertation, University of Florida, Florida.

Schuman, J., & Ice, P. (2011, October). *The art of using online analytics tools from Adobe.* Paper presented at Educause Annual Conference, Philadelphia, PA.

Schwartz, B. L., & Perfect, T. J. (2004). Introduction: Toward an applied metacognition. In Perfect, T. J., & Schwartz, B. L. (Eds.), *Applied metacognition* (pp. 1–14). Cambridge, UK: Cambridge University Press.

Schwier, R. A., & Balbar, S. (2002). The interplay of content and community in synchronous and asynchronous communication: Virtual communication in a graduate seminar. *Canadian Journal of Learning and Technology, 28*(2).

Scriven, M., & Paul, R. (2008). *Defining critical thinking.* Retrieved October 23, 2011, from http://www.criticalthinking.org/aboutCT/define_critical_thinking.cfm

Seals, B., & Glasgow, Z. (1998). *Making instructional design decisions* (2nd ed.). Upper Saddle River, NJ: Prentice Hall.

Segers, M., Van den Bossche, P., & Teunissen, E. (2003). Evaluating the effects of redesigning a problem-based learning environment. *Studies in Educational Evaluation, 29*, 315–334.

Sengupta, S. (2001). Exchanging ideas with peers in network-based classrooms: An aid or a pain? *Language Learning & Technology, 5*(1), 103–134. Retrieved from http://llt.msu.edu/vol5num1/sengupta/

Sharp, A. M. (1987). What is a community of inquiry? *Journal of Moral Education, 16*(1), 37–45.

Sharp, A. M. (1993). The community of inquiry: Education for democracy. In Lipman, M. (Ed.), *Thinking children and education* (pp. 337–345). Dubuque, IA: Kendall-Hunt.

Shattuck, K. (2005). *Cultures meeting cultures in online distance education: Perceptions of international adult learners of the impact of culture when taking online distance education courses designed and delivered by an American university.* Unpublished doctoral dissertation, The Pennsylvania State University, University Park.

Shattuck, K. (2007). Quality matters: Collaborative program planning at a state level. *Online Journal of Distance Learning Administration, 10*(3), 1–10.

Shea, P. J., Pickett, A. M., & Pelz, W. E. (2004). Enhancing student satisfaction through faculty development: The importance of teaching presence. In J. Bourne & J. C. Moore (Eds.), *Elements of quality online education: Into the mainstream:* Vol. 5 in the Sloan-C Series (pp. 39-59). Needham, MA: Sloan Center for Online Education.

Shea, P., Frederickson, E., Pickett, A., & Peltz, W. (2003). A preliminary investigation of "teaching presence" in the SUNY learning network. In Bourne & C.J. Moore (Eds.), *Elements of quality online education: Practice direction, Vol. 4,* (pp. 279-312). Needham, MA: Sloan Center for Online Education.

Shea, P., Pickett, A., & Li, C. S. (2006). Increasing access to higher education: A study of the diffusion of online teaching among 913 college faculty. *The International Review of Research in Open and Distance Learning, 6*(2). ISSN 1492-3831

Shea, P. J. (2006). A study of students' sense of learning community in online environments. *Journal of Asynchronous Learning Networks, 10*(1), 35–44.

Shea, P. J., Fredericksen, E. E., Pickett, A. M., & Pelz, W. E. (2004). Faculty development, student satisfaction, and reported learning in the SUNY learning network. In Duffy, T. M., & Kirkley, J. R. (Eds.), *Learner-centered theory and practice in distance education: Cases from higher education* (pp. 343–377). Mahwah, NJ: L. Erlbaum.

Shea, P. J., Li, C. S., & Pickett, A. (2006). A study of teaching presence and student sense of learning community in fully online and web-enhanced college courses. *The Internet and Higher Education, 9*(3), 175–190.

Shea, P. J., Pickett, A. M., & Pelz, W. E. (2003). A follow-up investigation of "teaching presence" in the SUNY learning netowrk. *Journal of Asynchronous Learning Networks, 7*(2), 61–80.

Shea, P., & Bidjerano, T. (2009). Community of inquiry as a theoretical framework to foster "epistemic engagement" and "cognitive presence" in online education. *Computers & Education, 52*(3), 543–553.

Shea, P., Fredericksen, E., Pickett, A., & Pelz, W. (2004). Faculty development, student satisfaction, and reported learning in the SUNY learning network. In Duffy, T., & Kirkley, J. (Eds.), *Learner-centered theory and practice in distance education* (pp. 343–377). Mahway, NJ: Lawrence Elrbaum Associates.

Shea, P., Hayes, S., Smith, S. U., Vickers, J., Bidjerano, T., & Pickett, A. (in press). Learning presence: Additional research on a new conceptual element within the Community of Inquiry (CoI) framework. *The Internet and Higher Education*.

Shea, P., Hayes, S., Vickers, J., Gozza-Cohen, M., Uzuner, S., & Mehta, R. (2010). A re-examination of the community of inquiry framework: Social network and content analysis. *The Internet and Higher Education, 13*(1-2), 10–21.

Shea, P., Li, C. S., & Picket, A. (2006). A study of teaching presence and student sense of learning community in fully online and web-enhanced college courses. Retrieved March 28, 2011, from http://gpc.edu/~onlineis/teaching_presence.pdf. *The Internet and Higher Education, 9*, 175–190. Retrieved March 28, 2011 doi:10.1016/j.iheduc.2006.06.005

Shea, P., Li, C. S., Swan, K., & Pickett, A. (2005). Developing learning community in online asynchronous college courses: The role of teaching presence. *Journal of Asynchronous Learning Networks, 9*(4), 59–82.

Shea, P., Li, C. S., Swan, K., & Pickett, A. (2005). Teaching presence and establishment of community in online environments: A preliminary study. *Journal of Asynchronous Learning Networks, 9*(4).

Shea, P., Pickett, A., & Li, C. S. (2005). Increasing access to higher education: A study of the diffusion of online teaching among 913 college faculty. *International Review of Research in Open and Distance Learning, 6*(2).

Sheridan, K., & Kelly, M. A. (2010). The indicators of instructor presence that are important to students in online courses. *Journal of Online Learning and Teaching, December*.

Sherry, L. (1996). Issues in distance learning. *International Journal of Educational Telecommunications, 1*(4), 337–365.

Shin, J. K. (2008). *Building an effective community of inquiry for EFL professionals in an asynchronous online discussion board* (Unpublished doctoral dissertation). University of Baltimore County, Baltimore.

Shipman, S., & Shipman, V. C. (1985). Cognitive styles: Some conceptual, methodological, and applied issues. In Gordon, E. W. (Ed.), *Review of research in education* (Vol. 12). Washington, DC: American Educational Research Association. doi:10.2307/1167151

Short, J., Williams, E., & Christie, B. (1976). *The social psychology of telecommunications*. London, UK: John Wiley & Sons.

Siemens, G., & Long, P. (2011). Penetrating the fog: Analytics in learning and education. *EDUCAUSE Review, 46*(5).

Sikora, A. C., & Carroll, C. D. (2002). *A profile of participation in distance education: 1999–2000. Postsecondary education descriptive analysis reports (NCES 2003-154). US Department of Education, National Center for Education Statistics*. Washington, DC: US Government Printing Office.

Simonson, M., & Schlosser, C. (2009). We need a plan – An instructional design approach for distance education courses. In Orellana, A., Hudgins, T. L., & Simonson, M. (Eds.), *The perfect online course: Best practices for designing and teaching*. Charlotte, NC: Information Age Publishing Inc.

Slagter van Tryon, P. J., & Bishop, J. M. (2006). Identifying e-mmediacy strategies for Web-based instruction. *Quarterly Review of Distance Education*, 7(1), 49–62.

Slavin, R. E. (1985). An introduction to cooperative learning research. In Slavin, R. E., Sharan, S., Kagan, S., Lazarowitz, R. H., Webb, C., & Schmuck, R. (Eds.), *Learning to cooperate, cooperating to learn* (pp. 5–15). New York, NY: Plenum Press.

Sloan Consortium. (2010). *Blended/hybrid courses*. Retrieved November 20, 2011, from http://commons.sloanconsortium.org/discussion/blendedhybrid-courses

Smith, B. (2002). The use of communication strategies in computer-mediated communication. *System*, 31, 29–53. doi:10.1016/S0346-251X(02)00072-6

Smith, H. (2008). Assessing student contributions to online discussion boards. *Practitioner Research in Higher Education*, 2(1), 22–28.

So, H.-J., & Brush, T. A. (2008). Student perceptions of collaborative learning, social presence and satisfaction in a blended learning environment: Relationships and critical factors. *Computers & Education*, 51(1), 318–336.

Soller, A. L. (2001). Supporting social interaction in an intelligent collaborative learning system. *International Journal of Artificial Intelligence in Education*, 12, 40–62.

Song, L., & McNary, S. (2011). Understanding students' online interaction: Analysis of discussion board postings. *Journal of Interactive Online Learning*, 1(1), 1–13. Retrieved from www.ncolr.org/jiol

Son, L. K., & Schwartz, B. L. (2004). The relation between metacognitive monitoring and control. In Perfect, T. J., & Schwartz, B. L. (Eds.), *Applied metacognition* (pp. 15–38). Cambridge, UK: Cambridge University Press.

Sorg, S. E. (2002). *Blended learning: Experiences at the University of Central Florida*. PowerPoint presentation. Retrieved August 14, 2011, from http://commons.ucalgary.ca/~lcportal/documents/sorg/Blended%20Learning%20U%20of%20Calgary%2012-04-02.htm

Sotillo, S. (2000). Discourse functions and syntactic complexity in synchronous and asynchronous communication. *Language Learning & Technology*, 4(1), 82–119.

Splitter, L., & Sharp, A. M. (1995). *Teaching for better thinking: The classroom community of inquiry*. Melbourne, Australia: ACER.

Stacey, E. (2002). Social presence online: Networking learners at a distance. *Education and Information Technologies*, 7(4), 287–294.

Stahl, G. (2000c). *A model of collaborative knowledge-building*. Paper presented at the Fourth International Conference of the Learning Sciences (ICLS 2000), Ann Arbor, MI.

Stahl, G. (2006). *Group cognition: Computer support for building collaborative knowledge*. Cambridge, MA: MIT Press.

Stavredes, T. (2011). *Effective online teaching: Foundations and strategies for student success*. San Fransicso, CA: Jossey-Bass.

Stein, D. S., & Wanstreet, C. E. (2008, August). Effects of coaching on cognitive presence in communities of inquiry. *Proceedings of the 24th Annual Conference on Distance Teaching and Learning*, Madison, WI.

Stein, D. S., Wanstreet, C. E., Slagle, P., & Trinko, L. A. (2011, August). E-coaching and feedback practices to promote higher order thinking online. *Proceedings of the 27th Annual Conference on Distance Teaching and Learning*, Madison, WI.

Stein, D. S., Wanstreet, C. E., Calvin, J., Overtoom, C., & Wheaton, J. E. (2005). Bridging the transactional distance gap in online learning environments. *American Journal of Distance Education*, 19(2), 105–118.

Stein, D. S., Wanstreet, C. E., Glazer, H. R., Engle, C. E., Harris, R. A., & Johnston, S. M. (2007). Creating shared understanding through chats in a community of inquiry. *The Internet and Higher Education*, 10(2), 103–115.

Sternberg, R. (2001). Metacognition, abilities and developing expertise: What makes an expert student? In Hartman, H. J. (Ed.), *Metacognition in learning and instruction* (pp. 247–260). Netherlands: Kluwer Academic Publishers.

Sternberg, R. J. (1988). *The nature of creativity: Contemporary psychological perspectives*. Cambridge: Cambridge University Press.

Stewart, S. (2008). *A study of instructional strategies that promote learning centered synchronous dialogue online*. Unpublished doctoral dissertation, University of South Florida, Florida.

Stewart, B. L. (2004). Online learning: a strategy for social responsibility in educational access. *The Internet and Higher Education*, *7*(4), 299–310. doi:10.1016/j.iheduc.2004.09.003

Stewart, T. (2001). *The wealth of knowledge: Intellectual capital and the 21st century organization*. New York, NY: Currency Books.

Stodel, E. J., MacDonald, C. J., & Thompson, T. L. (2006). Learners' perspectives on what is missing from online learning: Interpretations through the community of inquiry framework. *International Review of Research in Open and Distance Learning*, *7*(3), 1–24.

Straus, S. G., & McGrath, J. E. (1994). Does the medium matter? The interaction of task type and technology on group performance and member reactions. *The Journal of Applied Psychology*, *79*(1), 87–97.

Strauss, A., & Corbin, J. (1998). *Basics of qualitative research: Techniques and procedures for developing grounded theory*. Thousand Oaks, CA: Sage Publications.

Strijbos, J. W., Martens, R. L., Jochems, W. M. G., & Broers, N. J. (2004). The effect of functional roles on group efficiency: Using multilevel modeling and content analysis to investigate computer-supported collaboration in small groups. *Small Group Research*, *35*(2), 195–229.

Strijbos, J.-W., & De Laat, M. F. (2010). Developing the role concept for computer-supported collaborative learning: An explorative synthesis. *Computers in Human Behavior*, *26*(4), 495–505.

Strijbos, J.-W., Martens, R. L., Prins, F. J., & Jochems, W. M. G. (2006). Content analysis: What are they talking about? *Computers & Education*, *46*(1), 29–48.

Stringer, E. T. (2007). *Action research* (3rd ed.). London, UK: Sage Publications.

Suzuki, K., & Keller, J. M. (1996). Applications of the ARCS model in computer-based instruction in Japan. Annual Meeting of the Japanese Educational Technology Association, Kanazawa, Japan.

Swain, M. (1995). Three functions of output in second language learning. In Cook, G., & Seidhofer, B. (Eds.), *Principle and practice in applied linguistics* (pp. 125–144). Oxford, UK: Oxford University Press.

Swan, K. (2004). *Relationships between interactions and learning in online environments*. Retrieved December 21, 2008, from http://www.sloan-c.org/publications/books/interactions.pdf

Swan, K., & Shih, L. F. (2005). On the nature and development of social presence in online course discussions. *Journal of Asynchronous Learning Networks*, *9*(3), 115–136.

Swan, K., Shea, P., Richardson, J., Ice, P., Garrison, D. R., Cleveland-Innes, M., & Arbaugh, J. B. (2008). Validating a measurement tool of presence in online communities of inquiry. *E-Mentor*, *2*(24), 1-12. Retrieved June 23, 2010, from http://www.e-mentor.edu.pl/e_index.php?numer=24&all

Swan, K. (2002). Building learning communities in online courses: The importance of interaction. *Education Communication and Information*, *2*(1), 23–49.

Swan, K. (2002). Immediacy, social presence, and asynchronous discussion. In Bourne, J., & Moore, J. C. (Eds.), *Elements of quality online education* (*Vol. 3*, pp. 157–172). Needham, MA: Sloan Center for Online Education.

Swan, K. (2003). Developing social presence in online discussions. In Naidu, S. (Ed.), *Learning and teaching with technology: Principles and practices* (pp. 147–164). London, UK: Kogan Page.

Swan, K., Garrison, D. R., & Richardson, J. (2009). A constructivist approach to online learning: The community of inquiry framework. In Payne, C. R. (Ed.), *Information technology and constructivism in higher education: Progressive learning frameworks* (pp. 43–57). Hershey, PA: IGI Global.

Swan, K., Matthews, D., Bogle, L., Boles, E., & Day, S. (2011). Linking online course design and implementation to learning outcomes: A design experiment. *The Internet and Higher Education.* doi:doi:10.1016/j.iheduc.2011.07.002

Swan, K., & Shea, P. (2005). The development of virtual learning communities. In Hiltz, S. R., & Goldman, R. (Eds.), *Asynchronous learning networks: The research frontier* (pp. 239–260). New York, NY: Hampton Press.

Swan, K., & Shih, L. F. (2005). On the nature and development of social presence in online course discussions. *Journal of Asynchronous Learning Networks, 9*(3), 115–136.

Swann, J. (2009). A dialogic approach to online facilitation. In Same Places, Different Spaces, Proceedings ASCILITE Auckland 2009. Retrieved from http://www.ascilite.org.au/conferences/auckland09/procs/swann.pdf

Sweet, R. (1986). Student dropout in distance education: An application of Tinto's model. *Distance Education, 7*(2), 201–213. doi:10.1080/0158791860070204

Tallent-Runnels, M. K., Thomas, J. A., Lan, W. Y., Cooper, S., Ahern, T. C., Shaw, S. M., & Liu, X. (2006). Teaching courses online: A review of the research. *Review of Educational Research, 76*(1), 93–35.

Tangney, B., FitzGibbon, A., Savage, T., Meehan, S., & Holmes, B. (2001). Communal constructivism: Students constructing learning for as well as with others. In J. Price et al. (Eds.), *Proceedings of Society for Information Technology & Teacher Education International Conference 2001* (pp. 3114-3119). Chesapeake, VA: AACE.

Taylor, J. C. (2001). Fifth generation distance education. *Higher Education Series, 40.* Received April 10, 2008, from http://www.dest.gov.au/archive/highered/hes/hes40/hes40.pdf

Teaching, L., & the Technology (TLT) Group. (2011). *Rubrics: Definition, tools, examples, references.* Retrieved from http://www.tltgroup.org/resources/flashlight/rubrics.htm

Tekiner Tolu, A. (2010). *An exploration of synchronous communication in an online preservice ESOL course: Community of inquiry perspective.* Unpublished Dissertation, University of South Florida, Tampa, Florida.

Tempelaar, D. T., Niculescu, A., Rienties, B., Giesbers, B., & Gijselaers, W. H. (2012). How achievement emotions impact students' decisions for online learning, and what precedes those emotions. *The Internet and Higher Education, 15*(3), 161–169. doi:10.1016/j.iheduc.2011.10.003

Teng, T., & Taveras, M. (2004). Combining live video and audio broadcasting, synchronous chat, and asynchronous open forum discussions in distance education. *Journal of Educational Technology Systems, 33*(2), 121–129.

Terenzini, P. T., & Pascarella, E. T. (1997). Voluntary freshman attrition and patterns of social and academic integration in a university: A test of a conceptual model. *Research in Higher Education, 6*(1), 25–43. doi:10.1007/BF00992014

Terenzini, P., Rendon, L. I., Upcraft, M. L., Millar, S. B., Allison, K. W., Gregg, P. L., & Jalomo, R. (1994). The transition to college: Diverse students, diverse stories. *Research in Higher Education, 35*(1), 57–73. doi:10.1007/BF02496662

Tham, C., & Werner, J. (2005). Designing and evaluating e-learning in higher education: A review and recommendations. *Journal of Leadership & Organizational Studies, 11*(2), 15–24.

Thistlethwaite, J. (2006). More thoughts on `assessment drives learning'. *Medical Education, 40*(11), 1149–1150. doi:10.1111/j.1365-2929.2006.02638.x

Thompson, L. F., & Coovert, M. D. (2003). Teamwork online: The effects of computer conferencing on perceived confusion, satisfaction and postdiscussion accuracy. *Group Dynamics, 7*(2), 135–151.

Thompson, M. M. (2004). Faculty self-study research project: Examining the online workload. *Journal of Asynchronous Learning Networks, 8*(3).

Thompson, T. L., & MacDonald, C. J. (2005). Community building, emergent design and expecting the unexpected: Creating a quality eLearning experience. *The Internet and Higher Education, 8*(3), 233–249. doi:10.1016/j.iheduc.2005.06.004

Tinto, V. (1987). *Leaving college: Rethinking the causes and cures of student attrition.* Chicago, IL: University of Chicago Press.

Tinto, V. (1998). Colleges as communities: Taking research on student persistence seriously. *Review of Higher Education, 21*(2), 167–177.

Tippens, B., Brockhaus, A., Chan, E., Estes, R., Fletcher, B., Fukuda, M., Goldstein, Hiebert, McKittrick, Rhoades & Wille, L. (2011). *University of Washington Bothell Technology Advisory Committee FY11 annual report.* Retrieved November 20, 2011, from http://www.uwb.edu/getattachment/it/tac/tacdocs/FY11-Annual-Report.pdf

Tobias, S., & Everson, H. (2002). *Knowing what you know and what you don't: Further research on metacognitive knowledge monitoring. College Board Report, No. 2002-3.* NY: College Board.

Tobias, S., & Everson, H. T. (2009). The importance of knowing what you know: A knowledge monitoring framework for studying metacognition in education. In Hacker, D. L., Dunlosky, J., & Graesser, A. (Eds.), *Handbook of metacognition in education.* New York, NY: Routledge, Taylor, and Francis.

Tobin, K. (1987). The role of wait time in higher cognitive level learning. *Review of Educational Research, 57*(1), 69–95.

Tofade, T. (2010). Coaching younger practitioners and students using components of the co-active coaching model. *American Journal of Pharmaceutical Education, 74*(3), 51.

Tolu, A. T. (2010). *An exploration of synchronous communication in an online preservice ESOL course: Community of inquiry perspective.* Unpublished doctoral dissertation, University of South Florida, Florida.

Tomei, L. (2004). The impact of online teaching on faculty load: Computing the ideal class size for online courses. *International Journal of Instructional Technology & Distance Learning, 1*(1). Retrieved from http://www.itdl.org/journal/Jan_04/article04.htm

Torras, M. E., & Mayordomo, R. (2011). Teaching presence and regulation in an electronic portfolio. *Computers in Human Behavior, 27*, 2284–2291.

Tu, C. (2002). The measurement of social presence in an online learning. *International Journal on E-Learning, 1*(2), 34–45.

Tu, C. (2004). *Twenty-one designs to building an online collaborative learning community.* Westport, CT: Library Unlimited.

Tu, C. H., & McIsaac, M. (2002). The relationship of social presence and interaction in online classes. *American Journal of Distance Education, 16*(3), 131–150.

Tu, C., & Corry, M. (2003). Building active online interaction via a collaborative learning community. *Computers in the Schools, 20*(3), 51–59.

Tu, C.-H. (2000). On-line learning migration: From social learning theory to social presence theory in a CMC environment. *Journal of Network and Computer Applications, 2*, 27–37. doi:10.1006/jnca.1999.0099

Uljens, M. (1997). *School didactics and learning.* Hove, UK: Psychology Press. doi:10.4324/9780203304778

Underwood, J., & Underwood, G. (1999). Task effects on co-operation and collaborative learning with computers. In Littleton, K., & Light, P. (Eds.), *Learning with computers.* London, UK: Routledge.

University of Washington Bothell. (2008). *21st century campus initiative.* Retrieved November 11, 2011, from http://www.uwb.edu/getattachment/21stcentury/21cci-c.pdf

Uribe, D., Klein, J. D., & Sullivan, H. (2003). The effect of computer-mediated collaborative learning on solving ill-defined problems. *Educational Technology Research and Development, 51*(1), 5–19.

Uzener, S. (2007). Educationally valuable talk: A new concept for determining the quality of online conversations. *Journal of Online Learning and Teaching, 3*(4), 400–410.

Uzner, S. (2009). Questions of culture in distance learning: A research review. *International Review of Research in Open and Distance Learning, 10*(3).

Valcke, M., De Wever, B., Zhu, C., & Deed, C. (2009). Supporting active cognitive processing in collaborative groups: Potential of Bloom's taxonomy as a labelling tool. *The Internet and Higher Education, 12*, 165–172.

Van den Bossche, P., Gijselaers, W. H., Segers, M., & Kirschner, P. A. (2006). Social and cognitive factors driving teamwork in collaborative learning environments. Team learning beliefs & behaviour. *Small Group Research, 37*, 490–521.

Van der Maren, J.-M. (1996). *Méthodes de recherche pour l'Education* (2nd ed.). Montréal, Canada: Presses de l'Université de Montréal.

Van der Pol, J., Admiraal, W., & Simons, P. (2006). The affordance of anchored discussion for the collaborative processing of academic texts. *International Journal of Computer-Supported Collaborative Learning, 1*(3), 339–357.

Van Deusen-Scholl, N., Frei, C., & Dixon, E. (2005). Co constructing learning: The dynamic nature of foreign language pedagogy in a CMC environment. *CALICO Journal, 22*(3), 657–678.

van Merrienboer, J. J. G., Clark, R. F., & deCroock, M. B. M. (2002). Blueprints for complex learning: The 4C/ID model. *Educational Technology Research and Development, 50*(2), 39–64.

Vandergrift, K. E. (2002). The anatomy of a distance education course: A case study analysis. *Journal of Asynchronous Learning Networks, 6*(1), 76–90.

Vansieleghem, N. (2012). Philosophy with children as an exercise in parrhesia: An account of a philosophical experiment with children in Cambodia. In Vansieleghem, N., & Kennedy, D. (Eds.), *Philosophy for children in transition: Problems and prospects* (pp. 152–169). London, UK: Blackwell.

Varnhagen, S., Wilson, D., Krupa, E., Kasprzak, S., & Hunting, V. (2005). Comparison of student experiences with different online graduate courses in health promotion. *Canadian Journal of Learning and Technology, 31*(1), 99–117.

Vaughan, N. D., & Garrison, D. R. (2006a). A blended faculty community of inquiry: Linking leadership, course redesign and evaluation. *Canadian Journal of University Continuing Education, 32*(2), 67-92. Retrieved May 12, 2010, from http://www.extension.usask.ca/cjuce/articles/v32pdf/3223.pdf

Vaughan, N. (2004). Technology in support of faculty learning communities. *New Directions for Teaching and Learning,* (97): 101–109.

Vaughan, N. D. (2004). Technology in support of faculty learning communities. In Cox, M. D., & Richlin, L. (Eds.), *Building faculty learning communities: New directions for teaching and learning, No. 97* (pp. 101–109). San Francisco, CA: Jossey-Bass. doi:10.1002/tl.137

Vaughan, N. D. (2010). A blended community of inquiry approach: Linking student engagement and course redesign. *The Internet and Higher Education, 13*(1-2), 60–65. doi:10.1016/j.iheduc.2009.10.007

Vaughan, N. D. (2010). Student engagement and Web 2.0: What's the connection? *Education Canada, 50*(2), 52–55.

Vaughan, N. D., & Garrison, D. R. (2006). A blended faculty community of inquiry: Linking Leadership, course redesign and evaluation. *Canadian Journal of University Continuing Education, 32*(2), 67–92.

Vaughan, N., & Garrison, D. R. (2005). Creating cognitive presence in a blended faculty development community. *The Internet and Higher Education, 8*(1), 1–12.

Vaughan, N., & Garrison, D. R. (2006). How blended learning can support a faculty development community of inquiry. *Journal of Asynchronous Learning Networks, 10*(4), 139–152.

Veerman, A. L., & Veldhuis-Diermanse, E. (2001). Collaborative learning through computer-mediated communication in academic education. In P. Dillenbourg, A. Eurelings, & K. Hakkarainen (Eds.), *European Perspectives on Computer-Supported Collaborative Learning: Proceedings of the 1st European Conference on Computer-Supported Collaborative Learning* (pp. 625-632). Maastricht, The Netherlands: University of Maastricht.

Vesely, P., Bloom, L., & Sherlock, J. (2007). Key elements of building online community: Comparing faculty and student perceptions. *MERLOT Journal of Online Learning and Teaching, 3*(3), 234–246.

Vignare, K. (2007). Review of literature - Blended learning:Using ALN to change the classroom: Will it work? In Picciano, A. G., & Dziuban, C. D. (Eds.), *Blended learning: Research perspectives* (pp. 37–63). Needham, MA: Sloan Consortium.

Visser, J. (2000). Faculty work in developing and teaching web-based distance courses: A case study of time and effort. *American Journal of Distance Education, 14*(3), 21–32.

Vogler, K. E. (2008, Summer). Asking good questions. *Educational Leadership, 65*(9). Retrieved from http://www.ascd.org/publications/educational-leadership/summer08/vol65/num09/Asking-Good-Questions.aspx

Volet, S., Summers, M., & Thurman, J. (2009a). High-level co-regulation in collaborative learning: How does it emerge and how is it sustained? *Learning and Instruction, 19*, 128e143.

Volet, S., Vauras, M., & Salonen, P. (2009). Self- and social regulation in learning contexts: An integrative perspective. *Educational Psychologist, 44*(4), 215–226.

Volet, S., Vauras, M., & Salonen, P. (2009b). Psychological and social nature of self- and co-regulation in learning contexts: An integrative perspective. *Educational Psychologist, 44*, 1–12.

Voos, R. (2003). Blended learning - What is it and where might it take us? *Sloan-C View, 2*(1), 3–5.

Vygotsky, L. S. (1978). *Mind in society: The development of higher psychological processes*. Cambridge, MA: Harvard University Press.

Wade, S. E., & Fauske, J. R. (2004). Dialogue online: Prospective teachers' discourse strategies in computer-mediated discussions. *Reading Research Quarterly, 39*(2), 134–160.

Walker, S. E. (2003). Active learning strategies to promote critical thinking. *Journal of Athletic Training, 38*(3), 263–267.

Walters, W. (2004-2005). Infusing technology into any instructional program. *Virginia Society for Technology in Education Journal, 19*(1), 17-24.

Wang, A. Y., & Newlin, M. H. (2002). Integrating technology and pedagogy: Web instruction and seven principles of undergraduate education. *Teaching of Psychology, 29*, 325–330.

Wang, C. H. (2005). Questioning skills facilitate online synchronous discussions. *Journal of Computer Assisted Learning, 21*, 303–313.

Wang, C. M., & Reeves, T. C. (2007). The meaning of culture in online education: Implications for teaching, learning, and design. In Edmundson, A. (Ed.), *Globalized e-learning cultural challenges* (pp. 1–17). Hershey, PA: Information Science.

Wang, F., & Hannafin, M. J. (2005). Design-based research and technology enhanced learning environments. *Educational Technology Research and Development, 53*(4), 5–23. doi:10.1007/BF02504682

Wang, S. K., & Hsu, H. (2008). Use of the webinar tool (Elluminate) to support training: The effects of webinar-learning implementation from student-trainers' perspective. *Journal of Interactive Online Learning, 7*(3), 175–194.

Wang, S.-K. (2008). The effects of a synchronous communication tool (Yahoo Messenger) on online learners' sense of community and their multimedia authoring skills. *Journal of Interactive Online Learning, 7*(1), 59–74.

Wang, Y., & Sun, C. (2001). Internet-based real time language education: Towards a fourth generation distance education. *CALICO Journal, 18*(3), 539–561.

Wanstreet, C. E., & Stein, D. S. (2011a). Presence over time in synchronous communities of inquiry. *American Journal of Distance Education, 25*(3), 1–16.

Wanstreet, C. E., & Stein, D. S. (2011b). Gender and collaborative knowledge building in an online community of inquiry. In Wang, V. C. X. (Ed.), *Encyclopedia of information communication technologies and adult education integration* (pp. 707–722). Hershey, PA: IGI Global.

Warkentin, M. E., Sayeed, L., & Hightower, R. (1997). Virtual teams versus face-to-face teams: An exploratory study of a web-based conference system. *Decision Sciences, 28*(4), 975–996.

Weasenforth, D., Biesenbach-Lucas, S., & Meloni, C. (2002). Realizing constructivist objectives through collaborative technologies: Threaded discussions. *Language Learning & Technology, 6*(3), 58–86. Retrieved from http://llt.msu.edu/vol6num3/weasenforth/

Webb, N. M., & Palincsar, A. S. (1996). Group processes in the classroom. In Berliner, D., & Calfee, R. (Eds.), *Handbook of educational psychology* (pp. 841–873). New York, NY: Macmillan.

Wegner, S. B., Holloway, K. C., & Garton, E. M. (1999). The effects of internet-based instruction on student learning. *Journal of Asynchronous Learning Networks, 3*(2), 98–106.

Weigel, M., Straughn, C., & Gardner, H. (2010). New digital media and their potential cognitive impact on youth learning. In Khine, M. S., & Saleh, I. M. (Eds.), *New science of learning: Cognition, computers and collaboration in education* (pp. 2–22). New York, NY: Springer.

Weinberger, A., Reiserer, M., Ertl, B., Fischer, F., & Mandl, H. (2005). Facilitating collaborative knowledge construction in computer-mediated learning environments with cooperation scripts. In R. Bromme, F. W. Hesse, & H. Spada (Ed.), *Barriers and biases in computer-mediated knowledge communication and how they may be overcome* (5 ed., pp. 15-38). New York, NY: Springer.

Weller, M., & Mason, R. (2000). Evaluating an open university web course: Issues and innovations. In Asensio, M., Foster, J., Hodgson, V., & McConnell, D. (Eds.), *Networked learning 2000: Innovative approaches to lifelong learning and higher education through the internet* (pp. 361–368).

Wells, G. (2000). Dialogic inquiry in education: Building on the legacy of Vygotsky. In Lee, C. D., & Smagorinsky, P. (Eds.), *Vygotskian perspectives on literacy research: Constructing meaning through collaborative inquiry* (pp. 51–85). New York, NY: Cambridge University Press.

Wenger, E. (2002). Cultivating communities of practice: a quick start-up guide. Retrieved from http://www.ewenger.com/theory/start-up_guide_PDF.pdf

Wenger, E. (2006). Communities of practice: A brief introduction. Retrieved from http://www.ewenger.com/theory/

Wenger, E. (1998). *Communities of practice: Learning, meaning, and identity.* New York, NY: Cambridge University Press.

Wenger, E., McDermott, R., & Snyder, W. (2002). *Cultivating communities of practice: A guide to managing knowledge.* Boston, MA: Harvard Business School Press.

Wheatley, M. (2005). *Finding our way: Leadership for an uncertain time.* San Francisco, CA: Berrett-Koehler Publishers, Inc.

Wheatley, M. (2006). *Leadership and the new science: Discovering order in a chaotic world* (3rd ed.). San Francisco, CA: Berrett-Koehler Publishers, Inc.

Whelan, R. (2005). *Instructional technology and theory: A look at past, present and future.* Connect: Information Technology at NYU. Retrieved March 13, 2008, from http://www.nyu.edu/its/pubs/connect/spring05/whelan_it_history.html

Whipp, J., & Lorentz, R. (2009). Cognitive and social help giving in online teaching: An exploratory study. *Educational Technology Research and Development, 57*(2), 169–192.

White, A., Roberts, V. W., & Brannan, J. (2003). Returning nurses to the workforce: Developing an online refresher course. *Journal of Continuing Education in Nursing, 34*(2), 59–63.

White, B. Y., Frederikson, J. R., & Collins, A. (2009). The interplay of scientific inquiry and metacognition: More than a marriage of convenience. In Hacker, D., Dunlosky, J., & Graesser, A. (Eds.), *Handbook of metacognition in education* (pp. 175–205). New York, NY: Routledge.

Whitman, L. E., Malzahn, D. E., Chaparro, B. S., Russell, M., Langrall, R., & Mohler, B. A. (2005). A comparison of group processes, performance, and satisfaction in face-to-face versus computer-mediated engineering student design teams. *Journal of Engineering Education, 94*(3), 327–333.

Whitworth, L., Kimsey-House, K., Kimsey-House, H., & Sandahl, P. (2007). *Co-active coaching: New skills for coaching people toward success in work and life* (2nd ed.). Palo Alto, CA: Davies-Black Publishing.

Wildner-Bassett, M. E. (2005). CMC as written conversation: A critical social-constructivist view of multiple identities and cultural positioning in the L2/C2 classroom. *CALICO Journal, 22*(3), 635–656.

Wilen, W. (1986). *Questioning skills for teachers* (2nd ed.). Washington, DC: National Education Association.

Wilen, W. (1990). Forms and phases of discussion. In Wilen, W. (Ed.), *Teaching and learning through discussion: The theory, research and practice of the discussion method* (pp. 3–24). Springfield, IL: Charles Thomas Publishers.

Williams, E. A., Duray, R., & Reddy, V. (2006). Teamwork orientation, group cohesiveness, and student learning: A study of the use of teams in online distance education. *Journal of Management Education, 30*(4), 592–616.

Wise, A., Chang, J., Duffy, T., & del Valle, R. (2004). The effects of teacher social presence on student satisfaction, engagement, and learning. *Journal of Educational Computing Research, 31*(3), 247–271.

Witkin, H. A., & Goodenough, D. R. (1981). *Cognitive styles: Essence and origins.* New York, NY: International Universities.

Wittgenstein, L. (1953). *Philosophical investigations.* Oxford, UK: Blackwell Publishing.

Wood, A., & Smith, M. (2005). *Online communication: Linking technology, identity, and culture* (2nd ed.). Mahwah, NJ: Lawrence Erlbaum Associates.

Wu, A. (2003). Supporting electronic discourse: Principles of design from a social constructivist perspective. *Journal of Interactive Learning Research, 14*(2), 167–184.

Wu, D., & Hiltz, S. R. (2004). Predicting learning from asynchronous online discussions. *Journal of Asynchronous Learning Networks, 8*(2), 139–152.

Yamada, M. (2009). The role of social presence in learner-centered communicative language learning using synchronous computer-mediated communication: Experimental study. *Computers & Education, 52*(4), 820–833. doi:10.1016/j.compedu.2008.12.007

Yick, A., Patrick, P., & Costin, A. (2005). Navigating distance and traditional higher education: Online faculty experiences. *International Review of Research in Open and Distance Learning, 6*(2). Retrieved from http://www.irrodl.org/index.php/irrodl/article/view/235

Yin, R. K. (2009). *Case study research: Design and methods* (4th ed.). Thousand Oaks, CA: Sage Publications, Inc.

Yorke, M. (2003). Formative assessment in higher education: moves towards theory and the enhancement of pedagogic practice. *Higher Education, 45*(4), 477–501. doi:10.1023/A:1023967026413

Yukawa, J. (2006). Co-reflection in online learning: Collaborative critical thinking as narrative. *International Journal of Computer-Supported Collaborative Learning, 1*(2), 203–228. doi:10.1007/s11412-006-8994-9

Yukselturk, E., & Bulut, S. (2007). Predictors for student success in an online course. *Subscription Prices and Ordering Information, 71*.

Zawacki-Richter, O., Bäcker, E. M., & Vogt, S. (2009). Review of distance education research (2000 to 2008). Analysis of research areas, methods, and authorship patterns. *International Review of Research in Open and Distance Learning, 10*(6), 1-30. Retrieved June 14, 2010, from http://www.irrodl.org/index.php/irrodl/article/view/741/1461

Zhang, Z., & Kenny, R. F. (2010). Learning in an online distance education course: Experiences of three international students. *International Review of Research in Open and Distance Learning, 11*(1).

Zhao, N., & McDougall, D. (2008). Cultural influences on Chinese students' asynchronous online learning in a Canadian university. *Journal of Distance Education, 22*(2).

Zimmerman, B. J. (1989). A social cognitive view of self-regulated academic learning. *Journal of Educational Psychology, 81*, 329–339. doi:10.1037/0022-0663.81.3.329doi:10.1037/0022-0663.81.3.329

Zsohar, H., & Smith, J. A. (2008). Transition from the classroom to the Web: Successful strategies for teaching online. *Nursing Education Perspectives, 29*(1), 23–28.

About the Contributors

Zehra Akyol is a researcher and practitioner with interest in teaching and learning online and blended learning environments. She got her PhD degree in the field of Educational Technology. She conducted her doctoral research at University of Calgary focusing community development in online and blended learning environments and the factors affecting the development of communities of inquiry in these learning environments. Recently, she is studying metacognitive development in a community of inquiry environment in relation to learning and cognition. She is a member of the community of inquiry research group and on editorial review boards of several journals in the distance education and educational technology.

D. Randy Garrison is a Professor in the Faculty of Education at the University of Calgary. Dr. Garrison has published extensively on teaching and learning in adult, higher and distance education contexts. He has authored, co-authored or edited nine books and over 100 refereed articles/papers. His recent books are Blended Learning in Higher Education (2008); An Introduction to Distance Education: Understanding Teaching and Learning in a New Era (2010); and E-Learning in the 21st century (2nd Ed.) (2011). He has also won several awards including the 2009 Sloan-C Award for Most Outstanding Achievement in Online Learning by an Individual.

* * *

Dodzi J-A Amemado's research is focused on blended learning, distance education, e-learning approaches, virtual universities, and higher education transformation. In his recent PhD research completed at the University of Montreal, Dodzi examined the institutional changes and subsequent pedagogical innovations in the current evolving learning environment of universities, influenced by online education. Previously, Dodzi wrote a Master's thesis on the issues faced by virtual universities, and then prepared a research report for the International Development Research Center (IDRC) on the accessibility and efficiency of virtual universities. Dr. Amemado regularly presents research papers at various scientific conferences in Canada, the United States and Europe.

Douglas Archibald is the educational researcher scientist at the C.T. Lamont Centre for Research in Primary Care, Bruyère Research Institute and the Department of Family Medicine, University of Ottawa. Dr. Archibald has a PhD in Education (University of Ottawa) and a Master's of Arts in Education (Ontario Institute for Studies in Education). His program of research incorporates various facets of medical education which include interprofessional education, research methodology, and eLearning. Some recent projects have included the assessment of an online training program involving simulation to improve medical residents' knowledge and skills to manage patients with inflammatory arthritis; and the development and validation of assessment instruments for interprofessional education. Doug has recent publications in the fields of eLearning and health care education.

Bridget Arend, PhD is Director of University Teaching in the Office of Teaching and Learning at the University of Denver. She is involved in faculty development in the areas of teaching excellence, educational technology, and online and hybrid learning. Her research interests are centered on teaching strategies and assessment in online and technology-enhanced environments, and specifically on the interaction and thinking that occurs in online asynchronous discussions. She teaches courses about education, assessment, and educational technology in the Morgridge College of Education and University College at the University of Denver.

David T. Bentz, Ph.D. is an Assistant Professor in the College of Business at Bellevue University (Bellevue, NE, USA) where he serves as a Professor in the school's Master's of Instructional Design and Development program. Dr. Bentz's research interests include exploring social aspects of learning within online learning environments. His broad research interests encompass the Community of Inquiry framework, specifically the teaching presence and social presence components. Dr. Bentz's most recent research explores online students' perceptions of instructional immediacy behaviors. In addition to his teaching experience Dr. Bentz's practical experience includes more than a decade of service providing online learning instructional design and development within a variety of higher education settings.

Rebecca Bliquez is Education Librarian and Online Learning Coordinator at the Campus Library serving University of Washington Bothell and Cascadia Community College. She received her Master's degree in Information Resources and Library Science from the University of Arizona. Bliquez is a member of the Hybrid Course Development Institute instruction team at UW Bothell and her research interests include online and hybrid course design and delivery, assessment of student learning, and use of emerging technologies in instruction.

Leonard Bogle has 34 years of experience as an educator in the public schools of Illinois with the last 28 years served as an administrator to include Assistant and Head Middle School Principal, Elementary Principal, Director of Adult Education, Grant Writer, and School Superintendent. Dr. Bogle joined the Department of Educational Leadership at the University of Illinois Springfield in 2005 and currently teaches courses in the areas of educational administration and research. National presentations and publications focused on the delivery of on-line and blended classes to graduate students, the identification of quality on-line programs, effective delivery of online instruction using a variety of tools, and the development and delivery of school-wide cooperative instructional programs. A current research focus is on the design of online classes to improve student achievement and access.

Emily Boles is an instructional developer in the Center for Online Learning, Research and Service (COLRS) at the University of Illinois Springfield. At COLRS, she mentors faculty members in effective practices in online learning and technology integration. She coordinates several grant projects for the Center and is leading new UIS Continuing Education Online initiative. Emily teaches online courses for UIS and facilitates online workshops and webinars for the Sloan Consortium. Her experience in the field spans community colleges and four-year institutions. She has presented at regional, national, and international conferences on online teaching, learning, and technologies.

Andreas Brockhaus is the Director of Learning Technologies at the University of Washington Bothell. He has an M.A. in English from the University of Washington, Seattle, and is affiliate faculty in the School of Interdisciplinary Arts and Sciences. He provides support for the integration of technology in teaching and learning for faculty and staff in accordance with the University's mission of using the best of educational technology. His research and professional interests revolve around online learning, digital media, instructional design, faculty development, and assessment. He has been instrumental in promoting hybrid learning initiatives campus-wide as well as creating and running faculty development programs for online learning. Other projects he has led include launching lecture capture in all UW Bothell classrooms, implementing a campus-wide ePortfolio initiative using Google apps, and launching a digital media classroom and lab.

Melissa Burgess is the Director of Research Methodology at American Public University System. Dr. Burgess has an EdD in Education (Sam Houston State University) and a Masters of Arts in Education (University of Missouri-Columbia). Her focus of research spans the practical, theoretical, and policy-related areas of distance education. Specifically, recent research and subsequent publications include topics on adaptive learning, on-demand eLearning, cyberbullying, and institutional/program/course eStructuring.

M. Cleveland-Innes is Professor and Program Director in the Center for Distance Education at Athabasca University in Alberta, Canada. She teaches Research Methods and Leadership in the graduate programs of this department. Martha has received awards for her work on the student experience in online environments and holds a major research grant through the Canadian Social Sciences and Humanities Research Council. In 2011 she received the Craig Cunningham Memorial Award for Teaching Excellence and in 2009 she received the President's Award for Research and Scholarly Excellence from Athabasca University. She is currently part-time Guest Professor of Education Media Technology at The Royal Institute of Technology in Stockholm, Sweden. Her work is well published in academic journals in North America and Europe. Current research interests are in the areas of leadership in open and distance higher education, online teaching and learning and the effects of emotion on learning.

Scott Day is Associate Professor and Chair of the Department of Educational Leadership at the University of Illinois at Springfield (UIS). Dr. Day was one of two founding faculty to develop and teach one of the first courses in the online Master's in Teacher Leadership degree program ten years ago. The program was awarded the Sloan-C Outstanding Program of the Year in 2010. In 2010, Dr. Day was awarded the Pearson Faculty Award for Outstanding Teaching at UIS. His research publications includes work on blended learning, using design-based research to improve online courses and programmatic change, technology uses of at-risk students, and school district reorganization issues. Professor Day holds a Doctor of Education degree from the University of Illinois at Urbana-Champaign in Educational Organization and Leadership, in which he was awarded the Outstanding Dissertation Award from the University of Illinois' chapter of Phi Delta Kappa in 2000.

Sebastián Díaz serves as Associate Professor in the Department of Technology, Learning & Culture at West Virginia University, teaching in the areas of Statistics, Program Evaluation, Measurement, and Education Law. He also serves as a Strategic Planning and Evaluation Consultant for WVU's Office of International Student Affairs and Global Services. His research currently focuses on developing measurement instruments and evaluation methodologies germane to Intellectual Capital and Knowledge Management. As Senior Statistician for the PAR Framework project, funded by the Bill & Melinda Gates Foundation, he is conducting large-scale analytics on online course data from six colleges and universities. Before entering the tenure-track, Sebastián worked as a medical educator at both allopathic and osteopathic institutions. Sebastián earned a B.S. in Chemistry from Marietta College, a Ph.D. in Educational Research & Evaluation from Ohio University, and a law degree from the University of Akron.

Peggy A. Ertmer is a Professor of Learning Design and Technology in the College of Education at Purdue University. Her scholarship focuses on the impact that student-centered instructional approaches have on learning outcomes. She is particularly interested in the impact of student-centered instruction (problem-based learning, case-based learning) on higher-order thinking skills; the adoption of student-centered approaches by K-12 teachers; and strategies for facilitating higher-order thinking and self-regulated learning in online, problem-based learning environments. In addition, she explores the interplay between teacher beliefs and the use of student-centered instructional practices. Dr. Ertmer has published scholarly works in premier journals including the *American Educational Research Journal, Journal of Educational Psychology*, and *Educational Technology Research and Development*. She has co-edited three editions of the ID CaseBook: Case Studies in Instructional Design and is the founding Editor of the *Interdisciplinary Journal of Problem-based Learning*, published by Purdue University Press.

Linda Shuford Evans, PhD is an Assistant Professor of TESOL (Teachers of English to Speakers of Other Languages) in the Inclusive Education Department at Kennesaw State University. She holds B.S. and Ed.M. degrees in Elementary Bilingual Education from Boston University, and a PhD in Literacy and Language Arts from the University of South Florida, Tampa. She has worked as a bilingual teacher, ESL teacher, learning support specialist, and teacher educator. Her research interests include teacher education, language policy, dual/bilingual education, and migrant education. Dr. Evans has conducted numerous workshops and institutes for teachers and policy makers, and has presented at local, state, national, and international conferences.

Bas Giesbers obtained a Master's degree in Educational and Developmental Psychology at Tilburg University, the Netherlands. He gained experience as an educational technologist, teacher, and educational researcher through projects on remedial teaching via distance education, distance supervision (e.g. of internships and thesis writing), and teacher professionalisation in the field of technology use in education. Currently he works on his PhD research on the support of virtual team learning by synchronous communication means at the department of Educational Research and Development of the Maastricht University School of Business and Economics.

Yoshiko Goda is Associate Professor of Research Center for Higher Education and Instructional Systems Program Graduate School of Social and Cultural Sciences at Kumamoto University, Japan. She received her Ph.D. (Science Education) at Florida Institute of Technology in 2004 with partial support of a Fulbright scholarship. She has held teaching positions in various countries including as an instructor at

Applied Language Department at Shu-Te University, Taiwan (1999-2000), an adjunct faculty at graduate school of FIT (2004), US, a visiting scholar at Research Center for e-Learning Professional Competency at Aoyama Gakuin University (2005-2008), Japan, and an Associate Professor at Faculty of Social and Management Studies at Otemae University, Japan (2008-2010). She has co-authored "Technologies and Language Learning in Japan: Learn Anywhere, Anytime" (pp.38-54), in Levy, M., Blin, F., Siskin, C.B., & Takeuchi, O. (Eds.), 2011, WorldCALL: International perspectives on computer-assisted language learning, Routledge Studies and "Application of social presence principles to CSCL design for quality interactions" (pp.31-48), in Jia, J. (Ed.), 2012, *Educational stages and interactive learning: From kindergarten to workplace training*, IGI Global. Her current research interests include self-regulated learning for e-learning, online education program evaluation, computer-assisted language learning, and innovative community for global education.

David S. Goldstein is a Senior Lecturer in the School of Interdisciplinary Arts and Sciences at the University of Washington Bothell, where he serves as Director of the Teaching and Learning Center, overseeing faculty development, community-based learning, and student tutoring in writing and quantitative reasoning. He earned a Ph.D. in Comparative Culture from the University of California, Irvine, and has published widely in ethnic American literature, including a co-edited volume, *Complicating Constructions: Race, Ethnicity, and Hybridity in American Texts* (University of Washington Press, 2007) and in the scholarship of teaching and learning. Goldstein received the University of Washington's Distinguished Teaching Award in 2007.

Albert Gras-Martí is Emeritus Professor of Applied Physics at the University of Alacant. With a PhD in Physics (in the field of Atomic Collisions in Solids –ACIS-) and a background in Science Education, Gras-Martí is a member of the Catalan Academy of Sciences (IEC), and has published extensively in the field of ACIS and in PER (Physics Education Research). Present research interests include PER and Science Education Research at all educational levels, especially the applications of information and communication technologies to science education and e-learning in general, both in face to face and distant education.

Kim Hosler is an Educational Technology doctoral candidate at the University of Northern Colorado. She has presented at AECT conferences as well as at the Sloan-C Consortium annual conference on topics ranging from student perceptions of Quality Matters, the use of text messaging to enhance online communities, to engendering cognitive presence and critical thinking in online courses. She teaches online and face to face classes in technical writing and research methods as affiliate faculty for The Metropolitan State College of Denver, Regis University, and the University of Denver's University College. Previously, she managed several learning and professional development departments for technology and financial services companies. Kim's research interests include building learning communities in distance learning environments, mobile learning, and technology use in higher education.

Phil Ice is the Vice President of Research and Development at American Public University System. Dr. Ice has an EdD in Education with concentrations in Curriculum & Instruction and Instructional Technology. He is a three time recipient of the Sloan-C Effective Practice Award, the Adobe Excellence in Education Award and the Wagner Award for Innovation in Distance Education. His research focuses on the intersection of learning theory and emerging technologies.

Melissa Kelly is an Instructional Designer working on course development and research with faculty in the National College of Education at National Louis University. She is also working on completing a PhD in Educational Psychology. Over the past several years she has provided technical support for students enrolled in a wide range of online courses and has taught foundation courses.

David Kennedy is Professor in the Department of Educational Foundations, Montclair State University, and Fellow at the Institute for the Advancement of Philosophy for Children, also at Montclair State. He has contributed numerous chapter and journal articles on pedagogical, curricular and political aspects of community of philosophical inquiry in educational settings, eleven of which are collected in the recently published anthology, *Philosophical Dialogue with Children: Essays on Theory and Practice* (Mellen 2010). He is also the author of *The Well of Being: Childhood, Subjectivity, and Education* (SUNY Press, 2006), and *Changing Conceptions of the Child from the Renaissance to Post-Modernity: A Philosophy of Childhood* (Mellen, 2006).

Nadia Kennedy is Assistant Professor in the Department of Mathematics at Stony Brook University, where she teaches Mathematics Education, following 15 years of teaching math in elementary and secondary schools in her native Bulgaria. Her foci in community of inquiry studies include complexity and systems theory, argumentation theory, and dialogue theory. She is currently at work on a COI-based mathematics curriculum for middle-schoolers. Her recent papers include "Community of Philosophical Inquiry as a Discursive Structure, and its Role in School Curriculum Design" (*Journal of Philosophy of Education*, 2011) and "Between Chaos and Entropy: Community of Inquiry from a Systems Perspective" (*Complicity*, 2010), both co-authored with David Kennedy.

Kristine Korhumel currently serves as the Senior Programming Analyst for the NIH/HRSA Medical Education Partnership Initiative Coordinating Center (MEPI-CC) at the George Washington University (GWU) in Washington, DC. The MEPI-CC manages a series of institutional partnerships involving thirteen medical schools in Sub-Saharan Africa. Her primary work involves providing communications support between GWU and its African school partners, as well as designing and implementing the MEPI-CC's communications strategy. This includes programming and designing the MEPI website, developing a content management system, and providing technical support on web-based teleconferencing and communications platforms. Before joining the MEPI-CC, Ms. Korhumel earned her BS in Mechanical Aerospace Engineering with a minor in Fine Arts and a focus in Mathematics from GWU.

Carol Leppa is a Professor of Nursing at the University of Washington Bothell. Dr. Leppa has a Ph.D. from the University of Illinois at Chicago and has been on the Nursing faculty at UW Bothell since 1992, and received the UW Distinguished Teaching Award in 1998. Her nursing research interests focus on end-of-life care policy. Leppa has also been a leader on the UW Bothell campus in creating faculty development programs for hybrid teaching and learning.

Simon Lygo-Baker, PhD, has worked in academic development for the last ten years, most recently at King's College London. Whilst there he developed and delivered a range of accredited postgraduate programmes for staff across the university. In addition he established, in collaboration with academic staff, specific programmes and courses for departments and groups of staff aimed to enhance the learning opportunities for students. Currently he is involved in a range of research projects examining peer observation, student learning, and professionalism in higher education.

Daniel B. Matthews is an Associate Professor in the Department of Educational Leadership at the University of Illinois Spring (UIS) and a Fellow with the UIS Center for Online Learning, Research and Service (COLRS). His research is in the area of geographic diversity in online education, identifying factors related to success in online education, and improving online education through the use of the Quality Matters and Community of Inquiry frameworks. He is currently part of a research team that is using a multi-semester, collaborative design research approach to improve course processes and outcomes within a graduate program that is entirely online.

Katrina Meyer is Associate Professor of Higher and Adult Education at the University of Memphis and conducts research on a variety of topics related to online learning in higher education, such as online discussions, quality of and cost-efficiencies from online learning, student learning and faculty productivity online, as well as virtual universities. She also serves on the editorial boards of four research journals devoted to online learning and pioneered a methodology for studying institutional websites to determine a university's "virtual face."

Christine "Chris" Nickel works as an instructional designer at Regent University in Virginia Beach, VA, an occasional adjunct at Old Dominion University (Norfolk, VA) and freelances as an instructional design consultant. She received her Ph.D. in Instructional Design & Technology from Old Dominion University in 2010. Her research interests include cooperative and collaborative learning, online and blended learning environments, the community of inquiry framework, service learning, and creative and critical thinking strategies. Originally from the Rochester, NY area, Christine now enjoys warmer winters in Virginia. Every day she gets to experience love from her husband, son, dog, and cats in the home she affectionately calls "the petting zoo/crazy house."

Ana Oskoz is an Associate Professor of Spanish in the Department of Modern Languages, Linguistics and Intercultural Communication at the University of Maryland Baltimore County (UMBC). Her research focuses on the use of synchronous and asynchronous communication tools such as online chats, discussion boards, blogs, and wikis for second language learning to enhance second language writing and foster intercultural competence development. Ana Oskoz has chapters on the topics of error correction, collaborative writing and articles in the use of technology in the language classroom. Her articles have appeared in journals such as *Language Learning & Technology*, *Foreign Language Annals*, and *CALICO*. She is also co-editor of the 2012 *CALICO monograph*.

Luz Adriana Osorio is presently the Head of the Directorate in Information Technologies (DTI) of the Universidad de los Andes. A Professor in the Centro de Investigación y Formación en Educación (CIFE) of that University, she has a degree in Systems Engineering from the Universidad Autónoma de Manizales, and a Master's in System Engineering and Computation from the Universidad de los Andes. With a PhD in the Society of Information and Knowledge from the Universitat Oberta de Catalunya, she has also directed the Laboratorio de Investigación y Desarrollo sobre Informática y Educación (LIDIE).

Richard "Rick" Overbaugh is a Professor of Education at Old Dominion University in Norfolk, VA. He currently teaches graduate and undergraduate courses in instructional design and technology integration. Rick's current research interests include efficacy of instructional strategies and collaborative tools in distributed teaching/learning environments, and hierarchical assessment of knowledge acquisition. Rick designed a framework to coordinate and guide the development and subsequent investigation of educational environments based on certain aspects of the Sloan-C pillars of quality education. He has published more than 30 papers, counting 4 book chapters, and presented over 60 research papers. He has co-authored and co-presented with more than a dozen of his graduate students and a post-doctoral research assistant.

Ian Porter is a Learning Technologist in UW Bothell's Learning Technologies. He holds dual graduate degrees from the University of Washington, Seattle, in Library and Information Science and Digital Media Studies. In autumn of 2012, he will begin doctoral course work and research in communication, rhetoric, and media studies in the Department of Communication at UW. His professional interests include principled design of assignments and courses using technology. His research interests include media theory and history, rhetorical theory and criticism, and, specifically, rhetorical inquiry concerning new media and technology.

Jennifer C. Richardson is an Associate Professor in the Learning Design and Technology Program in the College of Education at Purdue University. Dr. Richardson's research focuses on distance learning, specifically the use of the Community of Inquiry Framework (CoI) and examining social presence and related strategies. She has also been working on developing professional development frameworks for mentoring graduate students to develop online courses and teach online. She has been teaching and doing research in distance education for the past eleven years and has been a recipient of the Sloan-C Effective Practices in Online Education Award, the AERA SIG Instructional Technology Leadership Award, and the Excellence in Distance Teaching Award from Purdue University. Jennifer is the past Chair for the AERA SIG Instructional Technology.

Bart Rienties is a Senior Lecturer at the University of Surrey. As economist and educational psychologist he conducts multi-disciplinary research on work-based and collaborative learning environments and focuses on the role of social interaction in learning, which is published in leading academic journals and books. His primary research interests are focused on computer-supported collaborative learning, the role of motivation in learning, the role of the teacher to design effective blended and online learning courses, and the role of social interaction in learning. Furthermore, Bart is interested in broader internationalisation aspects of higher education. He successfully led a range of national/European projects and received several awards for his educational innovation projects. Finally, he is chair of the international EDINEB Network.

Ayesha Sadaf is a Doctoral candidate in the Learning Design and Technology Program in the College of Education at Purdue University. She received Master's degree in Computer Graphics Technology from Purdue University. Her research focuses on technology integration, emerging technologies, creative and collaborative media, cognitive learning, critical thinking, and distance education. Ayesha is interested in exploring effective strategies to integrate emerging technologies in computer-supported collaborative environments for promoting student interaction, critical thinking, and cognitive learning. She has conducted several technology integration workshops and has presented her research at local, state, national and international conferences.

Annie Saint-Jacques, having done all her graduate studies at a distance, and holding a graduate diploma in multimedia instructional design and a master's degree in distance education, is currently writing the conclusion of her doctoral thesis "Effective Teaching Strategies for a Virtual Graduate Seminar: Developing a Community of Inquiry in Synchronous Mode within a Blended Online Learning Design Approach". A seasoned telecommuter, she has an extensive background in education as a Teacher, Lecturer, Senior Manager, Instructional Designer, and Academic Advisor. Her research interests include increased and open access in higher education, learning communities, synchronous (real time) online learning, efficient online teaching practices, and higher education policies. Annie has presented at major international conferences such as the *American Educational Research Association*, the *Association for the Advancement of Computing in Education*, and the *Association for Educational Communications and Technology*.

Kathleen M. Sheridan, Ph.D.is an Associate Provost and Professor at National Louis University. She received her PhD in Child and Family Studies from the University of Wisconsin–Madison in 1994. Her research interests include online learning and course development in higher education. She has published as well as presented keynote speeches, workshops, and papers at numerous national and international conferences.

David S. Stein, Ph.D., is Associate Professor in the College of Education and Human Ecology at The Ohio State University. His Doctorate in Adult Education is from the University of Michigan. He also received an M.S. in community health planning and administration from the University of Cincinnati. Dr. Stein specializes in adult teaching and learning. He has conducted workshops on principles of adult teaching and has served as a consultant to professional associations, the Ohio Board of Regents, the Supreme Court of Ohio Judicial College, and other universities on adult education. Presently, Dr. Stein is researching online learning and its influence on adult learning. He has presented at national and regional conferences on adult learning and has written extensively on how adults learn.

Karen Swan is the Stukel Professor of Educational Leadership at the University of Illinois Springfield (UIS) and a research associate in the UIS Center for Online Learning, Research and Service. Her research is in the area of media, technology, and learning on which she has authored over 100 publications, several hypermedia programs and two books. Dr. Swan has also been awarded several grants from such organizations as the National Science Foundation, the U.S. Department of Education, the New York City Board of Education, AT&T, and the Cleveland Foundation. Her current research interests include online learning, ubiquitous computing and learning analytics. Dr. Swan received the 2006 Sloan Consortium award for Outstanding Achievement in Online Learning by an Individual and in 2010 was inducted into the first class of Sloan-C Fellows. She also received a 2010 Distinguished Alumnus award from Teachers College, Columbia University, her alma mater.

Dirk Tempelaar, PhD, is Senior Lecturer at the Department of Quantitative Economics, Maastricht University. Next to teaching first year courses mathematics and statistics, and bridging courses to facilitate the transfer from high school to university, his research interests includes the investigation of student learning, and students' achievements in learning, from an individual difference perspective. Students' learning choices when learning in a blended learning environment, and the impact of individual differences on these preferred learning behaviours, is the main focus of his current research.

Aylin Tekiner Tolu, PhD is an Assistant Professor of in the English Language Teaching department at Yeditepe University, Turkey. She received her B.A. degree in Teaching English as Second Language and M.S. degree in Cognitive Science from Middle East Technical University in Turkey and a Ph.D. in Second Language Acquisition and Instructional Technology from the University of South Florida, Tampa. She worked as an ESL instructor and teacher educator. Her research interests include online education, ESL teacher education, and technology enhanced language education.

Maria Fernanda Aldana V has a psychology degree from the Universidad Javeriana and a Master's degree in Education and Community Development from CINDE, Universidad Surcolombiana. She works in the Centro de Investigación y Formación en Educación, CIFE, of the Universidad de los Andes.

Juny Montoya Vargas is presently the Head of the Centro del Investigación y Formación en Educación (CIFE) and directs the research group "Education in the disciplines." She is Associate Professor of the Universidad de los Andes, PhD in Education by the University of Illinois (Fulbright scholar), a lawyer and specialist in Business Law of the Universidad de los Andes. In this University she has directed the Centro de Investigaciones Sociojurídicas (CIJUS) from the Speciality in Finance Legislation and from the Undergraduate Law School; she coordinates the Sochrates Programme of teachers' formation of the Law Faculty and is a member of the Research Group in Interdisciplinary Studies of that Faculty.

Norm Vaughan, an Educator and Researcher with interests in blended learning, faculty development, and K to 12 schooling, is a Professor in the Department of Education, Faculty of Teaching and Learning at Mount Royal University in Calgary, Alberta. He is the co-author of the book *Blended Learning in Higher Education* (Jossey-Bass, 2008) and has published a series of articles on blended learning and faculty development. Norm is the Co-founder of the Blended Online Design Network (BOLD), a member of the Community of Inquiry Research Group, the Associate Editor of the *International Journal of Mobile and Blended Learning* and he is on the Editorial Boards of the *International Journal of Excellence in e-Learning*, *Canadian Journal of Learning and Technology*, the *Journal of Distance Education*, the *Journal on Centres for Teaching & Learning*, the *Learning Communities Journal*, and the *Journal of Information Fluency*.

Viviane Vladimirschi holds a Master of Education (M.Ed.) in Distance Education (Athabasca University, Canada) and a postgraduate degree in Educational Technologies (Pontifícia Universidade Católica de São Paulo, Brazil). She is also certified in Online Teaching (University of California Los Angeles, USA). Since 2002, she is director and owner of E-connection, a company that specializes in the design and delivery of online and blended education for corporate and academic enterprises. E-connection also renders consulting, project management, training of staff for online teaching, design, and implementation of Learning Management Systems (LMS) services for distance education. Viviane has presented keynote speeches, papers, and workshops at both International Conferences of Distance Education and National Conferences of Distance Education promoted by the Brazilian Association of Distance Education (ABED) in Brazil. Her current area of interest focuses on the implications of teaching, learning, and design for globalized e-learning.

Yianna Vovides is currently a Visiting Assistant Professor in the Communication, Culture, and Technology Program, Graduate School of Arts and Sciences, Georgetown University. Before joining Georgetown University in January 2012, Dr. Vovides was Director of Instructional Design at the George Washington University (GW). At the George Washington University she taught part-time in the International Education Program and the Educational Technology Leadership Program of the Graduate School of Education and Human Development. She currently serves as Communication Cluster Lead for the Medical Education Partnership Initiative Coordinating Center housed in GW's School of Public Health and Health Services. She has over 15 years of experience in instructional design and technology with a focus on designing online learning activities at both course and curriculum level. Her research interests include cyberlearning, technology acceptance, and metacognition. Her academic degrees include a BA and MA (focus: Development Support Communication) in Journalism and Mass Communication, and a PhD in Instructional Design and Technology from The University of Iowa.

Constance E. Wanstreet, Ph.D, is an Adjunct Assistant Professor in the College of Education and Human Ecology at The Ohio State University. Her doctorate from Ohio State is in workforce development and adult education. Dr. Wanstreet has developed and implemented training programs for adult learners in workplace settings and has served as a consultant to the Ohio Board of Regents and the Supreme Court of Ohio Judicial College. She has presented at national and regional conferences, primarily on how adults learn in online environments. Dr. Wanstreet's current research interests include electronic coaching in communities of inquiry and online knowledge building.

Masanori Yamada is Associate Professor in Research Center for Higher Education at Kanazawa University, Japan. He worked for NTT Comware Corporation where he was engaged in the research on the technology related to moving images from 2000 to 2003. He received M.A. and Ph.D in Human System Science from Tokyo Institute of Technology in 2005 and 2008 respectively. He has held project assistant professor at the University of Tokyo, where he managed various research projects about learning enviroment design, development and evaluation from 2006 to 2009. He is also a recipient of the outstanding young researcher award from Information Processing Society of Japan (2003), and Japan Society for Educational Technology (2010), and outstanding article award from the The Computer-Assisted Language Instruction Consortium (2011). His paper published by "Computers & Education" was selected as one of Top 25 Hottest Articles (April to June 2009). His current research centers on social software design and develpment for collaborative learning based on social psychology.

Index

U

undergraduate student research assistant (USRA) 338
United States Distance Learning Association (US-DLA) 46
university culture 427

V

virtual graduate seminar 84
visual stimulation 99
vital space 98, 101

W

wait-time 100, 154
Web 2.0 resources 50, 337
Wedemeyer, Charles 47
W(e)Learn Framework 185
Wilcoxon Sum Rank test 279, 282
workload 234
world wide web 441

Z

zone of proximal development 3, 15

CPSIA information can be obtained at www.ICGtesting.com
Printed in the USA
BVOW050216290812

298955BV00007B/2/P